# THE ENCYCLOPEDIA OF TRAINS AND LOCOMOTIVES

## THE COMPREHENSIVE GUIDE TO OVER 900 STEAM, DIESEL, AND ELECTRIC LOCOMOTIVES FROM 1825 TO THE PRESENT DAY

# THE ENCYCLOPEDIA OF TRAINS AND LOCOMOTIVES

THE COMPREHENSIVE GUIDE TO OVER 900 STEAM, DIESEL, AND ELECTRIC LOCOMOTIVES FROM 1825 TO THE PRESENT DAY

**GENERAL EDITOR: DAVID ROSS**

THUNDER BAY
P·R·E·S·S
San Diego, California

**Thunder Bay Press**
An imprint of the Advantage Publishers Group
5880 Oberlin Drive, San Diego, CA 92121-4794
www.thunderbaybooks.com



Library of Congress Cataloging-in-Publication Data available upon request.

ISBN 1-57145-971-5

Editorial and design by
Amber Books Ltd
Bradley's Close
74–77 White Lion Street
London N1 9PF
U.K.

Authors: David Ross, Colin Boocock, David Brown, Nick Lawford, Brian Solomon
Editor: Mariano Kälfors
Designer: Graham Curd
Picture research: Lisa Wren

Printed in Singapore

1 2 3 4 5 07 06 05 04 03

# CONTENTS

*The locomotives and trains featured in this book are arranged in date order, according to when they first went into service.*

**The renovated locomotive *Duchess of Hamilton* pulls a passenger charter through Birkett Common on the former Midland main line from Leeds to Carlisle in the early 1980s.**

# INTRODUCTION

**Regarded by many experts as the ultimate steam locomotive, a 4-8-8-4 'Big Boy' of the Union Pacific Railroad is preserved at Cheyenne, Wyoming.**

AMONG THE INVENTIONS that define the modern age, the railway train holds a prime position. The steam engine had already existed for over a hundred years when in 1804, as a locomotive engine, it first moved under its own power on land. By 1825 the train had come into its own, and with its appearance, the modern world truly begins. The era of mass travel, of bulk haulage, of rapid national and international distribution of goods and information had arrived. The transcontinental railway helped to weld the United States into a nation, and later facilitated the Russian Revolution. Railways were the vital infrastructure of trade and industry in the vast colonial domains of Africa and Australasia. Among the rival nations of Europe their strategic value was well understood from the beginning. The potential of the new machine released a flood of daring and ingenuity from engineers and technicians. Tunnels and viaducts, electrical communication, signalling techniques, grand public architecture - all demonstrated the revolution that railways brought to everyday life. Synchronised time was brought to communities that had previously set their clocks to suit themselves, or lived by the passage of the sun. But in less obvious ways too, in precision measurement, metallurgy, statistics, physics and dynamics, and business management, the existence and demands of railways drove experiment and knowledge forwards.

For more than a hundred years, steam power was the basis of the railway. Coal was the prime fuel, though other fuels were also used to make steam, from wood to powdered peat, from sugar-cane stalks to cotton waste and corn cobs, and, increasingly from the 1890s, oil. The great age of the railway was from 1850 to 1920 – during this period it dominated land transport. The invention of the internal combustion engine, enabling powered road transport, did not seem a major threat at first. Electric traction was particularly welcomed and developed by coal-less countries like Italy. Though electric trams put some suburban steam lines out of business, they often, as in France and Belgium, provided a complementary service to the railways. The First World War, with its speeding-up of motor car and truck technology, and Henry Ford's creation of the assembly line and the cheap motor car in the 1920s brought the car, coach and truck to the stage of real rivalry with railways in the industrialised nations. The railways fought back, themselves adopting the new technology and also building bigger, faster, more efficient steam locomotives. Nowhere was this process more apparent than in the United States of America, where the greatest titans of steam were built even as their glory was being eclipsed by the oncoming diesel-electrics.

By the 1950s steam traction was diminishing rapidly. Electric and diesel power gave more energy-efficient and cost-effective performance, enabling higher speeds and higher usage of prime routes, with less pollution by smoke and less risk of lineside fires. The locomotive itself became less and less used on passenger trains, as the multiple-unit, incorporating its own motive power, took over long-distance as well as local transit. Regression was still the operative word in most countries. Rail systems were cut back as the freeway and the jet plane took over more and more inter-city traffic. Only in China and India did the railways still remain the prime means of national transportation, and these were also the last major countries to have steam haulage. But later in the twentieth century, there was a change. Railways, from being an ashy Cinderella of the transport world, began to take on a new character. Road congestion had become a world-wide problem. A growing concern for the environment revealed trains as clean and efficient energy users. New technology enabled trains to compete with planes in medium-distance inter-city runs. France and Japan led the way in building new high-speed lines. Computer science helped to make rail freight competitive against road haulage. Great engineering ventures, like the Denmark–Sweden, Britain–France, and Japanese inter-island links, are based on the use of railways. New-built industrial railways like the West Australian ore lines ship vast tonnages in single train-loads several kilometres long. Rapid-transit rail links join airports to major cities like London, Oslo and Hong Kong, among many others.

There is no doubt that railways have a promising future as well as a fascinating past. In these pages, you can inspect both, as well as survey the full range of state-of-the-art motive power in each year. From the world's first steam-powered railway to the projects now in hand to construct magnetic-levitation lines that do away with the need for wheels, less than two hundred years have elapsed. Unique in its scope and range, this encyclopedia describes more than a thousand examples from all over the world as it charts the progress of those most visible and colourful elements of the railway, the locomotive and the train.

**A well-preserved New Zealand Railways Ka-class 4-8-4 No. 942 Nigel Bruce engine heads an Auckland-Rotorua special tour train, on 30 September 1991.**

PART ONE

# STEAM LOCOMOTIVES

Speaking of steam locomotives, American historian John H. White, Jr, wrote: 'Here was a machine that literally had fire in its belly. It roared down the track, a big clattering thing with a noisy bell and whistle. It was heavy and ponderous but cocksure: it rolled on, self-reliant and unafraid. Its only bad habits were drinking and smoking. It is no wonder, then, that thousands have been seduced by the charms and power of the steam locomotive.' Very many people have indeed been captivated. Even today, with its practical service at an end, the fascination continues, and not just because of nostalgia for the past. The steam locomotive is one of the very few machines which express both feeling and personality. From the very beginning, it made a profound impact on the imagination. At that time, this machine that moved on land had only one predecessor – the clockwork mouse. Some people were hostile, others terrified, but most saw it in a favourable light, and the affectionate nickname, 'the iron horse', was used from an early date.

**Above: The first bogie locomotive, John Jervis's 4-2-0 Experiment, built at West Point Foundry, USA, in 1832, and later renamed *Brother Jonathan*.**

**Left: Skirting the Indian Ocean coast, South African Railways Class 24 2-8-4s, Nos. 3669 and 3652, with a mail train on the Kaiman River viaduct, Cape Province, on 9 July 1983.**

By the year 1804, the steam engine had been a well-known and accepted fact of industrial life for almost a century. A few inventive pioneers had succeeded in driving ships with it. But on land, apart from one or two experiments with road vehicles, it had always been fixed in one place, driving pumps or other machinery. No self-propelling steam engine had ever pulled a load on land. Then, in February

There were five great 'schools' of steam locomotive design – the British, the American, the French, the German and the Russian ... dominating engine design in many other countries, and all building new types right up to the 1950s.

1804, Samuel Homfray of Penydarren Ironworks in South Wales wagered 500 guineas that a steam-powered 'travelling engine' set up on his mining tramroad by the Cornish engineer Richard Trevithick, would pull a load of 10t (11 tons) from Penydarren to Abercynon, a distance of just under 16km (10 miles). The bet was taken. The locomotive, the first in the world to run on rails, made the journey in four hours and five minutes, with seventy men clinging on to the wagons, which were loaded with pig-iron. The brittle, flanged cast-iron track was broken and cracked by the engine's wheels, however, and Penydarren went back to pony-hauling for thirty years. Trevithick's machine had shown the way, but it was not the direct ancestor of the later steam locomotives. Trevithick died in poverty in 1833, his pioneering machines obsolete, but by then the commercial railway was already a reality.

From its beginnings in Britain, the railway very soon became an international asset, and through the nineteenth century engineers and inventors in Europe and America contributed improvements. The first locomotive engineers were first and foremost practical men, even if some were also visionaries. They had to be: working in a new field, adapting old techniques to new needs, they were constantly discovering problems and devising solutions. Sometimes the same invention or improvement was made on both sides of the English Channel or the Atlantic Ocean; the Frenchman Marc Séguin was working on the tubular boiler at the same time as the Englishmen Henry Booth gave the idea to Robert Stephenson. Another Frenchman, Henri Giffard, invented the steam-powered injector. The Belgians Alfred Belpaire and Egide Walschaerts were responsible for improved fireboxes and valve gear. The American engineers John Jervis and Joseph Harrison provided the bogie, or pilot, and effective suspension; and another American, George Westinghouse, best solved the problem of how to brake a moving train automatically. The Scot James Urquhart, working in Russia, was first to succeed with an oil-fired steam locomotive. The German Wilhelm Schmidt developed the first really effective superheater. Decades before that, following some trouble with a herd of cows on the line, an Englishman had invented the first steam whistle. By the end of the nineteenth century, every new steam locomotive, however typically British, or Austrian, or American it might look, incorporated a range of features that had originated in other countries.

There were five great 'schools' of steam locomotive design - the British, the American, the French, the German and the Russian. Some experts would add to the number, citing the unique features of locomotives built in Austria between the 1880s and the 1920s, or the often-distinctive locomotives of Belgium. But the first five were by far the most influential, dominating engine design in many other countries, and all building

**Right: It may look primitive (here in replica form), but in 1829 Stephenson's *Rocket* represented a considerable advance in refinement and structure over previous locomotives.**

**Above: One of Britain's last steam locomotive types, a 'standard' 2-6-4T No. 80002, on the Keighley and Worth Valley Railway, on 12 October 1996.**

new types right up to the 1950s (or nearly so in the case of the USA). Russian influence was strong in China, the last large-scale builder and user of steam. Many countries like Spain, Australia, Czechoslovakia, South Africa and Japan borrowed aspects of design from two or more of these traditions, while adding details of their own in response to local needs or designers' tastes and ideas.

The total number of steam locomotives built is impossible to calculate. Including the many built for industrial and agricultural use on narrow-gauge tracks, it is probably in excess of 300,000. Today, the era of steam traction is over in every part of the world. But affection for the "iron horse" has ensured that in most countries, some are preserved by transport museums, tourist 'heritage' railways, and specialist societies. Though some of the finest steam locomotives are now just a memory that can be re-created only within the pages of this book, many others survive and are still able to arouse excitement and admiration in the era of the Space Shuttle.

*Note on Steam Locomotive specifications*:
The specification panels give, in metric and imperial measurements, the key dimensions of each locomotive type. In some cases, full information is not available. Details normally refer to the original engines of the class; especially in large classes, later modifications were frequent. The 'tractive effort' figures give an indication of relative pulling power. Based on the Gillot formula linking driving wheel diameter, cylinder measurement, and working boiler pressure, they are often referred to as 'nominal tractive effort' figures. A measurement of the energy exerted at the point where driving wheel meets rail, they give little guide to the actual performance of a locomotive. For example, if the wheel slips and spins, the tractive effort at that moment is zero. In the case of compound-and multi-cylinder locomotives, there is a more complex formula. In some cases, the builder's figure is given. The data listed include boiler pressure, cylinder diameter and stroke, diameter of driving wheels, grate area, evaporative heating surface of boiler, superheating surface (where fitted), tractive effort and total weight of engine plus tender. In one or two cases, estimated boiler pressure is given, and marked with an asterisk (*).

## *Locomotion No.1* 0-4-0 STOCKTON & DARLINGTON RAILWAY (S&D) GREAT BRITAIN: 1825

**Boiler pressure:** 3.5kg/cm² (50psi)
**Cylinders:** 241x609mm (9 ½ x24in)
**Driving wheels:** 1220mm (48in)
**Grate area:** 0.74m² (8sq ft)
**Heating surface:** 5.6m² (60sq ft)
**Tractive effort:** 861kg (1900lb)
**Total weight:** 6.9t (15,232lb)

The world's first public railway opened with a single locomotive, *Locomotion* No 1, on 27 September 1825. Built by Robert Stephenson & Co, of Newcastle upon Tyne, it was based on the colliery locomotives developed by the Stephenson family, and ran on their gauge of 1435mm (56 ½ in), which would eventually become the international 'standard'. The original boiler was a single flue, of wrought iron, continued into a tall chimney. It had two cylinders, centrally mounted, which drove the wheels by means of crossheads and connecting-rods. Their vertical placing was taken from stationary steam engines. The frame was of cast iron. No attempt was made to provide a cab or even a foot-plate. A four-wheel tender was provided, wooden-sided, with a sheet-iron water tank. The first boiler exploded in January 1828, after which the engine was substantially rebuilt by Timothy Hackworth, the S&D resident engineer. Later a third boiler was fitted. The speed of technical developments very soon made *Locomotion* obsolescent, but it worked regular services until 1841, and in deference to its primacy, was used to head ceremonial processions at the opening of new lines by the company. In the later 1840s, it was used as a pumping engine, and in 1857 was placed on a pedestal at North Road Station, Darlington. It was later moved to Bank Top station and since 1975 it has been in the Darlington Railway Museum. A replica of *Locomotion* participated in the 150th anniversary celebrations of the S&D in 1975, re-enacting the performance of the original.

***Locomotion* at Bank Top. Contemporary records show it took between 9 and 11 hours to pull 53-ton (58-ton) trains of coal on the 64km (40-mile) run from Darlington to Stockton.**

## *Royal George* 0-6-0 STOCKTON & DARLINGTON RAILWAY (S&D) GREAT BRITAIN: 1827

The 0-6-0 was to be the standard British freight locomotive type for many years, and this was the first to be built. Designed by Timothy Hackworth and built at the S&D Shildon works, it benefited from his two years of hard experience in running the motive power of the world's first public railway. He was less an innovator – though he would enter a locomotive, *Sans Pareil,* for the Rainhill trials of 1829 – than a meticulous practical engineer, concerned with providing enough steam, and getting effective traction on the rail. The first concern led him to more than double the heating surface of the 'Locomotion' type; the second to provide six coupled wheels, joined by connecting rods. In other respects, the engine retained many early features, including vertically-mounted cylinders, which drove directly on to the rear coupled wheels. The boiler, 3959mm (13ft) long and 1320mm (4ft 4in) in diameter, contained a single U-shaped return flue, as Trevithick had used in his engines. This was the first locomotive with a reduced opening to the blast pipe, a crucial feature in improving the draught. Engineers were already concerned about the cooling effects of cold water admitted to the boiler, and Robert Stephenson had devised a system of transferring some exhaust steam to heat a cistern containing the feed water; Hackworth adapted this for *Royal George.* Though the 0-6-0 engine would undergo many changes before its final design emerged, and Stephenson's 0-6-0 of 1834 would be the basic model, this engine gave an early example of reliability and sturdiness in the business of hauling slow goods trains. Engines of this wheel-arrangement continued to be the staple of goods haulage in Britain, France, Spain, India and many other countries through the nineteenth century; and many would still be at work half-way through the twentieth century.

**A drawing of *Royal George*. There is no frame: the boiler itself is still the main structural member. The bell with its rope is a piece of artistic licence: this was not a regular feature of British locomotives at any time.**

**Boiler pressure:** 3.65kg/cm² (52psi)
**Cylinders:** 279x507mm (11x20in)
**Driving wheels:** 1218mm (48in)
**Grate area:** not known
**Heating surface:** 13m² (141sq ft)
**Tractive effort:** 997kg (2200lb)
**Total weight:** not known

## SÉGUIN LOCOMOTIVE 0-4-0 — FRANCE: 1828

In 1827, the French scientist-engineer Marc Séguin built and patented a multi-tubular boiler, and he used it in a locomotive the next year. It had return flues, running to the end of the drum, then bending back to return to the firebox end, so that fire and chimney were at the same end. The firebox was beneath the boiler, not integral with the structure. Vertical cylinders drove the coupled wheels. The tender was pushed by the engine; one feature was the large bellows, driven from one of the tender axles and providing a forced draught to drew heat through the boiler tubes. The boiler itself was effective, producing 1500kg (3307lb) of steam per hour, compared to the 500kg (1100lb) achieved by previous boilers.

Specification: no details known

## *ROCKET* 0-2-2 LIVERPOOL & MANCHESTER RAILWAY (L&M) — GREAT BRITAIN: 1829

Robert Stephenson built this engine to conform with the terms of the trials organized at Rainhill in October 1829 to select the locomotive type for this new railway: to cost less than £550, to consume its own smoke, to weigh no more than 6 tons (6.6t), to draw a 20.3-ton (22-t) load at 16kph (10 mph), and to have a boiler pressure of not more than 3.5kg/cm$^2$ (50 psi). *Rocket* was the only contender to satisfy the conditions, and its triumph had a profound influence on British locomotive development. Already it incorporated great advances made in the five years since *Locomotion*. The chimney rose from a smoke box and was fitted with a blast pipe (perhaps a Timothy Hackworth borrowing fitted on the day before the trials), and the boiler itself was fitted with tubes – a simultaneous and parallel invention to that of the French engineer Marc Séguin (though it has been noted that Séguin visited Stephenson's factory in 1828). The cylinders were set beneath and behind the boiler, at an angle of 35°, and drove the rear wheels via connecting rods. The firebox was made of copper and the wheels were fitted with springs. The four-wheel wooden-framed tender was the first vehicle to have outside bearings. *Rocket* too was soon superseded; but its great contribution was to show that the steam locomotive could give consistent performance. The S&D sold the engine for £300 in 1837, and in much-altered form it can still be seen in the Science Museum of London.

**A modern replica of the *Rocket,* painted in the yellow livery worn at the Rainhill trials of 1829, and seen here on a visit to the heritage 'Bluebell' line in Kent, southeast England.**

**The replica *Rocket*, seen at an Open Day at the Doncaster Locomotive Works, June 1984. The tall chimney was intended to increase the draught; on later engines, much of it would be concealed within the smoke-box.**

**Boiler pressure:** 3.5kg/cm$^2$ (50psi)
**Cylinders:** 203x432mm (8x17in)
**Driving wheels:** 1435mm (56 ½in)
**Grate area:** 0.74kg/cm$^2$ (8sq ft)
**Heating surface:** 10.9m$^2$ (117.75sq ft)
**Tractive effort:** 1089kg (2405lb)
**Total weight:** 4.32t (9520lb)

## *PLANET* CLASS 2-2-0 LIVERPOOL & MANCHESTER RAILWAY (L&M) — GREAT BRITAIN: 1830

Robert Stephenson's *Planet* was the first locomotive which could be said to form a class. Up to then, engines had been one-offs, each incorporating improvements or experiments, as the designers and builders struggled with the business of making mobile steam power effective. By late 1830, with the construction of *Planet*, things settled down somewhat, and a whole series of locomotives was built in very much the same manner, some of them 0-4-0s, but the majority being 2-2-0. In particular, *Planet* confirmed what was to be the British style. The cylinders were now horizontal, set within the frames, and, unlike all previous engines, placed at the front. The aim was practical, to get better stability of running through better distribution of weight, though the 'invisible drive' stylistic effect also pleased the British engineers. Not all followed this policy: in 1834 George Forrester of Liverpool built the first engines with horizontal outside cylinders. These were 2-2-0 types for Ireland's first railway, the Dublin & Kingstown, but in general, inside cylinders would remain a hallmark of British locomotive design, despite their inconvenience of access and the

**A replica version of *Planet* with a replica train of contemporary open passenger vehicles. The distant warning signal on the left is set at danger for trains coming in the opposite direction.**

need to provide expensive crank axles. The outside 'sandwich' frame, of ash or oak planking, reinforced by iron plates on both sides, and with outside bearings, was another typical feature, and for the first time, the boiler was attached to the frame, rather than itself forming the main structural member. One of the main reasons for the outside frame was to provide support in the event – all too frequent – of the crank axle breaking. This axle was also protected by inside bearings. A small railed footplate was provided, but British designers saw no need to go to the expense of providing a cab to shelter the enginemen.

Although the 'Planets' established the basics, this was far from the end of experimentation and improvement. In 1831, Stephenson built two 0-4-0 'Planets' as heavy goods engines for the Liverpool & Manchester Railway, with coupled wheels of equal diameter. At 10.1t (11 tons), they were heavier than the passenger engines, and their names, *Samson* and *Goliath,* indicate how they were viewed at the time. Many others followed. Two of these were fitted with piston valves in 1832, the first examples of what would later become universal, but slide valves, less complicated in practice if less efficient in theory, remained standard for another six decades. Railway works were still little more than large blacksmith's shops, and men like Hackworth had to devise machine tools and work systems to cope with the steadily increasing workload of maintenance and repair on a growing fleet of locomotives. The fuel burned by these, as with all early British locomotives, was coke, the chief aim being to make the engines emit as little smoke as possible. A supply of coke was available as a by-product of gas manufacture, but all railway companies found it necessary to establish their own coking plants, and the tall chimneys of these rose beside the principal locomotive depots.

The 'Planet' design was elaborated into Stephenson's 'Patentee' class of 1833, on a 2-2-2 wheelbase, with trailing wheels set behind the firebox, which allowed for a somewhat longer boiler, reduced the axle-load on the driving axle, and gave the engine a more stable ride. This aspect was important, as the engines had rigid frames, with fixed wheels, and the four-wheelers especially were prone to pitch up and down and generally make life on the footplate highly uncomfortable. There was little understanding as yet of the problem of balancing in steam engines. Heavy cranks going round at high speed caused unsteadiness in lightweight locomotives. By 1837, John Braithwaite, on the Eastern Counties Railway in England, had begun to fit balance weights to the driving wheels to counteract the movement of the cranks. This method was continued and improved by William Fernihough on the same railway and the practice gradually became universal. The 'Patentees' and 'Planets', despite their full-length frames, used them only to support the boiler and the axle bearings. The cylinders were fixed to the boiler, and the tender drawbar was attached to the base of the firebox. In later designs, these would normally be attached to the frame.

One of the most imposing 'Planets' was the Great Western Railway's 2-2-2 *North Star.* Of larger dimensions but similar structure to the earlier ones, it was built by Stephensons in 1837 for the 1675mm (5ft 6in) gauge Virginia Railway in the USA, but was not shipped due to a contractual dispute, and was regauged to the GWR's 2138mm (7ft ¼in). It pulled the first train out of Paddington Station, London on 4 June 1838 and ran in service for 33 years, but was then stored and finally scrapped in 1906. By the late 1830s, the expanding railway system was creating great demand for new engines, not only in Britain but also in Europe. As well as being used on a number of British lines, locomotives of 'Planet' or 'Patentee' type were exported and became the basis of early locomotive design in the Low Countries, the German States, Russia, and the Italian States, among other countries. They were also influential in the USA. Stephenson's factory could not

**Notions of what constituted good style in the 1830s, as well as the urge to make railways visually acceptable, were responsible for such things as locomotive chimneys designed to resemble fluted classical columns.**

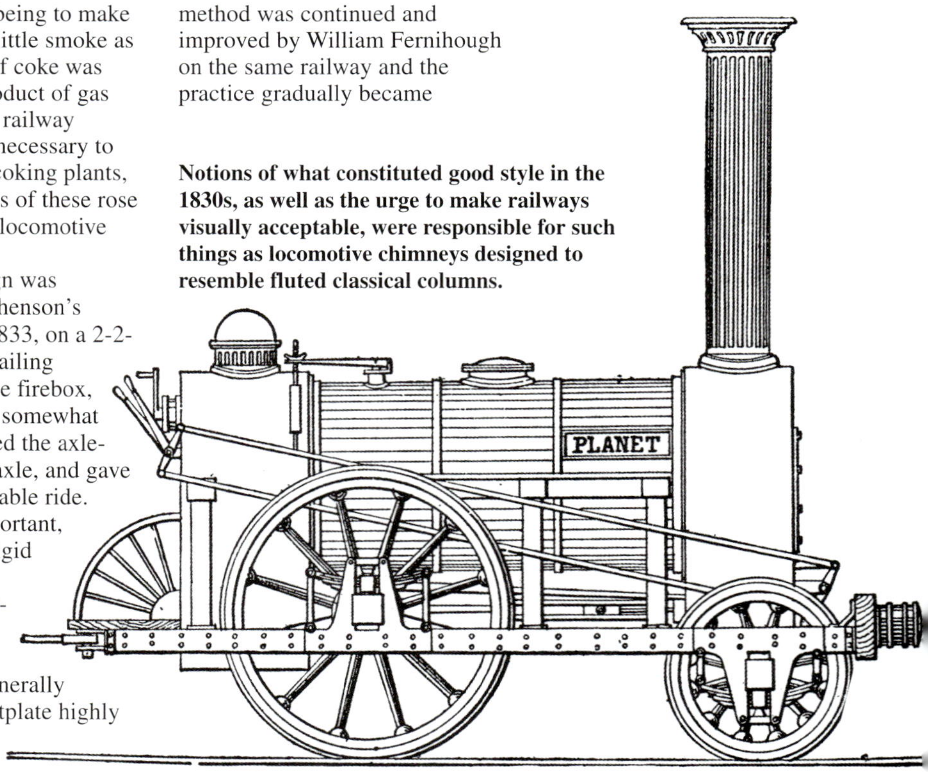

keep up with demand and others were licensed to produce locomotives to Stephenson design. Since every new railway had to set up its own workshops for maintenance and repair, local variants very soon began to appear.

In the early decades of railways, enginemen's cabs were usually notable by their absence. Drivers and their stoker assistants were considered the equivalent of coach drivers, who had no shelter, though more chance of wearing several layers of waterproof clothing. The trains hauled by the 'Planets' and other locomotives of the second railway decade were still made up of lightweight vehicles. Coaches and wagons were four-wheelers, joined at first by rigid hook or screw links, though chain links and buffers began to appear by 1830. Spring-loaded buffers were fitted to first-class carriages on the Liverpool & Manchester Railway from 1834. Brakes were rudimentary, fitted only to the locomotive's tender wheels and to those of the brake van. Originally based on the horse-drawn precedents of coach and cart, railway vehicles soon became longer and heavier, and carriage- and wagon-building became an important adjunct to the other aspects of railway management. The building of specialized vehicles like mail vans, tank wagons and cattle cars began quite early. In 1836, the Cumberland Valley Railroad in the USA was using 'bunk cars' on night-time journeys, an example followed in England in 1838 by 'bed carriages' on the London & North Western Railway. Refreshments were not available on board, and trains stopped for this purpose at stations where the railway company had franchised the catering. Trains also had no toilets, and the rush to the food and drinks counter was followed by the rush to the washrooms. Train heating was non-existent, and lighting, from the later 1830s, consisted of dim oil lamps placed from above into holes in the carriage roof.

**The replica *Planet*, photographed in front of 19th-century buildings at the Manchester Museum of Science and Technology, in 1994.**

Specifications are for the 'Planet' type.

**Boiler pressure:** 3.5kg/cm² (50psi)
**Cylinders:** 279x406mm (11x16in)
**Driving wheels:** 1525mm (60in)
**Grate area:** 0.74m² (8sq ft)
**Heating surface:** 46.8m² (504sq ft)
**Tractive effort:** 622kg (1371lb)
**Total weight:** 8.1t (17,920lb)

## *BEST FRIEND* OF CHARLESTON 0-4-0T CHARLESTON & HAMBURG RAILROAD USA: 1830

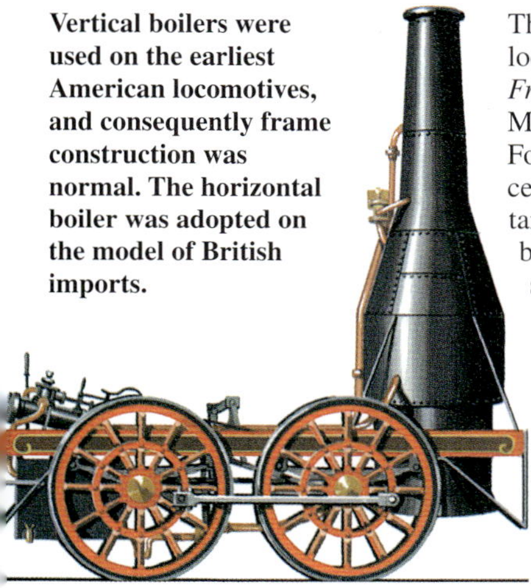

**Vertical boilers were used on the earliest American locomotives, and consequently frame construction was normal. The horizontal boiler was adopted on the model of British imports.**

The first home-produced steam locomotive in the USA, *Best Friend* was designed by E.L. Miller and built at the West Point Foundry, NY. It was the predecessor of all tank locos, with a well tank fitted inside the frame. The boiler was vertical, providing steam for two front-set cylinders driving the coupled wheels. *Best Friend* was recorded as hauling a five-car passenger train at 32kph (20mph). Public service on the line began in January 1831, the first American railroad to work a regular steam-powered schedule. On June 17, the boiler exploded and it was rebuilt as *Phoenix*.

**This working replica of *Best Friend* of Charleston was built in 1928 and incorporates certain twentieth century refinements, like a padded seat for the driver.**

**Boiler pressure:** 3.5kg/cm² (50psi)
**Cylinders:** 152x406mm (6x16in)
**Driving wheels:** 1371mm (54in)
**Heating surface:** not known
**Grate area:** 0.2m² (2.2sq ft)
**Tractive effort:** 206kg (452lb)
**Total weight:** 4t (8820lb)

## *JOHN BULL* 0-4-0 CAMDEN & AMBOY RAILROAD USA: 1831

The first locomotives to run in North America, imported from England by the Delaware & Hudson Canal Co. in 1829, were relatively primitive colliery types similar to *Locomotion No. 1*. From 1831, the new railway companies were able to benefit from the many improvements brought about in Britain. Nevertheless, the British models were often found unsatisfactory for American conditions. The consequent adaptations, and the rapid rise in demand, generated a home-grown locomotive-building industry which by the end of the 1840s was producing around 400 units a year, to distinctively American designs. *John Bull* was shipped in parts from Robert Stephenson & Co. to the Camden & Amboy, and assembled at Bordentown, NJ. Its cost was almost $4000. On 12 November 1831, it pulled a demonstration train for members of the New Jersey legislature, and went into regular service on partial completion of the line in September 1833, along with three other Stephenson types which had been built at Hoboken. *John Bull* was a four-wheel, inside-cylinder engine, of the 'Planet' goods class,

**This photograph of a replica *John Bull*, with the added pilot in position, shows clearly how American engineers could think of the front bogie as 'rolling out the road', and guiding the locomotive into a curve.**

built to the 1472mm (4ft 10in) gauge. It had not long been running before modifications were made. By 1832, a leading truck and pilot had been fitted, and later it was equipped with headlight, cab, bell and whistle. By the late 1840s, it was being used only on lightweight passenger trains, and in 1849 it was jacked up for use as a boiler-testing plant for new engines. By the 1850s, it was already regarded as an antique, and though most old engines went for scrap or drastic rebuild, *John Bull* survived, and in 1876 was shown as "America's first locomotive" at the Centennial Exhibition in Philadelphia. It was partially restored at this time. In 1885 the Pennsylvania Railroad, which had absorbed the C&A in 1871, presented the engine to the Smithsonian Museum. It made a run from New York to Chicago in April 1893. Since 1940, it has been a static exhibit. The tender is not the original, which was a four-wheeler adapted from a C&A car, but dates from the mid-nineteenth century. Built as an 8-wheeler, it was changed to its present 4-wheel form in order to better represent the original. But there is little left that is truly original about *John Bull,* except the boiler.

**Boiler pressure:** 3.5kg/cm$^2$ (50psi)
**Cylinders:** 228x508mm (9x20in)
**Driving wheels:** 1294mm (54in)
**Grate area:** 0.93cm$^2$ (10.07sq ft)
**Heating surface:** 27.5cm$^2$ (296.5sq ft)
**Tractive effort:** 575kg (1270lb)
**Total weight:** 10t (22,045lb)

## *DE WITT CLINTON* 0-4-0 MOHAWK & HUDSON RAILROAD — USA: 1831

The demands of US operation soon left the 0-4-0 type behind. This loco, designed by John B. Jervis, was not a great success, but incorporated three features unseen before. One was a protective roof for the crew, an early form of the cab; another was an integral tank built into the tender; the third was all-iron wheels – previous locos had had wooden wheel-centres. An early image of *De Witt Clinton* shows it hauling a set of cars closely modelled on the stage-coaches of the time. The dimensions are not known.

The *De Witt Clinton* was said to be capable of hauling five passenger carriages at a speed of 48kph (30mph) on level track. It weighed four tons in working order, and had a boiler pressure of 3.5kg/cm$^2$ (50psi).

**One of the first American-built locomotives with a horizontally set boiler, this was the shape of things to come, though it had inside cylinders on the British model, of dimensions 139x406mm (5.5x16in), driving crank axles.**

## *EXPERIMENT* 4-2-0 MOHAWK & HUDSON RAILROAD — USA: 1832

***Experiment,* showing Jervis's pioneering pivoted bogie. It must have been an uncomfortable locomotive to drive and fire, with the high footplate needed to clear the crank axle.**

Another John Jervis design, built by the West Point Foundry, this engine was the first to incorporate a leading truck, or bogie. The truck had an outside frame and bearings, with suspended springs. The 4-2-0 wheel arrangement was the first distinctively American type, and flourished between 1835 and 1842. In the USA, tracks were often lightly laid and twisting, and the swivelling truck kept engines on the road where a rigid wheel arrangement might have derailed. Nobly, Jervis did not patent this contribution to locomotive design. *Experiment* had other unusual features, including driving wheels in rear of the firebox. Among the fittings was 'a good and convenient hand force pump, with copper pipes to connect with the water tank on the tender waggon' – effective injection of feed water into the boiler was an as-yet unsolved problem of locomotive design. The engine had two inside cylinders and link motion modelled on a Stephenson 0-4-0. The outside frame was of seasoned white oak, strengthened with iron braces, and supporting outside bearings for the driving wheels. Originally built as an anthracite burner, poor steaming led to rebuilding of the firebox for wood-burning in 1833. Despite this, it was claimed that *Experiment* ran at 100kph (62mph) in 1832. Later renamed *Brother Jonathan*, the locomotive was rebuilt in 1846 as a 4-4-0.

**Boiler pressure:** 3.5kg/cm$^2$ (50psi)
**Cylinders:** 228x406mm (9x16in)
**Driving wheels:** 1524mm (60in)
**Grate area:** not known
**Heating surface:** not known
**Tractive effort:** 453kg (1000lb)
**Total weight:** 6.4t (14,175lb)

## *LANCASTER* 4-2-0 PHILADELPHIA & COLUMBIA RAILROAD USA: 1834

Matthias W. Baldwin (1795–1866), the son of a carriage builder, was a mechanic who turned locomotive builder in 1832. This was his third engine, one of five built that year in his Philadelphia works, based on Jervis's *Experiment* and sold to the Commonwealth of Pennsylvania for $5500, including the tender. It was a successful design and until 1842 Baldwin built only 4-2-0s, establishing a reputation for sticking to tried-and-true design. A notable feature was the half-crank axle, with the rods driving the wheels directly; but Baldwin dropped this from around 1840. *Lancaster* did not have a cab, and was wooden-framed without iron cladding. It did heavy duty until 1850, and was scrapped in 1851.

**Boiler pressure:** 8.4kg/cm² (120psi)
**Cylinders:** 228x406mm (9x16in)
**Driving wheels:** 1370mm (54in)
**Grate area:** not known
**Heating surface:** not known
**Tractive effort:** 1110kg (2448lb)
**Total weight:** 7.7t (16,975lb)

## *ADLER* 2-2-2 NÜREMBERG–FÜRTH RAILWAY BAVARIA (GERMANY): 1835

***Adler* was fitted with primitive buffers at the front end as well as on the tender: a necessity for shunting work, or for pulling when in reverse gear. A tender brake (not shown in the illustration) was also fitted.**

*Adler's* fame is as the first fully operational steam locomotive in Germany. Imported from Robert Stephenson's works in Newcastle, England, it was in most respects a standard 'Patentee' 2-2-2, ordered in a hurry when the plan for a home-built engine collapsed. The line, Germany's first, opened on 7 December 1835 and was accepted as one of, if not the best, passenger engine of the day. Details of *Adler* are somewhat unclear, though like most early Stephenson engines the design was simple, with outside frames throughout and a very tall chimney of small diameter. Two replicas were built in 1935 and 1950 respectively. It ran until 1857, when the wheels and motion were salvaged and the boiler sold for scrap. Although other Stephenson engines were supplied, as well as US engines, the German locomotive-building industry was well-established by the time of *Adler's* demise. One of the *Adler* replicas can be seen at the museum in Nüremberg, original terminus of the Nüremberg-Fürth line.

**Boiler pressure:** 4.2kg/cm² (60psi)
**Cylinders:** 229x406mm (9x6in)
**Driving wheels:** 1371mm (54in)
**Grate area:** 0.48m² (5.2sq ft)
**Heating surface:** 18.2m² (196sq ft)
**Tractive effort:** 550kg (1220lb)
**Total weight:** 11.4t (25,245lb)

## *DORCHESTER* 0-4-0 CHAMPLAIN & ST LAWRENCE RAILROAD CANADA: 1836

The Champlain & St Lawrence, opened on 21 July, 1836, was Canada's first railway. *Dorchester*, which pulled the first train, was a lightweight version of the Stephenson 'Samson' type, first built for the Liverpool & Manchester Railway in England in 1831. It was basically a 'Planet' with wheels of equal size joined by coupling rods, and intended to provide greater traction for the hauling of goods trains. Like the 'Planets', it had outside sandwich-type frames that held the main bearings, and the cylinders and motion were all inside. Railroad development was quite rapid in south-eastern Canada, linking inland towns to the St Lawrence harbours.

**Boiler pressure:** 3.5kg/cm² (50psi)
**Cylinders:** 228x355mm (9x14in)
**Driving wheels:** 1370mm (54in)
**Grate area:** 0.74m² (8sq ft)
**Heating surface:** not known
**Tractive effort:** 413kg (910lb)
**Total weight:** 5.7t (12,560lb)

## BURY LOCOMOTIVE 2-2-0 LONDON & BIRMINGHAM RAILWAY (L&B) GREAT BRITAIN: 1837

By 1837, railways in England had grown from links between towns into a national network. The first trunk route from the capital was the London & Birmingham, which opened in 1838. The contract for engines was placed with Edward Bury in 1837. He was an original designer, and his iron bar-frames (as distinct from plate-frames) reduced weight and became a standard in the USA, to which he exported a number of locos in the 1830s. His standard engine for the L&B was a bar-framed 2-2-0, with a circular outer firebox surmounted by a characteristic small 'haycock' copper dome, and was under-powered from the start. Four or more were needed on the heavier trains. Bury held on to the contract until 1847, by which time the traffic demands were beyond his engines. His business survived, however, for the small engines suited many lines. One of his 0-4-0 goods engines, built by Fairbairn & Sons for the Furness Railway in 1861 and affectionately known as *Coppernob*, has been preserved.

**Boiler pressure:** 3.5kg/cm² (50psi)
**Cylinders:** 280x415mm (11x16.5in)
**Driving wheels:** 1546mm (60.75in)
**Grate area:** 0.65 m² (7sq ft)
**Heating surface:** 33.2 m² (357sq ft)
**Tractive effort:** 629kg (1386lb)
**Total weight:** 10t (22,045lb)

**The small-but-cheaper engine philosophy maintained by Bury suited many buyers well at a time when most railways were only a few miles in length.**

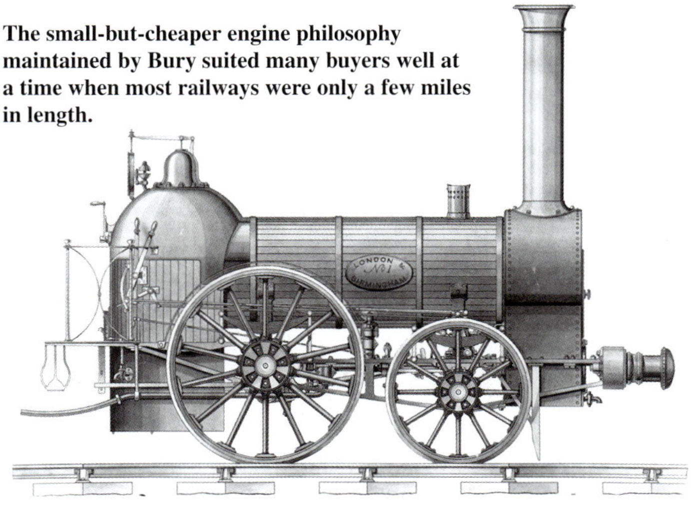

## NORRIS LOCOMOTIVE 4-2-0 BALTIMORE & OHIO RAILROAD (B&O) USA: 1837

**The Baltimore & Ohio's Mt Clare works built this replica of Norris's *Lafayette,* B&O No. 13, in 1927. The original was built in 1837. Note the bar linking the rear-wheel tender brakes.**

Baldwin's main rival in Philadelphia was William Norris, who set up as a locomotive builder in 1831. In 1837 he was the first US manufacturer to export to Europe (Austria). In the previous year, he had built a 4-2-0 with outside cylinders, *The Washington Country Farmer*, for the Philadelphia & Columbia; and eight on similar lines were ordered by the B&O. They represented a combination of British and American ideas, with Bury bar-frames and circular fireboxes, a front bogie with inside bearings, and outside cylinders. The Norris engines performed well on the B&O gradients. The longer, larger boiler saved them from the lack of power experienced by Bury's 2-2-0s in England. Their reputation as hill climbers was such that 15 were ordered by the Birmingham & Gloucester Railway in England, to work on its 1 in 37 Lickey incline.

**Boiler pressure:** 4.2kg/cm$^2$ (60psi)
**Cylinders:** 266x457mm (10.5x18in)
**Driving wheels:** 1220mm (48in)
**Grate area:** 0.8m$^2$ (8.6sq ft)
**Heating surface:** 36.6m$^2$ (394sq ft)
**Tractive effort:** 957kg (2162lb)
**Total weight:** 20t (44,090lb)

**The Norris locomotive had an impressive chimney but dispensed with a dome, and had a steam regulator inside the boiler.**

## 4-4-0 PHILADELPHIA, GERMANSTOWN & NORRISTOWN RAILROAD (PG&NRR) USA: 1837

Effective as it was, the American 4-2-0, with its single drivers, soon came to be considered as lacking tractive power, especially on freight trains. The natural remedy was to add another set of driving wheels, thus increasing the adhesive weight of the locomotive. This was first done by Henry R. Campbell, engineer of the Philadelphia, Germanstown & Norris Railroad. Cannier than Jervis, he patented his design for a 4-4-0 in 1836 and the first was built by James Brook of Philadelphia. Later it became known as the 'American Type' and was the most popular wheel arrangement in the USA and Britain in the nineteenth century. Campbell's engine was the biggest of its time and it was estimated that it could pull a 450-ton (457t) train at 15mph (24kph) on level track – a gain in tractive effort of over 60% on the standard Baldwin 4-2-0. The original engine was prone to derail, not because of its wheelbase but because of too-rigid suspension, something that was remedied in later engines of the type. In the 1850s, Campbell – essentially a civil engineer – would become an ardent advocate of the covered cab, but his 4-4-0 as first built did not have one: this may have been because lines that bought the basic engine liked to have the option of building their own cabs (at that time of wood).

Campbell was almost pipped to the post by two other Philadelphians, Andrew Eastwick and Joseph Harrison, who brought out a 4-4-0 for the Beaver Meadow Railroad in the same year (Campbell threatened to sue them for infringement of his patent). Their engine, *Hercules*, had the coupled wheels fitted to a truck frame in a partly successful attempt at equalizing the axles and thus enabling the wheels to ride dips and humps in the track. Harrison's patent equalizing lever of 1838 – a major step towards large locomotive design – solved the problem. The driving axles were connected by leaf springs and connecting levers, all attached to the main frame, spreading the effects of road shocks among the axles and ensuring that all wheels kept in contact with the rails. (As often happened in the early days, the English engineer Timothy Hackworth had devised a very similar leaf-spring equalizer on the locomotive *Royal George* in 1827). The railways were slow to take up the 4-4-0, however, and it was only after 1840 that production went up rapidly. From 1845, however, even the conservative Baldwin had to accept that it had superseded the 4-2-0.

**Boiler pressure:** 6kg/cm$^2$ (90psi)
**Cylinders:** 355x406mm (14x16in)
**Driving wheels:** 1370mm (54in)
**Grate area:** 1.1m$^2$ (12sq ft)
**Heating surface:** 67m$^2$ (723sq ft)
**Tractive effort:** 1995kg (4400lb)
**Total weight:** 12.2t (26,880lb)

## *Lion* 0-4-2 LIVERPOOL & MANCHESTER RAILWAY (L&M) GREAT BRITAIN: 1838

The L&M had its own works at Edgehill, Liverpool, but this, the oldest working locomotive in the world, was the first engine built by Todd, Kitson & Laird of Leeds. The 0-4-2 wheel arrangement did not become common, though it was used on some later British types. Now much-restored, the engine is typical of the epoch: the wood-lined boiler barrel, the tall 'haycock' shaped copper firebox, and the wheels set within the dual support of 'sandwich' frames.

***Lion* on the former LNWR Rugby-Warwick line in central England. Its spruce condition belies the many years spent as a stationary pumping engine in the Liverpool Docks. *Lion* is preserved at Liverpool.**

**Boiler pressure:** 3.5kg/cm$^2$ (50psi)
**Cylinders:** 304.5x457mm (12x18in)
**Driving wheels:** 1523mm (60in)
**Grate area:** not known
**Heating surface:** not known
**Tractive effort:** 888kg (1800lb)
**Total weight:** 29.8t (65,880lb)

## 2-2-2 NORTHERN RAILWAY (NORD) FRANCE: 1839

This modest machine was the first locomotive type built by André Koechlin at what would later become the great works of the *Société Alsacienne de Constructions Mécaniques*, with its headquarters at Mulhouse in Alsace. Twenty-three of these engines were built and sold to a variety of railway companies between 1839 and 1842, including three that went to the *Nord*. Stephenson's design influence was strong, as reflected by the inside cylinders and outside frames. Although several companies used single-wheelers up to the 1850s, and beyond in some cases, it never caught on to became a standard type in France as it did in Great Britain.

**Boiler pressure:** 6kg/cm$^2$ (85psi)
**Cylinders:** 330x462mm (13x18.2in)
**Driving wheels:** 1370.5mm (54in)
**Grate area:** 1.1m$^2$ (12sq ft)
**Heating surface:** 5.2m$^2$ (56.2sq ft)
**Tractive effort:** 1866kg (4115lb)
**Total weight:** 15.6t (34,495lb)

## *De Arend* 2-2-2 HOLLAND IRON RAILWAY COMPANY (HISM) NETHERLANDS: 1839

Linking Amsterdam and Haarlem, this was the first Dutch railway, laid at 2000mm (6ft 6in) gauge until 1866, when it was relaid to standard gauge. *De Arend*, 'The Eagle' was its second engine, built by Longridge & Co. of Bedlington, England. Like No. 1, *Snelheid*, 'Speed', it was essentially a Stephenson 'Patentee', of which many were being built for European railways at the time. Although *De Arend* was scrapped in 1857, a full-size working replica was built in 1938 for the centenary of the line. Across Europe, from Holland to Hungary, 'Patentee' type locomotives provided the first generation of locomotives on many of the new railways that spread across the continent.

**Boiler pressure:** 4kg/cm$^2$ (57psi)
**Cylinders:** 356x450mm (14x17.7in)
**Driving wheels:** 1810mm (71in)
**Grate area:** 1.1m$^2$ (11.8sq ft)
**Heating surface:** not known
**Tractive effort:** 1074kg (2367lb)
**Total weight:** 11.6t (25,640lb)

## GOWAN & MARX 4-4-0 PHILADELPHIA & READING RAILROAD (P&RR) USA: 1839

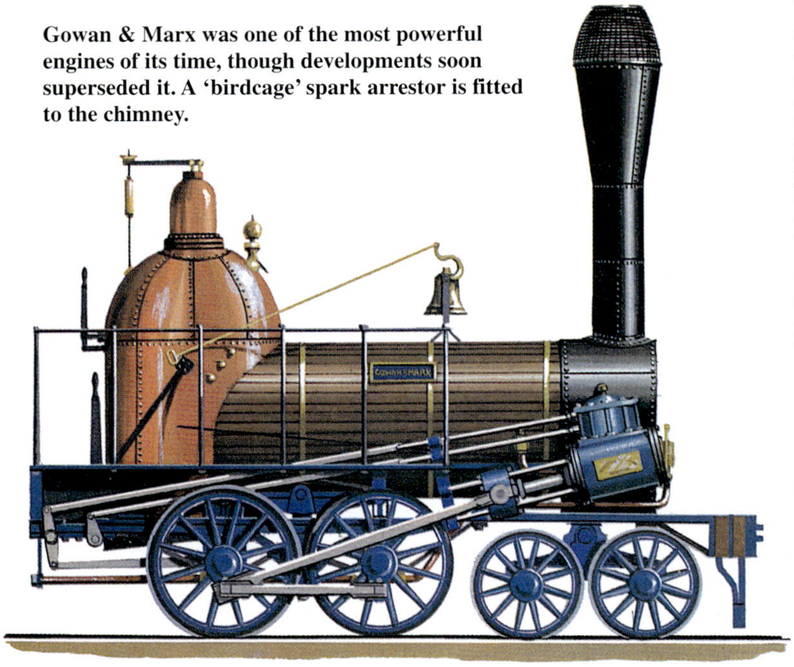


**Gowan & Marx was one of the most powerful engines of its time, though developments soon superseded it. A 'birdcage' spark arrestor is fitted to the chimney.**

The name of this early goods 4-4-0 came from a London banking firm that did business with the P&RR. The builders were Eastwick & Harrison of Philadelphia and the specification was for an engine to haul coal trains at slow speed. It had an equalizing lever linking the coupled axles, and was developed by Eastwick & Harrison in 1838 – a vital contributor to its general effectiveness, letting it ride a rough road without derailing. It had the Bury 'haycock' type of boiler, but with an oblong, not round firebox, giving it a larger grate than other engines, which helped it to develop more power. The boiler pressure is quoted at 5.6–9.1kg/cm$^2$ (80–130psi). Its valve gear, patented by Eastwick in 1835, was cumbersome, requiring movement of the valve ports, rather than of a sliding valve, in order to engage reverse gear, and this was later changed. A 6-ton tender was fitted.

On 5 December, 1839, it pulled the first train between Reading and Philadelphia, and on 20 February 1840 it hauled a 429t (472-ton) train of 101 cars on this line. Even at little more than walking pace, this was a great achievement. With further modifications, it was traded in to Baldwins against a new locomotive in 1859, having run 23,175km (144,000 miles) for the Reading. *Gowan & Marx* caused great interest in Europe, and inspired the invitation to its builders to set up their factory in St Petersburg, Russia.

**Boiler pressure:** 5.6kg/cm$^2$ (80psi)
**Cylinders:** 320x406mm (12.6x16in)
**Driving wheels:** 1066mm (42in)
**Grate area:** 1.1m$^2$ (12sq ft)
**Heating surface:** not known
**Tractive effort:** 2331kg (5140lb)
**Total weight:** 11t (24,250lb)

## *SAINT PIERRE* 2-2-2 PARIS–ROUEN RAILWAY FRANCE: 1843

Built at Rouen, this engine closely reflects the prevailing style at Crewe, England, on the Grand Junction Railway where its builder, William Buddicom had worked; and royalties were paid to Crewe's chief, the Scot Alexander Allan. Forty were built, of which 22 were later converted to well-tank types. It has the typical 'Crewe type' features: double frames, slightly inclined outside cylinders whose curve is incorporated into that of the firebox, and outside bearings on the leading and trailing axles. The reversing gear is a simple three-position gab gear. *Saint Pierre* worked until 1916, was fully restored in 1947, and is the oldest preserved locomotive in France.

**Boiler pressure:** 5kg/cm$^2$ (70psi)
**Cylinders:** 335x535mm (13.2x21in)
**Driving wheels:** 1720mm (68in)
**Grate area:** 0.97m$^2$ (10.5sq ft)
**Heating surface:** 65.8m$^2$ (709sq ft)
**Tractive effort:** 1460kg (3100lb)
**Total weight:** 18t (39,690lb)

**A Buddicom 2-2-2, engine number 3, at Bricklayer Arms depot in London, on loan from the SNCF for the South Bank Exhibition in 1951.**

## *BEUTH* 2-2-2 BERLIN–ANHALT RAILWAY PRUSSIA (GERMANY): 1843

In 1837–8, the American William Norris was making determined efforts to interest European railways in his engines. One of his contacts was a dynamic German industrialist, August Borsig, of Berlin, who brought out his own first engine, based on the Norris 4-2-2, in 1841. By 1843, his works produced their 24th engine, *Beuth*. With bar frames and a tall Norris-style firebox, it also showed strong English influence, notably in its 2-2-2 wheel arrangement and its use of the then new Stephenson's link motion.

The significant developments in locomotive building, like the injector, were picked up quickly by the international industry, while many others remained of purely local interest. Although the general form of the Stephenson link motion had been anticipated by the American William James in 1832, James's version had been forgotten, and it was this 1842 version (named for the company, though designed by William Williams and William Howe, employees of Robert Stephenson) that became used in locomotives all over the world. The first really effective locomotive valve gear, it was deliberately not patented. The 'link' was fixed in a curved slot that joined the ends of two connecting rods fixed to eccentrics on the driving axle, and simply raising or lowering it by means of a lever in the cab set the gear for forwards or backwards motion, and also provided intermediate cut-off positions to allow for steam expansion in the cylinders, though *Beuth* did not take advantage of this facility.

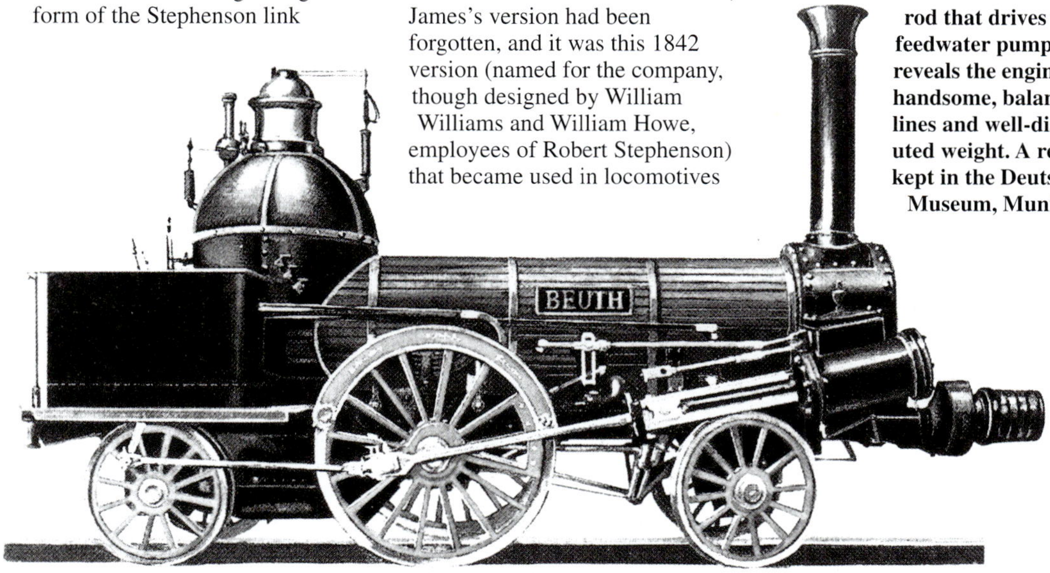


**This drawing of *Beuth* shows the connecting rod that drives the feedwater pump and reveals the engine's handsome, balanced lines and well-distributed weight. A replica is kept in the Deutsches Museum, Munich.**

Boiler pressure: 5.5kg/cm$^2$ (78psi)
Cylinders: 330x560mm (13.1x22.3in)
Driving wheels: 1543mm (60.75in)
Grate area: 0.83m$^2$ (8.9sq ft)
Heating surface: 47m$^2$ (500sq ft)
Tractive effort: 1870kg (4120lb)
Total weight: 18.5t (40,785lb)

## 2-6-0 MOSCOW & ST PETERSBURG RAILWAY — RUSSIA: 1843

The first ever Russian engine was an experimental one produced in 1833. The earliest Russian railways used British locomotives of the Stephenson type, but very soon American influence became increasingly strong. In 1843, the American engineers Eastwick & Harrison set up a factory in St Petersburg, northern Russia, at the invitation of the Tsar. Between then and 1862, they built several hundred engines. One of the first was an outside-cylindered 0-6-0, for goods haulage on the St Petersburg–Moscow line. A two-wheel front truck was soon added, making it the world's first 2-6-0 type. The dimensions are not known.

## *PHILADELPHIA* 0-6-0 PHILADELPHIA & READING RAILROAD (P&RR) — USA: 1844

The Philadelphia & Reading Railroad was a coalfield line, taking coal to the sea at Philadelphia, and its requirement was for reliable load-haulers. The downhill grade from the mining district permitted what were probably the heaviest trains in the world at that time, up to 600 tons (610t) or more. For this work, 0-6-0 engines were considered best. *Philadelphia* was not a wholly new engine in 1844: it was rebuilt from the remains of *Richmond*, which had blown up when still new in the same year. In 1848–9, it was virtually rebuilt again. The original builders were Norris of Philadelphia, for whom it was a standard design. Despite its freight, it was a wood-burner.

**Boiler pressure:** 8.4kg/cm$^2$ (120psi)
**Cylinders:** 365.5x508mm (14.4x20in)
**Driving wheels:** 1812mm (46in)
**Grate area:** 1m$^2$ (11.4sq ft)
**Heating surface:** 78.8m$^2$ (848 sq ft)
**Tractive effort:** 4081kg (9000lb)
**Total weight:** 18.5t (40,785lb)

## CRAMPTON LOCOMOTIVE 4-2-0 LIÈGE & NAMUR RAILWAY — BELGIUM: 1845

Thomas Russell Crampton was a gifted inventor and engineer whose influence was far greater in Belgium and France than in his native England. Trained on the broad-gauge Great Western under Daniel Gooch, his aim was to provide engines of comparable speed and stability on the 'standard' gauge.

One of his methods was to place very large driving wheels just behind the firebox, something not unknown in America. The Liège & Namur, a British-owned company, was the first to order Crampton's patent engine, and two were built by Tulk & Ley of Whitehaven, England.

These, named *Liège* and *Namur*, differed from Crampton's later practice by having domes, carrying the safety-valves, and inside frames. A large transverse spring spanned the footplate, serving the driver axle-boxes. The boiler was mounted very low, in deference to the prevailing view that a locomotive's centre of gravity should be as low as possible. The cylinders, each with a separate regulator, were placed between the front carrying wheels. A very similar engine was built by Tulk & Ley for the Dundee & Perth Railway in Scotland, in 1848. Even for the time, the footplate offered minimal protection, merely having a handrail.

Crampton engines could provide the speed and stability their designer sought, but no more than 25 were used in Britain, while over 300 ran in France, Germany and the Low Countries.

**_Namur_ is shown here. Both dome and boiler are lagged with polished wooden strips. On test in Britain, it was reported to be very fast, and a rough but basically stable rider.**

**Boiler pressure:** 6.3kg/cm$^2$ (90psi)
**Cylinders:** 406x507mm (16x20in)
**Driving wheels:** 2132mm (84in)
**Grate area:** 1.3m$^2$ (14.5sq ft)
**Heating surface:** 91.8m$^2$ (989sq ft)
**Tractive effort:** 2113kg (4660lb)
**Total weight:** not known

## *DERWENT* 0-6-0 STOCKTON & DARLINGTON RAILWAY (S&D) GREAT BRITAIN: 1845

As Crampton's example showed, even in the later 1840s, some constructors had not accepted the Stephensonian model, and built engines in their own way. This was one of a group of engines designed by W. and A. Kitching but still showing the influence of Timothy Hackworth on the Stockton & Darlington Railway. It was a triple unit, of tender, engine and water-cart, with the firebox under the chimney, and the boiler formed as a U-shaped return flue. The cylinders, set at the rear at a steep angle, drove the front coupled wheels, which were also of Hackworth's distinctive perforated pattern. The last of the type came out in 1848. *Derwent* has been preserved, and ran in steam for the Stockton & Darlington Railway centenary of 1925.

Although the Hackworth three-part locomotive seems to anticipate later designs, it was not an articulated unit: the engine, in the middle, pushed its tender and pulled its water cart.

***Derwent*, seen here at Bank Top station, Darlington, has been on exhibit since 1975 in that city's Railway Museum, on loan from the National Railway Museum at York.**

**Boiler pressure:** 5.25kg/cm² (75psi)
**Cylinders:** 362x609mm (14.5x24in)
**Driving wheels:** 1218mm (48in)
**Grate area:** 0.92m² (10sq ft)
**Heating surface:** 127m² (1363sq ft)
**Tractive effort:** 3038kg (6700lb)
**Total weight:** 22.7t (50,065lb)

## '*ODIN*' CLASS 2-2-2 ZEALAND RAILWAY COMPANY DENMARK: 1846

**The 'Sharpies' are believed to have been the first design of Charles Beyer, one of the founders of Beyer Peacock, who had emigrated from Saxony to Britain, and who began work with Sharps.**

Opened on 27 July 1847, Denmark's first railway ran from Copenhagen to Roskilde and was worked by five of these small single-driver engines, known as 'Sharpies' from their builder, Sharps of Manchester, England. With sandwich frames and inside cylinders, they had a very complicated crank axle, which had a total of 8 cranks to work the valve gear, the connecting rods, and two feedwater pumps for the boiler (two were usual in case one should break down). Four were reboilered; *Odin* was scrapped in 1876 and the other pioneers were gone by 1888. The 'Sharpie' design exemplifies the care and artistry that went into so many early locomotives.

**Boiler pressure:** 4.9kg/cm² (70psi)
**Cylinders:** 381x507.6mm (15x20in)
**Driving wheels:** 1523mm (60in)
**Grate area:** 0.99m² (10.7sq ft)
**Heating surface:** 77m² (830sq ft)
**Tractive effort:** 1952kg (4305lb)
**Total weight:** 22.1t (48,800lb)

## *JENNY LIND* 2-2-2 E.B. WILSON, LEEDS GREAT BRITAIN: 1846

The 2-2-2 was a standard British type of the 1840s, but this was an unusual version, as it was not designed by the railway using it. The London & Brighton Railway asked E.B. Wilson, of Leeds, to supply a passenger engine. This was the result, designed by David Joy. John Gray of the Hull & Barnsley Railway had established the design, with inside bearings for the driving wheels, and inside cylinders. Named after a popular Swedish singer (the railways were quick to capitalize on public taste), the high boiler pressure made the engine an excellent performer, and Wilson's went on to build more for home and foreign lines.

**The slots in the wheel-splasher, modelled on ships' paddle-boxes, had a practical function, to cool and ventilate the inside bearings.**

**Boiler pressure:** 8.4kg/cm² (120psi)
**Cylinders:** 381x508mm (15x20in)
**Driving wheels:** 1827mm (72in)
**Grate area:** 1.1m² (12sq ft)
**Heating surface:** 74.3m² (800sq ft)
**Tractive effort:** 2211kg (4876lb)
**Total weight:** 40.3t (88,928lb)

## *ATLAS* 0-8-0 PHILADELPHIA & READING RAILROAD (P&RR) USA: 1846

**Boiler pressure:** not known
**Cylinders:** 393x508mm (15.5x20in)
**Driving wheels:** 1167.5mm (46in)
**Grate area:** not known
**Heating surface:** not known
**Tractive effort:** not known
**Total weight:** 20.3t (44,800lb)

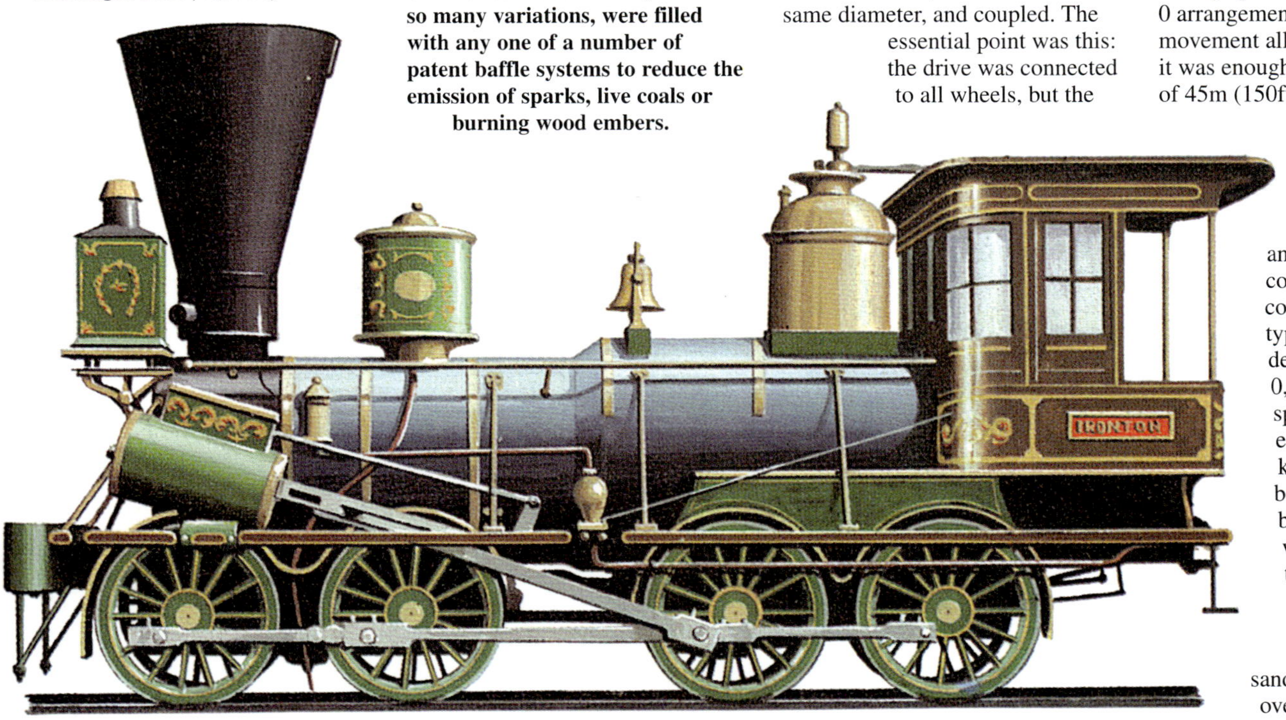


**The wide bell-mouthed chimneys of American locomotives, seen in so many variations, were filled with any one of a number of patent baffle systems to reduce the emission of sparks, live coals or burning wood embers.**

In the 1840s, American locomotive design continued to focus on the problem of reconciling heavier loads with uneven track and sharp curves. Despite his conservative reputation, Matthias Baldwin came up with an approach in 1837 (perhaps as a means of getting around Campbell's patent for the 4-4-0 type). He rebuilt one of his 4-2-0s as 0-6-0, all wheels of the same diameter, and coupled. The essential point was this: the drive was connected to all wheels, but the front truck wheels could move laterally, independently of each other and of the rear drivers, while all axles remained in parallel. This was the 'flexible beam truck', allowing the wheels to be more widely spaced than the normal 0-6-0 arrangement; and though the movement allowable was limited, it was enough to negotiate a curve of 45m (150ft) radius. Baldwin extended the concept to 8-wheel freight engines, with a wide space between the front and back pair of coupled wheels, and continued to build the type until 1866. The development of the 4-6-0, with its superior speed and good tractive effort, effectively killed off the flexible beam truck, which had been effective only with slow-speed trains. These, incidentally, were Balwin's first engines equipped with sandboxes and roofed-over cabs.

## *IRON DUKE* 4-2-2 GREAT WESTERN RAILWAY GREAT BRITAIN: 1847

**Boiler pressure:** 7.05kg/cm² (100psi)
**Cylinders:** 457x609mm (18x24in)
**Driving wheels:** 2440mm (96in)
**Grate area:** 2m² (21.5sq ft)
**Heating surface:** 166.2m² (1790.2sq ft)
**Tractive effort:** 3084kg (6800lb)
**Total weight:** 24.4t (53,760lb)

England, home of the 'standard gauge' of 1435mm (56.5in) was also from 1835 to 1892 the home of a rival, the 2138mm (84.25in) gauge of the GWR. This was not unusual; different gauges were found in other countries too, causing disruption to through traffic. Break of gauge was long a major irritation to travellers between New South Wales and Victoria, in Australia. In Britain, a Royal Commission examined the two gauges in 1845–6 and came down in favour of the 'standard gauge', though the GWR was allowed to continue to use the broad gauge in its own territory. The 'battle of the gauges' stimulated both locomotive design and running, as the exponents of each strove to prove their superiority. GWR 'broad gauge' was among the widest, and its engines consequently had a massive look, even though they did not utilize the full potential of the gauge. After an uncertain start, caused by excessively rigid track and some highly experimental engines, the GWR had become a line by which others were judged. The stability of the engines and the solidity of the permanent way, combined with excellence of locomotive design, made it one of the fastest railways in the world in its main-line expresses. The Locomotive, Carriage & Wagon Superintendent was Daniel Gooch, who had been with the company, as colleague to the great Isambard Kingdom Brunel, from its beginning. He had tested the way in 1846 with a 2-2-2, *Great Western*, of similar working dimensions to the subsequent 'Iron Dukes', which was reputed to have run from London Paddington to Swindon, 124.3km (77.25 miles), in 78 minutes, in June 1846. The only significant alteration was to fit a second set of front carrying wheels to spread the weight.

Twenty-two locomotives of the 'Iron Duke' class were built at the company's new Swindon works in 1847–51. It was a tribute to their quality (as well as to the GWR's later complacency) that when the older engines were scrapped in the 1870s they were replaced by almost identical designs, differing only by having cabs and

**Massive as they seemed at the time, the GWR broad-gauge engines could have been larger if the overhead and lateral constraints had been less. But the cost of line construction would have been much greater.**

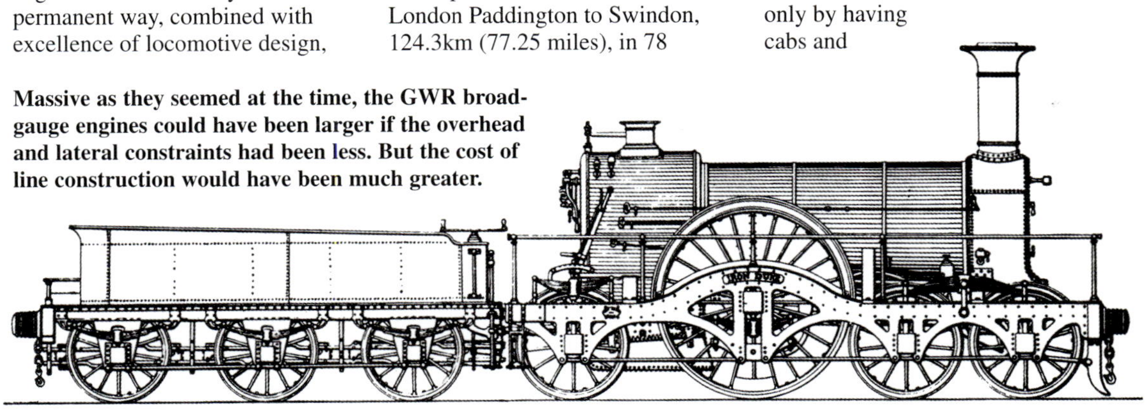

9.8kg/cm² (140psi) pressure – the pressure in the original locos had been increased to 8.4kg/cm² (120psi). They were built with outside sandwich frames and three plate frames inside, running from the back of the two inside cylinders to the front of the firebox. All five held bearings for the driving axle, though the carrying wheels were supported by the outer frames only. The front carrying wheels were on independent axles: the bogie had not yet come into use in England. The boiler was domeless, and steam was taken from a perforated pipe that ran to a regulator box inside the smoke-box. When new, the big driving wheel was flangeless, though replaced later by flanged wheels.

In 1847, these were the uncontestable giants and champions of British railroading. From then until 1880, they ran the country's fastest trains. In 1848, the 9.50 Paddington–Bristol mail train was allowed 56 minutes to travel the 85km (53 miles) from Paddington to Didcot, non-stop; and 29 minutes for the next 39km (24.25 miles) to Swindon. Speeds over 112kph (70mph) must have been common to maintain such a schedule. As in other countries, it was the demands of the mail service that forced up the speeds of the fastest trains. With such speeds, braking may be supposed to have assumed some importance.

However, until the 1870s, British and American engines had no brakes unless the tender was so equipped. Reliance was placed on the guard's brake in his van – passenger trains were still very light-weight in the 1840s. The driver could shut off steam, but otherwise had little control apart from applying the clumsy gab-gear reverser. For a long time, it was believed that driving wheel brakes would force the driving axles out of line and overstress the connecting rods.

**From a very early stage, railways carefully controlled such 'image' matters as typography, colour and logos. They were the first business to invent 'public relations'.**

No engines survive from Britain's broad gauge era. The GWR held on to *Lord of the Isles*, of the 'Iron Duke' class, from its withdrawal in 1884 until 1905, when G.J. Churchward, a great but unsentimental locomotive designer, had it summarily scrapped.

**A twentieth-century replica of *Iron Duke* trundles along a specially laid track in central England. The old 'baulk road' of the Great Western Railway was laid on long wooden blocks beneath the rails.**

## *LIMMAT* 4-2-2 NORTHERN RAILWAY — SWITZERLAND: 1847

The oldest Swiss locomotive was one of two engines built by Emil Kessler in Karlsruhe, Germany. It was to run between Zurich, Switzerland and Baden Baden in Germany, and the line opened on 19 August 1847. *Limmat* shows American influence in its wheel arrangement and high firebox, with a steam collector and safety valve placed on top. The tall chimney was of the bonnet type, with inner spark arrestors as well as a lid. Reboilered in 1866, it ran until 1882. A full-size working replica was built in 1947 for the Swiss railways' centenary, and is kept in the *Verkehrshaus*, Lucerne.

**Boiler pressure:** 5.5kg/cm² (78psi)
**Cylinders:** 340x500mm (14x20in)
**Driving wheels:** 1300mm (51.2in)
**Grate area:** 1.1m² (11.8sq ft)
**Heating surface:** 63.1m² (679.4sq ft)
**Tractive effort:** 2302kg (5076lb)
**Total weight:** 30t (66,150lb)

**The carrying wheels of *Limmat* help to support a longer boiler. They are fixed to the frame; the pivoted bogie had not yet been adopted in Europe.**

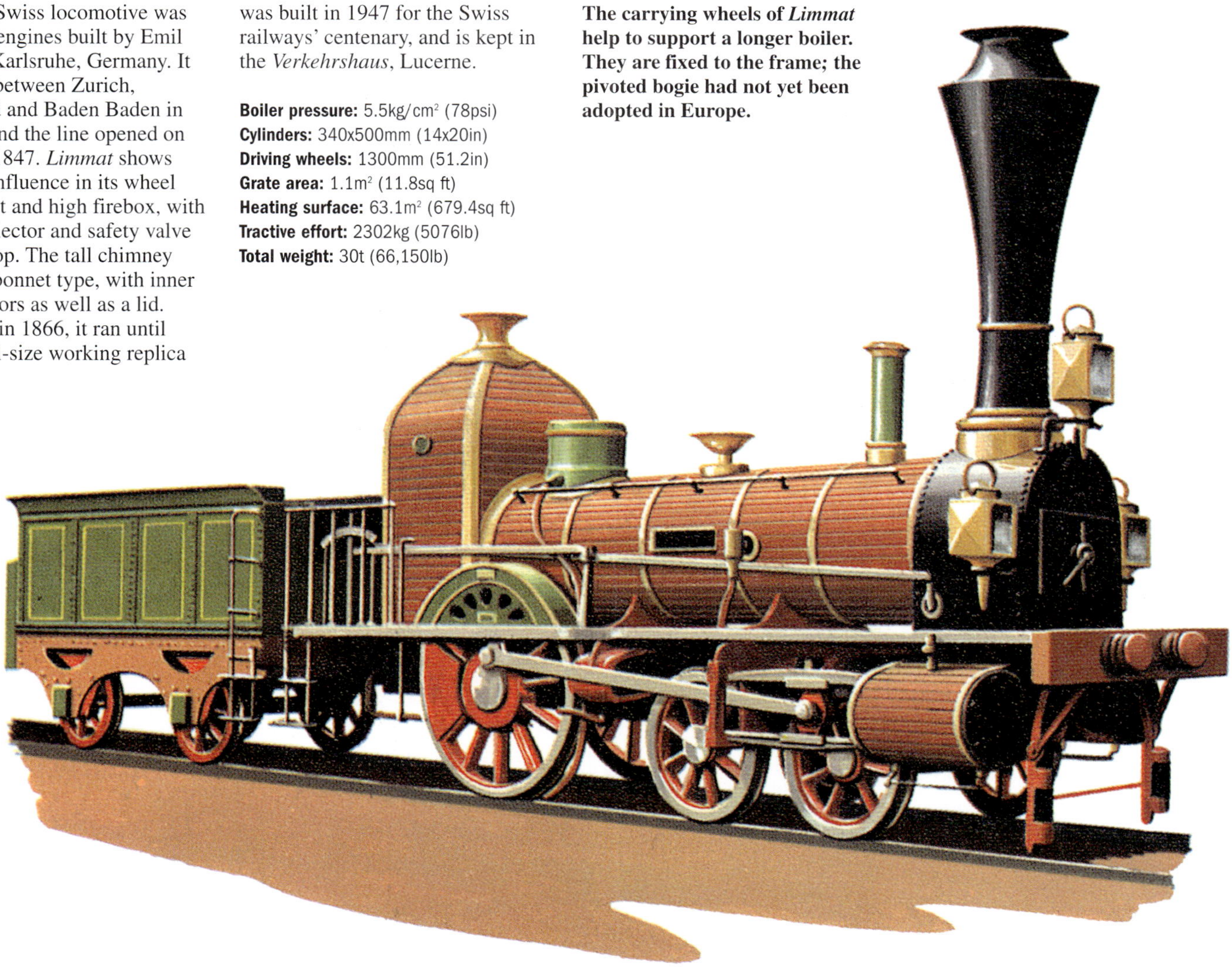

## *STEINBRUCK* 4-4-0 VIENNA-GLOGGNITZ RAILWAY — AUSTRIA: 1848

The mechanical engineer of this line was a Scot, John Haswell, but here he borrowed not on his home tradition but on the American designs being built at Norris's works in Vienna. The firebox behind the wheelbase and the closely placed wheels are Norris trademarks, but the radial bogie was Haswell's own, and anticipates the American patent Bissell truck. The huge chimney contains a spark-arrestor. The Vienna-Gloggnitz railway ultimately became part of the *Südbahn*, which eventually sold this engine to the Graz-Köflach Railway, where it ran from 1860 to 1910. It has been preserved and is now on display in the Vienna Railway Museum.

**Boiler pressure:** 5.5kg/cm² (78psi)
**Cylinders:** 369x790mm (14.5x31in)
**Driving wheels:** 1422mm (55.75in)
**Grate area:** 1.0m² (10sq ft)
**Heating surface:** 70.6m² (760sq ft)
**Tractive effort:** 2610kg (5750lb)
**Total weight:** 31.75t (70,000lb)

## *ELEPHANT* 4-4-0 SACRAMENTO VALLEY RAILROAD (SVR) — USA: 1849

When it was bought by the SVR in 1855, *Elephant* had already had a varied career. With two inside cylinders, and external valve gear operated through cylindrical-cased valve boxes set at an angle to the frame, it was a product of John Souther's Globe Works in Boston, and built to the 1524mm (5ft) gauge, probably for a Norfolk, Virginia, line. It was shipped to San Francisco in July 1850 and used briefly on the waterfront by a land-clearing contractor before the city authorities banned it. But it was the first steam engine to run in California. The Sacramento Valley, the state's first railway, bought it in 1850 to supplement two smaller engines, and it was renamed *Garrison* after the line's president. It ran well for ten years, an 1863 derailment causing little damage; and in 1865 it was regauged to the standard 1435mm (56.5in) when the SVR became the western end of the transcontinental line. In original form, it had handrails fixed on a riveted external bar frame. In 1869 it was rebuilt and modernized, with link motion valve gear, though it retained its inside cylinders. Again renamed, as *Pioneer*, it ran until 1879, when it was taken out of regular service. In 1849, it had been a big engine for the time, but things had moved on. It was use occasionally until 1886 when, despite its historic interest, it was broken up for scrap.

**Boiler pressure:** not known
**Cylinders:** 381x508mm (15x20in)
**Driving wheels:** 1802mm (71in)
**Grate area:** 0.9m² (9.63sq ft)
**Heating surface:** 66m² (710sq ft)
**Tractive effort:** not known
**Total weight:** 25.4t (56,000lb)

## 'BLOOMER' 2-2-2 LONDON & NORTH WESTERN RAILWAY GREAT BRITAIN: 1851

J.S. McConnell designed this engine to provide express motive power for London-Birmingham trains. Ultimately there were forty of them, though 36 'Small Bloomers' were also built from 1853, with 1980mm (78in) drivers, for secondary services. The 'Bloomers' had notably high pressure for British engines of their time, though McConnell's 10.5kg/cm$^2$ (150psi) was reduced to 8.4kg/cm$^2$ (120psi) in regular service. He set the boilers high, ignoring the theory that claimed this would make the engines topple over. It was a very successful class, surviving – with added cabs – for many years. The unofficial class name celebrates Mrs Amelia Bloomer, pioneer of women's dress reform. The 'Bloomers' showed plenty of leg, or rather wheel.

***Apollo*, with a southbound express, takes on water at Coventry station, around 1879. A Ramsbottom class DX 0-6-0 waits with a short freight on the through track.**

**Boiler pressure:** 10.6kg/cm$^2$ (150psi)
**Cylinders:** 406x558mm (16x22in)
**Driving wheels:** 2130mm (84in)
**Grate area:** 1.33m$^2$ (14.5sq ft)
**Heating surface:** 106.6m$^2$ (1448.5sq ft)
**Tractive effort:** 3854lb (8500lb)
**Total weight:** 30t (66,080lb)

## CRAMPTON TYPE 4-2-0 PARIS–STRASBOURG RAILWAY FRANCE: 1852

This Crampton design was built by J.F. Cail's works at Lille, in a first batch of 12. They had the typical domeless boiler with outside steam pipes and regulator box. Later variants had dome-fitted regulators. Crampton engines ran the main services on this line, later the *Chemin de Fer de l'Est*, into the late 1890s. No 80, *Le Continent*, was withdrawn in July 1914 after 62 years, then was reprieved for wartime work. In 1925 the engine was restored, and in 1946 was rebuilt to working order, with the discreet addition of an injector and a steel firebox instead of the original copper one. Such was the impact of the Crampton type in France that for a while the term *prendre le Crampton* became an alternative to *prendre le train,* 'take the train', at the time.

**The preserved but slightly modified Paris-Strasbourg Crampton 4-2-0 No. 80 locomotive, *Le Continent*, and train standing in yard at Culmont whilst en route to Tarare on 15 September 1966.**

**Boiler pressure:** 8kg/cm$^2$ (154lb[psi?])
**Cylinders:** 400x560mm (15.5x22in)
**Driving wheels:** 2300mm (90.75in)
**Grate area:** 1.31m$^2$ (13.3sq ft)
**Heating surface:** 100.4m$^2$ (1081sq ft)
**Tractive effort:** 3457kg (7620lb)
**Total weight:** 26.75t (58,983lb)

## 'BOURBONNAIS' 0-6-0 PARIS–LYONS RAILWAY FRANCE: 1854

First built by J.F. Cail of Lille, this became a standard freight engine on the PLM railway, with 1057 constructed between 1854 and 1882. By the latter date, boiler pressure had gone up to 10kg/cm$^2$ (142psi), the boilers had domes, and cabs were provided. Otherwise, little changed. The engines are based on the Stephenson 0-6-0, with outside cylinders and inside Stephenson link motion actuating slide valves. From the 413rd to be built, locomotive No. 1814 of 1868, a new boiler was fitted to the PLM 0-6-0s, pressed at 9kg/cm$^2$ (128psi).

Between 1907 and 1913, 215 were converted to 0-6-0 side tanks for shunting work. 'Bourbonnais' was a collective name rather than that of a single engine. The first one is preserved at Mulhouse.

**Boiler pressure:** 10kg/cm$^2$ (142.5psi)
**Cylinders:** 450x650mm (17.75x25.5in)
**Driving wheels:** 1300mm (51.2in)
**Grate area:** 1.34m$^2$ (14.4sq ft)
**Heating surface:** 85.4m$^2$ (919.6sq ft)
**Tractive effort:** 8616kg (19,000lb)
**Total weight:** 35.56t (78,400lb) (engine only)

## 4-4-0 NORTH-EAST RAILWAY (*NORD-OST BAHN*) SWITZERLAND: 1854

The Maffei works at Munich, Germany built these eight engines between 1854 and 1856, primarily for goods train work, with a maximum speed of 50kph (31mph). The N-OB was based at Zürich, Switzerland, where numerous trunk converged. They were small-boilered engines, with no dome, tall chimneys and a very short-wheelbase front bogie. Most of them received new boilers at the railway's own Zürich works between 1871 and 1876, and they were scrapped between 1887 and 1889. For a locomotive doing regular main-line work, a life-span of some 30-35 years was usual, if it was a reliable performer; though at least one new boiler would be fitted in this time.

**Boiler pressure:** 7kg/cm$^2$ (100psi)
**Cylinders:** 380x559mm (15x22in)
**Driving wheels:** 1676mm (66in)
**Grate area:** 1.1m$^2$ (11.8sq ft)
**Heating surface:** 83m$^2$ (893.6sq ft)
**Tractive effort:** 2890kg (6375lb)
**Total weight:** 43.7t (96,358lb)

## *SUSQUEHANNA* 0-8-0 PHILADELPHIA & READING RAILROAD (P&RR) USA: 1854

**Boiler pressure:** 6.3kg/cm² (90psi)
**Cylinders:** 482x558mm (19x22in)
**Driving wheels:** 1091mm (43in)
**Grate area:** 2.2 m² (23.5sq ft)
**Heating surface:** c 93 m² (1000sq ft)
**Tractive effort:** 6970kg (14120lb)
**Total weight:** 27.43t (60,480lb) (engine only)

Ross Winans was a maverick among American locomotive suppliers. Around 1840, he established himself at Baltimore, next door to the Baltimore & Ohio's workshops. He was preoccupied by the need to develop a good coal-burning firebox (a universal problem at the time) and in 1848 he built the oddly shaped 'Camel' type locomotive, with a sloping firebox at the rear and the driving cab perched above the boiler. This was the only type of locomotive that Winans' factory built; the total was around 300. The first coal-burning locomotive to be produced in quantity, its large and wide grate, placed behind the locomotive's frame and wheels, was able to take up the full width available. The fireman stood on the tender. The first of the line, *Camel*, was supplied in 1848 to the Boston & Maine, but was rejected after road tests; it was then sold to the Reading Railroad. Its performance seems to have been good, but apart from its appearance, it had a number of idiosyncrasies unlikely to appeal to a Master Mechanic. Winans persevered with steadily larger fireboxes. He found regular customers in the B&O (in which he was a large shareholder) and P&R lines, both of which ran slow-speed, heavy coal trains (the 'Camel' was ill-suited to speeds over 24kph/15mph) but few others expressed interest in the 'Camels'. By 1862, demand had ceased, and Winans closed his factory.

*Susquehanna* was a typical 'Camel', looking rather as if it had carried off a signal cabin from somewhere. The front tube of the apparent double funnel was an ash container, with a door at the base. Firing the huge box was a fireman's nightmare; Winans had incorporated feed-hoppers into his design, to get the coal to the front of the fire, but the firemen objected to the double task of shovelling coal from the floor up to the firing platform of the tender, and then into the hopper. The driver, perched high, had an unusually good view, though partly obscured by the very large dome, but did not have the advantage of the fireman's help as a lookout. There were significant shortcomings in the design. The main structural problem was the link between the firebox, which tended to sag, and the boiler. The boiler itself was weakened by the steam dome, which probably accounts for the relatively low pressure employed. The feedwater pump injected cold

**B&O No. 65, built by Winans in 1850, shows the type, though it has lost, or did not have, the apparent 'double funnel'. The fireman could scramble up the steps to take occasional refuge in the cab.**

water at the side of the firebox, unnecessarily reducing the heat of the hottest part of the boiler. The placing of the firebox made the tender-locomotive drawbar link a difficult one. The drawbar, passing through the ashpan, would frequently become red-hot in operation.

Even in its time, the 'Camel' was widely derided by rival builders. Winans' claim was for simplicity and ruggedness, but the engines were poorly finished and lacked items like boiler lagging, regarded as essential on most lines. At around $10,000 per locomotive, they were not cheap. Its main influence on later design was the 'Camelback' locomotive with Wootten firebox, but that was designed to burn anthracite waste, not coal, and was at least partly supported by wheels. In service, Winans' design had its merits. John H. White Jr quotes a run recorded around 1859, when *Susquehanna* took a train of 110 four-wheel coal cars from Pottsville to Philadelphia, 95 miles (152.8km), at 8 mph (13kph). It used 4.5 tons (4.t) of coal, costing $2.50 per ton. The fuel cost, of 11.74 cents a mile, compared very well against those of a wood-burner, which could run to 25 cents a mile. Oddly enough, wood-burning Camels were built by Winans for the Erie road in 1851. For all their drawbacks, the Camels went on performing their slow, steady duties almost to the end of the century. The last, on the B&O, went for scrap at the Mt. Clare shops in 1898.

## *THE GENERAL* 4-4-0 WESTERN & ATLANTIC RAILROAD USA: 1855

**Boiler pressure:** 9.8kg/cm² (140psi)
**Cylinders:** 381x558mm (15x22in)
**Driving wheels:** 1523mm (60in)
**Grate area:** 1.15m² (12.5sq ft)
**Heating surface:** 72.8m² (784.4sq ft)
**Tractive effort:** 3123kg (6885lb)
**Total weight:** 22.8t (50,300lb)

By 1855, the 'American' type 4-4-0 had developed into the brightly painted form, with shiny brass and copper-work, often with balloon spark-arrester smokestack and a big headlamp, familiar from many illustrations and Western movies. *The General*, built at Rogers Locomotive Works, Patterson, NJ, was famously hijacked during the US Civil War at Big Shanty, Ga, where the great engine chase took place. Apart from its shared adventure with the *Texas*, it was typical of many others that led less dramatic lives as the basic work-horse of the rapidly growing American railway network. Basic features of the design were level-set cylinders, a long-wheelbase truck, a deep, narrow wood-burning firebox, bar frames, big wooden cab, and an eight-wheel tender. Valve gear was much improved, with Stephenson's link motion normally replacing the old gab gear, which had permitted only 'backwards' or 'forwards'. Designers were very conscious of the aesthetic aspect of their engines: William Mason, a Massachusetts builder, wrote in 1853: 'We want them, of course, strong workers, but we want them also good lookers… we shall hope to see something soon on the rails that does not look exactly like a "cooking stove on wheels".' *The General*, much restored and now discreetly oil-fired, is preserved at Chattanooga.

**The relative lightness of American bar-frame construction is shown in this print of *The General;* there is no running plate alongside the boiler and 'the works' are on view (and easily accessible for repair and maintenance).**

## CLASS Q34 2-4-0 GREAT INDIAN PENINSULA RAILWAY (GIPR) INDIA: 1856

**Nineteenth-century Indian locomotives were usually British-built and their design followed British practice until the later 1940s.**

The first main-line engines supplied to India were small 2-4-0s built in England by the Vulcan Foundry for the Bombay-Thana 1675mm (5ft 6in) gauge line, India's first public railway, which opened on 16 April 1853. The 1856 engines were of similar design but larger, built by Kitson & Co, of Leeds, (who also built the East Indian Railway's restored 2-2-2 *Fairy Queen* of 1855). They were standard English 2-4-0s, with inside frames and bearings, but in India were fitted with long-canopy cabs to ward off sun and monsoon rain. For the next 20 years, engines of this type, usually with larger cylinders, would run most of the passenger trains on India's rapidly developing railway system. Two survived as works shunters and one, *Sindh*, is preserved.

**Cylinders:** 381x533mm (15x21in)
**Driving wheels:** 1675mm (66in)
Other details not available

## CLASS 030 0-6-0 MADRID-ZARAGOZA–ALICANTE RAILWAY (MZA) SPAIN: 1857

Very English in appearance, apart from the boiler-mounted sandbox and stovepipe chimney, these engines ran the goods trains on the MZA for many years, several of them attaining more than a century in service. The first ten were built by Ritson, Wilson of Leeds, England, in 1857; the others came from Kitson and from Cail in Lille, France. The only real change made to most of them was to provide air brake equipment and wooden cabs. They had inside cylinders and valve gear, and small four-wheel tenders. No 030.213, of the first batch, has been preserved.

**Seen here shunting at Atocha station, Madrid, this Cail-built 0-6-0, No. 2041, of 1858, was still in vigorous action in February 1956.**

**Boiler pressure:** 8kg/cm$^2$ (114psi)
**Cylinders:** 440x600mm (17.3x23.6in)
**Driving wheels:** 1430mm (56in)
**Grate area:** 1.3m$^2$ (14sq ft)
**Heating surface:** not known
**Tractive effort:** 5532kg (12,200lb)
**Total weight:** 49.2t (108,486lb)

## 'PROBLEM' CLASS 2-2-2 LONDON & NORTH-WESTERN RAILWAY GREAT BRITAIN: 1859

By mid-century, Crewe in England had one of the world's biggest locomotive works, owned by the LNWR. This Crewe-built class of 60 engines, also known as the 'Lady of the Lake' class, was designed by John Ramsbottom. Short and lightweight, they were also straightforward and reliable in operation and all survived (though rebuilt in the 1890s) into the twentieth century. The first 10 supplied feed water through crosshead pumps; the rest of the class, from November 1860, were fitted with Henri Giffard's still-new injector from France, invented in 1859. The speed with which this device was taken up internationally shows its importance. Until then, boiler feed was done through a pump driven from the crosshead or crank, and so could work only when the engine was in motion. The steam injector enabled water to be admitted when the engine was stationary. Like all such patent devices, a number of variants soon appeared, but the old feed-pumps soon vanished. (The feed pumps installed on many later locomotive types were needed because they had feedwater heaters, and injectors do not work with very hot feedwater). This class were also the first locomotives to be fitted with a screw-operated reverser, and among the first to have water pick-up apparatus, from track troughs, both invented by Ramsbottom.

**Boiler pressure:** 8.4kg/cm$^2$ (120psi)
**Cylinders:** 406x609mm (16x24in)
**Driving wheels:** 2322mm (91.5in)
**Grate area:** 1.4m$^2$ (14.9sq ft)
**Heating surface:** 102m$^2$ (1098sq ft)
**Tractive effort:** 3102kg (6840lb)
**Total weight:** 27.43t (60,480lb)

**By the late 1850s, a spectacle board finally gave some shelter to enginemen, though its purpose was more to facilitate fast running. Ramsbottom also patented an improved safety-valve, used on the 'Problems' and taken up by several other railways.**

## 4-4-0 TARRAGONA–BARCELONA & FRANCE RAILWAY SPAIN: 1859

Built by Slaughter, Gruning in Bristol, England, the two express locomotives of this type were the first of the British inside-cylinder 4-4-0s, the dominant passenger engine of the later nineteenth century. The line, absorbed in 1891 into the Madrid Zaragoza & Alicante Railway (MZA), was 1675mm (5ft 6in) gauge. The engines had inside plate frames, and an outside-framed front bogie. They ran into the 1890s, though Spanish railways had relatively few locomotives of this 4-4-0 configuration. Slaughter, Gruning are best known for their inside-cylinder 4-4-0 tank engines for the North London Railway, but these TB&F locomotives seem to have been a tender design from the start.

**Boiler pressure:** 9.8kg/cm$^2$ (140psi)
**Cylinders:** 393x558mm (15.5x22in)
**Driving wheels:** 1903mm (75in)
**Grate area:** 1.3m$^2$ (14.5sq ft)
**Heating surface:** 92.4m$^2$ (995sq ft)
**Tractive effort:** 3803kg (8386lb)
**Total weight:** 36.83t (81,200lb)

## 2-2-2 EXPRESS PASSENGER LOCOMOTIVE — EGYPT: 1862

Built at the Caledonian Railway's St Rollox Works in Glasgow, this goes back to a Caledonian design of 1859, by Benjamin Conner, based in turn on the 'Crewe type' with its curvaceous front-end view, but horizontally set cylinders. By this time, engines were being fitted with steel tyres and axles, the tyres introduced by Krupps of Germany. It is notable that a cab was provided – more common at the time on Scottish than English locomotives. One was shown at the London Exhibition of 1862, which led to an order from the Viceroy of Egypt; these were built by Neilson & Co. With lightweight trains on the level Nile Valley and Delta tracks, they gave adequate performance on undemanding schedules.

**Boiler pressure:** 8.4 kg/cm² (120psi)
**Cylinders:** 438x609mm (17.25x24in)
**Driving wheels:** 2487mm (98in)
**Grate area:** 1.29m² (13.9sq ft)
**Heating surface:** 108.6m² (1169sq ft)
**Tractive effort:** 3370kg (7430lb)
**Total weight:** 31.14t (68,656lb)

## CLASS Y43 4-6-0T GREAT INDIAN PENINSULA RAILWAY (GIPR) — INDIA: 1862

Designed by J. Kershaw and built by Sharp, Stewart in Manchester, these engines (5 in all) served on the 1 in 37 Ghat inclines of the GIPR. The gauge was 1675mm (5ft 6in). They were unusual engines, with the saddle tanks set at the front, and sandwich-type outside frames. The very short bogie (wider than it is long) could slide laterally. The inside cylinders were the largest yet fitted to a British-built locomotive. Sledge brakes, operating on the rails, were fitted. As first supplied, they had no cabs, despite the Indian climate. They were indifferent performers in service: handling traffic on the Ghat inclines remained a problem until the introduction of electric locomotives in the next century.

**Boiler pressure:** 8.4kg/cm² (120psi)*
**Cylinders:** 508x609mm (20x24in)
**Driving wheels:** 1318mm (52in)
**Grate area:** 2.4m² (25.9sq ft)
**Heating surface:** 133.5m² (1438sq ft)
**Tractive effort:** 8540kg (18,830lb)*
**Total weight:** 49.79t (109,760lb)

## 250 CLASS 2-6-0 ERIE RAILWAY — USA: 1862

The Erie wanted to increase the power of its freight hauling, previously done by 4-4-0s, and chose the 2-6-0 type for its 1827mm (6ft) gauge line. Ten were ordered from Danforth, Cooke & Co. of Paterson, NJ, in 1862, and were successful; this led to further orders. With two outside cylinders in typical American fashion, it was an anthracite burner. The grate was formed of iron tubes linking the water spaces at the front and rear of the firebox, a device invented by James Millholland of the Philadelphia & Reading Railway, and used on other coal-burning lines. The first American 2-6-0 had appeared in 1850, with a rigid wheelbase: the first with pivoted carrying wheels was built by Millholland in 1860, though the 'Mogul' name for this wheel-formation was not used until 1872.

**Boiler pressure:** 8.4kg/cm² (120psi)
**Cylinders:** 431x558mm (17x22in)
**Driving wheels:** 1370mm (54in)
**Grate area:** 1.95m² (21sq ft)
**Heating surface:** 116.5m² (1255sq ft)
**Tractive effort:** 4805kg (10,596lb)
**Total weight:** 36.07t (79,520lb) (engine only)

## NO. 1 4-4-0 GREAT NORTHERN RAILROAD (GNR) — USA: 1862

Railways were spreading fast in the American mid-west, and the first train to run in Minnesota was pulled by this engine, on the St Paul & Pacific Railroad, a constituent line of the Great Northern, and ultimately to become a sector in the transcontinental railway. No 1, bearing the name *William Crooks*, is preserved, but in a much-restored form. It was built in 1861, by Smith & Jackson, of Paterson, NJ, and taken by barge up the Mississippi to St Paul from the railhead at La Crosse, though the line was not yet open and it did not enter service until 1862. 4-4-0s were the typical motive power of the St Paul & Pacific. The railway did not reach the Pacific until 1893.

**Boiler pressure:** 8.4kg/cm² (120psi)
**Cylinders:** 304x558mm (12x22in)
**Driving wheels:** 1599mm (63in)
**Grate area:** not known
**Heating surface:** not known
**Tractive effort:** 2267kg (5000lb)
**Total weight:** 46.27t (102,000lb)

## 0-6-6-0 FREIGHT LOCOMOTIVE NORTHERN RAILWAY (*NORD*) — FRANCE: 1863

Jules Petiet, of the *Nord*, designed this engine, which though an unsatisfactory performer, was in some ways ahead of its time. Petiet used the Belpaire firebox, and the engine had a notably large grate area. Its 'duplex' drive was fixed in the frame, and some lateral motion of the coupled wheels at each end did not give enough flexibility. Articulation had yet to arrive. Another remarkable feature was a long exhaust flue carried back above the boiler, terminating in a funnel in front of the cab, and incorporating steam drier and feedwater heater. Steaming was poor and it was said to be able to pull only 630 tons (640t). Twenty were built, but were converted into a series of 40 shunting tanks.

**Boiler pressure:** 9kg/cm² (128psi)
**Cylinders:** 440x440mm (17.3x17.3in)
**Driving wheels:** 1065mm (42in)
**Grate area:** 3.3m² (35.5sq ft)
**Heating surface:** 197.3m² (2124sq ft)
**Tractive effort:** 10,798kg (21,866lb)
**Total weight:** 59.71t (131,638lb)

## 0-6-0 MIDLAND RAILWAY (MR) — GREAT BRITAIN: 1863

**Boiler pressure:** 9.8kg/cm² (140psi)
**Cylinders:** 431x609mm (17x24in)
**Driving wheels:** 1586mm (62.5in)
**Grate area:** 1.56m² (16.8sq ft)
**Heating surface:** 101.5m² (1093sq ft)
**Tractive effort:** 5980kg (13,200lb)
**Total weight:** 35.56t (78,400lb)

In the late 1850s, work was going ahead both in Britain and the USA on how to make coal burn better in locomotives and produce less smoke. Coke was expensive, while both countries had large reserves of coal, both bituminous and anthracite. Oddly enough, the same solution was patented by different inventors in each country, at much the same time. It was far more simple than any of the many previous efforts, which had involved double fireboxes and special devices of various kinds. An arch of flame-resistant firebricks was built across the upper area of the firebox, and a deflector plate was attached to the fire-door. These deflected and lengthened the flames from the fire, increased the heat of combustion, improved steam generation, and reduced the production of smoke. The pioneer line in Britain was the Midland Railway, and the engineer responsible was Charles Markham, who perfected the method by the end of 1859. In the USA, George S. Griggs had patented a brick arch in December 1857, though the idea seems to have been first employed a few years earlier in some Baldwin locomotives. From 1860 onwards, the firebrick arch was incorporated into fireboxes, and coal became the standard fuel on most lines.

This inside-cylinder, outside-framed 0-6-0 design of 1863 incorporated the brick arch firebox from the start. Up to 1874, 315 of this class were built, and they were the mainstay of the MR goods traffic. The outside frames, with rippled footplate and deep slots, were modelled on an 0-6-0 built in 1862 by Sharp Stewart in Manchester for Egypt. Many of the class ran until the late 1940s and the last was withdrawn in 1951.

## *THATCHER PERKINS* 4-6-0 BALTIMORE & OHIO RAILROAD (B&O) USA: 1863

The origins of the 4-6-0 go back to the late 1840s. In March 1847, the Norris Works of Philadelphia constructed a "ten-wheeler", *Chesapeake*, for the Philadelphia & Reading Railroad. Its design is generally credited to Septimus Norris, who certainly later tried to enforce a patent on the 4-6-0 wheel arrangement. Despite good reports of performance, the design was slow to catch on. Baldwin was still wedded to the 4-2-0 at this time, and did not offer a 4-6-0 design in his catalogue – widely circulated among railway companies - until after 1852. Many engineers felt that the four-wheel front truck bore too little weight and was liable to jump the rails, and that the design offered no real advantage over the 4-4-0. The leading coupled wheels, and sometimes the second set also, were invariably unflanged on the early 4-6-0s. The earliest 4-6-0s were designed as freight engines, but by the mid-50s, this model was established on several lines as a useful mixed-traffic type, which was able to haul both fast passenger and goods trains.

Thatcher Perkins had been designing locomotives from the 1840s. Large ones were his speciality, including an 0-8-0 for the B&O in 1848, of which line he was Master Mechanic at the time. In 1851, he became a partner in the Smith, Perkins loco works of Alexandria, Virginia. They built a ten-wheeler, *Wilmore*, for the Pennsylvania Railroad in 1856. In 1863, the B&O commissioned a 4-6-0 design from Thatcher Perkins for its Allegheny Mountain section between Piedmont and Grafton. Built at the B&O Mount Clare shops, they were intended for passenger service, and their weight was such that they could not be introduced until track and bridges had been strengthened. No 117 of this class operated until 1890, when it was taken out of service. Shown at various exhibitions, it was steamed and ran at the B&O's centennial celebration in 1927. Though heavily restored, it has survived and remains preserved at the B&O's Baltimore Museum. Although neither a mechanical or stylistic trend-setter, nor a specially distinguished performer, it well represents the handsome style of its period, and now bears the name of its designer. The boiler pressure, at 5.25kg/cm$^2$ (75psi), was curiously low and there must have been some difficulties feeding the cylinders. Perkins designed other 4-6-0s, including a 1524mm (5ft) gauge engine for the Louisville & Nashville Railroad, of which he became Master Mechanic in 1868; quite different to No 117, it was on a long wheelbase (7614mm/25ft) with 1497mm (59in) wheels; this was the 4-6-0 as freight hauler.

Though many US 4-6-0s were built, it remained overshadowed by the 4-4-0 in the ninetheenth century and by the 'Pacific' and eight or ten-coupled locomotive after around 1910. Across the Atlantic it was a different story, though adoption of the 4-6-0 tender engine in Britain and Europe was slow. In Italy, Cesare Frescot had brought out Europe's first 4-6-0 (the *Vittorio Emanuele* class) in 1884, but there and in other countries the 2-6-2 was often preferred. Northern Europe was more receptive to the 'ten-wheeler'. The first built in Britain were the celebrated L class for the Indus Valley State Railway (1884), but it was 1894 before the first 4-6-0s for home service were built, for the Highland Railway. It was not until the twentieth century that English lines employed the 4-6-0 type, but by the 1930s it was the most widely used tender locomotive type in Great Britain, as hundreds of the Stanier 'Black Fives' came into service on the LMS Railway. It remained among the 'British standard' types up to the end of steam.

**Boiler pressure:** 5.25kg/cm$^2$ (75psi)
**Cylinders:** 482x660mm (19x26in)
**Driving wheels:** 1472mm (58in)
**Grate area:** 1.8m$^2$ (19.4sq ft)
**Heating surface:** 103.4m$^2$ (1114sq ft)
**Tractive effort:** 4670kg (10,300lb)
**Total weight:** not known

## TYPE 1 2-4-2 BELGIAN STATE RAILWAYS (EB) BELGIUM: 1864

**Boiler pressure:** 12kg/cm$^2$ (171psi)
**Cylinders:** 430x560mm (17x22in)
**Driving wheels:** 2000mm (79in)
**Grate area:** not known
**Heating surface:** not known
**Tractive effort:** 5306kg (11,700lb)
**Total weight:** 33.5t (73,867lb)

This express passenger locomotive was one of the first major designs of Alfred Belpaire as chief mechanical engineer on the *Etat Belge*. It had the boiler and firebox he had designed, and which would be used by many others for almost a century to come. This was of distinctive appearance – a tall, high-shouldered box at the end of the boiler barrel, requiring the latter to taper outwards to meet it. Its purpose was to provide the maximum space for steam generation at the hottest part of the boiler – around and above the fire. The first examples were built by Cockerill of Seraing, and most other Belgian and some French constructors supplied later engines. In all, 153 were built, up to 1884. There were two inside simple-expansion cylinders, and the running plate was raised over the wheels to clear the coupling rod cranks. A stovepipe chimney was originally fitted, with the dome placed right behind it.

Other modern equipment included Giffard injectors, though later engines had Rongy's injector. Westinghouse brakes and pumps were fitted from 1878, and roofed cabs provided from 1882. Between 1889 and 1896, the Type 1s were re-boilered and a massive square chimney was added, a unique feature on express locomotives, though a number of other Belgian types were similarly equipped. Later, this was exchanged for an almost equally huge elliptical funnel. Until 1890, they ran express trains on all lines except that to Luxembourg; from then to the 1920s, they were on secondary services. All were scrapped by 1926.

**The EB Type 1 2-4-2 was originally fitted with the distinctive stovepipe chimney.**

## METROPOLITAN TANK 4-4-0T METROPOLITAN RAILWAY GREAT BRITAIN: 1864

**A Metropolitan 4-4-0T in latter-day form, in London Transport livery, photographed at Verney Junction, northern end of the Metropolitan–Great Central joint line.**

'As we grope our way into a mirk wherein the gas jets serve only to emphasize an ever-deepening gloom, the brimstone breath of the tunnels engulfs us. . .' So wrote the historian Hamilton Ellis about the world's first underground railway, beneath central London. Its first custom-built engines, supplied by Beyer Peacock of Manchester, were built to this 4-4-0 tank design. The leading truck was a Bissell-type bogie, that swung from a pivot set 2030mm (80in) behind its centre line. The most distinctive feature was the condenser apparatus, intended for use in the tunnels. Exhaust steam was blown from the blast pipe, through long lateral tubes, into the tank. This helped dissipate steam, and warmed the water, but did nothing for smoke emission. With numerous modifications over the years, including replacement of the Bissell truck by an Adams bogie, these engines, 120 in number, served the system well. Their coal capacity was 1 ton. When the first was broken up, in 1897, it had run 1,689,810km (1,050,000 miles). Others survived the 1905 electrification of the line by being sold to other companies, and some, sold to the Cambrian Railway in Wales, were converted to tender engines. One of the class, No 23, survives in preservation. The Metropolitan type was also built for some other lines, including five in 1871 for the Rhenish Railway of Germany.

**The original cab-less appearance of the Metropolitan tank engine, with narrow copper-capped chimney, and dome placed on the first boiler ring.**

**Boiler pressure:** 9.16kg/cm$^2$ (130psi)
**Cylinders:** 432x609mm (17x24in)
**Driving wheels:** 1753mm (69in)
**Grate area:** 2.7 m$^2$ (19sq ft)
**Heating surface:** 94m$^2$ (1013.8 sq ft)
**Tractive effort:** 5034kg (11,000lb)
**Total weight:** 42.83t (94,416lb)

## NO. 148 0-6-0 RUSE-VARNA RAILWAY BULGARIA: 1865

Bulgaria's first railway opened on 7 November 1865, with four locomotives from Sharps of Manchester, England, shipped direct to Varna's harbour on the Black Sea. It was in the north-east corner of the country, a standard-gauge line, 224km (139 miles) long. The engines were typical inside-cylinder English 0-6-0s of the period and did both passenger and freight work.

**No. 148, now kept at Ruse. Built in 1869, bought by the Chemins de Fer Orientaux of Turkey in 1873, it returned to Bulgaria in 1888.**

**Boiler pressure:** 8kg/cm$^2$ (114psi)
**Cylinders:** 432x610mm (17x24in)
**Driving wheels:** 1371mm (54in)
**Grate area:** 1.3m$^2$ (13.9sq ft)
**Heating surface:** 92.6m$^2$ (997sq ft)
**Tractive effort:** 5347kg (11,790lb)
**Total weight:** 30.6t (67,473lb)

## *CONSOLIDATION* 2-8-0 LEHIGH & MAHANOY RAILROAD USA:1866

**Boiler pressure:** 8.4 kg/m$^2$ (120psi)*
**Cylinders:** 507x609mm (20x24in)
**Driving wheels:** 1218mm (48in)
**Grate area:** 2.3m$^2$ (25sq ft)
**Heating surface:** not known
**Tractive effort:** 10,070kg (20,400lb)*
**Total weight:** 38.88t (85,720lb)

The Lehigh & Mahanoy was a new coal-carrying line with severe gradients, and its Master Mechanic Alexander Mitchell designed for it a "super freight" locomotive in 1865, with eight coupled wheels and a front Bissell pony truck, with solid wheels. Some trouble was found in getting a builder, but eventually Baldwins took on the job, in April 1866. By August, the engine was in service. During construction, the line merged with the Lehigh Valley Railroad, and the name of the new locomotive was chosen to celebrate the event. The newest developments were incorporated, including steel tyres from Krupps in Germany, who had pioneered this improvement, and a steam injector. The engine cost $19,000 to build, plus $950 war tax, but the railway was eminently satisfied with its investment. James I. Blakslee, the Superintendent, wrote to Baldwins: '*She is a perfect success . . .* I am satisfied she can out pull any machine ever built of her weight.'

The real success of *Consolidation* was not in tractive power, which could be matched by an 0-8-0; but in its ability to operate with a heavy load on a sharply curving track at higher speeds than any railway had dared to attempt before, and with a maximum axle load of 8.5t (8.4 tons). Nevertheless, in all respects this was a locomotive at the leading edge of design. Its truck was not a Bissell one but a new patent one by William Hudson, superintendent of the Rogers Locomotive Works, with a heavy equalizing lever linking the truck frame to the leading coupled wheel spring hangers. The long boiler, 4568mm (15ft) from firebox to smoke box, could make plenty of steam, and its big cylinders delivered the power to the wheels, with a long rod driving the third coupled wheels. Its single injector was supplemented by feedwater pumps on both sides, worked off return cranks on the last coupled wheels. It burned high-quality anthracite coal. The eight-wheel tender, mounted on two trucks, had a high canopy roof over the coal compartment.

Further engines of the class were ordered and considerable interest was aroused in other companies. But they were cautious about purchasing, partly because of its unusual length and greater cost, which left little change out of $20,000. But steadily the 2-8-0 won its reputation as a heavy freight hauler. It was found to be as advantageous on narrow gauge as it was on standard gauge. In 1873, Baldwins built a 913mm (3ft) gauge 'Consolidation' for the Garland extension of the Denver & Rio Grande Railway, which, as the Superintendent reported, 'moved up the 211-feet [65-m] grades and around the 30-degree curves seemingly with as much ease as our passenger engines on 75-feet [23-m] grades with three coaches and baggage cars.' From 1876, when it became the Pennsylvania Railroad's standard freight locomotive, the type grew very rapidly in popularity. Its greater capital cost was soon offset by the work it did. On the Erie Railroad, the managers calculated in 1878 that 55 2-8-0s did the work of 100 4-4-0s. The success of the 'Consolidation' launched the American trend towards ever-larger and more powerful locomotives.

Ultimately many thousands of the 'Consolidation' configuration would be built and used all over the world. Although it would be complemented by larger and more powerful designs, it would nevertheless remain a standard, and 2-8-0s continued to be built until the last years of steam operation.

**The Denver & Rio Grande Railroad was an early user of 'Consolidations' and the performance of its locos did much to publicize the virtues of the 2-8-0 on mountain lines.**

**A later D&RG 2-8-0. The drive is on the second coupled axle, as became most common with two-cylinder, simple-expansion 'Consolidation' locomotives.**

## *LANDWÜHRDEN* 0-4-0 OLDENBURG STATE RAILWAYS (OSB) — GERMANY: 1867

This influential design was the first locomotive to be built by Georg Krauss in Munich, Germany. One of his associates was Richard von Helmholtz, and together they designed the Krauss-Helmholtz leading bogie that came to be used in many European locomotives. The company eventually merged with Maffei to become Krauss-Maffei. *Landwührden* was shown at the Paris Exhibition of 1867 and won a gold medal for design and workmanship. Among its features was a well tank incorporated in the riveted box-frame, for heating feed water. Taken out of service in 1900, it is preserved (without a tender) in the Nürnberg transport museum.

**Boiler pressure:** $10kg/cm^2$ (142psi)
**Cylinders:** 355x560mm (14x22in)
**Driving wheels:** 1500mm (59in)
**Grate area:** $0.98m^2$ (10.5sq ft)
**Heating surface:** not known
**Tractive effort:** 4350kg (8820lb)
**Total weight:** not known

## CLASS G 0-6-0 SWEDISH RAILWAYS (SJ) — 1867

Between 1866 and 1874, Beyer Peacock of Manchester, England, and the Swedish builders Nydquist & Holm of Trollhättan, supplied 57 locomotives of this design , which was classed as Ga. English in appearance, they had two inside cylinders, actuated by slide valves through Stephenson's link motion. They were effective freight movers, and some lasted until 1921. Rebuilding with new boilers produced subclasses Gb and Gc. One of the earliest, though reboilered as Gc, is preserved. Its airy cab makes little concession to Swedish winters. In Sweden as in other countries, engine crews had to form trades unions in order to win significant improvements in working practices and hours.

**Boiler pressure:** $8.5kg/cm^2$ (121psi)
**Cylinders:** 406x610mm (16x24in)
**Driving wheels:** 864mm (34ins)
**Grate area:** $1.4m^2$ (15sq ft)
**Heating surface:** not known
**Tractive effort:** 8425kg (18,580lb)
**Total weight:** not known

## CLASS 335 0-6-0 HUNGARIAN RAILWAYS (MÁV) — HUNGARY: 1869

Although part of Austria's Hapsburg empire until 1918, Hungary, as an ancient kingdom, retained many elements of independence, including her own railway system. The MÁV state system began in 1867 and progressively enfolded lesser railways. Inevitably, a wide variety of locomotive types were inherited, all very similar in general respects but completely unstandardized, making repairs and the provision of spare parts extremely difficult. A start on standardized locomotive classes was made, and this goods engine, with the series 238 2-4-0 passenger engine of the same year, was the first fruit of that policy. The class 335 engines handled most of the country's freight, working on independent lines as well as those of the MÁV. With outside frames, simple expansion working through two outside cylinders, and Stephenson link motion actuating inside valves, it was in most respects typical of the older Austrian tradition, and constructed by Austrian builders. Though with slightly smaller wheels, and slightly different dimensions, it was very similar to the class 33 0-6-0 of the Austrian *Staats Eisenbahn Gesellschaft*, built at the StEg's own works from 1866. The boiler diameter was quite small, and a considerable array of domes and water-treatment cylinders was placed on top, together with a tall stovepipe chimney, usually with some form of spark arrester fitted at the base or the top. One is preserved.

**Boiler pressure:** $8.5kg/cm^2$ (121psi)
**Cylinders:** 460x632mm (18x25in)
**Driving wheels:** 1220mm (48in)
**Grate area:** $1.65m^2$ (17.7sq ft)
**Heating surface:** $128.4m^2$ (1382.4sq ft)
**Tractive effort:** 8570kg (17,355lb)
**Total weight:** 39.6t (87,318lb)

## CLASS 2 4-4-0 '*OUTRANCE*' NORTHERN RAILWAY (*NORD*) — FRANCE: 1870

**Boiler pressure:** $10kg/cm^2$ (145psi)
**Cylinders:** 462x609mm (18.2x24in)
**Driving wheels:** 2087.5mm (82.25in)
**Grate area:** $1.95m^2$ (21sq ft)
**Heating surface:** $99m^2$ (1066sq ft)
**Tractive effort:** 5400kg (11,900lb)
**Total weight:** 42.16t (92,960lb) (engine only)

*Outrance* means 'utmost' and these engines gave their utmost on the long gradients of the rolling country north of Paris, taking over from Crampton types on heavy passenger trains from the Channel coast and the north-eastern cities, until they were themselves displaced by new de Glehn compounds from 1891. The *Nord's* chief engineer, Jules Pétiet, took as his model Archibald Sturrock's 2-4-0 class of 1866, built for the English Great Northern Railway. Sturrock's successor, Stirling, later rebuilt these engines as 2-2-2s, but the '*Outrances*' with their four carrying axles and slightly larger dimensions were very successful and continued to be built up to 1885. They had outside frames, two inside simple expansion cylinders and long Belpaire fireboxes. An un-British feature was the forward-angled outside steam pipes running between a header behind the chimney and the steam-chests. The cab was little more than a frame for the spectacle-glasses. The original 4-wheel tenders were later replaced by larger six-wheelers. '*Outrances*' were widely admired. The same design was used by the Madrid Caceres & Portugal Railway in Spain (though built by Hartmann in Chemnitz, Germany), and the French-owned Rosario & Puerto Belgrano Railway in Argentina. The latter, class 21, built in 1910 by Schwarzkopff in Berlin, were the first Argentinian locomotives fitted with superheaters.

**Jules Pétiet, an innovative designer, was one of the first to use the higher, wider Belpaire firebox, which boosted the *Outrances'* steam-raising capacity.**

## No 1 4-2-2 GREAT NORTHERN RAILWAY (GNR) GREAT BRITAIN:1870

**The preserved No 1 hauls on the heritage Great Central Railway, between Loughborough and Rothley, on 9 May 1982.**

British railways retained use of the 'single driver' locomotive long after most other countries had adopted multiple-coupled types. The reasons for this attachment to what foreigners saw as an archaic wheel arrangement included the insularity and conservatism of the railway company engineers and managements, most of whom controlled their own building shops. Independent British builders, dependent on export orders, were constructing six and eight-coupled engines for other countries long before these came into home service. But some other factors favoured the single driver. Distances in Britain were relatively short: the GNR's main line was just over 322km (200 miles) long; and carriages were still relatively lightweight in the 1870s. All the stabling equipment, particularly turntables, was built for short engines. The quality of the track was generally high, so that the relatively heavy axle-load of a single-wheeler, in this case 15.2t (15 tons) was not a great problem. A single-wheeler was also cheaper to build than an engine with more axles. Nevertheless, there was a certain fashion for minimalism that had nothing directly to do with efficiency. One of the designers in whom this was most apparent was Patrick Stirling, a Scot who had come to the GNR at the end of the 1860s from the Glasgow & South Western Railway, and was to remain there until his death in 1895.

Stirling's engines were almost obsessively plain and simple. He disliked any sort of appendage and few of his engines had domes; he also disliked bogies, and greatly preferred the cylinders to be inside and out of sight. He likened an outside cylinder engine to 'a laddie running with his breeks down'. Soon after his arrival at the Doncaster Plant, he introduced the locomotive which was to be his classic, the 4-2-2 with 2436mm (8ft) drivers, of which No 1 still survives in preservation. It went against its designer's cherished prejudices by having a front bogie – necessary to bear the weight – and outside cylinders, which were required by the height of the driving axle. Despite these 'blemishes', this was Stirling's favourite among his numerous designs, and he watched over its performance very closely. Another of his prejudices was against double-heading; his engines were supposed to be able to do their work on their own, and a shed foreman who put two of them on a job was asking for trouble.

**No 1 with a special train in Kings Cross Station, London, 1938. Alongside is class N2 0-6-2 suburban tank No 4766.**

The work undertaken by the GNR singles, and by their numerous equivalents on other English lines, was by no means a matter of dainty little trains. The Kings Cross-Leeds expresses weighed up to 254t (250 tons) in the early 1880's, and these trains were allowed 12.5 minutes for the 13km (eight mile) climb at 1 in 200 from the start to Potter's Bar. In October 1875, No 22 ran from Kings Cross to Peterborough, 122.7km (76.25 miles), in 92 minutes with an 18-carriage train, an average speed of 80kph (50mph). In the 1890s, with steel-tyred wheels and heavier rails, the eight-footers turned in some remarkable performances, with speeds up to 133kph (83mph) recorded. To do this, the engines had to be 'thrashed' along by the drivers, and the simplicity and

**With seven vintage GNR six-wheel carriages, No 1 is prepared for departure for London from the bay at Cambridge station, with a special excursion on 24 August, 1938.**

robustness of the design allowed this to happen time after time. One writer likened the passage of a Stirling single at full speed to a volcanic eruption. Such fire-throwing, though wasteful and dangerous, was the only way to extract enough performance. But it would not have been possible without well-designed steam passages and a very fine and careful working out of the balance of the moving parts: Stirling's singles rarely indulged in wheel slipping.

The success of these locomotives, and of the GNR's slightly smaller 2309mm (7ft 7in) singles, some of which worked on express trains until the end of their careers, prompted other English lines to revive single-drivers. Scrapping began in 1899. No 1 ended its career as station pilot at Doncaster, and was retired in 1907. Now resident at York Railway Museum, it is still capable of being steamed.

**In this drawing of No. 93, the attention to design elements can be seen in the many different curves incorporated harmoniously in the overall structure of the locomotive.**

**Boiler pressure:** 9.9kg/cm² (140psi)
**Cylinders:** 457x711mm (2x18x28in)
**Driving wheels:** 2460mm (97in)
**Grate area:** 1.6m² (17.6sq ft)
**Heating surface:** 108m² (1165sq ft)
**Tractive effort:** 5034kg (11,000lb)
**Total weight:** 39t (86,128lb)

## *ICHIGO* 2-4-0T IMPERIAL JAPANESE RAILWAYS — JAPAN: 1871

**Japan opted for a narrower gauge, but in most detail respects, such as coupling and buffing gear, and signalling, the first Japanese railways were based on British practice.**

The first railway in Japan opened from Shimbashi Station, Tokyo, to Yokohama – 28km (17 miles) of 1065mm (3ft 6in) gauge – on 14 October 1872. It was worked by engines imported from Britain, ten small 2-4-0Ts, from five manufacturers. Their lack of cabs surprised the Japanese, though British weather is hardly better than Japan's. Cabs were added, and a famous print of 1875 shows a train in action at the Tokyo waterfront. No 1 was produced by the Vulcan Foundry. In 1911, it was sold to the Shimabara Railway Company in Kyushu. In 1936, it was bought for the Tokyo Transport Museum, where it still resides.

**Boiler pressure:** 8.4kg/cm² (120psi)
**Cylinders:** 304.5x456.8mm (12x18in)
**Driving wheels:** 1294mm (51in)
**Grate area:** 97m² (9sq ft)
**Heating surface:** 52.5m² (565.2sq ft)
**Tractive effort:** 2350kg (5180lb)
**Total weight:** 18.8t (41,440lb)

## FAIRLIE 0-4-4-0 FESTINIOG RAILWAY — GREAT BRITAIN: 1872

Articulated engines for use on narrow-gauge, twisting, hilly lines had been experimented with from an early stage. The American designer Horatio Allen had built some double engines, with back-to-back boilers and a central firebox, the two sets of driving wheels mounted in trucks, for the South Carolina Railroad in 1832. Francis Trevithick, son of Richard, was one of several designers to build back-to-back tank locomotives, for the Cornwall Minerals Railway. The Anglo-Belgian Cockerill company built an 0-4-4-0 double-boiler, double-firebox engine in 1852 for the Semmering gradient trials. So when Robert Fairlie patented his articulated double-engine design in 1865, it was not a new concept. Several British builders constructed Fairlies, mostly for export to Latin America and Russia. Most had a

**The Festiniog Railway's oil-burning Fairlie, seen here at the company's Boston Lodge works in the Welsh mountains.**

single firebox, though some had two. Compact power and a very tight turning circle were the key merits of the design; disadvantages were lack of fuel storage, cramped cab space on each side of the boiler, and weakness in the flexible steam-tube between the boiler and the bogie-mounted driving wheels. In Britain, Fairlies flourished best on the Welsh narrow gauge lines, where the tourist Festiniog Railway (600mm/23.5in gauge) built an oil-burning one as recently as 1979, more than 100 years after their 1872 model. But by 1911 the articulated principle was being pursued only on the Mallet and Beyer-Garrat systems.

**Steam pressure:** 9.9kg/cm$^2$ (140psi)
**Cylinders:** 216x355mm (4x8.5x14in)
**Driving wheels:** 812mm (32in)
**Grate area:** 1m$^2$ (11.2sq ft)
**Heating surface:** 66.2m$^2$ (713sq ft)
**Tractive effort:** 3400kg (7500lb)
**Total weight:** 20.37t (44,912lb)

## 'TERRIER' 0-6-0T LONDON BRIGHTON & SOUTH COAST RAILWAY GREAT BRITAIN: 1872

In the 1870s, many of the commuter lines of south London were in poor condition, still laid with the original lightweight rails. Fifty of this small inside-cylinder tank type were built between 1872 and 1880 to serve these routes. With a maximum axle load of 8 tons (8.3t), they rode well on the light track. The designer was William Stroudley, locomotive engineer for the London Brighton & South Coast Railway, renowned both for his artistry as well as the more utilitarian qualities of his engines. Nicknamed 'Terriers', the engines performed very well and many survived far into the next century. Two have been preserved in steaming condition.

**Several coats of paint lie between Stroudley's 'improved engine green' as applied by the London Brighton &South Coast Railway, and the British Railways lined-out black livery of the late 1950s, as 'Terrier' No. 32636 stands on shunting duty at Newhaven station on 13 April, 1958.**

**Boiler pressure:** 9.9kg/cm$^2$ (140psi)
**Cylinders:** 330x508mm (13x20in)
**Driving wheels:** 122cm (48in)
**Grate area:** 1.4m$^2$ (15sq ft)
**Heating surface:** 49m$^2$ (528sq ft)
**Tractive effort:** 3810kg (8400lb)
**Total weight:** 25t (55,104lb)

## 2-4-2 PARIS-ORLEANS RAILWAY (PO) FRANCE:1873

The 2-4-2 configuration was popular in France for express passenger services until the last decade of the nineteenth century, when many were converted to 4-4-0s. This was the first to appear. Other lines followed the pattern, with the *Etat* converting older 2-4-0s and the PLM building 390 new. The front carrying wheels were behind the outside cylinders, and the rear carrying wheels were under the cab. External Allan link motion was fitted. This motion was known as 'straight link' compared to the curved expansion link used in the Stephenson motion. The 2-4-2 tender locomotive enjoyed some vogue in Belgium and Germany, but was little used elsewhere.

**Boiler pressure:** 100kg/$cm^2$ (142psi)
**Cylinders:** 441.6x652.3mm (17.4x25.7in)
**Driving wheels:** 1999mm (78.75in)
**Grate area:** 1.6m2 (17.4sq ft)
**Heating surface:** 142.7$m^2$ (1537sq ft)
**Tractive effort:** 5408kg (11,925lb)
**Total weight:** 42.47t (93,630lb)

## *PRECEDENT* CLASS 2-4-0 LONDON & NORTH WESTERN RAILWAY (LNWR) GREAT BRITAIN: 1874

**Veteran of the 1895 'Race to the North' between the East and West Coast routes from London to Scotland, and painted in LNWR 'blackberry black', is No. 790 Hardwicke, at the Dinting Railway Centre on 3 October 1982.**

Nicknamed 'Jumbos', this inside-cylinder class was designed at Crewe, under F.W. Webb, to provide motive power on the London–Crewe–Manchester section of the LNWR. A valuable and long-lived addition to the stud, it proved its worth on the steep gradients of the Crewe–Carlisle section. By 1874, Crewe Works was a vast plant, reorganized on the most modern lines by John Ramsbottom: in 1876, it would build its 2000th locomotive. Its engines were painted a shiny black without ornamentation (at the time, there was a similar trend to utilitarian appearance in the USA).

Like many British express types, the 'Jumbos' had to make up by hard thrashing what they lacked in maximum boiler capacity, and they managed well, though at a high cost in fuel usage. One of the class, *Charles Dickens*, employed only on the Euston–Manchester run, recorded 3,218,500km (2 million miles) between 1882 and 1902; and continued on secondary duties until 1912. But as the locomotive historian E.H. Ahrons remarked, 'it would be interesting to learn how much of the original engine remained in it'. Would frames only 22mm (7/8-inch) thick be able to withstand such intensive pounding for 20 years?

**The 'Precedents' were designed early in F.W. Webb's tenure as Chief Mechanical Engineer of the LNWR, before his disastrous series of attempts with compound engines; and they outlived all the compounds.**

## CLASS DIV 0-4-0T ROYAL BAVARIAN STATE RAILWAYS (KBSTB) GERMANY 1875

Between 1875 and 1897, 132 of this lightweight well-tank design were produced by the Munich firms of Krauss and Maffei, which had yet to merge. Amendments to the design increased the maximum axle load from 12 to 14t. Carriage shunting was their major activity. When the DRG was formed, they became class $88^{71-72}$, but by 1930 all had been scrapped. The Palatinate Railway had 31 almost identical engines from 1892, DRG class $88^{73}$, of which one survived as a works engine until 1961. Such engines, lightly employed in moving 'dead' locos about the works, and sometimes treated almost as 'pets', account for some of the oldest survivals among steam locomotives.

**Boiler pressure:** 10kg/cm$^2$ (142.5psi)
**Cylinders:** 330x508mm (13x20in)
**Driving wheels:** 1006mm (39.6in)
**Grate area:** 1m$^2$ (10.8sq ft)
**Heating surface:** 64.3m$^2$ (692.3sq ft)
**Tractive effort:** 4671kg (10,300lb)
**Total weight:** 21.3t (46,966lb)

## F CLASS 0-6-0 INDIAN STATE RAILWAYS INDIA: 1875

Many hundreds of these locomotives were built and they were the standard freight model on metre-gauge (39.4in) Indian railways for decades. The first were supplied by Dübs & Co of Glasgow, and other manufacturers followed. The outside frames were typically British; the outside cylinders less so. Hall's patent cranks were fitted to the wheels, and the connecting rod was attached inside the coupling rods. The 'Fs' were powerful engines for their size, and train loads of up to 609t (600 tons) were claimed, though operating speeds were very slow. The original 6-wheel tenders had running-boards and hand-rails.

The 0-6-0 design was the most common form of motive power on all Indian railways in the late nineteenth century. On the 1676mm (5ft 6in) gauge, the Great Indian Peninsula Railway bought 102 of two different classes, K and L, between 1877 and 1884, while the East Indian railway built more than 470 of classes C and CA between 1886 and 1906. The broad-gauge engines were coal burners, but many of the metre-gauge F-class were wood-burners, with high-railed tenders. Up to 1882, 164 were built. From 1882 to 1922, a further 871 were built for the metre gauge. The later ones had larger wheels (1079mm/42.5in) and cylinder diameter increased to 355mm (14in). In 1902, F-class locos were the first to be built at the new Ajmer works of the Rajputana Malwa Railway. Ajmer's first F-class is preserved at Delhi.

**Over fifteen hundred 0-6-0 locomotives ran on the Indian Railways, coming from a variety of builders. This is one of two preserved metre-gauge (39.4in) F-class engines.**

**Boiler pressure:** 9.8kg/cm$^2$ (140psi)
**Cylinders:** 343x508mm (13.5x20in)
**Driving wheels:** 1028mm (40.5in)
**Grate area:** 1.1m$^2$ (12sq ft)
**Heating surface:** 60m$^2$ (648.2sq ft)
**Tractive effort:** 4858kg (10,700lb)
**Total weight:** 21.54t (47,488lb) (engine only)

## COMPOUND TANK 0-4-2T BAYONNE–BIARRITZ RAILWAY FRANCE: 1876

The first compound engines were designed in France by Anatole Mallet, who is most often associated with articulated locomotives; and built at Le Creusot. Small side-tank engines, they worked lightweight trains on this short line, which linked two neighbouring cities in the south-west. The two cylinders were outside, and whether for aesthetic or commercial reasons, the small high-pressure cylinder had a false casing to match the large one. At the Paris Exposition of 1878, Mallet, whose enthusiasm for compounding was well-known, was complimented on having produced a 'normal' engine. A contrast to the later compound locomotives associated with him, these diminutive engines were the precursors of an important aspect of locomotive design.

**Boiler pressure:** 10kg/cm$^2$ (145psi)
**Cylinders:** hp 241x450mm (9.5x17.75in); lp 340x450mm (15.75x17.75in)
**Driving wheels:** 1199mm (47.25in)
**Grate area:** 1m$^2$ (10.8sq ft)
**Heating surface:** 91m$^2$ (981sq ft)
**Tractive effort:** 1895kg (4180lb)
**Total weight:** 33.78t (74,480lb)

## CLASS H 0-4-2T NEW ZEALAND RAILWAYS (NZR) NEW ZEALAND: 1876

**One of the last Fell-powered trains climbs the hill in 1955, before opening of the detour. Up to four engines were used, at the head and tail, and inserted between the cars, on a 9-car train.**

The Fell traction system, invented by Englishman J.B. Fell, consisted of a large, double-headed centre rail set between the running rails. Horizontally set wheels, driven by two independent inside cylinders, were pressed against each side of this rail by powerful springs, and helped the normal running wheels to climb very steep gradients. Downhill, sledge-type brakes could be engaged against the the third rail. This system was used on the famous 1 in 15 Rimutaka Incline. The first New Zealand Fell locomotives were built in England, at the Avonside works, to H.W. Widmark's design, and delivered in 1876. Two more were built by Neilsons of Glasgow in 1886; all had outside cylinders driving the road wheels, but these had Joy's outside radial valve gear, not Stephenson's link motion of the first four.

The horizontal wheels exerted a pressure equivalent to 30 tons and the coupled wheels bore 32 tons. Each locomotive could haul 66t (65 tons) at about 4.8kph (3mph) up the hill; and as the heaviest train was 264t (260 tons), this was usually divided into sections, with four locomotives put to work. In the 1950s, the incline was replaced by an 8.8km (5.5 mile) tunnel and the Fell engines retired.

**Boiler pressure:** 11kg/cm$^2$ (160psi)
**Cylinders:** outside 355x406mm (14x16in); inside 304.5x355mm (12x14in)
**Driving wheels:** 812mm (32in)
**Grate area:** not known
**Heating surface:** not known
**Tractive effort:** 6044kg (13,328lb) (adhesion only)
**Total weight:** 44t (97,112lb)

## 93 CLASS 0-6-0 NEW SOUTH WALES GOVERNMENT RAILWAYS AUSTRALIA: 1877

**The last two regularly working members of Class 93, Nos 1904 and 1923, were kept at Waratah shed, Newcastle, until mid-1972, where they were used to push coal wagons up onto the wooden trestles of the coaling stage.**

Albeit with later modifications, including new Belpaire-type boilers from the late 1890s, this was perhaps Australia's longest-lived locomotive type, with some still operating into the 1970s. Reclassed as A-93 in 1889, they were based on the 17-Class Robert Stephenson 0-6-0 of 1865, and eventually numbered 78 engines. In the early 1900s, 14 were converted at Eveleigh to 2-6-4T, but their capacity to deal with the hilly Batlow and Oberon routes kept other tender-fitted trains in service.

**Boiler pressure:** 9.8kg/cm$^2$ (140psi)
**Cylinders:** 457x609mm (18x24in)
**Driving wheels:** 1218mm (48in)
**Grate area:** 1.66m$^2$ (17.9sq ft)
**Heating surface:** 120.2m$^2$ (1294sq ft)
**Tractive effort:** 8960kg (18,144lb)
**Total weight:** 57.5t (126,784lb)

## CLASS 97 0-6-0T KAISERIN ELISABETH BAHN (KEB) AUSTRIA: 1878

On its formation from the KEB and smaller lines in 1884, the Imperial Austrian Railways classed this side tank type as 97. It eventually had 225, and others were built up to 1913 for privately owned railways throughout the empire. The main dimensions remained the same, although there were many individual variations and alterations in detail of domes, chimneys, and so on. They were simple-expansion engines with outside cylinders and Stephenson's link motion, actuated by slide valves. One of this class was the first locomotive to be built in Czechoslovakia, by the PCM works, in 1900. They did a wide variety of work, from short-haul passenger trains to yard shunting.

**Boiler pressure:** 11kg/cm² (156psi)
**Cylinders:** 345x480mm (13.6x19in)
**Driving wheels:** 930mm (36.6in)
**Grate area:** 1m² (10.7sq ft)
**Heating surface:** 59.1m² (636sq ft)
**Tractive effort:** 5770kg (12,730lb)
**Total weight:** 30t (66,150lb)

## CLASS 2131 0-8-0 NORTHERN RAILWAY (*NORTE*) SPAIN: 1879

**Up to the 1980s, Spain was the prime European country in which to find nineteenth-century steam locomotive types, of varying degrees of 'quaintness', still in full-time work.**

British, French and German builders shared the work on this class of 47 locomotives built between 1879 and 1891. Thirty bore the names of Spanish rivers. With simple-expansion outside cylinders, Stephenson's link motion, low running plates with wheel splashers, outside steam pipes, and variously shaped pots and domes on the boiler, they had a typically Spanish blend of characteristics. Until the introduction of 2-8-0s in 1909, they were the *Norte's* main freight engines and almost all survived at work into the mid-1960s.

**Boiler pressure:** 9kg/cm² (128psi)
**Cylinders:** 500x660mm (19.7x26in)
**Driving wheels:** 1300mm (51in)
**Grate area:** 1.72m² ((19sq ft)
**Heating surface:** not known
**Tractive effort:** 9762kg (21,500lb)
**Total weight:** 73.86t (162,839lb)

## 'CAULIFLOWER' 0-6-0 LONDON & NORTH WESTERN RAILWAY (L&NWR) GREAT BRITAIN: 1880

In Britain, the standard freight locomotive was the 0-6-0, and every main-line company had its own variant on the theme, in considerable numbers. In 1913, there were 7204 of them, 46% of the entire British locomotive stock. Since Hackworth's *Royal George*, the basic type had developed as a solid, uncomplicated machine, usually inside-framed and almost invariably with two inside cylinders, adaptable to different track conditions, able to slog along the main line and to shunt in colliery and factory sidings. If more power were needed, another engine was added. From the 1870s, most 0-6-0s had cabs of some sort, and also steam brakes, steel fireboxes, and steel tyres. The LNWR had substantial coal and other freight traffic, and in 1880 F.W. Webb introduced a new 0-6-0, the first main line engine to use Joy's valve gear. It gained the name of 'Cauliflower', probably from the LNWR coat of arms on the rear splasher. Over 300 were built up to 1902, and they won particular fame because the poor performance of Webb's subsequent compound engines made their simple virtues shine all the more brightly, not least to the drivers and firemen. In the 1920s, a 'Cauliflower' was recorded as reaching 119kph (74mph) with a passenger train on the downhill grades between Penrith and Carlisle on the LMS main line.

**Already 40 years old by the formation of the London Midland & Scottish Railway in 1922, the 'Cauliflowers' were classified '2F' in the system's new power classification, indicating lightweight freight service.**

**Boiler pressure:** 9.9kg/cm² (140psi)
**Cylinders:** 457x609mm (18x24in)
**Driving wheels:** 1560mm (61.5in)
**Grate area:** 1.6 m² (17sq ft)
**Heating surface:** 112 m² (1208sq ft)
**Tractive effort:** 6800kg (15,000lb)
**Total weight:** 33.88t (74,704lb)

**No 28585 stands in the coaling and watering line at Willesden depot, London, on 17 September, 1932. Note the toolbox on the tender.**

## L-CLASS 4-6-0 INDUS VALLEY STATE RAILWAY (IVSR) INDIA: 1880

This class is both the first 4-6-0 tender locomotive to be built in Great Britain (by Neilson of Glasgow) and the first to run in India, though the Great Indian Peninsula Railway had a 4- 6-0T side tank type back in 1862. Built for the 1675mm (5ft 6in) gauge, it had two simple expansion outside cylinders and the usual capacious Indian cab. The maximum axle load was 11.1t (11tons) which may have given inadequate adhesion, as the 149 class L were supplemented by the 77 mechanically identical 'Heavy L' with a 12.4t (12.25-ton) axle load and 1294mm (51in) coupled wheels. The IVSR was absorbed into the North Western Railway in 1886, but the Ls served with distinction for 50 more years.

**Boiler pressure:** 11.2kg/cm$^2$ (160psi)
**Cylinders:** 457x660mm (18x26in)
**Driving wheels:** 1269mm (50in)
**Grate area:** 2m$^2$ (22sq ft)
**Heating surface:** 117.3m$^2$ (1263sq ft)
**Tractive effort:** 10,390kg (22,900lb)
**Total weight:** 41.4t (91,280lb)

## CLASS B50 2-4-0 STATE RAILWAYS (SS) DUTCH EAST INDIES (INDONESIA): 1880

This class of 17, the longest-lived tender engines in Indonesia, was built by the Manchester firm of Sharp, Stewart, between 1880 and 1885. Designed as passenger engines for short-haul journeys, they had modest four-wheel tenders. The two simple expansion cylinders were outside, operated by internal valve gear. Ninety years after their arrival, all – except 3 sent to Sumatra – were still in service. By the end of the 1980s, they were gone.

**Some engines of this class were used in Java until the 1980s. B5004 stands at Madinam shed on 2 March 1983.**

**Boiler pressure:** 10kg/cm$^2$ (140psi)
**Cylinders:** 381x457mm (15x18in)
**Driving wheels:** 1413mm (55.6in)
**Grate area:** 1.1m$^2$ (11.8sq ft)
**Heating surface:** 50m$^2$ (538.3sq ft)
**Tractive effort:** 3930kg (8668lb)
**Total weight:** 22.47t (49,532lb) (engine only)

## 4-2-2 PHILADELPHIA & READING RAILROAD (PRR) USA: 1880

A single set of driving wheels was used in this engine, the 5000th locomotive built at the Baldwin works in Philadelphia. It was intended for lightweight passenger trains to be run at the then high speed of 96.5kph (60mph) on the Bound Brook line between Philadelphia and New York. A special feature was an auxiliary steam cylinder just in front of the firebox, which bore down on the fulcrum of an equalizing lever joining the driving and trailing axles. The aim was to transfer weight to the drivers when starting, then redistribute it. The locomotive was later sold on, and is best known as sharing the name of its new owner, *Lovett Eames*. inventor of a vacuum brake, who sent the engine to England to demonstrate his system. It was broken up at Wood Green, London, in 1883.

**Boiler pressure:** 9.5kg/cm$^2$ (135psi)
**Cylinders:** 457x609mm (18x24in)
**Driving wheels:** 1980mm (78in)
**Grate area:** not known
**Heating surface:** 130m$^2$ (1400sq ft)
**Tractive effort:** 5187kg (11,439lb)
**Total weight:** 21t (63, 949lb)

## SHAY TYPE USA: 1880

**A three-truck Shay, from the cylinder side, showing the flexible drive. This is the same model as the preserved engine shown below.**

Ephraim Shay designed the first really effective geared locomotive. He sold his first one in 1880 and took out a patent in June 1881. He wanted to make an engine that could draw lumber cars on temporary hillside tracks, applying maximum haulage power to low-speed operation. His solution was to transmit the power from vertically mounted cylinders by means of a piston-driven crankshaft, which in turn operated drive shafts via universal joints, turning the axles of four-wheel trucks on which the engine rode. The first Shay ran on two trucks; the last, built for the Western Maryland Railroad's Chaffee branch in 1945, had three; the biggest, Class D, weighing 150 tons (152.4t), had four. All axles were powered and a Shay could take its load up a 1 in 10 grade relying on its own adhesion. Apart from the drive system, the most distinctive feature was the off-centre boiler barrel, placed to left of centre to balance the cylinders, both or all three of which were placed on the right-hand side.

In 1882, Shay assigned manufacturing rights to what was to become the great Lima Locomotive Company, and Lima included standard models of two, three or four trucks in its catalogue. Though Shay locomotives went all over the world, the great majority were bought by logging companies in North America, and of the several different types of geared locomotives for forestry work, the Shay was by far the most frequently used.

The specification here is for a three-truck superheated Shay of the 1930s.

**Boiler pressure:** 14kg/cm$^2$ (200psi)
**Cylinders:** 330x381mm (13x15in)
**Driving wheels:** 914mm (36in)
**Grate area:** 2.6m$^2$ (27.75sq ft)
**Heating surface:** 84m$^2$ (905sq ft)
**Superheater:** 17.5m$^2$ (189sq ft)
**Tractive effort:** 17,324kg (38,200lb)
**Total weight:** 85.28t (188,000lb)

**A well-preserved 3-cylinder, 3-truck Shay photographed in Maryland, the United States, in September 2000.**

## CLASS 220 4-4-0 HUNGARIAN RAILWAYS (MÁV) AUSTRO-HUNGARY:1881

Once the Budapest Locomotive Works were opened in 1880, MÁV and other Hungarian companies bought most of their locomotives there. This was one of the earliest, and the first 4-4-0. Between 1881 and 1905, 201 were built. To help spark retention, they had smoke-boxes extended to the buffer-beam and two outside simple expansion cylinders. An express passenger class, it was capable of relatively high speed with lightweight trains. Most were scrapped by 1939, but one from 1900 is preserved. Although MÁV also operated mountain lines, most of the system was in the Danube valley and on the great Hungarian plain, where fast running was possible, as on the stretch between Esztergom and Budapest, on the line between the Austrian and Hungarian capitals.

**Boiler pressure:** 12kg/cm² (171psi)
**Cylinders:** 450x650mm (17.75x25.6in)
**Driving wheels:** 1826mm (72in)
**Grate area:** 2.1m² (22.6sq ft)
**Heating surface:** 135.6m² (1460sq ft)
**Tractive effort:** 7380kg (16,280lb)
**Total weight:** 48.8t (107,604lb) (engine only)

## *ROCKET OF CHINA* 2-4-0T KAIPING TRAMWAY CHINA: 1881

The first railway in China opened between Shanghai and Wusung, in 1876 – a distance of 8km (5 miles) – and closed in 1877 after a fatal accident. The Kaiping Tramway, a narrow-gauge coal line, was next. Traction was intended to be by mule-power, but the British resident engineer built this small engine without permission. Prejudice against steam locomotion was strong in China at this time, and riots accompanied the building of early railways. When an inspection team was due to come, the engineer concealed his locomotive in a hastily dug pit.

**Cylinders:** 362x558mm (14.25x22in)
Other details not available

## 'VITTORIO-EMANUELE' CLASS 4-6-0 UPPER ITALIAN RAILWAYS (SFAI) ITALY: 1884

The many steep slopes between Turin and Genoa on this network (later the Mediterranean Railway Network), and particularly the Giovi Pass, had always required multiple engine power. It was to work the relief line to the Giovi incline that Europe's first 4-6-0 was designed by Cesare Frescot, chief mechanical engineer of the company. Even this line had a continuous gradient of 1 in 62 for 23.5km (14.6 miles) and a tunnel of 8.3km (5.1 miles). Perhaps due to the long tunnel, the line used Welsh steam coal, producing relatively little smoke compared with soft coal. On the new line, the class could climb at a steady 40kph (25mph) with a 130t (128-ton) train. It was a two-cylinder, simple expansion, mixed traffic engine. Fifty-five were built, designated as class 650 by the FS from 1905. The first was named to honour the united Italy's first king, and built at the Turin works; others were built by private constructors, Ansaldo of Sampierdareno and Miani & Silvestri of Milan, with 12 coming from Maffei in Munich. The firebox had an early form of combustion chamber. The front bogie was unusual, its wheelbase only 1200mm (47.3in), with the cylinders set behind it and the steam pipes sharply angled backwards. Frescot was concerned to keep the wheelbase of the locomotive within turntable and stabling limits, at 13,660mm (44ft 10in). By 1914, both the Giovi line and the relief line were electrified and the 4-6-0s were withdrawn.

**Boiler pressure:** 11kg/cm² (156.75psi)
**Cylinders:** 470x620mm (18.5x24.4in)
**Driving wheels:** 1675mm (66in)
**Grate area:** 2.25m² (24sq ft)
**Heating surface:** 124m² (1720sq ft)
**Tractive effort:** 6,960kg (15,335lb)
**Total weight:** 59.9t (132,079lb)

## CLASS 7 2-6-0 BUENOS AIRES GREAT SOUTHERN RAILWAY (BAGS) ARGENTINA: 1885

Destined for freight service, 28 of this class were built by Beyer Peacock in Manchester. Simple-expansion outside cylinders were fitted, in some of the class with a diameter of 457mm (18in). Oil was not yet the common fuel in Argentina and these engines had an extended smokebox to help prevent sparks when burning wood. A larger mixed traffic 2-6-0 from the same builders followed in 1901.

By 1924, only four of the class 7s remained in action, and all were withdrawn by 1926. The increasing length and weight of goods trains was a severe test for the class 7s, and from 1903, the class 11 2-8-0 compounds of 1903 relieved them of much of their heavy work.

**Boiler pressure:** 10.5kg/cm² (150psi)
**Cylinders:** 431x609mm (17x24in)
**Driving wheels:** 1269mm (50in)
**Grate area:** 1.9m² (20.1sq ft)
**Heating surface:** 100.8m² (1086sq ft)
**Tractive effort:** 6825kg (15,050lb)
**Total weight:** 78.7t (173,484lb)

## L-304 CLASS 2-6-0 NEW SOUTH WALES GOVERNMENT RAILWAYS AUSTRALIA: 1885

Unsurprisingly, as a British colony, with British-owned and run railways, Australia's early engines were almost entirely British in origin. But Baldwins were on the scene by 1885, when 10 of these neat 2-6-0s were supplied from Philadelphia to haul passenger trains over the Blue Mountains route west of Sydney. Later, they were moved to western New South Wales. The original class had domeless boilers, an un-American design feature presumably requested by the NSWGR. It was a hardworking class, and most went through three boilers in their time. The last was withdrawn in 1939. A further ten class L, with domed boilers, were supplied by Baldwins at the same time.

**Boiler pressure:** 9.8 kg/cm² (140psi)
**Cylinders:** 457x660mm (18x26in)
**Driving wheels:** 1548mm (61in)
**Grate area:** 1.5m² (16.9sq ft)
**Heating surface:** 120.9m² (1302sq ft)
**Tractive effort:** 7014kg (15,467lb)
**Total weight:** 48.26t (106,400lb)

## FORNEY TANK LOCOMOTIVE 0-4-4T MANHATTAN RAILWAY USA: 1885

Matthias Forney, who was both a technical journalist and a practising mechanic, was one of the few American advocates of the tank engine. In 1866 he took out a patent on a tank locomotive, arguing that the concentration of weight would improve traction. But while tank engines were widely used elsewhere, they found little favour on American railways, chiefly because of their heavy axle-load and restricted water capacity. Few customers appeared for the Forney type until, in 1878, the New York Elevated Railroad took it up. The 'El' had opened in 1868 as one of the first inner-city rapid-transit lines, going overhead while London went underground. The iron-framed trestles could not support heavy locomotives, and the line's first tiny engines lacked power to pull long trains. The

**Built by Vulcan in 1913 for the 609mm (2ft) gauge Monson Railway, this Forney was photographed at the Edaville 'Family Fun Park' Railway in Massachusetts. It is now at Portland, Mass.**

Forney type served the system well until electrification was completed in 1903, by which time the NY system had over 300 of them. Many were sold on to other lines.

The first elevated Forney weighed just under 15 tons (15.25t), and this gradually crept up to around 24 tons (24.4t) in later engines. Carried on four axles, this did not overstress the track supports. Built for stop-start work, and painted bright red, these were among the first US engines to have brakes, using the Lovett Eames vacuum system. They were also, in John H. White's words, 'put in diapers' in order to minimize ash, oil and water falling through the trackwork; for a similar reason, they burned only the best hard steam coal.

**Boiler pressure:** 8.4kg/cm² (120psi)
**Cylinders:** 304.5x456.8mm (12x18in)
**Driving wheels:** 1294mm (51in)
**Grate area:** 97m² (9sq ft)
**Heating surface:** 52.5m² (565.2sq ft)
**Tractive effort:** 2350kg (5180lb)
**Total weight:** 18.8t (41,440lb)

**A Manhattan Forney, with its slim chimney, closed-in cab, Belpaire firebox, and small bunker, typical of the first 'Elevated' engines. Bells and cow-catchers were not needed.**

**Forney locomotives ran on numerous lines apart from the 'El', some in Europe but mostly in the United States. No 3 of the Berkeley Railroad, South Carolina, was a wood-burner.**

## R-CLASS 4-6-0 SOUTH AUSTRALIAN RAILWAYS — AUSTRALIA: 1886

The first Australian 4-6-0s were the F (later B-13) freight class of the Queensland Government Railways. The Rs were a classic mixed-traffic version which were the staple of the SAR system up to the 1920s. Ultimately 84 were built, some at home by James Martin and the SAR's own Islington works, others in Scotland. From 1925, a number of the class were equipped with superheaters. They operated on all kinds of service from the crack Adelaide–Melbourne expresses to local freights. The front-cowled cab, generally fitted to Australian locos, was an attempt to reduce sun-glare and improve look-out. The Rs worked into the 1960s and several are preserved.

**Steam pressure:** 10kg/$cm^2$ (145psi)
**Cylinders:** 457x609mm (18x24in)
**Driving wheels:** 1370mm (54in)
**Grate area:** 1.9$m^2$ (20.3sq ft)
**Heating surface:** 120.2$m^2$ (1294sq ft)
**Tractive effort:** 7575kg (16,704lb)
**Total weight:** 65t (143,360lb)

## 'DECAPOD' 2-10-0 DOM PEDRO SEGUNDO RAILWAY — BRAZIL: 1886

Baldwins built this first 2-10-0 for shipping to Brazil. Its coupled wheelbase was 5178mm (17ft), and care was taken with the wheel design. The second and third sets of coupled wheels had no flanges, and the fifth set was allowed 6.3mm (0.25in) extra lateral movement; thus the 3858mm (12ft 8in) wheelbase between axles 1 and 4 in effect formed the rigid wheelbase, and curves of 12.7m (42ft) could be negotiated at the slow speeds intended.

Although it would in time become a staple freight locomotive, there was no rush to acquire 'Decapods' at this time: most lines looking for a bigger engine chose an articulated type. Much later, of course, it became a universally used freight engine wheel arrangement throughout the world.

**Boiler pressure:** $cm^2$)
**Cylinders:** 558x660mm (22x26in)
**Driving wheels:** 1142mm (45in)
**Grate area:** $m^2$)
**Heating surface:** $m^2$)
**Tractive effort:**
**Total weight:** 64t (141,000lb) (engine only)

## 4-CYLINDER 2-4-0 NORTHERN RAILWAY (*NORD*) FRANCE: 1886

Designed by Gaston du Bousquet, this express engine was the first 4-cylinder compound locomotive in France. The high-pressure cylinders, inside the frame, drove the first leading axle, and the outside, low-pressure cylinders drove the second axle (the other way round to the *Nord's* subsequent de Glehn 4-cylinder engines). At first, the driving wheels were not coupled, but coupling rods were later added, and the engines were also converted, by the addition of a leading bogie, to 4-4-0s.

The success of the Du Bousquet compounds was assisted by the French method of driver training, which included tuition on the theoretical aspects of steam power. As a result, the drivers had a clear understanding of compounding and of how it should be used for best results. The tradition thus established lasted right up to the last days of French steam.

**Boiler pressure:** 11kg/cm$^2$ (157psi)
**Cylinders:** hp 330x609mm (13x24in); lp 462x609mm (18.2x24in)
**Driving wheels:** 2113mm (83.25in)
**Grate area:** 2.4m$^2$ (25.6sq ft)
**Heating surface:** 103m$^2$ (1109sq ft)
**Tractive effort:** N/A
**Total weight:** 41.4t (91,280lb) (engine only)

## CLASS 56 0-6-0 IMPERIAL & ROYAL STATE RAILWAYS (KKSTB) AUSTRIA: 1888

From its formation in 1884, the kkStB set about a standardization policy and this goods engine formed a class of 153. Built between 1888 and 1890 at the Floridsdorf, StEG, and Wiener Neustadt works, they were distributed quite widely over the imperial system, and in 1918 examples were inherited by the new Polish, Yugoslavian and Czech railways, alongside those that remained in Austrian hands. They continued to operate on lightweight goods trains and as station pilots until the 1950s. Like other long-lived Austrian types, they went through a range of modifications under new ownership. Successive boiler changes, new blast pipes and chimneys, and other rebuildings produced new profiles, though the engines' basic role itself never changed.

**Boiler pressure:** 11kg/cm$^2$ (156psi)
**Cylinders:** 450x632mm (17.75x25in)
**Driving wheels:** 1258mm (49.5in)
**Grate area:** 1.8m$^2$ (19.4sq ft)
**Heating surface:** 119.4m$^2$ (1285.5sq ft)
**Tractive effort:** 9524kg (21,000lb)
**Total weight:** 41.5t (91,507lb) (engine only)

## LARTIGUE'S MONORAIL LISTOWEL & BALLYBUNION RAILWAY IRELAND: 1888

François Lartigue claimed that his patent monorail was easy and economical to build and operate. Technically, it was not a monorail, since it was supported on A-shaped iron trestles that bore a carrying rail on the apex, and a guide rail on each side, a quarter of the way from the ground. After failures in Belgium and France, he went to Ireland. The town of Ballybunion had been agitating for a line from Listowel, 14.9km (9.25 miles) away. Lartigue offered his system, and the L&B was formed. The first train ran on 29 February 1888.

The line ran three engines, the designs of Anatole Mallet and built by Hunslet of Leeds, England. Double units, with a boiler and firebox on each side of the carrying rail, they could pull 142.2t (140 tons) on the level or 71.1t (70 tons) up a 1 in 100 gradient. Three coupled wheels, double-flanged, engaged the top rail between the boilers. A booster cylinder was fitted to the tender, but was later removed. Dual controls were fitted, and the driver worked on the right, where he had also to feed his fire. Sections of track could be swung to one side to allow for crossings, and track joinings were managed in a similar way. The main problem was balance: when the line transported a grand piano, a cow was used to offset the load on the other side. Perhaps the most remarkable thing was that it lasted 36 years, until a damage in the civil war and a deficit of cash forced its closure. The last train ran to Listowel, on 14 October 1924, and the railway was then dismantled for scrap.

**Nothing remains of the monorail, but this photograph of a train at the Liselton station and crossing loop indicates how it operated.**

**Boiler pressure:** 10.5kg/cm$^2$ (150psi)
**Cylinders:** 178x304.5mm (7x12in)
**Driving wheels:** 609mm (24in)
**Grate area:** 0.46m$^2$ (5sq ft)(two boxes)
**Heating surface:** 6.6m$^2$ (71.75sq ft)
**Tractive effort:** 998kg (2200lb)
**Total weight:** 11.07t (24,4000lb) (engine only)

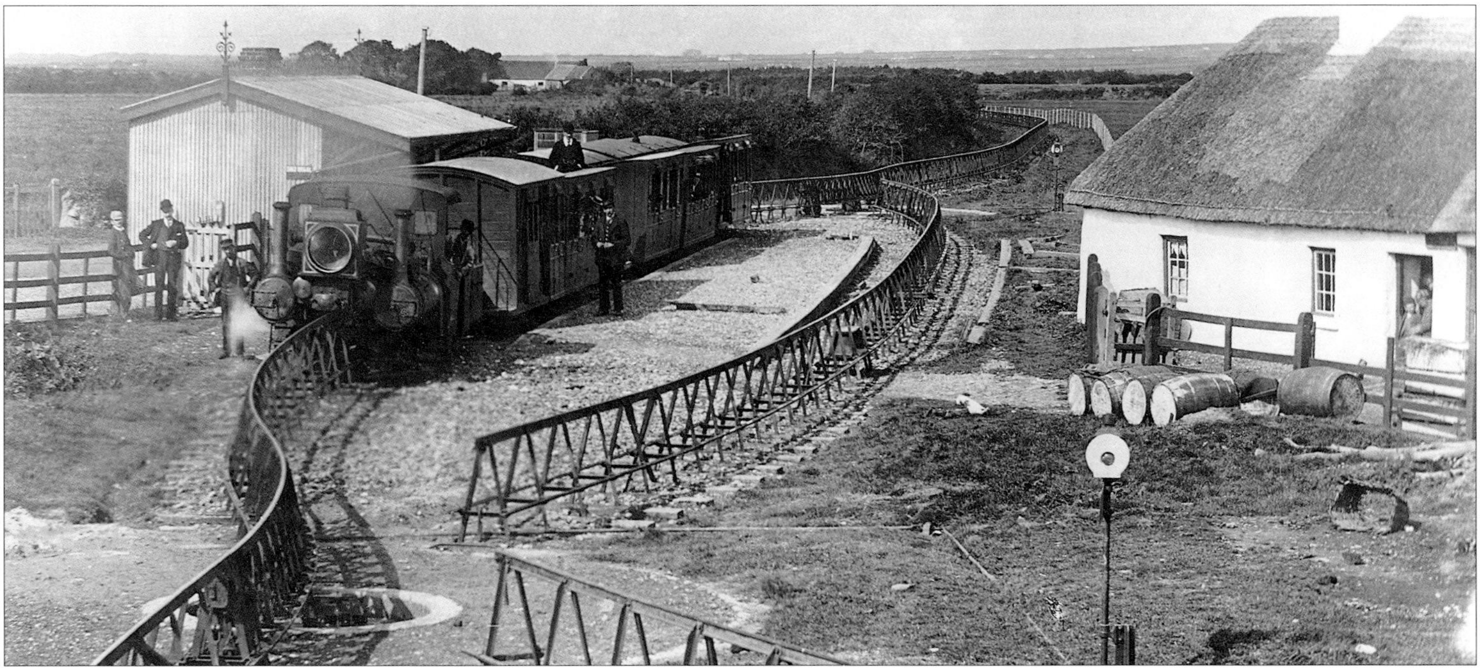

## 2-4-2T LANCASHIRE & YORKSHIRE RAILWAY (L&YR) GREAT BRITAIN: 1889

**An Aspinall 2-4-2T at Manchester in 1961, with British Railways number 50850. This is from the 1905 version, with larger bunker, Belpaire firebox and an extended smoke-box. A third version was produced in 1912.**

Designed by Sir John Aspinall and built at the company's Horwich Works, this was Britain's biggest 2-4-2T and it was the staple of passenger traffic on this busy inter-city provincial line. To enable it to run commuter expresses into Manchester, it was fitted with a water scoop, and engines from 1898 had coal and water capacity increased from the original 2.5 tons and 1340gals (1609 US gals). The leading and trailing wheels were mounted radially, the pivoting points being behind and ahead of the axles respectively, allowing good flexibility, and several other lines had 2-4-2Ts on the same principle.

**Boiler pressure:** 11.3kg/cm$^2$ (160psi)
**Cylinders:** 457x660mm (18x26in)
**Driving wheels:** 1720mm (67.8in)
**Heating surface:** 113m$^2$ (1216.4sq ft)
**Grate area:** 1.7m$^2$ (18.75sq ft)
**Tractive effort:** 7664kg (16,900lb)
**Total weight:** 56.85t (125,328lb)

## *TEUTONIC* 2-2-2-0 LONDON & NORTH WESTERN RAILWAY (LNWR) GREAT BRITAIN: 1889

In 1878, the Swiss engineer Anatole Mallet exhibited his compound tank engine at the Paris Exhibition. Among those who were impressed was F.W. Webb, the Chief Mechanical Engineer of the LNWR. Webb experimented with compound engines from 1879, and between 1882 and 1890 he brought out four different compound classes, all intended as express engines. The 'Teutonics' were the final class, and 10 were built. Like their predecessors, they had three cylinders, the two outer ones being high-pressure, and the inner one low-pressure. The outer cylinders drove the rear wheels, the inside cylinder drive the front set. The wheels were not coupled.

Complex and expensive, the compound engines reversed Crewe's previous policy of building cheap and simple designs. They were not a success. The 'Teutonics' were the most reliable in service. No 1304 *Jeanie Deans* ran the 'Scotch Express' between Euston and Crewe between 1891 and 1899, loading up to 305t (300 tons), at an average speed of just under 80kph (50mph) in the down direction, and 84kph (52mph) on the more favourably graded up service; and kept good time. No 1306, *Ionic*, achieved 1,140,240km (708,512 miles) up to 1904. But it does not compare with the 3,218,500km (two million miles) of the 2-4-0 'Precedent' *Charles Dickens*. The compounds were heavy coal users, and needed more repair and maintenance than simple-expansion engines. Webb retired, unwillingly, in 1903. By 1907, all his compounds had been scrapped.

**Boiler pressure:** 12kg/cm$^2$ (175psi)
**Cylinders:** hp 355x609mm (14x24in); lp 761x609mm (30x24in)
**Driving wheels:** 2157mm (85in)
**Grate area:** 1.9m$^2$ (20.5sq ft)
**Heating surface:** 126.5m$^2$ (1362sq ft)
**Tractive effort:**
**Total weight:** 46.23t (101,920lb)

***Jeanie Deans*, as delivered new from Crewe Works. The driving wheels, disconcertingly, sometimes turned in opposite directions on starting.**

## CLASS B 0-4-0ST DARJEELING HIMALAYAN RAILWAY (DHR) INDIA: 1889

**DHR No. 797 rounds a curve below Sonada, climbing with a train from Kurseong to Darjeeling, on 2 December 1984.**

**Boiler pressure:** 9.8kg/cm² (140psi)
**Cylinders:** 279x355mm (11x14in)
**Driving wheels:** 660mm (26in)
**Grate area:** 0.8m² (9sq ft)
**Heating surface:** 29.3m² (316sq ft)
**Tractive effort:** 3515kg (7750lb)
**Total weight:** 15.5t (34,160lb)

Sharp, Stewart were the first to build this saddle tank class, which formed the basic motive power of the celebrated 610mm (2ft) gauge mountain line, which still operates (now partly diesel-powered), climbing over 2000m (6560ft) to a summit level of 2258m (7407ft) at Ghum, in the course of a highly scenic 87km (54 mile) run with a series of spectacular loops and zig-zags. Thirty-four engines of class B were built over a 40-year period, mostly imported from Britain, though three came from the USA and three were assembled at the DHR Tindharia workshops.

**The summit station at Ghum, with DHR No 795 on a train from Darjeeling to New Jalpaiguri, on 29 January 2002.**

## CLASS W 2-6-2T NEW ZEALAND RAILWAYS (NZR) NEW ZEALAND: 1889

**On the rising grade, a class Wa 2-6-2T crosses a trestle with a coal train, running on Fell track but with central rail only for braking, near Paparoa on South Island, NZ.**

The two locomotives of this class were the first to be designed and built at the NZR's own workshops at Addington, and they survived in service into the 1950s. They were based on the dimensions of the 1874 class J 'Canterbury Goods' 2-6-0, and both were used on steeply graded track, at Upper Hutt, in the Wellington District, and on the celebrated Rimutaka incline, where they assisted the rack-fitted Fell locomotives.

Although the Class W had no third-rail traction, brakes were fitted to work on the centre rail. From the early 1900s, they worked on steep South Island colliery branches. The elder, No. 192, is preserved.

**Boiler pressure:** 12kg/cm² (170psi)
**Cylinders:** 355x508mm (14x20in)
**Driving wheels:** 926mm (36.5in)
**Grate area:** 1.1m² (12sq ft)
**Heating surface:** 63m² (683sq ft)
**Tractive effort:** 7040kg (15,500lb)
**Total weight:** 37.5t (82,656lb)

## MALLET 0-4-4-0T SWISS CENTRAL RAILWAY (SZE) SWITZERLAND: 1889

Anatole Mallet obtained his patent for an articulated engine in 1885, and the very first was an 0-4-4-0T of metre-gauge (39.4in) in 1888, for the Corsican Railways. In 1890, the Gotthard Railway commissioned a single 0-6-6-0T, and this class of 26 followed on the SZE. Sixteen were built between 1891 and 1893 by Maffei in Munich, and the others in 1897–1900 by SLM, Winterthur (these had slightly differing dimensions). All had the standard Mallet semi-articulation, the front (low-pressure) power unit mounted on a pivot set behind the wheels; the rear, high-pressure power unit being fixed to the frame. They were intended for heavy haulage, and fitted for steam heating to pull passenger as well as goods trains. Maximum service speed was 55kph (34mph). The four cylinders, outside-set, were operated by slide valves. As Mallet drivers all over the world would learn, care had to be exercised on starting: despite the presence of a valve to admit live steam to the low-pressure cylinders on starting, the fact that the two sets of wheels were independently coupled made the 'high pressure' wheels more likely to slip. Rather to Mallet's chagrin in later life, the giant locomotives that bore his name would be simple-expansion types: he was a firm believer in compounding. Over 5000 Mallets would be built, of wildly varying size, up to 1961.

The first of the SZE engines were withdrawn in 1910; the last was taken out of service in 1936. The longest survivors worked on the Pont-Brassus section of the Swiss Federal Railways (SBB).

**Boiler pressure:** 12kg/cm² (171psi)
**Cylinders:** hp 355x640mm (14x25in); lp 550x640mm (21.6x25in)
**Driving wheels:** 1280mm (50.4in)
**Grate area:** 1.8m² (19.4sq ft)
**Heating surface:** 113m² (1216.6sq ft)
**Tractive effort:** N/A
**Total weight:** 60.41t (133,182lb)

## HEISLER GEARED LOCOMOTIVE USA: 1889

**Its works code-name 'Arctic', the two-truck Heisler could pull 800t (787 tons) on level track, or 15.5t (15 tons) up a 1 in 10 grade. Built for the W.H. Eccles Lumber Co, this is one of numerous preserved examples.**

**Boiler pressure:** kg/cm² (160psi)
**Cylinders:** mm (9.5x10in)
**Driving wheels:** 76mm (30in)
**Grate area:** not known
**Heating surface:** not known
**Tractive effort:** 15,875kg (7200lb)
**Total weight:** 16.33t (36,000lb)

The Heisler locomotive shared the same general purpose as the Shay type, that of operating lumber trains over steep, twisting and lightly laid tracks. It too delivered a drive to four-wheel trucks via a crankshaft. But the boiler was centrally mounted in conventional fashion, and the cylinders set in a V formation on each side, balancing each other, and driving the centrally-mounted crankshaft. One axle of each truck was driven, the other was linked by an outside connecting rod. Charles Heisler's first locomotive was built in 1891, by the Dunkirk Engineering Co of New York, and he patented his design the following year. Regular production was from

1894 at the Stearns Locomotive Co , of Erie, Pennsylvania. This company was liquidated in 1904, and in 1907 became the Heisler Locomotive Works. They continued to build engines until 1941, when lack of demand forced the closure of the works.

Though speed was hardly a requisite, Heislers were reckoned to be the fastest of the geared locomotives. They were used mostly by US logging and mining companies, and approximately 625 were built. Specifications are for the two-truck smallest model, code-name 'Arctic', from the 1908 catalogue, which could pull 800t (787 tons) on the level, or 15.5t (15 tons) up a 1 in 10 grade.

**Appropriately a wood burner, No. 3 of the Eccles engines still does demonstration runs. Unlike the Shay locos, the actual means of propulsion is concealed on the Heisler type.**

## P-6 Class 4-6-0 NEW SOUTH WALES GOVERNMENT RAILWAYS AUSTRALIA: 1892

**Boiler pressure:** 11.2kg/cm² (160psi)
**Cylinders:** 508x660mm (20x26in)
**Driving wheels:** 1523mm (60in)
**Grate area:** 2.5m² (27sq ft)
**Heating surface:** 177.9m² (1916sq ft)
**Tractive effort:** 10,062kg (22,187lb)
**Total weight:** 90.12t (198,688lb)

Queensland Railways were the first in Australia to operate 4-6-0s, from 1883, and the South Australian and New South Wales systems followed suit. The first NSWGR 4-6-0s were twelve standard-pattern Baldwins ordered in a hurry and delivered in 1891 to ease the shortage of express motive power resulting from the late arrival of the P class engines. The first 50 finally arrived from Beyer Peacock's Manchester works in 1892. The design was the NSWGR's own: simple expansion engines with two outside cylinders operated by slide valves and internal sets of valve gear. The only exception were the last two of the first batch, which were built as 3-cylinder compounds, having two low pressure cylinders on one side and a single high pressure cylinder on the other. The arrangement was not successful and both were converted to 2-cylinder simple working in 1901. All had Belpaire fireboxes. Other characteristic features were the downwards slope of the running plate towards the buffer beam, and the sandbox combined in the splasher of the first coupled wheels. The class as a whole was very successful, and ultimately 191 were built for the NSWGR, 106 from Beyer Peacock, 20 from Baldwins, and the rest from

**Although designed by staff of the New South Wales Government Railway, the British ancestry of the P6 is clearly revealed in its simple lines and minimum of external features.**

Australian builders – 45 from Clyde Engineering and 20 from Eveleigh Works. Between 1911 and 1939, the class was fitted with Schmidt superheaters and piston valves. In 1924, it was re-classified C-32. Most were also given bogie tenders, though some, operating to country terminals where the turntables could not accommodate the big tenders, kept the original six-wheelers. During the 1930s, many of the class were also fitted with reinforced frames.

A further 26 were built as Class G for the Commonwealth Railways, between 1914 and 1917, to work on the new 1691km (1050 miles) transcontinental line, including the celebrated straight section of 456km (283 miles) across the Nullarbor Plain. Four came from Clyde Engineering in Sydney, 12 from Baldwins in Philadelphia, and the final 10 from Toowoomba Foundry, Queensland. A supplementary water tank was added behind the tender for the long dry sections. No G21 worked the first trans-Australia express, of 10 cars, out of Port Augusta at 9.32 pm on 22 October 1917. Two engine changes were made before arrival at Kalgoorlie, at 2.50 pm, on 24 October. Here the new line met the narrow-gauge Western Australian line, and the passengers had to change trains to continue to Perth. Seven Gs were later superheated as Class Ga, but their transcontinental work was taken over by C-class 4-6-0s in 1938.

The P class had a longer career. Even when displaced from express main-line work, they were kept busy on local and semi-fast passenger and fast goods services on lines in the Blue Mountains, the South Coast, and the Newcastle area. All 191 were still running in 1956, though many were withdrawn from then onwards. Forty-seven engines in the class achieved lifetime mileages in excess of 3,200,000km (2,000,000 miles), and No 3242 held the record for any Australian steam locomotive, of 3,802,024km (2,362,468 miles), a record that few engines anywhere could emulate. Another of the class, No 3246, operated the last scheduled steam service in Australia, between Newcastle and Singleton, in July 1971, when it was finally transferred to diesel working. Four of the class, plus No G1, have been preserved.

## CLASS 7 4-8-0 CAPE GOVERNMENT RAILWAYS (CGR) — SOUTH AFRICA: 1892

The 4-8-0 became a standard mixed-traffic type on the CGR and later the SAR system. This was the first to be introduced, followed by numerous sub-classes and the larger-dimensioned Class 8. Freight haulage was always the prime task of this type of engine, and in their later years they were mostly employed in marshalling yards.

Several were fitted with Belpaire boilers by the SAR. A long-lived type of engine, there were still eight of the original Class 7 at work in 1969.

**Eight of the original Class 7s were still in operation as late as 1969. In this photograph, taken on 4 February 1978, No. 975, built by Neilsons as long ago as 1892, stands in storage in the sidings at Germiston depot, on the outskirts of Johannesburg.**

**Boiler pressure:** 11kg/cm$^2$ (160psi)
**Cylinders:** 431.5x584mm (17x23in)
**Driving wheels:** 1079mm (42.5in)
**Grate area:** 1.6m$^2$ (17.5sq ft)
**Heating surface:** 93.8m$^2$ (1010sq ft)
**Tractive effort:** 8462kg (18,660lb)
**Total weight:** 46.23t (101,920lb) (engine only)

## CLASS CC SWEDISH STATE RAILWAYS (SJ) SWEDEN: 1892

The bogie coach was introduced into Sweden in 1891 and Class Cc was designed to cope with the heavier trains that followed. Designed by F.A. Almgren and built by Nydquist & Holm, it numbered 79 by 1903. Some were fitted for wood-burning and one burned powdered peat. A typical Swedish spark-arrester collar was fitted at the chimney base. Forty-eight were later superheated as Class Cd. Satisfactory on light trains, the Ccs were not strong performers, despite reboilering in the 1900s, but nevertheless the last of the class were retired only in 1956. In latter years, they were used mainly on branch services, where heavy hauling or high speed were not required.

**Boiler pressure:** 11kg/cm$^2$ (156psi)
**Cylinders:** 420x560mm (16.5x22in)
**Driving wheels:** 1880mm (74in)
**Grate area:** 1.86m$^2$ (20sq ft)
**Heating surface:** 108m$^2$ (1162.8sq ft)
**Tractive effort:** 4860kg (10,730lb)
**Total weight:** 41t (90,405lb) (engine only)

## K-CLASS 2-8-4T WESTERN AUSTRALIAN GOVERNMENT RAILWAYS (WAGR) AUSTRALIA: 1893

Suburban railway networks developed around the Australian cities, and this big engine was built by Neilsons of Glasgow for work in the Perth area. The gauge was 1065mm (3ft 6in). Twenty-four were built, though six were requisitioned by the British government in 1899 for war use in South Africa. Like many other Australian engines, it shows a basic British style with a number of American features, notably the cow-catcher (front and rear) and the central buffer-coupling. An attempt at superheating the class was a failure, but new boilers were fitted in the later 1930s. Most were withdrawn in the 1940s, but a few survived as yard shunters until 1964.

**Boiler pressure:** 8.3kg/cm$^2$ (120psi)
**Cylinders:** 431x533mm (17x21in)
**Driving wheels:** 964mm (38in)
**Grate area:** 1.55m$^2$ (16.7sq ft)
**Heating surface:** 90.4m$^2$ (973sq ft)
**Tractive effort:** 6953kg (15,332lb)
**Total weight:** 53.85t (118,720lb)

## CLASS S3 4-4-0 ROYAL PRUSSIAN UNION RAILWAYS (KPEV) GERMANY: 1893

Although the Prussian Railways were to be trend-setters in the early twentieth century, this successful class of 1027 engines, built up to 1904, owes much to a visit made by their chief engineer August von Borries to the USA, as the bar frames and long wheelbase show. Two-cylinder compounds, they used von Borries' own system developed previously. The valve gear was modern (Heusinger's version of the Walschaerts gear), but slide valves were still used. Much of Wilhelm Schmidt's experimentation with superheaters was carried out on this class.

Though von Borries was later well known for four-cylinder compounds, operated by only two sets of valve gears, his two-cylinder compounds had already attracted interest in England, where the cylinders could be inside, fitting in with the designers' preference for the moving parts of locomotives to be kept unseen, and led to the Worsdell-von Borries compounds on the Great Eastern and North Eastern Railways, between 1884 and 1893; and in Ireland on the Belfast & Northern Counties Railway between 1890 and 1908.

**Boiler pressure:** 12kg/cm$^2$ (171psi)
**Cylinders:** hp 480x600mm (18.9x23.6in); lp 680x600mm (26.6x23.6in)
**Driving wheels:** 1980mm (78in)
**Grate area:** 2.3m$^2$ (25sq ft)
**Heating surface:** 117.7m$^2$ (1267sq ft)
**Tractive effort:** N/A
**Total weight:** 50.8t (112,000lb) (engine only)

**At Strasbourg in December 1912 (a time when Alsace was annexed to Germany), a superheated S3 begins to get under way with an eastbound express.**

## CLASS C12 2-6-0T STATE RAILWAYS (SS) DUTCH EAST INDIES (INDONESIA): 1893

The Dutch management of the SS tended to follow European continental practice, and all 43 of the C12 2-cylinder compound, like its simple-expansion predecessor the C11, came from the German firm of Hartmann, in Chemnitz. Some of the class were fitted with extended smokeboxes. In the 1970s, 13 were still active, operating mixed-train services on branch lines in East Java.

**Still with copper chimney cap and dome, the well-maintained No. C12 06 gleams against a brilliant Javanese sunset.**

**Boiler pressure:** 12kg/cm² (171psi)
**Cylinders:** hp 380x509mm (15x20in); lp 580x509mm (22.8x20in)
**Driving wheels:** 1106mm (43.5in)
**Grate area:** 1.1m² (11.8sq ft)
**Heating surface:** 61.1m² (658sq ft)
**Tractive effort:** N/A
**Total weight:** 34.14t (75,264lb)

## 2-4-2T JAPANESE NATIONAL RAILWAYS (JNR) JAPAN: 1893

This was the first locomotive built in Japan, though 'assembled' might be more accurate, since most of its parts were prefabricated in Britain. The project was supervised by R.F. Trevithick, the grandson of Richard Trevithick, and carried out at the railway's Kobe workshops. It was a two-cylinder compound, and the cylinders were cast in Japan. Numbered 860, it was a one-off. Illustrating the struggle for the Japanese market, the next home product was a Mogul, made from parts supplied from Baldwins in the USA. From such tentative and late beginnings, the Japanese locomotive industry grew rapidly in scale and confidence. From 1912, it announced that it could now cater for all home demand, and by the 1920s and 30s, Japan had become an exporter of locomotives.

**Boiler pressure:** (cm²)
**Cylinders:** hp 381x508mm (15x20in); lp 572x508mm (22.5x20in)
**Driving wheels:** 1346mm (53in)
**Grate area:** 1.1m² (11.8sq ft)
**Heating surface:** 71.5m² (769.8sq ft)
**Tractive effort:** N/A
**Total weight:** not known

## CLASS 6 4-6-0 CAPE GOVERNMENT RAILWAYS (CGR) SOUTH AFRICA: 1893

South Africa's first 4-6-0s, designed by H.M. Beatty, and running on the 1065mm (3ft 6in) gauge, had two simple-expansion outside cylinders operated by internal Stephenson's link valve gear. Used for main-line work on Cape Town-Johannesburg mail trains, they reduced the schedule to 48 hours. The original Class 6 had many variants, up to 6L in 1904. The first ones came from the North British Locomotive Co, and most were British-built, though the 6K came from Baldwins.

**Struggling to get a long freight train on the move at night, this Class 6 puts on a spectacular fireworks display, and no doubt makes plenty of noise too. Engines of this class remained in service into the 1970s.**

**Boiler pressure:** 12.6kg/cm² (180psi)
**Cylinders:** 431x660mm (17x26in)
**Driving wheels:** 1370mm (54in)
**Grate area:** 1.6m² (17sq ft)
**Heating surface:** 96.7m² (1041sq ft)
**Tractive effort:** 8517kg (18,780lb)
**Total weight:** 75.2t (165,760lb)

## No 999 4-4-0 NEW YORK CENTRAL & HUDSON RIVER RAILROAD (NYC&HRR) USA: 1893

Designed to be a racer, this one-off locomotive ran the eastern leg of the 'Empire State Express' between New York and Chicago. Built at the line's own West Albany works, it was a typical American 4-4-0 with bar frames and two simple expansion outside cylinders, except for its unusually large coupled wheels.

These wheels carried it to a claimed world speed record of 180kph (112 mph) on 10 May 1893, running with a four-car train down a 1 in 350 gradient. On the previous day, it had also been timed at a sustained maximum of 166kph (103mph), but both speeds, timed by the train's conductor, remain unverified. Speed records must be confirmed by an experienced recorder or dynamometer car equipment.

It was wonderful publicity for the train and the line, however, and there is no doubt that No 999 was a very fast locomotive. Its performance in 1893 laid the basis for the celebrated 'Twentieth Century Limited' express. No 999, with some modifications, including standard 1981mm (78in) coupled wheels, is preserved at Chicago.

**With a handsome wood-bodied vestibule car attached, No 999 poses for the camera. The 'Empire State Express' was an early and trend-setting exercise in combined locomotive-and-train styling.**

**Boiler pressure:** 12.6kg/cm$^2$ (190psi)
**Cylinders:** 483x610mm (19x24in)
**Driving wheels:** 2184mm (86in)
**Grate area:** 2.8m$^2$ (30.7sq ft)
**Heating surface:** 179m$^2$ (1927sq ft)
**Tractive effort:** 7378kg (16,270lb)
**Total weight:** 92.53t (204,000lb)

## Class K DANISH STATE RAILWAYS (DSB) DENMARK: 1894

**The original look of the Class K before rebuilding. This was one of Denmark's largest locomotive classes.**

The first Danish 4-4-0, designed by O.F.A. Busse, ran in 1882. The designer's K class of 1899 was similar both in outline and in works, but with a bigger boiler and cylinders. Between 1894 and 1902, 100 were built and were to be found all over the DSB system. With outside cylinders and outside Allan link motion, they presented a complicated set of cranks, eccentrics and reciprocating rods. Superheaters were fitted to all the class between 1915 and 1925, and 50 were rebuilt between 1925 and 1932. Snow deflectors and the national colours on the chimney were typical Danish features.

**Boiler pressure:** 12kg/cm$^2$ (171psi)
**Cylinders:** 430x610mm (17x24in)
**Driving wheels:** 1866mm (73.5in)
**Grate area:** 1.8m$^2$ (19.3sq ft)
**Heating surface:** 87.9m$^2$ (947sq ft)
**Tractive effort:** 6220kg (13,716lb)
**Total weight:** 42.67t (94,080lb)

## 'BIG GOODS' 4-6-0 HIGHLAND RAILWAY — GREAT BRITAIN: 1894

**The first of the class, preserved No 103 stands at the western terminus of Kyle of Lochalsh, with the Isle of Skye in the background. In Highland Railway days the 'Big Goods' rarely operated on the Kyle line.**

The first 4-6-0 on a British railway, it was designed by David Jones of the HR and built by Sharp, Stewart of Glasgow. Fifteen were ordered straight off the drawing board, which seems risky, but the railway historian Brian Reed has noted that the HR's chief draughtsman, David Hendrie, had worked with Dübs in Glasgow on the class A 4-6-0 of the Nizam's State Railway in India, itself an enlarged version of the Indus Valley L-class 4-6-0 of 1880. The family resemblance is distinct. In any case, the 'Big Goods' were an instant success. Tasked to haul goods trains on the main line between Inverness and Perth, with its long steep gradients, they were often deployed in the peak summer season for passenger trains. This engine was a sign of what was to come, as British companies moved towards the big-engine philosophy that prevailed in other countries.

The two simple expansion cylinders were outside, operated by internal Allan valve gear. A Jones trademark was the louvred chimney, to help lift exhaust steam and smoke high up, particularly on the long downhill sections; and spark arresters were fitted in the chimney bases. Counter-pressure brakes of the Le Chatelier type were originally fitted. The class served for over 50 years, latterly as banking and pilot engines. The first to be delivered, No 103, is preserved.

**No 104 on a mixed goods train in 1894. Note the louvred chimney. Another Jones touch was the hinged-back vacuum brake pipe.**

**Boiler pressure:** 12.3kg/cm$^2$ (175psi)
**Cylinders:** 508x660mm (20x26in)
**Driving wheels:** 1600mm (63in)
**Grate area:** 2m$^2$ (22.6sq ft)
**Heating surface:** 155m$^2$ (1672.5sq ft)
**Tractive effort:** 11,050kg (24,362lb)
**Total weight:** 56.9t (125,440lb)

## TYPE 5500 4-4-0 JAPANESE NATIONAL RAILWAYS (JNR) JAPAN: 1894

**No. 8 of the Tobu Railway, at Tatebayashi depot in February 1962. An air-brake cylinder has been fitted alongside the smoke-box, and the high-sided tender is a later feature, but in most respects the appearance is original.**

Up to 1911, when the decision was made that Japan should rely on home-constructed locomotives, both Britain and the USA exported engines to Japanese railways. This Beyer-Peacock product, intended for main-line trains, had a long working life of over 60 years, latterly on branch-line duties.

Essentially British in appearance, its upward-canted footplate, angled to clear the outside cylinders, was distinctive, as was the equalizing spring mounted between the outside bearings of the front bogie. The buffer beam was supported by the inside frames with no lateral attachment to the running plate.

**Boiler pressure:** 12kg/cm² (171psi)
**Cylinders:** 406x559mm (16x22in)
**Driving wheels:** 1400mm (55in)
**Grate area:** 1.33m² (14.3sq ft)
**Heating surface:** 73m² (786sq ft)
**Tractive effort:** 6750kg (14,880lb)
**Total weight:** 55.81t (123,039lb)

## CLASS F3 4-6-0 MEXICAN RAILWAYS (FCM) MEXICO: 1894

Mexico's first 4-6-0 was the Class F1 of 1882, from Baldwins; the Class F3, from Neilsons in Glasgow, Scotland, was much more powerful. Much British capital had gone into the Mexican railways, and the USA and Britain were still competing for sales to Mexico. Soon, US types became universal, except for Fairlies. Two-cylindered, with inside Stephenson's link gear, the class numbered four in total. A large bogie tender reflected the complexities and difficulties of lineside water supply.

They were scrapped 30 years later, in 1927. The 4-6-0 remained a fairly common Mexican locomotive type; proportionately more so than in the USA, which otherwise exercised a huge influence on Mexican steam development.

**Boiler pressure:** 12.3kg/cm² (175psi)
**Cylinders:** 469.5x660mm (18.5x26in)
**Driving wheels:** 1370mm (54in)
**Grate area:** 2.2m² (24sq ft)
**Heating surface:** 123.3m² (1328sq ft)
**Tractive effort:** 11,116kg (24,512lb)
**Total weight:** 58.16t (128,219lb) (engine only)

## 0-6-6-0 JAROSLAV-VOLOGDA-ARCHANGEL RAILWAY RUSSIA: 1895

This 1065mm (3ft 6in) gauge line was first of many in Russia to use Mallet articulated compound tender engines. The pull of these wood-burners was so strong that they were liable to yank out the draw-hooks of goods wagons, and extra 'towing' cables were fitted to long freight trains. The frames were inside the front coupled wheels but outside the rear set, to make more room for the firebox. All four cylinders were outside, the valves actuated by Walschaerts gear. The engines featured the running plate railings ordered by Tsar Alexander II in the 1870s to be fitted on all locomotives for the crews' protection. This strategically located line was later converted to the normal Russian gauge of 1523mm (5ft) and integrated with the rest of the Russian system.

**Boiler pressure:** 12kg/cm² (170psi)
**Cylinders:** hp 330x550mm (13x21.7in); lp 194x550mm (18x21.7in)
**Driving wheels:** 1091mm (43in)
**Grate area:** 1.8m² (19.5sq ft)
**Heating surface:** 111.5m² (1200sq ft)
**Tractive effort:** 10,712kg (23,620lb)
**Total weight:** 71.9t (158,480lb)

## 'ATLANTIC' NO 153 ATLANTIC COAST LINE USA: 1895

**Boiler pressure:** kg/cm²)
**Cylinders:** 482x609mm (19x24in)
**Driving wheels:** 1827mm (72in)
**Grate area:** 2.4m² (26.25sq ft)
**Heating surface:** 190m² (2047.2sq ft)
**Tractive effort:** not known
**Total weight:** not known

Baldwins built this first 'Atlantic', and the 4-4-2 soon became widely used, not only in the USA but in Britain and France, as it answered a general need for more power. The essence of the design was outside cylinders and a large firebox supported on the trailing wheels. This enabled the firebox to be some 304mm (12in) deeper and also wider, though the first 'Atlantic' took little advantage of this. Baldwin's historian also noted that the type provided greater riding comfort and safety for the crew, with the cab behind, instead of on top of, the driving wheels. No 153 was a substantial locomotive, with a boiler of 1523mm (60in) in diameter, of parallel rather than the common wagon-top type. The smokebox was extended forward and provided space for a headlamp mounting in front of the chimney. The cylinders drove the rear pair of coupled wheels, and were operated by slide valves positioned on top. The valve gear was inside, operating the valves by means of rocker shafts.

It was an effective engine, and a similar type was built for the Concord & Montreal Railway in the following year, still with a narrow firebox. Very soon, however, the advantages of the type were being better deployed (see the 'Camelback' of 1897).

**In this first 'Atlantic', the firebox was about 305mm (12in) deeper than would have been possible without the pony wheels. The effulgence of the boiler barrel was achieved by using highly polished 'Russia iron' for the lagging plates.**

## T-524 CLASS 2-8-0 NEW SOUTH WALES GOVERNMENT RAILWAYS (NSWGR) AUSTRALIA:1896

The NSWGR had used 2-8-0s (first of all the J-483 from Baldwins) since 1891. This class, eventually numbering 280, became the line's basic freight locomotive, and won a high reputation for reliability. Though designed in Australia, all were built in Britain, 151 by Beyer Peacock of Manchester, the others by Glasgow-based builders, between 1896 and 1916. In 1924, they were reclassed as D-50, and in the 20s many were reboilered with superheaters. Though their main task was on heavy coal trains from the mining district around Newcastle, they were deployed all over the system. The same design was used by the Commonwealth Railways in 1916 for freight on the new Trans-Australia route. Ten were requisitioned from the builders in that year by the Railway Operating Division of the British Government and used for war service; from 1918 they went to the Belgian State Railways.

Although their heavy freight duties were taken over by later and more powerful types, there were still 114 of the class in service in 1964, employed chiefly on pick-up freight and marshalling yard work. The last in service, the non-superheated No 5069, was retired in 1973. It and three others have been preserved.

**The Ts barely changed in appearance, though superheated versions had longer smoke-boxes, and electric fitted.**

**Boiler pressure:** 11kg/cm$^2$ (160psi)
**Cylinders:** 533x660mm (21x26in)
**Driving wheels:** 1294mm (51in)
**Grate area:** 2.7m$^2$ (29sq ft)
**Heating surface:** 204.1m$^2$ (2198sq ft)
**Tractive effort:** 13,050kg (28,777lb)
**Total weight:** 113t (249,200lb)

**No 5112 was never superheated but did receive a new high-capacity tender. It is seen here shunting at Goulburn, in September 1969. Behind rises the trestle of the locomotive coaling plant.**

## CLASS 170 2-8-0 IMPERIAL & ROYAL STATE RAILWAYS (KKSTB) AUSTRIA: 1897

The design of this class was prompted by the building of the Arlberg mountain line from Switzerland into Austria. Reliable traction was needed on the grades and in the long summit tunnel. Karl Gölsdorf based his design on the class 73 0-8-0 and the class 63 2-6-0. A two-cylinder compound, it proved to be extremely successful. Up to 1918, 908 were built and used all over the Austrian empire. With its flat 'baker's oven' smokebox doors, wide-topped spark-arrester chimney and Clench steam drier pipe between its two lofty domes, it was an engine of striking rather than handsome appearance, typical of this period of Gölsdorf's work, before his visit to Britain. In mechanical terms it was both up to date and powerful, with the largest heating surface of any locomotive in Europe. Examples were built at all the main Austrian and Czech locomotive works. Even when

**At the time of its building, this was Europe's most powerful and advanced steam locomotive.**

**A well-preserved class 170 2-8-0, with the distinctive wide spark-arrestor chimney, at Vienna Süd depot, in May 1969.**

superseded as an express type, it found varied employment on local passenger and freight services. Many were converted to superheat, a process that continued in Czechoslovakia until 1947. From 1917, Gölsdorf's successor on the kkStB, Rihosek, had also produced a simple expansion version, class 270, with superheat, and this too was built in large numbers.

With the disintegration of Austria's Hapsburg Empire in 1918, members of the class were to be found in most of the former constituent parts, including North-east Italy, Yugoslavia, Poland and Czechoslovakia. The last known to be in service were on the Graz-Köflacher Bahn in Austria, from where they were withdrawn in the 1970s. One from the GKB has been preserved, and Czechoslovakia and Slovenia have one each.

**Boiler pressure:** 13kg/cm² (185psi)
**Cylinders:** hp 540x632mm (21x25in); lp 800x632mm (31.5x25in)
**Driving wheels:** 1298mm (51in)
**Grate area:** 3.9m² (42sq ft)
**Heating surface:** 240.7m² (2591sq ft)
**Tractive effort:** not known
**Total weight:** 68.5t (151,042lb)

## No 776 'Dunalastair II' 4-4-0 CALEDONIAN RAILWAY GREAT BRITAIN: 1897

The 4-4-0, established as the standard passenger locomotive on the late-Victorian railways of Britain, took a great step forward with the introduction of the Dunalastair I class in 1895. The new step was simple, the provision of a boiler of 1421mm (56in) diameter, larger than any previously fitted to a British engine. The designer was J.F. McIntosh, the Caledonian's Chief Mechanical Engineer, a practical-minded former driver, and the 1895 'Race to the North' between the East and West Coast routes from London to Edinburgh was perhaps the spur he needed. The big boiler was matched by a larger firebox and grate than on its predecessors, and the diameter of the inside cylinders was also enlarged. The result was a strong and free-steaming engine that proved its value in service immediately. The pioneer speed-recorder Charles Rous-Marten noted in 1896 that it could maintain the racing schedule of the previous year, but

**The final development: the Caledonian Railway's 'Dunalastair IV' of 1904.**

with double the load. McIntosh went on to produce three successive enlarged and improved versions, culminating in the 'Dunalastair IV' of 1904. Their reputation was such that he was approached by the Belgian State Railways, which from 1898 to 1906 resembled a sort of colony of the Caledonian, with McIntosh 4-4-0 and 0-6-0 types manufactured in hundreds.

**The original Dunalastair of 1897 looks quite slender compared to its later sister, but it caused a sensation in 1897.**

**Boiler pressure:** 12.3kg/cm² (175psi)
**Cylinders:** 482x660mm (19x26in)
**Driving wheels:** 1980mm (78in)
**Grate area:** 1.9 m² (20.6sq ft)
**Heating surface:** 139m² (1500sq ft)
**Tractive effort:** 8095kg (17,850lb)
**Total weight:** 53.67t (118,328lb)

## 4-6-0 CLASS 321 HUNGARIAN RAILWAYS (MÁV) HUNGARY: 1897

Building 4-6-0s when Austria favoured the 2-6-2 may have been a typical sign of Hungary going its own way. This was the MÁV's second 4-6-0, following on from the outside-framed class 320 which had been introduced in 1891. Built at the Budapest locomotive works, this was a much more contemporary design: an inside-framed two-cylinder compound intended as a heavy-duty engine for main-line passenger trains. Eighteen were built between 1897 and 1899. At first classified as Category 1k, they were specifically designed for hauling fast trains in mountain districts, and powerful brakes were fitted to the coupled wheels and the six tender wheels. The bogie pin was set well to the rear, and they were the first Hungarian locomotives with a degree of side-play to the bogie. Running-plates of toe-hold width emphasized the bulk of the cylinders and valve chests.

**Boiler pressure:** 13kg/cm² (185psi)
**Cylinders:** hp 510x650mm (22.8x25.6in); lp 750x650mm (29.5x25.6in)
**Driving wheels:** 1606mm (63.25in)
**Grate area:** 2.6m² (28sq ft)
**Heating surface:** 163.6m² (1761.4sq ft)
**Tractive effort:** 8210kg (18,103lb)
**Total weight:** 57.7t (127,228lb) (engine only)

## 'MIKADO' 2-8-2 NIPPON RAILWAYS JAPAN: 1897

Originally described as a 'modified Consolidation', these first 2-8-2s were built by Baldwins for Japan's 1065mm (3ft 6in) gauge. The key to the design was the need for a large, wide firebox to burn low-grade coal. This was placed behind the driving wheels, and a two-wheel truck inserted to support it and to balance the locomotive. In other respects, it was a conventional engine, with two outside simple-expansion cylinders driving on to the third coupled wheels.

The Japanese 'Mikado' (one of the titles of the Japanese emperor) was successful, and by 1902, Baldwins were building 2-8-2s for US lines, at first for those like the Bismarck Washburn & Great Falls, which also used low-grade coal. But soon the advantage of the big firebox in a heavy freight engine was recognized by lines which used good steam coal, and Mikados of considerably greater tractive power were produced. It was a particularly successful type on narrow-gauge tracks (see the 'MacArthur' 2-8-2 of 1942), but was frequently used on the standard gauge in both passenger and freight forms, the latter often assisted by a booster engine fitted to the trailing bogie.

**Boiler pressure:** (cm²)
**Cylinders:** 469x609mm (18.5x24in)
**Driving wheels:** 1117mm (44in)
**Grate area:** 4.2m² (45.1sq ft)
**Heating surface:** not known
**Tractive effort:** not known
**Total weight:** 54.25t (119,600lb) (engine only)

## 'CAMELBACK' 4-4-2 PHILADELPHIA & READING RAILWAY USA:1897

The wide Wootten firebox, patented by John H. Wootten in 1877 and intended for burning culm (waste anthracite coal from colliery dumps), was ideal for the 'Atlantic' type. Culm was much cheaper than normal coal, though it required some care in use, with a 'thin fire and a light draft' recommended to prevent the engine from blowing it all out of the stack before it was half-burned. This firebox left no room for the normal front look-out windows of a cab, and consequently the cab was moved, first on top of the firebox, then later further along the boiler. Though this helped the driver's look-out, it was a happy consequence rather than a prime reason. Baldwins built a 4-4-2 for the Atlantic City Railroad of New Jersey in 1896, just before it was taken over by the Philadelphia & Reading Railroad. It was provided with a massive Wootten firebox, and the driver's cab was placed astride the boiler in the fashion known as 'Mother Hubbard' or 'Camelback', which was very popular in the USA in the 1890s, and used on many different locomotive types from express engines to yard switchers. The term should not be confused with

Ross Winans' 'Camel' engines of

**The Pennsylvania Railroad was America's leading operator of 'Atlantics'. Most were rear-cab, but three 'Camelbacks' were built, with a grate area of 6.3m² (68 sq ft) – vast for the time.**

**A later version of the 'Camelback' form: Erie Railroad 4-4-2 class E2, No 934, takes coal at the Jersey City depot in January 1931. A compound class of 1907, it was rebuilt as simple expansion. The air cylinder is set above the wide firebox.**

an earlier generation. A very modern touch on this loco was that the driver and fireman communicated with each other by telephone. In the summer of 1897, this class was put on the 'Atlantic City Flyer', then the fastest scheduled service in the world, 90km (56miles) from Camden to Atlantic City in 50 minutes. The train despatcher's times, proudly shown in Baldwins' official history, show that the engines consistently beat this timing, with the best average speed being 114.5kph (71mph) with six cars behind the tender. The load varied between five and six cars, with around four hundred and twenty passengers. 'Atlantics' became synonymous with speed. On the New York Central in 1901, a class of Alco-built 'Atlantics' easily beat a three-and-a half-hour schedule between Albany and Syracuse (237.8km/147.8 miles) with sleeping-car trains loading up to 996t (980 tons).

The P&RR 'Camelback' was a Vauclain compound, using a system patented by Samuel M. Vauclain, formerly Baldwins' works superintendent, now a partner in the business, ultimately to be its Chairman and one of the USA's great railroad men. It had 4 cylinders, all outside, with the high-pressure cylinders set above the low-pressure ones, and formed in a single casting with the steam chests and half of the smoke box saddle. Both piston rods drove a single crosshead and connecting road on each side; and a single piston valve actuated both cylinders on each side. It thus obviated the need for internal drive (American engineers had detested crank axles from the very first). A bypass valve allowed live steam to enter the low pressure cylinders on starting. The tender was mounted on two four-wheel trucks, and its capacity was 9.14t (9 tons) of coal and 4958 gals (5954 US gals) of water. Despite the success of the P&RR 'Atlantics', the compounding system did have its problems, partly caused by the heavy reciprocating masses required to counteract the piston thrust, and partly by difficulty in balancing the work of the high and low pressure cylinders. Vauclain would continue to develop his ideas on compounding. He was an inventive engineer, with many patents to his name, including those for a flexible locomotive boiler, which was fitted, though not for long, to six locomotives of the Santa Fe in 1910–11.

**Boiler pressure:** 14kg/cm$^2$ (200psi)
**Cylinders:** hp 381x609mm (15x24in); lp 634x609mm (25x24in)
**Driving wheels:** 2134mm (84.25in)
**Grate area:** 7.5m$^2$ (80.75sq ft)
**Heating surface:** 236m$^2$ (2541sq ft)
**Tractive effort:** 10,390kg (22,900lb)
**Total weight:** 99t (218,000lb)

## 384 CLASS 2-6-0 EGYPTIAN RAILWAY ADMINISTRATION EGYPT: 1898

Formed in 1877, the ERA normally bought its engines from Britain and Europe, but 18 of this class were built by Baldwins in 1898. The Locomotive Superintendent was F.H. Trevithick, grandson of Richard Trevithick, and as so often, the American purchase was the result of British and French builders being too busy to guarantee a supply date. No more were bought at the time, but 2-6-0s, including another batch from Baldwins, were the staple mixed-traffic engines used on the system between 1920 and 1940. The trains themselves were relatively light: the international services arriving via Istanbul and Aleppo consisted of no more than a couple of Wagons-Lits cars.

**Boiler pressure:** 12.6?cm$^2$ (180psi)
**Cylinders:** 457x679mm (18x24in)
**Driving wheels:** 1529mm (60.25in)
**Grate area:** 2.35m$^2$ (23.35sq ft)
**Heating surface:** 184.5m$^2$ (1990sq ft)
**Tractive effort:** 7900kg (17,423lb)
**Total weight:** not known

## *Henry Oakley* 4-4-2 Great Northern Railway — Great Britain: 1898

Britain was not slow in importing the 'Atlantic' concept. The first was introduced by H.A. Ivatt, who had succeeded Patrick Stirling on the GNR and badly needed more express motive power to replace the old single-drivers. The class, nicknamed 'Klondykes' after the gold rush of the time, did not take full advantage of the possibilities of the 4-4-2, with a notably narrow firebox and a smallish boiler. In fact, several contemporary 4-4-0s had more heating surface.

**The preserved No 990 Henry Oakley, here seen receiving expert maintenance on an outing to the Keighley and Worth Valley Railway in Yorkshire, England, on 11 September 1977.**

**Boiler pressure:** 12.3kg/cm$^2$ (175psi)
**Cylinders:** 476x609mm (18.75x24in)
**Driving wheels:** 2020mm (79.5in)
**Grate area:** 2.5m$^2$ (26.75sq ft)
**Heating surface:** 134m$^2$ (1442 sq ft)
**Tractive effort:** 8160kg (18,000lb)
**Total weight:** 58.93t (129,920lb)

## Class C '*Coupe-Vent*' 4-4-0 Paris-Lyons-Mediterranean Railway (PLM) — France: 189

**Boiler pressure:** 15kg/cm$^2$ (213psi)
**Cylinders:** hp 340x620mm (13.6x24.6in); lp 540x620mm (21.25x24.6in)
**Driving wheels:** 2000mm (79in)
**Grate area:** 2.48m$^2$ (26.7sq ft)
**Heating surface:** 190m$^2$ (2040sq ft)
**Tractive effort:** 10,990kg (24,256lb)
**Total weight:** 101.38t (223,500lb)

Unlike some later streamliners, the partial casing on this striking class had a practical purpose, devised to minimize the effects of the 'Mistral' wind that sweeps down the Rhône valley, hence the nickname 'Wind-Cutter'. The designer was M. Ricour of the PLM, but the origins of the C-(compound) class went back to 1888, when A. Henry began to convert some 2-4-2 simples to four-cylinder compounds. These were the first engines with four cylinders driving two coupled

**Gallic styling: the original form of the 4-cylinder C class, with its 'armour-plated' look, is shown in this drawing.**

**The larger version of Class C, with streamlined casing between chimney and dome. The long wheelbase, with the outside cylinders in rear of the bogie, is evident, as is the sharp 'vee' of the cab.**

axles. Henry built two new 4-4-0s as compounds and his successor, Charles Baudry, built 40 more, of larger dimensions and introducing the streamlined casing. The high-pressure cylinders were inside, driving the leading coupled axle, and the outside low-pressure cylinders, set behind the bogie, drove the second axle. Between 1899 and 1902, 120 C-class engines with boilers further increased in capacity, and slightly modified casing including that between the chimney and the very substantial dome, were built by several different constructors, including the PLM's own *ateliers* at Arles. In these engines, the low-pressure cylinders had a fixed cut-off of 63 per cent, and the preceding 40 were converted to this format. A live steam valve to the lp cylinders was installed in most, but not all, to help in starting. They performed very well on Paris–Lyon–Marseille expresses, loading up to 200t (197 tons) and maintaining 100kph (62mph). A maximum test speed of 150kph (93mph) was recorded. One is preserved at Mulhouse.

## CLASS T9 4-4-0 LONDON & SOUTH WESTERN RAILWAY — GREAT BRITAIN: 1899

**Preserved Class T9 in its final British Railways livery, as No 30120 of the Southern Region. It is seen at Ropley, Hampshire, on the 'Watercress' line between Alton and Alresford, on 26 April 1986.**

An interesting comparison can be made between this class, known as the 'Greyhounds', and the Caledonian 4-4-0 of 1897. Dugald Drummond, its designer, had been McIntosh's predecessor on the Caledonian. Sixty-six T9s were built, in three series. All had two inside cylinders, the main modification being cross-water-tubes in the fireboxes, adding 15.3m² (165sq ft) of heating surface, after the first 20 had been built. They performed well for half a century and one has been preserved.

**Boiler pressure:** 12.3kg/cm² (175psi)
**Cylinders:** 470x660mm (18.5x26in)
**Driving wheels:** 2000mm (79in)
**Grate area:** 2.2 m² (24sq ft)
**Heating surface:** 124m² (1335sq ft)
**Tractive effort:** 7574kg (16,700lb)
**Total weight:** 51.2t (112,896lb) (engine only)

## CLASS G3 2-8-0 MEXICAN RAILWAYS (FCM) — MEXICO: 1899

The 2-8-0 was by far the predominant steam locomotive type on the standard gauge throughout Mexico.

First introduced in 1881, this type of engine proved their value on the lightly laid, curving and heavily graded lines (one of the first batch worked until 1956), and there was a great variety, some being wood or oil burners.

The FCM bought its engines in small batches, and this class of 10 was delivered by Baldwins between 1899 and 1908. All two cylinder simples, they underwent various changes in the course of long working lives, some exchanging their original inside Stephenson's link valve gear for the US Baker type.

Most of the Class G3 2-8-0 types were scrapped around 1960 onwards.

**Boiler pressure:** 12.2kg/cm² (175psi)
**Cylinders:** 507.6x660mm (20x26in)
**Driving wheels:** 1117mm (44in)
**Grate area:** 3m² (33.2sq ft)
**Heating surface:** 187.3m² (2047.2sq ft)
**Tractive effort:** 14,047kg (30,975lb)
**Total weight:** 64.8t (142,884lb) (engine only)

## CLASS 180 0-10-0 IMPERIAL & ROYAL AUSTRIAN STATE RAILWAYS (KKÖSTB) AUSTRIA: 1900

A two-cylinder compound for hauling trains from the Bohemian coalfield, this was Karl Gölsdorf's first 0-10-0, with a bold front end design, despite the disparate size of the outside-set high- and low-pressure cylinders. It had a Clench steam drier, forming a pipe between the two domes. It fulfilled the requirement of a light axle-loading (maximum 13.7t, 13.4 tons) and negotiation of 200m (200yd) curves, helped by lateral play allowed in axles 1, 3 and 5; the drive was on axle 4. A great success, 239 were built, leading to other 10-coupled types. No 180.01 is preserved in Vienna.

**The photograph below shows a Yugoslavia State Railway 28 Class 0-10-0 between Jesenice and Nova Gorica. First built in neighbouring Austria at the beginning of the 20th century, these former Austrian State Railway 80 Class engines included two cylinder compounds.**

**Boiler pressure:** 14.3kg/cm² (205psi)
**Cylinders:** hp 560x635mm (21.8x24.7in); lp 850x635mm (33.1x24.7in)
**Driving wheels:** 1258mm (49in)
**Grate area:** 3.4m² (36.6sq ft)
**Heating surface:** 202.1m² (2176sq ft)
**Tractive effort:** not known
**Total weight:** 65t (143,325lb) (engine only)

## COMPOUND CLASS 2.6 4-4-2 NORTHERN RAILWAY (*NORD*) FRANCE 1900

**As the first really effective compound express engines, the class 2.6 attracted exceptional interest throughout the railway world.**

The compounding system developed on the *Nord* line by the English-born Alfred de Glehn and the Frenchman Gaston du Bousquet dates back to 1885. It used four cylinders, with high-pressure outside, driving the second of two axles; low-pressure inside, driving the leading axle. Each cylinder had an independent set of valve gear, and cut-off could be adjusted independently for high and low pressure, through two regulators. There were two sets of reversing gears. The driver could also close off the low-pressure cylinders and send all exhaust steam up the blast pipe. Expertly applied, it meant that the engine could exert almost 50 per cent additional tractive effort on starting. It was a system of great flexibility, to cope with different loads and conditions, but it was undeniably complex to maintain and operate. The French tradition of highly trained drivers is partly owed to the need to manage compounding properly. Although other compounding systems were also used in France – the only country that made compounding work for express services – it was the de Glehn/du Bousquet system, as improved by André Chapelon from 1928, that became the nearest thing to a national standard.

Their first product was a 2-2-2-0, of 1885, rebuilt as a 4-2-2-0 in 1892 (the driving wheels were originally not coupled; in effect, each axle was driven by a separate 'engine', hence the unusual notation). The system first attracted real attention with the appearance of two prototype 4-cylinder compound 4-4-2s in 1900, rapidly followed by line production, the class ultimately numbering 35. The first were built by the *Société Alsacienne de Constructions Mécaniques* at Mulhouse, where de Glehn was director of engineering; others were built by the J.F. Cail shops at Lille. The production engines had coupled driving wheels, but retained other features of their predecessors, including the Belpaire firebox and the outside bearings on the front bogie. From the beginning they were star performers, though they achieved their full potential after 1912, with Schmidt superheating and enlarged high-pressure cylinders with piston valves. One (non-French) authority wrote: 'their hill-climbing capabilities have probably never been excelled by any locomotive of comparable size and power.' Such abilities were essential on the heavy Calais boat trains, often loading to 400t (393.6 tons). Apart from the Paris traffic, co-operation among international railways meant that through carriages were run from the Channel ports to Berlin, Vienna, Rome, Bucharest, and – with the inception of the Orient Express – to Athens and Istanbul. On level track, the 'Atlantics' ran these trains at 120kph (75mph).

The English Great Western Railway paid the French a compliment by buying three of the compounds, and derived much benefit though it did not adopt compounding. The great Pennsylvania Railroad in the USA bought one for similar reasons. The Royal Prussian Railway bought 79; and the Egyptian State Railways, 10. At home, the *Nord* 'Atlantics' ran into the 1930s, some of them by then fitted with wide-diameter chimneys and Lemaître blast pipes, and with eight-wheel bogie tenders holding 7t (6.88tons) of coal and 5070gals (6088 US gals) of water. But by then express train loads had increased further, beyond the capacity of a four-coupled locomotive, and these splendid engines were worthily succeeded by the *Nord* 'Pacifics'. No 2.670, as modified in 1912, is preserved at the National Railway Museum, Mulhouse.

**Boiler pressure:** 16kg/cm² (228psi)
**Cylinders:** hp 390x640mm (13.5x25.25in); lp 560x640mm (22x25.25in)
**Driving wheels:** 2040mm (80.25in)
**Grate area:** 2.76m² (33.4sq ft)
**Heating surface:** 138m² (1485sq ft)
**Superheater:** 39m² (420sq ft)
**Tractive effort:** 7337kg (16,178lb)
**Total weight:** 120t (264,500lb)

## CLASS 1900 *CLAUD HAMILTON* 4-4-0 GREAT EASTERN RAILWAY GREAT BRITAIN: 1900

Designed by Fred Russell of the GER, this was a 'big boiler' 2-cylinder simple 4-4-0 emulating the trend-setting Caledonian type of 1895. It ran most of the line's main expresses, including the summer 'Norfolk Coast Express' as well as the tightly timed Liverpool Street-Norwich trains. The first 'Clauds' had round-topped boilers; later ones had Belpaire boilers. A number of the class were fitted with the 'liquid fuel apparatus' introduced by James Holden on the GER in 1893; the fuel was liquid tar, a gas-works by-product. The system was successful, but was dropped when the price of coal fell.

**No 1870 of the first version pauses at Cambridge with a London express in 1900, and tops up the tender tank.**

**Boiler pressure:** 12.7kg/cm² (180psi)
**Cylinders:** 483x660mm (19x26in)
**Driving wheels:** 2130mm (84in)
**Grate area:** 1.9 m² (21.3sq ft)
**Heating surface:** 151 m² (1630sq ft)
**Tractive effort:** 7755kg (17,100lb)
**Total weight:** 51t (112,448lb)

## COMPOUND 4-4-0 MIDLAND RAILWAY (MR) GREAT BRITAIN: 1900

**Compound 1028 in LMS livery on the turntable in Derby Works. This is one of the 30 engines in R.M. Deeley's first batch, produced in 1905–6; like some others, it had a slightly extended smoke-box compared to the type-model, No 1000. The superheated boiler was fitted in 1923.**

Compounding was tried by several British railways, but only the Midland made it a success. The system was developed by Walter Smith of the North Eastern Railway, using three cylinders, the high-pressure one being inside, all driving the leading coupled wheels. A key feature was a valve, devised by Smith, which enabled the engine to start moving using the outer, low-pressure, cylinders only. In fact, the engine could be worked simple, compound, or 'reinforced compound' – in this case, with live steam admitted to the low-pressure cylinders. The Midland's Chief Mechanical Engineer was S. W. Johnson, known for the elegant finish of his engines. The NER did not pursue Smith's work, but Johnson was attracted by its potential for getting high performance and efficiency out of small engines. The first Midland compounds needed skilled driving, but they performed well. Critics commented on the lightweight trains they normally drew, but when given a stiffer task and a trained driver, the Midland compounds rose easily to the challenge. When R.M. Deeley took over from Johnson at the beginning of 1904, he got rid of Smith's change-valve in the interests of simplicity and general utility, sacrificing 'reinforced compounding' but using a special regulator to preserve the low-pressure start. Deeley's modifications of the type reduced power but made the engines easier to drive. Until the end of the Midland, these engines ran all the main expresses; and even after the formation of the London Midland & Scottish Railway in 1923, a new batch of 'Midland Compounds' was built, mostly for passenger service on southern Scottish lines.

**Boiler pressure:** 15.5kg/cm² (220psi)
**Cylinders:** hp 482x660mm (19x26in); lp 514x660mm (21x26in)
**Driving wheels:** 2134mm (84in)
**Grate area:** 2.6 m² (28.4sq ft)
**Heating surface:** 159.75 m² (1720sq ft)
**Tractive effort:** 10,884kg (24,000lb)
**Total weight:** 60.8t (134,176lb)

## *PRINCESS OF WALES* 4-2-2 MIDLAND RAILWAY (MR) GREAT BRITAIN: 1900

A factor helping to revive 'single-driver' engines in Britain was the invention of steam sanding gear, which let a stream of fine sand be jetted at the point where the wheel met the rail, helping adhesion, especially when starting off or on a greasy rail. This engine, No 2601, designed by Samuel W. Johnson, could feed sand to its huge driving wheels from both sides. It was one of the last, and the most powerful, single-driver express types to be built. Its big eight-wheel tender was almost as long as the engine.

**No 2601 at the head of the 1.30 pm Scotch express at St Pancras Station, London, on 2 September 1901. There were 10 of this class, though the Midland had altogether 95 4-2-2s.**

**Boiler pressure:** 12.6cm² (180psi)
**Cylinders:** 500x666mm (19.5x26in)
**Driving wheels:** 2397mm (93.5in)
**Grate area:** 2.3m² (24.5sq ft)
**Heating surface:** 113m² (1217sq ft)
**Tractive effort:** 7337kg (16,178lb)
**Total weight:** 51t (112,336lb)

## CLASS B51 4-4-0 STATE RAILWAYS (SS) DUTCH EAST INDIES (INDONESIA): 1900

Forty engines of this class were built between 1900 and 1909, the first from Hanomag, in Hanover, Germany; others from Hartmann in Chemnitz and from Werkspoor in the Netherlands. A two-cylinder compound, it was intended as an express passenger type on the main lines in Java. In the early 1970s, around 20 were still active on local services from Babat, Bodjonegoro and Tjepu depots; also from Rangkasbetung to Tanahabang station in Djakarta.

**B51.12 of PNKA, the Indonesian State Railways, in sparkling condition at Bodjonegoro depot, Java, on 29 December 1973.**

**Boiler pressure:** 12kg/cm$^2$ (171psi)
**Cylinders:** hp 380x510mm (15x20in); lp 580x510mm (22.8x20in)
**Driving wheels:** 1503mm (59in)
**Grate area:** 1.3m$^2$ (14sq ft)
**Heating surface:** 85.5m$^2$ (920.5sq ft)
**Tractive effort:**
**Total weight:** 35.4t (78080lb) (engine only)

## CLASS 500 4-6-0 ADRIATIC NETWORK (RA) ITALY: 1900

Designed by Giuseppe Zara, with the prototype built at the RA works in Florence, this was a cab-first design, with the unusual four cylinder compound arrangement devised by Plancher, having both high pressure cylinders to one side, and both low pressure ones to the other. All drove the second coupled axle. Walschaerts valve gear was fitted; one outside piston valve distributed steam to both cylinders on each side. The cylinders were mounted on an extension of the frame beyond the smoke box. In normal service, this back-to-front engine ran permanently 'backwards'. The valve layout allowed live steam to the low pressure cylinders on starting. Coal was carried in bunkers fitted alongside the firebox, and a six-wheel water-tank tender was attached at the cylinder end, with a flexible hose link to the injector.

A mixed-traffic type, it was recorded as hauling goods trains up to 830t (817 tons), and as maintaining 90kph (56mph) on passenger service. Although this engine solved the problem of a clear look-out, and also avoided any drifting steam or smoke, it did not start a fashion. Inequalities between high and low pressure steam supply caused the engine to 'hunt' from side to side; the Plancher system was really only suited to low speeds. The limited coal capacity also made long-distance running difficult. Designated Class 670 of the State system (FS), from 1905 (671 for superheated versions), the 43-strong class worked into the 1940s, stationed at Verona and Bologna.

**Boiler pressure:** 15kg/cm$^2$ (213psi)
**Cylinders:** hp 365x656mm (14.25x25.6in); lp 596x656mm (23.25x25.6in)
**Driving wheels:** 1938.5mm (75.6in)
**Grate area:** 3m$^2$ (32.47sq ft)
**Heating surface:** 153.5m$^2$ (1653sq ft)
**Tractive effort:** 6698kg (14,770lb)
**Total weight:** 100t (221,000lb)

## CLASS 7B 2-6-0 BUENOS AIRES GREAT SOUTHERN RAILWAY (BAGS) ARGENTINA: 1901

An enlarged, 2-cylinder compound version of the Class 7 of 1885, also from Beyer Peacock, the later history of this class shows the make-do and mend often required on cash-strapped systems. Most of the 28 were put in store from 1938, since maintenance of compounds was too problematic.

However, from 1949 an acute shortage of motive power brought a re-examination. Four were converted to oil burning, one of them fitted with cylinders from semi-derelict engines of another class; another with a cast-iron bush fitted inside a broken low-pressure cylinder.

The class as a whole was scrapped by 1967. No 3096 of this class hauled the first train into Carmen de Patagones, at the southern end of the Great Southern system, in 1921, and was the only one to be given a name, Maragata.

**The illustration shows a class 10 2-6-0, No. 85. Twenty-seven were built for the Western Railway (FCGOA) by Kitson and Beyer Peacock in 1902-3. It is emitting typical oil-burner smoke.**

**Boiler pressure:** kg/cm$^2$ (175psi)
**Cylinders:** hp mm (18x26in); lp 660x660mm (26x26in)
**Driving wheels:** 1726mm (68in)
**Grate area:** 1.9m$^2$ (20.1sq ft)
**Heating surface:** 48.8m$^2$ (1240sq ft)
**Tractive effort:** 6866kg (15,140lb)
**Total weight:** 79.5t (175,280lb)

## CLASS Q 4-6-2 NEW ZEALAND RAILWAYS (NZR) NEW ZEALAND: 1901

This was the first locomotive of the 'Pacific' type, so-called because it was shipped across that ocean to New Zealand. The NZR's Chief Mechanical Engineer, A.W. Beattie, wanted an engine with a wide firebox to burn lignite coal of low calorific value, mined on South Island, where they were intended to operate the 1065mm (3ft 6in) gauge main line passenger services. This need for combustive capacity, rather than anything else, prompted the placing of a trailing pony wheel to support the firebox. Thirteen were built by Baldwins in the USA. Beattie's specification was up to the minute in other ways. These were among the first engines outside continental Europe to have Walschaerts valve gear, and the outside-admission piston valves which it actuated were another modern feature; slide valves were still in general use. They had bar frames, a dome-shaped sandbox, and Westinghouse air brakes. Baldwin built 'Pacifics' for US use from 1902, beginning with one for the St Louis, Iron Mountain & Southern Railway. The usefulness of the wide supported grate, combined with six-coupled traction, was plain, and soon it became an international type. The original Q class was very successful in itself, running relatively leisurely schedules. Some were transferred to North Island lines, and the last one was retired from duty in 1957.

**Boiler pressure:** 14kg/cm² (200psi)
**Cylinders:** 406x559mm (16x22in)
**Driving wheels:** 1245mm (49in)
**Grate area:** 3.72m² (40sq ft)
**Heating surface:** 155m² (1673sq ft)
**Tractive effort:** 8863kg (19,540lb)
**Total weight:** 75t (165,000lb)

## 2-4-2 ROYAL SIAMESE RAILWAYS (RSR) — THAILAND: 1901

A 2-4-2 was an unusual configuration for the twentieth century, the RSR modelling this class of seven locomotives on the Paris-Orleans 2-4-2 of 1873. The builders were Krauss of Munich and the metre-gauge (39.4in) was the norm on Siamese railways. Like other engines on the system, they were wood-burners, and were durable, operating light passenger services into the 1940s. Four were delivered in 1901, two in 1902, and one in 1912. Though Krauss had built 2-4-2 compounds for Yugoslav narrow gauge work, the RSR rejected compounding: its 2-4-2s were simple-expansion engines. The pony wheel was set under the cab, allowing for a deep ashpan set between it and the driving wheels.

**Boiler pressure:** 12.4kg/m² (177psi)
**Cylinders:** 360x500mm (14x19.7in)
**Driving wheels:** 1350mm (53in)
**Grate area:** not known
**Heating Surface:** not known
**Tractive effort:** 3042kg (6707lb)
**Total weight:** 28t (61,740lb) (engine only)

## CLASS K9 4-6-0 PLANT SYSTEM (SAVANNAH, FLORIDA & WESTERN RAILWAY) — USA: 1901

This class was built for high-speed passenger work by Alco's Rhode Island Locomotive Works. A speed of 193kph (120mph) was claimed (but not substantiated) for No 111 in 1901. The Seaboard Line and the Plant System were competing for the US Mail contract from Washington to the West Indies. An eight-car mail train was split between the two lines at Savannah, and the first to reach its own terminus at Jacksonville, Fla, was to get the contract. The Plant System's first engine, No 107, was delayed by a hot axle box. No 111 took over the train and iran from Jesup to Jacksonville, 186km (115 miles), averaging 124kph (77mph). No 111 was broken up in 1942.

**Boiler pressure:** 12.6cm² (180psi)
**Cylinders:** 487x718mm (19x28in)
**Driving wheels:** 1846mm (72in)
**Grate area:** 3m² (3sq ft)
**Heating surface:** not known
**Tractive effort:** 9633kg (21,240lb)
**Total weight:** 114.7t (252,900lb)

## CLASS 18 4-4-0 STATE RAILWAYS (EB) — BELGIUM: 1902

In 1898, Neilson, Reid & Co of Glasgow had built five 4-4-0s for the EB that were virtually identical to J.F. McIntosh's Caledonian Railway 'Dunalastair II' design. Another 719 Caledonian-type 4-4-0s and 0-6-0s were built – all in Belgium - during the EB's 'McIntosh phase' which lasted until 1906. One hundred and forty were of this express passenger class, operating mostly between Brussels and Antwerp. The last six were built with Schmidt superheaters, some time before their Scottish sisters were so equipped; also piston valves. One has been preserved, with its Caledonian-type bogie tender.

**Looking for all the world as if it had just come up from Glasgow, the preserved Class 18 stands with a train of vintage vehicles at Brussels Nord Station. The triple-window cab is the one un-Caledonian feature.**

**Boiler pressure:** 13.5kg/cm² (195psi)
**Cylinders:** 482x660mm (19x26in)
**Driving wheels:** 1980mm (79in)
**Grate area:** 2.2m² (22sq ft)
**Heating surface:** 126.8m² (1365.5sq ft)
**Tractive effort:** 8930kg (19,690lb)
**Total weight:** 50.3t (110,880lb) (engine only)

## CLASS D1 2-6-0 DANISH STATE RAILWAYS (DSB) DENMARK: 1902

The DSB was formed in 1892 with Otto Busse (formerly of the Jutland-Funen Railways) as chief mechanical engineer until 1910. He began a policy of widespread standardization, and his D-class goods 2-6-0s engines eventually totalled 100, of which the D1 class accounted for 41. Built mostly between 1902-06 by Henschel and Hartmann in Germany, with eight from Nydquist & Holm of Sweden in 1908, these engines were 2-cylinder simples.

Busse was conservative and still used slide valves, though with Walschaerts valve gear. The engines were given superheaters between 1914 and 1920, and rebuilt with new boilers as class $D_{IV}$ between 1925 and 1940. Withdrawals began in the 1950s, but 18 were still at work in the early 1960s.

**Boiler pressure:** 12kg/cm² (170psi)
**Cylinders:** 431.4x609mm (17x24in)
**Driving wheels:** 1383mm (54.5in)
**Grate area:** 207.8m² (19.3sq ft)
**Heating Surface:** 106.7m² (1149sq ft)
**Tractive effort:** 8340kg (18,390lb)
**Total weight:** 44.7t (98,560lb) (engine only)

## CLASS G8 0-8-0 ROYAL PRUSSIAN RAILWAYS (KPEV) GERMANY: 1902

In the Prussian Railways' classification, G stood for *Güterzuglokomotive*, 'goods train locomotive'. The 8 had originally been a power classification, and though by this time G8 meant this specific locomotive type, the fact it had eight wheels was a coincidence. A true classic, it became a standard workhorse on many railways. It was a modernized version of the G7 0-8-0 of 1893, which itself continued in production as the $G7^2$ until 1917. The first G8 was built by the East Prussian Vulkan works at Stettin, to kPEV design. Unlike the G7, which had both simple and compound expansion versions, this was a simple expansion type only, with two outside cylinders, piston valves, outside Walschaerts valve gear, and an early version of the Schmidt superheater. In all these respects, it showed the way forward. The Prussian Railways had been experimenting with superheating since 1897. With the completion of his work, Dr Wilhelm Schmidt, a physicist, brought about the most significant development in steam locomotive design of the twentieth century. The superheater, installed at the front end of the boiler, took live steam from the upper part of the main steam pipe, and brought it to a header, from where it was redirected through a series of small pipes, or elements, through the upper part of the boiler to be further heated to super-high temperature before being brought to a second superheater header, or one linked to the first, from where it was passed through the main steam pipes to the cylinders. Although others were later to

**A long-surviving G8 is prepared for work at Burdur locomotive depot in Turkey. G8s were used here on local passenger services until the late 1980s.**

develop their own patent versions, some of which, like the French Houlet version, gave even higher temperatures (others perhaps merely sought to evade Schmidt's patent), Schmidt's work was decisive. From around 1910, no modern locomotive, except the smallest, could be without a superheater. All 'saturated' types became obsolescent, and thousands would be rebuilt to incorporate the new piping. The chief benefit was that the hot dry steam continued to expand in the cylinders and so not only provided more power for every ounce of steam produced, but also greater economy in working. 'Saturated' steam, by comparison, was liable to condense in the cylinders and form water. Among the disadvantages of superheating was that the hotter the steam was, the drier it was, and so more and better lubricant was needed where metal surfaces moved together in superhot conditions. Another effect of using superheated steam was to speed up the abandonment of flat slide valves in favour of piston valves in the operation of the cylinders: flat surfaces and dry steam created too much friction. Schmidt himself developed a broad-ring piston valve, which many railways used until the narrow-ring piston valve was introduced in the 1920s (another German innovation) and soon became universally used.

In the next ten years, over 1000 G8s were built, and it became the standard freight engine of the kPEV. Like the P8, it had a round-topped firebox and a narrow grate. With a maximum axle-load of 14.2t (13.9 tons) and a compact wheelbase, it was a go-anywhere engine. In 1913, a heavier $G8^1$ version was introduced, built first by the Hanomag works at Hanover but also by virtually every other German builder, 12 in all. Wartime service between 1914 and 1918 proved the value of this engine. The G8s hauled unprecedented loads and ran to far more demanding schedules than had been required of freight engines in peacetime. By 1921, a total of 5087 had been constructed. In the period 1933-41, 688 were rebuilt as 2-8-0s and classified $G8^2$.

Like that other Prussian classic, the P8 4-6-0, the G8 was widely exported. German war reparations in 1918 spread them even further across European and Middle Eastern systems, as far east as Syria. It was not the cheapest 0-8-0 to build but its performance, economy and reliability were outstanding. They were also built to last. G8s were still working on heavy coal trains for the Turkish State Railways into the 1970s. In Germany, the *Deutsche Reichsbahn Gesellschaft* (DRG) classified them as series $55^{25-57}$. From 1945, both the *Deutsche Bundesbahn* (DB) and the *Deutsche Reichsbahn* (DR) operated the engines. Several are preserved, in Germany and other countries.

**Boiler pressure:** 14kg/cm² (200psi)
**Cylinders:** 600x660mm (23.4x25.75in)
**Driving wheels:** 1350mm (52.6in)
**Grate area:** 2.66m² (28.6sq ft)
**Heating surface:** 139.5m² (1502.7sq ft)
**Superheater:** 40.4m² (435sq ft)
**Tractive effort:** 20,660kg (45,569lb)
**Total weight:** 55.7t (122,752lb) (engine only)

## 'SAINT' CLASS 4-6-0 GREAT WESTERN RAILWAY (GWR) GREAT BRITAIN: 1902

**'Saint' class No. 2941 Easton Court, on a stopping train service, at Wolverhampton Low Level Station in September 1932. 'Star' class No. 4027 is edging into view on the left.**

George Jackson Churchward became Locomotive, Carriage & Wagon Superintendent of the GWR in 1902, but even before that he had, as the No 2, influenced mechanical developments, and he was a strong influence on later British design. A careful planner and a keen student of best practice elsewhere, he understood the need for engines that provided haulage power as well as speed. Starting from basics, he developed a new boiler, No 1 of the GWR series, without a dome, its gentle taper owing something to the American wagon-top design, linked to a high-shouldered Belpaire-type firebox. With an operating pressure of 14kg/cm² (200psi) or more, this assured plenty of steam. Another feature of this boiler was the top-feed system, through one-way clack valves. Though British designers generally avoided using feedwater heaters, this system, sending the feedwater forward through a series of trays, did allow for a degree of heating before it mixed with the steam and boiling water around the firebox; and it was later used on British Railways standard locomotives.

Apart from one or two pre-1900 experiments, Churchward's first 4-6-0 appeared in 1902, No 100, *Dean*. It set the pattern for the GWR's subsequent mixed-traffic 4-6-0s, with outside cylinders, having a long 762mm (30in) stroke, and Stephenson's link

**Around 1923, Saint Helena enters Exeter St David's on the North-to-West 'tea and luncheon car' train, from Carlisle to Plymouth.**

motion inside the frame. This was a composite frame of British-style plate construction to hold the driving axles, and with an American touch in the combination of each cylinder with half of the smokebox saddle, resting on a bar bolted to the main plates. Still exercising caution, Churchward rebuilt one of the 4-6-0s, *Albion*, as an 'Atlantic' for purposes of comparison, both with the 'Deans' and the bought-in de Glehn 'Atlantic' *La France*. It was 1906 before line production of the 4-6-0s got under way, by which time superheaters were fitted (first of Schmidt, later of Swindon type). The GWR preferred a moderate degree of superheating, but Churchward, and other designers, soon realized that to use the full potential of superheating, a reappraisal of the working of the valve gear was needed. The old form of Stephenson link motion, still widely used, relied on short-travel valves, which restricted the ease with which steam could be got in and out of the cylinders. The most efficient modern engines were now fitted with larger valves with a longer range of travel, opening wider steam ports and allowing for admission of more steam. At the same time, they made possible a shorter 'cut-off' of the steam, to 20 per cent of the piston's stroke, or even less: very necessary with the expansive potential of superheated steam. On the GWR two-cylinder engines, the Stephenson's link motion was adapted to allow for a short cut-off. On his four-cylinder 4-6-0s of the 'Star' and subsequent classes, Churchward used Walschaerts valve gear. This had been invented in 1844, but it was from around 1906 that this radial valve gear, or adaptations of it, came into general use beyond continental Europe, since it facilitated the management of steam admission from valve chest to cylinder. With the superheater, longer pistons, longer valve travel, and shorter cut-off, the driver had both more steam, more expansion of the steam, and greater control over its use. This was the beginning of an era in which the performance and potential of a locomotive could be assessed more precisely, as well as dramatically increased.

Up to 1911, 77 'Saints' were built, and with their successors, the smaller-wheeled GWR 'Grange' and 'Hall' classes, two-cylinder types, totalling almost 490 locomotives, were by far the most numerous of the Great Western 4-6-0s. Although designated as mixed-traffic engines, their performance on express services could match that of the 4-cylinder 'Star' and 'Castle' classes. The 'Saints' lasted until the 1950s, the last of them being scrapped in 1953.

**'Saint' class No. 2933 Bibury Court setting off from Worcester Shrub Hill Station with a Hereford train. This engine had its chimney moved slightly forwards during smoke-box experiments in 1924.**

**Boiler pressure:** 15.75cm$^2$ (225psi)
**Cylinders:** 461.5x769mm (18x30in)
**Driving wheels:** 2064mm (80.5in)
**Grate area:** 2.5m$^2$ (27sq ft)
**Heating surface:** 199m$^2$ (2143sq ft)
**Superheater:** 24.4 m$^2$ (263sq ft) (from 1906)
**Tractive effort:** 11,066kg (24,395lb)
**Total weight:** 71.3t (157,248lb) (engine only)

## CLASS B2 0-6-0 CENTRAL MEXICAN RAILWAY (FCC) MEXICO: 1902

Class B were Mexico's only 0-6-0 shunting engines, 31 in all, of which 24 were of class B2, a wholly American type with bar frames and two outside cylinders. Fourteen came from the Alco-Brooks Rhode Island works between 1902 and 1904, and 10 from Baldwins in 1907; these had Belpaire boilers and were oil burners. The bogie tenders sloped down towards the back in classic switcher fashion. In the normal way of operations, shunting in Mexican yards was carried out by the same 2-8-0s that usually hauled the freight trains. The volume of freight, and the financial position of the railways, did not warrant large numbers of shunting engines, and the class B2 locos were found only in the largest yards. Like other locomotives of this kind, they had long working lives.

**Boiler pressure:** 12.6kg/cm$^2$ (180psi)
**Cylinders:** 482x609mm (19x24in)
**Driving wheels:** 1269mm (50in)
**Grate area:** 3m$^2$ (32sq ft)
**Heating surface:** 154m$^2$ (1660sq ft)
**Tractive effort:** 9900kg (21,830lb)
**Total weight:** 57t (126,000lb) (engine only)

## 2-6-0 CORDOVA AND HUATUSCO RAILWAY (FCCH) MEXICO: 1902

Mexico had numerous narrow gauge lines in addition to the standard-gauge systems, either acting as servers to main lines or operating in remote districts. Typical motive power was these three little 2-6-0s built by Baldwins for this 609mm (24in) gauge line in Vera Cruz province, which linked a hill district with the main line from Vera Cruz to Mexico City. It was absorbed by the Central Mexican Railway in 1909. With a height of 2893mm (9ft 6i), these were scaled-down versions of the standard outside-cylinder US 'Mogul'. Almost from the time that these engines were built, the Mexican branch lines began to suffer from the competition of roads.

**Boiler pressure:** 11kg/m$^2$ (160psi)
**Cylinders:** 304x457mm (12x18in)
**Driving wheels:** 774mm (30.5in)
**Grate area:** 66m$^2$ (7.1sq ft.)
**Heating Surface:** 38.5m$^2$ (415sq ft)
**Tractive effort:** 4541kg (10,014lb)
**Total weight:** 37.6t (82,906lb)

## CLASS MA 2-8-0 SWEDISH STATE RAILWAYS (SJ) SWEDEN: 1902

These engines were designed specifically for the iron ore trains running from Kiruna in Swedish Lapland to Narvik in Norway, which loaded to around 1016t (1000 tons). Built by Nydquist & Holm as two-cylinder compounds, they were not particularly effective performers. They had plate frames and large boilers, with the cylinders set behind the smoke box and driving the third axle. Slide valves were originally fitted, though the best performers of the class were two engines fitted with larger cylinders and piston valves. An insulated closed-in cab was provided for working this line, beyond the Arctic Circle.

**All Swedish locomotives had spark arrestors; in class Ma, one was incorporated in the 'choker' ring set at the base of the chimney. This was the most frequent method used, and typified a Swedish engine.**

**Boiler pressure:** 14kg/cm$^2$ (200psi)
**Cylinders:** hp 530x640mm (21x25in); lp 810x640mm (32x25in)
**Driving wheels:** 1296mm (50.5in)
**Grate area:** 2.9m$^2$ (31.2sq ft)
**Heating surface:** 211.7m$^2$ (2280sq ft)
**Tractive effort:** 16,780kg (37,000lb)
**Total weight:** 107.7t (237,440lb)

## A3/5 4-6-0 SWISS FEDERAL RAILWAYS (SBB) SWITZERLAND: 1902

**Boiler pressure:** 15kg/cm$^2$ (213psi)
**Cylinders:** hp 360x660mm (14x26in); lp 570x660mm (22.5x26in)
**Driving wheels:** 1780mm (69.4in)
**Grate area:** 2.6m$^2$ (28 sq ft)
**Heating surface:** 155.6m$^2$ (1676sq ft)
**Tractive effort:** N/A
**Total weight:** 105t (231,840lb)

Built by SLM at Winterthur for the Jura-Simplon Railway, these four-cylinder de Glehn compounds had high-pressure cylinders outside, driving the middle coupled wheels. The low-pressure cylinders drove the leading axle; both sets of cylinders had independent valve gear. Eventually numbering 111, the class was designed to take a 300t (295-ton) train up a grade of 1 in 100 at 50kph (31mph), but consistently exceeded this, often with trains up to 400t (393 tons). From 1913, half the class received Schmidt superheaters. One engine is preserved.

**This was one of the many new or recent locomotive types 'overtaken' by the development of the superheater. From 1913, about half the class were fitted with the Schmidt equipment.**

## CLASS S 4-6-4T NEW SOUTH WALES GOVERNMENT RAILWAYS (NSWGR) AUSTRALIA: 1903

**Preserved, restored, and still in steam – Class S tank No 3112 photographed at Alumatta loop, Wangaratta, on the Albury–Sydney main line, on 15 October 1988.**

Between 1903 and 1917, 145 of these large tank engines were supplied, partly by Beyer Peacock in Manchester and partly by the NSWGR Eveleigh Works. They dominated Sydney commuter services, but also worked from Wollongong and Newcastle in the heyday of suburban train operations. A roller-type destination indicator was mounted on the buffer-beam. In 1924, they were reclassed as C-30. After electrification of the Sydney lines in 1928, they were transferred to country depots. Their power and reliability were considered too valuable to lose, and 77 were converted to tender-engine 4-6-0s, as Class C-30T, to operate country branch lines where greater fuel and water capacity were needed. Some 29 were provided with superheaters.

With the decline of suburban and local services, the class became largely used for freight and for carriage shunting, though even in 1960 they were still running passenger trains out of Newcastle and Wollongong. In the 1960s, most were withdrawn and only three of the tank types remained in service in 1971. Several of this useful class, both tank and tender versions, are preserved.

**Boiler pressure:** 11.2kg/cm² (160psi)
**Cylinders:** 474x615.4mm (18.5x24in)
**Driving wheels:** 1410mm (55in)
**Grate area:** 2.3m² (24sq ft)
**Heating surface:** 144.2m² (1453sq ft)
**Tractive effort:** 9211kg (20,310lb)
**Total weight:** 72.3t (159,421lb)

## CLASS 206 4-4-0 IMPERIAL & ROYAL AUSTRIAN STATE RAILWAYS (KKÖSTB) AUSTRIA: 1903

**Few designers stamped such a clear identity on their locomotives: the Gölsdorf style was unmistakable. Its robustness and apparent simplicity concealed a high degree of sophistication.**

Gölsdorf's 4-cylinder compounds replaced the 4-4-0s on the international expresses. Air brakes were fitted, in addition to the original vacuum brake equipment. By 1945, some were being withdrawn and all were out of service by 1950.

This marks the culmination of Karl Gölsdorf's 4-4-0 express designs, which had begun in 1894 with the Class 6, and continued in 1898 with the class 106, used to haul the 'Orient Express' and the Ostend-Athens 'Tauern Express' through Austria. All were two-cylinder compounds, the cylinders outside, hp on the right and lp on the left, operated by an adapted form of Heusinger gear. Unlike its predecessors, the 206 had only a single dome and an exterior devoid of pipes – on a visit to Britain, the designer was impressed by the uncluttered look of English locomotives. Between 1903 and 1907, 70 of the class were built at Floridsdorf, StEG (the *Staats Eisenbahn* works) and Wiener Neustadt, and at PCM in Prague, and they were employed in express passenger service chiefly on lines in Bohemia and Moravia. The limitations of two-cylinder compounding and the demands of heavier trains on the often steeply graded routes were impelling the kkStB towards larger types, and

**Boiler pressure:** 13kg/cm² (185psi)
**Cylinders:** hp 500x680mm (19.7x26.8in); lp 760x680mm (30x26.8in)
**Driving wheels:** 2100mm (82.75in)
**Grate area:** 3m² (32.3sq ft)
**Heating surface:** 150m² (1615sq ft)
**Tractive effort:**
**Total weight:** 54.2t (119,511lb) (engine only)

## CROSS-COMPOUND 2-8-0 FRANCO–ETHIOPIAN RAILWAY (CFE) ETHIOPIA: 1903

Begun in 1897, the 785km (488-mile) metre-gauge (39.4in) Djibouti–Addis Ababa railway did not reach the Ethiopian capital until 1917.

However, by 1902, 309km (192 miles) were built and a regular service was operating. The first two 2-8-0s came from SLM in Winterthur, Switzerland, and a further two were built by the *Société Alsacienne* at Mulhouse. They were cross-compounds, with the high-pressure cylinder on the right, low-pressure on the left. Until the advent of superheated 2-8-0s after 1910, they were the most powerful engines on the line.

**The bar-framed construction of the Franco–Ethiopian cross-compound 2-8-0 engine is demonstrated in the photograph. No 22 bears the name *Puissant*, 'Powerful', in French and Amharic. Useful supplementary water tanks are fitted on each side of the tender.**

**Boiler pressure:** 13kg/cm$^2$ (185psi)
**Cylinders:** hp 420x550mm (16.5x21.6in); lp 630x550mm (24.8x21.6in)
**Driving wheels:** 1000mm (39.4in)
**Grate area:** 1.3m$^2$ (13.8sq ft)
**Heating surface:** 91.5m$^2$ (985sq ft)
**Tractive effort** not known
**Total weight:** 34.5t (76,072lb) (engine only)

## CLASS TK 2 2-8-0 FINNISH RAILWAYS (VR) FINLAND: 1903

The 2-8-0 suited the lightly laid tracks of most Finnish lines. Class Tk1 was imported from Baldwins in 1900, but the Tk2 two-cylinder compounds were home-built at the Tampella Works. Its axle loading was 8.3t (8.2 tons). The gauge was the Russian standard 1524mm (5ft). Finland was rich in wood, so most locomotives burned wood, unusual for Europe. Balloon-style, spark-arrester chimneys and high-railed tenders were therefore common. The class was withdrawn between 1957 and 1960.

**No 411, a Tk2 of 1903, heads a goods train at Kajaani in August 1952. Typical wooden-sided passenger cars of the period, with recessed doors, are on either side.**

**Boiler pressure:** 12.5kg/cm$^2$ (178psi)
**Cylinders:** hp 410x510mm (16x20in); lp 590x510mm (23.25x20in)
**Driving wheels:** 1120mm (43.7in)
**Grate area:** 1.4m$^2$ (15sq ft)
**Heating surface:** 84.8m$^2$ (913sq ft)
**Tractive effort:** 4660kg (10,275lb)
**Total weight:** 37.6t (82,900lb) (engine only)

## CLASS 242.12 2-8-0 EASTERN RAILWAY (EST) FRANCE: 1903

These were France's first 2-8-0s, two prototypes coming from the *Société Alsacienne*, at Mulhouse. Production began in 1905 and eventually the class numbered 175. Consisting of four-cylinder compounds, they had high-pressure cylinders inside the frames (unlike most French locomotives), driving the second pair of coupled wheels. To allow for the coupling rods, there was a gap between the first and second coupled axles. Slide valves were worked by Walschaerts gear on the outside cylinders and Stephenson's link on the inside. It was the *Est's* prime freight locomotive until 2-10-0s came in 1926.

**The hardy Class 242.12 2-8-0 grew to 75 in number in the first decade of the Twentieth century.**

**Boiler pressure:** 16kg/cm² (227psi)
**Cylinders:** hp 391x650mm (15.4x25.6in); lp 599x650mm (23.6x25.6in)
**Driving wheels:** 1396mm (55in)
**Grate area:** 2.8m² (30.1sq ft)
**Heating surface:** 242m² (2282.5sq ft)
**Tractive effort:** 12,702kg (28,008lb)
**Total weight:** 72.8t (160,720lb)

## 'CITY' CLASS 4-4-0 GREAT WESTERN RAILWAY (GWR) GREAT BRITAIN: 1903

The GWR 'City' class shows the old tradition in its double frames and inside cylinders, with springs mounted above the running plate; together with the new-style tapered and domeless boiler with Belpaire firebox, introduced by G.J. Churchward. The class was designed for use on lightweight, fast passenger trains; at this time the GWR and the London & South Western Railway were competing for traffic from Plymouth and Exeter to London. They established an immediate reputation for speed. On 14 July 1903, *City of Bath* took a special train from Paddington via Bristol to Exeter

**The preserved *City of Truro* steams at speed through Harbury Cutting with a special train from Derby to London Paddington.**

(311km/193 miles) in 172.5 minutes, maintaining a steady 120.7kph (75mph) on level track.

On 9 May, 1904, heading the 'Ocean Mail' of 145.6t (148 tons) on the hilly Plymouth to Bristol section, *City of Truro* ran 205.6km (127.8 miles) in 123.25 minutes. During this run, a speed of 164kph (102mph) was recorded by Charles Rous-Marten during the descent of Wellington Bank. For long, it was considered the first authenticated occasion of 100mph plus, but later research has thrown serious doubt on the achievement. The true speed is likely to have been just under 100mph (169kph). *City of Truro* was in service until 1931 and saved from scrapping by a press campaign. It was restored to in 1957, when it reached 135kph (84mph) on an 8-coach special train on Wellington Bank, scene of its triumph 53 years before. It is kept at the GWR Museum, Swindon.

**Great Western nameplates are sought after and can sell for more than the entire locomotive cost.**

**Boiler pressure:** 12.6kg/cm² (180psi)
**Cylinders:** 457x660mm (18x26in)
**Driving wheels:** 2045mm (80.5in)
**Grate area:** 1.91m² (20.56sq ft)
**Heating surface:** 169m² (1818sq ft)
**Tractive effort:** 8070kg (17,790lb)
**Total weight:** 94t (207,000lb)

## STEAM RAILCAR GREAT WESTERN RAILWAY (GWR) GREAT BRITAIN: 1903

The self-contained steam railcar goes back to 1847, inspired by an inspection car built by W. Bridges Adams at Bow, London, for the Eastern Counties Railway. In the following year, he built a steam-car for passenger service on the Bristol & Exeter Railway. The notion lapsed until 1903, when it was revived for light branch traffic. Engine unit and carriage shared a frame, and the GWR version extended the coachwork around the small boiler, so that to the casual eye it looked like a coach without visible means of propulsion. Most of these units were later converted to 'auto-train' or push-pull working, with a small tank loco, whereby the engine's main controls could be activated, in 'push' mode, from a driving position at the front of the carriage.

**One of the 99 GWR rail-motors, No 11, built in 1903, passes through Acton, West London in 1905. Driven from the coach end, it has no passengers, which suggests a special working.**

## 4-6-0 CAPE GOVERNMENT RAILWAYS (CGR) SOUTH AFRICA: 1903

**Boiler pressure:** 12.6kg/cm² (180psi)
**Cylinders:** 474x666mm (18.5x26in)
**Driving wheels:** 1384mm (54in)
**Grate area:** 1.7m² (18.75sq ft)
**Heating surface:** 99m² (1068sq ft)
**Superheater:** 28.8m² (310sq ft)
**Tractive effort:** 7806kg (17,212lb)
**Total weight:** 86.9t (194,811lb)

Constructed in Glasgow to the design of H.M. Beatty, Chief Locomotive Superintendent of the CGR, this was the first British-built locomotive to have a Schmidt superheater, and the first superheated engine in South Africa. Of 1065mm (3ft 6in) gauge, it shows another modern feature in the piston valves (using the version patented by Dr Schmidt) set above the two outside cylinders. The valves were actuated by Stephenson's link motion. The class was used for mixed traffic working in the Western Cape, though eventually it was deployed as far north as Bulawayo in Rhodesia.

**In South Africa, rail tracks were unfenced, and the locomotives' headlight served more to warn stray people or animals than to aid the driver.**

## 'SANTA FE' CLASS 900 2-10-2 ATCHISON TOPEKA & SANTA FE RAILROAD USA: 1903

In 1902, Baldwins built their 20,000 locomotive, and also their heaviest yet, a 2-10-0 freight class for the Santa Fe. It was also the first tandem compound, in which the four cylinders are mounted outside in pairs, low pressure behind high pressure, each pair sharing a common piston rod. The enlarged 2-10-2 version – first of its kind – followed in 1903. The drive was to the middle coupled wheel, which was flangeless. This compound system, another brainchild of Samuel Vauclain, proved popular for a time, being used on locomotives in Russia and other countries as well as on other US locomotives. But it was not a lasting solution; like his vertically-mounted paired cylinders, any inequalities of steam distribution set up stresses, which affected the riding of the locomotive as well as reducing its efficiency. The powerful double thrust on the connecting rods, though it provided a strong tractive effort, had its own problems of stress. Seventy-six of the class were built in 1903–4, all for freight service; the first 40 were coal burners; the

**'Santa Fe' became the type-name for the 2-10-2 locomotive, at least in America. At this time, the tenders of US locomotives had not yet developed into huge vehicles.**

rest were oil-fuelled. All were later converted to two-cylinder, simple expansion types. With large cylinders, 718x820mm (28x32in), their nominal tractive effort was raised to 33,922kg (74,800lbs). After this time, compounding became rarer on American railroads, except on articulated locomotives. A big boiler and efficient simple-expansion cylinders could develop the necessary tractive power, with far fewer operational and maintenance problems.

**Boiler pressure:** 15.75kg/cm² (225psi)
**Cylinders:** hp 482x812mm (19x32in); lp 812x812mm (32x32in)
**Driving wheels:** 1461mm (57in)
**Grate area:** 5.43m² (58.5sq ft)
**Heating surface:** 445.4m² (4796sq ft)
**Tractive effort:** 28,480kg (62,800lb)
**Total weight:** 130.2t (287,240lb) (engine only)

## CLASS U 4-6-0 STATE RAILWAYS — RUSSIA: 1903

Engineer A.O. Delacroa designed this passenger class, built between 1903 and 1910. It was a four-cylinder de Glehn-type compound, with the outside cylinders driving the middle coupled wheels, and a top speed of 105kph (65mph). The Class Us served on the railways of Ryasan-Ural and Tashkent. One headed the train that took Lenin from Finland to St Petersburg in 1917; another pulled his funeral train in 1924. Both are preserved, in Finland and Russia respectively.

**The steam locomotive as national icon. U-class No. 127, preserved at Moscow: the engine which drew Lenin's funeral train in 1924.**

**Boiler pressure:** 14kg/cm² (199psi)
**Cylinders:** hp 370x650mm (14.5x25.6in); lp 580x650mm (22.8x25.6in)
**Driving wheels:** 1730mm (68in)
**Grate area:** 2.8m² (30sq ft)
**Heating surface:** 182m² (1959.5sq ft)
**Tractive effort:** N/A
**Total weight:** 72.1t (158.980lb) (engine only)

## 'PRAIRIE' TYPE 2-6-2 LAKE SHORE & MICHIGAN SOUTHERN RAILROAD — USA: 1903

**Boiler pressure:** 14kg/cm² (200psi)
**Cylinders:** 525.6x718mm (20.5x28in)
**Driving wheels:** 2076mm (81in)
**Grate area:**
**Heating surface:**
**Tractive effort:** 11,337kg (25,000lb)
**Total weight:** 145t (320,000lb)

In 1901, Baldwins sold the first 'Prairie'. This was meant to offer greater power than the 2-6-0, but many lines preferred the 4-4-2 'Atlantic' for passenger trains. The front four-wheel bogie, as opposed to a two-wheel truck, was more secure at high speed, and with its large-diameter driving wheels, it was intended for tightly timed passenger trains of light weight. But the 'Prairie' was versatile and other lines used it for freight. This model was built by Alco for the Lake Shore, and is one of the most elegant American locomotives of its time. In 1906–7, the Northern Pacific acquired 150 2-6-2s from the Brooks Works, with 1615mm (64in) drivers. These were lighter than the Lake Shore engines, but their tractive effort was 50 per cent greater. Many survived as yard switchers into the 1950s. The 'Prairie' also spread to Europe, especially Italy and Eastern Europe. Some were built in 'Camelback' versions, including one for the Leigh Valley in 1902.

**With smaller front and larger rear carrying wheels, the 'Prairie' combined six-wheel traction with the big firebox of the 'Atlantic'.**

## CLASS S9 4-4-4 ROYAL PRUSSIAN RAILWAYS (KPEV) — GERMANY: 1904

Famous engine producers Henschel & Sohn, of Kassel, always at the cutting edge of German steam technology, built this semi-streamlined cab-first locomotive as an experiment in 1904.

The boiler and tender were encased in a carriage-like body, with the chimney protruding from the roof. The driver's controls were mounted in a vee-shaped cab. The fireman sweated in an enclosed compartment in the middle of the loco-tender unit, which incidentally included the world's first corridor-tender. The engine was a 3-cylinder compound, intended for express passenger work, but the concept was not pursued in Germany.

**Boiler pressure:** 14kg/cm² (200psi)
**Cylinders:** 526x636mm (20.6x24.8in)
**Driving wheels:** 2226mm (86.8in)
**Grate area:** 4.4m² (47.3sq ft)
**Heating surface:** 258m² (2796.6sq ft)
**Tractive effort:** 9348kg (20,610lb)
**Total weight:** 85.5t (188,496lb)

## SERIES C4/5 2-8-0 SWISS FEDERAL RAILWAYS (SBB) — SWITZERLAND: 1904

Ten thousand kilograms (22046 pounds) of nominal tractive effort, or the ability to haul 200t (196.8 tons) up a 1 in 38 gradient at 20–25kph (12–15mph) were required when this four-cylinder compound locomotive was specified. SLM at Winterthur built the class between 1904 and 1906. It shared a tender with the A3/5 of 1902. The cylinders were in line, high-pressure inside, but with two driven axles. The last to be withdrawn in 1959, was one of the oldest No. 2701 of 1904. It was a typically Swiss procedure that a locomotive design should begin with a set of clear performance parameters. Few other railway systems would have dictated their requirements with such precision. In the case of Switzerland, steep gradients and heavy international traffic made it imperative that performance should be predictable and reliable. But the same could have been said for other railways.

**Boiler pressure:** 14kg/cm$^2$ (200psi)
**Cylinders:** hp 370x600mm (14.5x23.6in); lp 600x640mm (23.6x25.2in)
**Driving wheels:** 1330mm (52.4in)
**Grate area:** 2.8m$^2$ (30sq ft)
**Heating Surface:** 174.2m$^2$ (1875.5sq ft)
**Tractive effort:** 10,000kg (22,050lb)
**Total weight:** 109t (240,345)

## MALLET 0-6-6-0 BALTIMORE & OHIO RAILROAD (B&O) — USA: 1904

Affectionately known as 'Old Maud', and the world's largest in its day, the first US Mallet-type loco portended even mightier things to come. Built by Alco, it served on freight trains in the Western Pennsylvania mountains. A compound type, with low pressure cylinders driving the first, articulated set of wheels, and high pressure cylinders driving the rear, fixed wheels, it satisfied the American railroads' desire to get maximum adhesive grip in banking heavy trains on the long, curving mountain grades without the difficulties of a long rigid wheelbase. About 80 of this type were built, of which some were converted to 2-6-6-0. Early American Mallet users generally preferred the 2-6-6-2 configuration, allowing the use of a wide, deep firebox. They were very slow, but at this time sheer slogging power was most important, to move the heaviest possible trains.

**Boiler pressure:** 16.45kg/cm (235lb)
**Cylinders:** hp 513x820mm (20x32in); lp 820x820mm (32x32in)
**Driving wheels:** 1436mm (56in)
**Grate area:** 6.7m$^2$ (72.2sq ft)
**Heating surface:** 518.8m$^2$ (5586sq ft)
**Tractive effort:** 32,426kg (71,500lb)
**Total weight:** 151.7t (334,500lb) (engine only)

## BESA PASSENGER LOCOMOTIVE 4-6-0 WESTERN RAILWAY (WR) — INDIA: 1905

Only Brazil had a larger metre-gauge (39.4in) network than India., whose route mileage stood at 25,845km (16,060 miles) in 1969. Only the gauge was metric; other measurements were imperial. The first line opened in 1873, and the system grew under both state and corporate enterprise. Locomotive purchase was controlled by state governments initially, but from 1886, individual lines could order their own engines. This led to a variety of types and standards, though the old 0-6-0 'F' type

**A strong wind blows back the smoke as Northern Railway BESA 'Heavy Mail' No 2441 is prepared for duty. On the left is 'F' class 0-6-0 No 36809.**

**A superheated BESA 'Heavy Mail', with outside steam pipes fitted, stands at Waltair Shed on 13 January 1978. Over 100 were still at work at this time.**

predominated. As traffic increased, modern motive power was needed. In 1902, the Bengal & North-Western ordered two 4-6-0s from Neilson & Co of Glasgow. Class A had 1523mm (60in) coupled wheels and inside valve gear; Class B, 1218mm (48in) driving wheels and Walschaerts valve gear. In 1903, the British Engineering Standards Association (BESA) set out a range of standard designs for Indian locomotives on the metre gauge; those for broad gauge engines followed in 1905. BESA produced two 4-6-0 designs, one a mixed-traffic type, and this one, known as the 'Heavy Mail' engine. Accessible machinery, simple operation, and a light axle load (10.16t/10 tons) were the keynotes. The tenders had front canopies, Indian-style. The standard designs served the Indian railways well for many years, though often modified over time. Many engines from the Indian metre gauge lines were sent for war work in Mesopotamia and East Africa between 1914 and 1918. Despite new standard types (Indian Railway Standard) being formulated after the war, new engines were built to the BESA specification (with the addition of superheaters and piston valves) as late as 1939. 'Pacifics' later took over most heavy express duties, but some Indian lines, like the Rohilkund & Kumaon, kept to 4-6-0s until the end of steam.

The metre-gauge lines of India covered virtually every terrain to be found on the sub-continent. Most were rural lines, single-track, carrying agricultural produce or mineral traffic. Passengers were served by mixed trains operating at low speeds, averaging 19kph (12mph). But there were some long-distance services, like the 'Delhi Mail', running over a 965km (600-mile) route from Ahmadabad to the capital, which in the 1970s took just under 24 hours, with 22 intermediate stops.

BESA designs were constructed by various overseas – mostly British – workshops, as well as by Indian ones like the Ajmer plant. The 4-6-0s numbered many hundreds, and many were still in service into the 1970s.

**Boiler pressure:** 11.2kg/cm$^2$ (160psi)
**Cylinders:** 423x564mm (16.5x22in)
**Driving wheels:** 1461mm (57in)
**Grate area:** 1.5m$^2$ (15.6sq ft)
**Heating surface:** 90.5m$^2$ (975sq ft)
**Tractive effort:** 6481kg (14,290lb)
**Total weight:** 37.5t (82,880lb)

**Another variant on the basic theme. No 254, a 4-6-0 of the Bengal-Nagpur Railway, photographed in 1944.**

## CLASS 21 2-6-0 NORWEGIAN STATE RAILWAYS (NSB) NORWAY: 1905

Traffic on longer branch lines was handled by the 45-strong class 21 2-6-0s, which were lightweight locomotives with a maximum axle load around the 10t mark. The first batch, 21a, were two-cylinder compounds, which used the Prussian Railways' von Borries system and had slide valves. The sub-classes which followed, from 21b to 21e (1919), were super-heated two-cylinder simples with piston valves. Some were equipped for wood-burning, with spark-arrester chimneys. Built to haul wooden cars, the Class 21s were under-powered for the heavier trains of the 1920s and were subsequently replaced by 4-6-0s on all but the most lightweight services.

**Boiler pressure:** 12kg/cm$^2$ (171psi)
**Cylinders:** 432x610mm (17x24in)
**Driving wheels:** 1445mm (57in)
**Grate area:** 1.8m$^2$ (19.4sq ft)
**Heating surface:** 78.1m$^2$ (841sq ft)
**Tractive effort:** 8020kg (17.680lb)
**Total weight:** 58.9t (119,272lb)

## CLASS 12B 4-6-0 BUENOS AIRES & GREAT SOUTHERN RAILWAY (BAGS) ARGENTINA: 1906

British capital investment built most Argentinian railways, and British influence on all aspects of design and management was strong. Vulcan Foundry of Manchester built this class of eight 2-cylinder compounds as an express type for the 1675mm (5ft 6in) gauge line. Its low running plate and wheel splashers are typically British. All were later converted to oil burning and superheaters were fitted from 1924. The maintenance difficulties of compound engines caused their withdrawal in 1937.

**Boiler pressure:** 15kg/cm$^2$ (220psi)
**Cylinders:** hp 355x660mm (14x26in); lp 698x660mm (23x26in)
**Driving wheels:** 1827mm (72in)
**Grate area:** 2.6m$^2$ (28sq ft)
**Heating surface:** 156.9m$^2$ (1690sq ft)
**Tractive effort:** N/A
**Total weight:** 116.8t (257,600lb)

**Argentina had few known coal reserves at this time, and imported steam coal was prohibitively expensive. The discovery of oil in Chubut Province prompted the conversion of coal burning locomotives to oil burning ones on a large scale.**

## CLASS P8 4-6-0 ROYAL PRUSSIAN RAILWAYS (KPEV) GERMANY: 1906

The P8 was one of the most numerous and successful locomotive classes ever built. There was nothing especially remarkable or breathtakingly new about the design, though they were thoroughly modern for their time. They did have the Schmidt super-heater, by far the most effective device of its kind; and Walschaerts valve gear fitted externally, with piston valves set above the two simple-expansion outside cylinders. The construction was robust, and the maximum axle-load was 17.2t (16.9 tons), relatively low for a big engine. The firebox was round-topped, with a long, narrow grate, and the boiler was straight-topped, with a dome and sandbox. Its mountings would vary later, with some engines equipped with a second dome housing the top feed from a Knorr feed water pump and heater. The tender, on two four-wheel interior-sprung bogies, held 4700gals of water (5640 US gals) and 5t (4.92 tons) of coal. The first P8s were built by Schwartzkopff in Berlin, but other builders were involved before long. The total number built for the kPEV up to 1921 (when it was absorbed into the *Deutsche Reichsbahngesellschaft*) was 3370. The DRG built a further 101. Other railways in Germany and elsewhere bought it: Latvia, Lithuania, Romania and Turkey operated P8s, as did the Mecklenburg, Oldenburg and Baden lines in Germany. The Polish State Railways bought 100, with larger grates. The total number built was little short of 4000. Many ended up in France, Belgium and some Eastern European countries as a result of war reparations, both in 1918 and in 1945.

As the engines were already superheated, few significant changes were made during the lifetime of the class. New boilers generally increased the heating surface available. In DRG days, post-1926, they were fitted with smoke deflectors, initially large ones fitted to the running plate, later replaced by smaller ones fitted to the smoke box sides. In later life, many acquired the bathtub-style *Kriegslok* tenders, in replacement of their original straight-sided tenders, and some on the East German DR were fitted with Giesl ejector chimneys. As with other numerous classes, various engines were equipped with experimental valve gears in the 1920s and 30s. But essentially the P8 remained as it had been first designed.

It was a mixed-traffic engine, with wide route availability, and served as such, operating every kind of service from main line expresses to local goods trains. Its basic criteria of performance were to haul 700t (689 tons) on level track at 80kph (50mph) and 300t (295 tons) up a 1 in 100 grade at 50kph (31mph). Often it exceeded these, but that was not the point. It broke no speed records, but it was that darling of the railway accountant, a 'general user' or 'pool' engine which needed no specialist driver, used standard parts, and could undertake almost any task.

After the end of World War II, the surviving usable P8s were divided, with the rest of the DRG assets, between the *Deutsche Bundesbahn* in the Federal Republic, and the *Deutsche Reichsbahn* in the Democratic Republic, of Germany. By January 1975, the last to work in Germany (on the DB) was withdrawn, but P8s were still in service in other countries. At least eight of the class have been preserved.

**Wing-type smoke deflectors were fitted to most of the P8s working on the later Deutsche Reichsbahn Gesellschaft and Deutsche Bundesbahn.**

**As DB No 038.3551, a P8 with 'bathtub' tender stands with a three-car local train at a station on southern Germany, in July 1968.**

**Boiler pressure:** 12kg/cm² (170.6psi)
**Cylinders:** 575x630mm (22.6x24.8in)
**Driving wheels:** 1750mm (68.9in)
**Grate area:** 2.6m² (27.8sq ft)
**Heating surface:** 143.3m² (1542sq ft)
**Superheater:** 58.9m² (634sq ft)
**Tractive effort:** 12,140kg (26,769lb)
**Total weight:** 78.5t (172,500lb)

## *CARDEAN* 4-6-0 CALEDONIAN RAILWAY (CR) GREAT BRITAIN: 1906

Intended to haul Anglo-Scottish expresses over the Caledonian's main line, including the 314m (1030ft) Beattock Summit between Carlisle and Glasgow, this small class of five engines was as far as J.F. McIntosh could take his 'big boiler' policy. Built at the CR St Rollox works, it was really an expanded 'Dunalastair' with six coupled wheels; and compared to what was being built at Swindon, and also in its native Glasgow (for export), it was a distinctly old-fashioned machine, in appearance and in mechanism. But No 903 *Cardean* in particular had great prestige with the travelling public, as the regular engine of the 'Corridor', the 2 pm Glasgow Central-Euston express. Its big eight-wheel tender, with a 5000 gallon (6000 US gal) capacity enabled it to run over 161km (100 miles) non-stop. No exceptional speeds are recorded, but it was a reliable performer on the long ascents, apart from one occasion when a crank axle broke and it lost a wheel. Tested against a LNWR 'Experiment' 4-6-0 on the Preston-Carlisle section in 1909, it showed superior power output. The class was fitted with superheaters in 1911–12. One engine, No 907, was wrecked in the Quintinshill crash of 22 May 1915 (Britain's worst railway disaster) – the others were withdrawn by 1930.

**Publicity pictures like this, of Cardean racing along with the 'Corridor' past a signal at clear, seduced a whole generation of schoolboys with the glamour of steam power.**

**Cardean's workload was a daily round trip of approximately 354km (220 miles), from Glasgow to Carlisle and back again. It had a regular driver, who was almost as famous as his locomotive.**

**Boiler pressure:** 14kg/cm² (200psi)
**Cylinders:** 527x660mm (21x26in)
**Driving wheels:** 1981mm (78in)
**Grate area:** 2.4m² (26sq ft)
**Heating surface:** 223m² (2400sq ft)
**Tractive effort:** 10,282kg (22,672lb)
**Total weight:** 133.5t (294,000lb)

## CLASS 835 0-6-0T STATE RAILWAYS (FS) ITALY: 1906

In 1903, the Ernesto Breda works in Milan built a class of outside cylinder side tank engines for the Mediterranean Railway, which was the prototype for the larger-cylindered 835s. This was the standard Italian shunting tank, and eventually numbered 370. Like similar engines elsewhere, they were called 'coffee pots'. When their boilers wore out, some were rebuilt, with the same frames and wheels, as electric shunters. No 835.106, from 1910, is preserved.

**Boiler pressure:** 12kg/cm² (170psi)
**Cylinders:** 410x580mm (16x22.6in)
**Driving wheels:** 1310mm (51in)
**Grate area:** 1.4m² (15 sq ft)
**Heating surface:** 78m² (840sq ft)
**Tractive effort:** 7434kg (16,390lb)
**Total weight:** 45t (99,225lb)

**When their boilers wore out, a number of 835s were resurrected as DC electric shunting engines of Group E321, using the old frames and wheels.**

**Dockside work was a typical task for the Class 835. Its short wheelbase enabled it to work round tight curves. Sparks were not tolerated in dockside areas, and a special spark-arresting chimney has been fitted.**

## CLASS P1 4-4-2 DANISH STATE RAILWAYS (DSB) DENMARK: 1907

**DSB No. 52 – every inch an express design. Sandbox and dome were combined, and the safety valves emerged through the vee-point of the cab. The unusual ribbed construction of the tender is apparent.**

Although Denmark had its own locomotive works in Frichs of Aarhus, the DSB generally turned to Germany, and this Atlantic (the DSB's first large express engine) was built by Hanomag (who made 19 in total). It was a 4-cylinder compound of Vauclain type, the inner high pressure cylinders driving the leading axle, and the outer low pressure cylinders driving the second axle. Two sets of inside Walschaerts gear operated piston valves were shared by the hp and lp cylinders on each side. A further 14, with superheaters, were built by Schwartzkopff in 1910 and classed P2. Some were 'stretched' into 'Pacifics' in the late 1940s. Two 4-4-2s are preserved.

**Boiler pressure:** 15kg/cm$^2$ (214psi)
**Cylinders:** hp 360x640mm (14x25in); lp 620x640mm (24x25in)
**Driving wheels:** 1984mm (77.4in)
**Grate area:** 3.2m$^2$ (34.5sq ft)
**Heating surface:** 192.5m$^2$ (2072sq ft)
**Tractive effort:** 18,140kg (40,000lb)
**Total weight:** 119t (262,500lb)

## CLASSES 4500 & 3500 4-6-2 PARIS-ORLEANS RAILWAY (PO) FRANCE: 1907

**Boiler pressure:** 16kg/$cm^2$ (232psi)
**Cylinders:** hp 390x650mm (15.3x25.6in); lp 640x650mm (25.2x25.6in)
**Driving wheels:** 1846mm (72.75in)
**Grate area:** 4.33$m^2$ (36sq ft)
**Heating surface:** 195$m^2$ (2100sq ft)
**Tractive effort:** not known
**Total weight:** 99.6t (219,600lb)

**The class 4500 was a very large engine by European standards and this may have prompted the PO management to buy from America, where the 'Pacific' type had first been built.**

With long inter-city runs through sparsely inhabited countryside, the French railways needed large passenger engines, and this was the first 'Pacific' design to run on a European railway, developed by the PO and *Société Alsacienne* at Belfort. A four-cylinder compound of de Glehn-du Bousquet type, the class numbered 70 by 1908, and in 1910 a further 30, with superheaters, were delivered. Thirty of the first set were built in the USA by Alco at Schenectady, NY, the rest in Belfort. A further 90, with coupled wheels of 1948mm (76.75in), and designated class 3500, were built between 1909 and 1918. Piston valves, still quite new, worked the high pressure cylinders, traditional slide valves worked the low pressure ones. In 1926, a decision was made to rebuild a 3500 engine to the design of André Chapelon, a brilliant young PO engineer. Feed water heating, the installation of a thermic syphon in the firebox, enlarging and redesign of the superheater, improved steam flow, improved valve control with poppet valves, greater draught from a new kind of double chimney, and smoke deflectors – all this transformed the engines inside and out. Performance improved radically, startling the engineering world and initiating a new era in internal design for steam locomotives. Rebuilding of the other 3500s began at once, and eventually 102 were either rebuilt or built new. Dimensions are for the original non-superheated 4500 class.

## CLASS 640 2-6-0 STATE RAILWAYS (FS) ITALY: 1907

Italy's first 2-6-0 was the compound Class 600 of 1904. It became a popular type on the many long secondary lines in hilly country. Class 640 comprised 173 engines. Compounding was dropped but superheating adopted: 640.01 was Italy's first superheated locomotive.

**In Italy, as in most other countries, the advent of effective superheating brought about a loss of interest in compound expansion. In the 640 class, unusually, the cylinders and motion were inside the frames and the valve gear was on the outside.**

The cylinders were inside, operated by outside piston valves actuated by Walschaerts gear off the middle driving wheels. To assist with flexibility on tight curves, the leading axle is combined in a Helmholtz truck with the front coupled axle.

The first 48 Class 640s came from the Schwartzkopff works, Berlin, while the rest were produced in Breda and other Italian engine builders. No 640.106 has been preserved.

**Boiler pressure:** 12kg/$cm^2$ (170psi)
**Cylinders:** 540x700mm (21x28in)
**Driving wheels:** 1850mm (73in)
**Grate area:** 2.4$m^2$ (26sq ft)
**Heating surface:** 108.5$m^2$ (1168sq ft)
**Superheater:** 33.5$m^2$ (360sq ft)
**Tractive effort:** 10,830kg (23,890lb)
**Total weight:** not known

## CLASS 470 0-10-0 STATE RAILWAYS (FS) ITALY: 1907

One of the 12 FS standard types, this Plancher-type 4-cylinder compound had high and low pressure cylinders on right and left sides respectively, one outside and one inside the frame.

The first 12 were built by Maffei in Munich, the remaining 131 were from Italian shops. Banking and heading heavy freights on mountain grades was the reason for the development of this engine. Their fuel arrangements were unusual. Four tonnes of coal were carried in a bunker built on the left hand running plate and the rear top of the boiler, while water was carried in a four-wheel tender. One hundred and nine were rebuilt with conventional six-wheel tenders in the 1920s and 30s. The last in service were withdrawn at Terni in 1970. No 470.092 is preserved. In this form, they continued to give useful service on freight trains for another three decades.

**Boiler pressure:** 16kg/$cm^2$ (230psi)
**Cylinders:** hp 375x650mm (14.6x25.6in); lp 610x650mm (23.8x25.6in)
**Driving wheels:** 1360mm (53.5in)
**Grate area:** 3.5$m^2$ (38sq ft)
**Heating surface:** not known
**Tractive effort:** not known
**Total weight:** 67t (147,735lb)

## 0-6-0T CHUGOKU RAILWAY JAPAN: 1907

Kerr Stuart of Stoke on Trent, England, built this 1065mm (3ft 6in) gauge 0-6-0T and then shipped it to Japan in 1907. A side-tank engine with two outside cylinders, it was one of their standard types for export and for home industrial lines, with similar engines going to metre-gauge (39.4in) lines in Argentina and Colombia, and standard gauge colliery lines in England and Wales. A powerful engine for its size, it could move 606t (600 tons) on the level. The Japanese engine long outlived its manufacturers' demise in 1930. In 1952, it was sold to the Kawasaki Iron & Steel Co and worked there until it was finally condemned for scrap in 1966. Its career was typical of a host of small industrial engines, in Japan and other countries, which might change ownership, location and even gauge several times over in the course of a working life measured in decades.

**Boiler pressure:** 11.2kg/$cm^2$ (160psi)
**Cylinders:** 368x508mm (14.5x20in)
**Driving wheels:** 1067mm (42in)
**Grate area:** 1.67$m^2$ (18sq ft)
**Heating surface:** 59.2$m^2$ (638sq ft)
**Tractive effort:** 6170kg (13,600lb)
**Total weight:** not known

## CLASS A 4-4-2 SWEDISH STATE RAILWAYS (SJ) SWEDEN: 1907

Twenty-five engines of this inside-cylinder type were built by the Swedish firms Nydquist & Holm and Motala for fast passenger services in the south of Sweden. Its distinctive features included an elongated dome (holding the sandbox) and a wedge-fronted cab. The leading bogie had outside bearings; the pony wheel, inside bearings. The firebox was narrow, spurning one advantage of the 'Atlantic' format. Four of the class were rebuilt as 4-6-0s.

**Dome and sandbox are combined within a single casing on the boiler top, to warm the sand, keeping it dry and ready-flowing. The Class A, like most Atlantics, was prone to wheel-slip, so this was useful.**

**Boiler pressure:** 12kg/cm² (170psi)
**Cylinders:** 500x600mm (19.5x23.4in)
**Driving wheels:** 1880mm (73in)
**Grate area:** 2.6m² (28sq ft)
**Heating surface:** 133m² (1439sq ft)
**Tractive effort:** 7980kg (17,600lb)
**Total weight:** not known

## MALLET COMPOUND 2-6-6-0 EASTERN RAILWAY (EST) FRANCE: 1908

In 1890, Anatole Mallet had built the first of his patent semi-articulated locomotives, an 0-6-6-0 for the Swiss Gotthard Railway, and a number of small similar engines followed, all built by the Maffei works in Munich. In 1904, his system was taken up in a bigger way by the Baltimore & Ohio Railroad in the USA, and the Mallet type became associated with large American locomotives as well as with rather smaller Alpine ones. In a form of re-export from the USA to Europe, the *Est* ordered the two engines of this class from Alco in Schenectady. In standard Mallet form, the front truck, supported by the carrying and first set of coupled wheels, was articulated. The second set of coupled wheels was attached to the main frame. Again as Mallet intended, they were compounds, with two outside high pressure cylinders driving the rear axle of the rear set of coupled wheels, and the two low pressure cylinders driving the corresponding axle of the front set. These were very large engines for their day, in European terms at least. They were intended for use as banking engines and for short-distance freight haulage on steep grades in the industrialized but hilly country around Nancy and Mulhouse, and consequently had quite small 4-wheel tenders, with a capacity of 4.75t of coal and 2900gals (3480 US gals) of water

**Boiler pressure:** 15kg/cm² (213psi)
**Cylinders:** hp 444x660mm (17.5x26in); lp 802.3x660mm (28x26in)
**Driving wheels:** 1274mm (50.2in)
**Grate area:** 3.8m² (40.9sq ft)
**Heating surface:** 124.9m² (1345sq ft)
**Tractive effort:** not known
**Total weight:** 103t (227,165lb) (engine only)

## CLASS S 3/6 4-6-2 ROYAL BAVARIAN STATE RAILWAYS (KBSTB) GERMANY: 1908

**A typical shot from the *Deutsche Reichsbahngesellschaft* era, of a Bavarian compound 'Pacific' running at speed through the picturesque South German countryside, with the 'Rheingold' express.**

Josef Anton Maffei had established a locomotive works in the Bavarian capital, Munich, in 1837, and in the early 1900s the firm was flourishing, with engineer-designers of great ability in Anton Hammel and Heinrich Leppla. They had purchased and explored Vauclain and de Glehn compounds from the USA and Germany before developing their own family of compound locomotives. These had bar frames, with the low-pressure cylinders outside. The first 'Pacific' of this type was built in 1907 for the Baden State Railways. The S 3/6 for the Bavarian Railways followed in 1908, and 159 of this class were built between then and 1931, all at Maffei's Hirschau works except for the final 18, built by Henschel at Kassel. There were some variants, with 18 engines of 1912–13 having larger-diameter, 2000mm (79in) wheels. The positioning and type of ancillary equipment like brake pumps and feed water heaters also varied. All 4 cylinders drove the second coupled axle, with the inside cylinders operated by the outside valve gear by means of rocker shafts. The big low-pressure cylinders, forged in a single block with the steam pipes, combined with the conical smoke box door and a tallish, well-shaped chimney, gave the front end a distinctive and powerful appearance, though the overall effect was of elegance rather than muscle. They were indeed quite light-footed, with a maximum axle load of 18t (17.7 tons). This quality, combined with an impressive reputation for power, speed, economy and reliability, induced the *Deutsche Reichsbahn Gesellschaft* to order 40 new S 3/6s for service on other lines. The DRB also fitted smoke deflectors to the class.

The S 3/6 has been described as one of the truly great designs of the early twentieth century. It had the ability often sought but not always achieved, to haul heavy trains at a consistent and high speed. One of those built in 1927, DRG No 18.518, was recorded as having pulled a 670t (659-ton) train up the 1 in 128 bank between Treuchtlingen and Donauwörth at a sustained 70kph (43.5mph), and maintained 116kph (72mph) on the level track to the south.

Five engines were destroyed in the course of World War II, but the rest remained in post-war service. Thirty were rebuilt with larger, all-welded boilers between 1952 and 1956. Their final duties were hauling express trains on the Ulm–Friedrichshafen and Munich–Lindau lines, and most famously the 'Rheingold Express' operated by Mitropa (Middle European Sleeping & Dining Car Company – German's rival to the Wagons-Lits company) between Hook of Holland and Basel; and the last were withdrawn from Lindau in 1966. Thirteen have been preserved.

**Boiler pressure:** 16kg/cm$^2$ (228 psi)
**Cylinders:** hp 425x610mm (16.7x24in); lp 650x670mm (25.6x26.4in)
**Driving wheels:** 1870mm (73.6in)
**Grate area:** 4.5m$^2$ (48.8sq ft)
**Heating surface:** 197.4m$^2$ (2125sq ft)
**Superheater:** 74.2m$^2$ (798sq ft)
**Tractive effort:** not known
**Total weight:** 149t (328,500lb)

## *The Great Bear* 4-6-2 GREAT WESTERN RAILWAY (GWR) GREAT BRITAIN: 1908

Britain's first 'Pacific' type was built by G.J. Churchward at Swindon, and remained a one-off. A stretched version of his 4-6-0 'Star' class, with four simple-expansion cylinders, a long domeless boiler and a straight-sided Belpaire firebox , it was an engine of austere appearance. The Locomotive Superintendent's intentions for it are unclear: it was too long (10.5m/34ft 6in) and heavy to operate on any route other than London–Bristol, and its performance was not such an improvement over the GWR 4-6-0s to justify the building of further examples. In 1924, as the British LNER company was developing its new 'Pacifics', the GWR quietly rebuilt their monster as a 'Castle' class 4-6-0.

**Boiler pressure:** 15.75kg/c m$^2$ (225psi)
**Cylinders:** 381x660mm (15x26in)
**Driving wheels:** 2043mm (80.5in)
**Grate area:** 3.9 m$^2$ (41.8sq ft)
**Heating surface:** 263 m$^2$ (2831.5sq ft)
**Superheater:** 50.5 m$^2$ (545sq ft)
**Tractive effort:** 13,346kg (29,430lb)
**Total weight:** 99t (218,400lb) (engine only)

**In 1924, the frame was shortened, a new boiler fitted, and the engine rebuilt, becoming a 'Castle' 4-6-0, with a new name, *Viscount Portman.***

## Class AP 4-4-2 EAST INDIAN RAILWAY (EIR) INDIA: 1908

'Atlantics' were not conspicuous in India; in 1920, there were 117, compared to 847 4-4-0s and 812 4-6-0s on the 1675mm (5ft 6in) gauge. The EIR, 'India's premier line', linking Calcutta to Delhi, had the most (45), built by the North British Locomotive Co and the Vulcan Foundry in 1908–9, with outside cylinders, Belpaire fireboxes, and raised front caps on the chimneys. AP stood for 'Atlantic Passenger' and the class was an express passenger engine.

**This 1944 view of EIR AP 'Atlantic' No. 127 shows the diagonal supply pipe between the injector and the top-feed valve. The train appears to be suffering a prolonged stand-still.**

**Boiler pressure:** 12.6kg/cm$^2$ (180psi)
**Cylinders:** 482x660mm (19x26in)
**Driving wheels:** 2005mm (79in)
**Grate area:** 2.9m$^2$ (32sq ft)
**Heating surface:** 184.8m$^2$ (1990sq ft)
**Tractive effort:** 8244kg (18,177lb)
**Total weight:** 67,809kg (149,520lb)

## MALLET TYPE 0-4-4-0 MADAGASCAR RAILWAYS (CFM) MADAGASCAR: 1908

This configuration of Compound Mallets dominated services on the metre-gauge (39.4in) Madagascar Railways until the arrival of diesel *autorails*. Most were built by the *Société Alsacienne* of Mulhouse, but Baldwin supplied six in 1916. Fifty-six locomotives of this type were in use, the majority saturated, and about 18 superheated. They were tank-tender engines, with side tanks alongside the boiler but also a four-wheel tender fitted with wood rails, as all were wood-burners with high spark-arrester chimneys. A few were active in the late 1950s, on shunting duties. In steam days, travel in Madagascar was interesting but uncomfortable. The far-travelled railway enthusiast C.S. Small described the Tamatave-Tananarive train as 'consisting of wooden cars with wooden axles and square wheels.'

**Boiler pressure:** 12kg/cm² (171psi)
**Cylinders:** hp 280x500mm (11x19.7in); lp 425x500mm (16.7x19.7in)
**Driving wheels:** 1000mm (39.4in)
**Grate area:** 1.2m² (12.9sq ft)
**Heating Surface:** 71.4m² (768.7sq ft)
**Tractive effort:** N/A
**Total weight:** 35.4t (78,080lb)

## K-CLASS BEYER GARRATT 0-4-0+0-4-0 TASMANIAN RAILWAYS AUSTRALIA: 1909

**Boiler pressure:** 13.6cm² (195psi)
**Cylinders:** hp 282x410mm (11x16in); lp 436x410mm (17x16in)
**Driving wheels:** 799mm (31.5ins)
**Grate area:** 1.4m² (14.8sq ft)
**Heating surface:** 52.7m² (568sq ft)
**Tractive effort:** 6521kg (14,380lb)
**Total weight:** 34t (75,040lb)

**The first Beyer Garratt K-1, photographed at the National Railway Museum, York, England. It is currently being restored at the Festiniog Railway's works in Wales.**

This was the first patent Beyer-Garratt type of articulated locomotive; H.W. Garratt was the patentee and Beyer Peacock of Manchester were the builders. The principle was of two engines, each a complete mechanical unit, sharing a boiler. This was mounted on a girder frame and supported by pivoting links to the engine units. Ball-joint connections were used for the steam pipes. Its advantages were that the boiler could be large, sufficient to power both engines; and the entire machine, with its double joints, could negotiate tight curves. It also lent itself well to narrow gauge use. Later Garratts were giants, but this first one, built for the 610mm (2ft) gauge, was a pocket giant. At the purchasers' request, it was a compound, with the high-pressure cylinders driving the rear bogie and the low-pressure ones forward. The rear cylinders, under the cab, gave the enginemen very hot feet, and all subsequent Garratts had cylinders at the outer ends of the power bogies. The engines did an excellent job in general, working nickel ore trains from 1910 to 1930, when they were put into store. Beyer Peacock bought back K-1, as a historic locomotive to restore it, incorporating many parts cannibalized from K-2. When Beyer Peacock closed in 1965, it was bought by the Festiniog Railway in Wales.

## CLASS 429 2-6-2 IMPERIAL & ROYAL AUSTRIAN STATE RAILWAYS AUSTRO-HUNGARY: 1909

**Boiler pressure:** 14kg/cm² (199psi)
**Cylinders:** hp 450x720mm (17.7x28.4in); lp 690x720mm (27x28.4in)
**Driving wheels:** 1574mm (62in)
**Grate area:** 3m² (32.3sq ft)
**Heating surface:** 131.7m² (1418sq ft)
**Superheater:** 23.8m² (256sq ft)
**Tractive effort:** not known
**Total weight:** 61.2t (engine only)

**As 35.233 of the Austrian Federal Railway, a superheated class 429 assembles its train of four-wheelers at the junction station of Selzthal in southern Austria.**

The 2-6-2 was a popular wheel arrangement in eastern Europe, and with various modifications this class ran under several designations in different countries of the former Austrian empire after 1918. Intended to operate secondary passenger services, it began as a superheated 2-cylinder compound, with slide valves to operate the low-pressure cylinder and piston valves for the high-pressure, and 57 were built in this form. From 1911, however, it was built only as a simple-expansion engine, class 429.9 of the Imperial Railways, eventually numbering 197.

Building took place at the Austrian workshops of Floridsdorf, StEG, and Wiener Neustadt, also at PCM in Prague. In Poland, it became class Ol.12; in Czechoslovakia, class 354.7; and in Yugoslavia, class 106. Each country modified these engines, many compounds being rebuilt as simples. Double domes connected by steam pipe were fitted in Czechoslovakia. Withdrawals began during the 1950s and the numbers dropped steadily with the arrival of more up-to-date 2-6-2 and 4-6-0 locomotives, but only in the 1970s did the last of the class disappear; and one of the Czech engines has been preserved. Specifications are for the original compound form.

## CLASS 324 2-6-2 HUNGARIAN STATE RAILWAYS (MÁV) HUNGARY: 1909

With modifications, this mixed-traffic class was built (and in cases, substantially rebuilt) at the Budapest Locomotive Works for 34 years, up to 1943 – 900 in all. Some were built for the Imperial & Royal State Railways as Austrian class 329. It began as a non-superheated 2-cylinder compound and finished as a superheated 2-cylinder simple. Many were fitted with Brotan boilers with water-tube firebox, and Pecz-Rejto water-purifiers. The class performed well, and the last to run were withdrawn in 1970. Specifications are for superheated simple engines with the original boiler.

**Pecz-Rejto water-purifying equipment is fitted to the boiler top of the 324. The conical door increased smoke-box air capacity, though it also helped to suggest speediness.**

**Boiler pressure:** 12kg/cm$^2$ (171psi)
**Cylinders:** 510x650mm (20x25.6in)
**Driving wheels:** 1440mm (56.75in)
**Grate area:** 3.1m$^2$ (33.4sq ft)
**Heating surface:** 159.2m$^2$ (1714sq ft)
**Superheater:** 37.9m$^2$ (408sq ft)
**Tractive effort:** 11,895kg (26,228lb)
**Total weight:** 60.1t (132,520lb)

## CLASS B 4-6-0 SWEDISH STATE RAILWAYS (SJ) SWEDEN: 1909

With 98 locomotives, this was the largest passenger class in Sweden. The main frames were of bar construction, but the bogie had plate frames outside the wheels. Its two cylinders were outside, worked by Walschaerts valve gear actuated by piston valves, and were superheated – up-to-date for 1909. Its conical smoke box door was typical of Swedish new passenger engines, as was the vee-fronted cab, its doors opening on to the running plate. A spark arrester, *de rigeur* on Swedish engines, was fitted inside the chimney.

**The Class B, modelled from Prussia's P8, was built until 1944, and its locomotives were some of the last steam engines in Sweden. Several have been preserved. No 1379 of 1916 hauls a train of 1950s stock between Nykøping Syd and Oxeløsund, on 4 June 2002.**

**Boiler pressure:** 12kg/cm$^2$ (170psi)
**Cylinders:** 590x620mm (23x24in)
**Driving wheels:** 1750mm (68.25in)
**Grate area:** 2.6m$^2$ (28sq ft)
**Heating surface:** 143.3m$^2$ (1542sq ft)
**Superheater:** 58.9m$^2$ (634sq ft)
**Tractive effort:** 12,190kg (26,880lb)
**Total weight:** 8t (178,605lb) (engine)

## Class 1500 4-6-2 Buenos Aires & Pacific Railway (BAP) Argentina: 1910

**Boiler pressure:** 10.5kg/cm² (150psi)
**Cylinders:** 533x660mm (21x26in)
**Driving wheels:** 1701mm (67in)
**Grate area:** 2.5m² (27sq ft)
**Heating surface:** 148m² (1597sq ft)
**Superheater:** 40.5m² (435sq ft)
**Tractive effort:** 11,995kg (26,450lb)
**Total weight:** 53.5t (361,000lb)

**The BAP line suffered more than most Argentinian railways from bad water, and corroded boilers were a major problem.**

Built for the 1675mm (5ft 6in) gauge, this sturdy 'Pacific'class, from the North British Locomotive Co, Glasgow, gave stalwart if slow service for over 50 years. A two-cylinder simple, it had a Belpaire boiler and firebox, Walschaerts valve gear and a superheater. Since the BAP ran through cattle-rearing *pampas* country, the front buffers tilted back when out of use to minimize damage to animals (the cow-catcher was made of wood). Like most Argentinian engines, they were oil-fired, from a tank fitted inside the bogie tender.

## Type 10 4-6-2 Belgian State Railways (EB) Belgium: 1910

**A type 10 in its final form, in the late 1950s. No 10018 is on the line between Brussels Nord and Midi, backing with a train of empty stock. The tender is stacked with a typical mixture of briquettes and dusty slack.**

'Space to mount a cannon' was one comment on the empty platform in front of the smokebox of J.B. Flamme's 'Pacific', with the outside cylinders slung on either side and two further cylinders concealed within. But the Belgians had never baulked at engines that looked strange to the foreigner. Flamme, in charge of the EB's motive power since 1904, had looked long and hard at the French compounds, and like his English contemporary Churchward, ended up by saying yes to four cylinders and no to compounding for his express engines. The inside cylinders drove the front coupled wheels; hence their far-forward placement. The Type 10 shared a boiler with the Type 36 2-10-0 freight locomotive, built at the same time – an American-looking wagon-top design with a sharp taper. The firebox was built high in order to burn poor-quality coal, and the boiler had to be expanded to fit. Twenty-eight were built between 1910 and 1912, and proved their worth on heavy boat trains from Ostend into central Europe. By 1914, there were 58 of them. The second batch had minor modifications resulting in a 4t drop in weight. After 1918, a number of alterations were made, including double chimneys, larger superheaters, the fitting of ACFI-type feed water heaters, and smoke deflectors. German bogie tenders acquired as war reparations replaced the original small six-wheel tenders. Changes continued through the late 1930s, with a Kylchap double-blast chimney and further enlargement of the superheater. The modernized Type 10s hauled expresses on the Luxembourg line until electrification in 1956; they were finally withdrawn in 1959.

**Boiler pressure:** 14kg/cm² (199psi)
**Cylinders:** 500x660mm (19.7x26in)
**Driving wheels:** 1980mm (78in)
**Grate area:** 4.6m² (49.2sq ft)
**Heating surface:** 232m² (2500sq ft)
**Superheater:** 76m² (816sq ft)
**Tractive effort:** 19,800kg (43,800lb)
**Total weight:** 160t (352,640lb)

## CLASS 375 2-6-2T HUNGARIAN STATE RAILWAYS (MÁV) HUNGARY: 1910

MÁV built a large number of 2-6-2 side tank 2-cylinder compound locomotives for branch-line work between 1907 and 13, including 305 of this class, with a maximum axle-load of only 9 tons (9.1t). Although not superheated, they had piston valves and did useful work for many decades. When Croatia was ceded to Yugoslavia in 1945, 65 were transferred to the JDZ system, plus 40 built as superheated simple expansion engines. All were designated as class 51, and some worked into the 1970s.

**The former Yugoslavia was the last haunt of the original 375 class, and as class 51 they were used on local trains and pick-up freights. One of their last locations was on the line from Zagreb through the coastal mountains to the Dalmatian Sea at Rijeka, now in Slovenia.**

**Boiler pressure:** 14kg/cm² (199psi)
**Cylinders:** hp 410x600mm (16x23.5in); lp 590x600mm (23.25x23.5in)
**Driving wheels:** 1180mm (46.5in)
**Grate area:** 1.85m² (19.9sq ft)
**Heating surface:** 81.7m² (879.6sq ft)
**Tractive effort:** N/A
**Total weight:** 52.1t (114,880lb)

## CLASS 27 4-6-0 NORWEGIAN STATE RAILWAYS (NSB) NORWAY: 1910

In 1900, the NSB began operating 4-6-0s. The first, Class 18, were a mix of compound and simple mixed-traffic engines and were supplied by Hartmann of Chemnitz, Germany. Class 27 had bigger driving wheels and was a passenger version, 15 being built between 1910 and 1921. In 1927, two Class 18b compounds were rebuilt as Class 27. These simple two-cylinder engines, with piston valves and superheaters, were built by the NSB works at Hamar. The NSB ran long-distance trains from Oslo to Stavanger, Bergen, Trondheim and even Bodø in the far north, as well as to the Swedish border. Services were infrequent and slow on the single-track main lines. The 4-6-0s hauled all the heavier passenger trains, including sleeper trains, until the advent of larger engines in the 1930s.

**Boiler pressure:** 12kg/cm² (171psi)
**Cylinders:** 450x600mm (17.7x23.6in)
**Driving wheels:** 1600mm (63in)
**Grate area:** 1.5m² (16sq ft)
**Heating surface:** 76.4m² (822sq ft)
**Superheater:** 22.7m² (244sq ft)
**Tractive effort:** 7730kg (17,060lb)
**Total weight:** 72t (158,760lb) (engine)

## CLASS N1 2-6-0 CENTRAL RAILWAY OF URUGUAY (CUR) URUGUAY: 1910

Uruguay's largest railway, with 1569km (975 miles) of standard-gauge track, the CUR was English-owned and English builders supplied most of its locomotives; the eight Class N1s came from Beyer Peacock in Manchester. They were used on cross-country services, both passenger and freight, capable of hauling fifteen wooden-bodied carriages, around 381t (375 tons), at 80kph (50mph). From 1938, they were reboilered with superheaters, and classed as N3. One is preserved in working order.

**The preserved N-class No 120 of the CUR, gets steam up for a night-time picture. Converted to oil burning and superheater-fitted in 1942, it is actually No 119, renumbered while still in service.**

**Boiler pressure:** 12.6kg/cm² (180psi)
**Cylinders:** 457x609mm (18x24in)
**Driving wheels:** 1523mm (60in)
**Grate area:** 1.8m² (20sq ft)
**Heating surface:** 101.5m² (1093sq ft)
**Tractive effort:** 8993kg (19,830lb)
**Total weight:** not known

## CLASS E6 4-4-2 PENNSYLVANIA RAILROAD (PRR) USA: 1910

**A Pennsylvania Atlantic in action: a preserved class E7, No. 8063, piloting a D16sb 4-4-0, at Middletown, PA, on 23 August 1985. This class antedated the E6 by eight years.**

The 'Atlantic' type was already going into decline in the USA when this class appeared, but unlike other lines, the Pennsylvania retained 4-4-2s rather than building a lightweight 'Pacific'. Eighty-two of class E6 were built in 1910–14, at the PRR Juniata works, the wide Belpaire firebox making the most of the space above the pony wheels. The prototype had no superheater, but superheaters were fitted to the others. They had a long career in passenger service; the original engine being withdrawn in 1950 and the others following by 1953.

**Boiler pressure:** 14.4kg/m$^2$ (205psi)
**Cylinders:** 558x660mm (22x26in)
**Driving wheels:** 2030mm (80in)
**Grate area:** 5.8m$^2$ (62sq ft)
**Heating Surface:** 266.3m$^2$ (2867sq ft)
**Tractive effort:** 14,186kg (31,275lb)
**Total weight:** 105t (231,500lb) (engine only)

## SERIES 310 2-6-4 IMPERIAL & ROYAL AUSTRIAN STATE RAILWAYS (KKÖSTB) AUSTRIA: 1911

Karl Gölsdorf was a locomotive designer of great originality and flair who left his mark on a whole generation of Imperial Austrian locomotives. Between 1884 and his death in 1916, he was Chief Mechanical Engineer of the state railways, formed from various private railway companies in 1884. Particularly in the pre-superheater era, pre-1906, compounding attracted many designers as a means of extracting more power from a given amount of steam, and thus reducing fuel costs. Gölsdorf was among those who applied themselves to making this system work in practice as well as on paper. The 4-cylinder compound design of this imposing class marks the peak of Austrian compounding practice. All cylinders were in line under the smoke box, high-pressure inside, driving on to the second coupled axle. In full forward (for starting) or reverse gear, live steam was admitted to the low-pressure cylinders, through ports that were not uncovered when valve travel was shortened as the driver notched up.

Before 1911, Gölsdorf's locomotives had been characterized by a steam drier, often exposed above the boiler, placed between two domes, but he abandoned this in favour of a superheater once its performance had been established. Ten 2-6-4s of Series 210 were built

**Bereft of its tender, a Series 310 2-6-4 stands in a scrap line at the Vienna Süd depot, October 1965. A typically sculptural-looking Gölsdorf tender stands behind the interposed tank locomotive.**

**Unlike many locomotive engineers of his time, Gölsdorf had no hesitation in using both compounding and superheating, in this respect anticipating the work of later designers like André Chapelon.**

in 1908–10, followed by 111 of Series 310 between 1911 and 1916, the later version being fitted with a 24-element Schmidt superheater instead of a steam drier. The leading wheels formed a Krauss-Helmholtz bogie with the front coupled wheels, and the rear bogie – anticipating American 'superpower' practice by about 17 years – supported the big broad firebox needed to burn the often poor-grade coal used by the Austrian Railways. The 2-6-4 configuration was sometimes referred to as the 'Adriatic'. Three Austrian and one Czech builders were involved – Floridsdorf, *Staats Eisenbahn Gesellschaft* (StEG) and Wiener Neustadt, of Vienna, and PCM, of Prague. The large-diameter driving wheels suggested high speeds, but their purpose was in fact to reduce piston speed and consequent wear in the single large piston valve that served both cylinders on each side: the maximum speed was 100kph (62mph). This was dictated by the lightweight track and steep gradients that prevailed throughout much of the system, and the 310s had a maximum axle load of only 14.4 tons (14.6t).

**Even when found dumped on a siding, the visual impact of the front end of the 2-6-4s is highly impressive.**

Apart from Austria, they were stationed in depots in what later became Poland, Czechoslovakia and Hungary, in all cases working on main-line passenger expresses into the 1930s. Vienna was a staging-point for many expresses, partly because the Austrian Railways forbade international trains on its tracks unless they went via the capital. The Berlin–Budapest–Orient Express passed through the city, as did the Bucharest-bound Ostend–Vienna–Orient Express, and the St Petersburg–Vienna–Nice–Cannes Express, among others. Some of these expresses were at times no more than a *Wagon-Lits* through carriage added to another train; others were long rakes of sleeping and dining cars. World War I disrupted these services, but most were resumed in the 1920s. In the 1930s, the 310s were increasingly diverted to secondary trains. Various forms of modernization were applied to the engines on different systems. Three remained in service on the Czechoslovak State Railways into 1954. With their lofty aspect and big acetylene headlamps, they were most handsome engines. No 310.23 has been preserved.

**Boiler pressure:** 15kg/cm$^2$ (213psi)
**Cylinders:** hp 390x720mm (15.4x28.3in); lp 660x720mm (24.4x28.3in)
**Driving wheels:** 2100mm (82.7in)
**Grate area:** 4.6m$^2$ (49.7sq ft)
**Heating surface:** 193m$^2$ (2077sq ft)
**Superheater:** 43m$^2$ (463sq ft)
**Tractive effort:** not known
**Total weight:** 146t (322,000lb)

## 2-8-0 GREAT CENTRAL RAILWAY (GCR) — GREAT BRITAIN: 1911

The 2-8-0 had been introduced to Great Britain in 1903 on the Great Western Railway, but no other company took it up until this one was designed. The GCR opened its trunk line from the Midlands to London in 1903, but its major business was further north and it needed a heavy engine for freight traffic in its Yorkshire–Nottinghamshire industrial heartland. The engine, designed by J. G. Robinson, had two simple-expansion outside cylinders driving the third pair of coupled wheels. Inside admission piston valves were placed between the frames, operating a version of the Stephenson's link motion.

During World War I, when the need for military trains and locomotives to support overseas campaigns arose, this was the type chosen by the government's Railway Operating Department, which had 521 built by several builders as well as the GCR's

**A Class 04 2-8-0 stands in the yard of the former Great Central locomotive shed at Retford, on the GC Nottingham-Lincoln line, in May 1964.**

**As British Railways No 63893, an ex-Great Central 2-8-0 waits with a coal train in a crossing loop on the Woodhead Tunnel line between Sheffield and Manchester.**

own Gorton works at Manchester. They were fitted with Westinghouse brake pumps to work French and Belgian stock, and also with steam heating apparatus for use in troop trains. After 1918, a number of British railways acquired the ex-ROD engines, and others remained in foreign service, both in Europe and in Mesopotamia and Iran (Persia).

**Boiler pressure:** 11.2kg/cm² (160psi)
**Cylinders:** 533x660mm (21x26in)
**Driving wheels:** 1436mm (56in)
**Grate area:** 2.4m² (26.25sq ft)
**Heating surface:** 125m² (1348sq ft)
**Superheater:** 23.7m² (255sq ft)
**Tractive effort:** 12,630kg (27,840lb)
**Total weight:** 75t (1625,424lb)

## CLASS Z530 2-6-0T PIRAEUS-ATHENS-PELEPONNESUS RAILWAY (SPAP) GREECE: 1911

Over 750km (466 miles) of metre-gauge railways were operated by the SPAP, with a variety of locomotive types of which the 2-6-0T was the most common. This class, built by Krauss-Maffei in Munich, was the first in Greece to be fitted with superheaters. Some previous examples had been compounds, but this was a two-cylinder simple expansion type, with Walschaerts valve gear and internal piston valves. They were very up-to-date engines in their time, and eventually the class, through acquisition of other lines, and rebuilds of the compounds, numbered 25.

**A Z530, No 552, stands alongside an older 2-6-0T, Z508, the latter fitted with Stephenson link valve gear, at Kalamai station on the SPAP system.**

**Boiler pressure:** 12kg/cm² (171psi)
**Cylinders:** 420x500mm (16.5x19.7in)
**Driving wheels:** 1200mm (47.25in)
**Grate area:** 1.2m² (12.9sq ft)
**Heating surface:** 56.1m² (604sq ft)
**Superheater:** 16.5m² (177.6sq ft)
**Tractive effort:** 7480kg (16,500lb)
**Total weight:** 37.2t (82,026lb)

## FAIRLIE LOCOMOTIVE 0-6-6-0 MEXICAN RAILWAY — MEXICO: 1911

Mexico, with steeply graded, curving lines in many parts, was one of the countries which took most strongly to the Fairlie type, even on standard-gauge lines. One displayed its road-holding qualities by running away after a brake failure, back down a violently curved 1 in 25 gradient, for 11km (7 miles), reaching 96kph (60mph) without derailing. This was the largest Fairlie locomotive, 4416mm (14ft 6in) high, and with a 10,812mm (35ft 6in) wheelbase, built by the Vulcan Foundry, Manchester, to haul 304.8t (300 ton) loads up gradients of 1 in 25, relying on adhesion only.

This was the kind of task at which these double-ender engines excelled.

**Boiler pressure:** 12.6kg/cm$^2$ (180psi)
**Cylinders:** 482x634.5mm (19x25in)
**Driving wheels:** 1218mm (48in)
**Grate area:** 4.4m$^2$ (47.75sq ft)
**Heating surface:** 271.6m$^2$ (2924sq ft)
**Tractive effort:** 26,096kg (57,534lb)
**Total weight:** 140.2t (309,120lb)

## CLASS PO$^3$ 4-6-0 STATE RAILWAYS (SS) — NETHERLANDS: 1911

Quietly powerful, this class was designed by Beyer Peacock in Manchester, England, who built 36, the rest of the total of 120 coming from Werkspoor in the Netherlands and from German builders. Four simple-expansion cylinders in line drove the leading coupled axle and two sets of Walschaerts gear drove the inside cylinder piston valves. Up until 1929, they handled the heaviest express traffic. Five were streamlined in 1936. No 3737, now preserved, was the last steam locomotive to operate in scheduled service on the Dutch railways.

**Boiler pressure:** 12kg/cm$^2$ (170psi)
**Cylinders:** 400x660mm (15.6x26in)
**Driving wheels:** 1850mm (73in)
**Grate area:** 2.8m$^2$ (30sq ft)
**Heating surface:** 145m$^2$ (1561sq ft)
**Superheater:** 41m$^2$ (441sq ft)
**Tractive effort:** 8900kg (19,624lb)
**Total weight:** 72t (158,760lb) (engine only)

**With big headlamps and air brake equipment, the class was a blend of English and Continental design. For 20 years, it was the mainstay of Dutch express passenger services.**

## CLASS E 2-4-6-0T PORTUGUESE RAILWAYS (CP) — PORTUGAL: 1911

A number of Mallet types were used in Portugal from 1905 on metre-gauge (39.4in) lines through the winding valleys. Henschel of Kassel, Germany, built this tank version between 1911 and 1923 to operate on the route from Regua to Vila, in the Douro Valley, and other branches. The distribution of coupled wheels was unusual, but the class worked very efficiently. There were 18 in total, without superheating but fitted with piston valves. One was later fitted with a Giesl ejector, but no further modernization was carried out, though the class worked on into the late 1970s.

By this time they were more than half a century old, but were well adapted to working at slow speeds on these twisting routes with short but steep gradients.

**Boiler pressure:** 14kg/cm$^2$ (199psi)
**Cylinders:** hp 350x550mm (14x21.6in); lp 500x550mm (20x21.6in)
**Driving wheels:** 1000mm (39.4in)
**Grate area:** 2m$^2$ (21.5sq ft)
**Heating surface:** 137m$^2$ (1475sq ft)
**Tractive effort:** N/A
**Total weight:** 59.5t (131,197lb)

## CLASS S 2-6-2 RUSSIAN STATE RAILWAYS — RUSSIA: 1911

More than 3700 locomotives of this class were built, and it was the staple motive power for passenger trains on most Russian trunk lines until the 1960s. It developed from an Imperial Ministry specification of 1908, which set out the requirement for a 2-6-2 with a Krauss leading truck, a wide grate, and a Notkin-type superheater. Produced in 1910 by the Sormovo Works in St Petersburg, it was used around that city and was the basis of the excellent S class design. By 1918, some 900 had been built, and construction continued under the Soviet regime, at various builders,

**No 250.74 with a passenger train. A door opened from the cab front on to the railed running plate.**

including the Kolomna works, which produced the Su in 1925, a longer-wheelbased version. Other sub-classes appeared as the S was adapted for various requirements, including Class Sv ($C^B$), built in 1915 to standard gauge and lower clearance for the Warsaw-Vienna line, later widened to the 1524mm (5ft) gauge and converted to oil burning for the Moscow–Kursk line. Production continued until 1951. The S locos were seen on every kind of passenger service, and their capacity for speed was shown in 1936, when a series of them covered the 650km (404 miles) between Moscow and Leningrad with a light train in 6hrs 20mins, including stops to change engines.

**Boiler pressure:** 13kg/cm$^2$ (185psi)
**Cylinders:** 575x700mm (22.6x27.5in)
**Driving wheels:** 1850mm (72.75in)
**Grate area:** 4.7m$^2$ (50.9sq ft)
**Heating surface:** 198m$^2$ (2131sq ft)
**Superheater:** 89m$^2$ (958sq ft)
**Tractive effort:** 13,650kg (30,100lb)
**Total weight:** 85.3t (188,160lb) (engine only)

**A green-liveried Su locomotive, No 251.86, passes a crossing loop with the international express between Helsinki and Leningrad (now St Petersburg).**

## SERIES EB 3/5 2-6-2T SWISS FEDERAL RAILWAYS (SBB) SWITZERLAND: 1911

Increased traffic on suburban and country routes was the reason for this class, made for start-stop workings on steeply graded lines. A Maffei 2-6-2T had been introduced successfully on the Bodensee–Toggenburg Railway in 1910, and the SBB decided to adopt the same type. The boiler and motion of the B 3/4 2-6-0 were used, but the cylinder diameter was reduced, to improve the tank locomotive's tractive effort. Thirty-four were built, by SLM, between 1911 and 1916. Three have been preserved.

The numerals of the Swiss locomotive notation indicated powered and carrying axles; thus a 3/5 locomotive had three coupled axles and two carrying axles – five in total. This class proved highly effective in service, especially in winter conditions.

**Boiler pressure:** 12kg/cm$^2$ (170psi)
**Cylinders:** 520x600mm (20x23.4in)
**Driving wheels:** 1520mm (59.25in )
**Grate area:** 2.3m$^2$ (25.75sq ft)
**Heating surface:** 120m$^2$ (1294sq ft)
**Superheater:** 33.5m$^2$ (360sq ft)
**Tractive effort:** 10,350kg (22,820lb)
**Total weight:** 57.8t (127,449lb)

## CLASS 34 2-6-(2)-0 OTTOMAN-ANATOLIAN RAILWAY (CFOA) TURKEY: 1911

The locomotives of this unique wheel arrangement were, in fact, some of a class of 22 2-6-0s built in Germany by Hanomag and Borsig for this line, then under German management. It later became the Turkish Railway (TCDD) main Istanbul–Ankara connection.

Some of the CFOA lines were lightly laid and the 15.25t (15.5-ton) maximum axle load was too great for them. As there was sufficient space between the second and third coupled axles, an extra carrying axle was inserted there, reducing the loading by 2 tons.

In all other respects, they remained conventional German-style engines. Although adaptations of this kind are unusual, it was less uncommon for wheel arrangements to be changed by reduction of the number of axles rather than by the addition of further axles.

**Boiler pressure:** 12kg/cm² (171psi)
**Cylinders:** 540x630mm (21.3x24.8in)
**Driving wheels:** 1500mm (59in)
**Grate area:** 2.25m² (24.2sq ft)
**Heating surface:** 130.1m² (1401sq ft)
**Superheater:** 39.3m² (423sq ft)
**Tractive effort:** 12,570kg (27,717lb)
**Total weight:** 59.6t (131,418lb) (engine only)

## CLASS 109 4-6-0 SOUTHERN RAILWAY (SÜDBAHN) AUSTRO-HUNGARY: 1912

Forty-four of this class were built between 1912 and 1914, a sturdy 2-cylinder simple design, with piston valves and superheaters. Much of the *Südbahn* was in Hungary, and after 1918, the Hungarian Railways inherited 12 and built another four at Budapest, as class 302. Four were passed on to Yugoslavia as Class 33 of the JDZ. The Austrian engines had a single dome with safety valves mounted on top; the Hungarian ones were fitted with two additional domes for water purifying and steam collecting. One has been preserved in Austria. They were excellent mixed-traffic locomotives and were often used on fast freights. On level track, their operating speed was 100kph (62mph) with 270t (266 tons), and 90kph (56mph) with 355t (349 tons).

**Boiler pressure:** 13kg/cm² (185psi)
**Cylinders:** 550x660mm (21.6x26in)
**Driving wheels:** 1700mm (67in)
**Grate area:** 3.6m² (38.8sq ft)
**Heating surface:** 237m² (2552sq ft)
**Superheater:** 52.8m² (568sq ft)
**Tractive effort:** 12,910kg (28,470lb)
**Total weight:** 66.9t (147,514lb)

## CLASS H-6-G 4-6-0 CANADA NORTHERN RAILWAY CANADA: 1912

Unusually for a North American line, the Canada Northern went in for 4-6-0s in a big way, with over 330 in several different classes. The H-6-g numbered 66, all built by the Montreal Locomotive Works during 1912–13 for the opening of the transcontinental through route to Vancouver in British Columbia. The Canada Northern was absorbed into the Canadian National system soon after World War I.

Withdrawal of this class began in 1954, but they survived to the end of the steam era, working on the CN, with the last one going out of service in 1961.

Class H-6-g No 1932 of the Canada Northern, built 1913, is preserved at the Alberta Railway Museum, Edmonton, though with a tender of later date, and is still capable of being steamed.

**Boiler pressure:** 12.6kg/cm² (180psi)
**Cylinders:** 558x660mm (22x26in)
**Driving wheels:** 1599mm (63in)
**Grate area:** not known
**Heating surface:** not known
**Superheater:** N/A
**Tractive effort:** 13,860kg (30,500lb)
**Total weight:** 87.9t (193,760lb)

## CLASS 231C 4-6-2 PARIS LYONS & MEDITERRANEAN RAILWAY (PLM) FRANCE: 1912

**A shiny 231-C four-cylinder compound, No 68 stands outside the workshops at Fives–Lille, France, after receiving a service and modification.**

Not to be confused with the later 231C 'Super Pacific' of the *Chemin de Fer du Nord*, this PLM class (462 in total) was a mix of compound and simple-expansion engines, all – except the first compound prototype – with four in-line cylinders. But from 1913 all were built as compounds, or converted to compound working. By 1921, 177 had been built. After Chapelon's work, post-1928, had revolutionized French ideas about locomotive performance, about half the class were modified, 30 receiving new boilers and steam passages. Some of the class were in service as late as 1969, and four have been preserved.

**Boiler pressure:** 16kg/cm² (228psi)
**Cylinders:** hp 440x660mm (3x25.6in); lp 25. 650x650mm (17.6x25.6in)
**Driving wheels:** 2000mm (78.7in)
**Grate area:** 4.3m² (45.7sq ft)
**Heating surface:** 203m² (2185sq ft)
**Superheater:** 65m² (694sq ft)
**Tractive effort:** N/A
**Total weight:** 145.5t (320,500lb)

## CLASS T18 4-6-4T ROYAL PRUSSIAN RAILWAYS (KPEV) GERMANY: 1912

Up to 1927, Vulkan of Stettin and Henschel of Kassel produced over 500 of these engines, which were in effect a tank version of the P8 mixed-traffic 4-6-0, though not identical in dimensions.

With similar characteristics of economy and reliability, they handled suburban passenger services around Berlin and other Prussian cities. Building continued under DRG auspices until 1927.

The 4-6-4 was a notoriously unsteady side-tank type, but the T18s seem to have had no problems. Seven were bought by Turkey in 1925. Classed as $78^{0\text{-}5}$, the last were withdrawn from the DR in 1972. Two are preserved.

**A T18, as No. 078 235-9 stands above the inspection pit in Deutsche Bundesbahn paintwork, Germany.**

**Boiler pressure:** 12kg/cm² (170psi)
**Cylinders:** 560x630mm (22x24.5in)
**Driving wheels:** 1650mm (64.3in)
**Grate area:** 2.4m² (26sq ft)
**Heating surface:** 138.3m² (1489sq ft)
**Superheater:** 49.2m² (529.7sq ft)
**Tractive effort:** 12,085kg (26,648lb)
**Total weight:** 105t (231,525lb)

## 4-6-2T LONDON BRIGHTON & SOUTH COAST RAILWAY (LBSCR) GREAT BRITAIN: 1912

No 326 Bessborough at London Bridge Station. Built in 1912, with Walschaerts valve gear, it was classed J2.

By now, it was not unusual for six-coupled tank engines to run main-line express services over distances up to 130km (80 miles). The distance from London to the south coast towns served by the LBSCR was 80–130km (50–80 miles). The LBSCR was the second in Britain to use the Schmidt superheater, and did so to great effect. In 1908, one of its Class I 3 4-4-2T had beaten a tender engine of the LNWR in competitive fuel economy trials, again on a 130km (80 mile) route. These 4-6-2Ts were the second set designed by D. Earle Marsh for the LBSCR, built at the line's Brighton works, and fitted with Walschaerts valve gear. Their water capacity was 2000gals (2400 US gals), and they carried 3.04t (3 tons) of coal, less than some tender engines. They ran the fastest London–Brighton services until replaced on the 'Brighton Belle' Pullman by a larger 4-6-4T in 1914.

**Boiler pressure:** 12kg/cm² (170psi)
**Cylinders:** 533x660mm (21x26in)
**Driving wheels:** 2038mm (79.5in)
**Grate area:** 2.5m² (26.7sq ft)
**Heating surface:** 141m² (1523sq ft)
**Superheater:** 31.8 m² (342sq ft)
**Tractive effort:** 9450kg (20,840lb)
**Total weight:** 87.4t (192,640lb)

**No 325 Abergavenny, built in 1910, was the unique J1, seen here outside the LBSCR terminus at Brighton. Both class Js were scrapped in 1951.**

## CLASS F10 2-12-2T STATE RAILWAYS (SS) DUTCH EAST INDIES (INDONESIA): 1912

**Boiler pressure:** 12kg/cm² (171psi)
**Cylinders:** 540x510mm (21.3x20in)
**Driving wheels:** 1106mm (43.5in)
**Grate area:** 2.6m² (28sq ft)
**Heating surface:** 122.2m² (1316sq ft)
**Superheater:** 40.7m² (438sq ft)
**Tractive effort:** 14,970kg (30,320lb)
**Total weight:** 80t (176,288lb)

Twenty-eight locomotives of this superheated two-cylinder simple class were built up to 1920. Eighteen, including the first one, were from Hanomag of Hanover in Germany, the others from Werkspoor in the Netherlands. The cylinders drove the third coupled wheels, which were flangeless. The coupled wheelbase was a long one, 6250mm (20ft 6in) and side-play was allowed for in the first and sixth axles, similar to the arrangement in a contemporary 0-12-0T designed by Karl Gölsdorf for the Vordenberg rack line in Austria. Nevertheless, jacks were carried on the running plate, suggesting that derailing was not unexpected. The side tanks were of modest size, with further tank capacity also within the frame and below the coal bunker. Operating mostly in eastern Java, the F10s hauled lengthy mixed trains in the fertile and densely populated but hilly districts around Malang and Blitar. Several were also stationed at Solok depot in western Sumatra around 1970. Of fine appearance, it was the only 12-coupled engine on the Indonesian system, and a sparklingly polished No F10.18 led the locomotive parade at the PNKA (Indonesian State Railway) 25th anniversary parade in September 1970.

**A less well-kept F10. In latter years, steam maintenance standards on the Indonesian PNKA system varied widely from depot to depot, but the larger locomotives tended to be most neglected.**

## CLASS 685 2-6-2 STATE RAILWAYS (FS) ITALY: 1912

**One of the Crosti-boilered class 685s, seen at Venice in September 1950. Streamlining reduces the visual impact of the 'missing' front chimney.**

In 1906, Italy introduced the 'Prairie', a 4-cylinder compound design by S. Plancher, of the Southern Adriatic Railway, later FS class 680, built in Italy by Breda and Ansaldo (except for 20 built by Schwarzkopff in Berlin). Compounding was dropped, and from 1912, new 2-6-2s were built as 4-cylinder simples, redesignated Class 685. The class eventually numbered 241. The four cylinders, in line, drove the second coupled axle, each pair of cylinders operated by a common piston valve. The class had a complex history. In 1924, four were rebuilt with rotary-cam Caprotti valve gear and classed as 686. In 1926, 30 were built with Caprotti valve gear; of these, five were rebuilt in 1939–41 with streamlining and Franco-Crosti boilers, and classed s685. From 1918, 119 of the pre-1912 compound 2-6-2s were rebuilt as 685s, with superheaters; some were later fitted with Caprotti valve gear, some with Friedmann injectors worked by exhaust steam. The rebuilding programme continued into the 1930s; by then, the older engines were being equipped with four high pressure cylinders, as well as triple blast-pipe chimneys, Knorr feed water pumps and pre-heating gear, and Caprotti valve gear. One from 1908, s685.600, is the 1000[th] engine built by the Ernesto Breda works in Milan, and is preserved.

**Boiler pressure:** 12kg/cm$^2$ (170psi)
**Cylinders:** 420x650mm (16.5x25.5in)
**Driving wheels:** 1850mm (72.75in)
**Grate area:** 3.5m$^2$ (38sq ft)
**Heating surface:** 178.6m$^2$ (1922sq ft)
**Superheater:** 48.5m$^2$ (516sq ft)
**Tractive effort:** 12,586kg (27,741lb)
**Total weight:** 120.4t (265,362lb)

**No 685 568 leaves Milan Central with a local train in August 1955, passing NE636 118, one of a very numerous articulated six-axle electric loco class.**

## CLASS E 0-10-0 RUSSIAN STATE RAILWAYS RUSSIA: 1912

From early in the 20[th] century, the centralized Russian railway bureaucracy had been wondering how to fulfil the growing need for more powerful freight engines. The design that finally appeared in 1912 has been chiefly credited to V.I. Lopushinsky, and the first examples were built under his direction at the Lugansk works. They had two simple-expansion cylinders, fitted outside, operated by piston valves which were actuated by Walschaerts gear. The first ones were oil burners, intended for the Far-Caucasus line. Coal burners, with larger cylinders, followed for the Northern Donetz line. With a maximum axle load of 16.2t (15.9 tons) they were adaptable to a wide variety of track conditions. From 1915, following successful performance of the first engines, production of the E class got under way at several different workshops, and this became by far the most numerous locomotive class ever to exist. By 1923, about 2800 had been built. By 1960, the

**An E-class on passenger service – in this September 1973 picture, the locomotive is slowly backing to be coupled to its train.**

total number exceeded 13,000.

The 1917 Revolution temporarily halted locomotive production; the Soviet government placed huge orders with builders in Sweden and Germany for E class engines, 500 from Nydquist & Holm of Trollhättan, Sweden and 700 from 19 assorted German builders. These were built to the specification of Lugansk engines of 1917, and were said to have been paid for with gold bullion. By 1926, the state-run locomotive industry had been established in Russia, and an improved version had been brought out by the Bryansk works, designated Eu (*usilenny* = 'more powerful'). Between then and 1933, some 3350 were built there and at the re-named Lugansk, now Voroshilovgrad; also at Kolomna, Sormovo and Kharkov. Its boiler pressure was 12kg/cm$^2$ (171psi) and its maximum axle load was 16.4 tons (16.7t). A further version appeared in 1931: Em 710xx, with a higher power-to-weight ratio, boiler pressure at 14kg/cm$^2$ (199psi) and maximum axle load 17t (16.7 tons) – about 2700 of these were built up to 1936. Many of these acquired a supplementary cylindrical water tank on the tender to increase their range; some E-types were also fitted as condensing engines. In the early 1930s, the Murom repair works developed the Er as a heavier version and around 850 of this were built at Bryansk and Voroshilovgrad. In 1944, some of the Er locomotives were rebuilt with 13kg/cm$^2$ (185psi) boilers designed for the Su 2-6-2, and designated Esu. In these, the twin domes and sandbox were combined in a single boiler-top housing, and a clerestory-style cab was fitted. This style continued in post-war building. After the end of World War II, with many locomotives destroyed or in dire need of reboilering or other major repair, Er types were built in great numbers, up to 1952. Most of these were built not in Russia but in Poland, Czechoslovakia, Hungary and Romania. Their total number is not certain, but is at least 2200 and perhaps over 3000.

**A driver oils the motion of his engine. The relatively small wheels seem dwarfed by the locomotive's bulk.**

Freight movement was the chief priority of the Soviet Russian railway system, and the E-class was to be seen virtually everywhere, on the basic duties of yard shunting and short distance goods trains. For travellers, it was the most frequently seen locomotive on Russian railways. Even in 1959, engines first built in 1912 were seen in use, and the class remained in service until the final abolition of steam power on the Soviet Railways. Specifications given are for the 1915 engines.

**Preserved No 799-36 of class Er on a branch train excursion service in the Ukraine, July 1995.**

**Boiler pressure:** 12kg/cm$^2$ (171psi)
**Cylinders:** 647x705mm (25.5x27.75in)
**Driving wheels:** 1333mm (52in)
**Grate area:** 4.2m$^2$ (45.2sq ft)
**Heating surface:** 207m$^2$ (2231 sq ft)
**Superheater:** 50.8m$^2$ (547sq ft)
**Tractive effort:** 22,675kg (50,000lb)
**Total weight:** 80t (176,400lb) (engine only)

## NO. 101 2-8-0 SMYRNA-KASSABA & EXTENSION RAILWAY (SCP) TURKEY: 1912

Twelve of these two-cylinder superheated engines, eventually to become Class 45.121 of the Turkish State Railways (TCDD), were supplied from Humboldt in Germany for this Anatolian line. The design was a Maffei one, and very similar engines were also supplied to Syria. Compact and powerful, with a maximum axle load of 12.5t (12.2 tons), it was a useful mixed-traffic locomotive. The Oriental Railway (CO), joining Istanbul to the European network, bought 22 from French builders between 1924 and 1927; these were absorbed with the CO itself into the TCDD in 1937.

**Between 1910 and 1950, 2-8-0s were the mainstay of all long-distance traffic on most Middle Eastern lines, both passenger and freight. They offered just the right balance of power, weight and size.**

**Boiler pressure:** 12kg/cm² (171psi)
**Cylinders:** 530x660mm (20.8x26in)
**Driving wheels:** 1400mm (55in)
**Grate area:** 2.4m² (25.8sq ft)
**Heating surface:** 173.9m² (1872.3sq ft)
**Superheater:** 32m² (344.5sq ft)
**Tractive effort:** 13,480kg (29,000lb)
**Total weight:** 60.1t (132,520lb)

## CLASS 20 2-6-0 SERBIAN STATE RAILWAYS (SDZ) SERBIA (YUGOSLAVIA): 1912

With its somewhat 'British' looks, this class shows its parentage at the Borsig works in Berlin. The first five were built for the Ottoman Railway in Turkey, but taken by the Serbs in the Balkan War of 1912.

The Serbian Railways then ordered an additional 40, of which 23 had arrived before the outbreak of World War I. Another 200 were supplied by Germany in post-war reparations. It was a useful, modern design, with two simple expansion cylinders, piston valves and superheater, and fitted with a substantial bogie tender.

**A wayside station in the former Yugoslavia, with a Borsig class 20 2-6-0 on a four-carriage local service.**

**Boiler pressure:** 12kg/cm² (171psi)
**Cylinders:** 520x630mm (20.5x24.8in)
**Driving wheels:** 1350mm (53in)
**Grate area:** 2.4m² (25.8sq ft)
**Heating surface:** 113.8m² (1225sq ft)
**Superheater:** 48.9m² (526.5sq ft)
**Tractive effort:** 12,960kg (28,580lb)
**Total weight:** 55.2t (1217,716lb) (engine only)

## CLASS 629 4-6-2T SOUTHERN RAILWAY (*SÜDBAHN*) AUSTRIA: 1913

First built for the *Südbahn*, by StEG, this 'Pacific' tank became a standard class on the Imperial railways and 45 were built up to 1918. The design featured two simple-expansion cylinders, superheaters, and piston valves. A further 55 were built in Austria by 1927; and 35, with modifications, were built in Czechoslovakia. Many of the Austrian engines received Giesl ejectors, and several were still at work in 1970. Perhaps the least altered were those which ran as Class 18 in Yugoslavia.

**Boiler pressure:** 13kg/cm² (185.25psi)
**Cylinders:** 475x720mm (18.7x28.4in)
**Driving wheels:** 1625mm (64in)
**Grate area:** 2.7m² (29sq ft)
**Heating surface:** 142.7m² (1536.4sq ft)
**Superheater:** 29.1m² (313.3sq ft)
**Tractive effort:** 11,080kg (24,430lb)
**Total weight:** 80.2t (176,841lb)

**No 18.003 of the Yugoslav State Railways, a former class 629 4-6-2T locomotive, makes a smoky evening departure on a local passenger service. The engines retained in the former Yugoslavia were the longest-lived and least-altered members of the original class. First built in Austria before World War I, these effective and long-lasting locos were exported to Czechoslovakia and Yugoslavia.**

## 0-6-6-0 ARICA-LA PAZ RAILWAY BOLIVIA: 1913

On a gauge of 39.6in (1005mm) this line connects the capital of landlocked Bolivia, high in the Andes, with the sea at Arica in Chile. Mallet-type compound engines were supplied in 1913-18 to haul both passenger and freight traffic, by Hanomag in Germany and Baldwins in the USA; though both were without superheat, the US-built engines were more up-to-date, with piston valves rather than slide valves, and power reversing gear. The Andean railways were among the most demanding in the world in terms of operation as well as construction. Snow, landslides and washouts were added to the difficulties of operating single-line routes with severe gradients, tight curves and frequent reversals. Fortunately, high altitude has no adverse effect on steam engines, unlike diesels.

**Boiler pressure:** 14kg/cm² (200psi)
**Cylinders:** hp 406x558.5mm (16x22in); lp 634.5x558.5mm (25x22in)
**Driving wheels:** 1104mm (43.5in)
**Grate area:** 2.9m² (31.3sq ft)
**Heating surface:** 136.4m² (1469sq ft)
**Tractive effort:** N/A
**Total weight:** 69t (152,320lb)

## CLASS 900 2-10-0 BULGARIAN STATE RAILWAYS (BDZ) BULGARIA: 1913

The BDZ was first set up in 1888 and Bulgarian locomotive practice, though strongly influenced by Austria and Germany, was distinctive in many ways despite the country having no large locomotive works of its own. With the four in-line cylinder tail-rods protruding in front like gun barrels, this freight engine had a rugged, uncompromising appearance. It used the Maffei compounding system, though the 70 locomotives built in the class were manufactured between 1913 and 1917 by Hanomag in Hanover. These were the most powerful Bulgarian engines before the modernization policy introduced in 1930. The high-pressure cylinders were inside, and a common piston valve drove the high- and low-pressure cylinder on each side. All cylinders drove the third coupled wheels, which had no flanges. Many of the class were fitted with chimney lids and a backwards-angled smoke-deflecting semi-collar behind the chimney. In the renumbering programme of 1935, the class was redesignated as 19. By this time, more modern freight types had displaced them from main-line services, but some of the class survived on remoter lines of the Central and Eastern operating districts into the 1960s.

**The post-war catenary for electric traction is already in position as this locomotive backs on to a local train in its final years of service.**

**Boiler pressure:** 15kg/cm$^2$ (214psi)
**Cylinders:** hp 430x720mm (17x28.3in); lp 660x720mm (26x28.3in)
**Driving wheels:** 1450mm (57in)
**Grate area:** 4.5m$^2$ (48.4sq ft)
**Heating surface:** 201.8m$^2$ (2172.7sq ft)
**Superheater:** 50m$^2$ (538.3sq ft)
**Tractive effort:** N/A
**Total weight:** 83.8t (188,550lb)

## 4-4-2 EGYPTIAN STATE RAILWAYS (ESR) EGYPT: 1913

'Atlantics' had worked in Egypt in small numbers since 1900, but a superheated type dominated main-line passenger traffic from Cairo to Alexandria and to distant Upper Egypt between the two world wars.

Between 1913 and 1926, 80 were built, in Germany, America and Scotland, of generally similar appearance and dimensions, though after Nos 1–5, from Schwartzkopff, the cylinder stroke went up to 28in (711mm). The two cylinders were outside, simple-expansion, driving the rear coupled axle, worked by Walschaerts gear with piston valves. In the 1930s, two were experimentally converted into 4-6-0s, but this was not taken further. The 'Atlantics' were scrapped by 1940.

**Cylinders:** 507.6x660mm (20x26in)
**Driving wheels:** 1980mm (78in)

Other data not available

## CLASS VR1 0-6-0 STATE RAILWAYS (VR) FINLAND: 1913

This was the first specifically designed shunting engine on the VR, and 43 were built up to 1927. Up to 1925, they were not superheated, but from then on superheaters were fitted to the whole class. Six ended up in Russia after 1918; in 1928, four returned. Coal burners, all were built at Tampere by Tampella, except for 10 built by Hanomag in 1921–23. Fitted with German Heusinger valve gear and piston valves, this useful class worked up to 1970 and was to be found at depots all over the country.

**Boiler pressure:** 12kg/cm$^2$ (171psi)
**Cylinders:** 430x550mm (17x21.6in)
**Driving wheels:** 1270mm (50in)
**Grate area:** 1.44m$^2$ (15.5sq ft)
**Heating surface:** 52.9m$^2$ (566.3sq ft)
**Superheater:** 15.4m$^2$ (162.5sq ft)
**Tractive effort:** 8230kg (18,147lb)
**Total weight:** 44.8t (98,784lb)

**Vr1 No 670, one of a batch of five built in 1923 by Hanomag. Four engines of the class are preserved, though not this one.**

## Class T161 0-10-0T ROYAL PRUSSIAN RAILWAYS (KPEV) GERMANY: 1913

Classed as $94^{5-17}$ when taken into the DRG, this was a large class, numbering 1250 when construction ceased in 1924. Similar in dimensions to the G10 0-10-0, it had two outside cylinders, Walschaerts valve gear, a Schmidt superheater and a long, narrow grate. The leading and trailing coupled wheels were allowed a degree of side-play, and with all wheels contributing to the adhesive weight, it made a powerful and efficient heavy shunting engine. Several examples survived in use until 1973.

**One of the last T161 locomotives on shed in Germany, as Class 94 of the Deutsche Bundesbahn. To the delight of local enthusiasts, a single engine is still preserved in good operating condition, DB No 94 249, at the Heiligenstadt railway museum.**

**Boiler pressure:** 12kg/cm² (171psi)
**Cylinders:** 610x660mm (24x26in)
**Driving wheels:** 1350mm (53in)
**Grate area:** 2.3m² (24.8sq ft)
**Heating surface:** 129.4m² (1393.2sq ft)
**Superheater:** 45.3m² (487.7sq ft)
**Tractive effort:** 18,594kg (41,000lb)
**Total weight:** 84.9t (187,204lb)

## Class 429 'Director' 4-4-0 GREAT CENTRAL RAILWAY (GCR) GREAT BRITAIN: 1913

**The preserved 'Director', No 506 Butler-Henderson on the heritage Great Central Railway at Loughborough Central Station, in March 1984. The oval-shaped buffers were a GC trademark.**

Though bigger than most, this was a classic British 4-4-0 design, by J.G. Robinson, with two inside cylinders and inside motion, a low, unbroken running plate, and a double splasher hiding the upper halves of the driving wheels. The first batch consisted of ten engines; eleven more, 'Improved Directors', were built in 1920–23, and a further 24 were put in service in 1924, after the GCR had been amalgamated into the London & North Eastern Railway. These last worked in Scotland and were modified to fit a tighter loading gauge on the former North British Railway, with reduced boiler fittings.

**Boiler pressure:** 12.6kg/cm² (180psi)
**Cylinders:** 513x660mm (20x26in)
**Driving wheels:** 2077mm (81in)
**Grate area:** 2.4m² (26sq ft)
**Heating surface:** 154m² (1659sq ft)
**Superheater:** 28.2m² (304sq ft)
**Tractive effort:** 8910kg (19,644lb)
**Total weight:** 62t (136,640lb) (engine only)

## TYPE 9600 2-8-0 JAPANESE NATIONAL RAILWAYS (JNR) JAPAN: 1913

In 1912, the JNR announced that in future, except in special cases, all locomotives would be home-produced.

By this time, a variety of types, both British and American had been imported, but it was the American form of design that prevailed in domestic types built by Kawasaki Zosen Shipyard, Kisha Seizo Kaisha, and JNR's own workshops at Kokura. It was a first essay at a Japanese-designed and built big freight engine. The American influence is plain in the style and design.

The design was a success and 770 were built up to 1926, making it Japan's first 'mass-produced' engine. It was the main-line goods engine until the introduction of the D51 in the 1930s, after which it was more often found on branch and yard work.

**Boiler pressure:** 13kg/$cm^2$ (185psi)
**Cylinders:** 508x610mm (20x24in)
**Driving wheels:** 1250mm (49.25in)
**Grate area:** 2.32$m^2$ (25sq ft)
**Heating surface:** 154.5$m^2$ (1663sq ft)
**Superheater:** 35.2$m^2$ (350sq ft)
**Tractive effort:** 13,900kg (30,650lb)
**Total weight:** 94.85t (209,144lb)

## CLASS C 5/6 2-10-0 SWISS FEDERAL RAILWAYS (SBB) SWITZERLAND: 1913

**Boiler pressure:** 15kg/$cm^2$ (215psi)
**Cylinders:** hp 470x640mm (18x23.5in); lp 690x640mm (27x23.5in)
**Driving wheels:** 1330mm (52in)
**Grate area:** 3.7$m^2$ (40sq ft)
**Heating surface:** $m^2$)
**Superheater:** $m^2$)
**Tractive effort:** 20,408kg (45,000lb)
**Total weight:** 128t (282,240lb)

This was the most powerful steam locomotive to operate in Switzerland. Between 1913 and 1917, 30 were built for passenger and goods trains over the Gotthard line, with a requirement to work trains of 300t (295 tons) tare up a gradient of 1 in 40 at 25kph (15mph). The first two were 4-cylinder simples, later rebuilt as compounds; the rest were built as compounds, with the high-pressure cylinders inside the frames. These drove the second coupled axle; the low-pressure cylinders drove the third.

Like other European locomotives, the front carrying wheels formed a Krauss–Helmholtz bogie with the front coupled wheels.

Several have been preserved.

**Reliability was the prority for Swiss main-line locomotives. By 1913, electrification had just begun, and steam had a virtual monopoly of the mountain lines.**

## CLASS MS 2-6-4T UGANDA RAILWAY (UR) UGANDA: 1913

The Uganda railway, later absorbed into the East African Railways, was formed as early as 1895; the eight unsuperheated locomotives of the MS class were built in England by Nasmyth Wilson as a larger and more powerful version of the Class S 2-6-2T.

Intended for shunting and branch work, some were fitted with supplementary tenders, partly because they lacked adhesion with empty side tanks.

They had two outside simple-expansion cylinders and Belpaire fireboxes, and in branch service hauled 152.4t (150-ton) trains at 48kph (30mph). Reclassed as EE in 1929, they survived in action to the mid-1960s.

**Boiler pressure:** 11kg/$cm^2$ (160psi)
**Cylinders:** 381x558.5mm (15x22in)
**Driving wheels:** 1091mm (43in)
**Grate area:** 1.18$m^2$ (12.8sq ft)
**Heating surface:** 95.1.5$m^2$ (1024sq ft)
**Tractive effort:** 7100kg (15,655lb)
**Total weight:** 53.2t (117,376lb)

## CLASS 11B 2-8-0 BUENOS AIRES GREAT SOUTHERN RAILWAY (BAGS) ARGENTINA: 1914

Earlier 2-8-0s on this line had been two-cylinder compounds, but this large class of 100, built up to 1932, was simple-expansion. The first order was divided between British and German builders. Though designated goods engines, they often worked branch passenger trains, as well as running freight over most of the BAGS lines. In 1965, the ASTARSA company in Buenos Aires carried out a renovation programme on the class, which ran until steam was phased out on Argentine Railways. Over 100 steam locomotives were renovated at the ASTARSA workshops at La Plata, which closed only in 1997. Argentina was the home of L.D. Porta, whose contributions to steam locomotive theory and practice became more widely appreciated in the later twentieth century.

**Boiler pressure:** 11.2kg/$cm^2$ (160psi)
**Cylinders:** 482x660mm (19x26in)
**Driving wheels:** 1409mm (55.5in)
**Grate area:** 2.3$m^2$ (24.5sq ft)
**Heating surface:** 141.4$m^2$ (1522sq ft)
**Superheater:** not known
**Tractive effort:** 9818kg (21,650lb)
**Total weight:** 106.4t (234,528lb)

## CLASS 601 2-6-6-0 HUNGARIAN RAILWAYS (MÁV) AUSTRO-HUNGARY: 1914

Built in the Budapest locomotive works, this was the biggest engine to run on the MÁV system, and was designed for the difficult Zagreb-Rijeka line in what is now Slovenia, though they also ran on lines in the Carpathians and other mountain regions.

In all, 63 were built, including three supplied to the Turkish Oriental Railway. They were Mallet-type 4-cylinder compounds, with Brotan boilers and Pecz-Rejto water purifying equipment. It was said that two firemen had to be carried to cope with their fuel demands, but some survived on the Yugoslavian JDZ until 1960, working as bankers on the line from Split to Zagreb.

This was natural Mallet country, and this, together with the relative infrequency of services over the largely single-track route, and Yugoslavia's lack of capital for investment in new equipment, accounts for the longevity of a locomotive type that was expensive to run and complex to maintain and repair.

**Boiler pressure:** 15kg/$cm^2$ (214psi)
**Cylinders:** hp 520x660mm (20.5x26in); lp 850x660mm (33.5x26in)
**Driving wheels:** 1440mm (56.75in)
**Grate area:** 5.1$m^2$ (55sq ft)
**Heating surface:** 275.2$m^2$ (2963sq ft)
**Superheater:** 66$m^2$ (710.6sq ft)
**Tractive effort:** N/A
**Total weight:** 106.5t (234,832lb) (engine only)

## CLASS HS 2-8-0 BENGAL–NAGPUR RAILWAY (BNR) INDIA: 1914

As part of the innovative BESA programme (see 1905), a 2-cylinder, heavy goods type (HG) was introduced to the Indian railways in 1906.

This was a superheated version of that engine, with Schmidt superheaters at first, then Robinson's adaptation later.

The Bengal-Nagpur had 174, making it the most numerous class on the line.

The North Western had 132 of the HS class, and it was also built for the Great Indian Peninsula Railway, the Madras & Southern Mahratta, and the East India Railway, between 1913 and 1920.

**A 'Heavy Goods' 2-8-0 sets off with a train of loaded coal waggons from a colliery railhead, while others are filled from the conveyor system.**

Builders were Kitson of Leeds, North British, Vulcan Foundry, and Robert Stephenson.

**Boiler pressure:** 12.6kg/cm$^2$ (180psi)
**Cylinders:** 558.3x660mm (22x26in)
**Driving wheels:** 1434mm (56.5in)
**Grate area:** 2.9m$^2$ (32sq ft)
**Heating surface:** 164.4m$^2$ (1770sq ft)
**Superheater:** 36.1m$^2$ (389sq ft)
**Tractive effort:** 15,419kg (34,000lb)
**Total weight:** 74.4t (164,080lb) (engine only)

## CLASS F 4-6-2 SWEDISH STATE RAILWAYS (SJ) SWEDEN: 1914

The first 'Pacifics' in Scandinavia, they formed a class of 11, built by Nydquist & Holm between 1914 and 1916, and hauled main-line expresses from the Norwegian border and on the Gothenburg-Stockholm line. Big headlights and snow deflectors dominated the front end of what was anyway an imposing engine. They were four-cylinder in-line compounds on the Vauclain model, all driving the second pair of coupled wheels. The high-pressure cylinders were

**One of the later Swedish double-chimney versions, No 978, stands at Dybbølsbro locomotive depot, Copenhagen, on 5 October 1971. It has been fitted with a German-style 'bathtub' tender, and the chimney is ringed with the national colours.**

inside the frame and the low-pressure ones outside; each set worked by a single piston valve operated by Walschaerts outside valve gear. The leading bogie and the trailing wheels ran on outside bearings. On the boiler top, a large cover went over both regulator dome and sandbox. The cabs had wooden sides, a typically Swedish feature intended to provide better winter insulation than metal.

The class did excellent work until electrification made them redundant in 1937. They were sold to the Danish State Railways, reconditioned, refitted for right-hand drive, and put into service as DSB Class E.

Between 1942 and 1950, the Danish Frichs works built a further 25, with steel cabs and an additional dome housing a steam drier; 15 of these also had double chimneys with Lemaître blast pipes.

The first of the original set, No 1200, was returned to Sweden where it is preserved.

**Boiler pressure:** 13kg/cm² (185psi)
**Cylinders:** hp 420x660mm (16.4x26in); lp 630x660mm (24.5x26in)
**Driving wheels:** 1880mm (73.3in)
**Grate area:** 3.6m² (38.75sq ft)
**Heating surface:** 184.5m² (1987sq ft)
**Superheater:** 63.5m² (684sq ft)
**Tractive effort:** N/A
**Total weight:** 86.8t (191,520lb) (engine only)

## P1 TRIPLEX LOCOMOTIVE 2-8-8-8-2 ERIE RAILROAD — USA: 1914

**Boiler pressure:** 14.7kg/cm² (210psi)
**Cylinders:** 923x820mm (36x32in)
**Driving wheels:** 1615mm (63in)
**Grate area:** 8.3m² (90sq ft)
**Heating surface:** 639.5m² (6886sq ft)
**Superheater:** 147m² (1584sq ft)
**Tractive effort:** 72,562kg (160,000lb)
**Total weight:** 392t (864,400lb)

**The cab of the 'Triplex' was noisy and hot, with a set of cylinders on either side of it. The exhaust vent at the rear of the tender can be also be seen in this photograph.**

Four of these engines were built by Baldwins, three for the Erie and one for the Virginian Railroad. The latter differed from the Erie engines in having smaller driving wheels and a four-wheel truck supporting the tender. The order was placed in 1913, and designed according to patents granted to George R. Henderson, Consulting Engineer to Baldwins. His aim was to maximize the adhesive weight, and hence the pulling power, of a big road engine. The six cylinders were of identical size and cast from the same pattern. Steam went direct from the boiler to the middle pair, which acted as high-pressure cylinders; they exhausted into the front and rear, low-pressure, cylinders. The front cylinders then exhausted into the stack in order to create a draught for the fire; exhaust from the others passed through a feedwater heater and out through a pipe behind the tank. Total length was 32,005mm (105ft). The first Erie engine was named *Matt H. Shay*, in honour of its oldest living engineman. In a test, it hauled a train of 250 loaded cars, weighing 18,203t (17,912 tons) and 2.5km (1.6 miles) long. The Triplexes were intended as pushers on the Gulf Summit grades. Unfortunately, the steam distribution system was inadequate and performance was below expectations. They were dismantled between 1929 and 1933, and the Virginian engine was converted to a 2-8-8-0.

**The theory behind the 'triplex' design was sound, but supplying steam from a single boiler to three sets of cylinders was impractical in working conditions.**

## K4 4-6-2 PENNSYLVANIA RAILROAD (PRR) — USA: 1914

'An engine among engines' wrote A.F. Staufer, author of *Pennsy Power* (1957), and indeed this was one of the largest and most successful classes of 'Pacific' among the railways of the world. The brief given to motive power chief J.T. Wallis was to produce a main passenger engine for the line, and the prototype of the design was built in 1914. Based on the E6 'Atlantic' type, it was a compact locomotive even by the American standards of the time, but with a tractive effort rated at 20,166kg (44,460lb) it had ample power packed into it. It was superheated but hand-fired, and a screw reverser was fitted. Line production began in 1917. Only minor changes were made in the first 14 years, testifying to the thoroughness with which the design had been prepared and tested at the

**Stopping by the water tower on a snowy evening – K4 No 5354 at Fort Wayne, Indiana, with a passenger train bound for Grand Rapids, in December 1947.**

**During the mid-30s streamlining vogue, five of the class were streamlined, but the cladding was removed in the early 1940s.**

Altoona test plant and on the road. They gave excellent main line service through the 1920s and 30s, and lasted on secondary duties into the 1950s. Eventually, 425 K4s were built, all but 74 of them at the PRR's Juniata shops; the others were built by Baldwin. The decision to order a further 100 in 1927–8 aroused controversy: critics said a more powerful 'Hudson' type should have been brought in. By the mid-1930s, all K4s were fitted with power reversers and automatic stokers: that 6.5m² (70sq ft) grate was a very big one for a fireman to keep supplied on a long run.. Over the years, eight tender types were fitted, ranging upfrom type 70-P 75, holding 12.7t (12.5 tons) of coal and 7000gals (5800 US gals) of water, to 130-P 75 with almost double the capacity.

The K4 could maintain 96–120kph (60–75mph) with a 1016t (1000-ton) train over level or gently rolling terrain; its top recorded speed of 148kph (92mph) was achieved in test operations with No 5354. As cars became heavier, they were often used in double-headed formation. In 1917, air conditioning had not figured among the luxuries provided for passengers, but 20 years later, air-conditioned cars were helping to maintain the 'Limited's' prestige. K4s hauled this great train in four stages between New York and Chicago: Manhattan Transfer to Harrisburg (301km/187 miles); Harrisburg to Pittsburgh (394km/245 miles); Pittsburgh to Crestline (304km/189 miles); Crestline to Chicago (449km/279 miles). The last of the class in passenger service, No 5351, was retired in November 1957. The first of the K4s, No 1737, was due to be preserved, but its condition was too bad, and by a piece of engineering sleight of hand its plates were transferred to No 3750.

**Boiler pressure:** 15kg/ cm² (205psi)
**Cylinders:** 692x718mm (27x28in)
**Driving wheels:** 2051mm (80in)
**Grate area:** 6.5m² (69.9sq ft)
**Heating surface:** 375m² (4041sq ft)
**Superheater:** 87.6m² (943sq ft)
**Tractive effort:** 20,163kg (44,460lb)
**Total weight:** 140.5t (309,890lb)

## 4-6-2 FRANCO–ETHIOPIAN DJIBOUTI–ADDIS ABABA RAILWAY (CICFE) — ETHIOPIA: 1915

Some locomotive classes led surprising lives. Locomotive No 231 of this African line was built at Haine St-Pierre in Belgium as part of an order of six for a Spanish metre-gauge (39.4in) railway. The outbreak of war meant it was not delivered. Stored for over 20 years, it was finally sold in 1936 for passenger service on the Djibouti–Addis line, where it was liked well enough for three more to be ordered from new and supplied in 1938. The train took two days, with an overnight stop, and though the little 'Pacifics' boasted smoke deflectors, the operating speed scarcely required them. Like other Ethiopian steam locomotives, they ran on oil fuel. They showed a hint of the Belgian preference for large chimneys, mounted well-forward on the smoke-box, but were otherwise quite normal smaller-scale 'Pacifics' with simple expansion, two outside cylinders, and Walschaerts valve gear.

**Boiler pressure:** 8.4kg/cm² (120psi)
**Cylinders:** 400x560mm (15.6x22in)
**Driving wheels:** 1000mm (39.4in)
**Grate area:** not known
**Heating surface:** not known
**Superheater:** N/A
**Tractive effort:** 5546kg (12,230lb)
**Total weight:** 48t (105,840lb) (engine only)

## CLASS HV 1 4-6-0 FINNISH RAILWAYS (VR) — FINLAND: 1915

This was a very efficient mixed-traffic type of engine for the 1524mm (5ft) gauge, a class of 43 with superheater and Heusinger valve gear; similar engines of classes Hv 2 and Hv 3 were built up to 1941.

Most were coal burners, with stovepipe chimneys topped by a mesh spark-arrester. Hv 1 No 575 was the first locomotive to be built at the Lokomo Works in Tampere; some were also built by Tampella in the same city.

Finland did not use the 'Pacific' type until as late as 1937, so 4-6-0s pulled all long-distance passenger trains.

The Hv1s had a maximum operating speed of 95kph (60mph) – fast for the period.

The busiest route, Helsinki-Tampere, consisting of about 160km (100 miles) was covered in just under three hours, with all services making several stops for junction connections.

**Boiler pressure:** 12kg/cm² (170psi)
**Cylinders:** 510x600mm (20x23.4in)
**Driving wheels:** 1750mm (68.25in)
**Grate area:** 1.9m² (21sq ft)
**Heating surface:** 108.6m² (1169.2sq ft)
**Superheater:** 30.7m² (330.5sq ft)
**Tractive effort:** 8985kg (19,800lb)
**Total weight:** 55.2t (121,716lb) (engine only)

## CLASS AB 4-6-2 NEW ZEALAND RAILWAYS (NZR) NEW ZEALAND: 1915

**Boiler pressure:** 12.6kg/cm$^2$ (180psi)
**Cylinders:** 431x660mm (17x26in)
**Driving wheels:** 1370mm (54in)
**Grate area:** 2.6m$^2$ (28.3sq ft)
**Heating surface:** 106.6m$^2$ (1148sq ft)
**Superheater:** 17m$^2$ (183sq ft)
**Tractive effort:** 9639kg (21,250lb)
**Total weight:** 54.3t (119,728lb) (engine only)

**Despite the country's isolation and small population, and their narrow-gauge track, New Zealand railways were generally up to date with steam locomotive designs; a tradition that remained until the end of steam.**

The first class A 'Pacifics' were compounds designed by A.L. Beattie and built in 1906 in time to run on the new Main Trunk Railway joining Auckland and Wellington. The Ab was its direct successor, but Beattie's successor H.H. Jackson wanted a simple-expansion engine, and it was designed as such by S.H. Jenkinson in the NZR drawing office. In 1909, the NZR had experimented with a Cole-type superheater bought in from Alco in the USA, and finding it satisfactory, dropped compounding for superheating in future designs. Meanwhile, a shortage of motive power had also brought in ten 'Pacifics' from the ever-ready Baldwin works of Philadelphia in 1914; designated class Aa, they were produced within 60 days of the order being placed. The Ab was New Zealand's most numerous 'Pacific' class, with 141 built between 1915 and 1926. Two outside cylinders were operated by Walschaerts valve gear. It had the spacious cab typical of NZ engines, and the other standard features of a cowcatcher and a large headlight. Slightly under half were home-built, with 83 coming from the North British Locomotive Company of Glasgow (another two were lost in a shipwreck, joining the several hundred locomotives which now lie in various places on the bottom of the sea). Unlike the first Q-class 'Pacifics', these were intended to burn good quality bituminous coal and had smaller fireboxes. Between 1947 and 1957, another 11 were built at the NZR Hillside Works by converting class Wab 4-6-4 tank engines. Vanderbilt-type tenders were fitted to the class, the first to be used in New Zealand. As on some Scottish lines, semi-automatic tablet exchangers were fitted to the cab sides, to enable them to run at higher speed through crossing loops on the largely single-tracked routes. The Ab has been described as a 'maid of all work' engine, and it was to be found in most parts of the country, working both passenger and freight traffic. Its prime purpose was that of an express passenger engine, and like many very successful types, a special claim to fame was found for it. It was said to be the first engine capable of developing one horse-power for every 45.3kg (100lb) of engine weight. On test in the South Island, No 608 ran with a 429t (423-ton) train on the Timaru-Christchurch line (160km/ 99.5 miles) in 147 minutes, and at a maximum speed of 96.5kph (60mph). On the same line in 1948, No 611 reached a peak speed of 107kph (66.5mph) between Orari and Temuka, with a train of 391t (385 tons). These were excellent performances for engines on the 1065mm (3ft 6in) gauge, and with coupled wheels of 1370mm (54in) diameter. In 1924, when the 'Limited' express was

**Preserved Class Ab No 795 stands with some vintage vehicles at Kingston, terminus of a branch from Invercargill, South Island, in February 1997.**

introduced between Auckland and Wellington, its average speed, inclusive of stops, was 48kph (30mph).

When displaced from express trains by the K and J classes, the Abs were transferred to freight haulage, handling train-loads up to 762t (750 tons) on gently graded routes. The majority were stationed at South Island depots. Disposals began in 1956.

**The precursor of class Ab, the compound 'Pacific' class A, at Auckland. Leaking steam and no polish suggest this is the 1930s.**

## CLASS 32A 2-6-2T NORWEGIAN STATE RAILWAYS (NSB) NORWAY: 1915

**Boiler pressure:** 12kg/cm² (170psi)
**Cylinders:** 525x600mm (20.5x23.4in)
**Driving wheels:** 1600mm (62.5in)
**Grate area:** 1.9m² (21sq ft)
**Heating surface:** 88m² (948sq ft)
**Superheater:** 27m² (290.7sq ft)
**Tractive effort:** 10,310kg (22,735lb)
**Total weight:** 66.6t (146,853lb)

Norwegian-built, by Hamar, this compact engine was typical of the NSB's fleet of suburban tank engines which served chiefly on the lines converging on Oslo. It has an American air, and engines of the sister 32c class were built by Baldwins and had bar frames. This one, however, is plate-framed. A substantial pair of outside cylinders were operated by piston valves, driven by Walschaerts gear. A single long housing on top of the boiler housed sandbox and dome.

**Typical services for the class 32A were of the outer-suburban sort, to outlying towns of the Oslo region like Drammen, Lillestrøm and Ski.**

## CLASS YE 2-10-0 RUSSIAN STATE RAILWAYS RUSSIA: 1915

In 1914 and 1915, S.M. Vauclain, then vice-president of the Baldwin Locomotive Works, visited Russia in the pursuit of sales. In the early years of World War I, Imperial Russia fought on the Allied side. Between 1915 and 1917, 1300 of these locomotives were ordered, and 881 were delivered before the Soviet revolution stopped trade between the two countries. One consignment is believed to have been lost at sea. One hundred embargoed engines were bought by the US government, converted to standard gauge and sold on to the Erie, the Seaboard, and other US lines. The rest were cancelled. Alco at Schenectady, and the Canadian Locomotive Company at Montreal, worked with Baldwins in the building programme.

The class was employed on lines in Siberia and the Far East, and a large number were used in China, where the Chinese Eastern Railway was under Russian control, and converted to standard gauge in 1935–36. They gave good service, and when Russia was again on the Allied side in World War II, arrangements under the 'Lease-Lend' scheme were made to rebuild the same design, denoted as class Ye,a. Between them, Alco and Baldwins built a further 2120 of this class between 1944 and 1947. After US-Soviet relations deteriorated after thewar, the last 20 were diverted to Finland. Some engines of the earliest vintage were still operating in Siberia into the late 1950s.

**Boiler pressure:** 12.6kg/cm² (180psi)
**Cylinders:** 634.5x710.6mm (25x28in)
**Driving wheels:** 1320mm (52in)
**Grate area:** 6m² (64.5sq ft)
**Heating surface:** 210m² (2261sq ft)
**Superheater:** 63.6m² (684.75sq ft)
**Tractive effort:** 17,780kg (39,200lb)
**Total weight:** 90t (201,600lb)

## 2-8-0 STATE RAILWAYS (*ETAT*) FRANCE 1916

**Boiler pressure:** 12kg/cm$^2$ (171psi)
**Cylinders:** 590x650mm (23.25x25.6in)
**Driving wheels:** 1450mm (57in)
**Grate area:** 3.1m$^2$ (34sq ft)
**Heating surface:** 170m$^2$ (1830.3sq ft)
**Superheater:** not known
**Tractive effort:** 16,000kg (35,280lb)
**Total weight:** 74.9t (165,132lb)

**The 2-8-0 locomotives served in the war, running supply and heavy munition trains from the Atlantic ports to the Flanders battlefields.**

Many locomotives were sent from Britain to France during World War I, including 50 of the Highland Railways 'Castle' passenger class of 1905. This 2-8-0 class, also Scottish-built (North British Loco Co), remedied a shortage of freight engines on the *Etat*. The French design was parallel-boilered, with round-topped firebox, and two simple-expansion outside cylinders, operated by Walschaerts gear. The cylinders were set in rear of the smokebox.

## CLASS DD50 MALLET 2-8-8-0 STATE RAILWAYS DUTCH EAST INDIES (INDONESIA): 1916

Among the few American engines to run in Dutch Indonesia were these great Mallets, of which eight were built by Alco, with another 12 of the very similar class DD51 following in 1919. Superheated compounds, they were built to haul heavy freight trains on the 1065mm (3ft 6in) gauge. The high-pressure cylinders were operated by piston valves, with slide valves on the low-pressure ones. All the DD50s were withdrawn and scrapped by the late 1960s. By the mid-70s, the only 2-8-0 Mallets still in use on the Indonesian PNKA system were some of the German and Dutch-built DD52s.

Freight was the main revenue earner of the Indonesian railways in steam days. Coal, mineral ore, and tropical forest products all required heavy haulage power, and the various Mallets served the system well. Even then, parts were cannibalised to keep some of the class going.

**Boiler pressure:** 14kg/cm$^2$ (199 psi)
**Cylinders:** hp 445x610mm (17.4x24in); lp 711x610mm (28x24in)
**Driving wheels:** 1106mm (43.5in)
**Grate area:** 4.2m$^2$ (45.2sq ft)
**Heating surface:** 213.4m$^2$ (2297sq ft)
**Superheater:** 64.4m$^2$ (693.4sq ft)
**Tractive effort:** N/A
**Total weight:** 95.4t (210,375lb)

## CLASS C27 4-6-4T STATE RAILWAYS (SS) DUTCH EAST INDIES (INDONESIA): 1916

The first 14 C27s were built by the Swiss SLM works at Winterthur; 20 came from Werkspoor in the Netherlands, and another five from Armstrong Whitworth in Newcastle, England. These last were delivered in 1922, by which time the enlarged C28, a 58-strong, German-built class, had come into service. Both types were employed on fast short-haul passenger service on the Javanese network.

**The low-set side tanks of the Class C27 are noticeable in this picture. The locomotive is also fitted with a chimney cowl.**

The C27 had minimal side tanks, with most of its water capacity in a bunker tank, while the C28 had more conventional side tanks with downward-angled tops, though the tanks were not extended back alongside the wide firebox. Large smoke deflectors also distinguished the C28, which was one of the fastest locomotives on the SS: its 1503mm (59in) wheels took it up to 113kph (70mph) and more on the 1065mm (3ft 6in) gauge tracks. It was said to be the Indonesian locomotive men's favourite engine type. Both classes were superheated two-cylinder simples, with piston valves operated by Walschaerts gear. Many examples of both survived until the last days of steam on the national PNKA system, working on slow-speed mixed-train services typical of the Javanese rural lines.

**Boiler pressure:** 12kg/cm$^2$ (171psi)
**Cylinders:** 450x550mm (17.7x21.6in)
**Driving wheels:** 1350mm (53in)
**Grate area:** 1.9m$^2$ (20.4sq ft)
**Heating surface:** 99.9m$^2$ (1075.5sq ft)
**Superheater:** 30.8m$^2$ (331.6sq ft)
**Tractive effort:** 8416kg (18,560lb)
**Total weight:** 66t (145,530lb)

## CLASS TV1 2-8-0 STATE RAILWAYS (VR) FINLAND: 1917

Between 1917 and 1944, the VR acquired 144 of this class, mostly from Tampella and Lokomo in Finland, but also from Nohab in Sweden and Hanomag in Germany. A wood-burning main-line freight engine with two simple-expansion cylinders, its 13t (12.8-ton) axle load allowed it to operate on the lightly laid northern tracks. Over its 27-year building period, numerous different fitments by way of feedwater heaters were tried, and in post-1938 engines the boiler pressure went up to 13kg/cm$^2$ (185psi). All had electric lighting by the 1950s. They were taken out of service between 1965 and 1969.

**Some of the Tv 1 2-8-0s were still operating in 1972. This winter scene from that year shows one pulling a sand train near Hyrynsalmi, close to the Russian border.**

**Boiler pressure:** 12kg/cm$^2$ (171psi)
**Cylinders:** 560x650mm (22x25.6in)
**Driving wheels:** 1400mm (55in)
**Grate area:** 2.3m$^2$ (24.8sq ft)
**Heating surface:** 123.8m$^2$ (1332.9sq ft)
**Superheater:** 38.6m$^2$ (415.6sq ft)
**Tractive effort:** 11,350kg (25,026lb)
**Total weight:** 61.5t (135,607lb) (engine only)

## CLASS C53 4-6-2 STATE RAILWAYS (SS) (DUTCH EAST INDIES) INDONESIA: 1917

This 1065mm (3ft 6in) gauge 'Pacific' design came from Werkspoor in the Netherlands. An oil-fired 4-cylinder compound, its cylinders, unusually for a six-coupled engine, drove the first coupled axle. Twenty were built, chiefly to run the Batavia (Djakarta)–Surabaya North Coast line, on which they are reputed to have reached 120kph (75mph) on occasions. Sixteen were removed to the Siamese and Malayan railways by the Japanese during World War II. The last two were withdrawn at Surabaya in 1973; one is preserved.

**To clear out the tubes of an oil-fired locomotive, shovelfuls of coarse sand were thrown into the firebox. Sucked through by the draught, this invariably resulted in a great plume of smoke.**

**Boiler pressure:** 14kg/cm$^2$ (200psi)
**Cylinders:** hp 340x580mm (20.5x22.8in); lp 520x580mm (20.5x22.8in)
**Driving wheels:** 1600mm (62.5in)
**Grate area:** 2.7m$^2$ (29sq ft)
**Heating surface:** 123m$^2$ (1324sq ft)
**Superheater:** 43m$^2$ (463sq ft)
**Tractive effort:** N/A
**Total weight:** 66.5t (147,000lb) (engine only)

## CLASS 56 2-10-0 TURKISH STATE RAILWAYS (TCDD) TURKEY: 1917

The 'Decapod' was to be the most typical of modern Turkey's steam locomotives, and these were the first. In 1917, Turkey, as the Ottoman Empire, and Germany were war allies, and these engines were German-built and based broadly on the Prussian Railways' G12 class, two-cylinder simples, but with smaller wheels and cylinders, also a round-topped instead of Belpaire boiler.

Fifteen were built, of which ten were supplied to the Ottoman army for war use. With formation of the TCDD in 1927, under the new Turkish Republic, they were designated class 56.

They were scrapped in the early 1950s. The five retained engines outlived them, ending up in Luxembourg.

In Turkey, a variety of more modern 2-10-0s and 2-8-0s replaced these old engines, from German, American and British builders.

**Boiler pressure:** 16kg/cm$^2$ (228psi)
**Cylinders:** 650x660mm (25.6x26in)
**Driving wheels:** 1450mm (57in)
**Grate area:** 4m$^2$ (43sq ft)
**Heating surface:** 222.9m$^2$ (2400sq ft)
**Superheater:** 106m$^2$ (1141sq ft)
**Tractive effort:** 23,180kg (51,000lb)
**Total weight:** 105.9t (233,509lb) (engine only)

## CLASS 328 4-6-0 HUNGARIAN STATE RAILWAYS (MÁV) HUNGARY: 1918

'Proud, gaunt, yet rakish' wrote an observer of this first post-1918 passenger class. It was in fact a pre-war design, ordered in 1914, but work was put off during World War I. Henschel of Kassel, Germany, built 100 up to 1920 and the Budapest works (known after 1945 as MÁVAG) built 58 in 1919–22. One of the features of this engine, as with many other Hungarian locomotives up to the mid-1920s, was a Brotan boiler. This was the 1906 invention of a Czech engineer who worked for the Imperial Austrian Railways: a double boiler with a steam drum placed above a fire-tube drum, and a firebox whose side walls (and sometimes also back wall) were lined with water tubes. The Hungarian Railways took up the idea. Some engines were fitted with this double-barrelled boiler; the 'steam drum', of smaller diameter than the 'fire drum', bearing also the various domes, and creating engines of a remarkable appearance. This form was not wholly satisfactory in operation, and MÁV engineers adapted the concept as a single combined fire-tube and water-tube boiler. Brotan's aim had been to minimize the corrosive effect of highly sulphurous coal on a copper-lined firebox, and as this was Hungary's prime type of fuel, there was a good reason for employing the Brotan system. Outside central Europe, the Brotan boiler was almost wholly ignored. It required to be set above the fire-grate and was partly responsible for the lofty look of the Class 328, which, unusually, had it as standard. With its 60 water-pipes, the firebox was also a very wide one. Normally only a proportion of engines in any class might be Brotan-boilered; it was estimated that around a quarter of MÁV engines were so fitted in the 1920s, after which the proportion steadily declined. Another even more frequent Hungarian feature was a water purifier, fitted to reduce the amount of calcium salts and other impurities in the feed water. Most typical at this time was the cylindrical Pecz-Rejto purifier, fitted on the boiler top of the class 328s, and which also functioned to some degree as a feedwater heater, with a valve for steam admission. Later types more generally used the circular Titan type, enclosed in a dome.

The 328s were distinctive in other ways. A large dome was mounted on the first boiler ring, with safety valves protruding from its sides, and just in front of it, outside steam pipes emerged from the superheater header and descended to the steam chests above the outside cylinders. The smokebox door was conical (like one or two other Hungarian classes, and some Italian types), the chimney had a flared back, and the outer front edges of the cab were angled back, all presumably to accentuate the engine's 'express' status. The cylinders were operated by piston valves, actuated by outside Walschaerts valve gear. As with other modern Hungarian engines, the cab was roomy and the front-end of the tender was also built up to make a more weather-proof structure. In later years, some of the class were modified in various ways, receiving smoke deflectors and Ister-type exhausts, and often having the water purifiers removed.

On international trains, engines were normally changed at the frontier stations. An unusual service worked by the new 328s was the 'military train' inaugurated in February 1919, which ran from Paris through Vienna and Budapest to Bucharest, for the benefit of military and diplomatic staff of the victorious Allied powers. Although it was one of the first 'native' classes of independent Hungary, engines of class 328 did run in other countries. Seventeen of the original 100 had been diverted to France as German war reparations; these turned out to exceed the loading gauge and the French sent them to Czechoslovakia, where they became class 375.1. It was on Czech rails that their maximum recorded speed was noted, of 120kph (74.5mph). Eight of these were returned to MÁV in 1939. Five of the class were sent to Yugoslavia in 1943. After 1945, the class was less often used on express duties, but 328s continued to work local services until the mid-1960s.

Even in their latter years, with a maximum permitted haulage capacity of 485t (477 tons), at a maximum of 75kph (47mph), they could handle stopping trains of up to fourteen or so cars.

**Boiler pressure:** 12kg/cm$^2$ (171psi)
**Cylinders:** 570x650mm (22.4x25.6in)
**Driving wheels:** 1826mm (72in)
**Grate area:** 3.25m$^2$ (35sq ft)
**Heating surface:** 164.7m$^2$ (1450.2sq ft)
**Superheater:** 45.2m$^2$ (486.6sq ft)
**Tractive effort:** 11,760kg (25,930lb)
**Total weight:** 69t (152,145lb) (engine only)

## CLASS 740 2-8-0 STATE RAILWAYS (FS) ITALY: 1918

Italy's most numerous locomotive type, with 470 built up to 1923, this two outside-cylinder simple took over, as a standard, from the 393-strong North American-built Class 735 of 1917–19, and these two types ran most main-line freight services. The 740s also operated on lines in Sicily and Sardinia. As with other large classes, various adaptations were made, especially to the draughting system, which was poor in the original design. No 740.324 was the first locomotive ever to be fitted with Caprotti rotary cam valve gear, in 1922. Five of the class were given Franco-Crosti boilers in 1942. As late as 1980, around 80 were still in traffic.

The bulk of FS freight operations were concentrated in the Milan–Turin–Genoa triangle in the north of the country, with heavy gradients between the first two cities and Turin, and the majority of the 740s were stabled in this area, which also generated most northbound international freight services. But internal long-distance freight was also a feature, particularly on the Milan–Florence-Rome–Naples route. On this line speed was important, as inter-city freights had to be fitted in with high-speed passenger services. Italy had few quadruple-track sections or overtaking loops, and the class 740 therefore had to produce a good speed as well as pulling-power, with 80kph (50mph) where the track allowed.

**Boiler pressure:** 12kg/cm$^2$ (171psi)
**Cylinders:** 540x700mm (21.25x27.6in)
**Driving wheels:** 1370mm (54in)
**Grate area:** 2.8m$^2$ (30sq ft)
**Heating surface:** 152.9m$^2$ (1646sq ft)
**Superheater:** 41.2m$^2$ (443.6sq ft)
**Tractive effort:** 13,424kg (29,600lb)
**Total weight:** 66t (145,505lb)

# MIKA I CLASS 2-8-2 KOREAN GOVERNMENT RAILWAYS (KGR) KOREA: 1918

**MIKA 2-8-2 No 161 at the head of a train of US Army hospital cars, at Yong Ling Po, in 1954. The Korean War disrupted rail services, but the railways were used on both sides for supply and relief duties.**

Alco of Schenectady, NY, were the first builders of this powerful freight class, though later ones were built in Japan by Shakakou, Kisha and Kawasaki. As industrialization developed in Korea, larger and heavier steel-framed bogie wagons were used; and the need for greater tractive power became urgent. The design was wholly American, with bar frames, two outside cylinders, and simple expansion. It was highly efficient, and over 400 were built of the MIKA type, up to MIKA 7 in 1951–52. South Korea's last 2-8-2s were Chinese Sys, built up to 1994.

**Boiler pressure:** 13.4kg/$m^2$ (191psi)
**Cylinders:** 584x711mm (23x28in)
**Driving wheels:** 1370mm (54in)
**Grate area:** 5$m^2$ (53.8sq ft)
**Heating Surface:** 337.8$m^2$ (3637sq ft)
**Superheater:** 66$m^2$ (710.6sq ft)
**Tractive effort:** 20,195kg (44,530lb)
**Total weight:** 98.7t (217,677lb) (engine only)

**The American design of the MIKA-01 is clear in this picture of No 150, of the South Korean Railways, taken some time around 1954.**

## CLASS 434.2 2-8-0 CZECHOSLOVAK STATE RAILWAYS (CSD) CZECHOSLOVAKIA: 1920

No 2246 of class 434 is turned at Prague Tesnoo depot in October 1966. The tender is built up with wooden boards to hold additional coal.

Czechoslovakia became independent of the Austro-Hungarian Empire after World War I and the origin of this class goes back to the Imperial Railways, as the Class 170 2-cylinder non-superheated compound design by Karl Gölsdorf. The CSD inherited 368 of these rugged but by then somewhat obsolescent engines, and nine of them were used for development into the 434.2 class. Rebuilding was extensive, involving new boilers, superheating, and simple expansion, but succeeded in giving the engines a power boost of the order of 25 per cent. From 1930, the whole class was rebuilt, piecemeal, with further improvements being added at various times up to 1947.

Larger superheaters were fitted from 1939. The steam drier, with its pipe between two domes, was retained. Three workshops were involved in the rebuilding, Louny, Plzen and Nymburk. After 1945, 127 of the class were fitted with Giesl ejector chimneys and rocking grates. They were used on freight trains loading up to 1400t (1380 tons), but were versatile enough to be employed on passenger services also. All were still in service during the 1960s. Withdrawals began in the 1970s, but even in 1978 some were still in use as station pilots and on local passenger trains.

Several have been preserved. Dimensions given are for the small-bore superheater version, pre-1939.

**Boiler pressure:** 13kgcm$^2$ (185psi)
**Cylinders:** 570x632mm (22.4x25in)
**Driving wheels:** 1308mm (51.5in)
**Grate area:** 3.9m$^2$ (42sq ft)
**Heating surface:** 163m$^2$ (1755sq ft)
**Superheater:** 77.3m$^2$ (832.2sq ft)
**Tractive effort:** 17,370kg (38,300lb)
**Total weight:** 69.5t (153,247lb) (engine only)

A Class 434 shunts at Plzen, now in the Czech Republic, on 15 May 1967. This locomotive has been fitted with a Giesl ejector chimney, as was done with many other Czech locomotives after 1945.

## CLASS K1 2-6-0 GREAT NORTHERN RAILWAY (GNR) GREAT BRITAIN: 1920

A Class K1 as British Railways No 61809, at Doncaster on 30 August 1959, where it was built almost 30 years before.

**Boiler pressure:** 12.6kg/cm$^2$ (180psi)
**Cylinders:** 474x666mm (18.5x26in)
**Driving wheels:** 1744mm (68in)
**Grate area:** 2.6m$^2$ (28sq ft)
**Heating surface:** 176.5m$^2$ (1901sq ft)
**Superheater:** 37.8m$^2$ (407sq ft)
**Tractive effort:** 12,018kg (26,500lb)
**Total weight:** 117.4t (258,944lb)

The restricted loading gauge in Britain, allowing a maximum height of 3959mm (13ft) on locomotives designed for wide availability, restricted modern locomotive design. It was difficult to place a big boiler on big wheels, so boiler-top mountings had to be reduced. This class was the first in Britain to have a boiler of 1829mm (6ft) diameter, and the resultant low chimney enhanced its massive front-end appearance. Intended chiefly for fast freight traffic, it had three simple-expansion cylinders, all driving the second coupled axle. The class was first to use the conjugated valve gear developed by H.N. (later Sir Nigel) Gresley, in which two outside sets of Walschaerts valve gear also drive the inside cylinder by means of cross-levers placed ahead of the cylinders and linking the valves.

**A Great Northern 'Klondike' 4-4-2 waits its turn as No 114 stands on the manually operated turntable.**

The end product was a very powerful engine for its size. From 1923, the Great Northern was amalgamated into the new London & North Eastern Railway, with Gresley as Chief Mechanical Engineer, and a number of further 2-6-0 types stemmed from this design, the 2-cylinder K2 and the 3-cylinder K3 and K4. Gresley was a strong advocate of 3-cylinder drive, though his conjugated gear was a perennial problem for maintenance crews. The first engines had tenders holding 3500 gals (4200US) and 7.6t (7.5 tons)of coal.

## CLASS 12M 4-6-2 STATE RAILWAY (FCS) ARGENTINA: 1921

The State Railway was built between 1921 and 1934, from Patagones to Bariloche, on the 1675mm (5ft 6in) gauge, to open up the Rio Negro province. Most traffic was worked by the 18 'Pacifics' of this class, 13 of them built by Maffei in Germany, four by Cockerill and one by Haine St Pierre, of Belgium. Two-cylinder simples, built German-style, with bar frames and boiler-top sandboxes, they served on this difficult line for over 30 years. The best timing over the 827km (514 mile) route was 22 hours. In 1953, they were withdrawn after the introduction of diesel traction. Like most later Argentinian steam locomotives, these burned heavy fuel oil. They always took a supplementary water tank wagon on the arid stretch between San Antonio and Ingeniero Jacobacci stations.

**Boiler pressure:** 12kg/cm$^2$ (170psi)
**Cylinders:** 500x629mm (19.7x24.8in)
**Driving wheels:** 1599mm (63in)
**Grate area:** 3m$^2$ (32.3sq ft)
**Heating surface:** 215.3m$^2$ (2319sq ft)
**Superheater:** not known
**Tractive effort:** 9433kg (20,800lb)
**Total weight:** 123.9t (273,280lb)

## CLASS 940 2-8-2T STATE RAILWAYS (FS) ITALY: 1921

This was a side tank version of the 2-8-0 class 740. Four were built by *Officine Meccaniche*, Milan, for the FS and 46 built in Naples and Reggio Emilia. Three more were built for the independent Santhia-Biella Railway. It was designed for use in mountain areas, and remained in service around Como and Sulmona into the early 1980s. The side tanks slope forwards in order to reduce water movement and to improve forward vision. No 940.001 is preserved at Milan.

**The preserved 940.022 at Cismon del Grappa, on a special charter train from Grieno to Carpane-Valstaena, on 9 May 2001.**

**Boiler pressure:** 12kg/cm$^2$ (170psi)
**Cylinders:** 540x700mm (21.25x27.5in)
**Driving wheels:** 1370mm (54in)
**Grate area:** 2.8m$^2$ (30.1sq ft)
**Heating surface:** 152.9m$^2$ (1646sq ft)
**Superheater:** 41.2m$^2$ (443sq ft)
**Tractive effort:** 15,065kg (33,220lb)
**Total weight:** 87t (192,464lb)

## CLASS 31B 4-8-0 NORWEGIAN STATE RAILWAYS (NSB) NORWAY: 1921

Norway's first 4-8-0s came from SLM in Switzerland in 1910 (class 26); this 4-cylinder compound class was the largest and heaviest, built for passenger service on the trunk line between Oslo and Bergen, and with a maximum axle load of 14t (13.8 tons). Twenty-seven were built between 1921 and 1926. The cylinders were in line, low-pressure outside, and all drove the second coupled axle. Piston valves were driven by Walschaerts gear. Interestingly, four simple-expansion predecessors of this class had been built in 1915–21, but the combination of compounding plus superheating was chosen for the production run.

**No 452 stands in the locomotive yard at Trondheim in 1966, still in service; but note the fuelling depot already installed for the diesels.**

**Boiler pressure:** 16kg/cm$^2$ (228psi)
**Cylinders:** hp 420x600mm (16.5x23.6in); lp 630x600mm (24.8x23.6in)
**Driving wheels:** 1350mm (53in)
**Grate area:** 3m$^2$ (32.29sq ft)
**Heating surface:** 166m$^2$ (1788sq ft)
**Superheater:** 45.5m$^2$ (489sq ft)
**Tractive effort:** not known
**Total weight:** 118t (260,631lb)

## CLASS S 2-8-0 CENTRAL RAILWAY OF URUGUAY (CUR) URUGUAY: 1921

Hawthorn Leslie of Newcastle on Tyne, England, built this 3-cylinder simple-expansion type for the CUR in the pre-depression heyday of South American railways, when freight traffic was substantial and trains the chief means of conveyance, with cattle and agricultural products brought from the interior to the docks at Montevideo. As elsewhere in South America, the 2-8-0 was the standard freight type. The CUR was nationalized in 1949. One of the Class S is preserved at the Peñarol roundhouse.

**The last surviving S-class locomotive, No 139, makes an evening departure with a freight train. Although preserved by the Circle of Railway Studies of Uruguay, this last surviving engine is no longer in working condition.**

**Boiler pressure:** 12.6kg/cm$^2$ (180psi)
**Cylinders:** 431.5x660mm (17x26in)
**Driving wheels:** 1523mm (60in)
**Grate area:** 1.8m$^2$ (19.5sq ft)
**Heating surface:** 133.7m$^2$ (1440sq ft)
**Superheater:** not known
**Tractive effort:** 8690kg (19,160lb)
**Total weight:** not known

## CLASS K 2-8-0 VICTORIAN RAILWAYS (VR) AUSTRALIA: 1922

Traffic demands often seemed to take railway managements by surprise: but since they had to rely on past statistics to project future trends, and as most new locomotives took at least a year from drawing board to actuality, they should not be blamed too harshly. Engines could be built very fast sometimes, but not always. It was a shortage of freight power in 1919 that prompted the Victorian Railways to invest in a new light freight locomotive. The K class took to the rails three years later, but the investment proved to be a good one – some of them were still at work in 1972. Ten were initially built at the VR Newport shops. In 1940, in a similar shortage, another 43 were ordered, and all were in service by 1946.

Running on the VR 1600mm (5ft 3in) gauge, though built for freight, the Ks were often used on passenger services. They were sturdy, reliable 2-cylinder simple engines with Belpaire boilers, and though the boiler pressure was relatively low, they were very free steamers. All were fitted with staff exchangers for non-stop single-line working. The final seven of the 1940 batch had Boxpok wheels. Withdrawal of the class began in 1958, but nevertheless at least 12 remained in service in 1972, mostly on station pilot duty. Several are preserved.

**K153 at Geelong, on 7 December 1980. Their reliability and pulling power makes the K-class popular choices for 'heritage' trains.**

**Preserved No K160 climbs with a train of wooden-bodied cars on the heritage Castlemaine & Maldon Railway, on 23 August 1987.**

**Boiler pressure:** 12.25kg/cm$^2$ (175lb)
**Cylinders:** 508x660mm (20x26in)
**Driving wheels:** 1397mm (55in)
**Grate area:** 2.4m$^2$ (25.75sq ft)
**Heating surface:** 134.4m$^2$ (1447sq ft)
**Superheater:** 26m$^2$ (281sq ft)
**Tractive effort:** 12,756kg (28,127lb)
**Total weight:** 104.6t (230,643lb)

## CLASS 22 2-8-2 GERMAN STATE RAILWAYS (DRG) GERMANY: 1922

Classified 22 on formation of the DRG, this 3-cylinder simple express locomotive was a long-lived class. All 85 were inherited by the East German *Deutsche Reichsbahn* after 1945, and from 1958 to 1962 they were rebuilt as *Rekoloks* ('reconstructed locos'), ending up longer and larger, and fitted with Russian Trofimov piston valves.

In this form, they continued to work up to the early 1970s. The rebuilding was on such a scale as to constitute virtually new locomotives, and they handled main-line expresses within East Germany and to its eastern and southern borders.

Up to 1992, only one line linked East and West Germany, worked by the Deutsche Bundesbahn, via Helmstedt and Magdeburg, to West Berlin.

**Boiler pressure:** 16kg/cm$^2$ (228psi)
**Cylinders:** 520x660cm (20.5x26in)
**Driving wheels:** 1750mm (69in)
**Grate area:** 4.23m$^2$ (45.5sq ft)
**Heating surface:** 206.3m$^2$ (2221sq ft)
**Superheater:** 83.8m$^2$ (902.2sq ft)
**Tractive effort:** 13,918kg (30,700lb)
**Total weight:** 107.5t (237.037lb)

## CLASS A1 4-6-2 GREAT NORTHERN RAILWAY (GNR) GREAT BRITAIN: 1922

During the World War I, British railways were government-controlled. When the run-down system was returned to private ownership, the government insisted on a new structure, with four major companies replacing the previous hundred-plus. A great deal of rationalization of jobs and functions resulted when the changes took effect from the end of 1922. The Chief Mechanical Engineer of the GNR, H.N. Gresley, found himself in charge of locomotives for four of the larger old companies and several smaller ones, all incorporated in the London & North Eastern Railway. One of the great British engineers, his first 'Pacific' design, which speedily became the LNER's standard heavy express engine, though it had numerous problems and flaws, was essentially a fast, free-steaming locomotive.

Built at the GNR's Doncaster Plant, the first one entered service in 1922. A handsome, fluid-lined engine, which set the basic look of LNER 'Pacifics' – except the A4 streamliners – for 25 years, it showed Gresley's qualities as a stylist as well as his limitations in failing to modify design defects. Three simple-expansion cylinders drove the second coupled wheels, using the conjugated valve gear that was first employed on the K1 2-6-0 of 1920, and which caused frequent problems. Other details also gave trouble. It would be 1928 before most of these were resolved and its successor class, the LNER's A3, could be reasonably called Britain's 'Super-Pacific', capable of running non-stop between London and Edinburgh (632km/393 miles).

**Engine no. 60154 sits in the sidings at Leeds, 1963.**

**Boiler pressure:** 12.6kg/cm² (180psi)
**Cylinders:** 508x660mm (20x26in)
**Driving wheels:** 2032mm (80in)
**Grate area:** 3.8m² (41.25sq ft)
**Heating surface:** 272m² (2930sq ft)
**Superheater:** 49m² (525sq ft)
**Tractive effort:** 13,333kg (29,385lb)
**Total weight:** 151t (332,000lb)

**A restored LNER engine no. 4472, *The William Shakespeare*, passes through the Oxfordshire countryside in 1993.**

## North Eastern Railway (NER) 'Pacific' — Great Britain: 1922

The NER brought out this Darlington-built 'Pacific', designed under the auspices of Sir Vincent Raven, just before the great set of railway mergers that made it a constituent part of the London & North Eastern Railway. It was a three-cylinder simple, all cylinders driving the first coupled axle, making the engine so long that crewmen called it the 'skittle alley'. Minor variations within the class included outside bearings on the trailing wheels of the last three engines. Comparative tests with the almost-simultaneous Gresley 'Pacific' of the Great Northern were judged to be in favour of the GN design, and the five engines of this class had a relatively short life in service.

**North Eastern Railway Raven 'Pacific' *City of Durham*, here with a high-sided LNER tender, and the number 2403. The class was withdrawn for scrap in 1937.**

**Boiler pressure:** 14kg/cm$^2$ (200psi)
**Cylinders:** 482x660mm (19x26in)
**Driving wheels:** 2032mm (80in)
**Grate area:** 3.8m$^2$ (41sq ft)
**Heating surface:** 225m$^2$ (2422.2sq ft)
**Superheater:** 36.75m$^2$ (695.6sq ft)
**Tractive effort:** 9045kg (19,945lb)
**Total weight:** 98.5t (217,280lb)

## Class E10 0-10-0T — State Railways Sumatra (SSS) — Dutch East Indies (Indonesia): 1922

The vast and climatically steamy equatorial island of Sumatra was the home of the first 19 E10 class, later E10$^1$, built by Esslingen in Germany. They worked the steeply graded, part-rack railway which had opened in 1891 from the port of Padang on the west coast into the mountainous interior. Coal deposits made the railway an economic proposition, but also required powerful locomotives. The gauge was 1065mm (3ft 6in). Most of the engines were stabled at the junction of Padang Pandjang, close to the steepest sections. They were four-cylinder compounds, superheated, with external valve gear and the inside cylinders driving the wheels that engaged on the central rack rail. Clearly they were effective load haulers: even as they were wearing out in the 1960s, a further 16 E10s were built between 1964 and 1967, as class E10$^2$: 10 from Esslingen and 6 from Nippon Sharyo in Japan. Mechanically the new engines were very similar to those of 1920s vintage, though more modern in appearance and with some significant modifications, including the fitting of Giesl ejectors and chimneys. These were the last rack and adhesion locomotives to be built for regular service. Dimensions given are for E10$^1$.

**A Class E102, of the 1964 batch, made in Esslingen, Germany, No E10.53, in steam against a Sumatran background, in August 1982.**

**No E1053 at Padang Pandjang locomotive yard on 11 August 1982. Like all the 1960s locos, it came equipped with a Giesl ejector.**

**Boiler pressure:** 14kg/cm$^2$ (199psi)
**Cylinders:** all 450x520mm (17.7x20.5in)
**Driving wheels:** 1000mm (39.4in)
**Grate area:** 1.9m$^2$ (20.4sq ft)
**Heating surface:** 71.6m$^2$ (771sq ft)
**Superheater:** 30.8m$^2$ (331.6sq ft)
**Tractive effort:** 12,504kg (27,572lb)
**Total weight:** 54.3t (119,840lb)

## CLASS 741 2-8-0 STATE RAILWAYS (FS) ITALY: 1922

**The last of class 741 stayed in service until 1980. Here a preserved example, No 741.120, stands at Pistoia locomotive depot, on 7 May 2001.**

One of the most unusual locomotive profiles ever seen was that of the Italian Franco-Crosti-boilered conversions, of which the majority were 2-8-0 freight engines. Tourists were often startled by this engine that seemed to have no chimney. Italian class numbering grouped wheel configurations together, and the various 2-8-0 types were all between 720 and 745. Some were sub-classes, and there was much renumbering as engines of one sub-class were given different boilers or rebuilt with different valve gear. Class 741 comprised two separate categories. The first was five class 740s of 1918, fitted with Caprotti valve gear, which were later returned to class 740. The larger group, of 81 engines, were also rebuilds from class 740, fitted with Crosti boilers between 1955 and 1960. By this time, the FS system was committed to electrification, with diesel power on non-electrified lines; and the policy with steam traction was to convert and maintain existing types rather than to build anything new.

The system was devised by the Italian engineer Attilio Franco, and though first tried out in Belgium in 1932, its real development was undertaken by Franco in association with Dr Piero Crosti on the FS in the late 1930s. It was based upon deflecting the hot exhaust steam back through a large drum or drums set parallel with the boiler, before being ejected from a rearward chimney or vent at the right-hand side of the firebox. These drums were virtually secondary boilers, through which feedwater from the tender was passed, and converted into steam at sufficient pressure to make its way into the main boiler. The effect was to maintain the boiler steam at a more consistent and also higher temperature than when cold or partly warmed feedwater was sporadically admitted. Secondary benefits, though important in hot, dry terrain, were reduction in the ejection of sparks and burning cinders, and conservation of water. The first Italian experiment was made with a cab-front Class 670, with the auxiliary boiler mounted on the water-cart tender. In 1940, some Class 685 2-6-2s were built with an auxiliary pre-heater drum on each side of the boiler, and these locomotives were also given streamlined casings. Similar treatment was applied to five of the 740 class 2-8-0s in 1942, with rather rough-and-ready sheet metal casing. Between 1951–53, another 88 of class 740 were rebuilt as Franco-Crostis, without streamlining, as class 743. The final form, developed by Crosti, was to have the pre-heater as a single drum placed beneath the main boiler, inside the locomotive's frame. This was the method used with the 741s. The smokebox was placed behind the pre-heater drum, and the chimney was attached to the right-hand side of the boiler, just in front of the firebox.

Substantial savings in fuel compared to conventionally boilered engines of class 740 were claimed, up to 25 per cent. Mechanically the engines were unchanged, and there was no difference in the power output. The Crosti-boilered engines were used interchangeably on the same schedules as the 740s. One expert commentator suggested that the improvements owed almost as much to better boiler proportions and internal draughting as they did to the pre-heating system. Nevertheless, the potential of the system attracted interest and numerous state railways built one or two prototypes. British Railways engineers built 10 of the BR standard 9F 2-10-0s with Crosti boilers at Crewe works in 1955. It was also used in Germany. But like all other post-1945 technical improvements to steam traction, it came too late to be seriously developed. The class 743 conversions were withdrawn in the late 1970s and the last of the class 741s survived until 1980.

**Boiler pressure:** 12kg/cm$^2$ (171psi)
**Cylinders:** 540x700mm (21.25x27.6in)
**Driving wheels:** 1370mm (54in)
**Grate area:** 2.8m$^2$ (30sq ft)
**Heating surface:** 112.6m$^2$ (1212sq ft)
**Superheater:** 44m$^2$ (473sq ft)
**Tractive effort:** 14,700kg (29,767lb)
**Total weight:** 68.3t (150,600lb)

## Class Ok-22 4-6-0 Polish State Railways (PKP) — Poland: 1922

The Prussian P-8 was the model for the PKP's first passenger engine. Five were built by Hanomag in Hanover, with a larger and higher-set boiler than the P8 but placed on a P8-type frame and wheels. After a pause, a further 185 of the class were built by the Polish Chrzanov works between 1928 and 1934. Until the advent of the Po-29 4-8-2 and the Pt-31 2-8-2, in 1930 and 1932, they ran all types of passenger service, but from 1932 were employed largely on stopping trains. Some were still in service up to the mid-1960s.

**Boiler pressure:** 12kg/cm$^2$ (171psi)
**Cylinders:** 575x630mm (22.6x24.8in)
**Driving wheels:** 1750mm (69in)
**Grate area:** 4m$^2$ (43sq ft)
**Heating surface:** 182.1m$^2$ (1960.6sq ft)
**Superheater:** 61.6m$^2$ (663.2sq ft)
**Tractive effort:** 12,100kg (26,680lb)
**Total weight:** 78.9t (173,974lb) (engine only)

**A preserved Ok-22, No 31, on a two-car train. The tall aspect of Polish engines is clear, notably in the lofty cab, with its ventilated clerestory roof.**

## Class 8E 2-6-4T Buenos Aires Great Southern Railway (BAGS) — Argentina: 1923

**At first, the class 8E engines were equipped with Weir feed-water heaters and feed pumps, and mechanical lubrication, but these were abandoned as maintenance costs outweighed fuel savings.**

In the early 1920s, with Argentina's population growing fast, the BAGS greatly developed commuter traffic to the capital, remodelling the terminus at Plaza Constitution, and quadruple-tracking its 1675mm (5ft 6in) gauge main line out for 18.5km (11.5 miles) to Temperley. New motive power was supplied by 61 of this three-cylinder simple expansion tank built at the Vulcan Foundry works, Manchester. Water (1953gals/2344 US gals), was carried in a back tank, and 4.1t (4 tons) of coal were in the short side bunkers, though all were also fitted for oil burning from the start.

**Boiler pressure:** 14kg/cm$^2$ (200psi)
**Cylinders:** 444x660mm (17.5x26in)
**Driving wheels:** 1726mm (68in)
**Grate area:** 2.3m$^2$ (25sq ft)
**Heating surface:** 113.6m$^2$ (1223sq ft)
**Superheater:** 28m$^2$ (302sq ft)
**Tractive effort:** 29,859lb (kg)
**Total weight:** 102.6t (226,240lb)

## Class 231C 4-6-2 Northern Railway (Nord) — France: 1923

The *Nord* had used 'Pacifics' since 1912, almost all of them de Glehn compounds. Resumption of peacetime services increased passenger traffic and a new, improved type was ordered. Known for a time as the 'Super-Pacifics', the first 40 of these locomotives were built at the Blanc-Misseron shops at Lille. They had Belpaire boilers, but unusually, they did not take advantage of the Pacific's ability to carry a wide firebox; theirs was narrow and entirely between the frames. They became familiar to cross-Channel travellers as motive power for the 'Golden Arrow/*Flèche d'Or*' London–Paris Pullman express, and on the first leg of such grand international trains as the 'Arlberg–Orient Express' with through carriages all the way to Bucharest, and the

**No 231C.57, showing some of the later modifications to the class, stands on the lateral transporter in front of the La Chapelle works, Paris, in August 1958.**

Rome express, all superb spectacles as the long trains of blue and gold *Wagon-Lits* coaches moved out behind the gleaming locomotives.

These engines could be worked compound, semi-compound, or simple, depending on how the driver chose to admit steam to the cylinders. Two were built as two-cylinder simples in experiments with Caprotti and Dabeg valve gear.

Eventually, the class totalled 86. Later modifications included the fitting of Lemaître blastpipes and chimneys, the raising of the running plate to allow access to the low-pressure cylinders, and the addition of smoke deflectors.

Although a reliable and popular class of engine, its 'super' designation was undermined by the arrival on the *Nord* of Chapelon 'Pacifics' and the 231Cs were displaced from the heaviest expresses.

**Boiler pressure:** 16kg/cm$^2$ (227psi)
**Cylinders:** hp 440x660mm (17.6x26in); lp 620x690mm (24.4x27.2in)
**Driving wheels:** 1700mm (74.9in)
**Grate area:** 3.5m$^2$ (37.5sq ft)
**Heating surface:** 249m$^2$ (2680sq ft)
**Superheater:** 57m$^2$ (616sq ft)
**Tractive effort:** N/A
**Total weight:** 160t (353,000lb)

## 'CASTLE' CLASS 4-6-0 GREAT WESTERN RAILWAY (GWR) GREAT BRITAIN: 1923

By 1907, the formula for GWR passenger engines was established with the 'Star' class, as four cylinders, simple expansion, with internal Walschaerts valve gear. But work continued in the Swindon works on the application of valves and valve gear, and in 1923 a heavier locomotive was made possible by a combination of improved track and better understanding of the stress imposed by the 'hammer-blow' of reciprocating motion. The resulting design, equipped with a new taper boiler (No 7, made specially for this class), gave sharply increased performance combined with a remarkable economy in coal consumption.

The 'Castles' aroused intense interest among other British companies and set a benchmark for performance when tested against engines of the LMS and LNER during 1925–26. The class eventually numbered 171, including 15 which were rebuilds of earlier 4-6-0 types, and was the standard for fast passenger services throughout the GWR system. Perhaps its most famous – though not its hardest – service was on the 'Cheltenham Flyer', a lightweight afternoon express

**No 5029 Nunney Castle with the Loughborough–Leicester North train, on the heritage Great Central Railway, 12 March 1995.**

**No 7029 Clun Castle, with twin headlamps and double chimney, seen at Swindon, during the GWR 150th celebrations in August 1985.**

which ran between Swindon and Paddington non-stop. On 5 June 1932, hauling 198.2t (195 tons) No 5006 *Tregenna Castle* covered this 124km (77 mile) section in 56 minutes, 47 seconds. At 2km (1.3 miles) from the terminus, the train was still travelling at 130kph (80mph). Between 1957 and 1960, a number of the class were given double chimneys and larger superheaters, which enhanced their performance, but withdrawal began in 1962 and was complete by 1965. Seven have been preserved, including the first one, *Caerphilly Castle*.

**Boiler pressure:** 15.75 kg/cm$^2$ (225psi)
**Cylinders:** 406x660mm (16x26in)
**Driving wheels:** 2045mm (80.5in)
**Grate area:** 2.8 m$^2$ (30.3sq ft)
**Heating surface:** 190.4 m$^2$ (2049.3sq ft)
**Superheater:** 30 m$^2$ (324 sq ft)
**Tractive effort:** 14,285kg (31,500lb)
**Total weight:** 81.1 tonnes (178,864lb)

## CLASS 01 2-6-2 SERBIAN, CROATIAN & SLOVENIAN RAILWAYS (SHS) YUGOSLAVIA: 1923

These German-built engines were designed in 1912 but delivered after World War I, in 1923, to the SHS, which after 1928 became the Yugoslav State Railways (JDZ). There were 126 in the class. Four-cylinder compound and simple versions of almost identical appearance had been built in 1912–13, with outside Walschaerts gear and piston valves, operating both cylinders on each side.

**Modern engines in their period, the Class 01 was a good enough locomotive type to serve well into the 1980s. Here, a wide-chimneyed model leaves Belgrade pulling a suburban train.**

**Here the simple-expansion No 75, of the Yugoslav State Railways, heads an inter-city stopping train.**

**Boiler pressure:** 12kg/cm$^2$ (171psi)
**Cylinders:** 410x650mm (16x25.6in)
**Driving wheels:** 1850mm (73in)
**Grate area:** 3m$^2$ (32.3sq ft)
**Heating surface:** 126.5m$^2$ (1362sq ft)
**Superheater:** 38.6m$^2$ (415.6sq ft)
**Tractive effort:** 6444kg (13,000lb)
**Total weight:** 67t (147,735lb) (engine only)

## 1400 CLASS 2-8-2 MISSOURI PACIFIC RAILROAD (MOPAC) USA: 1923

**In the livery of the Louisville and Nashville Railroad, an associate company of the Missouri Pacific, class 1400 No 1906 stands at the head of a mixed freight. Sister L&N engine No 1901 stands on an adjacent road.**

A standard freight type on the MoPac until the end of steam, with 171 built, it handled virtually every kind of freight service from long-distance fast freight to cattle cars or perishable goods. Built by Alco, with the drive on the third set of coupled wheels, and a slightly tapered round-top boiler, about half were fitted with steam boosters to the trailing wheels, adding a tractive effort of 2030kg (4475lb) on starting. Most were coal burners, though some were oil-fired. The bogie tenders had a brakeman's cabin built over the water tank. They survived in large numbers into the 1950s, by which time pick-up freights and yard duties were their main tasks.

**Boiler pressure:** 14kg/cm² (200psi)
**Cylinders:** 685x812mm (27x32in)
**Driving wheels:** 1599mm (63in)
**Grate area:** 6.2m² (66.7sq ft)
**Heating surface:** 369.6m² (3900sq ft)
**Superheater:** 97.6m² (1051sq ft)
**Tractive effort:** 28,548kg (62,950lb)
**Total weight:** 138.4t (305,115lb)

## CLASS M1 4-8-2 PENNSYLVANIA RAILROAD (PRR) USA: 1923

**Boiler pressure:** 17.5kg/cm² (250lb)
**Cylinders:** 685x761mm (27x30in)
**Driving wheels:** 1827mm (72in)
**Grate area:** 6.2m² (66.8sq ft)
**Heating surface:** 379m² (4087sq ft)
**Superheater:** 97.6m² (1051sq ft)
**Tractive effort:** 29,274kg (64,550lb)
**Total weight:** 254t (560,000lb)

**The drawing shows a locomotive of class M1a, No 6707, built by Baldwins to PRR specification in 1930. Typical features include the wide saddle-type sandbox, power reversing gear, and the Belpaire firebox.**

The first engine of the 'Mountain' wheel arrangement was built in 1911 by Alco (at Schenectady, NY, for the Chesapeake & Ohio Railway) to haul passenger trains over its Clifton Forge Division in the Allegheny Mountains. At the time, it was claimed as the most powerful non-articulated engine in the world, and the design was recognized as valuable where adhesion and tractive power were needed as well as speed. In 1918, it was one of eight standard types designated by the wartime US Railroad Administration, and many were built for lines with mountain sections. The PRR built its first as a test engine, at its Juniata workshops in Altoona, and 200 others of Class M1 followed. Following US practice, it was a 2-cylinder simple, with Walschaerts valve gear operating piston valves. The boiler tapered up from 2144mm (84.5in) behind the chimney to 2436mm (96in) and the long Belpaire firebox was supplied by duplex stokers. The running plate was stepped up to accommodate the air compressor equipment. On these locomotives, braking power was as vital as traction, as they negotiated the long descents with trains of 140 coal hopper cars loading up to 4776t (4700 tons).

The 4-8-2 remained a popular type in the USA and Canada until the end of the 1920s, when most lines took up the 4-8-4, with its even bigger firebox. The M1s were withdrawn in 1950.

## CLASS 11C 4-8-0 BUENOS AIRES GREAT SOUTHERN RAILWAY (BAGS) ARGENTINA: 1924

Argentina's first 4-8-0, this three-cylinder simple was one of the heaviest and most powerful engines to run on the country's 1675mm (5ft 6in) gauge. Their arrival marks the high point of the foreign-run railways in Argentina, about to go into steady decline through the 1930s and 40s. Between 1924 and 1929, 75 were built by Armstrong Whitworth in Newcastle and Beyer-Peacock in Manchester; all were oil-fired. Weir feed-water heaters and pumps were fitted to 40, but later removed due to maintenance difficulties. These engines could handle 2032t (2000-ton) trains over the level plains and their 16.2t (16-ton) axle load gave good route availability. Overhauled by the ASTARSA company in 1957, they were still giving good service 10 years later.

**Though in store at Tolosa depot on 21 March 1972, this class 11C locomotive of the General Roca Railway in fact never ran again.**

**Boiler pressure:** 14kg/cm$^2$ (200psi)
**Cylinders:** 444x660mm (17.5x26 in)
**Driving wheels:** 1434mm (56.5in)
**Grate area:** 2.7m$^2$ (29.3sq ft)
**Heating surface:** 213.3m$^2$ (2297sq ft)
**Superheater:** not known
**Tractive effort:** 15,600kg (34,400lb)
**Total weight:** 85.3t (188,160lb) (engine only)

## CLASS S 2-6-4T DANISH STATE RAILWAYS (DSB) DENMARK: 1924

Borsig of Berlin designed this big three-cylinder simple-expansion suburban tank for work in the Copenhagen area, and built the first two engines; the remaining 18 were built in Denmark by Frichs. Condensing apparatus was fitted, with exhaust steam passing into side tanks, and a feedwater pump attached on the left side. Smoke deflectors were added in the 1930s. After some suburban lines were electrified, the class worked longer-distance passenger trains, with the coal capacity increased to 4.1t (4 tons), until the early 1960s.

**The lofty aspect of the class S is shown in this shot of No740, about to leave the Helsingør terminus with a stopping train for Copenhagen. Bunker capacity was increased to 4 tons (4.1t) of coal for longer-range services.**

**Boiler pressure:** 12cm$^2$ (171psi)
**Cylinders:** 431x672.5mm (17x26.5in)
**Driving wheels:** 1726mm (68in)
**Grate area:** 2.4m$^2$ (25.8sq ft)
**Heating surface:** 118.1m$^2$ (1272sq ft)
**Superheater:** 45.9m$^2$ (495sq ft)
**Tractive effort:** N/A
**Total weight:** 100.1t (220,864)

## CLASS 424 4-8-0 HUNGARIAN STATE RAILWAYS (MÁV) HUNGARY: 1924

'The most useful class in Hungary', this two-cylinder simple expansion was also described as 'a sound, simple, completely straight-forward mixed traffic design with no exotic features'. Only 26 were built at first, with a solitary 27th in 1929. But in the period 1940–44, a further 216 were built, with more following after 1945. Some were also built for Yugoslavia and the Slovakian Railways, and an unquantified number were built for export to China. After the war, large numbers ended up in Russia, though by the early 1960s, the survivors were being returned to Hungary. In all, about 365 were built, up to 1958, all at the Budapest locomotive works, with the later examples carrying large German-type smoke deflectors, and with Ister double blast pipes and chimneys (similar to the Giesl model). The base of the firegrate was above the coupled wheels, resulting in a high-set boiler. The third dome contained water-purifying apparatus, a necessity in Hungary. Until the termination of steam on the MÁV, these were the most frequently seen engines, handing passenger and freight work in a way comparable to the British 'Class 5' 4-6-0, as the duty roster prescribed.

**The Class 424 4-8-0 was the most useful type of engine in service in Hungary during and after World War II.**

**Boiler pressure:** 13kg/cm$^2$ (185psi)
**Cylinders:** 600x660mm (23.6x26in)
**Driving wheels:** 1606mm (63.25in)
**Grate area:** 4.45m$^2$ (47.9sq ft)
**Heating surface:** 162.6m$^2$ (1750sq ft)
**Superheater:** 58m$^2$ (624.5sq ft)
**Tractive effort:** 16,325kg (36,000lb)
**Total weight:** 83.2t (183,456lb) (engine only)

## C-36 CLASS 4-6-0 NEW SOUTH WALES GOVERNMENT RAILWAYS (NSWGR) AUSTRALIA: 1925

By this time, Australia had a well-established locomotive industry, and the 75 C-36s were designed by the NSWGR and built at its own Eveleigh and Clyde Engineering shops between 1925 and 1928. They replaced the NN 4-6-0s, of 1914 vintage, on main-line workings including the Brisbane, Wollongong and Werris Creek routes, and Victoria interstate expresses to Albury. Despite their by-name of 'pigs', they were very successful free-steaming engines with a good turn of speed. They had two outside cylinders, piston valves and Walschaerts valve gear. The original firebox was round-topped, but from 1953, 73 of the class were rebuilt with higher-pressure Belpaire boilers, and with smoke-box mounted throttle valves, as previously used on the C-38 'Pacifics'. In 1958, No 3616 was fitted with a Giesl ejector chimney and superheat booster. This improved performance, but by then, the system was then converting to diesel, and further modernization was abandoned.

The two unrebuilt engines were withdrawn in 1958, and the numbers gradually reduced over the next decade. In 1968, the class was withdrawn, but six were then reprieved, fitted with power reversers and other modifications demanded by the footplatemen's union, and ran until mid-1969. The last was withdrawn in September 1969. Three have been preserved.

**Boiler pressure:** 12.6kg/cm$^2$ (180psi)
**Cylinders:** 23x26in (584x660mm)
**Driving wheels:** 1751mm (69in)
**Grate area:** 2.8m$^2$ (30.5sq ft)
**Heating surface:** 184.8m$^2$ (1990sq ft)
**Superheater:** 60.4m$^2$ (650sq ft)
**Tractive effort:** 15,060kg (30,498lb)
**Total weight:** 159t (350,595lb)

**Preserved NSWGR No 3642 , with Belpaire firebox, is steamed for the first time after undergoing a complete rebuild. New or restored boilers must pass rigorous tests. This engine has been active since its official 'retirement' in 1969.**

**No 3642 stands at Sydney's Central Station, in green express livery. The cylinder of the power-reverser can be seen by the firebox. It is coupled to a class 59 2-8-2, painted in utilitarian freight-haulage black.**

## CLASS 241-A 4-8-2 EASTERN RAILWAY (EST) FRANCE: 1925

This was Europe's first 'Mountain' type, introduced on the *Chemin de Fer de l'Est*; a de Glehn/du Bousquet type four-cylinder compound built at the Fives-Lille works, with four sets of Walschaerts valve gear. There were two domes: that nearest the cab held a perforated steam-drier pipe. A larger-cylindered version was also built after 1928, for the *Etat* (Western) Railway, which eventually relinquished them to the old Eastern Railway (now the SNCF's Eastern Region – who had produced the original design). From 1933 onwards, 48 were rebuilt on Chapelon principles.

**Boiler pressure:** 16kg/cm$^2$ (290psi)
**Cylinders:** hp 425x720mm (16.75x28.4in); lp 660x720mm (26x28.4in)
**Driving wheels:** 1950mm (77in)
**Grate area:** 4.43m$^2$ (47.7sq ft)
**Heating surface:** 217m$^2$ (2342sq ft)
**Superheater:** 16m$^2$ (172sq ft)
**Tractive effort:** 11,205kg (24,707lb)
**Total weight:** 123.5t (272,384lb)

**In September 1955, No 241.A5 receives some last-minute attention from its driver at La Villette depot, Paris, while waiting at the head of the line of engines ready for service.**

## CLASS 01 4-6-2 GERMAN STATE RAILWAYS (DRG) GERMANY: 1925

Formed in 1920, the *Deutsche Reichsbahn Gesellschaft* (DRG) took over 212 different locomotive classes from the old state railways. There was, however, a serious lack of engines, since many had been ceded to other countries as war reparations. The DRG formed a Locomotive Committee with the principal manufacturers, to establish a set of standard types, or *Einheitslok.* Its chairman was Dr R.P. Wagner, a distinguished engineer. He had been with the Royal Prussian Railways and there was a strong Prussian influence on the standard types. For express passenger work, the 'Pacific' type was chosen, with a brief to haul a train of 800t (787 tons) at 100kph (62mph) on level track, or 500t (492 tons) at 50kph (31mph) on a rising grade of 1 in 10. Twenty went into service in 1925–6; of these, 10 were two-cylinder simple expansion engines and 10 were four-cylinder compounds. Following comparative tests, it was decided to proceed with the simple expansion type, Series 01. Between 1925 and 1938, 231 were built (the 10 compounds were also converted to simples in 1942).

**No 01.1082 at speed with an express train. This locomotive shows the 'wing'-type smoke deflectors. It is an oil-burner with the wide chimney fitted to later engines of the class.**

The 01s were bar-framed, with a copper firebox, a flush-topped boiler and two domes, the leading one being the boiler inlet for the Knorr feedwater supply system, the rear one holding a Wagner-designed regulator. Between them was a sandbox holding sand, to be applied to all coupled wheels in the event of slipping. One of the many similarities to American design was the cylindrical feedwater heater partly built into the upper section of the smoke box. Walschaerts valve gear actuated piston valves, with all the motion outside and easily accessible. The trailing wheels, with inside bearings, were set behind the firebox, under the cab. On the first engines, the running plate sloped down to the buffer beam, and large smoke deflectors were mounted on this. Later, Witte's smaller wing-type smoke deflectors were attached to the smoke-box sides, and the front sloping plates removed, further exposing the 'works'. The first 01s were built by Borsig and AEG, but Henschel and Krupp were also later involved. From 1930, they were supplemented by a light 'Pacific' type, of similar appearance, Series 03, of which 298 were built by 1937. With a maximum axle load of 17.5t (17.2 tons), it had a wider route availability, and once it went into production, no more of the Maffei S 3/6 'Pacifics' were built.

The maximum operating speed was first set at 130kph (80mph), though many lines had a speed limit of only 100kph (62mph) until the general train-speed increases from the mid-1930s. Two of the 03s were streamlined in 1934–35, but for really fast working, a 3-cylinder engine was required, and between 1939 and 1941, 115 of this type were built, classed $01^{10}$ and $03^{10}$ respectively. Of the 55 engines of the $01^{10}$ class, only one was streamlined; all 60 of the $03^{10}$ were streamlined, though the casings were removed after 1945.

From 1951, some of the original two-cylinder engines and some of the three-cylinder engines working on the *Deutsche Bundesbahn* were rebuilt with larger boilers, which contained combustion chambers as well. Wide chimneys were fitted, to allow for ejection of steam from auxiliary equipment like the Knorr feed pump.

Many of these rebuilds were converted to oil burning. Painted in DB black, with red wheels, they made an impressive spectacle. Such large classes inevitably meant that a number of variants appeared, and different eight-wheel tender types were fitted.

When Germany was partitioned in 1945, the stock was divided, 171 of the 01s to the *Deutsche Bundesbahn*, and 70 to East Germany, which kept the name of the *Deutsche Reichsbahn*. They worked express services until 1973 on the DB, and some of the DR engines were still operating as late as 1981.

Several examples of both the two- and three-cylinder engines of Groups 01 and 03 are preserved.

**This photograph of a well preserved 4-6-2 shows the original appearance of the 01s, with large smoke-deflectors and the sloped running-plate.**

**Boiler pressure:** 16kg/cm$^2$ (228psi)
**Cylinders:** 600x660mm (25.6x26in)
**Driving wheels:** 2000mm (78.7in)
**Grate area:** 4.3m$^2$ (46.3sq ft)
**Heating surface:** 23m$^2$ (2661sq ft)
**Superheater:** 85m$^2$ (915sq ft)
**Tractive effort:** 16,160kg (35,610lb)
**Total weight:** 109t (240,000lb) (engine only)

# 4F CLASS 0-6-0 LONDON MIDLAND & SCOTTISH RAILWAY (LMS) GREAT BRITAIN: 1925

Ubiquitous on the LMS system, these engines were scarcely altered from the Midland Railway's '3835' class, of 1914, of which 191 had been built by 1923, and 500 more were built. Larger boilers with Belpaire fireboxes, piston valves and superheaters were the main differences from the older 0-6-0 types. All the class were fitted with vacuum brake equipment. They hauled freight on main and secondary routes when speed was not essential, but were often seen on local passenger services and on piloting and banking duties.

**Re-enacting its most typical role in active service, preserved No 44422 in British Railways livery hauls a short pick-up goods train of four-wheel waggons and brake van on the Churnet Valley Railway, on 25 April, 1998. The lamp denotes 'empty waggon train'.**

**Boiler pressure:** 12.2 kg/cm$^2$ (175psi)
**Cylinders:** 507x660mm (20x26in)
**Driving wheels:** 1294mm (51in)
**Grate area:** 1.95m$^2$ (21sq ft)
**Heating surface:** 107.4m$^2$ (1157sq ft)
**Superheater:** 23.5m$^2$ (253sq ft)
**Tractive effort:** 9796kg (21,600lb)
**Total weight:** 91.4t (201,488lb)

## 2-8-2 NIGERIAN GOVERNMENT RAILWAYS (NGR) NIGERIA: 1925

Like other colonial African networks the Nigerian system, of 1065mm (3ft 6in) gauge, had lengthy single-track sections and maintained a pattern of infrequent heavy trains. This in turn required powerful engines, though with a limited maximum axle load, in this case 16.75t (16.5 tons). This British-built 2-8-2 class answered the need in 1925. Designed as three-cylinder simples, they had the conjugated valve gear developed by Gresley.

Combustion chambers extended the Belpaire fireboxes and reduced boiler-tube length: a consideration which much improved their steam-raising ability. By 1930, they were effectively superseded by a larger 4-8-2. Subsequently they were mostly employed on shorter runs in the vicinity of Lagos and Port Harcourt.

**Boiler pressure:** 12.6kg/cm² (180psi)
**Cylinders:** 457x711mm (18x28in)
**Driving wheels:** 1370mm (54in)
**Grate area:** 3.5m² (38sq ft)
**Heating surface:** 213m² (2290sq ft)
**Superheater:** 47m² (506sq ft)
**Tractive effort:** 17,487kg (38,560lb)
**Total weight:** 127.8t (281,904lb)

## CLASS 020 2-8-4T PORTUGUESE RAILWAYS (CFP) PORTUGAL: 1925

Henschel, responsible for much of the CFP locomotive stock, built two 2-8-4T classes for Portugal's broad gauge lines (1665mm/ 5ft 6in); Class 018 was lighter and used for services in the south of the country; the24 020s were used mainly around Lisbon and Oporto. They were of typical German bar-frame construction, with two outside simple-expansion cylinder. It was a reliable heavy suburban class, and most were still in service in the late 1960s.

**Boiler pressure:** 13kg/cm² (185psi)
**Cylinders:** 610x660mm (24x26in)
**Driving wheels:** 1350mm (53in)
**Grate area:** 3.6 m² (38.75sq ft)
**Heating surface:** not known
**Superheater:** not known
**Tractive effort:** 11,072kg (24,414lb)
**Total weight:** 103.7t (228,658lb)

**Shortly after receiving the final general overhaul of its career, No 0190 stands at Regua on 15 September 1973.**

Engine No 0187 at the head of a mixed train, the 09.48 from Barcelos to Moncao, on 25 May 1972 (note the station house's appropriate weather-vane at the top of the photograph).

In sad contrast, a derelict Class 18 is left rusting away on a siding. In southern European countries, there were few breakers' yards and long lines of dumped engines could often be found.

## CLASS 16D 4-6-2 SOUTH AFRICAN RAILWAYS (SAR) SOUTH AFRICA: 1925

When it came to exports, American companies could build to order, and this thoroughly British-looking 1065mm (3ft 6in) gauge 'Pacific' in fact came from Baldwins in Philadelphia. It received an 'Experimental' tag from the fact that a number of American features were incorporated, including hard-grease lubrication, self-cleaning front ends, and shaking grates. In terms of maintenance and turn-round times, American practice was well ahead of British. Four of these engines were built, with eight more in 1929.

They clipped 101 minutes off the 'Union Limited' Cape Town-Johannesburg route, 1538km (956 miles), running without change of engine at an average of 57kph (35.5mph).

A still serviceable Class 16D, No 860, is kept at Dal Josafat station, in Cape Province. 'Heritage' steam services are run to this station from Cape Town.

**Boiler pressure:** 13.7kg/$cm^2$ (195psi)
**Cylinders:** 558x660mm (22x26in)
**Driving wheels:** 1523mm (60in)
**Grate area:** 4.2$m^2$ (45sq ft)
**Heating surface:** 227.8$m^2$ (2453sq ft)
**Superheater:** 55$m^2$ (593sq ft)
**Tractive effort:** 15,206kg (33,530lb)
**Total weight:** 87.4t (192,650lb) (engine only)

## 'BERKSHIRE' 2-8-4 ILLINOIS CENTRAL RAILROAD USA: 1925

**Boiler pressure:** 16.8kg/$cm^2$ (240psi)
**Cylinders:** 710x761mm (28x30in)
**Driving wheels:** 1599mm (63in)
**Grate area:** 9.84$m^2$ (106sq ft)
**Heating surface:** 479$m^2$ (5157sq ft)
**Superheater:** 196$m^2$ (2111sq ft)
**Tractive effort:** 31,473kg (69,400lb)
**Total weight:** 174.6t (385,000lb) (engine only)

William E. Woodard, Lima Locomotive Company's chief engineer, led the design of the first 2-8-4. Built by Lima as an experiment and showpiece, it was sold later to the Illinois Central. The intention was to obtain high horsepower and economical use of fuel. In this it was largely successful and in its design details

**A later 'Berkshire', No. 2746 of the Chesapeake & Ohio Railroad, built by Lima in 1946, wheels a mainline freight under a signal gantry in 1948. The C&O had altogether 90 of these great locomotives, built between 1943 and 1947.**

was a model for all other 'super-power' engines to come. It was a two-cylinder, simple expansion locomotive, with a long firebox nearly a quarter the length of the boiler, supported by the four-wheel truck. The truck also had a steam booster, giving an additional 5986kg (13,200lb) of tractive effort at low speed. Lima 'super-power' led the way to a reassessment of steam performance: not simply brute dragging force, but force per unit of time, measured in horsepower in the cylinders and at the drawbar.

## CLASS 387 4-6-2 CZECHOSLOVAK STATE RAILWAYS (CSD) CZECHOSLOVAKIA: 1926

This was a handsome express passenger locomotive designed and built at the Skoda works, where a total of 43 were constructed up to 1937. Driven by three simple-expansion cylinders, it had Heusinger valve gear, that for the inside cylinder being worked by a rocking lever driven from the third coupled axle on the left side. The later models, Nos 387.022 to 387.043, had driving wheels of 1950mm (76.8in) diameter and somewhat reduced heating surface.

After 1945, fourteen of the class were given Kylchap double blast-pipes and chimneys, replacing the original British-style lipped chimney. The class operated until 1974, and the last one built, No. 387.043, is preserved.
The Heusinger valve gear is virtually identical to that of Walschaerts, but was developed independently in Germany by Edmund Heusinger as early as 1849.

**Boiler pressure:** 13kg/cm² (185psi)
**Cylinders:** 525x680mm (20.7x27in)
**Driving wheels:** 1900mm (74.8in)
**Grate area:** 4.8m² (51.7sq ft)
**Heating surface:** 260m² (2799sq ft)
**Superheater:** 93m² (1001sq ft)
**Tractive effort:** 11,030kg (24,320lb)
**Total weight:** 89.6t (197,568lb) (engine only)

## CLASS 44 2-10-0 GERMAN STATE RAILWAYS (DRG) GERMANY: 1926

**A Class 44 on a post-war freight. One of these was the last steam locomotive in service on the DB, in October 1977. Others ran on the DR into the 1980s.**

Like the Class 01 'Pacific', this was a 'standard engine' of the DRG, designed under the aegis of Dr R.P. Wagner. Intended as a general heavy freight hauler, it was another successful design, with 1753 built between 1926 and 1944. It was a three-cylinder simple expansion engine, bar-framed, with a copper firebox. Four-point suspension had been worked out, in order to make the ride easier, but its 20t (19.7 ton) axle load restricted it to main line services. The maximum operating speed was 70kph (43.5mph).

**Boiler pressure:** 16kg/cm² (228psi)
**Cylinders:** 600x660mm (23.6x26in)
**Driving wheels:** 1400mm (55in)
**Grate area:** 4.5m² (48.4sq ft)
**Heating surface:** 237m² (2551.6sq ft)
**Superheater:** 100m² (1076sq ft)
**Tractive effort:** 23,140kg (51,000lb)
**Total weight:** 114.1t (25,225lb) (engine only)

## 'LORD NELSON' CLASS 4-6-0 SOUTHERN RAILWAY (SR) GREAT BRITAIN: 1926

The reason for this 16-strong class was the need for an engine able to cope with heavy boat trains from London to Dover and Folkestone, and holiday expresses to the south-west of England; but it also let the company boast an engine which, briefly, had the highest tractive effort of any express locomotive in Britain. Designed by R.E.L. Maunsell, it was a four-cylinder

**The preserved SR No 850 *Lord Nelson* at the former 'Steamtown' railway centre at Carnforth, Lancashire, on 4 September 1980. In the background is the coaling tower, built of reinforced concrete.**

simple-expansion engine. Named after British admirals, they were effective locomotives but a poorly designed firebox made it hard to keep the fire hot enough. In the late 1930s, they were fitted with Lemaître multiple-jet chimneys, which helped considerably.

***Lord Nelson*** **heading for Carlisle with the 'Cumbrian Mountain Express' charter train, on 24 January 1981.**

**Boiler pressure:** 15.5kg/cm² (220psi)
**Cylinders:** 419x610mm (16.5x24in)
**Driving wheels:** 2007mm (79in)
**Grate area:** 3.1m² (33sq ft)
**Heating surface:** 18.5m² (1989sq ft)
**Superheater:** 35m² (376sq ft)
**Tractive effort:** 15,196kg (33,500lb)
**Total weight:** 142.5t (314,000lb)

## CLASS 12 4-8-2 RHODESIAN RAILWAYS (RR) RHODESIA: 1926

**Boiler pressure:** 13.3kg/cm² (190psi)
**Cylinders:** 507.6x660mm (20x26in)
**Driving wheels:** 1294mm (51in)
**Grate area:** not known
**Heating surface:** 187m² (2017sq ft)
**Superheater:** 33.6m² (362sq ft)
**Tractive effort:** 14,940kg (32,940lb)
**Total weight:** 86.4t (190,560lb)

Nineteen of this class were delivered in 1926 to the 1065mm (3ft 6in) gauge RR, and a further 11 in 1930. Some of the class had Lentz-actuated piston valves, but these were replaced by Walschaerts valve gear. Initially they worked over the Salisbury–Gwelo line. In 1944, three were rebuilt as class 12A with wider, shorter boilers and bigger tenders; two of these were sold to the Mozambique railways in 1964.

**A class 12A rebuild of the former Rhodesian, now Zimbabwean, Railways, this 1929 locomotive, like the other class 12s, was a product of the North British Locomotive Works, Glasgow. These had wider, shorter boilers and larger tenders**

**Class 12 No 247 in Bulawayo yard, on 14 May 1976.**

## 9000 CLASS 'UNION PACIFIC' TYPE 4-12-2 UNION PACIFIC RAILROAD (UPR) USA: 1926

Built by Alco's Brooks Works, these were until 1934 the longest and largest non-articulated locomotives in the world. The coupled wheelbase was 9340mm (30ft 8in). Eighty-eight were built and a company statement said the aim was 'to haul mile-long freights at passenger train speeds.'

Unusually for the USA, they were three-cylinder engines, though employing simple expansion. The first and last sets of coupled wheels were allowed lateral play – the fourth was originally flangeless, but this was later found to be unnecessary. Though no other lines used them, the 4-12-2s ran on the UP until 1956, and they represented the maximum power to be got from a rigid-framed locomotive. Originally deployed on the UP main line through Wyoming, they later worked in Kansas and Nebraska. The first engine, No 9000, is preserved.

**Boiler pressure:** 15.5kg/cm² (220psi)
**Cylinders:** 685x812mm (27x32in); inside cyl 685x787mm (27x31in)
**Driving wheels:** 1700mm (67in)
**Grate area:** 10m² (108.25sq ft)
**Heating surface:** 543.8m² (5853sq ft)
**Superheater:** 237.8m² (2560sq ft)
**Tractive effort:** 43,832kg (96,650lb)
**Total weight:** 354.6t (782,000lb)

**A 4-12-2 rolls its load across the plains: UP 9007 at Archer, Wyoming, on 4 September 1955. The westbound freight consists of 102 cars; the train is travelling at 40kph (25mph).**

## Class Tk3 2-8-0 STATE RAILWAYS (VR) FINLAND: 1927

**Woodburning Tk3 No 1163 in a winter landscape. The class was affectionately known as Pikku-Jumbo, 'Little Jumbo'. They often worked passenger and mixed trains as well as main-line freight.**

Increasing freight loads prompted the building of this class, with its maximum axle load of 10.7t (10.5 tons), intended to run on lightly laid track. Within 4 years, 100 were built and when construction ended in 1953, there were 158. It was a two-cylinder simple-expansion wood-burner. Twenty-four were claimed by the Russians after the 'Winter War' of 1939–40, and 70 were built after 1943, all in Finland except for 20 by Frichs of Aarhus in Denmark. Withdrawals began in the 1960s, but several of Finland's largest steam class have been preserved.

**Boiler pressure:** 14kg/cm$^2$ (199psi)
**Cylinders:** 460x630mm (18x24.8in)
**Driving wheels:** 1270mm (50in)
**Grate area:** 1.6m$^2$ (17.2sq ft)
**Heating surface:** 84.8m$^2$ (913sq ft)
**Superheater:** 26m$^2$ (279.9sq ft)
**Tractive effort:** 9550kg (21,058lb)
**Total weight:** 51.8t (114,219lb) (engine only)

**Another woodburner, with a well-stacked tender, No 1450 awaits departure with a local train from the northern station of Kemi, near the Swedish border, in September 1968.**

## 'KING' CLASS 4-6-0 GREAT WESTERN RAILWAY (GWR) GREAT BRITAIN: 1927

**The first of the 'Kings', No 6000 *King George V,* with boiler cladding partly removed, at Stafford Road Works, Wolverhampton, on 10 February 1962.**

1926–7 were years of significant locomotive development in Great Britain, stimulated by inter-company rivalry and a heightened sense of the value of good publicity. The GWR's contribution was the 4-cylinder simple 'King', dubbed 'Britain's most powerful express passenger locomotive' on its appearance. In effect, it was the culmination of the design policy that had begun in 1907. The domeless tapered boiler reached a maximum diameter of 2837mm (6ft). The heaviest 4-6-0 on British railways, it was intended to haul the main West of England and Birmingham expresses to and from Paddington.

A maximum axle load of 22.8t (22.5 tons) confined it to certain lines and despite that it cut the London-Plymouth timing of the 'Cornish Riviera Limited' to 4 hours for the 363km (225.5 mile) journey, it was not allowed over the Royal Albert Bridge west of Plymouth.

By 1930, the class numbered 30. The maximum recorded speed of a 'King' was 174.6kph (108.5mph), though its real value was in maintaining consistent speeds of the order of 96–105kph (60–65mph) with trains loading up to 508t (500 tons).

Under the nationalized regime from 1948, the 'Kings' had double chimneys fitted and a number of other technical refinements were made, with the result that their performance was further enhanced. They operated on express services until their final withdrawal in early 1963.

**Boiler pressure:** 17.6kg/ cm$^2$ (250psi)
**Cylinders:** 413x711mm (16.25x28in)
**Driving wheels:** 1980mm (78in)
**Grate area:** 3m$^2$ (34.3sq ft)
**Heating surface:** 204.4 m$^2$ (2201sq ft)
**Superheater:** 29 m$^2$ (313sq ft)
**Tractive effort:** 18,140kg (40,000lb)
**Total weight:** 90.4t (199,360lb) (engine only)

**A close-up of No 6000's front end, showing the bell which was presented on its US tour in 1927. The 'Welsh Marches Express' was a special charter service to Shrewsbury and Hereford, on 25 August 1985.**

**No 6005 *King George II* and two other 'Kings', in British Railways livery, ready for service at the Stafford Road locomotive depot, Wolverhampton.**

## 'ROYAL SCOT' 4-6-0 LONDON MIDLAND & SCOTTISH RAILWAY (LMS) GREAT BRITAIN: 1927

**No 6100 *Royal Scot*, uniquely bearing a nameplate also on the smokebox door. The bell was presented when the locomotive was sent on a visit to the USA in 1933, and removed when the engine was rebuilt in 1950.**

This designation effectively covers two different locomotive designs; the first 'Royal Scots' and the rebuilds from 1943–55. The class began as a very hurried order placed with the North British Locomotive Company of Glasgow for 50 locomotives, when it became plain that the LMS had no engine capable of pulling the new 'Royal Scot' London–Glasgow express on the 481.3km (299 mile) non-stop London–Carlisle stage. A compound 'Pacific' design was abandoned in the planning stage after tests made with a borrowed GWR simple-expansion 'Castle' 4-6-0. To assist with design, the Southern Railways agreed to supply a set of drawings of the new 'Lord Nelson' 4-6-0. The episode illustrates the absurdity of four companies each producing its own standard types within a relatively small country.

The class, designed as three-cylinder simples, was a successful one, able to take a 457t (450-ton) train unaided over the Shap summit, and 20 more were built. It was a massive-looking engine, 4022mm (13ft 2.5ins) high, with a tiny chimney and low dome, and a straight-sided Belpaire firebox. Its small original tender was later replaced by a standard LMS 4000gal (4800 US gals), 9.1t (9-ton) tender. After 13 years' intensive service, the older engines began to be rebuilt with taper boilers and double chimneys. This sometimes amounted to virtually a new engine, with little beside the cab and tender preserved – but the operation was a great success and gave the 'Royal Scots' another two decades of express work.

**The restricted height of chimney and dome, to keep within the loading gauge, is clear from this picture. The tender is the later standard LMS tender, which replaced the original one.**

**Boiler pressure:** 17.5kg/cm$^2$ (250psi)
**Cylinders:** 457x660mm (18x26in)
**Driving wheels:** 2056mm (81in)
**Grate area:** 2.9m$^2$ (31.2sq ft)
**Heating surface:** 193m$^2$ (2081sq ft)
**Superheater:** 41.3m$^2$ (445sq ft)
**Tractive effort:** 13,242kg (29,200lb)
**Total weight:** 86.2t (190,176lb)

## CLASS XC 4-6-2 INDIAN RAILWAYS (IR) INDIA: 1927

Some railways, like the Bengal–Nagpur, developed their own express types (in their case, a four-cylinder compound Pacific), but most followed the specifications of the Indian Railways Standards Committee of 1924, offering three levels of Pacific power, XA, XB and XC, all two-cylinder simples. The XC was the heavy express engine. The classes were built in large numbers, but were of only moderate quality. The leading bogies and the drawgear were badly designed, making them unstable, especially on track that was less than perfect. This was corrected only after an accident in 1937, when an XB overturned.

**A Class XC, No 22228, at Calcutta on 31 December 1976. All X-class engines were modified after an XB overturned on level track in 1937.**

**Boiler pressure:** 12.6kg/cm² (180psi)
**Cylinders:** 584x711mm (23x28in)
**Driving wheels:** 1880mm (74in)
**Grate area:** 4.75m² (51sq ft)
**Heating surface:** 226m² (2429sq ft)
**Superheater:** 59m² (636sq ft)
**Tractive effort:** 13,895kg (30,625lb)
**Total weight:** 178t (392,500lb)

## SWITCHING ENGINE 0-6-0 STATE BELT RAILROAD OF CALIFORNIA USA: 1927

Switching engines carried out the train marshalling operations at termini, and in carriage and freight yards, and often also hauled local pick-up freights from factory sidings and local depots. By this time, some were very large 10-coupled engines, with boosters on the tender wheels, needed to move trainloads of 1.6km (1mile) or more in length. More typically, switchers were of 0-8-0 or 0-6-0 wheel arrangement, often modified from 'Consolidation' or 'Mogul' types. Not normally used on the open road, and restricted to low speeds, they were not

**A preserved 0-6-0 switcher, No 4466 of the Union Pacific Railroad, with downwards-sloping tender. The weights of cylinders and firebox balanced each other, with the wheels in between.**

Yolo Shortline 0-6-0 No 1233 on the open road. Like the Southern Pacific class S-14 0-6-0, this engine has a Vanderbilt tender rather than the typical sloping switcher tender.

considered to need front trucks: good adhesion, with the weight on the driving wheels, and a tight turning circle were more important: frame length of these engines sometimes extended to more than double their coupled wheelbase. A Baldwin 0-8-0 switcher of the Illinois Central, also built in 1927, 11,167mm (36ft 8in) long, had a wheelbase of only 4568mm (15ft). With the American aversion to using tank engines, they usually had tenders, often sloped down towards the rear to give the driver a better view when reversing. By 1927, power-operated reversing gear, long pressed for by the labour unions, was almost always fitted in switchers, a great relief to drivers. Being relatively straightforward engines, and running up modest mileages, switchers often had a long working life, and examples from the early twentieth century survived on many lines into the last days of steam.

**Boiler pressure:** 13.3kg/cm$^2$ (190lb)
**Cylinders:** 508x609mm (20x24in)
**Driving wheels:** 1294mm (51in)
**Grate area:** 3m$^2$ (33.1sq ft)
**Heating surface:** 145.3m$^2$ (1564sq ft)
**Superheater:** 40.4m$^2$ (435sq ft)
**Tractive effort:** 15,000kg (30,400lb)
**Total weight:** 67t (147,700lb)

## CLASS J1 'HUDSON' 4-6-4 NEW YORK CENTRAL RAILROAD (NYC) USA: 1927

**Boiler pressure:** 15.75kg/cm$^2$ (225psi)
**Cylinders:** 634x711mm (25x28in)
**Driving wheels:** 2005mm (79in)
**Grate area:** 7.6m$^2$ (81.5sq ft)
**Heating surface:** 389m$^2$ (4187sq ft)
**Superheater:** 162.1m$^2$ (1745sq ft)
**Tractive effort:** 19,183kg (42,300lb)
**Total weight:** 256.3t (565,200lb)

The first 4-6-4s were significantly more powerful than the 'Pacifics', which they replaced on such NYC express services as the 'Empire State'. Built by Alco, the J1 class totalled 225. The type developed rapidly: by 1930, with the J1c, the boiler pressure had gone up to 19.3kg/cm$^2$ (275psi) and the cylinders had been modified to 571x736mm (22.5x29in) for better tractive effort. All were booster-fitted on the rear bogie, whose rear wheels at 1294mm (51in) were 381mm (15in) bigger than the front pair. From 1937, a considerably altered 'Hudson', classed J3, appeared, 10 of them streamlined for high-prestige duties.

The 4-6-4 proved excellent for high-speed passenger express work. The fastest was probably the F6 'Hudson' built by Baldwins for the Chicago Milwaukee St Paul & Pacific Railroad, in 1930. In July 1934, No 6402, hauling the 9 am 'Milwaukee Express', ran between Chicago and Milwaukee at an average 123.4kph (76.7mph), and maximum 166.5kph (103.5mph).

**Class J-1 No. 5271 poses with a 10-car train, typical of the NYC expresses, around the year 1935. The rugged building style, hidden in later streamlined engines, is visible here.**

## CLASS 3000 2-8-2 BUENOS AIRES PACIFIC RAILWAY (BAP) ARGENTINA: 1928

**Boiler pressure:** 14kg/cm² (200psi)
**Cylinders:** 622x761mm (24.5x30in)
**Driving wheels:** 1700mm (67in)
**Grate area:** 4.27m² (46sq ft)
**Heating surface:** 256m² (2760sq ft)
**Superheater:** 62.8m² (676sq ft)
**Tractive effort:** 18,272kg (40,290lb)
**Total weight:** 208.25t (459,200lb)

British works were used to building engines for export that were bigger than those ordered for home. This heavy two-cylinder simple 'Mikado' is a good example, built by Beyer Peacock to the 1675mm (5ft 6in) gauge and with a boiler of 2094mm (82in) outer diameter. For long-distance work across the plains, it had a large bogie tender holding 15.24t (15 tons) of coal, with one of the first steam coal pushers fitted in Britain.

**The bogie tender of the Class 3000 was the first built in Britain to be equipped with a steam-powered coal pusher, for transferring fuel forwards to the shovelling plate.**

## S-CLASS 4-6-2 VICTORIAN RAILWAYS (VR) AUSTRALIA: 1928

**Boiler pressure:** 14kg/cm² (200psi)
**Cylinders:** 520x710mm (20.5x28in)
**Driving wheels:** 1852mm (73in)
**Grate area:** 4.6m² (50sq ft)
**Heating surface:** 294m² (3166sq ft)
**Superheater:** 57.7m² (622sq ft)
**Tractive effort:** 17,786kg (39,220lb)
**Total weight:** 197.7t (436,016lb)

Four engines formed this small but famous class of 1600mm (5ft 3in) gauge 'Pacifics', designed to pull the Melbourne-Sydney 'Spirit of Progress' on the Melbourne-Albury section. The VR's Chief Mechanical Engineer, Alfred Smith, led the design team and they were built at the VR Newport Railway Workshops as three-cylinder simple expansion engines, with cast-steel frames, and outside Walschaerts valve gear, the inside cylinder operated by Gresley's conjugated lever arrangement. They were immediately put on to the 'Spirit', and when, with a great fanfare of publicity, an all-steel new carriage set was introduced in 1937, the 'S' class was transformed to match by a streamlined casing that completely hid the boiler and smoke-box, but left the wheels and motion uncovered. New, larger tenders mounted on two six-wheel bogies enabled them to make the 317km (197 mile) run to Albury non-stop. The engines were painted in the same blue livery as the train. Hand-firing made the run a supreme task for the fireman, who shovelled 6.1t (six tons) of coal in the course of three hours and fifty minutes, and was paid a special rate. The train was normally of 10 cars, weighing 508t (500 tons) but occasionally it was made up to 12. In 1951–52, the class was converted to oil-burning, but in the latter year they were displaced from the 'Blue' service by B-class diesel electrics. Years of hard work had taken their toll on the boilers, and all four were withdrawn and broken up between October 1953 and September 1954.

**The S-class is seen here in the original un-streamlined form, prior to the makeover of 1937 which transformed their appearance, though mechanically they were unchanged.**

## CLASS CC50 2-6-6-0 STATE RAILWAYS (SS) DUTCH EAST INDIES (INDONESIA): 1928

With winding mountain lines on 1065mm (3ft 6in) gauge, the main Indonesian islands were good territory for articulated locomotives. The SS favoured Mallets, and had at least eight classes, including the CC10 2-6-6-0T, built 1904–11; and the last Mallets ever built, the four BB81 0-4-4-2T, built in Japan by Nippon Sharyo in 1962. Class CC50 was a four-cylinder compound. Thirty were delivered in 1927–28, 16 from Werkspoor and 14 from SLM, Winterthur. Stationed across Java, they ran mixed-traffic services.

**Mallet CC5001, with an array of headlights, stands at Bayonbong on 3 December, 1980. This is one of the Werkspoor-built locos.**

**Boiler pressure:** 14kg/cm² (199psi)
**Cylinders:** hp 340x510mm (13.4x20in); lp 540x510mm (21.25x20in)
**Driving wheels:** 1106mm (43.5in)
**Grate area:** 3.4m² (36.6sq ft)
**Heating surface:** 150.8m² (1623.6sq ft)
**Superheater:** 50m² (538.3sq ft)
**Tractive effort:** N/A
**Total weight:** 74.6t (164,640lb) (engine only)

## CLASS 80 0-6-0T GERMAN STATE RAILWAYS (DRG) GERMANY: 1928

This superheated shunter was among the first *Einheitsloks*, 'standard engines' of the DRG. Many lines had used elderly main-line engines for this purpose, which though cheap on the capital account, was in reality expensive in maintenance and spares.

The 39 Class 80s built in 1928–9 were based at the major termini of Cologne and Leipzig.

Rarely has so much power been packed into a 3200mm (10ft 6in) wheelbase. They could move 900t (885 tons) at 45kph (28mph) on the level, and lasted with the DB right up to 1965 (and with the DR as late as 1977).

In their last years on the DR, these poerful engines were employed largely as works shunters, but emerged occasionally to haul specials, much to the delight of enthusiasts.

**Boiler pressure:** 14kg/cm$^2$ (199psi)
**Cylinders:** 450x550mm (17.7x21.6in)
**Driving wheels:** 1100mm (43.3in)
**Grate area:** 1.5m$^2$ (16.1sq ft)
**Heating surface:** 69.6m$^2$ (749sq ft)
**Superheater:** 25.5m$^2$ (274.5sq ft)
**Tractive effort:** 11,988kg (26,435lb)
**Total weight:** 54.4t (119,952lb)

## CLASS 86 2-8-2T GERMAN STATE RAILWAYS (DRG) GERMANY: 1928

An *Einheitslok* like the previous type, this was a more numerous class, with 774 built up to 1943; most German builders had a share in the construction. Designed to run in either direction, it was meant for mixed-traffic local trains on lines with a 15t (14.7 ton) maximum axle loading, and had a maximum operating speed of 70kph (44mph). Two horizontal outside cylinders, simple-expansion, operated by Heusinger valve gear, drove the third coupled wheels. Two sand domes with a compressed-air spray system helped with adhesion on slippery rails. Two other domes contained the feed-water valve and the steam regulator. A Knorr feedwater heater was fitted, with a Knorr-Tolkien feedwater pump. As with all DRG classes, electric lighting was fitted, driven by a steam-powered dynamo. The later engines, built during the war, were 5.5t (5.4 tons) lighter than the first ones.

The first went to the hilly regions of the Moselle and Swabia, and the first 16 were fitted with counter-pressure brakes for downhill work. Over 20 were wrecked during the war; after it, 184 were retained on Czech, Polish, Austrian and Russian railways, while the DB received 385 and the DR around 175. The last to go, ran on the DR system until 1976, mostly in Saxony – but also on the causeway line from Heringsdorf to the island of Usedom, for which they were fitted with smoke deflectors against the almost-permanent east wind.

**Boiler pressure:** 14kg/cm$^2$ (199psi)
**Cylinders:** 570x660mm (22.4x26in)
**Driving wheels:** 1400mm (55in)
**Grate area:** 2.3m$^2$ (24.8sq ft)
**Heating surface:** 117.3m$^2$ (1262.9sq ft)
**Superheater:** 47m$^2$ (506sq ft)
**Tractive effort:** 18,195kg (40,000lb)
**Total weight:** 88.5t (195,142lb)

**One of the efficient, multi-domed Class 86 standard tank engines of the *Deutsche Bundesbahn*, operating in typically hilly country.**

## CLASS 22 2-4-2T HUNGARIAN STATE RAILWAYS (MÁV) HUNGARY: 1928

In Hungary as elsewhere, competition from road transport began to bite into the railways' business from the mid-1920s. For the works and repair shops whose investment was in steam power, there was also a threat of competition from diesel railcars. To provide faster local services that could compete with the opposition, the MÁV introduced this small superheated tank class, with two simple-expansion outside cylinders, and by 1939, it numbered 136, plus 35 supplied to the Yugoslavian Railways. In 1948, the class was redesignated 275.

**No 275.038 at Balatan. Its chimney lip hides a spark arrestor. The lack of a running plate was not a usual feature of MÁV tank engines.**

**Boiler pressure:** 13kg/cm$^2$ (185psi)
**Cylinders:** 355x460mm (14x18in)
**Driving wheels:** 1220mm (48in)
**Grate area:** 1.25m$^2$ (13.5sq ft)
**Heating surface:** 49.2m$^2$ (529.7sq ft)
**Superheater:** 16.7m$^2$ (180sq ft)
**Tractive effort:** 5240kg (11,550lb)
**Total weight:** 34.4t (75,852lb)

## 'CAB-FIRST' CLASS AC-5 4-8-8-2 SOUTHERN PACIFIC RAILROAD (SPR) USA: 1928

The 'cab-first' concept goes back to railways in Germany and Italy, but the SPR took it up in the biggest way. In the long snow-sheds and tunnels of its Sierra Nevada line, an engine whose cab was free from back-blown smoke was a great boon to the crew. Between Truckee and Blue Canyon, there were 61km (38 miles) of snow-sheds, designed to prevent drifts 15–60m (50–200ft) deep from blocking the line. As the engines burned oil, the problem of access to the fuel supply was easily dealt with: oil and water were towed in a 12-wheel double bogie tender, with oil supplied at 2.2kg (5lb) pressure to the burners. The first AC (articulated consolidation) locomotives had been Mallet compounds turned back-to-front in 1910; these were rebuilt from 1927 as simple expansion engines, and the AC-5s were four-cylinder simples from the start, of greater mechanical dimensions than the AC-1s. Ten of this new type were built by Baldwins in 1928, with a further 16 in the following year, and 25 more in 1930, when the boiler pressure was raised to 17.5kg/cm$^2$ (250psi). In all, the SP had over 200 AC locomotives, constructed up to 1937, of which only class AC-9 was not cab-forward. Their original intended route was the mountain stretch between Roseville, California, and Sparks, Nevada, but they were also used on other divisions of the SP where their power and smoke-free driving position were of value.

Like the Italian class 671, these locomotives ran permanently 'backwards'. The last in action was 4274 in December 1956; the last of the line, 4294, is preserved.

**The view was fine, but crews worried at first about collisions. Southern Pacific No 4100 belonged to class AC-4, identical in leading dimensions with AC-5. AC-4 was numbered 4100–4109; AC-5, 4110–4125.**

**Boiler pressure:** 16.5kg/cm$^2$ (235psi)
**Cylinders:** 609x812mm (24x32in)
**Driving wheels:** 1612mm (63.5in)
**Grate area:** 12.9m$^2$ (139sq ft)
**Heating surface:** 604.1m$^2$ (6505sq ft)
**Superheater:** 277.5m$^2$ (2988sq ft)
**Tractive effort:** 46,848kg (106,300lb)
**Total weight:** 278.4t (614,000lb) (engine only)

## X-CLASS 2-8-2 VICTORIAN RAILWAYS (VR) AUSTRALIA: 1929

**Boiler pressure:** 14.3kg/cm² (205lb)
**Cylinders:** 558x710mm (22x28in)
**Driving wheels:** 1548mm (61in)
**Grate area:** 3.9m² (42sq ft)
**Heating surface:** 242.8m² (2615sq ft)
**Superheater:** 38.3m² (412sq ft)
**Tractive effort:** 17,556kg (38,712lb)
**Total weight:** 188.3t (415,184lb)

For heavy mineral traffic, the VR opted for the 2-8-2 on its 1600mm (5ft 3in) gauge. Between 1929 and 1947, 29 were built at the line's own Newport shops. All but two had a booster fitted to the pony truck, to aid in starting, and contributed 4083kg (9000lb) of tractive effort. The X-class managed a fine turn of speed: X-32 once hauled the crack 'Spirit of Progress' passenger express without losing time. This engine was fitted with a coal-pulverizing plant. Some early engines received new Belpaire boilers with combustion chambers. Smoke deflectors were also fitted. The class was scrapped between 1957 and 1961. One is preserved.

**The illustration shows a rebuilt X-class loco with Belpaire firebox. The smoke deflectors were fitted at the same time, and the draughting system was changed, with stove-pipe chimney fitted (in Australian parlance, a 'basher' front end).**

## BEYER GARRATT 4-6-2+2-6-4 LEOPOLDINA RAILWAY BRAZIL: 1929

The first two of these engines were built primarily for passenger service on the twisting metre-gauge (39.4in) tracks between Campos and Victoria, and a further 12 were supplied, also from Beyer Peacock, in 1937 and 1943. They had Belpaire boilers, Walschaerts valve gear, and piston valves. Although built to burn low-grade coal, the tender rails show that they often burned wood as fuel, and the capacious ashpans would have coped effectively with this.

The Brazilian railways were very much freight-oriented. Apart from an interesting flirtation with French practice in the late 1940s, they tended to buy from American locomotive builders, and US-type 2-8-0s and 2-8-2s predominated. The Leopoldina system, with its Manchester-built Garratts, was an exception.

**Boiler pressure:** 12.3kg/cm² (175psi)
**Cylinders:** 393x558mm (15.5x22in)
**Driving wheels:** 1015mm (40in)
**Grate area:** 3.1m² (34sq ft)
**Heating surface:** 157.6m² (1697sq ft)
**Superheater:** 31.1m² (335sq ft)
**Tractive effort:** 13,300kg (29,330lb)
**Total weight:** 113.3t (249,760lb)

## CLASS T1 'SELKIRK' TYPE 2-10-4 CANADIAN PACIFIC RAILWAY (CPR) CANADA: 1929

The origins of the 2-10-4 are with the Texas & Pacific Railway, which had 10 locomotives of this configuration built by the Lima Locomotive Works in 1925, and it was duly known as the 'Texas' type. It proved an excellent heavy freight engine, and the T&P had acquired another 60 by 1929. Like the 'Berkshire' type also built by Lima, but even more so, it was a 'super-power' locomotive. Henry Blaine Bowen, CPR's head of motive power, also opted for 2-10-4s, and offered $20 to staff as a prize for the best class name: 'Selkirks' was chosen, after the range in the Rocky Mountains

**The Canadian Transcontinental – a 'Selkirk' 2-10-4, having negotiated the spiral tunnels, the steep grades, and the bends, emerges into the open air and on to level track.**

through which they would operate. Nos 5900–5919 were built by the Montreal Locomotive Works in 1929; 5920–5929 in 1938; and the final batch, 5930–5935, in 1949: the last steam locomotives built for the CPR. These semi-streamlined two-cylinder simple-expansion engines operated both passenger and freight services through the Rockies between Calgary and Revelstoke. On the long and spectacular climb from Banff to Beavermouth, through the twin spiral tunnels of the Kicking Horse Pass, they took up to 14-car trains on the transcontinental 'Dominion', of around 1016t (1000 tons), unaided. All services were turned over to diesel haulage by 1954. The last two 'Selkirks' to be built have been preserved.

**CP No 5935 poses when new in 1949. This locomotive is preserved at the Canadian Railway Museum, near Montreal.**

**Boiler pressure:** 20kg/cm$^2$ (285psi)
**Cylinders:** 634x812mm (25x32in)
**Driving wheels:** 1599mm (63in)
**Grate area:** 8.7m$^2$ (93.5sq ft)
**Heating surface:** 453.8m$^2$ (4886sq ft)
**Superheater:** 196.1m$^2$ (2112sq ft)
**Tractive effort:** 34877kg (76,905lb)
**Total weight:** 202.7t (447,000lb) (engine only)

## Southern Railway 0-8-0T (SR) GREAT BRITAIN: 1929

Intended for hump and yard shunting, with a wheelbase of only 8274mm (17ft 6in) against a length of 11,989mm (39ft 3in), this was the only eight-coupled design built by the Southern. A 3-cylinder simple, it had a small grate and firebox, reducing fuel consumption during the 'stand-by' periods typical of shunting engines. The class, eight in total, was built at the Southern's Brighton works. A useful fitting, for the driver, was a steam reverser.

**The unequal spacing between the driving wheels is to make enough length for the coupling rod of the inside cylinder, which drove the second coupled axle. The side tanks were small, but it was rarely far from a water supply.**

**Boiler pressure:** 12.6kg/cm$^2$ (180psi)
**Cylinders:** 406x711mm (16x28in)
**Driving wheels:** 1421mm (56in)
**Grate area:** 1.72m$^2$ (18.6sq ft)
**Heating surface:** 118.8m$^2$ (1279sq ft)
**Tractive effort:** 14,568kg (29,500lb)
**Total weight:** 72.7t (160,384lb)

## Class PO4 4-6-0 DUTCH STATE RAILWAYS (NS) NETHERLANDS: 1929

Thirty-six engines of this four-cylinder simple-expansion class were built, by Henschel of Kassel, in 1929 and 1930, as express passenger locomotives to handle the heaviest trains made up of the NS's new steel carriages and *Wagons-Lits* stock, taking over from the class 3700 4-6-0s. With an 18t (17.7-ton) maximum axle load, they initially suffered from some route restrictions, being unable to use the Ijssel bridge between Utrecht and Groningen. As a relatively small network, the NS sought to spread its costs, and this class shared its bogie tender design with the older 3700 of the SS and the 3600 of the NCS (State Railways and Central Railways prior to the formation of the NS), and its boiler with the later 6300 4-8-4Ts of 1930-31. The two outside cylinders drove the first set of coupled wheels, with internal Walschaerts valve gear. Maximum service speed was 110kph (68mph). Plans for electrification and dieselization meant that it became clear this would be the last Dutch express steam locomotive. Even steam engines were being put to intensive use, with three crews manning each locomotive in three daily shifts. But its effectiveness was such that the 6300 tank version was ordered, with 22 delivered in 1930–31. Among the international trains hauled by this class were the weekly 'Rotterdam Lloyd', Rotterdam-Marseille, linking with the Mediterranean steamers; and the 'Netherlands-Lloyd' from The Hague to Genoa, via Paris and the Mont Cenis tunnel, both inaugurated in 1936.

**Boiler pressure:** 14kg/cm$^2$ (199psi)
**Cylinders:** 420x660mm (16.5x26in)
**Driving wheels:** 1850mm (73in)
**Grate area:** 3.2m$^2$ (34.4sq ft)
**Heating surface:** 150m$^2$ (1615sq ft)
**Superheater:** 53m$^2$ (570.6sq ft)
**Tractive effort:** 13,575kg (29,940lb)
**Total weight:** 84t (185,220lb) (engine only)

## Class S 0-8-0 SOUTH AFRICAN RAILWAYS (SAR) SOUTH AFRICA: 1929

Around 100 of Classes S, S1 and S2 were built between 1929 and 1953, two-cylinder simple-expansion engines of varying power and axle load; the S1 being the strongest and the S2 the lightest. The original 11 engines

**A class S, with 12-wheel Vanderbilt-type tender, shunts boxcars at Port Elizabeth docks on 23 June 1971.**

were built in Germany by Henschel; S1 was the first locomotive type built at the SAR's own Salt River works, Cape Town, in 1947. Shunting and train marshalling was their work, and they were based at the major yards, including Germiston (Johannesburg), Kimberley, Durban and Cape Town. Specifications are for Class S.

**Boiler pressure:** 15kg/cm$^2$ (215psi)
**Cylinders:** 590x634.5mm (23.25x25in)
**Driving wheels:** 1218mm (48in)
**Grate area:** 3.7m$^2$ (40sq ft)
**Heating surface:** 157m$^2$ (1690sq ft)
**Superheater:** 40.3m$^2$ (434sq ft)
**Tractive effort:** 20,590kg (45,400lb)
**Total weight:** 62.9t (138,878lb) (engine only)

**A Class S, with original tender, on shunting duty in the huge yards at Germiston, to the east of Johannesburg.**

## 'NORTHERN' CLASS S1 4-8-4 GREAT NORTHERN RAILWAY (GN) USA: 1929

The 4-8-4 first ran on the Northern Pacific Railroad in 1927, but when the GN's new train, the 'Empire Builder', cut five hours from the transcontinental schedule, six of this configuration were built by Baldwins for the long haul over the continental divide in Montana. The maximum westbound grade was 1.8 per cent and they took 14-car trains up without assistance, enjoying a tractive effort 22 per cent greater than that of the 4-8-2 'Mountain' types they replaced. The boiler was of 2487mm (98in) diameter and had a Belpaire firebox. Both front and rear bogies ran in outside frames, and all axles had roller bearings. As often with US engines, compressor pumps were mounted on the smoke-box front. Apart from one, No 2552, they were oil burners, with tenders of the 'Vanderbilt' type, running on two six-wheel bogies, and holding 4800gal (5800 US gal) of oil and 18,300gal (22,000 US gal) of water. These 'Northerns' 4874mm (16ft) high and 33,071mm (108ft 7in) long, were imposing engines and the company exploited them vigorously for their promotional value as well as for their service in action. But with the arrival of the GN's class S2 4-8-4, with 80in (2030mm) driving wheels, they were soon switched to freight haulage, and the S2s took over the passenger express work.

**Boiler pressure:** 17.5kg/cm$^2$ (250psi)
**Cylinders:** 710x761mm (28x30in)
**Driving wheels:** 1853mm (73in)
**Grate area:** 8.7m$^2$ (94sq ft)
**Heating surface:** 423m$^2$ (4560sq ft)
**Superheater:** 188.3m$^2$ (2028sq ft)
**Tractive effort:** 30,385kg (67,000lb)
**Total weight:** 418.7t (847,900lb)

## 'SCHOOLS' CLASS 4-4-0 SOUTHERN RAILWAY (SR) GREAT BRITAIN: 1930

The first 10 of this compact 'pocket express' class, named after well-known schools, were built at the Southern's Eastleigh works, mainly for London–Hastings trains, a route with severe loading restrictions. So successful was it that 30 more were built, claimed as the most powerful 4-4-0s in Europe. Three simple-expansion cylinders, each with a set of Walschaerts valve gear, drove the first coupled wheels. The 'Schools' were able to compete with the 'Lord Nelson' 4-6-0s on express trains of 356–366t (350–360 tons). Wide-chimney exhausts with Lemaître blast pipes were fitted to 20 of the class.

**Boiler pressure:** 15.5kg/cm$^2$ (220psi)
**Cylinders:** 419x660mm (16.5x26in)
**Driving wheels:** 2005mm (79in)
**Grate area:** 2.6 m$^2$ (28.3sq ft)
**Heating surface:** 149 m$^2$ (1604sq ft)
**Superheater:** 26 m$^2$ (280 sq ft)
**Tractive effort:** 11,396kg (25,130lb)
**Total weight:** 68t (150,080lb)

**The preserved 'Schools' 4-4-0 No 928 *Stowe*, hauls the 11.30 from Sheffield Park to Horsted Keynes, through Three Arches Cutting on the heritage 'Bluebell' Line in Kent, on 7 September 1986.**

## No 10000 4-6-4 LONDON & NORTH EASTERN RAILWAY (LNER) GREAT BRITAIN: 1930

**As British Railways No 60700, with a conventional boiler, the unique ex-LNER 4-6-4 10000 passes Hornsey in the London suburbs with a northbound express from London Kings Cross.**

The only 4-6-4 to run in Britain, this experimental compound engine had a high-pressure water-tube boiler. Nigel Gresley, CME of the LNER, wanted to explore the potential of the marine boiler, and a bulbous streamlined casing was designed to cover it. A four-cylinder compound, its main aim was to deliver power comparable to the LNER 'Pacifics' but with greatly reduced fuel consumption. It worked a number of scheduled services, but was expensive and troublesome to maintain, and was rebuilt with a conventional A4 locomotive boiler in 1938, though retaining its extra set of trailing wheels.

**Boiler pressure:** 31.5kg/cm$^2$ (450psi)
**Cylinders:** hp 304.5x660mm (12x26in); lp 507.6x660mm (20x26in)
**Driving wheels:** 2030mm (80in)
**Grate area:** 3.2m$^2$ (34.9sq ft)
**Heating surface:** 184.4m$^2$ (1986sq ft)
**Superheater:** 13m$^2$ (140sq ft)
**Tractive effort:** 14,510kg (32,000lb)
**Total weight:** 168.6t (371,840lb)

## CLASS GTO3 4-8-4T DUTCH STATE RAILWAYS (NS) NETHERLANDS: 1930

Moving bulk coal trains from the South Limburg coalfield to the west of the country was the main task of this heavyweight back-tank type, and in 1930–31 Henschel and Berliner Maschinenbau (formerly Schwartzkopff) built 22. Like the PO4 4-6-0, they had four simple expansion cylinders to drive the first coupled axle, bar frames and Belpaire fireboxes. To let it take passenger trains, if required, the maximum operating speed was 90kph (56mph). The most powerful and heavy tank type in Europe when new, it was exceptionally long at 17,385mm (57ft). Coal capacity was 4.5t (4.4 tons); water capacity 3090gal (3710US). One is preserved.

**No 6321 at Dordrecht, around 1935. It was unusual for a four-coupled engine to have the drive on the first axle. The copper-capped chimney was a long-maintained Dutch tradition.**

**Boiler pressure:** 14kg/cm² (171psi)
**Cylinders:** 420x660mm (16.5x26in)
**Driving wheels:** 1550mm (61in)
**Grate area:** 3.2m² (34.4sq ft)
**Heating surface:** 150m² (1615sq ft)
**Superheater:** 50m² (538.3sq ft)
**Tractive effort:** 14,720kg (32,457lb)
**Total weight:** 127t (280,035lb)

## 15CA CLASS 4-8-2 SOUTH AFRICAN RAILWAYS (SAR) SOUTH AFRICA: 1930

The long distances and heavy mineral loads of South African railways required powerful freight engines, despite the 1065mm (3ft 6in) gauge, and from the 1920s, a new generation of heavy steam traction was developed. 4-8-2s had been in use since 1904, and new, larger classes, like the '12' and its derivatives in the mid-1920s, produced a tractive effort of around 18,594kg (41,000lb) with a maximum axle load of 17.8t (17.5 tons). By 1930, these had been overtaken by the 15CA class, the 'Big Bills'. The SAR always took an interest in American practice, and the first of these engines were built by Baldwins, though Breda (Milan) and the North British Locomotive Company (Glasgow) also constructed them. Maximum axle load was 18.8t (18.5 tons), but the tractive effort was significantly higher than the '12'. With a maximum height of 3959mm (13ft), and a width of 3045mm (10ft), permitting a lateral overhang of 1576mm (3ft 4in) on each side, these engines were of massive appearance. They were two-cylinder simple expansion types, with piston valves actuated by Walschaerts gear.

In 1935 the 'Big Bills' were themselves superseded by the 15E, which had a larger boiler and whose cylinders were operated by rotary cam poppet valves, and which bore many resemblances to the German-produced 16E class 'Pacific'.

**No 2826 at the coaling stage of the depot at De Aar, where the Cape Town–Kimberley–Johannesburg main line met lines to East London and Southwest Africa.**

**Boiler pressure:** 14kg/cm² (200psi)
**Cylinders:** 609x710.6mm (24x28in)
**Driving wheels:** 1447mm (57in)
**Grate area:** 4.5m² (48.3sq ft)
**Heating surface:** 257.7m² (2775sq ft)
**Superheater:** 64.6m² (696sq ft)
**Tractive effort:** 21,809kg (48,090lb)
**Total weight:** 176.2t (388,528lb)

**With close on 4535kg (100,000lb) of tractive effort between them, two Class 15CA 4-8-2s haul a mixed freight. Their relatively heavy maximum axle load meant that they were restricted to main-line service.**

## GARRATT TYPE 4-6-2+2-6-4 CENTRAL ARAGÓN RAILWAY SPAIN: 1930

The driving wheels of this express class were the largest yet used on a Garratt locomotive. Six were built by Euskalduña at Bilbao, to haul passenger trains between Valencia and Calatayud. On the mountain sections, they were able to haul 300-ton trains at 40kph (25mph) up gradients of 1 in 46 with curves of 300m radius. They had Walschaerts valve gear with piston valves, Belpaire fireboxes and ACFI feedwater heaters. Originally coal-fired, they were later converted to oil. The only Garratts used for passenger work in Europe, they were very effective, and remained in service on the RENFE until 1970. One is preserved, at the Barcelona Railway Museum. Euskalduña built one other Garratt class under licence, a 2-6-2+2-6-2 for the mineral line worked by the Compania Minera de Sierra Minera.

**Boiler pressure:** 14kg/cm$^2$ (200psi)
**Cylinders:** 482x660mm (19x26in)
**Driving wheels:** 1751mm (69in)
**Grate area:** 4.9m$^2$ (53sq ft)
**Heating surface:** 298.9m$^2$ (3218sq ft)
**Superheater:** 68.9m$^2$ (742sq ft)
**Tractive effort:** 18,540kg (40,880lb)
**Total weight:** 183.4t (404,320lb)

## CLASS Z-5 2-8-8-4 NORTHERN PACIFIC RAILROAD (NP) USA: 1930

Until the advent of the Union Pacific 'Big Boys' in 1941, this was the biggest locomotive in the world, and in terms of grate area, evaporative heating surface and superheating surface, they were never exceeded. The prototype was built by the American Locomotive Co in 1928; and 11 were ordered in 1930, but from Baldwin. These 'Yellowstones' were designed to haul 4064t (4000-ton) freight trains on the 347.6km (216-mile) sector of the transcontinental route through the 'Badlands' between Mandan, North Dakota and Glendive, Montana, up grades of 1.1 per cent, and they worked into the late 1940s. The engines stood 5228mm (17ft 2in) from the rails to the chimney lip, and were built Mallet-fashion, with the pilot and front coupled wheels forming an articulated truck; the rear coupled axles fixed to the frame, and a pivoted four-wheel trailing truck, but the four cylinders were simple-expansion only. The long firebox was intended to burn lignite, or 'Rosebud coal', from a NP-owned mine. A booster engine was fitted to the trailing truck to assist with starting off, and delivering an additional 6077kg (13,400lb) of tractive effort. All were later fitted with roller bearings, something in which the NP was a pioneer. Cladding was applied to the boiler from a point between the chimney and the first dome, giving it a smooth skin in contrast to the exposed pipework around the smokebox.

**Boiler pressure:** 17.5kg/cm$^2$ (250psi)
**Cylinders:** 660x812mm (26x32in)
**Driving wheels:** 1599mm (63in)
**Grate area:** 17m$^2$ (182sq ft)
**Heating surface:** 712.6m$^2$ (7673sq ft)
**Superheater:** 299m$^2$ (3219sq ft)
**Tractive effort:** 63,492kg (140,000lb)
**Total weight:** 499t (1,010,475lb)

## CLASS 78 4-6-4T AUSTRIAN FEDERAL RAILWAYS (ÖBB) AUSTRIA: 1931

This large side-tank class was employed on shorter-range express duties, like the Vienna–Linz trains. Between 1931 and 1936, 16 were built at the Floridsdorf works, Vienna, and 10 more were built in 1938–9 after the German annexation of Austria. These were built with German (DRG) style cabs and boiler fittings; like the earlier models, they were given smoke deflectors. As two-cylinder simple-expansion engines, they had Lentz oscillating cam poppet valves to operate the cylinders, and the whole class was fitted with Giesl ejector chimneys in the late 1930s.

**Boiler pressure:** 16kg/cm² (230psi)
**Cylinders:** 500x720mm (19.7x28.3in)
**Driving wheels:** 1619mm (63.8in)
**Grate area:** 3.6m² (38.75sq ft)
**Heating surface:** 170m² (1830sq ft)
**Superheater:** 52m² (560sq ft)
**Tractive effort:** 15,260kg (33,650lb)
**Total weight:** 109t (240,345lb)

**Giesl ejector-fitted No 78.614 at Seltzthal, in the Austrian Alps, in October 1966. The sandbox appears to be a wooden crate. A feedwater heating pipe leads back from the smoke-box to the water tank.**

**With more conventional boiler fittings, a Class 78 runs past narrow gauge tracks with turntables, laid for ore-carrying tubs whose cargo would be transferred to main-line waggons here.**

## CLASS 46.01 2-12-4T BULGARIAN STATE RAILWAYS (BDZ) BULGARIA: 1931

An era of modern and large-scale design began in 1930 on the BDZ. These were the largest non-articulated tank engines in the world, a class of 12 built to German design by the Cegielski works in Poland, and intended for heavy mineral traffic over mountain lines, particularly between the Pernik coalfield and the capital, Sofia. They had two outside cylinders driving the third coupled axle, which (like the fourth) had no flanges on the wheels. The leading bogie and the first coupled axle formed a Krauss-Helmholtz truck, and the sixth coupled axle was allowed a lateral

**The driver looks out at steam issuing from the injector as No 46.12 pulls slowly up-hill with a long line of empty coal waggons, on the Pernik loop near Sofia. A brake-man can be seen perched on the tenth waggon.**

movement of 25mm (1in) either way. These refinements appear to have been enough to get the locomotive safely round curves at the low operating speeds maintained. The maximum axle load was 17t (16.7 tons). The array of domes on the long boiler top held a Wagner regulator, a Wagner top-feed system, sand (two domes), and the main regulator valve. Walschaerts gear and piston valves operated the massive cylinders. Their coal capacity of 10.16t (10 tons) and water capacity, in side and back tanks, of 4000gals (4800 US gals) were greater than that of many tender locomotives. In 1943, these mammoth tanks were supplemented by class 46.13, eight three-cylinder 2-12-4Ts, built by Schwarzkopff in Berlin. Their cylinders measured 550x700mm (21.6x27.6in) and their calculated tractive effort, 29,922kg (65,966lb) was somewhat less than that of the two-cylinder engines.

**Withdrawn from service, two-cylinder engines of class 46 stand on a siding at Vakerel. Technically regarded as being in storage, some engines were kept for years, but very few ever ran again.**

**Boiler pressure:** 16kg/cm² (228psi)
**Cylinders:** 700x700mm (27.6x27.6in)
**Driving wheels:** 1340mm (52.8in)
**Grate area:** 4.9m² (52.7sq ft)
**Heating surface:** 224m² (2412sq ft)
**Superheater:** 83.9m² (903.3sq ft)
**Tractive effort:** 31,836kg (70,200lb)
**Total weight:** 149.1t (328,765lb)

## CLASS 4.1200 2-8-2T NORTHERN RAILWAY (NORD) FRANCE: 1931

**Boiler pressure:** 18.3kg/cm² (261psi)
**Cylinders:** 641x700.5mm (25.25x27.6in)
**Driving wheels:** 1548mm (61in)
**Grate area:** 3.1m² (33.4sq ft)
**Heating surface:** 166.4m² (1791.5sq ft)
**Superheater:** 45m² (484.5sq ft)
**Tractive effort:** 25,609kg (56,000lb)
**Total weight:** 104.2t (229,783lb)

Since 1910 most of the main French companies favoured the 2-8-2 tank locomotive for short-haul passenger and express suburban services. The Paris-Orleans line had an excellent version, class 141.TA, with two sand domes, of which 37 went to the Moroccan Railways in 1924–26. In 1930–31, the concept was updated on the *Est, Etat* and *Nord* lines with new designs. The *Nord* class, 141.TC in SNCF coding, built at the line's La Chapelle shops, was a high-powered machine, which on one occasion, in July 1932, took a 490t (482-ton) train from Paris to Creil, 50km (31 miles) in 30 minutes, start to stop. This class worked the last steam trains out of the *Gare du Nord*, on 12 December 1970.

**The larger French passenger tank locomotives looked every bit as much like express engines as did their tender-fitted sisters, and performance was in a comparable league.**

## CLASS FD 2-10-2 SOVIET RAILWAYS RUSSIA: 1931

In 1931, the Soviet Union (in the middle of Stalin's rapid industrialization programme) was facing a transport crisis, due to a lack of motive power. A number of strategic main lines were quickly upgraded to take locomotives of 20-ton (20.2t) axle load and this class, named for Felix Dzerzhinsky (who had reorganized the Russian railways in 1921) was designed (by engineers arrested by the OGPU secret police) to haul heavier and faster freight trains.

**FD class No 2714. The leading vehicle appears to be a train-heating car. Originally, the engine would have supplied steam heating to the train.**

**No 2714 gets its train under way. The tall, built-up chimney can be clearly seen.**

A two-cylinder simple, it shows numerous American features, including bar frames, a mechanical stoker, and thermic syphon in the firebox. In 1933, series production began at Voroshilovgrad and over 3000 were built. In the late 1950s and early 60s, around 1250 of these locomotives were transferred to China and regauged to standard gauge, as Chinese class FD.

**Boiler pressure:** 15kg/cm$^2$ (215psi)
**Cylinders:** 672x761mm (26.5x30in)
**Driving wheels:** 1497mm (59in)
**Grate area:** 7m$^2$ (76sq ft)
**Heating surface:** 294m$^2$ (3163.4sq ft)
**Superheater:** 148.1m$^2$ (1595sq ft)
**Tractive effort:** 29,251kg (64,500lb)
**Total weight:** 137t (302,085lb) (engine only)

## 240.P1 4-8-0 PARIS–ORLEANS RAILWAY (PO) FRANCE: 1932

To speed up express schedules on the Paris–Toulouse service, the PO was considering various motive power options from 1930. At the suggestion of André Chapelon, then employed in the line's research department, the former PO 4-cylinder compound 'Pacific' No 4521 was rebuilt as a 4-8-0 to his design. He had already transformed the PO 3500 class 'Pacifics'. Between October 1931 and August 1932, radical alterations were made at the Tours workshops. The new boiler came from the *Nord* 'Super-Pacific', with a long narrow Belpaire firebox, into which a Nicholson thermic syphon was incorporated. The handsome lines of the original were transformed by an accumulation of pipes, domes, pumps and cylinders into a husky-looking double-chimneyed engine of very different appearance. Inside, the changes were equally drastic.

Performance was also increased by an astonishing degree. The free steaming circuits, the draught and blast arrangements, the excellent boiler and firebox allowed the engine to develop 2984kW (4000hp) in the cylinders at a speed of 112.6kph (70mph) with a train of 584t (575 tons). A further eleven were rebuilt in 1934, followed by 25 in 1940. These had mechanical stokers. The 240P.1 could run on grades or on the flat to the kind of schedule that post-war planners devised for electric traction, and with heavier trains. It is one of the mysteries of railway life that the SNCF, when established in 1938, did not build more of these remarkable locomotives.

**The typical Chapelon look: steam-pipes and external fittings were integrated into the overall working of the machine and contributed to its performance.**

**Boiler pressure:** 20.5kg/cm$^2$ (292psi)
**Cylinders:** hp 17.3x25.6 in (mm); lp 25.2x25.6in
**Driving wheels:** 1846mm (72.75in)
**Grate area:** 3.75m$^2$ (40sq ft)
**Heating surface:** 213m$^2$ (2290sq ft)
**Superheater:** 68m$^2$ (733sq ft)
**Tractive effort:** 14,026kg (32,029lb)
**Total weight:** 110.7t (244,160lb)

## CLASS 85 2-10-2T GERMAN STATE RAILWAYS (DRG) GERMANY: 1932

The German designation 1'E1'h3 describes this three-cylinder superheated 2-10-2. It was a standard engine, sharing numerous parts with other standard DRG classes. In all, 10 were built, by Henschel of Kassel. They had the standard German Heusinger valve gear, with the inside cylinder, which drove the second coupled wheels, worked from an eccentric on the third coupled wheels. At each end, a Krauss-Helmholtz bogie linked the pony wheels to the end coupled wheels, enabling the engine to run at 80kph (50mph) in either direction. A powerful type for use in hilly country, all were first based at Freiburg in the Black Forest. They were cut up in 1961, except for one, on static display at the Konstanz engineering school.

**On the Deutsche Reichsbahn, a Class 85. Small numbers of several 'standard' DRG classes were built; some were never built at all.**

**Boiler pressure:** 14kg/cm$^2$ (200psi)
**Cylinders:** 600x660mm (23.6x26in)
**Driving wheels:** 1400mm (55in)
**Grate area:** 3.5m$^2$ (37.7sq ft)
**Heating surface:** 195.8m$^2$ (2108sq ft)
**Superheater:** 72.5m$^2$ (780.5sq ft)
**Tractive effort:** 20,299kg (44,759lb)
**Total weight:** 133.6t (294,588lb)

## CLASS K 4-8-4 NEW ZEALAND RAILWAYS (NZR) NEW ZEALAND: 1932

Apart from a 1065mm (3ft 6in) wide gauge, the New Zealand railways were restricted by a tight loading gauge, with a maximum height of 3502mm (11ft 6in) and width of 2589mm (8ft 6in). The impressive class K was a triumph of design, shoe-horning unprecedented power into a narrow space. Trainloads and traffic requirements needed something bigger than the Ab 'Pacifics' on certain trains, and the K class was designed for these services. A 4-8-2 had been first planned, but a 4-wheel truck under the firebox was needed to keep the maximum axle loading to a modest 14.2t (14 tons). Thirty were built at the NZR Hutt Workshops between 1932 and 1936, working mostly on the Main Trunk Auckland–Wellington line. Many up-to-date features were incorporated, including power reversing gear, a

**Class Kb No 970 moves on to a crossing loop on the Christchurch–Greymouth 'Midland' line, linking the east and west of South Island. The train is largely composed of double-deck sheep waggons.**

mechanical lubricator, and an air-operated fire-door. They ran both passenger and freight services, maintaining 80kph (50mph) with 508t (500 ton) trains, and 48kph (30mph) with 1016t (1000-ton) trains on level track. The normal maximum service speed was 88.5kph (55mph) which was often well exceeded. Ka and Kb types followed, with modifications including roller bearings throughout; Ka types were built up to 1950 and there were 71 assorted Ks in total.

**The final version: Ka class No 942 at Huntley, North Island; the Ka locomotives had a redesigned front end and 'skyline' casing.**

**Boiler pressure:** 14kg/cm² (200psi)
**Cylinders:** 508x660mm (20x26in)
**Driving wheels:** 1370mm (54in)
**Grate area:** 4.4m² (47.7sq ft)
**Heating surface:** 179.5m² (1933sq ft)
**Superheater:** 45m² (485sq ft)
**Tractive effort:** 14,850kg (32,740lb)
**Total weight:** 88t (194,208lb) (engine only)

## CLASS 464 4-8-4T CZECHOSLOVAK STATE RAILWAYS (CSD) CZECHOSLOVAKIA: 1933

Locomotive building in what was to become Czechoslovakia began with the establishment of the PCM works in 1900. After the formation of the Czech Republic in 1918, the industry expanded considerably. Skoda, already a major industrial concern, set up locomotive works in the early 1920s. The other major manufacturer, CKD, was an amalgamation of PCM and two other smaller firms, Breitfeld & Danek, and Emil Kolben. Naturally enough, the CSD embarked on a home-production policy. Its method of steady development through successive types is shown by this powerful tank type. In 1924, the class 455.1 2-8-0 was introduced, itself a development of an earlier six-coupled design. In turn, it became the basis of a large 2-8-4 tank locomotive, Class 456.0, dating from 1927. At the time, this was the most powerful tank engine on the CSD, and proved very successful in service; some lasted into the 1970s. In

**The imposing front end of a beautifully maintained and cleaned preserved class 464 locomotive, fitted with German Witte-type smoke deflectors, in September 1980.**

**A more workaday 464 leaves the shed for service before the elimination of steam in Czechoslovakia. This engine is fitted with a Giesl ejector.**

1933, an enlarged version was produced as class 464, a heavier and more powerful engine but with a smaller water and coal capacity than the 455. It was a two-cylinder, simple-expansion design, with Heusinger valve gear, and inside bearings on all axles. Like all Czech designs, it had a wide firebox to burn low-grade lignite 'brown coal' from the Bohemian coalfield. At first, only 3 of the type were constructed, though by 1938 the class numbered 76, with larger superheaters and smoke deflectors added from the fourth onwards (deflectors were also fitted to Nos 001–3). They were built by Skoda in Plzen and CKD in Prague.

Though Czechoslovak railways inherited, and often rebuilt, many locomotives from the Austrian and Hungarian tradition, its locomotive practice in the 1920s and 30s was independent and distinctive. The country's location in central Europe meant its engineers were familiar with work in Germany and Russia, as well as British, French and American developments. The plain smokebox doors with flared and lipped chimneys had a British air. The last nine to be built had Russian Trofimov-type piston valves, and Swedish SKF roller bearings on the front and rear bogie axles. Development continued after 1945, though Czechoslovakia was turned into a Soviet satellite state from 1948. Steel fireboxes replaced the original copper ones, and larger superheaters were fitted. Many of the class acquired pneumatically operated firedoors and Giesl double blast ejectors and chimneys: indeed, tthis latter feature was almost as common in Czechoslovakia as in its native Austria.

Heavy passenger trains, often international expresses, and some relatively short main lines made the eight-coupled tank engine an appropriate one for express work. Indeed, the last steam locomotives to be built for CSD would be 4-8-4 express tank engines, of the 464.2 class, in 1955. The 464.0s were employed on main-line express services on mountainous routes, notably on that between Chomutov and Cheb in the north-west. Some were based at Klatov, south of Plzen, but others of the class also operated in Slovakia. During World War II, 15 were commandeered by the German DRG, but were retrieved in 1945. In the 1970s, the 464s began to be withdrawn, and the last in service was withdrawn from Klatovy shed in 1981. Along with the first one, No. 464.001, it has been preserved.

Further development of the 4-8-4T began in 1940, when CKD built two engines classed 464.1. Of almost identical appearance to the 464.0, they had a boiler pressure of $18kg/cm^2$ (256psi), cylinders of 500mm (19.7in) diameter, and a large-bore superheater. Wartime conditions put a stop to further work, and after 1945, attention was concentrated on developing the already-built 464.0 class.

**Boiler pressure:** $13kg/cm^2$ (185psi)
**Cylinders:** 600x720mm (23.6x28.3in)
**Driving wheels:** 1624mm (64in)
**Grate area:** $4.38m^2$ (47.1sq ft)
**Heating surface:** $194m^2$ (2088.7sq ft)
**Superheater:** $62.1m^2$ (668.6sq ft)
**Tractive effort:** 17,560kg (38,720lb)
**Total weight:** 114.5t (252,472lb)

## MALLET TYPE R441 0-4-4-0T ERITREAN RAILWAYS (FE) ERITREA: 1933

The FE used Mallet tank engines on its 950mm (37.4in) gauge track which climbed 2175m (7135ft) in 117.5km (73 miles) from Massawa to Asmara, a 10-hour trip. The first were compounds from Maffei in 1910. This later class of 15, built in Italy, were simple-expansion engines, 10 with Walschaerts valve gear and five with Caprotti poppet valve gear. A further eight engines supplied by Ansaldo in 1938 reverted to compound expansion. In 1954, only one of the R441s that had been converted to compound, was still working, though five of the 1911 vintage were still in steam.

**In typical scrubland terrain, an 0-4-4-0 'Mallet' of the FE pulls a low-level flat car, probably for permanent-way maintenance equipment.**

**Boiler pressure:** 12kg/$cm^2$ (171psi)
**Cylinders:** 330x500mm (13x19.7in)
**Driving wheels:** 900mm (35.5in)
**Grate area:** not known
**Heating surface:** not known
**Tractive effort:** 11,636kg (25,660lb)
**Total weight:** 46t (101,430lb) (engine only)

## 'PRINCESS ROYAL' AND 'DUCHESS' CLASSES 4-6-2 GREAT BRITAIN: 1933

The years between 1933 and 1939 saw great advances in power and performance in British express locomotives – as illustrated by the LMS 'Pacifics', all designed and built under the control of W.A. (later Sir William) Stanier. The first two 'Princess Royals' were introduced in 1933 (Nos 6200 and 6201) and a further 10 were built in 1935, all at Crewe works. Experience with the prototypes led to several modifications. All had a taper boiler, 1903.5mm (6ft 3in) at its widest; small wheel splashers were needed to fit the big wheels and big boiler into the loading gauge. All were 4-cylinder simple-expansion engines, the inner cylinders driving the first coupled wheels, the outer ones driving the second pair. Each cylinder had an independent set of Walschaerts valve gear, and the outside cylinders covered the rear wheel of the front bogie. This bogie had inside bearings and the pony wheels had outside bearings. As in the 'Royal Scots', the boiler fittings were notably low, giving the engines a long, smooth profile. Most of the improvements between 1933 and 1935 related to increased superheating and improved steam passages. The LMS designers had observed with keen interest the work of André Chapelon in France, but the LMS had also developed its own considerable expertise in metallurgy, which was of great value in producing high-performance locomotives while reducing the need for expensive maintenance and replacement parts. The small tenders of the first two engines were replaced by standard large LMS tenders with capacity for 10.16t (10 tons) of coal and 4000 gals (4800 US gals) of water. All the main lines were well

**'Pacific' No 46229 *Duchess of Hamilton*, with the headboard for the 'Caledonian' London–Glasgow express, at Steamtown, Carnforth, on 10 April 1982.**

***Duchess of Hamilton* crosses Birkett Common, on the former Midland main line from Leeds to Carlisle, with the charter 'Cumbrian Mountain Pullman', on 27 February 1982.**

supplied with water-troughs, and the coal capacity was just enough for the London-Glasgow run.

Competition on the main London–Scotland lines was fierce in the 1930s, and for the first time there were also air services to contend with: the railway was no longer the speediest form of travel. In 1937, the LMS brought out a revised, streamlined 'Pacific' design for the new 'Coronation' express; and this, slightly modified, was also the basis of the non-streamlined 'Duchess' class of 1938. The principal difference between these and the 1935 engines was a substantial increase in evaporative heating surface from [of?] 215m$^2$ (2314sq ft) and in superheater area from 60.6 m$^2$ (652sq ft); this was accompanied by a 76mm (3in) increase in driving wheel diameter and an additional 0.46 m$^2$ (5sq ft) of grate area. The outside valve gear also operated the inside cylinders through rocker arms, and the outside cylinders were placed just ahead of the rear bogie wheel. Due to the employment of nickel steel, the weight increase over the 'Princess Royals' was only 748kg (1650lb). The cab fronts were angled to improve night vision, and the new engines had steam-operated coal pushers to help in the fireman's arduous task, and some were fitted with Kylchap double chimneys. The streamlining of the 'Coronation' engines, always something of a public-relations exercise, was removed between 1945 and 1949. Altogether, 38 'Duchesses' were built, up to 1948.

Theywere formidable performers. The maximum speed recorded was 183.4kph (114mph), by 6220 *Coronation*, hauling 274.3t (270 tons), on 29 June 1937; the same engine on the return trip ran the 254km (158 miles) from Crewe to London Euston at an average speed of 128kph (79.5mph) with 160kph (100mph) again being exceeded. They regularly ran the 645km (401 mile) London–Glasgow journey at an average of 93kph (58mph), including a crew-change stop. On a 614t (604 ton) test train in February 1939, No 6234 *Duchess of Abercorn* developed a maximum indicated kW in the cylinders of 2486 (3333hp), probably a record for any British locomotive. They worked on main-line expresses until 1964. Three of the 'Duchesses' have been preserved. Dimensions given are those of the non-streamlined engines of 1938.

**Boiler pressure:** 17.5kg/cm$^2$ (250psi)
**Cylinders:** 419x711mm (4x16.5x28in)
**Driving wheels:** 2057.5mm (81in)
**Grate area:** 4.6 m$^2$ (50sq ft)
**Heating surface:** 260 m$^2$ (2807sq ft)
**Superheater:** 79.5 m$^2$ (856sq ft)
**Tractive effort:** 18,140kg (40,000lb)
**Total weight:** 164t (362,000lb)

## CLASS YA-01 4-8-2+2-8-4 SOVIET RAILWAYS — RUSSIA: 1933

Russian railways had used articulated Fairlie and Mallet engines quite extensively in the pre-Revolutionary period.

In 1932, the Soviet Railways ordered a Garratt-type articulated locomotive from Beyer Peacock of Manchester, England, for testing on 2540t (2500-ton) coal trains. This was the largest steam locomotive ever built in Europe, though it was kept to a maximum axle load of 20.3t (20 tons).

Shipped to Leningrad, it was tested on the Sverdlovsk-Chelyabinsk line in the rough and demanding terrain of the South Ural mountains.

Allegedly because its maintenance requirements did not suit the Russian operating conditions, the Ya remained a single-engine class, and the prototype was broken up in 1937.

**Boiler pressure:** 14kg/cm$^2$ (220psi)
**Cylinders:** 568.5x741mm (22.4x29.2in)
**Driving wheels:** 1497mm (59in)
**Grate area:** 7.98m$^2$ (86sq ft)
**Heating surface:** 337.1m$^2$ (3630sq ft)
**Superheater:** 90m$^2$ (970sq ft)
**Tractive effort:** 35,692kg (78,700lb)
**Total weight:** 270.2t (595,840lb)

## 4-8-0 DELAWARE & HUDSON RAILROAD (D&H) — USA: 1933

Under its President, L.H. Loree, the D&H pursued a progressive design and maintenance policy. At this time railways in several countries were experimenting with very high pressure.

This locomotive, named for Loree, was the third in a D&H series begun in 1924. It was a four-cylinder triple-expansion compound, with front and rear cylinders driving the same set of coupled wheels. The high-pressure cylinder on the right of the cab discharged to the intermediate-pressure cylinder on the left, and the steam finally was piped to the two front low-pressure cylinders. Rotary cam poppet valves were also fitted, and the firebox had over-fire air jets to improve combustion. A six-wheel rear bogie on the tender was fitted with a booster engine. With so many innovative features, it unsurprisingly remained a one-off. Fortunately the D & H also possessed a stud of well-designed and maintained conventional locomotives.

**Boiler pressure:** 35kg/cm$^2$ (500psi)
**Cylinders:** hp 507.6x812mm (20x32in); intermediate 698x812mm (27.5x32in); lp 837.5x812mm (33x32in)
**Driving wheels:** 1599mm (63in)
**Grate area:** 7m$^2$ (75.8sq ft)
**Heating surface:** 311m$^2$ (3351sq ft)
**Superheater:** 99.9m$^2$ (1076sq ft)
**Tractive effort:** 53412kg (108,000lb)
**Total weight:** (t) (engine only)

## CLASS KF1 4-8-4 CHINESE GOVERNMENT RAILWAYS — CHINA: 1934

**Boiler pressure:** 15.5kg/cm$^2$ (220psi)
**Cylinders:** 530x750mm (20.8x29.5in)
**Driving wheels:** 1751mm (69in)
**Grate area:** 6.3m$^2$ (67.8sq ft)
**Heating surface:** 277.6m$^2$ (2988.8sq ft)
**Superheater:** 100m$^2$ (1076sq ft)
**Tractive effort:** 14,930kg (32,920lb)
**Total weight:** 118.9t (engine only)

**The KF1s worked on main lines into the late 1970s, latterly stabled at the Changchun steam shed, which retained its coaling tower until 1996. Apart from the York one, an example is preserved at the Beijing Railway Museum.**

China's only 4-8-4 type was built by the Vulcan Foundry at Manchester, England; the class totaled 24. They were long two-cylinder engines, 30.8m (101ft 1in) including the bogie tender, built on bar frames, with the firebox supported by an outside-framed bogie. The original valve gear was an adaptation of Walschaerts' similar to the American Baker gear.

The class was used in express passenger service, though despite its imposing appearance it was not particularly powerful for a 4-8-4. No KF17 is preserved at the British National Railway Museum in York.

## CLASS 05 4-6-4 GERMAN STATE RAILWAYS (DRG) — GERMANY: 1934

A class of three, built by Borsig and intended for the haulage of light trains at very high speeds, the 05s showed Germany's steam engineers responding to the new fast diesel railcars. The DRG had asked for a locomotive to pull a 250t (246-ton) train at 150kph (93mph) in normal service on level track, with a maximum operating speed of 175kph (108mph). Such a train would match the performance of the diesel railcars working between Berlin, Hamburg and Frankfurt, but with much greater passenger capacity and comfort. (The thought process was exactly that of the LNER in Britain at the same time). Three simple-expansion cylinders drove the first coupled wheels (inside) and the second pair (outside), and three sets of Walschaerts valve gear were provided. The boilers were of the same diameter as the 01 Pacifics, but made of molybdenum steel plates, and the first two engines were bar-framed. The third was different in many respects, built originally as a cab-front engine, to run on pulverized coal fuel. All three were almost completely enclosed in a streamlined casing, which was painted in a red livery with a black, gold-lined band at footplate level. A platform-level view of one of these approaching at speed would have been awe-inspiring. Double brake blocks were fitted to all wheels except the front wheels of the bogie, which had single blocks only, at the trailing end. In every detail, 05.001 and 002 were thoroughly planned and built to sustain high speeds over long distances. Surprisingly perhaps, the copper-lined firebox was hand-fired: but it was an experimental engine, and careful measurement of coal input was a necessary part of the testing process. The tender was a large, seven-axle one, mounted on a four-wheel bogie with outside bearings, and three fixed axles with outside bearings set in the frame. Its capacity was 10t (9.8 tons) of coal and 8200gals (9848 US gals) of water. Germany did not use water troughs.

On 11 May, 1936, during a test run with a 197t (194 ton) train, No 05.002 took the world record for steam with a speed of 200.4kph (124.5mph). This was achieved on virtually level track, a point not ignored by the Germans when the British class A4 'Pacific' *Mallard* two years later snatched the record by doing 201.2kph (125mph) on a 1 in 200 falling gradient. The 05.001 and 002 were magnificent engines, and achieved other fast runs, but if a production run been made, it would have been difficult to adjust their full speed potential to the other traffic on a busy main line like Berlin–Hamburg. This problem was not resolved until Japan and France began building dedicated high-speed lines in the 1970s. Nevertheless, from October 1936 until the outbreak of war in 1939, they operated Europe's fastest scheduled steam service – 2hrs 24mins for the 286km (178.1 mile) Hamburg–Berlin route, requiring an average speed of 118.7kph (74.mph), which implied long stretches run at substantially higher speeds.

In 1950, 05.001 and 002 were rebuilt by Krauss-Maffei, and the streamlining was removed. No. 003, which had not been a success and had been rebuilt conventionally in 1944-45, was also rebuilt. All three then participated in passenger express duties on the *Deutsche Bundesbahn* (DB), until 1957. No 05.001 has been preserved, with its streamlined casing partly restored, but leaving the wheels and motion visible.

**Boiler pressure:** 20kg/cm$^2$ (284psi)
**Cylinders:** 450x660mm (17.75x26in)
**Driving wheels:** 2300mm (90.5in)
**Grate area:** 4.71m$^2$ (51sq ft)
**Heating surface:** 256m$^2$ (2750sq ft)
**Superheater:** 90m$^2$ (976sq ft)
**Tractive effort:** 14,870kg (32,788lb)
**Total weight:** 213t (475,064lb)

## 2-6-4T LONDON MIDLAND & SCOTTISH RAILWAY (LMS) GREAT BRITAIN: 1934

Built at Derby, this was the LMS's standard large suburban tank type. A 3-cylinder version was built in 1934, but this two-cylinder engine (built from 1935 with 15% greater superheating surface) inspired later developments, and it served major cities in LMS territory. Intensive use was required, and mechanical lubrication of the pistons, piston valves, and piston rod packings was introduced. Hardened manganese-molybdenum steel was used for the coupling and connecting rods. It carried 3.5 tons of coal and 2000gals (2400US) of water: water pick-up gear extended its operating range.

**Former LMS 2-6-4T as British Railways No.45128, taking on coal at Edinburgh's St Margarets depot. A partially missing cover exposes the top-feed's clack valve.**

**Boiler pressure:** 14kg/cm$^2$ (200psi)
**Cylinders:** 497x660mm (19.6x26in)
**Driving wheels:** 1751mm (69in)
**Grate area:** 2.5 m$^2$ (26.7 sq ft)
**Heating surface:** 126.8m$^2$ (1366sq ft)
**Superheater:** 22.75m$^2$ (245sq ft)
**Tractive effort:** 9886kg (21,800lb)
**Total weight:** 96.8t (196,000lb)

# Class P2 2-8-2 London & North Eastern Railway (LNER) Great Britain: 1934

Britain's only eight-coupled passenger express engine was designed and built at Doncaster in accordance with the LNER 'horses for courses' policy to work heavy express trains between Edinburgh and Aberdeen, a main line more steeply graded than the Edinburgh-London route. Two prototypes, both 3-cylinder simples, explored different valve arrangements; the first, No 2001 *Cock o' the North*, having camshaft-operated poppet valves; the second, *Earl Marischal*, having Gresley's conjugated Walschaerts valve gear; and this was also used on the other four members of the class, built in 1936. Two forms of streamlining were also tried, settling on one similar to that designed in 1935 for the A4 'Pacific'. These were the first British engines to have the Kylchap double-blast chimney. There was considerable liaison between Gresley and Chapelon, and No 2001 was sent to France, for testing at the Vitry plant. Imposing though they were, the P2s showed none of the French compounds' economy, and substantially less power. With a grate at the maximum size for hand-firing, they were also heavy coal users, requiring the fireman to shovel in about 36kg (80lbs) per mile, or over 4.06t (4 tons) on a 161km (100-mile) journey. They suffered from wear in the axle-boxes and hot bearings were common. During World War II, and following the death of Sir Nigel Gresley, all six were rebuilt as rather ungainly 'Pacifics', A2/2.

**A view from above, showing the Kylchap double chimney and the streamlined casing of No 2001 in its original form. The whistle is in front of the chimney.**

**No 2001 *Cock o' the North* in original condition, on its first visit to Kings Cross Station, London, in May 1934.**

**Boiler pressure:** 15.5kg/cm$^2$ (220psi)
**Cylinders:** 533x660mm (21x26in)
**Driving wheels:** 1880mm (74in)
**Grate area:** 4.6m$^2$ (50sq ft)
**Heating surface:** 324.m$^2$ (3490sq ft)
**Superheater:** 59m$^2$ (635sq ft)
**Tractive effort:** 19,955kg (44,000lb)
**Total weight:** 111.7t (246,400lb)

## 2-8-2T GREAT WESTERN RAILWAY (GWR) GREAT BRITAIN: 1934

Steam locomotives are potentially long-lived and all railway companies shared the urge to make the most of their potential, if necessary by rebuilding. This was a typical example, in which the GWR 4200 and 5200 2-8-0T classes, built to pull coal trains, were adapted from 1934 to 2-8-2T and transferred to slow main-line goods work following a decline in coal exports from Wales. The boiler was a GWR standard used on other types as well, and the truck inserted beneath the extended bunker was also of standard type.

**Ex-GWR 2-8-2 No 7238, extended from a 2-8-0T, stands at Oxley locomotive shed, Wolverhampton, in May 1952.**

Thus a useful engine was kept in service, at far less cost than a new one.

**Boiler pressure:** 14kg/cm² (200psi)
**Cylinders:** 482x761mm (19x30in)
**Driving wheels:** 1408mm (55.5in)
**Grate area:** 1.9m² (20.5sq ft)
**Heating surface:** 137m² (1479sq ft)
**Superheater:** 17.8m² (192sq ft)
**Tractive effort:** 13,288kg (29,300lb)
**Total weight:** 94t (207,424lb)

## CLASS 5P5F 4-6-0 LONDON MIDLAND & SCOTTISH RAILWAY (LMS) GREAT BRITAIN: 1934

**The original form of the 'Black Five' in 1934, with domeless boiler, painted in LMS black.**

From the early 1930s, the LMS followed a policy of locomotive standardization. Its philosophy of 'scrap and build' was not shared by all British engineers – on the LNER, engines continued to be designed for specific routes. Later designated 5MT (mixed traffic), this was the most numerous tender class to run on British rails, with 842 built by 1948, and it was crucial to the company's plan. This general utility 'pool' engine was meant to be worked by any driver over any part of the LMS system. Designed under the auspices of W.A. (later Sir William) Stanier, it had the coned boiler design with Belpaire firebox that he had brought from

**Under the scrutiny of three schoolboys in the 1950s, No 44870, with domed boiler, stands at Crewe with a south-bound express. The 2a code indicates Rugby as its home depot (this coding system was introduced in 1950).**

the Great Western, and two simple-expansion outside cylinders, operated by piston valves with outside Walschaerts valve gear. Large piston valves of 254mm (10in) diameter helped their free-steaming quality. The original version had a domeless boiler, with the regulator fitted to the super-heater header in the smoke-box, and a top feed system mounted on the second ring; later examples retained the top feed, but were built with domed boilers. From 1935, a larger number of super-heating elements were fitted, 24 as opposed to 14, producing an increase of almost 9.3m$^2$ (100sq ft) of heating surface; from 1938, this was increased again to 28. The design also promoted easy maintenance: the running plate was above the wheels, and the cab, similar to that of the 5XP 'Jubilee' class, was more spacious than in most British locomotives. But there was no electric lighting, and a manual screw reverser was fitted. The first order was for 70, 50 from the Vulcan Foundry and 20 from the LMS's Crewe Works. Later they were also built at the Derby and Horwich works, and by Armstrong Whitworth in Newcastle. A popular engine with crews and maintenance teams, it accelerated the scrapping of older types. The chief duties of the 'Class 5s' were on medium-distance passenger and freight trains, but they often ran express services. The first 10 were sent to Perth in Scotland, where their hill-climbing abilities were welcomed on the former Highland main line. Here they operated everything other than local services, running double-headed on the heavier trains like the Inverness–London 'Royal Highlander' sleeper. Loading up to 660t (650 tons), this was one of the few British passenger trains to be regularly triple-engined, with a banking engine provided at the rear for the northbound ascent of Druimuachdar Pass from Blair Atholl, 24km (15 miles) with a maximum gradient of 1 in 70. But the 'Class 5's' were an equally familiar sight on the Somerset & Dorset line in southwest England, the Central Wales line, and at very many points in between.

The engines had a sturdy appearance conveying something of their reliability. To the end of 1939, they averaged 233,340km (145,000 miles) between general repairs; in the 1950s, this increased to 257,500km (160,000 miles). Despite a reputation for being rough riders at speed, they were 'clocked' on numerous occasions at speeds in excess of 145kph (90mph) and were capable of sustained speeds around 120kph (75mph). In 1936, a non-stop run from Crewe to Euston was timed at 254km (158 miles) in 159.5 minutes with a 386t (380-ton) train. In 1947–48, 30 of the class were fitted experimentally with various permutations of Caprotti valve gear, double chimneys and roller bearings. The first two features were not adopted on the British standard 4-6-0s, which were in most respects a second-generation of the 'Class 5', but roller bearings became standard. All were fitted with a standard LMS 6-wheel tender with high turned-in sides, a capacity for 9.15t (9 tons) of coal and 4000 gallons (4800US) of water, and water pick-up apparatus.

The class operated until the final days of steam on British Railways, in 1968, hauling the last scheduled steam passenger expresses in Britain. There are 15 preserved.

**Steam pressure:** 15.75kg/cm$^2$ (225psi)
**Cylinders:** 470x711mm (18.5x28in)
**Driving wheels:** 1830mm (72in)
**Grate area:** 2.6m$^2$ (28.7sq ft)
**Heating surface:** 135.6 m$^2$ (1460sq ft)
**Superheater:** 33.3 m$^2$ (359sq ft)
**Tractive effort:** 11,790kg (26,000lb)
**Total weight:** 72.1 tonnes (159,040lb)

**In LMS livery, No 5248, one of the last to be built, provides its own vacuum-power to the turntable at Holyhead, terminus for boat trains to Dun Laoghaire in Ireland.**

## SATA I CLASS 2-10-2T KOREAN GOVERNMENT RAILWAYS (KGR) KOREA: 1934

Twenty-four of these powerful tank locomotives were built in Japan between 1934 and 1939, 14 by Nippon Sharyo and 10 by Keijo. They were intended for heavy short-range freight work, chiefly in marshalling yards.

Following the division of the peninsular in 1947, eight were in South Korea and 16 in the North. The southern engines were all derelict by the early 1950s, but the fate of those in North Korea is still not known outside of the country.

The locomotives in the first batch were numbered 1801–1810 by the KGR. In 1951, American Don Ross, the expert on Korean steam, discovered four engines of Class SATA 1 in a partially dismantled state at Susaek, once an important marshalling yard on the main north-south line, north of Seoul, but then used as a dumping ground for engines made redundant by the Korean War.

**Boiler pressure:** 14kg/$cm^2$ (199psi)
**Cylinders:** 560x710mm (22x28in)
**Driving wheels:** 1450mm (57in)
**Grate area:** 4.75$m^2$ (51sq ft)
**Heating surface:** not known
**Superheater:** not known
**Tractive effort:** 19,860kg (40,200lb)
**Total weight:** 110t (242,550lb) (engine only)

## AA 20-1 4-14-4 SOVIET RAILWAYS RUSSIA: 1934

As a rule, Russian locomotive engineering was eminently practical, and even experimental designs were entered into in a spirit of serious scientific enquiry. Consequently the one and only class AA20, the largest non-articulated locomotive in Europe, and with the longest rigid wheel-base ever built, was something of an embarrassment. Named after its sponsor, Andrei Andreyev, it was intended to demonstrate the maximum freight locomotive dimensions and performance within the Russian gauge, with the recently increased maximum axle loading of 20 tons. Numerous engineers opposed the proposal, saying that 2-10-2s would be far more useful. The original design was for a 2-14-4, to be built by Krupps in Germany, but a front bogie was substituted and it was built at the Voroshilovgrad works. Although intended for coal trains from the Donbass region to Moscow, it never entered revenue-earning service. A publicity visit to Moscow was made in January 1935, and the engine was duly hailed as a triumph of Soviet technology. A veil was drawn over its further activities, and it was three decades before the Russian technical press were able to admit that the AA20 was a complete failure. It spread the tracks, damaged points, and was excessively prone to derailment. At some point, without publicity, it was scrapped.

**Boiler pressure:** 17kg/$cm^2$ (242psi)
**Cylinders:** 741x807mm (29.2x31.8in)
**Driving wheels:** 1599mm (63in)
**Grate area:** 12$m^2$ (129sq ft)
**Heating surface:** 448$m^2$ (4823sq ft)
**Superheater:** 174$m^2$ (1873.4sq ft)
**Tractive effort:** 40,286kg (88,830lb)
**Total weight:** 211.3t (465,920lb) (engine only)

## CLASS S-3 2-8-4 NEW YORK CHICAGO & ST LOUIS RAILROAD (NICKEL PLATE ROAD) USA: 1934

Lima Works built 70 of the S-3 'Berkshire' for the Nickel Plate Road, essentially similar to a range of others built during the 1930s for other lines with heavy freight traffic, all two-cylinder simples, fitted with the US standard Type E superheater. Differences in dimension and detail were relatively small. Some types had trailer boosters. Engines of this configuration were the backbone of general long-distance freight. They normally ran with 12-wheel tenders with a capacity around 16,600gals (20,000US) of water and 22.35t (22 tons) of coal. The Nickel Plate's first 15, of 1934, were classed as S-1. Over a fifteen-year period, virtually nothing changed in the design of the S-3: for the line's purpose, a sufficient point of steam development had been reached. Forty were built up to 1943, then 10 S-2s followed in 1944 and 10 S-3s in 1949. Dimensions are for S-3.

**Boiler pressure:** 17kg/$cm^2$ (245psi)
**Cylinders:** 634.5x863mm (25x34in)
**Driving wheels:** 69in (1751mm)
**Grate area:** 8.4$m^2$ (90.3sq ft)
**Heating surface:** 443.2$m^2$ (4772sq ft)
**Superheater:** 179.4$m^2$ (1932sq ft)
**Tractive effort:** 29,070kg (64,100lb)
**Total weight:** 201.5t (444,290lb) (engine only)

## CLASS 1 4-6-2 BELGIAN NATIONAL RAILWAYS (SNCB) BELGIUM: 1935

Designed by M. Notesse of the SNCB, and built in Belgium by Cockerill, this was among the heaviest European Pacific types, with a maximum axle load of 23.7t (23.3 tons). In accordance with contemporary fashion, the front end was partly air-smoothed. Four simple-expansion cylinders were set in line, the inside ones driving the leading coupled wheels; the outside ones the second pair. Kylchap double blast pipes discharged through a Legein-type chimney, and ACFI feed water pumps and heaters were fitted. The class, totalling 35, was used on the heaviest main line expresses. One is preserved.

**Boiler pressure:** 18kg/$cm^2$ (260psi)
**Cylinders:** 420x720mm (16.5x28.4in)
**Driving wheels:** 1980mm (78in)
**Grate area:** 4.9$m^2$ (52.75sq ft)
**Heating surface:** 234$m^2$ (2527sq ft)
**Superheater:** 111.6$m^2$ (1202sq ft)
**Tractive effort:** 9935kg (22,000lb)
**Total weight:** 126t (277,760lb)

**The front end design of the Belgian Class 1 is modelled on that of the British P2 2-8-2 of a year earlier.**

## CLASS JF 'STANDARD' 2-8-2 SOUTH MANCHURIA RAILWAY CHINA: 1935

Until the establishment of a Communist government, Chinese locomotives were imported, chiefly from the USA, Britain and Germany. Fom 1932, after the Japanese occupation of Manchuria, Japanese designs predominated, though these were usually based on American originals. After 1945, Japanese practice prevailed, to be replaced by Soviet influence in the 1950s. JF was the Chinese notation for a 2-8-2, and this very numerous 'standard' type, later named the 'Liberation' class, was based on an Alco 'Mikado' supplied in 1918 to the South Manchurian Railway. Over 2500 were built between 1935 and 1957, at first in Japan at several shops, including Kawasaki, Kisha Seizo Kaisha, Hitachi and Nippon Sharya, later in China at Dalian and Qingdao. In the 1930s, independent Chinese railway companies imported various other 2-8-2s, all denoted as sub-classes of JF. From 1957, a modified standard version was built at the Chinese works, of identical main dimensions but with longer piston valve travel – 161mm (6.3in) as against 152mm (6in). From 1958, the JS 2-8-2, built to a Soviet design, superseded it. But the 'standard' JF locomotives continued to work freight over most of the network. They were two-cylinder simple-expansion engines, with Walschaerts valve gear actuated by piston valves. Many were adapted for shunting, with sloping-backed tenders.

**Boiler pressure:** 14kg/cm$^2$ (200psi)
**Cylinders:** 580x710mm (22.8x28in)
**Driving wheels:** 1370mm (54in)
**Grate area:** 5.1m$^2$ (54.9sq ft)
**Heating surface:** 209.4m$^2$ (2254sq ft)
**Superheater:** 64.9m$^2$ (698.7sq ft)
**Tractive effort:** 20,737kg (45,725lb)
**Total weight:** 103.8t (228,879lb) (engine only)

## SERIES 60 2-4-2T LÜBECK-BÜCHEN RAILWAY (LBE) GERMANY: 1935

In the 1930s, Germany built some remarkable high-speed tank engines. The LBE was taken into the DRG in January 1936, by which time the two Henschel-built streamlined engines of this class were running the 84km (52 mile) Hamburg–Travemünde service in one hour, with a stop at Lübeck. Fast acceleration was essential, and they went from 0 to 120kph (75mph) in 5.5 minutes. It was a specially fitted push-pull train; on the return trip, the driver sat in a cab in the front coach with electrically powered links to the controls. He communicated with the fireman by telephone. A third engine, with some modifications, was also built. These engines were an important step towards the 4-6-6T 'super-tanks' of 1939, but the diesel multiple-unit was to end the line of development.

**Boiler pressure:** 16kg/cm$^2$ (228psi)
**Cylinders:** 400x660mm (15.8x26in)
**Driving wheels:** 1980mm (78in)
**Grate area:** 1.4m$^2$ (15sq ft)
**Heating surface:** 75.4m$^2$ (812sq ft)
**Superheater:** 26m$^2$ (280sq ft)
**Tractive effort:** 7310kg (16,120lb)
**Total weight:** 69t (152,145lb)

## 8F 2-8-0 LONDON MIDLAND & SCOTTISH RAILWAY (LMS) GREAT BRITAIN: 1935

**Preserved 8F 2-8-0 No 48305 nowadays more often hauls passenger trains than freight, operating on 'heritage' lines throughout England.**

The typical LMS 'look' of standardized designs was continued in this, the company's main-line heavy freight locomotive. The first batch were classified 7F, but later ones were uprated to 8F. Early in World War II, the British Ministry of Supply selected this as the standard engine for military use at home and abroad. They were fitted with Westinghouse brake pumps to the right of the smokebox, to work air-braked stock.

By 1945, over 700 had been built, and virtually every locomotive works in the country had contributed some. Many remained in the Middle East after the war, and some were still working in Turkey 20 years after steam was finished in Britain. Experience with these contributed to the remarkable series 61 tank engines of 1939.

**Boiler pressure:** 15.75kg/cm² (225psi)
**Cylinders:** 470x711mm (18.5x28in)
**Driving wheels:** 1435mm (56.5in)
**Grate area:** 2.6 m² (28.7sq ft)
**Heating surface:** 136m² (1463sq ft)
**Superheater:** 21.8m² (235.25sq ft)
**Tractive effort:** 14,965kg (33,000lb)
**Total weight:** 72.1t (159,040lb)

## A4 4-6-2 LONDON & NORTH EASTERN RAILWAY (LNER) GREAT BRITAIN: 1935

Even without its claim to the world speed record for steam, the A4 would be among the most notable of locomotives, not only for its distinctive wedge-fronted shape but also for the quality of its performance over 30 years of main-line service.

Under its Chief Mechanical Engineer, H.N. Gresley, the LNER had been building 'Pacifics' since 1923 and had had ample time to study the formula, and make the most of it. Since 1928, LNER had been building the A3 'Super-Pacific' in large numbers, and these engines, typified by No 4472 *Flying Scotsman* (rebuilt from A1) were giving excellent service, particularly since the early problems with Gresley's conjugated valve gear had been resolved. Now something different was needed. The spark was lit by the high-speed *Fliegende Hamburger* two-car diesel express unit developed in Germany in 1933. At first, the LNER management contemplated something like this for a four-hour London–Newcastle service, 429km (266 miles). But the best that the diesel could offer was 4 hours,

**The striking silver and grey pre-war livery is shown here on an A4 representing the original No 2509 Silver Link, photographed at the National Railway Museum, York, on 2 July 1988.**

15 minutes, and test runs with the A3s indicated a steam locomotive could take a heavier train in less time. However, something special in the way of locomotive power was thought necessary for the new train, to be called the 'Silver Jubilee' in honour of George V's 25 years on the throne. A new 'Pacific' was drawn up, modifying the A3 design in order to improve tractive effort and power output. Only six months elapsed between approval of the project and the delivery of the first A4, No 2509 *Silver Link*, on 5 September 1935. At this time, as the railways faced up to motor and air competition, streamlining was widely practised, often of a crudely cosmetic sort, though Raymond Loewy was sculpting great engines in the USA. Gresley enlisted the aid of the Italian car designer Ettore Bugatti, and the streamlining of the A4s was done on a scientific basis, with a significant claimed reduction in air resistance. The angle-fronted cab also gave better vision to the driver. But undoubtedly the most significant streamlining was inside, where the casing concealed a $17.5kg/cm^2$ (250psi) taper boiler with very carefully designed steam passages feeding three simple-expansion cylinders slightly smaller than those of the A3s. Here the LNER designers put into effect what they had learned from earlier work with André Chapelon in connection with the P2 2-8-2s.

Unveiling of the new train, with streamlined articulated coaches and its gleaming wedge-fronted silver engine, was a sensation in itself, duly crowned by *Silver Link* breaking the British speed record with two maxima of 181kph (112.5mph) on the demonstration run, and exceeding 160.9kph (100mph) for 25 miles at a stretch. The 4-hour London–Newcastle service was inaugurated on 30 September 1935. Between 1936 and 1938 a further 31 A4s were built at the LNER's Doncaster plant, mainly for use on other extra-special services like the 6-hour London-Edinburgh 'Coronation' train of 1937. This train had Britain's fastest-ever steam timing, requiring an average 71.9mph (116kph) for the non-stop London-York section. The nine-coach train weighed 312t (307 tons) tare. But some of the glory of the A4s was taken by the rival 'Coronation Scot' of the LMS, whose demonstration run established a new British record of 184.2kph (114.5mph).

In early 1938, a number of new A4s were fitted with Kylchap double chimneys, following successful experiment on an A3 'Pacific'. One of these was No 4468 *Mallard*. On 4 July that year, in the course of braking tests, this engine was authorized by Gresley to try for a maximum speed. He was after not only the British record, but the world record, held since May 1936 by the German State Railway (DRG) 4-6-4 No 05.002 with 200.4kph (124.5mph). With six 'Coronation' articulated coaches, and a dynamometer car, the train weight totalled 243.9t (240 tons). On the East Coast main line south of Grantham, the train came over the low summit at Stoke at 119kph (74mph) and with the engine at full regulator and first 40 per cent, then 45 per cent cut-off in the cylinders, accelerated down the 1 in 200 gradient until a maximum sustained speed of 201.1kph (125mph) was reached. The record was – just – beaten. Since that day, debate has gone on. The Germans pointed out that their record was reached on level track, with no help from gravity. The suggestion that *Mallard* actually touched 202.7kph (126mph) has recently been discounted, but computer-aided reviews of the dynamometer car records leave no doubt that the A4 attained the fastest verified speed of any steam locomotive.

**In blue LNER livery, preserved No 4468 Mallard stands with a special charter train, 'The South Yorkshire Pullman', at the south end of York Station, on 4 October 1986.**

**The plaque proudly fixed on Mallard's side by the LNER claims that 126 miles (203km) per hour was achieved.**

The work of this class and of its LMS 'Duchess-Coronation' rivals represents the high point of British express steam operation. The constraints of the British loading gauge were among the factors inhibiting the development there of larger steam locomotives, though some were planned. The feedwater heaters, thermic syphons, generator sets and other items used on high-speed engines in other countries were very hard to fit into the limited space available, and it was in other countries that post-war steam development went on to greater things.

But, from 1957, all the single-chimney A4s were fitted with double Kylchap chimneys, and even in those twilight years of steam power, the class was still attaining speeds in excess of 161kph (100mph). The exploits of the A4s are legion, both in high speeds and in powerful traction. A notable feat, again by *Mallard*, was the ascent of Stoke Bank, in the opposite direction to its record-breaking run, with a 421.6t (415-ton) train, at speeds up to 132kph (82mph) and breasting the summit at 125.5kph (78mph). In 1961 the 2462kW (3300hp) 'Deltic' diesel-electrics began to relieve the A4s on East Coast main-line services, but for several years they enjoyed an 'Indian summer' in Scotland, working Glasgow-Aberdeen expresses.

**Boiler pressure:** 17.5kg/cm$^2$ (250psi)
**Cylinders:** 470x660mm (18.5x26in)
**Driving wheels:** 2030mm (80in)
**Grate area:** 3.8m$^2$ (41.3sq ft)
**Heating surface:** 239m$^2$ (2576sq ft)
**Superheater:** 70m$^2$ (751.6sq ft)
**Tractive effort:** 16,326kg (36,000lb)
**Total weight:** 104.6t (230,720lb)

## 'TURBOMOTIVE' 4-6-2 LONDON MIDLAND & SCOTTISH RAILWAY (LMS) GREAT BRITAIN: 1935

Experimental and one-off engines often ended up under tarpaulins at the back of a shed, but this one spent years in revenue service, on express trains. Built by the LMS at Crewe, in collaboration with Metropolitan Vickers, it incorporated the Swedish-designed Ljungström non-condensing turbine with the frames and boiler of a 'Princess Royal' 4-6-2. The turbines were at the front, forward or main drive on the left, and backward on the right. Main drive delivered its maximum hp output at around 99kph (62mph), showing that the design was meant for hauling heavy trains at moderately fast speeds. A double blast-pipe chimney was fitted from the start, and three different boilers were used up to 1939. Test results both in tractive power on gradients and in coal and water consumption were favourable, and if war had not intervened, more might have been done with turbine traction.

The engine was normally employed on the London–Liverpool expresses and up to

**This drawing of the 'turbomotive' shows the right-hand side with the smaller reversing turbine, which did not in fact extend back to cover the first wheel splasher. The smoke deflectors were a later addition.**

A broadside view of LMS No 6202 as originally built, in June 1935. It was classed as 7P, the same power rating as the conventional 'Princess Royals'.

1939 its annual distance in service was just over 87,200km (54,180 miles), compared with about 128,740km (80,000 miles) for its non-turbine 'Princess Royal' sisters. Delays in spare part production, inevitable with a single-model engine, were partly responsible. In 195,1 the engine was rebuilt as a conventional reciprocating one, but that same year was destroyed in a disastrous crash at Harrow, north London.

**Boiler pressure:** 17.5kg/cm$^2$ (250psi)
**Cylinders:** None
**Driving wheels:** 1981mm (78in)
**Grate area:** 4.2m$^2$ (45sq ft)
**Heating surface:** 215m$^2$ (2314sq ft)
**Superheater:** 61m$^2$ (653sq ft)
**Tractive effort:** 18,150kg (40,000lb)
**Total weight:** 166.5t (367,000lb)

## CLASS 49 'DOVREGUBBEN' 2-8-4 NORWEGIAN STATE RAILWAYS (NSB) NORWAY: 1935

The first 2-8-4, or 'Berkshire' type was built in 1925 by the Lima Locomotive Works in the USA, as an experiment and proved highly successful. The placing of a four-wheel truck under the firebox enabled a large expansion of the combustion area, with a grate area of 9.3m$^2$ (100sq ft). It remained an American exclusive until the NSB, looking for a powerful locomotive to work through the Dovrefjell mountains between Oslo and Trondheim (particularly the steep Dombas-Trondheim section), opted for it and designed and built the first examples in Europe. The first three were built by Thunes

**No 472, one of the Krupp engines, standing at the head of an Oslo-bound train at the terminus in Trondheim, in August 1956. The pitched roof of the coal bunker can be seen behind the cab.**

**The drawing represents the original appearance of the Norwegian-built double-chimneyed 'Dovregubben' engines of 1935.**

Mekaniske Vaerksted of Oslo; 463 and 464 were classed 49a, and 465, with detail differences, including a Dabeg feed water heater, was 49b. No. 463 was named *Dovregubben*, 'Dovre Giant'. They were four-cylinder compounds, with the high pressure cylinders inside. Walschaerts valve gear, positioned outside, served both cylinders on each side. These engines had double blast pipes and chimneys, and thermic syphons in the fireboxes. Axle weight was an important consideration, and plate frames and welded construction were used, in order to get a maximum loading of no more than 15.5t (15.25 tons). The fire-door was opened by air pressure. Despite the large grate, firing was done manually. The tenders were of Vanderbilt type, frameless, and mounted on outside-framed double bogies, with a covered coal bunker set on top of the water tank.

From the first, the class was put into intensive use and despite the teething troubles inevitable with a new and complicated locomotive design, soon operated very satisfactorily. High speed was not a requirement and the maximum running speed was 100kph (62mph), but they proved to have excellent adhesion and acceleration.

After the German occupation of Norway in 1940, four more were delivered, two from Krupp in Essen and two from Thune, classed 49c. These had single chimneys and smaller-diameter cylinders, and German-type smoke deflectors. Intensive wartime use with inadequate lubricants, fed with superheated steam at almost 440°C (824°F), left the engines in poor condition. They worked on until the 1950s, when Class Di3 diesel-electrics replaced them in service, and six were scrapped in 1958. One of the Krupp-built engines is preserved, though the number and name-plates of the very first, No 463, have been transferred to it.

**Boiler pressure:** 17kg/cm$^2$ (240psi)
**Cylinders:** hp 440x650mm (17.5x25.5in); lp 650x700mm (25.5x27.5in)
**Driving wheels:** 1530mm (60in)
**Grate area:** 5m$^2$ (55.5sq ft)
**Heating surface:** 255m$^2$ (2742sq ft)
**Superheater:** 101m$^2$ (1092sq ft)
**Tractive effort:** N/A
**Total weight:** 151.5t (334,000lb)

## 'ANDES' CLASS 2-8-0 CENTRAL RAILWAY (FCC) PERU: 1935

Peruvian railways had been ordering locomotives from the USA since the 1870s, but though this famous 'Consolidation' type looks American, it was built in England by Beyer Peacock. Its formidable task was to operate trains on the FCC's mountain line between Lima and Huancayo, which goes almost from sea level to a height of 15,693ft (4783m). And though downhill loads of copper ore were heavier, the ascent, whether with freight or the daily passenger service, was one of the hardest tasks for a steam locomotive relying only on wheel-to-rail adhesion. With six 'Z' sections on the route, it was a forwards-backwards progress. The steepest grade is 1 in 22 (4.5 per cent).

**'Andes' 2-8-0 No 221 halts with a mixed train at Rio Blanco, in December 1952. The station bell, to announce approaching trains, and the disc signal are both notable features.**

**The preserved 'Andes' 2-8-0 No. 206 in action on level terrain. The locomotive has a supplementary water tank car behind the tender.**

There were 29 locomotives of this class, delivered between 1935 and 1951. They were oil-fired two-cylinder simples, solidly built on bar frames and with short boilers to avoid exposing the crown sheet when the line plunged downhill. Braking was of prime importance and a double-pipe air brake was fitted, so that pressure was maintained at all times. To help maintain traction, sand was air-blasted to the coupled wheels. Diesel haulage took over in the 1960s, but No 206 was preserved and is still capable of being steamed.

**Boiler pressure:** 14kg/cm² (200psi)
**Cylinders:** 508x711mm (20x28in)
**Driving wheels:** 1321mm (52in)
**Grate area:** 2.6m² (28sq ft)
**Heating surface:** 160m² (1717sq ft)
**Superheater:** 32m² (341sq ft)
**Tractive effort:** 16,600kg (35,600lb)
**Total weight:** 113t (250,000lb)

## CLASS 16E 4-6-2 SOUTH AFRICAN RAILWAYS (SAR) SOUTH AFRICA: 1935

Designed by A.G. Watson of the SAR, the six engines of this class were built for the 1065mm (3ft 6in) gauge by Henschel of Kassel. Delivered in parts and assembled at the Salt River works, they were very fast runners. The SAR's only exclusively passenger locomotive, it was a two-cylinder simple, with rotary cam gear operating poppet valves. Two firemen kept the big grate fed. On a test run in 1935, No 854 reached 112kph (70mph), but the class is said to have often exceeded this on the Kimberley–Bloemfontein 'Orange Express'.

**The German origins of the Class 16E are apparent in this view of No 857, taken at Bloemfontein on 5 July 1971. Engines of this class hauled the Kimberley–Bloemfontein 'Orange Express' at high speeds, frequently in excess of 112kph (70 mph).**

**Boiler pressure:** 14.7kg/cm² (210psi)
**Cylinders:** 609x710.6mm (24x28in)
**Driving wheels:** 1827mm (72in)
**Grate area:** 5.8m² (63sq ft)
**Heating surface:** 249m² (2682sq ft)
**Superheater:** 55m² (592sq ft)
**Tractive effort:** 16000kg (35,280lb)
**Total weight:** 169.8t (374,416lb)

# CLASS A 4-4-2 CHICAGO MILWAUKEE ST PAUL & PACIFIC RAILROAD (CMSTP&PRR) USA: 1935

**America's 'Super-Atlantic', No 2 of Class A. Despite their distinctive appearance and exceptional performance, none of the four were preserved. All were cut up in 1951–52.**

Travellers between Chicago and Minneapolis–St Paul had a choice of three routes, which competed fiercely, offering high standards of speed and service. There was no climbing to do, so high speeds were possible, and Alco built four specialized oil-burning locomotives with streamlined casings to pull the 'Hiawatha' flyer on a timing of 6hrs, 30mins for its 663km (412mile) route, averaging a speed of 106kph (66mph). On a test outing, one made one of the fastest-ever steam runs, 227km (141 miles) from Milwaukee to New Lisbon in 113mins. The 'Hiawatha' timing was later cut to 6hrs 15mins, despite five intermediate stops. Sustained speeds in excess of 161kph (100mph) were necessary to maintain time. Engine and train were painted in a striking livery of yellow, orange, maroon and brown. It was not a lightweight train: with nine cars, it weighed 419.1t (412.5 tons). These were the biggest, heaviest 'Atlantics' built, and larger tenders later increased their weight. In 1938, the streamlined F7 4-6-4s replaced them, able to maintain the schedule with a 12-car train, and from 1940 the Atlantics were diverted to the new 'Mid-West Hiawatha' operating between Chicago, Omaha and Sioux Falls.

By 1948, diesel locomotives had taken over, and the 4-4-2s, not adaptable to other types of use, were retired by 1951, their prestige and superb performance forgotten; all were scrapped.

**Boiler pressure:** 21kg/cm$^2$ (300psi)
**Cylinders:** 483x711mm (19x28in)
**Driving wheels:** 2134mm (84in)
**Grate area:** 6.4m$^2$ (69sq ft)
**Heating surface:** 301.5m$^2$ (3245sq ft)
**Superheater:** 96m$^2$ (1029sq ft)
**Tractive effort:** 13,900kg (30,600lb)
**Total weight:** 265.18t (537,000lb)

**It is 2.21 pm by the station clock at Milwaukee, Wisconsin, and 'Atlantic' No. 4, Chippewa, is coupled up to the 'Hiawatha'. The 'hoghead', US railroad slang for the driver, looks all set to let her roll for Chicago.**

## CLASS J3 4-8-4 CHESAPEAKE & OHIO RAILROAD (C&O) USA: 1935

Fifteen of these passenger engines were built by Lima between 1935 and 1948; the later ones classed as J3a had roller bearings and other improvements but the same dimensions. The last to be built, No 614, which had been preserved for special excursion work, was hastily overhauled and used for the ill-judged ACE (American Coal Enterprises) display runs in the winter of 1984–5. This scheme, intended to promote the production of new-generation, 'clean coal' steam locomotives, though initially backed by the Chessie System and US coal interests, expired in 1985 without having produced a prototype engine, though plans for an ACE 3000 and 6000 had been drawn up.

Unfortunately, the J3, not properly adapted, put up anything but a 'clean' performance and on one demonstration trip in January 1985 it also, embarrassingly, ran completely out of coal.

**Boiler pressure:** 17.2kg/cm² (245psi)
**Cylinders:** 699x762mm (27.5x30in)
**Driving wheels:** 1829mm (72in)
**Grate area:** 9.3m² (100sq ft)
**Heating surface:** 514m² (5534sq ft)
**Superheater:** 218m² (2347sq ft)
**Tractive effort:** 33,179kg (67,187lb)
**Total weight:** 216t (476,280lb) (engine only)

## CLASS F-2A 4-4-4 CANADIAN PACIFIC RAILWAY (CPR) CANADA: 1936

**A Toronto landmark rises behind the preserved CPR 4-4-4 No 2928 of class F-1a, standing in the city's main station.**

By the mid-1930s, as road transport grew ever more popular, many railways developed 'super-trains' of one kind or another to protect their traffic. The CPR was well to the fore in this, and introduced four inter-city services in 1936 on its more vulnerable routes. These were Toronto–Detroit, Edmonton–Calgary, and two services between Montreal and Quebec. The 4-car trains weighed about 200 tons, lightweight in North American terms, and a 'lightweight' locomotive was designed to help run them. 4-4-4 was an unusual wheel formation, for a tender engine at least, though the Philadelphia & Reading in the USA had briefly had some in 1915. They were built at Montreal Locomotive Works, and had the kind of features normally associated with much larger engines. The two simple-expansion cylinders drove the leading coupled axle. The firebox, larger than that of most European large 'Pacifics', was fed by a mechanical stoker. All axles ran on roller bearings. To celebrate 50 years of CP transcontinental service, the class was referred to in line publicity as the 'Jubilees'.

The F-2a probably brought more weight and power to its task than was really needed, and a second batch, classed F-1a, were slightly smaller, and the cylinders drove on the rear coupled axle. Twenty-eight of those were built in 1938, and one is preserved. The rest of both classes were scrapped in 1957–58.

**Boiler pressure:** 21kg/cm² (300psi)
**Cylinders:** 438x711mm (17.25x28)
**Driving wheels:** 2032mm (80in)
**Grate area:** 5.2m² (55.6sq ft)
**Heating surface:** 263m² (2833sq ft)
**Superheater:** 102m² (1100sq ft)
**Tractive effort:** 12,000kg (26,500lb)
**Total weight:** 209t (461,000lb)

## CLASS ET6 0-8-0 CHINESE GOVERNMENT RAILWAYS CHINA: 1936

Four of this class,designed for shunting and banking, were built by Armstrong Whitworth of Newcastle, England; in 1949–50, further engines were supplied by the North British Locomotive Company of Glasgow. Despite the British origin, it was an American-style design, fitted with a US E-type superheater. The prototype had a bell in front of the chimney, not a standard fitting on Chinese locomotives. Locomotives of this class operated not on main lines, but on industrial railways and complexes. With a maximum axle load of 13.7t (13.5 tons), they ran on lightly laid track and trestles. Designed to burn low-grade coal, they had deep ashpans between the rear driving wheels. Since they operated in yards and work-places, they were fitted with bells. The 1936 engines had US-style sloping tenders, those of 1949 had back-sloping tanks but built-up coal bunkers set in from the tank sides.

**Boiler pressure:** 15.5kg/cm² (221psi)
**Cylinders:** 420x600mm (16.5x23.6in)
**Driving wheels:** 1200mm (47in)
**Grate area:** 3m² (32.3sq ft)
**Heating surface:** 104m² (1119.7sq ft)
**Superheater:** 40.8m² (439.3sq ft)
**Tractive effort:** 11,646kg (25,680lb)
**Total weight:** 51.8t (114,219lb) (engine only)

## CLASS V2 2-6-2 LONDON & NORTH EASTERN RAILWAY (LNER) GREAT BRITAIN: 1936

In the 1930s, the LNER was the most adventurous of Britain's 'big four' railway companies where wheel arrangements were concerned. Intended for passenger and fast freight work on main lines, this Doncaster-built 'Prairie' of which four were built for testing in 1936, became a class of 188. Three-cylindered, with simple expansion, it closely resembled the Gresley A3 'Pacifics', with the same conjugated valve gear and the same extension behind the chimney to accommodate the superheater header. But its cylinders, smoke-box saddle, steam and exhaust passages were all a single casting, with the outside steam pipes. The 'banjo dome' was in fact a steam collector. A useful feature was the angled cab front, taken from the A4 design. Although British designers avoided the Helmholtz-type linking of front truck and leading coupled wheels, common elsewhere, this class had a good reputation for smooth running. Only the first engine had a name, *Green Arrow*, given in connection with a new fast freight service.

**The name plate of No 4771 *Green Arrow*; the 'Green Arrow' service was an express freight from London to the North, instituted in 1936.**

From the first, the V2s did regular passenger turns, notably on the Kings Cross to Doncaster section of the Leeds and Harrogate 'Yorkshire Pullman', typically loading to around 406t (400 tons) and averaging 96.5kph (60mph) over the 251km (156 miles). As very long runs were not anticipated, it had a smaller tender than the 'Pacifics', with capacity for 7.7t (7.6 tons) of coal and 4200 gals (5044US) of water; and, of course, the water scoop standard on LNER main line engines.

**Boiler pressure:** 15.5kg/cm² (220psi)
**Cylinders:** 470x660mm (18.5x26in)
**Driving wheels:** 1880mm (74in)
**Grate area:** 3.8m² (41.2sq ft)
**Heating surface:** 226m² (2431sq ft)
**Superheater:** 63 m² (680sq ft)
**Tractive effort:** 13,514kg (29,800lb)
**Total weight:** 94.5t (208,544lb)

**No 4471 runs past the rugged ruins of Conwy Castle, North Wales, on the former LNWR line from Chester to Holyhead, with a special excursion train. This route is at the other side of the country from the engine's 'East Coast' origins.**

## CLASS 42.01 2-8-2 TRANS-IRANIAN RAILWAY IRAN: 1936

A Scandinavian consortium oversaw the building of this long and mountainous route, linking the Persian Gulf to the Caspian Sea, via Teheran; and though the bulk of the locomotive stock was two-cylinder German 2-8-0s, Nohab of Trollhättan, Sweden, supplied the eleven 2-8-2s of Class 42.01 These three-cylinder engines were intended chiefly for passenger trains. Intense wartime traffic was probably responsible for the early demise of a class that needed too-careful maintenance for emergency conditions.

The Class 42 were handsome locomotives, whose appearance clearly showed their Swedish origins, with round-topped boiler, two elongated domes combining sand-boxes, and conical smoke-box door. The cab had a slight vee-front and was completely enclosed.

A large-capacity eight-wheel tender was provided for working on this 1392km (865-mile) line, largely through the sparse desert country in the south.

**Boiler pressure:** 12.5kg/cm$^2$ (178psi)
**Cylinders:** 497.5x660mm (19.6x26in)
**Driving wheels:** 1350mm (53.2in)
**Grate area:** 4.2m$^2$ (45sq ft)
**Heating surface:** 216m$^2$ (2325sq ft) (including superheater)
**Superheater:** not known
**Tractive effort:** 12,882kg (28,406)
**Total weight:** 87.3t (192,640lb) (engine only)

## CLASS D52 2-8-2 JAPAN: 1936

With 1115 built between 1936 and 1945, this 'Mikado' was the classic Japanese goods locomotive. Twelve plants were involved in building it, including Kawasaki Sharyo, Kisha Seizo Kaisha, Nippon Sharyo Seisakusho, and Hitachi Seisakusho, as well as JNR workshops. Lighter and shorter but with greater tractive power than its predecessor, the D51, it had a long boiler housing typical of Japanese locomotives, and a flowerpot chimney. In North American style, a feedwater heater cylinder was fixed crosswise in front of the chimney, and various pumps for brakes and lubrication were fixed on the sides. Two outside simple-expansion cylinders were operated by piston valves actuated by Walschaerts gear. It was also the first Japanese locomotive to have Boxpok-type wheels. After the first 96 had been built, some modifications were made, making the later ones 0.9t (0.88 tons) heavier. Engines built in 1943–46, when steel was in short supply due to the war, had wooden smoke deflectors and running plates, and were often weighed down with concrete; these were rebuilt after 1945. Also after 1945, some of the class were fitted with smoke collection devices and others were adapted to burn oil as well as coal. Belonging unashamedly to the 'let it all hang out' school of design, the D52 was a robust and workmanlike engine, but in the words of one Japanese writer, 'the truly representative steam locomotive of Japan.'

**Boiler pressure:** 14kg/cm$^2$ (213psi)
**Cylinders:** 550x660mm (21.6x26in)
**Driving wheels:** 1400mm (55in)
**Grate area:** 3.3m$^2$ (35.5sq ft)
**Heating surface:** m$^2$)
**Superheater:** m$^2$)
**Tractive effort:** 18,110kg (39,930lb)
**Total weight:** 76.8t (169,344lb)

## CLASS 142 2-8-4 RUMANIAN RAILWAYS (CFR) RUMANIA: 1936

**A few years after retirement from daily working, surviving Class 142 No 044 stands in the yard at Halta Desmir, in May 1971.**

This design came from Austria, but whereas the ÖBB built only 13 as class 214, the CFR built 79 at the workshops of Malaxa and Resita, between 1936 and 1940. With two simple-expansion cylinders, they were Rumania's largest passenger engines, working most main passenger trains until the mid-1960s. They were distinguished by long smoke deflectors set high on the smoke-box sides, a 'skyline casing' that concealed the domes, and a downwards extension of the running plate over the upper part of the cylinders. The rear four-wheel truck had inside bearings. Most of the class had Lentz over-head cam poppet valves to work the cylinders, though some were for a

**Class 142 No 044, fully restored and with a short but rather miscellaneous train. The front vehicle is a baggage van.**

time fitted with Caprotti gear.

No mechanical stoker was fitted in the firebox, but, like most other Rumanian large locomotive types, this class was equipped to burn a coal-oil mixture for hard work. This system was invented by a Rumanian engineer, H. Cosmovici; heavy oil was sprayed into the firebox, then ignited, giving another heat source. Used in Bulgaria, it was also tested on some large German engines. The oil tanks were fitted in the tender, or above the side water tanks in tank locomotives.

**Boiler pressure:** 15kg/cm$^2$ (213.75psi)
**Cylinders:** 650x720mm (25.6x28.4in)
**Driving wheels:** 1940mm (76.5in)
**Grate area:** 4.72m$^2$ (50.8sq ft)
**Heating surface:** 262m$^2$ (2820sq ft)
**Superheater:** 77.8m$^2$ (837.6sq ft)
**Tractive effort:** 20,040kg (44,190lb)
**Total weight:** 123.5t (272,317lb) (engine only)

## 'UNION' CLASS 0-10-2 UNION RAILROAD — USA: 1936

By this time, big American locomotives were in a class of their own, rivalled only by the attempts of the Soviet railways to outbuild their capitalist rivals. This class, though only three in number, is interesting partly because it can be more easily compared to European and other 10-coupled types. The Union Railroad was a short but strategically placed line, providing links between six trunk line railroads in the busy Pittsburgh area. It had less than 72km (45 miles) of track but the usage was extremely intensive and some of the lines were steeply graded. To provide greater traction than the company's 2-8-0s, this engine was commissioned from Baldwins, the first 0-10-2. The wheelbase was also restricted by the need to fit the same turntables as the 2-8-0s. Since the locomotive would only ever operate at low speeds, a leading truck was dispensed with, though the end product looked oddly like an engine that had managed to mislay its front carrying wheels. To assist moving of heavy trains up the grades, a booster was fitted to the leading tender truck, whose wheels were coupled. It added a tractive force of 7780kg (17,150lb) to the locomotive's effort. The short-distance working of what was essentially a giant switching engine meant that the tender, though large by non-American standards, holding 14.2t (14 tons) of coal and 10,000gals (12,000US) of water, was quite a small one.

**Boiler pressure:** 18.25kg/cm$^2$ (260lb)
**Cylinders:** 711x812mm (28x32in)
**Driving wheels:** 1548mm (61in)
**Grate area:** m$^2$)
**Heating surface:** m$^2$)
**Superheater:** m$^2$)
**Tractive effort:** 41,220kg (90,900lb)
**Total weight:** 292.3t (644,510lb)

## 'CHALLENGER' CLASS 4-6-6-4 UNION PACIFIC RAILROAD (UP) — USA: 1936

**The long piston-road of the front cylinder and the massive dimensions of the boiler are clearly visible in this imposing shot of preserved UP No 3985.**

Both the Union Pacific and Northern Pacific put locomotives of this configuration on the road in 1936. They were two-in-one articulated engines, with a single huge boiler supplying steam to two power units, based on the Mallet principle, but with simple-expansion cylinders only. Walschaerts valve gear actuated the piston valves, and the cylinders drove the third pair of coupled wheels. Both on the UP and NP engines, the front cylinders were positioned further ahead of the coupled wheels than the rear ones; with an extra-long piston rod taking up the space. The UP engines, named 'Challengers', were designed as mixed-traffic engines, though most of their activity was on fast freights. Considered as passenger engines, they were the largest and most powerful ever to run. Forty were ordered from Alco in 1936, and a further 65, incorporating some modifications, were built between 1942 and 1945. The type proved excellent for high-speed freight trains, and other lines quickly followed the example. Baldwins built 4-6-6-4s for the Denver & Rio Grande Western in 1938, and for the Western Maryland in 1939. But the 'Challengers' were the only ones to operate regular passenger services, notably between Salt Lake City, Las Vegas, and Los Angeles.

Some were converted to oil burning but the great majority were coal burners, the huge grates fed by automatic stokers. They remained in service until 1958, by which time the UP's diesel programme had advanced far enough to deprive them of any suitable duties. One is preserved in working order (No 3985).

**Boiler pressure:** 17.9kg/cm$^2$ (255psi)
**Cylinders:** 533x813mm (21x32in)
**Driving wheels:** 1753mm (69in)
**Grate area:** 10m$^2$ (108sq ft)
**Heating surface:** 431m$^2$ (4642sq ft)
**Superheater:** 162m$^2$ (1741sq ft)
**Tractive effort:** 44,100kg (97,400lb)
**Total weight:** 486t (1,071,000lb)

**No 3985 gets on the move, heading towards San Jose for a railway history convention in 1992. The length of the boiler severely limited the engineer's forward look-out.**

**The huge size of the 'Challengers' is appreciated when one realises that the driving wheels are as tall as the average man. They could turn at a speed of 110kph (70mph), with a 20-car passenger train.**

## CLASS H1 'ROYAL HUDSON' 4-6-4 CANADIAN PACIFIC RAILWAY (CPR) CANADA: 1937

There was certainly something lionlike about the CPR 'Hudsons', caused by the styling of the big chimney, whose housing curved manelike back into the boiler top. But its 'Royal' tag came not from the king of the beasts but from No 2850's having headed the royal train during the visit of King George VI and Queen Elizabeth in 1939. The 4-8-4s were introduced to provide motive power of greater stamina on the long trans-continental run. They were built by the Montreal Locomotive Works to CPR specifications. Combustion chambers were incorporated, extending the firebox at the expense of some boiler length, and mechanical stoking was fitted. The boiler was round-topped, with no dome, but a safety-valve housing set just in front of the firebox.

Sixty-five were built in all, between 1937 and 1945, and a number of modifications produced sub-classes of H1. These included power reversers. Twenty engines had boosters fitted, driving the rear set of trailing wheels, which were larger than the front pair. The last five, built to operate in British Columbia, were oil-fired; and a number of others based in the prairie provinces were later converted to oil burning. The 'Royal Hudsons' worked on express duties into the mid-1950s, when the class began to be scrapped. By 1965, all had left the scene, but five have been preserved, of which two remain in operating condition.

**'Royal Hudson' No 2858 on static display at the Canadian Railway Museum, near Montreal.**

**Boiler pressure:** 19.3kg/cm$^2$ (275psi)
**Cylinders:** 559x762mm (22x30in)
**Driving wheels:** 1905mm (75in)
**Grate area:** 7.5m$^2$ (81sq ft)
**Heating surface:** 352m$^2$ (3791sq ft)
**Superheater:** 143m$^2$ (1542sq ft)
**Tractive effort:** 20,548kg (45,300lb)
**Total weight:** 299t (659,000lb)

**In mountain country, preserved 'Royal Hudson' No 2860 takes the 'Columbia' train up-grade. Each summer, a 'Hudson' runs excursions between North Vancouver and Squamish, BC.**

## CLASS HR1 4-6-2 STATE RAILWAYS (VR) FINLAND: 1937

**HR 1004, built by Lokomo in 1939, simmers gently at a country terminus. One Hr1, of 1940, is still preserved.**

Finland's only 'Pacific' type, on the 1524mm (5ft) gauge, 21 in all, was built between 1937 and 1957, at the Tampella and Lokomo works in Tampere. It was a successful, free-steaming engine and only detail modifications were made over two decades, the final version having roller bearings. Essentially it was a two-cylinder simple design, showing, like most Finnish engines, considerable German influence. Until 1963, they worked on passenger expresses in the south, but were then displaced by diesels to run fast freight on central Finnish lines, which they did into the 1970s.

**Boiler pressure:** 15kg/cm$^2$ (214psi)
**Cylinders:** 590x650mm (23.25x25.6in)
**Driving wheels:** 1900mm (75in)
**Grate area:** 3.5m$^2$ (37.7sq ft)
**Heating surface:** 195.4m$^2$ (2103.8sq ft)
**Superheater:** 68m$^2$ (732.1sq ft)
**Tractive effort:** 15220kg (33,562lb)
**Total weight:** 93t (205,065lb) (engine only)

## CLASS PM-36 4-6-2 POLISH STATE RAILWAYS (PKP) POLAND: 1937

In the 1930s, express services in Poland were both internal, between the major cities, and international, linking Germany and Czechoslovakia to the Russian frontier and its change of gauge from standard to 1524mm (5ft). Most of the heavy expresses were hauled by the class Pt-31 2-8-2, a powerful and efficient locomotive dating from 1932, but in 1937 it was decided to begin a two-cylinder 'Pacific' class for express work.

**Preserved locomotive 36.2, at Glogow on 19 July 1995. An unusual feature of these engines was cab access via a door set at the front end of the tender.**

Two were built at the Chrzanov works in Warsaw, Pm-36.1 as a streamliner, the second as a conventional engine, whose lines closely resembled those of the *Deutsche Reichsbahn's* class 03 light 'Pacific'. They were built in German fashion, with bar frames, as two-cylinder simples. Both were planned to run at speeds up to 140kph (87mph) and had the largest-diameter driving wheels of any Polish engine. As in all modern Polish locomotives, the driving cab was fully enclosed, but unusually its entrance was built into the tender frame. The German invasion and occupation of Poland in 1939 put a stop to any further development of the class, and during the war period the first engine had its streamlined casing removed.

**Boiler pressure:** 18kg/cm$^2$ (256.5psi)
**Cylinders:** 530x700mm (21x27.6in)
**Driving wheels:** 2000mm (79in)
**Grate area:** 3.9m$^2$ (42sq ft)
**Heating surface:** 198m$^2$ (2132sq ft)
**Superheater:** 71.2m$^2$ (766.5sq ft)
**Tractive effort:** 16,227kg (32,860lb)
**Total weight:** 94t (207,270lb) (engine only)

## CLASS 46 2-8-2 TURKISH STATE RAILWAYS (TCDD) TURKEY: 1937

Turkey's first modern express locomotive was a 2-cylinder 'Mikado' built by Henschel of Kassel, Germany. From the same builder came a mixed traffic 2-10-0, with a boiler and other parts. In 1937, 11 of the 2-8-2 were delivered, and 10 more were ordered in 1940 but not delivered. They were excellent engines, performing well on the Turkish section of trains like the 'Taurus Express', Istanbul-Baghdad, into the mid-1960s, often rostered along with the new diesel-electrics. In the 1950s, the 'Taurus Express' ran twice-weekly, the 2655km (1650-mile) journey taking 73hrs, 30mins going east, of which up to 10 were consumed by frontier checks. Usually, the 2-8-2s ran the Istanbul (Haydarpasa) to Ankara section. British and Czech 2-10-0, German 0-8-0, ex-British War Department 2-8-0, and the elegant Iranian 'Pacific' locomotives, were all found on later stages.

**Boiler pressure:** 16kg/cm$^2$ (228psi)
**Cylinders:** 650x660mm (25.6x26in)
**Driving wheels:** 1751mm (69in)
**Grate area:** 4m$^2$ (43sq ft)
**Heating surface:** 222.9m$^2$ (2340sq ft)
**Superheater:** 106m$^2$ (1141.2sq ft)
**Tractive effort:** 21,700kg (47,850lb)
**Total weight:** 104.5t (230,422lb) (engine only)

## CLASS F7 4-6-4 CHICAGO, MILWAUKEE, ST PAUL & PACIFIC RAILROAD (CMSTP&PRR) USA: 1937

**Boiler pressure:** 300psi (21kg/cm$^2$)
**Cylinders:** 597x762mm (23.5x30in)
**Driving wheels:** 2134mm (84in)
**Grate area:** 8.9m$^2$ (96.5sq ft)
**Heating surface:** 387m$^2$ (4166sq ft)
**Superheater:** 157m$^2$ (1695sq ft)
**Tractive effort:** 22,820kg (50,295lb)
**Total weight:** 359t (791,000lb)

**The Class F74-6-4 was introduced to haul heavier trains in the cold north of the United States.**

These were introduced to enable heavier trains to be hauled on the Chicago–Minneapolis–St Paul 'Hiawatha' expresses, while keeping the exceptionally fast schedule on this competitive line. Other lines were using 4-8-4s for similar purposes, like the Union Pacific's semi-streamlined GS type operating the San Francisco-Los Angeles 'Daylight' streamlined train. But it is unlikely that any 4-8-4 exceeded the speeds attained by the F7. With a streamlined front and boiler casing that covered the cylinders too, the F7s showed the tendency of American designers to play down the 'steamy' aspect of their passenger engines, though the wheels and running gear were left uncovered for easy access. Unlike their 4-4-2 predecessors, they were coal-burning. They ran trains of up to 12 cars, 559t (550 tons) at an average of 106kph (66mph), including 5 stops. There are accounts of these engines exceeding 193kph (120mph), but none are authenticated. In 1940, however, they did operate the fastest scheduled steam service anywhere, on the 'Hiawatha's' Sparta-Portage sector, 126.3km (78.5 miles) run at an average of 130.75kph (81.25mph), an interesting comparison with the English 'Cheltenham Flyer' of the 1930s on its Swindon–London stage.

## GS2 CLASS 4-8-4 SOUTHERN PACIFIC RAILROAD (SP) USA: 1937

**The 'Daylight Limited' restored – the replica train, hauled by preserved GS4 No 4449, swings round the bend at Brock, California.**

The 'Daylight' name of the San Francisco–Los Angeles streamlined train referred to its ability to do the 756km (470-mile) run within daylight hours; GS2 locomotives supplied the power. The design was introduced in 1930, built by Baldwins; GS2, built by Lima, was the first to be streamlined and had other modifications. In total, 74 GS types were built, up to 1943. They were all oil burners, and booster-fitted to help tackle the heavy 1 in 45 (2.2 per cent) grade of Santa Margarita Hill, up which they commonly hauled their 568-ton trains unaided. No GS2 survives, but a GS4 and GS6 have been preserved, the former in working order.

**Boiler pressure:** 21.1kg/cm$^2$ (300psi)
**Cylinders:** 648x813mm (25.5x32in)
**Driving wheels:** 2032mm (80in)
**Grate area:** 8.4m$^2$ (90.4sq ft)
**Heating surface:** 454m$^2$ (4887sq ft)
**Superheater:** 194m$^2$ (2086sq ft)
**Tractive effort:** 32,285kg (71,173lb)
**Total weight:** 400.5t (883,000lb)

## GARRATT 4-6-2+2-6-4 PARIS LYONS MEDITERRANEAN RAILWAY (PLM) ALGERIA: 1938

The PLM operated lines in Algeria until amalgamation with the state system created Algerian Railways (CFA) in 1938. This engine was a blended the Beyer-Garratt format with French design. Both elegant and muscular-looking, its cylindrical tank and tender had the same diameter as the boiler, giving it a more unified appearance than most Garratts. It incorporated a variety of refinements, including electrically operated, cam-worked Cossart valve gear, dual controls to help with driving in either direction, and fan ventilation for the enclosed cab. It was the fastest Garratt type on record, achieving a maximum speed of 132kph (82mph) on test between Calais and Paris. In scheduled service, it ran the 422km (262 miles) between Algiers and Oran in 7 hours. The North African lines ran

Classed as type 231-132 when it became the property of the CFA, No 4 of the PLM's Algerian Garratts enters the station at Algiers to be joined to its train, on 4 May 1939.

other fast expresses, often with *Wagon-Lits* stock, linking cities in Tunisia, Algiers and Morocco, and the Garratts ran the full length of the Algerian main line, 1368km (850 miles) from Ghardimaou on the Tunisian border to Oudja on the border with Morocco. But like all engines with complex details, these required skilled maintenance, and in the wartime conditions prevailing in North Africa between 1940–45, this was not possible. By the mid-40s, the Garratts were in a decrepit condition, and the CFA pressed ahead with the purchase of diesel-electric units. None survived after 1951.

**Boiler pressure:** 20kg/cm$^2$ (248psi)
**Cylinders:** 490x660mm (19.25x26in)
**Driving wheels:** 1800mm (71in)
**Grate area:** 5.4m$^2$ (58sq ft)
**Heating surface:** 260m$^2$ (2794sq ft)
**Superheater:** 91m$^2$ (975sq ft)
**Tractive effort:** 24,950kg (55,010lb)
**Total weight:** 216t (476,280lb)

## CLASS 56 4-6-2 MALAYAN RAILWAYS MALAYA: 1938

Built in Glasgow to haul the mail trains between Singapore and Kuala Lumpur, and Kuala Lumpur–Butterworth, this metre gauge (39.4in) 'Pacific' class had a maximum axle load of 12.95t (12.75 tons). To keep the weight as low as possible, bar frames were used, and the boiler shell and inner firebox were of nickel steel. They had three cylinders, operated by poppet valves through a rotary camshaft system. The bogie tender held 10.16t (10 tons) of coal and 3500gals (4200US) of water. Fifteen were delivered in 1938–39, and a further 51 in 1940 and 1945–46, all from North British in Glasgow. They ran until the late 1960s, though by then displaced by diesel units onto secondary passenger and freight services.

**No 564.36, having run forward to the water tower at Tapah Road station, is ready to reverse to be reconnected to its train.**

**Boiler pressure:** 17.5kg/cm$^2$ (250psi)
**Cylinders:** 317x609mm (12.5x24in)
**Driving wheels:** 1370.5mm (54in)
**Grate area:** 2.5m$^2$ (27 sq ft)
**Heating surface:** 123.25m$^2$ (1327sq ft)
**Superheater:** 20.2m$^2$ (218sq ft)
**Tractive effort:** 10,928kg (22,130lb)
**Total weight:** 58.9t (129,920lb) (engine only)

## 232 CLASS 4-6-4 SOVIET RAILWAYS — RUSSIA: 1938

This was intended as a small class of 10 streamlined engines, specially built to haul the *Krasnaya Strela* ('Red Arrow') express between Moscow and Leningrad (650km/404 miles) on an eight-hour schedule with two engine changes *en route*. Only three were built, two at Kolomna, one at Voroshilovgrad. The first, known as 232 No 1, reached the maximum recorded speed of any Russian steam locomotive, 170.5kph (106mph) near Kalinin on 29 June 1938. The German invasion put a stop to development, and work on the class was not resumed afterwards. Nos 2 and 3 remained in active service on the 'Red Arrow' into the late 1950s. The class was designed in emulation of such American 'Hudson' types as the Chicago and Milwaukee F-7; it was important to show the Soviet public that Russian technology was as good as that of the capitalist countries.

**Boiler pressure:** 15kg/$cm^2$ (213psi)
**Cylinders:** 579x700.5mm (22.8x27.6in)
**Driving wheels:** 1995mm (78.6in)
**Grate area:** 6.5$m^2$ (70sq ft)
**Heating surface:** 239$m^2$ (2573.2sq ft)
**Superheater:** 124.5$m^2$ (1340.4sq ft)
**Tractive effort:** 14,960kg (33,000lb)
**Total weight:** 148.8t (301,340lb) (engine only)

## CLASS 15F 4-8-2 SOUTH AFRICAN RAILWAYS (SAR) — SOUTH AFRICA: 1938

The first of this class came from Henschel and Berliner Maschinenbau; 30 were delivered by Beyer Peacock to SAR in 1944, and others by North British Locomotive Co. Eventually, 225 were built. SAR had been operating 4-8-2s since 1910 and this design reflected the results of that experience. The boiler, slightly tapered, had a maximum diameter of 2018mm (79.5in). At 3947mm (155.4in) high and 3045mm (120in) wide, they just squeezed into the loading gauge. The bogie and truck wheels, and the two four-wheel bogies of the tender, were all fitted with roller bearings. The smoke boxes had self-cleaning screens. Most had automatic stokers, though some were hand-fired. The fire-door was steam operated and the grate had a power shaker to clear ash.

**Boiler pressure:** 14.7kg/$cm^2$ (210psi)
**Cylinders:** 609x711mm (24x28in)
**Driving wheels:** 1523mm (60in)
**Grate area:** 5.8$m^2$ (62.5sq ft)
**Heating surface:** 317$m^2$ (3415sq ft)
**Superheater:** 61.3$m^2$ (660sq ft)
**Tractive effort:** 19,202kg (42,340lb)
**Total weight:** 180.3t (397,600lb)

**One of the SAR's largest classes, the 15F, was equipped with accessories that made it the most up-to-date locomotive of its time.**

**Smoke and steam rise in profusion and obscure the train behind, as a Class 15F passes under a bridge.**

## CLASS E-4 4-6-4 CHICAGO & NORTH WESTERN RAILROAD (CNW) — USA: 1938

Competing for passenger traffic with the Milwaukee Road's 'Hiawathas', the CNW had to come up with something special, and had nine streamlined 'Hudsons' built by Alco in a style not at all unlike the Milwaukee Road engines, also from Alco; but exposing the cylinders as well as the motion. A hard-coal burner, it had a smaller grate than the rival F-7 4-6-4, and larger-diameter cylinders gave it a higher nominal tractive effort (good for publicity), but the dimensions of the two were otherwise almost the same. In performance terms, the two types were evenly matched, though the Milwaukee Road set tighter schedules than the CNW. But the E-4 could exceed 160kph (100mph) with a 500t train on level track. Engines such as these achieved the peak of US steam performance; major developments would have been needed to go beyond this point; and these, of

**Boiler pressure:** 21kg/$cm^2$ (300psi)
**Cylinders:** 634.5x736mm (25x29in)
**Driving wheels:** 2132mm (84in)
**Grate area:** 8.4$m^2$ (90.7sq ft)
**Heating surface:** 369.5$m^2$ft (3979sq)
**Superheater:** 175$m^2$ (1884sq ft)
**Tractive effort:** 24,940kg (55,000lb)
**Total weight:** 186.8t (412,000lb) (engine only)

## CLASS J-3A 4-6-4 NEW YORK CENTRAL RAILROAD (NYC) USA: 1938

Alco built 39 of this class, as well as another nine in streamlined form, tailored for the 'Twentieth Century Limited', representing the peak development of the NYC's racing 'Hudsons' and bringing the line's stock of the type to 275. In 1941, another two were streamlined to run the 'Empire State Express'. The streamliners' casing added only 2494kg (5500lb) to the engine weight. A booster engine fitted to the trailing bogie could supply a further 5487kg (12,100lb) of tractive effort in starting.

**Boiler pressure:** 19.3kg/cm² (275psi)
**Cylinders:** 571x736mm (22.5x29in)
**Driving wheels:** 2005mm (79in)
**Grate area:** 81.9m² (82sq ft)
**Heating surface:** 388.9m² (4187sq ft)
**Superheater:** 162m² (1745sq ft)
**Tractive effort:** 19,700kg (43,440lb)
**Total weight:** 163.2t (360,000lb) (engine only)

**The 'Empire State' express, still a steam-hauled flyer in February 1952, seen here at Dunkirk, NY, its un-streamlined J-class 'Hudson' pumping a crisp white exhaust into the frosty air.**

## CLASS GS-6 4-8-4 SOUTHERN PACIFIC RAILROAD (SP) USA: 1938

**Boiler pressure:** 18.2kg/cm² (260psi)
**Cylinders:** 685x761.4mm (27x30in)
**Driving wheels:** 1865.5mm (73.5in)
**Grate area:** 8.4m² (90.2sq ft)
**Heating surface:** 450.6m² (4852sq ft)
**Superheater:** 193.75m² (2086sq ft)
**Tractive effort:** 29,115kg (64,200lb)
**Total weight:** 212.4t (468,400lb) (engine only)

Although the 4-8-4 is associated mainly with passenger trains, a number of lines acquired freight or mixed-traffic versions, usually with high-speed freight in mind. The GS-6 was tasked with hustling perishable Californian fruit and vegetables eastwards across the prairies in 12.2m (40ft) insulated and ice-packed refrigerator cars, each weighing up to 76.2t (75 tons) fully loaded, and with up to 30 in a trainload. In all, 23 were built, by Lima, and the dimensions of this locomotive compare interestingly with those of its express passenger sister of 1937. The nominal tractive force as stated by the builders was marginally less, and in most respects the engine was just slightly smaller. Notably the driving wheels were smaller and the steam pressure considerably lowered, reflecting a lower running speed. The freight model had more weight borne by the coupled wheels, 128.4t (126.4 tons) compared to the passenger engine's 125t (123 tons), a modest extra amount of adhesion in getting the drag on a lengthy train. Both were oil burners and were fitted with the same standard 'Type E' superheater. Though the tenders, on two six-wheel bogies, were identical in appearance, the GS-6's carried slightly less water and slightly more oil. Despite its lowlier role, the GS-6 was subjected to similar semi-streamlined styling, though painted in glossy black rather than the 'Daylight' livery.

**For all their size, the American 4-8-4s had a certain muscular compactness, certainly compared to the articulated locomotives. SP No 436, at San Francisco in June 1952, exudes power, but within a few years the SP would scrap all its remaining steam engines.**

## CLASS 12 4-4-2 BELGIAN NATIONAL RAILWAYS (SNCB) BELGIUM: 1939

The last 4-4-2 to be designed, this locomotive, on a more modest European scale, replicated the aim of engines like the CPR 4-4-4 in Canada: to operate lightly loaded high-speed inter-city services. Its outer shell provided effective streamlining while leaving working parts accessible, and yellow speed-stripes on its green background gave it the look of a flyer. Designed by M. Notesse, six were supplied in 1939, from Cockerill's shops. These had bar frames and inside cylinders, and four had Walschaerts valve gear with outside return cranks to the leading coupled wheels; the others had rotary cam valve gear, one Caprotti, the other Dabeg. The six-wheel tenders were cannibalized from redundant engines, and given a streamlined casing.

The 'Atlantics' began working 250t (246 ton) trains between Ostend and Brussels, 115km (71.5miles) in one hour, with a maximum speed of 140kph (87mph), though at high speed their ride was reputedly uncomfortable. World War II ended the service. When the Ostend line was electrified, they worked similar trains on the Brussels–Lille route, and were still doing so in 1960. One member of the class has been preserved.

**No 12.001, first of the class, in the yard at Lille, France, ready for the one-stop (at Tournai) return journey with the Brussels express.**

**Boiler pressure:** 18kg/cm$^2$ (256psi)
**Cylinders:** 480x720mm (18.8x28.4in)
**Driving wheels:** 2100mm (82.75in)
**Grate area:** 3.7m$^2$ (39.8sq ft)
**Heating surface:** 161m$^2$ (1729sq ft)
**Superheater:** 63m$^2$ (678sq ft)
**Tractive effort:** 12,079kg (26,620lb)
**Total weight:** 89.5t (188,500lb) (engine only)

## SERIES 61 4-6-6T GERMAN STATE RAILWAYS (DRB) GERMANY: 1939

This locomotive was the peak of Germany's streamlined tank operations. Its prototype, a 4-6-4T, No 61 001, had been built in 1935 by the Kassel firms of Henschel in partnership with Wagenfabrik Wegmann. Their aim was to design a steam train that would emulate the performance of the new diesel-powered lightweight expresses, and be as convenient to operate. The locomotive was wholly streamlined and the four-car train was also streamlined. A driving cab was installed at the end of the last coach, so that on a return journey it became the front of the train. The engine was a big one, a three-cylinder simple, though its shrouding was so complete that it was recognized as a steam locomotive only with difficulty.

The four-car *Henschel-Wegmann Zug*, as it was known, went into service in 1936 between Berlin and Dresden. In that year the solitary 60 001 ran a twice-daily express, doing the 176km (109-mile) journey in 100 minutes. It was clear, however, that its water and fuel capacity were limited. On many occasions it arrived at the terminus with a dry tank, and for this reason the 4-6-6T was conceived, with an outside-frame 6-wheel truck at the rear to carry 5t (4.9 tons) of coal and 1010gals (1210US) of water. The advent of war ended the service. The stock of the train was used, with an extra coach, for the post-war V-200-hauled *Blauer Enzian* express. No 61 001 was taken out of service in 1952; while the 4-6-6T was rebuilt by the *Deutsche Reichsbahn* in 1961 as a 4-6-2 tender locomotive for testing new rolling stock.

**Boiler pressure:** 20kg/cm$^2$ (285psi)
**Cylinders:** 390x660mm (15.3x26in)
**Driving wheels:** 2300mm (90.6in)
**Grate area:** 2.8m$^2$ (30sq ft)
**Heating surface:** 150m$^2$ (1615sq ft)
**Superheater:** 69.2m$^2$ (745sq ft)
**Tractive effort:** 7380kg (16,270lb)
**Total weight:** 146.3t (296,257lb)

## CLASS WM 2-6-4T EAST INDIAN RAILWAY (EIR) INDIA: 1939

For the 1675mm (5ft 6in) gauge suburban networks of the great Indian cities, a standard 2-6-4 passenger tank type was designed in the 1900s. The Bengal-Nagpur Railway had 30 2-6-4Ts of class FT dating from 1906; the East Bengal Railway had 53 class K or KS (superheated) from 1907–27, and the EIR had 15 of class BT from 1912–14. To supplement the older types on these and other lines, the large WM was designed as an Indian Railways standard, with outside cylinders and greater speed and haulage power.

**Class WM 13002 with a heavy commuter train (and a supercargo mounted on the front buffer-beam). The large angular casing of the steam pipes, a typical feature of many Indian locomotives, is very apparent.**

**Boiler pressure:** 14.7kg/cm$^2$ (210psi)
**Cylinders:** 406x710.6mm (16x28in)
**Driving wheels:** 1700mm (67in)
**Grate area:** 2.3m$^2$ (24sq ft)
**Heating surface:** 88.7m$^2$ (955sq ft)
**Superheater:** 22.3m$^2$ (240sq ft)
**Tractive effort:** 8660kg (19,000lb)
**Total weight:** 105.9t (233,630lb)

## 800 CLASS 4-6-0 GREAT SOUTHERN RAILWAY (GSR) IRELAND: 1939

***Maeve*, photographed at Adelaide, Belfast, in April 1964, the same year that the class 800 were taken out of service.**

Locomotive design on the 1524mm (5ft) gauge Irish railways was closely identified with the British tradition. Economic difficulties in the Irish Free State meant that there was little new building. By 1939, the main Dublin–Cork line was chronically short of adequate motive power, and the three '800s' were designed and built at the GSR Inchicore shops in Dublin to provide express services on this route, and named *Maeve*, *Macha* and *Tailte* after legendary Irish queens. Three-cylinder simples, with three sets of Walschaerts valve gear, and double chimneys, they were the largest and most powerful locomotives built in Ireland, their dimensions comparable with the English 'Castles' or 'Royal Scots'. They handled the traffic with ease, though their performance was soon constrained by the 'Emergency' years of 1939–45 and the fuel shortages in post-war Ireland. It was 1950 before they could shine again. In that year, the Belfast-Dublin express became a through train to Cork, reversing at the capital's Amiens Street terminus, from where it was hauled by an '800' via the link line under Phoenix Park on to the GSR main line. Although speeds of up to 161kph (100mph) were rumoured, nothing of this sort has been verified, though they were undoubtedly fast engines. *Tailte* was withdrawn in 1957, the two others in 1964, but *Maeve* is kept at the Ulster Transport Museum.

***Maeve*, photographed in November 1996 inside the Cultra transport museum, near Belfast in Northern Ireland.**

**Boiler pressure:** 15.75kg/cm$^2$ (225psi)
**Cylinders:** 470x711mm (18.5x28in)
**Driving wheels:** 2007mm (79in)
**Grate area:** 3.10m$^2$ (33.5sq ft)
**Heating surface:** 174m$^2$ (1870sq ft)
**Superheater:** 43.5m$^2$ (468sq ft)
**Tractive effort:** 14,970kg (33,000lb)
**Total weight:** 137t (302,500lb)

**The steam locomotive as an expression of national identity. The decorative cast name-plate is suitably spelled in its Gaelic form, *Maedb*.**

## CLASS 131 2-6-2T RUMANIAN STATE RAILWAYS (CFR) RUMANIA: 1939

Though mechanically similar to the Hungarian class 375 2-6-2T, which it replaced in service, this was one of the few steam locomotives designed in Rumania, which mainly bought in German and other central European designs. The Resita works built 65 between 1939 and 1942, and they were used in suburban and local passenger services.

They were fitted with the Cosmovici dual oil and coal burning system, with oil tanks above the side water tanks.

**Boiler pressure:** 12kg/cm$^2$ (171psi)
**Cylinders:** 510x650mm (20x25.6in)
**Driving wheels:** 1440mm (56.75in)
**Grate area:** 3.6m$^2$ (38.7sq ft)
**Heating surface:** not known
**Superheater:** not known
**Tractive effort:** 11,900kg (26,250lb)
**Total weight:** not known

## STEAM-DIESEL LOCOMOTIVE 2-8-2 SOVIET RAILWAYS RUSSIA: 1939

The marriage of the steam engine and the internal combustion engine turned out to be a forlorn hope. The British Kitson company built a 'diesel-steam' prototype in 1924. Known as the Kitson-Still, it had double-acting pistons, moved by diesel combustion at the inner end and by steam expansion at the outer end. Without a firebox, it started on steam via a burner placed in the boiler, and the acceleration eventually produced a compression rate at which the diesel fuel ignited and drove the cylinders, while the waste heat generated was used to heat the water which made the steam to operate the steam end. Ansaldo in Italy made a similar experiment. Kitsons went bankrupt in the post-1929 Slump, but the concept was revived in Soviet Russia, in the late 1930s, where it was known as the *Teploparovoz* type. The Kitson locomotive had eight inside cylinders, arranged in banks of four on opposite sides of a crankshaft set parallel to the axles. The much bigger Russian engines were a 2-8-2 and a 2-10-4, from the Voroshilovgrad works, and a 2-10-2 from Kolomna. These, for good measure, were also opposed-piston locomotives, in which a centrally mounted set of outside cylinders on each side drove the pistons in opposing directions, thereby obtaining (in principle at least) a balance of revolving forces which resulted in less hammer-blow effect on the track and less wear and tear on the moving parts of the engine.

The 2-10-2 burned gas rather than diesel, generating it from anthracite. It also had an anthracite pulverizer for steam fuel, and a tender condenser. These excessively complex designs were abandoned by 1948. Detailed specifications are not available.

## CLASS 19D 4-8-2 SOUTH AFRICAN RAILWAYS (SAR) SOUTH AFRICA: 1939

The Class 19 'Mountains', mostly German-built, were designed to haul branch traffic, goods, passenger and mixed, and did so until the final phasing-out of steam, by which time many were in poor condition. The first were delivered in 1928. Class 19D, built by Krupp and Borsig, was identical to the preceding 19C of 1933, except for having Walschaerts valve gear and piston valves, instead of rotary cam gear with poppet valves. A further delivery was made in 1948, and Vanderbilt 12-wheel tenders were fitted to these. One of the class was modernized with L.D. Porta's gas-producer system in 1979.

**A 19D at Mafeking in 1979. From 1937 to 1948, 235 were built. With a maximum axle load of 13.8t, they were used on branch lines.**

**Boiler pressure:** 14kg/cm$^2$ (200psi)
**Cylinders:** 533x660mm (21x26in)
**Driving wheels:** 1370mm (54in)
**Grate area:** 3.3m$^2$ (36sq ft)
**Heating surface:** 171.5m$^2$ (1847sq ft)
**Superheater:** 36.2m$^2$ (390sq ft)
**Tractive effort:** 16,370kg (36,096lb)
**Total weight:** 81.2t (179,088lb)

## CLASS FEF-2 4-8-4 UNION PACIFIC RAILROAD (UP) USA: 1939

The period from 1939 to 1944 marked the real heyday of the 4-8-4 as a passenger engine. A Norfolk & Western Class J reached 177kph (110mph) with a 1025 ton train on level track, and similar feats have been ascribed to the UP FEF ('four-eight-four'), of which 45 were built, with variations of design, between 1938 and 1944, all by Alco.

These engines attained a peak of power and efficiency, ironically, just as the General Motors EMD diesels began to eat seriously into the domain of steam.

Streamlining was no longer enough, and the FEFs were free both of cosmetics and gadgets – they were merely superb two-cylinder simple-expansion steam locomotives.

**Union Pacific No 844 is the last locomotive of the final series, FEF-3. Built in 1944, preserved, restored and still steaming, it attracts attention as it stands at Sacramento, California.**

**Boiler pressure:** 21kg/cm$^2$ (300psi)
**Cylinders:** 635x813mm (25x32in)
**Driving wheels:** 2032mm (80in)
**Grate area:** 9.3m$^2$ (100sq ft)
**Heating surface:** 393m$^2$ (4225sq ft)
**Superheater:** 130m$^2$ (1400sq ft)
**Tractive effort:** 28,950kg (63,800lb)
**Total weight:** 412t (908,000lb)

## CLASS S1 6-4-4-6 PENNSYLVANIA RAILROAD (PRR) USA: 1939

**No 6100 at Chicago, on 24 June, 1941, at the head of the PRR luxury train, *The General*. With six out of 10 axles not contributing to adhesive weight, one of the engine's problems can be seen.**

Not every design from the heyday of steam (the late 30s and early 40s) was a success. Despite a test run at 162.5kph (101mph) with a 1364t (1342-ton) train, this locomotive, was a one-off. A 32-ton maximum axle load limited its use, and its adhesive weight was only 26.5 per cent of the total, so both sets of driving wheels tended to slip at the same time on starting. Built at the PRR's Juniata shops, it was exhibited at the New York World's fair in 1939–40, but little used, and was broken up in 1949.

**Boiler pressure:** 21kg/cm$^2$ (300psi)
**Cylinders:** 558x660mm (22x26in)
**Driving wheels:** 2132mm (84in)
**Grate area:** 12.26m$^2$ (132sq ft)
**Heating surface:** 525.2m$^2$ (5660sq ft)
**Superheater:** 193.6m$^2$ (2085sq ft)
**Tractive effort:** 35,456kg (71,800lb)
**Total weight:** 523.4t (1,060,000lb)

## CLASS TR1 2-8-2 STATE RAILWAYS (VR) FINLAND 1940

The backbone of Finnish freight operation was the Tk and Tv 2-8-0 types, but a need for greater power to move heavier trains led to this design. It shared its boiler and tender with the Hr1 'Pacific' class of 1937, and other parts were interchangeable between the classes. The front carrying and coupled axles formed a Krauss-Helmholtz bogie and the trailing axle was an Adams radial one. Between 1940

**Right: A class Tr-1 No 1093 stands outside Helsinki station in 1963.**

**Below: A Lokomo-built engine of 1955, class Tr-1 No 1086 at Kouvola, a junction on the Helsinki–Leningrad main line, in 1970.**

and 1957, 67 Tr1s were built, mostly by Tampella and Lokomo in Tampere, Finland; but including 20 from the German firm of Jung. Over the 17 years, the design was slightly modified, and the final four engines had roller bearings on all axles. During World War II, some of the class ran on wood fuel.

They worked the heaviest main-line trains, but a maximum operating speed of 80kph (50mph) meant they were also used on long-distance passenger trains. After 1945, they were supplemented by the powerful 2-10-0s class Tr2. By the late 1960s, their use had declined, but they were used into the 70s hauling winter-season freight to ice-free harbours in the south.

**Class Tr1 No 1096 at Kouvola in in July 1967. One of the last to be built, in the mid-1950s, it has German-style smoke deflectors.**

**Boiler pressure:** 15kg/cm$^2$ (214psi)
**Cylinders:** 610x700mm (24x27.5in)
**Driving wheels:** 1600mm (63in)
**Grate area:** 3.5m$^2$ (37.7sq ft)
**Heating surface:** 195.4m$^2$ (2103sq ft)
**Superheater:** 68m$^2$ (732.1sq ft)
**Tractive effort:** 20,740kg (45,730lb)
**Total weight:** 95t (engine only)

## 160.A.1 2-12-0 FRENCH NATIONAL RAILWAYS (SNCF) FRANCE 1940

A six-cylinder steam locomotive might seem like a wild flight of imagination by a theory-obsessed designer. Two, three, or four were established as the standard forms. But this was no madcap design. It was a rebuild by André Chapelon of a 6000-class 2-10-0. This was a class of 4-cylinder compounds, which, with some modernizations, had been running freight trains on the Paris–Orleans system since 1909. The aim was to produce a big freight engine that would perform economically at low speeds – something steam locomotives were historically bad at doing. The six coupled axles were not for show, but because the long boiler and firebox required adequate support and a sufficiently low maximum axle loading. Six cylinders were considered necessary to provide the power and traction required; a single pair of low-pressure cylinders would have had to be so large as to break the loading gauge. Four in-line low-pressure cylinders were set ahead of the first coupled axle, with the inside pair driving the second axle and the outside pair the third. The high-pressure cylinders also inside, towards the middle of the locomotive, and receiving steam via a Houlet superheater, drove the fourth coupled axle. They had steam 'jackets' to keep the outer walls hot. The boiler was divided into two parts, an adaptation of the Italian Franco system, the front end being a pre-heating drum, from which almost-boiling water was fed by an overflow system into the main boiler. A Nicholson-type thermic syphon was fitted in the firebox. Every effort was made to generate, to conserve, and to make the most effective use of steam. Exhaust steam drove the ACFI feed pump that supplied the pre-heater. Steam was re-superheated in a Schmidt superheater between the high-pressure and low-pressure cylinders. Lentz poppet valves were used to work the pistons, actuated by oscillating cams driven by Walschaerts gear, all of it outside the frames, with the hp cylinders worked from the 4th coupled axle. Kylchap double exhaust pipes were fitted. The original frame was substantially reinforced as well as lengthened. The three driving axles were fixed, and the others had a degree of lateral movement to enable the long wheelbase to traverse curves.

The rebuilding began in 1936, in pre-SNCF days, but progress was slow, and it was completed in June 1940, just before the fall of France. The new engine was stored away at Brive, in the southwest, until after the war. Tests could not be undertaken until 1948, by which time Chapelon's other solitary masterpiece, the 4-8-4 No 242.A1, had undergone its own trials. As with the 4-8-4, the achievement of the 2-12-0, and the lessons learned from it, were never to be applied in France. The tests were made both on the Vitry static testing plant, and on the road; and the aim of the design was fully met. At low speeds, the locomotive showed no decline in thermal efficiency. Its fuel consumption went down, not up as had been the norm hitherto. A valuable result, not anticipated, was that the steam jackets on the high-pressure cylinders, combined with moderate superheat in the low-pressure cylinders, removed the need for super-hot superheating, whose extremely high temperatures were a constant source of expensive damage to castings, joints and lubricated surfaces.

Although speed was not a prerequisite, the engine recorded 95kph (59mph) on test. It took a train of 65 vehicles, 1686t (1660 tons) on level track between Laroche and Dijon at a steady 48kph (30mph). The maximum actual tractive effort recorded on the move in these tests was of the order of 22,200kg (48,940lb). On one occasion, starting a 1686t (1660 ton) train on a curving 1 in 125 gradient, the dynamometer car registered a tractive effort of 39,836kg (87,824lb). Tests were made with various proportions of superheat in the hp and lp cylinders and conclusively established its value. The 2-12-0 was inevitably a test engine; indeed its designer referred to it as a laboratory. But no further conversions were authorized, and it remained a single-engine class until it was scrapped in November 1955, two years after Chapelon had retired from the SNCF.

**Boiler pressure:** 18.3kg/cm$^2$ (261psi)
**Cylinders:** hp and inside lp 520x540.6mm (20.5x21.3in); lp outside 640x649.75mm (25.2x25.6in)
**Driving wheels:** 1396mm (55in)
**Grate area:** 4.4m$^2$ (47.4sq ft)
**Heating surface:** 218m$^2$ (2347sq ft)
**Superheater:** 174m$^2$ (1873sq ft)
**Tractive effort:** 25,167kg (55,490lb)
**Total weight**: 152.1t (335,500lb) (engine only)

## CLASS PC 4-6-2 IRAQ STATE RAILWAYS IRAQ 1940

Despite war conditions, three streamlined two-cylinder 'Pacifics' were delivered by Robert Stephenson & Hawthorns, of Darlington, England, to Iraq in 1940; a fourth was lost *en route*. Handsome engines, reminiscent of the British 'Coronation' and A4 classes, they were ordered originally for the completion of the line from Baghdad via Tel Kotchek into Turkey, the route of the 'Taurus Express' from Istanbul. The schedule was, however ,a distinctly slow one, taking 17hrs 30min to the border, and altogether three days and nights to make the 2603km (1617 mile) journey. The engines were still operating the service in the 1950s.

By that time they offered the weary passengers an elegant contrast to the German 0-8-0s and former British War Department 2-8-0s which hauled the train on the earlier sections of the long haul from Haydarpasa.

**Boiler pressure:** 15.4kg/cm$^2$ (220psi)
**Cylinders:** 533x660mm (21x26in)
**Driving wheels:** 1751mm (69in)
**Grate area:** 2.9m$^2$ (31.2sq ft)
**Heating surface:** 251.3m$^2$ (2706sq ft) (including superheater)
**Superheater:** not known
**Tractive effort:** 14,092kg (31,074lb)
**Total weight:** 100.2t (221,088lb)

## H-CLASS 'HEAVY HARRY' 4-8-4 VICTORIAN RAILWAYS (VR) AUSTRALIA 1941

The largest locomotive on the VR 1600mm (5ft 3in) gauge system, this one-off was also Australia's first 4-8-4, followed by the South Australian 520 class in 1943. Built at the Newport work-shops, with American-style bar frames, it was intended to haul the 'Overland' express between Melbourne and Adelaide, but did little passenger work. A mechanical rarity, this three-cylinder simple expansion engine also had separated double chimneys. Despite route restrictions, 'Heavy Harry' worked hard from 1941 to 1958, on fast goods trains on the line between Melbourne and Wodonga, running 1,314,976km (817,088 miles) in total. The tender was massive, running on two six-wheel bogies, and feeding into a mechanical stoker. 'Heavy Harry' is preserved at the Newport Railway Museum.

**Boiler pressure:** 15.4kg/cm$^2$ (220psi)
**Cylinders:** 546x711mm (21.5x28in)
**Driving wheels:** 1624mm (67in)
**Grate area:** 6.3m$^2$ (68sq ft)
**Heating surface:** 369.6m$^2$ (3980sq ft)
**Superheater:** 72.4m$^2$ (780sq ft)
**Tractive effort:** 24,946kg (55,008lb)
**Total weight:** 264.2t (582,512lb)

**The twin-chimneyed 'Heavy Harry' on 7 December 1980; it is the prime attraction in its place of retirement, the North Williamstown Railway Museum, Melbourne.**

## TYPE 97 2-12-2T GERMAN STATE RAILWAYS (DRG) AUSTRIA 1941

After the war, this locomotive became class 297 (two models only), built at the Floridsdorf works and fitted for working on the mineral line between Eisenerz and Vordenberg. Two outside cylinders drove the rail wheels and two on the inside drove the two rack wheels. These were governed by a separate regulator, operating only over the rack sections of the track. Steeply graded, the line rose 440m (1443ft) in 8km (5 miles), and was laid to standard gauge, to let iron-ore wagons be worked on to the Vienna–Villach main line. The engines could work trains of 400t (393.6 tons) unaided up the grades, more than double the tonnage taken by the previous class 197 0-12-0Ts. Maximum speed was 25kph (15.5mph). They were fitted with Giesl ejectors. In practice, the older engines were more reliable and the 297s spent a lot of time in the repair shops. One has been preserved.

**Boiler pressure:** 16kg/cm$^2$ (228psi)
**Cylinders:** outer 610x520mm (24x20.5in); inner 400x500mm (15.75x19.7in)
**Driving wheels:** 1030mm (40.5in)
**Grate area:** 3.9m$^2$ (42sq ft)
**Heating surface:** not known
**Superheater:** not known
**Tractive effort:** 25,620kg (56,500lb)
**Total weight:**

## Nos. 153-7 2-8-2 DONNA TERESA CHRISTINA RAILWAY BRAZIL 1941

Of moderate power, these five Mikados were built at the Alco works in Schenectady and shipped direct to Brazil.

Though scaled to the metre gauge (39.4in) of this predominantly freight-carrying line, they were standard US-style locomotives, with bar frames and two outside simple-expansion cylinders.

By the later 1950s, they were somewhat underpowered for the traffic requirements of the period, but were not officially withdrawn until 1984.

**No 153 shunting a line of coal trucks in the sidings at Tubarao, on 14 March, 1973. The engine is in very good external condition, looking as if it had recently been overhauled.**

**Boiler pressure:** 12.6kg/m$^2$ (180psi)
**Cylinders:** 406x558mm (16x22in)
**Driving wheels:** 1066mm (42in)
**Grate area:** 4.42m$^2$ (47.6sq ft)
**Heating surface:** 92.9m$^2$ (1000.5sq ft)
**Superheater:** 19.8m$^2$ (213sq ft)
**Tractive effort:** 9305kg (20,517lb)
**Total weight:** 57.8t (127,500lb) (engine only)

## Class 11 4-10-0 BULGARIAN STATE RAILWAYS (BDZ) BULGARIA 1941

This unusual wheel configuration was provided for the BDZ by German builders, 10 from Henschel in 1941 and 12 more in 1943 from Borsig and Skoda (then under German control).

It was intended for heavy trains of either passengers or freight, and followed the three-cylinder simple pattern established by the BDZ since 1935.

The main use was on the steeply graded international main line from Sofia to Belgrade in Yugoslavia, over the challenging Dragoman Pass. German smoke deflectors were fitted, but also a Bulgarian flared semi-collar chimney cap.

Highly considered in their own country, political separation from Europe made it difficult for the qualities of Bulgarian locomotives to be appreciated.

**Boiler pressure:** 16kg/cm$^2$ (228psi)
**Cylinders:** 520x700mm (20.5x27.5in)
**Driving wheels:** 1450mm (45in)
**Grate area:** 4.9m$^2$ (52.75sq ft)
**Heating surface:** 224m$^2$ (2411.7sq ft)
**Superheater:** 83.9m$^2$ (903.3sq ft)
**Tractive effort:** 22,570kg (49,770lb)
**Total weight:** 109.6t (241,668lb)

## Experimental Locomotive 19-1001 2-8-2 GERMAN STATE RAILWAYS GERMANY 1941

Henschel were developing this experimental type at their works in Kassel in the early stages of World War II. It was an eight-cylinder locomotive, each driving axle being turned by a two-cylinder V-format driving unit suspended from the main frame, outside the wheels. Piston valves operated the cylinders by means of eccentrics, the eccentric shaft chain-driven from a main crankshaft. After 1945, American forces removed the locomotive to Fort Monroe, USA, where it was broken up in 1952. Wartime conditions meant that this fascinating experimental engine was never completed or fully tested. At the end of the war, Kassel was included in the American-administered zone of Germany, and US engineers had it shipped to the USA, and kept at Fort Monroe. However, American interest in steam power was now waning fast; in 1952, after years of neglect, the engine was broken up.

**Boiler pressure:** (20kg/cm$^2$284psi)
**Cylinders:** 300x300mm (11.8x11.8in)
**Driving wheels:** 1244mm (49in)
**Grate area:** 4.5m$^2$ (49sq ft)
**Heating surface:** 239.7m$^2$ (2580.75sq ft)
**Superheater:** 100m$^2$ (1076.6sq ft)
**Tractive effort:** N/A
**Total weight:** 96.5t (212,782lb) (engine only)

## 'Merchant Navy' Class 4-6-2 SOUTHERN RAILWAY (SR) GREAT BRITAIN 1941

To avoid wartime restrictions on construction, this express passenger engine was described to the Ministry of Supply as a 'mixed traffic' type. In the eyes of its designer, Oliver Bulleid, it was a new-generation locomotive intended for an era when trains loading up to 610t (600 tons) would be hauled at average speeds of 113kph (70mph). It was a bold but prescient vision. Equally bold were some of the novelties incorporated inside the 'air-smoothed' casing. Bulleid was an authority on welding, and much weight was saved by welded construction of an all-steel firebox and boiler. The three simple-expansion cylinders were operated by piston valves, actuated in turn by a unique chain-driven valve gear enclosed within an oil-tight casing, which also enclosed the middle connecting-road, crosshead and crank. This feature was to present many repair and maintenance problems. The 'Merchant Navies' were followed by a lighter-weight 'West Country' class, 110 strong, of the same design, including the Boxpok wheels.

Eventually all the 'Merchant Navy' and many of the 'West Country' class were rebuilt without

**The engines were named after famous steamship lines, and the house flag of the line was incorporated in the nameplates of each locomotive, along with the class designation.**

the outer casing and with three sets of conventional Walschaerts gear. The episode illustrates the autocratic power, even into the 1940s, which a British Chief Mechanical Engineer possessed within his domain. No other country, nor Great Britain for much longer, would have accepted a situation in which some 200 new engines were built with an untried and inaccessible system for such a crucial part of the works.

**Rebuilt 'Merchant Navy' No 35007, Aberdeen Commonwealth Line, at Salisbury Station, in 1958. With conventional valve gear, they were more reliable performers and lost none of their power or speed.**

**Boiler pressure:** 19.75kg/cm$^2$ (280psi)
**Cylinders:** 457x609mm (18x24in)
**Driving wheels:** 1880mm (74in)
**Grate area:** 4.5m$^2$ (48.5sq ft)
**Heating surface:** 236m$^2$ (2451sq ft)
**Superheater:** 76.3m$^2$ (822sq ft)
**Tractive effort:** 17,233kg (38,000lb)
**Total weight:** 96.25t (212,240lb)

## USATC SWITCHER 0-6-0T UNITED STATES ARMY TRANSPORTATION CORPS USA 1941

**Boiler pressure:** 14.7kg/cm$^2$ (210psi)
**Cylinders:** 419x609mm (16.5x24in)
**Driving wheels:** 1370mm (54in)
**Grate area:** 1.8m$^2$ (19.4sq ft)
**Heating surface:** 81.3m$^2$ (876sq ft)
**Tractive effort:** 9810kg (21,630lb)
**Total weight:** 45.6t (100,650lb)

Three US builders, Davenport, Vulcan, and Porter, built 382 of this side-tank design, one of the USATC's standards, which became a familiar sight especially in Greek and Yugoslavian station yards after the end of World War II. It was built for service in Britain, Europe and the Middle East, and so had to conform to the British loading gauge. Two sandboxes and a dome on one short boiler, with the stovepipe chimney, gave them a characteristic look. The two outside cylinders were operated by Walschaerts gear. The first ones arrived in England in July 1942. Thirteen were acquired after the war by the Southern Railway, for working in Southampton Docks,

**No-one is around to supervise as an ex-USATC 0-6-0, now on the Hellenic State Railways, is rather splashily filled from a column that has lost the canvas tube which guided water into the filler-hole.**

and some of these remained active until 1967. It also appears to have influenced the design of the Great Western's 1948 0-6-0 with outside cylinders. Seventy-seven were bought by the SNCF, where some lasted until 1971. Yugoslavia received 120, and built 23 more to the same plans in 1956–57. Twenty went to Greece, where some were converted to tender 0-6-0s. During 1943, 30 engines, oil-fired, were sent for work in the Middle East, operating in Iraq, Palestine, and Egypt, and some of them remained in civilian service after 1945. Four were supplied to the Jamaican Government Railways in 1943–45. Several examples are preserved in Britain.

## CLASS J 4-8-4 NORFOLK & WESTERN RAILWAY (N&W) USA 1941

The Norfolk & Western's main business was moving vast tonnages of coal. It ran few passenger services and its stud of express engines was not large, but their quality was first class. Between 1941 and 1943, 11 of class J were built to handle the line's principal passenger trains, and by 1950, the first had run over 1,609,000km (1,000,000 miles). The monthly distance run varied from 24,000 to 29,000km (15,000–18,000 miles), and though the longest single run (from Roanoake, Virginia, to Cincinnati, Ohio) was 682km (424 miles), smart turn-round times at the terminal stations contributed most to this mileage. These engines were designed to run about 386,000km (240,000 miles) before a overhaul. To many operators of steam locomotives, such figures would have seemed impossible. But high standards of shed maintenance and preparation paid off for the N&W. Of all the American railroads, this one worked hardest to modernize and retain its steam fleet, striving to match the levels of availability and use promised by the diesel-electric builders. In the end, it could not buck the trend, but its steam services were all the more distinguished because of the hilly terrain in which they operated. The Class J was reached 177kph (110mph) on a test run with 1041t (1025 tons) on the Pennsylvania Railroad, near Crestline: at which speed, its 1776mm (70in) driving wheels were being turned at a rate which would have brought much greater speed with larger diameter. Speeds of up to 145kph (90mph ) in regular service with 14- or 15-car trains were also recorded. By the time the Js were taken out of service in 1959, two had exceeded 3,218,000km (2,000,000 miles).

**Boiler pressure:** 21kg/cm$^2$ (300psi)
**Cylinders:** 685x812mm (27x32in)
**Driving wheels:** 1776mm (70in)
**Grate area:** 10m$^2$ (107.7sq ft)
**Heating surface:** 489.6m$^2$ (5271sq ft)
**Superheater:** 202.2m$^2$ (2177sq ft)
**Tractive effort:** 39,506kg (80,000lb)
**Total weight:** 431t (872,600lb)

**The polished front end of preserved class J No. 611, seen at Roanoke, Va, in 2000. The pilot is designed as a snowplough rather than as the traditional cowcatcher.**

A water tower straddles the tracks, enabling locomotives to be replenished on both lines simultaneously, with gravity feed.

No 611 broadside-on, running at the head of a special service, near Roanoke, Va., in 1993.

## CLASS 4000 4-8-8-4 UNION PACIFIC RAILROAD (UP) USA 1941

**The scale of the 'Big Boys' can be judged by the size of the engineer of No 4024. One of the original 1941 locomotives, it is forging its way up-grade with a mixed train of freight cars.**

These were the 'Big Boys' – the name was chalked on a smokebox during construction by an unknown employee of Alco, and it stuck. The 25 engines of this class were the largest and most powerful steam locomotives ever built, surpassing the Northern Pacific 'Yellowstones' of 1928 in weight and with a length of 40,490mm (132ft 10in) compared to 37,185mm (122ft); though with a lesser nominal tractive effort. Although the Union Pacific was an early user of diesel locomotives for its passenger express trains, it did not begin to use diesels for freight until 1947. In this department, steam was still unchallenged. But the requirements were severe. The design was worked out by the Research & Standards department of the UP, in close association with the American Locomotive Company (Alco) which built the engines. The moving spirit was Otto Jabelmann, the UP's head of motive power and machinery since 1936, and vice-president in charge of research and mechanical standards since 1939. He had also overseen the design of the line's other giant steam locomotives, including the 'Challenger' 4-6-6-4s of 1936 which preceded the 'Big Boys'. The UP also operated the world's longest rigid-frame locomotives, the 88 three-cylinder 4-12-2s built between 1926 and 1930. However, it was clear that to obtain greater power, an articulated wheelbase would be necessary. The 'Challengers' provided the answer. Mallet-type engines, though with simple expansion only, their front coupled wheels formed an articulated truck while the rear coupled wheels were set in the frame. On the first engines of the type, the front truck was allowed vertical as well as lateral movement. This was one of the few unsatisfactory aspects of the design, giving the front set of coupled wheels a tendency to slip. Until now, articulation had been associated with low-speed slogging, but the 'Challengers' could and did run at 130km (80 miles) an hour, riding easily. As the Lima-built 'super-power' 2-8-4 of 1925 had done, the UP's and Alco's great 4-6-6-4 opened a door to further possibilities with steam traction. Other lines soon realized this, and a further eight bought engines of the same type. A total of 254 were built, of which 105 belonged to the UP.

Although it continued to order 'Challengers', the UP did not feel it had yet reached the ultimate point, and the 4-8-8-4 was soon on the drawing board. The new engines were enlarged 'Challengers', longer and heavier, with a vast firebox extending forward over the two rear coupled axles. The frame was a huge single cast steel piece. Welding was extensively used in the building, notably in the construction of the boiler, pressed to a higher level than the 'Challenger's' 19.7kg/ cm$^2$ (280psi). Multiple-jet exhausts fed out through a double chimney. All axles were fitted with roller bearings. A significant new feature was the redesign of the joint between the front truck and the frame, to allow lateral movement only. Any changes in gradient or unevenness in the track were absorbed by a highly effective suspension system. This solved the slipping problem, and a final batch of 'Challengers' incorporated the same feature. Although they could and did operate on any part of the system, the operating requirements of the 'Big Boys' were defined by the UP's mountainous Sherman Hill main line through the Wasatch Mountains between Ogden, Utah, and Green River, Wyoming, a 283km (176-mile) stretch rising from 589m (1933ft) to 2442m (8013ft) with a ruling grade of 1.14 per cent. They were not pushers; they were built to haul trains of up to 70 refrigerated fruit cars, weighing 3251t (3200 tons) over the road without assistance. By this stage of steam locomotive development, designers had ceased to be simply concerned by how many tons a locomotive could pull, probably at a low speed. Prompted by traffic managers anxious to combine haulage power with speed and efficiency, they were thinking in terms of what horsepower could be developed by a really big locomotive, working hard. In the case of the 'Big Boys', full power output was obtained at 112kph (70mph), though they could operate at up to 130kph (80mph). This maximum equated to around 7460kW (10,000hp) developed in the cylinders, an output beyond that of any other steam locomotive and far beyond that of contemporary diesel units. But at low speeds, they were less able to exert their power potential: this was the perennial problem of the steam locomotive. In a 1974 article in the American *Trains* magazine, W. Withuhn commented: 'Big Boy's *profitable* capacity was not so much determined by its 6200hp (4623kW) at 35 miles (56kph) as it was limited by its 5200hp (3877kW) at 20 miles (32kph).' In other words, at the crucial phases of starting off and accelerating with a heavy train, the 4000s were unable to put more than half their full power potential to use. Steam designers might have shrugged this off in previous years, but now it was a serious disadvantage in comparison with the competing diesel-electrics, which though individually much less powerful, could be worked multiple-unit, and could deploy full power over a much wider spectrum of speeds. Despite this, the 'Big Boys' were effective in service and the first batch, built in 1941, all achieved more than 1,609,000km (one million miles) of running. Wartime traffic gave them much heavier loads, and they often worked double-headed, a thrilling spectacle as they climbed the grade. Their last revenue-earning duties were done in July 1959, and withdrawal began from 1961. Four survived at Green River depot until July 1962. Eight of the 'Big Boys' are preserved as static museum and display items: in one bizarre experiment at the Los Angeles City Fairplex, it was found that the firebox of No 4014 could accommodate 32 school-children.

The longest turntables in the world were installed at Green River and Ogden, 41m (135ft) to turn the 'Big Boys'. Working hard, a 'Big Boy' consumed 9.9t (22,000lb) of coal in an hour, and the tenders, running on five fixed axles plus a four wheel bogie in front, held 28.45t (28 tons) of coal and 20,800gals (25,000 US gals) of water. Two mechanical stokers kept the vast grate supplied with coal.

**One of the preserved 'Big Boys', No 4012, at the railway museum at Scranton, Pa., on 2 May 1997.**

**Action on Sherman Hill, Wyoming – a 4-6-6-4 'Challenger' heads a 4-8-8-4 'Big Boy' on a lengthy freight rounding a bend.**

**Boiler pressure:** 21kg/cm$^2$ (300psi)
**Cylinders:** 603x812mm (23.75x32in)
**Driving wheels:** 1726mm (68in)
**Grate area:** 14m$^2$ (150.3sq ft)
**Heating surface:** 547m$^2$ (5889sq ft)
**Superheater:** 229m$^2$ (2466sq ft)
**Tractive effort:** 61,394kg (135,375lb)
**Total weight:** 350t (772,000lb) (engine only)

# CLASS 52 'KRIEGSLOKOMOTIVE' 2-10-0 GERMAN STATE RAILWAYS (DRG) GERMANY 1942

In 1938, the *Deutsche Reichsbahn Gesellschaft* introduced its Class 50 as a standard two-cylinder 2-10-0 heavy freight locomotive. It was very much in the DRG tradition, with bar frames, round-top boilers, and wide fireboxes. After the beginning of World War II in 1939, production was stepped up, and the design was modified to speed up building. The modified engines were classed as 50ÜK (*Übergangskriegslokomotive*, 'transitional war locomotive'), and a total of 3164 were built. In 1941, the war effort created a severe shortage of motive power, so a massive increase in locomotive production was begun. From this came Class 52, the 'war engine' proper, whose details were worked out by a technical group from the DRG and the principal manufacturers. The prototype 52.001 was built by Borsig, a two-cylinder engine, with simple expansion, and Walschaerts gear operating piston valves. Around 6700 were built between 1942 and 1945. Speed of construction, and the minimum of materials consistent with durability, were essential. Welding was used more than in any previous locomotive; they had completely welded boilers and welding was used wherever possible to join parts that would once have been riveted or bolted together. The square steam-pipes and steam chest above the cylinders emphasized the 'no frills' approach, though from 1943, light-weight smoke deflectors of the type developed by Friedrich Witte were fitted to the smokebox sides, making the engines look less gaunt. All German manufacturers except the bomb-damaged Krupps built the class 52, as did the Skoda works at Plzen in Czechoslovakia, Graffenstaden in France, and the Polish Chrzanov and Cegielski works. It was never a totally homogeneous class. The different makers, and a stream of revised detail instructions, ensured considerable variety, apart from the major amendments which formed effective sub-classes. Most of the 52s had plate frames, of steel 30mm (1.2in) thick, much thinner than the 80mm (3.1in) bar frames of the class 50.

**This illustration of a 'Kriegslok' shows the hinged chimney cowl, enclosed cab, and insulated pumps needed to operate in extremely low temperatures on the Russian front.**

The Germans found in 1941 that their locomotives were liable to break down in the extreme cold of Russian winters, and a number of special features, including a chimney cowl, insulation of outside-mounted pumps, fully enclosed cab, and in some cases insulated tender tanks, were fitted to some of the first *Kriegsloks*. Feedwater heaters, standard on the class 50, were not, however, fitted to the class 52s. The original version was coal-fired, but an oil-burner later appeared. This had a tank fitted in and around the coal bunker space on the tender. Another variant was fitted with a condensing tender: a number of the class were equipped in this way to run supply trains to the German armies fighting on the Russian front, as the retreating Russians had razed all their engine sheds and refuelling facilities. Armour plating was fitted to some of these engines. Some Russian lines were re-gauged to standard by the Germans, but around 1500 class 52s were fitted with axles for the Russian 1524mm (5ft) gauge.

**In the twilight of an Austrian locomotive shed, the uncompromising lines of a 'Kriegslok' are unmistakable, even though the new owners have replaced its original stove-pipe chimney with an oblong Giesl ejector.**

From 1943, the standard tender for the class 52 was the welded Type 914, known as the *Wanne*, or 'bath-tub' from its rounded sides. Riding on two four-wheel bogies, it could be built in one-third of the time of a conventional tender, held more coal and water, and used less metal in construction. Its capacity was 10t of coal and 7000gal (8400 US gals) of water. Cracks tended to develop around the bogie mountings, and in the post-war period these tenders were reinforced in this area.

Like the class 50s, the class 52s had a maximum speed of 80kph (50mph), running either forwards or backwards. They were involved in an intensive network of conventional freight trains running normal goods services, in addition to rostered or special supply trains carrying military equipment. They were also among the locomotives involved in the dark and secret business of hauling trainloads of human beings over new lines laid right into the concentration and death camps. Over a thousand operated under military direction in the eastern occupied territories; and some hundreds of others were sold or sent on loan to Croatia, Hungary, Rumania, Serbia and Turkey. The *Kriegsloks* were used in all German-controlled regions before May 1945, including Norway; and after the defeat of Germany, large numbers were taken over by the liberated nations, or commandeered by, or given in reparations to, the Russians. Construction on a limited scale went on until 1951, including 150 built in Poland, 100 in Belgium and 84 in West Germany. These had feedwater heaters but otherwise retained their austerity look.

As with the British and American war-effort locomotive designs, the *Kriegsloks* were built in the anticipation of a short if busy life, but as with the others, their construction proved robust enough to ensure many years of service. In Germany itself, the stock was divided between the Federal and Democratic Republics, operating the DB and DR systems respectively. The DB phased its class 52s out rapidly after 1954. Their life on the DR was much longer, with the rebuilding of 200 during 1960–67 as class $52^{80}$, with all-welded standard boilers, combustion chambers in the fireboxes, Heinl feedwater heaters, and rotating spectacle glasses. Some of these *Rekolok* rebuilds were also given Giesl blast pipes and double chimneys. Twenty-five other 52s were adapted to burn pulverized brown coal as fuel. The 52s formed the DR's most numerous steam class, and the last ones remained in service until the 1980s; 15 of the unrebuilt class 52 were still on the roster in 1986, and those of class $52^{80}$ worked right until the end of steam in East Germany, in 1989.

On most Eastern European systems, they ran into the 1970s or even later. Russia after the war held around 2130, as 'trophy' locomotives. Regauged, repaired, rebuilt, cannibalized (sometimes one locomotive was resurrected from the wrecks of three) as class TE, they were widely deployed in the western Soviet Union and its satellite states until the late 1950s. Many were converted to oil firing. In 1963, the Russians sold 100 oil-fired former class 52s to Czechoslovakia, where they were designated class 555. Two hundred went to Poland, 140 to Bulgaria, and another 100 to Hungary; in all, some 700 were redistributed as the Russian diesel and electric programmes began to take effect. On the Yugoslavian system, they were designated class 33 and were the largest single class on the JDZ; after the collapse of Yugoslavia, some were brought from storage into active use in Bosnia during the mid-1990s. The furthest-flung of the locomotives were 12 from Russia and Poland, which were supplied to North Vietnam around 1984. Some of the longest-lived specimens were in Turkey, where their 15.2t (15-ton) axle-load kept them useful on branch lines in eastern Anatolia, sometimes partnered with ex-US S-160 2-8-0s, until 1990. In the late 1990s, large numbers were still in store in several East European countries, and around 200 *Kriegsloks* have been selected for preservation in many countries.

**A post-war Class 52, and one of the last to run, No 052 6921 shunts at Merstheim, in 1971. The tender has a built-in brakeman's compartment.**

**Boiler pressure:** 16kg/cm$^2$ (228psi)
**Cylinders:** 600x660mm (23.6x26in)
**Driving wheels:** 1400mm (55in)
**Grate area:** 3.9m$^2$ (42sq ft)
**Heating surface:** 177.6m$^2$ (1912sq ft)
**Superheater:** 63.7m$^2$ (685.8sq ft)
**Tractive effort:** 23,140kg (51,000lb)
**Total weight:** 84t (185,220lb) (engine only)

## Q1 0-6-0 SOUTHERN RAILWAY (SR) — GREAT BRITAIN 1942

**Class Q1 No 33017, in British Railways livery, near Grately, on a Salisbury–Basingstoke goods train, in October 1962.**

Extravagantly austere in appearance, this wartime engine was Britain's most powerful 0-6-0 type, produced as a 'general utility' locomotive. The main reason for the lack of running plate, etc., was that the boiler and firebox were very large and proportionately heavy. As with his 'Merchant Navy' Pacifics, the designer Oliver Bulleid incorporated welding techniques to save on weight and building time. It also had cast steel Boxpok wheels of the same type as the larger engines. With its 18.8t (18.5-ton) maximum axle loading, the Q1 had 93 per cent availability over the entire Southern system.

The two cylinders, set inside, had piston valves actuated by Stephenson's link motion. The inward tapering dog-bowl chimney crowned a five-jet blast-pipe nozzle. Although chiefly intended for freight work, train heating equipment was fitted, and the Q1, though used only on local services, could attain good speed. Indeed it was rumoured to have travelled at 120kph (75mph) in reverse gear, with its designer sitting happily on the buffer-beam.

**Boiler pressure:** 16.1kg/cm$^2$ (230psi)
**Cylinders:** 482x660mm (19x26in)
**Driving wheels:** 1548mm (61in)
**Grate area:** 2.5m$^2$ (27sq ft)
**Heating surface:** 152.5m$^2$ (1642sq ft)
**Superheater:** 20.2m$^2$ (218sq ft)
**Tractive effort:** 13,086kg (26,500lb)
**Total weight:** 89.8t (182,000lb)

## CLASS V4 2-6-2 LONDON & NORTH EASTERN RAILWAY (LNER) GREAT BRITAIN 1942

This was intended to be a large class, but only two V4s were built following the death of their chief designer, Sir Nigel Gresley, and a sudden radical change in LNER locomotive policy. Its wide-availability mixed-traffic potential was instead taken up by the two-cylinder B1 4-6-0 of 1942. The V4 was a three-cylinder engine, with Gresley's conjugated valve gear working the inside cylinder. It incorporated other late-Gresleyan features, such as a steam collector behind the dome. The first two engines, as prototypes, had different fireboxes, the first of copper, the second of welded steel. They ran mostly in Scotland, and were withdrawn for scrapping in 1957 and 1958.

**Boiler pressure:** 17.5kg/cm$^2$ (250psi)
**Cylinders:** 380x660mm (15x26in)
**Driving wheels:** 1725mm (68in)
**Grate area:** 2.6m$^2$ (28.5sq ft)
**Heating surface:** 134m$^2$ (1444sq ft)
**Superheater:** 33m$^2$ (356sq ft)
**Tractive effort:** 11,950kg (24,200lb)
**Total weight:** 114.9t (253,456lb)

**The second V4, as British Railways No 61701, seen at Ferryhill locomotive depot, Aberdeen, in May 1957. The first was named Bantam Cock, and railwaymen christened this one, unofficially, *Bantam Hen*.**

## 151.3101 CLASS 2-10-2 SPANISH NATIONAL RAILWAYS (RENFE) SPAIN 1942

The Spanish firm La Maquinista built 22 of these large engines between 1942 and 1945. Originally numbered 5001–5022, they were soon afterwards renumbered as 151.3101–3122. Whilst locomotive students like to feel they can identify an unknown type as French, German or Italian, from certain characteristics, it is hard to define a Spanish look. French, British, American and German influence all played a part in Spanish locomotive design, but in this one, it is perhaps a French air that predominated.

It was a three- cylinder simple, all three in line, the inside cylinder driving the second coupled axle and the outside ones driving the third. The valve gear was Walschaerts, operating Lentz oscillating cam poppet valves. The double chimney had Kylchap blast pipes. The long 10-coupled wheelbase was given some flexibility by a Krauss truck, linking the front carrying axle and the leading coupled axle. ACFI feed water pumps and heaters were fitted, most of the equipment being on the running plate – with the Spanish gauge of 1674mm (65.9in), there was room to spare. Two had mechanical stokers. Seven were oil burners.

These were powerful heavy haulage units, which originally worked coal trains from the mining area of Ponferrada to the coast at La Coruña, and then were transferred to work between León and Venta de Banos.

**Boiler pressure:** 16kg/cm$^2$ (228psi)
**Cylinders:** 570x750mm (22.4x29.5in)
**Driving wheels:** 1560mm (61.5in)
**Grate area:** 5.3m$^2$ (57sq ft)
**Heating surface:** 267.6m$^2$ (2880sq ft)
**Superheater:** 140.9m$^2$ (1516.6sq ft)
**Tractive effort:** 21,150kg (46,640lb)
**Total weight:** 213.1t (470,000lb)

## 4-6-2 ROYAL SIAMESE RAILWAYS (RSR) THAILAND 1942

The RSR's first 'Pacifics' for the metre gauge (39.4in) came from North British in Glasgow in 1917. In 1942, during the Japanese occupation of Thailand, 10 new 4-6-2s were supplied, from Hitachi and Nippon Sharyo. They were finely finished compared

**Photographed on a goods train at Ron Phibun on 1 January 1974, No 823 of the post-war production batch bears the message 'Happy New Year 1974' in both English and Thai.**

with Japanese engines for home use at this time, even having copper chimney caps. Nippon Sharyo built 30 more of this wood-burning class between 1949 and 1950. Two-cylindered, simple expansion, with Walschaerts valve gear, these robust engines ran express services until steam was ended on the Thai railways in 1982.

**No 850, last of the post-war batch of Japanese-built 'Pacifics'. It was converted from wood- to oil-burning almost as soon as it was delivered in 1950.**

**Boiler pressure:** 13kg/cm$^2$ (185psi)
**Cylinders:** 450x610mm (17.7x24in)
**Driving wheels:** 1372mm (54in)
**Grate area:** (m$^2$)
**Heating Surface:** 134.5m$^2$ (1448sq ft)
**Superheater:** 40.7m$^2$ (438.2sq ft)
**Tractive effort:** 8780kg (19,360lb)
**Total weight:** 58t (127,890lb) (engine only)

## CLASS H8 2-6-6-6 CHESAPEAKE & OHIO RAILWAY (C&O) USA 1942

Lima Works's largest to date, the 'Allegheny' type was named after the mountains through which it worked. This articulated four-cylinder simple locomotive had outside bearings on all the carrying wheels. The six-wheel rear truck supported a firebox 4568mm (15ft) long. Between Hinton, West Virginia, and Clifton Forge, Virginia, they took trains of up to 5200t (5130tons) unaided. Up to 1949, 60 were built, but the last were soon withdrawn, in 1956. 'Where you want 6000, 8000, even 10,000 horsepower in one engine – the steam locomotive is unchallenged.' Thus claimed Lima, boasting 8000 horsepower for the 'Allegheny' class. In 1944, Lima built eight identical locomotives for the Virginian Railroad, Class AG, for use on coal trains through the mountains.

**Boiler pressure:** (260psi)
**Cylinders:** 571x837.5mm (22.5x33in)
**Driving wheels:** 1700mm (67in)
**Grate area:** 12.4m$^2$ (133.3sq ft )
**Heating surface:** 631m$^2$ (6794sq ft)
**Superheater:** 115m$^2$ (2922sq ft)
**Tractive effort:** 49,970kg (110,200lb)
**Total weight:** 498.3t (1,098,840lb)

## TC-S160 CLASS 2-8-0 US ARMY TRANSPORTATION CORPS (USATC) USA 1942

Commissioned as one of four standard steam types by the USATC, 2120 of the TC S160 class and its variants were built, to standard gauge, at the three major US loco works, Alco, Baldwins and Lima, between 1942 and 1945. A small engine by American standards, built to fit within the relatively tight British loading gauge, it was a typically US design, with bar frames, two outside simple-expansion cylinders, operated by piston valves, actuated by Walschaerts gear; a high-set boiler, and a wide, round-topped steel firebox. Driving position was on the right; on the fireman's side a tiny door opened frontwards on to the running plate. The engines had steam brakes plus

**An S-160 in the livery of the Southern Railway of India, at the important junction of Coimbatore, on 30 December 1979.**

**S-160s got as far as China, where they were classed KD6 and worked in mining areas at least into the 1980s. Note the extended upper cab sides.**

a Westinghouse air brake pump, with air cylinders placed under the running plate on each side. The compressor pump was fitted to the left of a narrowed smokebox door. On the engines used in Britain, dual air/vacuum brake equipment was fitted. Fireboxes were fitted with rocking grates and hopper ashpans. On the boiler top, dome and sandbox were in a single housing. The standard American three-point suspension system gave them a stable ride even over ill-maintained and bomb-blasted tracks. Despite a number of American 'convenience' fittings, which made the locomotives popular with British and European crews, there was no power reverser. The great majority were coal burners, though some oil-burners were built or converted, including 106 for the south-west region of France, which had oil-fuelling facilities. Two types of standard eight-wheel tender carried 8.1 or 10.1t (8 tons or 10 tons) of coal and 5400gals (6480US) of water. The design was a very sound one, with only one significant defect that emerged with time, a weakness in the screw fixing of the firebox roof stays, which caused a number of firebox collapses.

The first overseas destination for the S160s was Britain, partly to provide extra motive power under the Lease-Lend scheme, partly as a holding base for the invasion of Europe. In September 1943, the Great Western Railway's repair shops at Ebbw Junction, Newport, in South Wales, became the HQ of No 756 Railway Shop Battalion, US Army, and engines were readied here for use or storage. As back-up in the North African campaign, 139 were shipped to Oran by mid-July 1943. By late 1944, they were being shipped to the continent in large numbers, to operate in liberated and Allied territory. Two Military Railway Services control departments kept track of their locations and allocated their functions, together with those of other military locomotives like the British WD types. Apart from military use in troop, munitions and general supply trains, and ambulance trains, they were loaned to supplement deficiencies in available power on civilian services. Usage peaked in 1945; then, as hostilities ceased in Europe, many were gathered in a huge 'dump' at Louvain in Belgium and also at other depots. A vast redistribution took place. Almost the only country not to take some into permanent service was France, which had none working on the SNCF system by the end of 1946. Thirty went to the ÖBB in Austria, 244 to Italy (25 of these were sold to Greece in 1959) 27 to Greece, 65 to Yugoslavia, 40 to the DB in Germany, 50 to the TCDD in Turkey, around 500 to MÁV in Hungary and a similar quantity to PKP in Poland, 80 to Czechoslovakia, 101 to South Korea, and 25 to China. Around 30 engines remained at work on the Tunisian and Algerian railways. The remainder probably ended up in Russia, joining the 200 that had been sent directly there in the course of 1943 (these were built to fit the 1524mm/5ft gauge). Another 60 had been built to Indian broad gauge (1675mm/5ft 6in), shipped out in parts, and assembled at works near Bombay and Calcutta. They went into service with the Indian Government Railways from August 1944. Most were given fittings or adaptations normal to their new owners, most often taller chimneys, and in time some were more substantially rebuilt. Locomotives of the same type also went in small numbers to Jamaica and Peru (1943) and Mexico (1946). The S160s had been built as wartime engines, with no expectation of a long life, but in Poland

**No 611, the only S-160 to be fitted with poppet valves, still employed at the US army's Fort Eustis, Va, facility on 20 September 1965.**

and Hungary large numbers were still in regular service in the early 1970s. In these two countries particularly, the S160s were invaluable freight engines during the hard years of the later 1940s, running in service with their war-time rivals, the German class 50 and 52 2-10-0s. Numbers have been preserved in several different countries.

**Fifty-two of the S-160 class ended up in Greece, where they were a mainstay of freight haulage. Here, one survivor, as Thg 536 of the Hellenic State Railways, shunts at Eginion on 2 November 1972.**

**Boiler pressure:** 15.75kg/cm$^2$ (225psi)
**Cylinders:** 482x660mm (19x26in)
**Driving wheels:** 1447mm (57in)
**Grate area:** 3.8m$^2$ (41sq ft)
**Heating surface:** 164m$^2$ (1765sq ft)
**Superheater:** 43.7m$^2$ (471sq ft)
**Tractive effort:** 14,280kg (31,490lb)
**Total weight:** 73.6t (162,400lb) (engine only)

## CLASS TC S118 'MACARTHUR' 2-8-2 US ARMY TRANSPORTATION CORPS (USATC) 1942

Like the other USATC designs built in large numbers, this one not only performed valuable service during World War II, but was a staple engine on many systems for a long time after that. Designed by Alco for the metre (39.4in) or 1065mm (3ft 6in) gauges, 859 were built between 1942 and 1945, with Baldwins, Davenport, Porter and Vulcan all involved in building. It acquired the unofficial name of 'MacArthur', in honour of US General Douglas MacArthur, whose star was high at the time. Maximum route availability was

**A MacArthur on the metre gauge (39.4in) of the Southern Railway of India. The robustness and relative simplicity of the design are clearly apparent.**

demanded, so the heaviest axle load was 9.1t (9 tons) and it was built to clear even restricted loading gauges, while various different kinds of drawgear and braking equipment could be fitted, and it could easily be switched from coal to oil firing. It was intended to be as economical and simple as possible both in construction and in operation.

Most MacArthurs went to the Indian metre-gauge (39.4in) lines, delivered for assembly on arrival. In the later stages of the war some went to Burma, Malaya and Siam (Thailand). Others were in service – in some cases into the 1970s – in Iraq, Algeria, Tunisia, Nigeria, the Gold Coast (Ghana), the East African Railways system, the French Cameroons, the Manila railroad in the Philippines, the Queensland Government Railways in Australia, the United Fruit Co lines in Honduras, and the White Pass & Yukon Railroad in Alaska. After the war, some were built for the Peleponnesus Railway in Greece. One continent was without a 'MacArthur': rail-free Antarctica.

**An Indian Railways MacArthur working hard. The engine is well-kept, and, for an Indian loco, decorated in a restrained manner.**

**Boiler pressure:** 13kg/cm² (185psi)
**Cylinders:** 406x609mm (16x24in)
**Driving wheels:** 1218mm (48in)
**Grate area:** 2.6m² (27.7sq ft)
**Heating surface:** 127.3m² (1371sq ft)
**Superheater:** 34.7m² (374sq ft)
**Tractive effort:** 9900kg (20,100lb)
**Total weight:** 54t (119,000lb) (engine only)

## T 1 DUPLEX-DRIVER 4-4-4-4 PENNSYLVANIA RAILROAD (PRR) USA 1942

**In the early 1940s, with diesel competition now fierce, steam locomotive builders were looking for ways in which to pack more power into a single frame – regarded as a way for steam to beat the diesel.**

In 1942, the PRR was looking for a replacement for the now ageing K4 'Pacific' class. For some years, Baldwins had been promoting the concept of duplex, or divided, drive to produce power beyond that of a 4-8-4. They built two prototypes of the T 1, Nos 6110 and 6111, with two sets of outside cylinders each driving four big wheels. The advantages of this form were that the operating machinery could be lighter, the cylinders could be smaller and the stroke shorter, the stress on moving parts significantly less, and the piston thrust could be lower. In addition, the rigid frame promised more stable running at high speeds.

The styling was the famous 'shark-front'. In all respects, it was thoroughly up to date. Poppet valves worked the cylinders. All axles had Timken roller bearings. They were fitted with big 180-P-

84 tenders. The trials of the prototypes brought in good reports. Both could achieve 161kph (100mph) in service with 1036t (1020 ton) trains. Another 50 T 1s were ordered, 27 from Baldwins, the others from Juniata. But as the new engines came into service, problems began to mount. A major one was the lack of adhesion. Wheel-slip was endemic with the class, and drivers struggled (often in vain) to cure it. Other mechanical and operating problems arose. For all its robust appearance, the T 1 was not a successful design. One railroad historian described it as 'impressive in every way except grate area and boiler capacity.' Unfortunately, these were vital aspects. By 1953 they had all gone, most of them with less than 10 years' service.

**Boiler pressure:** 21kg/cm$^2$ (300psi)
**Cylinders:** 501x660mm (19.75x26in)
**Driving wheels:** 2032mm (80in)
**Grate area:** 8.5m$^2$ (92sq ft)
**Heating surface:** 391m$^2$ (4218sq ft)
**Superheater:** 132.8m$^2$ (1430sq ft)
**Tractive effort:** 31,925kg (64,650lb)
**Total weight:** 432.6t (4,000lb)

## CLASS C-38 4-6-2 NEW SOUTH WALES GOVERNMENT RAILWAY (NSWGR) AUSTRALIA 1943

**Boiler pressure:** 17.1kg/cm$^2$ (245psi)
**Cylinders:** 546x660mm (21.5x26in)
**Driving wheels:** 1751mm (69in)
**Grate area:** 4.4m$^2$ (47sq ft)
**Heating surface:** 243m$^2$ (2614sq ft)
**Superheater:** 70.2m$^2$ (755sq ft)
**Tractive effort:** 17,912kg (36,273lb)
**Total weight:** 222.5t (450,688lb)

The C-38 supplanted the C-36 4-6-0 on express services. Harold Young, Chief Mechanical Engineer of the NSWGR, designed the first five. Partially streamlined, these were built by Clyde Engineering; and the next 25, which were not streamlined, at the line's own Eveleigh and Cardiff shops. All had cast-steel frames, roller bearings on all axles, and Canadian-type 'Boxpok' unspoked wheels. Power reversers were fitted. All were in service by 1949, painted in a green livery, with buff and red lining out (replaced by black in the 1950s).

Manually fired, they worked the Sydney–Albury section of the 'Melbourne Limited' sleeping car train, loaded to 500t (492 tons), and with grades of up to 1 in 40 along the route. In 1955, diesel-electrics took over, and many C-38s were transferred to fast goods work, though they retained Sydney–Newcastle expresses until 1970; in December, No 3280, the last in regular service was withdrawn. Examples, both streamlined and unstreamlined, are preserved.

**Preserved No 3801 recalls the glory days of the 'Limited' as it rounds the curve towards Seymour, on 24 October 1988.**

**A Sydney depot scene from 1967. No 3828 has come in from hauling the 'Southern Highlands' express. Behind, No 3808 is coaled up ready to haul a fast freight to Moss Vale.**

**Triple 'Pacific' power draws a crowd at Moss Vale as three C-38s prepare for an excursion. The train engine is taking on water.**

## CLASS 520 4-8-4 SOUTH AUSTRALIAN RAILWAYS (SAR) AUSTRALIA 1943

**No 520, *Sir Malcolm Barclay-Harvey,* shows off the shark-nose line that was the height of fashion in the early 1940s. At this time, American influence on Australian railways was increasingly strong.**

Operating on the 1600mm (5ft 3in) gauge, and able to run on light 27.2kg (60lb) rails, the outline of this semi-streamlined mixed-traffic engine recalls the American PRR T-1. It was the SAR's last new steam design. Twelve were built at the SAR Islington shops, and used for passenger and freight trains between Adelaide and Port Pirie and Terowie and Tailem Bend, but also appeared on most other lines in the state. In 1948, all were converted to oil fuel, and ran until the early 1960s. Two have been preserved.

**Boiler pressure:** 14kg/cm$^2$ (200psi)
**Cylinders:** 521x711mm (20.5x28in)
**Driving wheels:** 1676mm (66in)
**Grate area:** 4.2m$^2$ (45sq ft)
**Heating surface:** 228m$^2$ (2454sq ft)
**Superheater:** 60.5m$^2$ (651sq ft)
**Tractive effort:** 14,800kg (32,600lb)
**Total weight:** 221.8t (449,120lb)

## CLASS L4-A 4-8-2 NEW YORK CENTRAL RAILROAD (NYC) USA 1943

This was a mixed-traffic locomotive, known by the NYC as the 'Mohawk' type: 'Mountain' was not deemed appropriate by the managers of the 'Water Level Route'. With the first in 1916, the NYC had over 350 in service. The 50 of class L4-a were built between 1942 and 1944 by Lima, by then a division of Lima-Hamilton (the steam firm of Lima had merged with the diesel engine Hamilton company); 25 of class L4-a and 25 of the almost identical L4-b. Capable of running at 130kph (80mph), they were able to deputize for 'Hudsons' in express service.

**Class L-4a No 3113 gets a heavy westbound freight on the move past Dunkirk, New York, on a crisp winter morning in early 1952. By this time, the class was almost wholly employed on freight traffic, with very little passenger work, due to the advent of more powerful engines.**

**Boiler pressure:** 17.5kg/cm$^2$ (250psi)
**Cylinders:** 660x761.4mm (26x30in)
**Driving wheels:** 1827mm (72in)
**Grate area:** 6.9m$^2$ (75sq ft)
**Heating surface:** 434.2m$^2$ (4675sq ft)
**Superheater:** 195.3m$^2$ (2103sq ft)
**Tractive effort:** 27,165kg (59,900lb)
**Total weight:** 181.9t (401,100lb) (engine only)

## Class U1-f 4-8-2 CANADIAN NATIONAL RAILWAYS (CNR) CANADA 1944

U1 was the CNR designation for 'Mountain' 4-8-2s, a design it had used since 1923. The 'f' was the ultimate model, 20 in number, constructed at the Montreal Locomotive Works. They had one-piece cast steel frames, Boxpok-type balanced coupled wheels, and a combined injector and feed water heater of novel design, mounted under the running plate. All were given Vanderbilt tenders, mounted on two six-wheel bogies. They operated fast passenger trains between Toronto and Montreal, a route which competed with the CPR line. Six members of the class are in preservation.

**Boiler pressure:** 18.3kg/cm$^2$ (260psi)
**Cylinders:** 610x762mm (24x30in)
**Driving wheels:** 1854mm (73in)
**Grate area:** 6.6m$^2$ (70.2sq ft)
**Heating surface:** 333m$^2$ (3584sq ft)
**Superheater:** 146m$^2$ (1570sq ft)
**Tractive effort:** 23,814kg (52,500lb)
**Total weight:** 290t (638,000lb)

**Maintained by the Rocky Mountain Railway Society as a static exhibition piece, and with the the Rockies as a background, CNR's 'Mountain' class U1-F No 6015 stands fenced off from the tracks at Stettler, Alberta.**

## 2-10-0 MINISTRY OF SUPPLY GREAT BRITAIN 1944

The previous 10-coupled engines to run in Britain had been two exceptional one-offs. But British builders had sent many hundreds abroad. Abroad was also the first destination of most of this special wartime two-cylinder design, bigger brother of a 2-8-0 produced from 1943 (which owed much to the LMS 8F, the first British military engine of World War II). The concept was for an engine with a light axle weight, 13.5t (13.3 tons), low enough to run on lightweight or improvised track, but with a good tractive effort. Also required was a tight turning circle, achieved here, despite a wheelbase of 6396mm (21ft), by making the third driving wheels flangeless, and allowing a degree of lateral play to the front and rear coupled axles, of 127mm (0.5in). The North British Locomotive Company dropped tank production to build it, and many features show its 'Austerity' background: the round-topped parallel boiler and firebox lent themselves to quantity production; fabricated parts were used instead of heavy forgings and castings; some wheels and wheel parts were cast-iron, not steel. The boiler pressure, cylinders, motion and wheel diameter were identical to those of the 2-8-0, but the capacity for making steam was much greater, as was the adhesive weight, so performance was significantly better. Vacuum and air brake equipment was fitted, as well as a steam brake. An 8-fixed-wheel tender carried 9.15t (9 tons) of coal and 5000 gals (6000 US gals) of water. Built for a short life, many of these engines ran on post-war freight duties into the 1960s, and the class provided a valuable basis for the excellent British standard 2-10-0 of the 1950s.

**Boiler pressure:** 15.75kg/cm$^2$ (225psi)
**Cylinders:** 482x711mm (19x28in)
**Driving wheels:** 1434mm (56.5in)
**Grate area:** 3.7m$^2$ (40sq ft)
**Heating surface:** 181m$^2$ (1951sq ft)
**Superheater:** 39.3m$^2$ (423sq ft)
**Tractive effort:** 14,913kg (30,200lb)
**Total weight:** 148t (299,712lb)

**One of the few to remain in military use after the war, WD No 600 Gordon, of the Longmoor Military Railway, now in preservation, awaits the whistle at Bridgnorth, Severn Valley Railway, on 30 April 1983.**

## CLASS Q2 4-4-6-4 PENNSYLVANIA RAILROAD (PRR) USA 1944

The Pennsy did not give up easily in the campaign to perfect the 'duplex drive' which had already produced the T1 4-4-4-4.

In 1942, a 4-6-4-4, class Q1, was built, but found unsatisfactory. The prototype Q2 followed, and trials were successful enough for the War Production Board to allow a production run of 25, built in 1944–45. A booster engine was fitted to the rear bogie.

Although the least problematic of the duplex drivers, these engines had surprisingly short careers, most being put into store in 1949; by this time the PRR diesel fleet was growing rapidly, and all the Class Q2s were scrapped between 1953 and 1956.

The shark-nose design was dropped, though the Q2 had a skyline casing along the boiler-top, partially enclosing the chimney.

The maximum axle load was 36t (35.5 tons), among the heaviest of any locomotive of the period, which restricted its route availability and caused some worries in locomotive yards.

**Boiler pressure:** 21kg/$cm^2$ (300psi)
**Cylinders:** front 502x711mm (19.75x28in); rear 603x737mm (23.75x29in)
**Driving wheels:** 1751mm (69in)
**Grate area:** 113$m^2$ (1216.6sq ft)
**Heating surface:** 573$m^2$ (6169.25sq ft)
**Superheater:** 337$m^2$ (3628.3sq ft)
**Tractive effort:** 45,722kg (100,800lb)
**Total weight:** 280.7t (619,000lb)

## CLASS 2900 4-8-4 ATCHISON TOPEKA & SANTA FE RAILROAD (ATSF) USA 1944

Thirty of this class were built by Baldwin, the Santa Fe's last fling with express steam. Fitted with roller bearings throughout, like some other 4-8-4s they were reputed to have operated at 161kph (100mph) and more. One of their racing grounds was between Los Angeles and San Diego, though they also ran the long haul between LA and Kansas City without change of engine. They later went on to run freight trains in Texas and Oklahoma but, still with much useful life ahead of them, they were all taken off in 1959–60. Some of them had the curious Santa Fe special feature of an extensible chimney that could be raised to improve draughting. Several are preserved.

**Boiler pressure:** $cm^2$)
**Cylinders:** 710x812mm (28x32in)
**Driving wheels:** 2030mm (80in)
**Grate area:** 10$m^2$)
**Heating surface:** 493$m^2$)
**Superheater:** 219$m^2$)
**Tractive effort:** 29,932kg (66,000lb)
**Total weight:** 231.4t (510,150lb)

**Santa Fe No 2928 pilots a triple-unit diesel-electric on the 'Super Chief', eastbound from San Bernardino, up the 2.2 per cent Cajon Pass grade in California. The smoke-stack is fully extended.**

## CLASS 534.03 2-10-0 CZECHOSLOVAK STATE RAILWAYS (CSD) CZECHOSLOVAKIA 1945

**With modified draught system and ejector chimney, No 534.0325 heads a train of tank cars at Beroun, on the main line between Prague and Plzen, in the former Czechoslovakia, in October 1972.**

This was essentially a pre-war design, hurriedly got under way in 1945 to provide badly needed new motive power. By the end of 1947, 200 had been built by the Skoda and CKD works. Class 534.1 goes back to 1923, and was based on an Austrian Gölsdorf design, complete with steam-drier pipe between the domes. Very capable and versatile, it was updated in many respects in 1937 as 534.02, and this, again updated, was the basis of the 534.03. Roller bearings and a power reverser were among the new fittings. Though overtaken in power by later classes, it remained valuable on secondary services until the end of steam on the CSD.

**Boiler pressure:** 16kg/$cm^2$ (185psi)
**Cylinders:** 580x630mm (22.8x24.8in)
**Driving wheels:** 1310mm (51.6in)
**Grate area:** 4.1$m^2$ (44.1sq ft)
**Heating surface:** 190.8$m^2$ (2054sq ft)
**Superheater:** 65.8$m^2$ (708.4sq ft)
**Tractive effort:** 17,810kg (39,280lb)
**Total weight:** 82.7t (182,353lb)

# 47-CLASS 0-8-0 DUTCH STATE RAILWAYS (NS) NETHERLANDS 1945

Anticipating the outcome of World War II, the Dutch government in exile ordered this three-cylinder simple-expansion freight class from Nohab in Sweden during 1944, and the first two were shipped to Rotterdam in August 1945. All 35 were in service by the end of 1946. They were modern machines with SKF roller bearings, electric generators and feedwater heating. The shortage of locomotives saw them first put in passenger service, before being transferred to the South Limburg coalfield for mineral freight work.

**On passenger duty at Amsterdam, in 1947, No 4703 stands ready to move off. The tender design was shared with Class 4001. Just behind is class 39 4-6-0 No 3913.**

**Boiler pressure:** 13kg/cm$^2$ (185psi)
**Cylinders:** 500x660mm (19.7x26in)
**Driving wheels:** 1350mm (53.2in)
**Grate area:** 3m$^2$ (32.3sq ft)
**Heating surface:** 135.8m$^2$ (1462sq ft)
**Superheater:** 48.5m$^2$ (522sq ft)
**Tractive effort:** 16,680kg (36,780lb)
**Total weight:** 74.8t (164,934lb)

**The Class 47 was based on the 0-8-0 freight engine of the Grängesberg–Oxelösund Railway in Sweden. It was the NS's first three-cylinder locomotive type; this one is shunting at Eindhoven in 1947.**

## 4001 CLASS 4-6-0 DUTCH STATE RAILWAYS (NS) — NETHERLANDS 1945

Simultaneously with the 47-class 0-8-0s, 15 of these passenger locomotives were ordered, also from Nohab, who ferried them to Denmark and delivered them by rail, in 1945 and 1946. Three-cylinder simples, their coned smokebox doors and vee-form cabs gave them a distinctly Swedish look. Though equipped with modern features like electric lighting, their boiler pressure was relatively low. The tenders were modelled on Gölsdorf's Austrian design. These engines hauled main-line expresses until electrics and diesels took over in the early 1960s. But they had always been regarded as something of a stop-gap, to make up for the ravages of war on the Dutch Railways' locomotive stock; electrification of almost the entire system had been the aim even in the 1930s.

**Boiler pressure:** 12kg/cm² (171psi)
**Cylinders:** 500x660mm (19.7x26in)
**Driving wheels:** 1890mm (74.5in)
**Grate area:** 3.25m² (35sq ft)
**Heating surface:** 147m² (1582.7sq ft)
**Superheater:** 50m² (538.3sq ft)
**Tractive effort:** 11,000kg (24,255lb)
**Total weight:** 83.6t (engine only)

## CLASS L 2-10-0 SOVIET RAILWAYS — RUSSIA 1945

'L' (originally P for *Pobyeda*, 'victory') was designed at the Kolomna works, under L.C. Lebedyanski, a two-cylinder design. Its 18t (17.7 ton) axle load let it run on temporary track, but it became a standard main-line goods engine, and 5200 were built over the next 10 years. The engine was 4873mm (16ft) high and there was a large space between frame and boiler. The casing between dome and chimney covered a steam drier pipe. This was the first Russian locomotive to have Boxpok-type wheels, which became a post-war standard. The L class remained in service until 1975.

**The last years of main-line steam, and No 3767 heads pressurized wagons. By now, the outer railings of earlier types had been replaced by a handrail along the boiler.**

**Boiler pressure:** 14kg/cm² (199psi)
**Cylinders:** 650x800mm (25.6x31.5in)
**Driving wheels:** 1150mm (59in)
**Grate area:** 6m² (64.5sq ft)
**Heating surface:** 222m² (2390sq ft)
**Superheater:** 113m² (1216sq ft)
**Tractive effort:** 27,690kg (61,000lb)
**Total weight:** 103.8t (228,879lb) (engine only)

**The L class was used in many of the constituent republics of the former USSR. Here, a pensioned-off member of the class has been set up as a static display item at Tapa, in Estonia.**

## S1 'NIAGARA' CLASS 4-8-4 NEW YORK CENTRAL RAILROAD (NYC) USA 1945

In theory designed for passenger and freight work, but in practice purely passenger engines, the S1s, far better known as 'Niagaras', were designed at a time when air competition scarcely existed, and the fast way from New York to Chicago was by express train. Ten years later, things looked very different. But these engines showed that the railroad's era of monopoly had not led to complacency. Massive as they were, they were built for consistent high speed and performance, to a degree that was probably never equalled with steam.

Twenty-five were built in 1945–46, by Alco, to the specifications of Paul Kiefer, the NYC's head of motive power. The 1493km (928-mile) New York–Chicago run, once requiring up to four locomotive changes, was to be run by the same engine, with a pause for a rapid top-up of the tender coal. Water could be picked up from troughs, 'pans' in the USA, laid between the tracks.

An annual distance run in excess of 442,000km (275,000 miles) could be expected. And average speeds were very high. The prime train was the 'Twentieth Century Limited' and its timing was 16 hours, requiring an average of 93kph (58mph) including stops. By this time, steam engines were not permitted within New York City limits, so electric locos hauled the fliers out to Harmon, where the 'Niagaras' took over. Mile after mile at 128kph (80mph) plus was needed to maintain the schedule. Sophisticated and swift work in the depots at each end was needed to keep the engines serviced to a peak of efficiency. For consistent heavy-duty performance, this class was unrivalled anywhere in the world.

**In a classic image of American passenger railroading with steam, Class S1 No 6016 fronts a passenger train formed from nine cars and a matching baggage car, at Oscawanna, NY, around the year 1947.**

**Boiler pressure:** 19.3kg/cm$^2$ (275psi)
**Cylinders:** 648x813mm (25.5x32in)
**Driving wheels:** 2007mm (79in)
**Grate area:** 9.3m$^2$ (100sq ft)
**Heating surface:** 4.48m$^2$ (48.27sq ft)
**Superheater:** 191m$^2$ (2060sq ft)
**Tractive effort:** 27,936kg (61,570lb)
**Total weight:** 405t (891,000lb)

## CLASS WP 4-6-2 INDIAN RAILWAYS (IR) INDIA 1946

**Most main-line expresses were likely to be WP-hauled, like the 'Punjab Mail', the 'Deccan Queen' or the 'Grand Trunk Express'. India still retains the taste for named expresses.**

Built to the Indian 1675mm (5ft 6in) broad gauge, the WPs were a significant change of locomotive policy on the IR. These were American-style engines, with the prototypes coming from Baldwin and nearly half of the class, 320 engines, from the USA or Canada. Chrzanov in Poland and Vienna Lokomotivfabrik of Austria each built 30. Unhappy experiences with pre-war 'Indian Standard' types meant these reliable engines came as a great relief. In all, 755 were built between 1947 and 1967, the last 435 at the new Chittaranjan works, set up in 1950. Given a massive appearance by their big boiler, small chimney, and bulbous smoke box front, they were built in the classic American manner, with bar frames, two simple-expansion cylinders, and Walschaerts valve gear actuating piston valves. The parallel boiler was topped by a long parallel casing hiding all fittings except the just-protruding

**The dipping steam bucket crane, moving ash or ballast, gets on with its work as a class WP goes majestically by, on its way from locomotive shed to terminus.**

chimney. Most of the class had Boxpok-type balanced wheels. Reliable, and easy to maintain, their suspension system was well-adapted to Indian tracks.

The bullet-headed green front end of a WP, with the eight-pointed silver star around the headlamp, was a familiar sight to travellers in India, though often in a neglected state in latter years. It was likely to be hauling such trains as the 'Punjab Express' and the Agra-bound 'Taj Mahal'; and even after class withdrawal in the 1990s, some are still in special service.

**Boiler pressure:** 14.7kg/cm² (210psi)
**Cylinders:** 514x711mm (20.25x28in)
**Driving wheels:** 1705mm (67in)
**Grate area:** 4.3m² (46sq ft)
**Heating surface:** 286.3m² (2257sq ft)
**Superheater:** 67m² (725sq ft)
**Tractive effort:** 13,884kg (30,600lb)
**Total weight:** 172.5t (380,000lb) (engine only)

## CLASS QR-1 4-8-4 MEXICAN NATIONAL RAILWAYS (NDEM) MEXICO 1946

**Boiler pressure:** 17.5kg/cm² (250psi)
**Cylinders:** 634.5x761mm (25x30in)
**Driving wheels:** 1777mm (70in)
**Grate area:** 7.1m² (77sq ft)
**Heating surface:** 388.8m² (4186sq ft)
**Superheater:** 154.8m² (1667sq ft)
**Tractive effort:** 25,814kg (56,920lb)
**Total weight:** 175.5t (387,00lb)

On the NdeM, 'Northerns' were known as 'Niagras'. Thirty-two were built, half each by Alco and Baldwin. These two-cylinder simples, US-style engines, were among the lightest in weight of North American 4-8-4s.

**QR No 3027 is turned at the Valle de Mexico roundhouse on 11 October 1961. By this time, the 'Niagras' were the last 4-8-4s in regular service in North America.**

Intended for freight train haulage, they were the last steam locomotives ordered for Mexico. They were also among the last to remain in service. Even after diesels had taken over most services, a few of the 'Niagras' remained as banking engines and on standby duty. The last were taken out of service in 1965.

## CLASS PT-47 2-8-2 POLISH STATE RAILWAYS (PKP) POLAND 1947

**A preserved PT-47 in action, steaming through the Polish countryside.**

The Pt (passenger 2-8-2) type had been introduced in Poland in 1932, and this was a post-war version, equipped with a welded firebox and mechanical stoking. Cegielski and Chrzanov built 180, which were used on express services. Large cylinders and coupled wheels of mixed-traffic diameter gave it powerful tractive effort. It was built to the 1435mm (4ft 8in) gauge, but Poland inherited a high clearance from Russian practice, and this engine stood 4670mm (15ft 4in) above the rails. On the standard gauge, international services linked Poland to Germany, Czechoslovakia and Hungary, and the Pt-47s hauled international expresses on non-electrified lines.

**Boiler pressure:** 15kg/cm² (214psi)
**Cylinders:** 630x700mm (24.75x27.5in)
**Driving wheels:** 1850mm (72.75in)
**Grate area:** 4.5m² (48.5sq ft)
**Heating surface:** 230m² (2476sq ft)
**Superheater:** 101m² (1087sq ft)
**Tractive effort:** 19,110kg (42,120lb)
**Total weight:** 173t (381,500lb)

## DD.17 CLASS 4-6-4T QUEENSLAND GOVERNMENT RAILWAYS (QGR) AUSTRALIA 1948

Brisbane had the only suburban network in Queensland (1067mm, 3ft 6in gauge), and this tank class of 12 – the last built in Australia - was introduced to replace older engines. Its looks are American, and though built at the QGR's Ipswich shops, it owes much to Baldwins' USATC-16 tender engines. Modern features included roller bearings, mechanical lubrication and self-cleaning smoke boxes. After diesels took over local passenger traffic, they were transferred to shunting duties. The last of the class to be taken out of service was No 1046 in October 1969. Four have been preserved.

**Boiler pressure:** 12.6kg/cm² (180psi)
**Cylinders:** 431x609mm (17x24in)
**Driving wheels:** 1294mm (51in)
**Grate area:** 1.7m² (18.5sq ft)
**Heating surface:** 98.8m² (1064sq ft)
**Superheater:** 13.9m² (150sq ft)
**Tractive effort:** 10,275kg (20.808lb)
**Total weight:** 68.5t (138,88lb)

**Preserved No 1047 at Bottom Points on the former NSWGR Zig-Zag railway line, near Lithgow, west of Sydney, with a two-car tourist train, on 14 December 1980.**

## CLASS 433 2-8-2T CZECHOSLOVAK STATE RAILWAYS (CSD) CZECHOSLOVAKIA 1948

**A modified class 423, with narrow Giesl chimney and oblong ejector, at the head of a typically varied selection of carriages on a Prague suburban service.**

A total of 231 were built up to 1946, incorporating various alterations made at different times. The main changes were the clerestory-type roof to the cab, extension of the tanks over the cylinders, and a rearward and upward extension of the bunker.

Dome arrangements came and went, so that 423s could be seen with a single great elongated housing, or three domes, or two domes. More importantly, boiler pressure was raised and larger superheaters fitted. All in all, it was a highly successful class, with the 433s as the final development. Several of both 423 and 433 are still preserved.

The history of this 60-strong class merges into that of the Class 423, of which it was essentially a modernized form: roller bearings were fitted to 20 ocomotives and some also had Giesl ejectors. Apart from an increase in boiler pressure from the original 13kg/cm² (185psi), the alterations were largely cosmetic. A shorter, wider chimney was substituted for the original tall one, and the combined sandbox and dome were separated into two domes and a sandbox. Class 423 was designed in 1921 as a standard type to replace a range of small, obsolescent engines on local lines. Some early models were non-superheated, for comparison purposes; the superheaters won (they usually did in such tests), and the saturated engines were later converted. The long dome on early models housed regulator, top feed and sandbox, and collar spark arresters were fitted to the chimneys.

**Boiler pressure:** 15kg/cm² (180psi)
**Cylinders:** 480x570mm (19x22.5in)
**Driving wheels:** 1150mm (45.2in)
**Grate area:** 2.1m² (22.6sq ft)
**Heating surface:** 97.6m² (1051sq ft)
**Superheater:** 33.8m² (364sq ft)
**Tractive effort:** 12,956kg (28,568lb)
**Total weight:** 70.6t (155,673lb)

## CLASS 241.P 4-8-2 FRENCH NATIONAL RAILWAYS (SNCF) FRANCE 1948

**One of the last of the class still in service runs past the marshalling sidings at Nevers with a three-car train, in April 1968. The locomotive weighs considerably more than its train.**

When new steam express power was required for the southeast region, the SNCF took a puzzling decision: ignoring the 242.A.1, it chose as the prototype an ex-PLM 4-8-2 type, 241.C, designed in 1931 and inferior in many respects. However, André Chapelon was asked to effect improvements before series construction began.

New cylinders (with an improved steam circuit) were made, and the frames were strengthened by transverse steel members. The external design closely followed Chapelon's established pattern. But it was impossible to incorporate the range of radical changes that marked his 'Pacific' rebuilds, and they were moderate performers in service. Between 1948 and 1952, 35 were built by the Le Creusot Company, replacing 40 2-8-2s of the 141.P class. The Paris–Dijon section was electrified by 1952, so the 241.Ps were first based at Marseille, hauling heavy expresses along the Rhône valley to Lyon and back; when this stretch too was put under catenary, they were dispersed to depots in the North, East and West regions. The last of the big four-cylinder compounds in regular service, they ran until 1970; their final service being between Nantes and Le Mans. The last three were taken out of service at Le Mans depot in May 1970, but have been preserved.

**Boiler pressure:** 20.5kg/cm$^2$ (292psi)
**Cylinders:** hp 447x650mm (17.6x25.6in); lp 675x700.5mm (26.6x27.6in)
**Driving wheels:** 2018mm (79.5in)
**Grate area:** 5m$^2$ (53.8sq ft)
**Heating surface:** 244.6 m$^2$ (2632.5sq ft)
**Superheater:** 108.4m$^2$ (1116.5sq ft)
**Tractive effort:** N/A
**Total weight:** 145.7t (321,348lb)

## 242 A.1 4-8-4 FRENCH NATIONAL RAILWAYS (SNCF) FRANCE 1948

The biographer of André Chapelon describes this as 'the greatest steam locomotive of all', and no-one would dispute that it has a strong claim to that title. If the design had been reproduced, it would have created a most formidable class of engines, but unfortunately, 242.A1 remained a solitary example of excellence. Its beginning was highly unpromising. Designed as a prototype 4-8-2 express passenger type for the *Etat*, and built at the Fives-Lille works in 1932, it proved to be a bad steamer and a rough rider. It was never put into regular service, and no others were constructed. In the late 1930s, the SNCF authorities were planning the future development of large engines, and permission was given for the 4-8-2 to be rebuilt under Chapelon's direction as a three-cylinder compound. Wartime delays meant that the work did not begin until 1942, at the *Forges et Aciéries de la Marine et d'Homecourt*, at St Chamond. The reconstruction was radical, beginning with the frames. Though Chapelon's ultimate aim was a single-piece steel chassis, as would be fitted to many post-war locomotives, he was obliged in this case to strengthen the frame by a combination of transverse steel stays and welded steel plates along the sides. This increased the weight to a point where the additional carrying axle was needed in order to keep the maximum axle load at 21t (20.6 tons), and the engine became a 4-8-4 (2-4-2 in French denomination). The high pressure cylinder, driving the first coupled axle, was fitted inside, in line with the external low pressure cylinders, each operated independently by Walschaerts valve gear, with that for the inside cylinder worked off the third left-hand coupled axle, as with some Czech locomotives. The low pressure cylinders drove the second coupled axle. Poppet valves in the original machine were replaced by double piston valves. Naturally, very close attention was paid to the size and positioning of steam passages and to the draughting and exhaust system. A triple Kylchap ejector and chimney were fitted. A large Houlet superheater was installed, and two Nicholson thermic syphons were fitted in the firebox, which was made of steel and mechanically stoked. Roller bearings were fitted to the front and rear bogies, inside Timken pattern in front and outside SKF in rear. Many minor details were attended to: in locomotives,

**A photograph taken in September 1959 shows the locomotive already out of service, standing on a storage siding at Le Mans depot.**

**Critics of the A.1 claimed that it spread the track at high speed, but there seems to be no published evidence to support the assertion.**

the chafing effect between axle boxes and the horn guides had always been a source of vibration and weakening of the frame; for the first time in Europe, American Franklin automatic wedges were fitted, to minimize the effect, which they did with great success. The big engine rode with remarkable ease and silence. The effect of the rebuild was to increase the weight by 20.3t (20 tons) but to virtually double its potential power output. The work was finished in May 1946.

Exhaustive tests followed, showing that there was nothing theoretical about this power. An experienced British recorder timed it from a dead stand to 100kph (62mph) over a distance of 10.9km (6.75 miles), with a train of 831t (818 tons). Drawing 950t (935 tons) it attained 120.7kph (75mph) on level track. On a climbing grade of 1 in 71, it maintained 65kph (40.5mph) with a train of 599t (590 tons). Its capacity for acceleration from a standing start was demonstrated on the 1 in 200 Survilliers bank. From a stop at Chantilly, and with a train of 867.6t (854 tons), it attained a speed of 98kph (61mph) in just over 3.2km (2 miles), and topped the summit at 106.5kph (66.2mph). Measuring the output in horsepower, this was the first European locomotive to sustain a continuous 2984kW (4000hp) or more at the tender drawbar, corresponding to more than 3730kW (5000hp) developed in the cylinders, while running at speeds of up to 120.7kph (75mph). It achieved these results without excessive use of fuel or water: its fuel economy was as great as that of the French four-cylinder compounds, and considerably greater than that of, for example, the most powerful British 'Pacifics' of the 'Coronation' class. A further important consideration was its ability to start off heavy trains on rising gradients without suffering that bugbear of so many steam locomotives, slipping of the coupled wheels. In such situations, a calculated tractive effort of 25,400kg (56,000lb) was produced. None of these were freak results or the product of specially favourable situations. The tests ran between 1946 and 1948, on some of France's most challenging main lines, in all seasons, including winter, when steam had also to be used to heat a long train of passenger cars. The consistency of performance was important, and impressive.

Whilst the 4-8-4 was a large engine in European terms, it was only of moderate size compared to American express engines. But with this engine, any former notion of correlation between dimensions and power output had to be set aside. The Southern Pacific's GS-4 class 4-8-4 weighed 215.4t (475,000lb), more than half as much again as the French engine. The New York Central's class S-1a 4-8-4 had 44 per cent more evaporative heating surface, 40 per cent more superheating surface, and almost double the grate area. These were regarded as first-rate express passenger locomotives, but the A.1 could at least match them in performance, and leave them far behind in economy.

But after the years, SNCF policy made a decisive shift towards electrification as the main source of motive power. The fact that Chapelon had demonstrated that a steam engine could out-perform the French electric designs was not a triumph, but an embarrassment. At this time, the delayed tests of his 2-12-0 were further reinforcing the steam case. The fuel economy of his engines also negated the argument that the capital costs of electrification would be balanced by lower running costs. The principal effect of the A.1 was to send the electrical engineers back to the drawing board to upgrade their new 2-D-2 locomotives to match its performance. Placed at the Le Mans depot, the A.1 took its turns with 'Pacifics' to run Paris expresses which were easily within its power. Its capacity could only be revealed when having to make up time after delays. In 1960 it was withdrawn from service and broken up.

**Boiler pressure:** 20.4kg/cm$^2$ (292psi)
**Cylinders:** hp 600x720mm (23.6x28.3in); lp 680x760mm (27x29.9in)
**Driving wheels:** 1950mm (76.75in)
**Grate area:** 5m$^2$ (54sq ft)
**Heating surface:** 253m$^2$ (2720sq ft)
**Superheater:** 120m$^2$ (1249sq ft)
**Tractive effort:** 25,400kg (56,000lb)
**Total weight:** 150.3t (331,520lb) (engine only)

## CLASS 1500 0-6-0T BRITISH RAILWAYS, WESTERN REGION — GREAT BRITAIN 1948

In 1948, the former Great Western Railway was still building inside-cylinder 0-6-0 tanks on a pattern that had hardly changed for more than twenty years. However, this pannier tank was a more up to date design, of largely welded construction, with innovative Belpaire boiler and Walschaerts valve gear, no running plate and a minimal buffer beam. These features were partly to reduce weight and partly to improve access for maintenance crews.

The GWR-style copper chimney band was kept, however. They were used as carriage shunters at London's Paddington station.

Withdrawal of the 10 engines of this class began in the autumn of 1959. 0-6-0Ts with a traditional inside-cylinder design and often much greater age survived this class by some years.

**Boiler pressure:** 14kg/cm$^2$ (200psi)
**Cylinders:** 444x609mm (17.5x24in)
**Driving wheels:** 1408mm (55.5in)
**Grate area:** 1.6m$^2$ (17.4sq ft)
**Heating surface:** m$^2$)
**Superheater:** 6.9m$^2$ (74sq ft)
**Tractive effort:** 10,204kg (22,500lb)
**Total weight:** 59.1t (130,368lb)

## CLASS A1 4-6-2 BRITISH RAILWAYS, EASTERN REGION — GREAT BRITAIN 1948

This class took over the designation A1 from the first LNER Pacifics. Designed by A.H. Peppercorn, 49 were built at Doncaster under the nationally-owned British Railways regime which began in 1948. One writer noted with satisfaction that it was 'every inch a Doncaster Pacific… The original theme first postulated by Gresley in 1922 was still substantially there in 1948.' Still, there were significant changes. The conjugated valve gear was replaced by three sets of Walschaerts gear. A larger though still manually fired grate was installed. A stubby, stovepipe-style double chimney and Kylchap blast exhaust were fitted, and electric lighting was provided. The boiler, with a steam collector in its 'banjo dome' was of the same dimensions as that designed for the previous class, A2. This had been something of a mixed bag, consisting of the rebuilt Gresley 'Mikados', designated A2/2; a 1944 Pacific, A2/1; and a

**Class A1 4-6-2 No 60128 *Bongrace* at London Kings Cross, in 1955. Many of the class were named after racehorses.**

1946 development of that, A2/3, later versions of which were heavily remodelled at the front end when Peppercorn took charge at Doncaster in mid-1946. Compared with the A4 boiler, it had a reduced heating surface despite the bigger firebox.

Peppercorn's A1 was an effective engine in service, free-steaming and relatively fault-free. The last five had roller bearings on all axles, and four of these ran over 1,609,000km (1,000,000 miles) in relatively short careers. The last one withdrawn was in June 1966.

**Boiler pressure:** 17.5kg/cm$^2$ (250psi)
**Cylinders:** 482x660mm (19x26in)
**Driving wheels:** 2030mm (80in)
**Grate area:** 4.6m$^2$ (50sq ft)
**Heating surface:** 228.6m$^2$ (2461.3sq ft)
**Superheater:** 64.8m$^2$ (679.7sq ft)
**Tractive effort:** 11,306kg (24,930lb)
**Total weight:** 105.6t (232,960lb)

**The *Queen of Scots* was an all-Pullman express between London, Leeds, Edinburgh and Glasgow. Here No 60141 Abbotsford of Copley Hill locomotive depot, Leeds, approaches Wortley South Junction, Leeds.**

## CLASS C62 4-6-4 JAPANESE NATIONAL RAILWAYS (JNR) JAPAN 1948

**Boiler pressure:** 16kg/cm² (228psi)
**Cylinders:** 520x660mm (20.5x26in)
**Driving wheels:** 1750mm (69in)
**Grate area:** 3.8m² (41.5sq ft)
**Heating surface:** 244.5m² (2632sq ft)
**Superheater:** 77.4m² (833sq ft)
**Tractive effort:** 13,925kg (30,690lb)
**Total weight:** 145.2t (320,166lb)

'C' in a Japanese locomotive indicated six coupled wheels, and the Japanese 'Hudsons' were seen as the follow-on to the C59 heavy 'Pacific' class. The first were the C61s, 33 of which were built in 1947. Class C62 followed speedily, with 49 built by the Hitachi Seisakusho, Kawasaki Zosenjo and Kisha Seizo Kaisha workshops. Japan had inaugurated its 'super-expresses' with the *Tsubame*, 'Swallow' in 1930, running between Tokyo and Kobe, 601.4km (373.7 miles) in 9 hours, drawn by a C51 'Pacific'. *Tsubame* was picked up as a byname for the C62s, which took over the train, and had a swallow device on the smoke deflectors.

**Post-war Japanese locos followed American design and building styles of the pre-war era, with bar frames and high-set running plates. Note the swallow sign on the smoke deflector.**

## 'RIVER' CLASS 2-8-2 NIGERIAN RAILWAYS (NR) NIGERIA 1948

In the post-war years the British Crown Agents, responsible for supplies to colonial governments, commissioned a 1065mm (3ft 6in) gauge 2-8-2 freight design for Nigeria. Between 1948 and 1954, virtually identical locomotives were built for the Tanganyika Railway and the East African Railways, the latter being metre gauge (39.4in). The original order was supplied by the Vulcan Foundry and the North British Locomotive Company. It was intended as a medium power freight engine, with a 13-ton (13.2t) axle-loading, able to work over lightweight rails and poorly-kept track. The Nigerian and Tanganyikan engines were intended to burn low-grade locally mined coal; the EAR followed its usual policy of the time in having oil burning engines that could readily be converted to coal burning if the need arose. The engines were bar-framed, two-cylinder simples, with outside Walschaerts valve gear. The boilers were of the parallel type, with straight-sided Belpaire fireboxes. Both the front and rear trucks were fitted with outside bearings; the EAR engines (class 29) had roller bearings on all axles. They were fitted with Giesl ejectors, with debatable benefits, in the 1960s. The Nigerian batch were given names after rivers of the country.

**Boiler pressure:** 14kg/cm² (200psi)
**Cylinders:** 533x660mm (21x26in)
**Driving wheels:** 1218mm (48in)
**Grate area:** 3.3m² (36sq ft)
**Heating surface:** 174.4m² (1878sq ft)
**Superheater:** 45.4m² (489sq ft)
**Tractive effort:** 14,716kg (29,800lb)
**Total weight:** 74.9t (165,312lb)

## 4-8-4 NATIONAL RAILWAYS DEPARTMENT (DNEF) BRAZIL 1949

In 1948 Brazil had the world's biggest metre-gauge (39.4in) network, over 35,200km (22,000 miles), much of it in poor condition and with out of date equipment. An order for new locomotives, both 4-8-4 and 2-8-4, was won by the French consortium GELSA, which appointed André Chapelon as designer. These metre-gauge (39.4in) 2-cylinder simple engines make an interesting comparison with the Indian Railways' YP and YG locomotives, built at the same time. They had Kylchap double exhausts and mechanical stokers, and Belpaire fireboxes fitted with two thermic syphons. Though some were still at work in the 1970s, not only in Brazil but also in Bolivia, they were not particularly successful in service.

**Boiler pressure:** 19.6kg/cm² (280psi)
**Cylinders:** 431x639mm (17x25.2in)
**Driving wheels:** 1523mm (60in)
**Grate area:** 5.4m² (58sq ft)
**Heating surface:** 167m²)
**Superheater:** 732m²)
**Tractive effort:** 15,894kg (35,056lb)
**Total weight:** 93t (205,030lb)

## CLASS 476.0 4-8-2 CZECHOSLOVAK NATIONAL RAILWAYS (CSD) CZECHOSLOVAKIA 1949

The Czech loading gauge allowed engines of a height of 4619mm (15ft 2in) and a width of 3096mm (10ft 2in), which gave designers useful scope.

This class of three 3-cylinder compound engines was a development of the 2-cylinder 475 class 4-8-2 of 1947, incorporating numerous features of engine designer André Chapelon's work in France. The high pressure cylinder was set inside the frame on the 476.0.

However, the compounding system was not a success, and after the first three, the remaining 12 of the class were built as three-cylinder simples, in which form they served well on long-distance east-west expresses.

Political separation from Western Europe made it difficult for the good qualities and superb performance of Czech locomotives to be appreciated outside of the Eastern Bloc.

**Boiler pressure:** 20kg/cm² (285psi)
**Cylinders:** hp 500x600mm (19.7x23.6in); lp 580x680mm (22.8x26.8in)
**Driving wheels:** 1624mm (64in)
**Grate area:** 4.3m² (46.3sq ft)
**Heating surface:** 201m² (2164sq ft)
**Superheater:** 63.3m² (681sq ft)
**Tractive effort:** N/A
**Total weight:** 108.4t (239,020lb)

## 232.U.1 4-6-4 NORTHERN RAILWAY/FRENCH NATIONAL RAILWAYS FRANCE 1949

This locomotive was born in the days of the *Nord* Railway in the 1930s, when a new generation of steam power to replace the 'Pacifics' was being planned. A 4-6-4 design by the *Nord* engineering chief, M. de Caso, was favoured because of its wide grate. For comparison purposes, it was decided to build engines both compound and simple, though both types would benefit from the principles of internal streamlining laid down by Chapelon. Four of each type were ordered from the *Société Alsacienne* of Mulhouse in 1938; three simples, class 232.R, were delivered by April 1940, and the four compounds, 232.S, were completed in late 1940. The unfinished simple was first of all to be converted to turbine drive, but this was not pursued and it was completed as a four-cylinder compound in 1949. A number of distinctive features ensured its separate classification, including a Houlet superheater, long-travel piston valves driven by Walschaerts gear, and SKF roller bearings on all axles. All eight engines were semi-streamlined with strong, sweeping lines that complemented their actual power. But although they gave impressive performance, and 232.U.1 could comfortably handle a Paris-Lille express of 576t (567 tons) at an average 114.25kph (71mph) for the round trip, they were neither as powerful nor as economic in running as Chapelon's 4-8-4 242A.1. For any locomotive other than a French one, this might be an unfair comparison. 242.U.1 is preserved.

**De Caso's locomotives were more streamlined than Chapelon's, though with his Class 232s, he was able to create a new – and effective – design.**

**The unique 232.U1 seen at La Chapelle locomotive depot, Paris, in 1960. This engine has been preserved.**

**Boiler pressure:** 20.5kg/cm² (292psi)
**Cylinders:** hp 447x700.5mm (17.6x27.6in); lp 680x700.5mm (26.8x27.6in)
**Driving wheels:** 1999mm (78.75in)
**Grate area:** 5.2m² (55.7sq ft)
**Heating surface:** 195m² (2099sq ft)
**Superheater:** 87.4m² (941sq ft)
**Tractive effort:** N/A
**Total weight:** 147.2t (324,520lb)

## 'LEADER' 0-6-6-0T BRITISH RAILWAYS, SOUTHERN REGION GREAT BRITAIN 1949

Oliver Bulleid's attempt to build a steam engine with the operating characteristics of a diesel was dogged by design troubles, and the single prototype was little used; work on three part-built engines was abandoned at Brighton Works after 1949. It was mounted on two articulated six-wheel bogies, each driven by a three-cylinder engine on the centre axle, with steam

**The prototype Leader, numbered 36001, outside Brighton Locomotive Works in 1949, during its trial period. The works shunter, a venerable Stroudley 'Terrier' 0-6-0, makes an intriguing contrast on the left.**

distribution by sleeve valves. All the motion and cranks were encased and automatically lubricated. There was a driving cab at each end, and a hot space for the fireman in the middle. Four thermic syphons were fitted in the firebox. The class was provisionally rated 5MT, for mixed traffic haulage. All were dismantled by 1951. The abandoning of the project caused some controversy among those who believed that a new generation of steam locomotives was possible and desirable.

But the problems caused by the 'Leader's' novel design features would have required a massive investment programme, with no clear view of success. The locomotive policy of the nationalised British Railways was to build standard steam types – so the 'Leader' was doomed.

**Boiler pressure:** 19.6kg/cm² (280psi)
**Cylinders:** 311x380mm (12.25x15in)
**Driving wheels:** 1548mm (61in)
**Grate area:** 4m² (43sq ft)
**Heating surface:** 221.7m² (2387sq ft)
**Superheater:** 42.1m² (454sq ft)
**Tractive effort:** 11,927kg (26,300lb)
**Total weight:** 132t (291,200lb)

## CLASS YP 4-6-2 INDIAN RAILWAYS (IR) — INDIA 1949

**A class YP hauling a cross-country Chitogarh–Ahmedabad passenger train, on 5 January 1981.**

This numerous express class was a standard type on the metre-gauge (39.4in) railways of India. The first came from North British in Glasgow and Krauss-Maffei in Munich; from 1956, they were built by the Telco works at Jamshedpur or by Chittaranjan, where the final ones were built between 1969 and 1972: the last express steam engines to be constructed in India. The class shared a boiler with the new 2-8-2 standard, class YG. These handsomely proportioned engines were only 3147mm (10ft 4in) high, with a maximum axle loading of 10.7t (10.5 tons). Their construction was to a similar specification as for the new standard broad gauge engines of Class WP, with a strong American influence: two cylinders, simple expansion; bar frames, with one-piece steel castings at each end; a substantial firebox incorporating combustion chamber, thermic syphon and arch tubes. Roller-bearing axle boxes were fitted to the pony and tender wheels. By this time, the value of large-diameter long-travel piston valves in ensuring the free passage of steam to the cylinders was appreciated, and those fitted to the YPs and actuated by the ubiquitous Walschaerts gear were of 228mm (9in) diameter. Smoke deflectors were fitted, but the engines did not have Boxpok wheels. Over 750 YP locomotives were still in service during 1974–75.

**Boiler pressure:** 14.7kg/cm² (210psi)
**Cylinders:** 387x609mm (15.25x24in)
**Driving wheels:** 2128mm (54in)
**Grate area:** 2.6m² (28sq ft)
**Heating surface:** 102.25m² (1101sq ft)
**Superheater:** 30.7m² (331sq ft)
**Tractive effort:** 8367kg (18,450lb)
**Total weight:** 58t (127,680lb) (engine only)

**By 1980, steam locomotives were often badly maintained, but YP No 269, here in that year, has shining paintwork and no leaky valves.**

## CLASS 15A 4-6-4+4-6-4 RHODESIA RAILWAYS (RR) RHODESIA 1949

Based on the RR class 15 Beyer-Garratt of the same wheel arrangement, which dated from 1930, the 15A was altered in various ways, of which the most obvious was the down-curved ends of the tank and tender – an aesthetic rather than a practical change, which greatly improved the look of these and later Garratts. Forty were delivered between 1949 and 1952, and ran both freight and passenger services on the 1065mm (3ft 6in) gauge route between Bulawayo and Mafeking. A number of these locomotives still survive in service in Zambia.

**Full speed across the veld – a class 15A, now of Zimbabwean Railways, on the line between Wankie and Bulawayo.**

**Boiler pressure:** 14kg/cm$^2$ (200psi)
**Cylinders:** 445x660mm (17.5x26in)
**Driving wheels:** 1448mm (57in)
**Grate area:** 4.6m$^2$ (49.6sq ft)
**Heating surface:** 216m$^2$ (2322sq ft)
**Superheater:** 46m$^2$ (494sq ft)
**Tractive effort:** 21,546kg (47,500lb)
**Total weight:** 189.5t (418,000lb)

**A broadside-on photograph offers a comprehensive view of the sleek shape and layout of a Class 15: this is an official portrait of No 403.**

## CLASS 12L 4-6-2 CENTRAL ARGENTINE RAILWAY ARGENTINA 1950

No less than 90 of this class were ordered from the Vulcan Foundry Co. in 1948, just before the Argentine railways were nationalized. Only 40 were delivered, the rest being cancelled in favour of 21 metre-gauge (39.4in) diesel-electrics, and it was Argentina's last steam type. Most worked on the Central Railway, though five went to the former Great Southern. Three-cylinder simples, they had Caprotti cam-operated valve gear and parallel boilers with wide round-topped fireboxes. Their big tenders, with two six-wheel bogies, weighed more than the locomotive, when full. Their design was based on the Armstrong Whitworth 12L 4-6-2s of 1930 (crews were said to prefer the older locos). The tenders allowed them to run from Buenos Aires to Rosario (303km/ 188 miles) without taking on more water. They were withdrawn in the late 1960s.

**Boiler pressure:** 15.8cm$^2$ (225psi)
**Cylinders:** 507.6x660mm (20x26in)
**Driving wheels:** 1903mm (75in)
**Grate area:** 4m$^2$ (43sq ft)
**Heating surface:** 232.8m$^2$ (2507sq ft)
**Superheater:** not known
**Tractive effort:** 11,460kg (25,270lb)
**Total weight:** 101.5t (224,000lb) (engine only)

## CLASS TKT 48 2-8-2T POLISH STATE RAILWAYS (PKP) POLAND 1950

Up to 1958, the Polish works of Cegielski and Chrzanov built about 195 of this tank type. Intended for freight haulage, it spent more time in passenger service. Extra power and adhesion weight and lighter axle loading gave it the edge over the heavyweight Ok1-27 2-6-2T. This class ran Warsaw's last steam-powered suburban trains. Without smoke deflectors initially, it later had standard ones fitted. As steam in Poland was being phased out, and with a useful service life left, 20 of these engines were sold to the Albanian State Railways.

**In the early 1970s, TKt tanks were still active in the Warsaw area. While its neighbours have their smoke-box doors open for cleaning, the TKt 48 in the foreground has steam up and is ready to leave the roundhouse.**

**Boiler pressure:** 15kg/cm$^2$ (213.75psi)
**Cylinders:** 500x700mm (19.7x27.6in)
**Driving wheels:** 1450mm (57in)
**Grate area:** 3m$^2$ (32.3sq ft)
**Heating surface:** 123.1m$^2$ (1325.3sq ft)
**Superheater:** 48.6m$^2$ (523.2sq ft)
**Tractive effort:** 15,420kg (34,000lb)
**Total weight:** 95t (209,475lb)

# Class 11 4-8-2 Benguela Railway (CFB) Angola 1951

**Boiler pressure:** 14kg/cm² (200psi)
**Cylinders:** 533x660mm (21x26in)
**Driving wheels:** 1372mm (54in)
**Grate area:** 3.7m² (40sq ft)
**Heating surface:** 165m² (1777sq ft)
**Superheater:** 39m² (420sq ft)
**Tractive effort:** 16,375kg (36,100lb)
**Total weight:** 133.5t (295,000lb)

Angola was a Portuguese colony, but the Portuguese locomotive industry was small, so the CFB looked elsewhere for its motive power. This sophisticated wood-burner for the 1065mm (3ft 6in) gauge was built by the North British Locomotive Company. Its fuel was quick-burning eucalyptus wood, specially planted adjacent to the tracks and split into 609x253mm (24x10in) chunks for hand firing. Modifications to the firebox included ashpan ventilation and a dust protection plate, and a spark arrester was fitted inside the smoke-box. Mineral haulage by Beyer-Garratts was the line's main business, and the 4-8-2s were largely used on passenger services, taking 500-ton trains over sections with a ruling gradient of 1 in 80.

**No 402 pulls out of Lobito with a short train, probably bound for Benguela, along the coast, on 21 May 1974.**

**With tender stacked, and a train of loaded, sheeted trucks waiting on an adjacent siding, No 404 looks ready for action.**

## CLASS R 4-6-4 VICTORIAN GOVERNMENT RAILWAYS (VGR) AUSTRALIA 1951

In the late 1940s, the VGR began 'Operation Phoenix', to modernize the somewhat run-down system, whose main passenger motive power was the A2 class 4-6-0 dating back to 1907. As part of the exercise, 70 of these Hudsons were ordered from the North British Locomotive Co.: two-cylinder simples, of very solid bar-frame construction, 127mm (5in) thick. A 'Pacific' had been the first plan, but the addition of mechanical stokers to the design necessitated the four-wheel bogies. Considerable care was put into cylinder, valve and steam circulation design, in order to make them free-steaming. Belpaire fireboxes were fitted, and they had large, 279.5mm (11in) diameter piston valves set above the cylinders. Running on the 1600mm (5ft 3in) gauge, provision was made for later conversion to standard gauge. The running plate was deepened and curved at each end; and with the smoke deflectors and buffer beam they were painted scarlet, though otherwise the engines were finished in unlined plain black.

The Rs performed excellently on express duty, but full use of the class's potential was much restricted by the simultaneous introduction of B-class diesel-electrics, and the Hudsons were transferred to secondary and freight work. At one time they were all to be fitted with 'Stug' apparatus for burning pulverized coal, but this plan was cancelled. Withdrawals began in 1961.

**Boiler pressure:** 14.7kg/cm² (210psi)
**Cylinders:** 546x711mm (21.5x28in)
**Driving wheels:** 1827mm (72in)
**Grate area:** 3.9m² (42sq ft)
**Heating surface:** 88.3m² (2243sq ft)
**Superheater:** 42.9m² (462sq ft)
**Tractive effort:** 16,197kg (32,800lb)
**Total weight:** 190t (418,880lb)

**A dramatic parallel demonstration run by the preserved express engines VGR Class R 4-6-4 No 761 and NSWGR C-38 'Pacific' No 3801, at Broadford, Victoria, on 19 October 1988.**

## W-CLASS 4-8-2 WESTERN AUSTRALIAN GOVERNMENT RAILWAYS (WAGR) AUSTRALIA 1951

**Boiler pressure:** 14kg/cm² (200psi)
**Cylinders:** 406x609mm (16x24in)
**Driving wheels:** 1218mm (48in)
**Grate area:** 2.5m² (27sq ft)
**Heating surface:** 103.7m² (1117sq ft)
**Superheater:** 28.3m² (305sq ft)
**Tractive effort:** 10,701kg (21,670lb)
**Total weight:** 102.7t (226,464lb)

**As in other Australian states, the transfer from steam to diesel cut short the life-span of engines built in the 1950s. The W-class might have been expected to work into the 1980s, but most had less than 20 years of service.**

Designed by the WAGR and built by Beyer Peacock in Manchester, England, for the 1065mm (3ft 6in) gauge, 60 of these engines were delivered in 1951–52. They were chiefly intended for branch freight work, but were versatile enough to operate main line passenger trains and all but the heaviest freight workings. Ease of operation and maintenance was by now increasingly important, and the class had self-cleaning smoke boxes, self-emptying ashpans, power reversers, and roller bearings on all axles. The last 11 of the class were taken out of service in December 1973, and several are preserved.

**Built in Manchester, England, the W-Class 4-8-2 was versatile enough to operate mainline passenger trains as well as freight work in the challenging terrain and climate of Australia.**

## CLASS 556 2-10-0 CZECHOSLOVAK STATE RAILWAYS (CSD) CZECHOSLOVAKIA 1951

Up to May 1958, Skoda built 510 of this class, a worthy finale to almost 60 years of Czech-built steam power. The welded boiler and firebox with thermic syphon, arch tubes and combustion chamber were now standard, as were Kylchap double blast pipe chimneys and mechanical stokers. These superb two-cylinder engines could haul 1200t (1180-ton) trains at 80kph (50mph) on the level and often took much heavier loads, up to 4000t (3930 tons). On 1 April 1981, No 556.0506 worked the last scheduled steam service on the CSD. Numerous examples remain in preservation.

**Boiler pressure:** 18kg/cm$^2$ (256psi)
**Cylinders:** 550x660mm (21.7x26in)
**Driving wheels:** 1400mm (55in)
**Grate area:** 4.3m$^2$ (46.3sq ft)
**Heating surface:** 187.2m$^2$ (2015.5sq ft)
**Superheater:** 72.2m$^2$ (777sq ft)
**Tractive effort:** 23,920kg (48,440lb)
**Total weight:** 95t (209,475lb)

**Class 556.0381, with a snow-plough fitted below the buffer beam, is turned at Tesnoo locomotive depot, Prague.**

## CLASS 477.0 4-8-4T CZECHOSLOVAK STATE RAILWAYS (CSD) — CZECHOSLOVAKIA 1951

The post-war locomotive development work of the CSD was greatly influenced by André Chapelon, and the first fruits of this were seen in the two-cylinder 4-8-2 class 475.1 of 1957. They were also reproduced in this remarkable tank design, which had three cylinders, all simple expansion, the inside valve gear driven off the left-hand third coupled wheel in typical Czech style. The boiler, already lofty, was covered by a 'skyline' casing holding the steam pipe, as in contemporary Russian engines. Originally designated 476.1, the class was redesignated following the addition of extra side-fitted water tanks (the third digit, plus 10, indicated maximum axle loading, which went up from 16t to 17t (16.7 tons). The last 22 of this 60-strong class had false side-tanks between these tanks and the cab-front. Uniquely for a tank engine, the 477s were all fitted with mechanical stoking apparatus.

The class was nicknamed *Papousek*, 'Parrots' after their colourful red white and blue livery. Czech engines were invariably well turned-out, with a variety of colour schemes for the most prestigious classes. The first of the class, originally numbered 476.101, was the 3000th engine built by CKD. This was the last steam type to be built by this company for CSD, and three are preserved.

**Boiler pressure:** 16kg/cm² (228psi)
**Cylinders:** 450x680mm (17.75x27in)
**Driving wheels:** 1624mm (64in)
**Grate area:** 4.3m² (46.3sq ft)
**Heating surface:** 201m² (2164sq ft)
**Superheater:** 75.5m² (813sq ft)
**Tractive effort:** 11,680kg (25,760lb)
**Total weight:** 130.7t (288,193lb)

## CLASS 65 2-8-4T GERMAN FEDERAL RAILWAYS (DB) — GERMANY 1951

**Boiler pressure:** 14kg/cm² (199psi)
**Cylinders:** 570x660mm (22.4x26in)
**Driving wheels:** 1500mm (59in)
**Grate area:** 2.7m² (29sq ft)
**Heating surface:** 139.9m² (1506.2sq ft)
**Superheater:** 62.9m² (677.2sq ft)
**Tractive effort:** 16,960kg (37,400lb)
**Total weight:** 107.6t (237,258lb)

**The Class 65 – design defects made it a poor performer. This example is at the country station of Bad Schwalbach, on the secondary line through the Taunus Mountains between Wiesbaden and Limburg.**

One of the first products of the DB's post-war new building programme, built by Krauss-Maffei in Munich, this was intended to be a standard type. Full advantage was taken of modern engineering techniques in the all-welded boiler and firebox, the latter with combustion chamber; Heusinger valve gear operated the two outside cylinders, driving the third coupled axle. Basic equipment included a Knorr feedwater heater, compressed air sanding gear operative either in forward or reverse gear (boxes not on the boiler-top but built into the side tanks), pressure lubrication, and electric turbo-generator.

It was a mixed-traffic engine, designed for frequent stops, rapid acceleration, and a top speed of 85kph (53mph) in either direction, though the relatively small wheels suggested an emphasis on freight haulage. Unfortunately, it was not as successful as anticipated. A maximum axle load of 17.5t (17 tons) restricted its use on minor lines. Water spilled from the tanks on braking. Its fuel bunker and tanks were on the small side for freight work. At speeds in excess of 50kph (31mph), it developed an increasingly strong hunting motion, caused by an imbalance in the reciprocating and revolving masses of the machinery. Whilst 87 of the 'rival' Class 65[10] of the DR were built, Class 65 numbered only 18. The first withdrawal was in 1966 and all were gone by 1972, while many older tank types worked on.

## 2-6-4T BRITISH RAILWAYS (BR) — GREAT BRITAIN 1951

Of the old companies, the one whose influence was most obvious on British 'standard' types was the London Midland & Scottish. The new 2-6-4, despite more fluid lines and features like an angled cab front, was clearly a smoothed-out version of the LMS 2-cylinder class of 1935. To handle the same type of suburban and local passenger traffic, 155 were built. The bunker coal capacity was 3.55t (3.5 tons) and the side tanks held 2000gals (2400 US gals).

**No 80182 at the terminus of Aberystwyth, West Wales, in 1964. The class was distributed widely over the British Railways network.**

**Boiler pressure:** 15.8kg/cm² (225psi)
**Cylinders:** 457x711mm (18x28in)
**Driving wheels:** 1599mm (63in)
**Grate area:** 2.5m² (26.7sq ft)
**Heating surface:** 126.8m² (1366sq ft)
**Superheater:** 33m² (248sq ft)
**Tractive effort:** 11,936kg (24,170lb)
**Total weight:** 88.4t (194,880lb)

**The well-preserved 2-6-4T No 80079 engine negotiates the historic cast-iron Victoria Bridge on the Severn Valley Railway, with a Bridgnorth–Bewdley train in tow, in the summer of 1982.**

## 'BRITANNIA' CLASS 7MT 4-6-2 BRITISH RAILWAYS (BR) — GREAT BRITAIN 1951

In 1948, a Locomotive Standards Committee began to set policy for future motive power on the nationalized British railways. Despite, or because of, the great variety of existing locomotive types, some quite new, it was decided to design a new set of standard locomotives which could cope with all traffic requirements. Many component parts were taken from, or modelled on, existing equipment, but the range of 'modern' features was greater than on any predecessor. Many of these were intended to be labour-saving, like self-cleaning smokeboxes, rocker grates, self-emptying ashpans, mechanical lubricators and roller bearings – nothing new in themselves. Some features of proved effectiveness, like the thermic syphon, were not employed. The cabs were mounted on the boiler, not on the frame as in previous British practice. For an

**'Britannia' 4-6-2 No 70025 Western Star, on the Carmarthen–London 'Red Dragon' express, photographed at Chipping Sodbury, in the early 1950s.**

engine designed by a committee, and at several different locations, the 'Britannia' class was a distinct success. The first, No 70000, was built at Crewe. Unlike any previous British 'Pacific' for home use, it had only two cylinders. Although designated as a mixed-traffic type, it was in effect an express passenger engine, intended to supplement the more powerful existing 'Pacifics'. Fifty-five were built, and after some initial problems with self-detaching driving wheels, they performed reliably in an era when maximum power output was rarely required. Their best service was on the London–Norwich route, whose slow timings were improved by 20 per cent. A larger and more advanced standard express 'Pacific' was also planned, but only the prototype was built.

**Boiler pressure:** 17.6kg/cm$^2$ (250psi)
**Cylinders:** 508x711mm (20x28in)
**Driving wheels:** 1880mm (74in)
**Grate area:** 3.9m$^2$ (42sq ft)
**Heating surface:** 229.8m$^2$ (2474sq ft)
**Superheater:** 65.4m$^2$ (704sq ft)
**Tractive effort:** 14,512kg (32,000lb)
**Total weight:** 95.5 tonnes (210,560lb)

## 2-8-2 RAILWAYS OF THE HASHEMITE KINGDOM OF JORDAN (JR) — JORDAN 1951

The 1050mm (41.4in) gauge Jordan Railway was formerly part of the Hedjaz Railway. Between 1908 and 1924, this linked Turkey, Syria, Lebanon, Jordan and Saudi Arabia, but currently it operates only in sections in Syria and Jordan. Mikados had always been the staple engines, and between 1951 and 1955 the JR bought nine 2-8-2s from three different makers, Robert Stephenson & Hawthorns in England, Jung in Germany and Haine St Pierre in Belgium. The basic model was the Indian Standard class YD, dating back to the 1920s.

**Boiler pressure:** 12.6kg/cm$^2$ (180psi)
**Cylinders:** 431.4x609mm (17x24in)
**Driving wheels:** 1218mm (48in)
**Grate area:** 2.4m$^2$ (26sq ft)
**Heating surface:** 129.2m$^2$ (1391sq ft)
**Superheater:** 28.8m$^2$ (310sq ft)
**Tractive effort:** 10,026kg (22,108lb)
**Total weight:** 57.9t (127,680lb)

**Jordanian 2-8-2 No 51, with supplementary water tank, on a special excursion from Amman in July 1992.**

## CLASS 01.49 2-6-2 POLISH STATE RAILWAYS (PKP) — POLAND 1951

**The aerodynamic design of the 'elephants' ears' smoke deflectors, beside the chimney, can be seen on this Class 01.4981. In Poland, 14 engines of this class are preserved.**

**Here, the fully enclosed Polish cab can be seen. In 1997, engines of this class were still working from the Wolsztyn locomotive shed, in Poznan.**

A modernized variant of the Russian Su 2-6-2, this class was designed for mixed-traffic use, but mainly used on passenger trains. Between 1951 and 1954, 112 were built by Chrzanov. Welding was used extensively in the construction of boiler and firebox. They were 2-cylinder simple expansion engines, reputed to have a high turn of speed, and were the first to be fitted with the PKP 'elephant's ear' smoke deflectors, mounted high up alongside the chimney.

**Boiler pressure:** 14kg/cm$^2$ (199.5psi)
**Cylinders:** 500x630mm (19.7x25in)
**Driving wheels:** 1750mm (69in)
**Grate area:** 3.7m$^2$ (40sq ft)
**Heating surface:** 159.4m$^2$ (1716sq ft)
**Superheater:** 68.3m$^2$ (735.3sq ft)
**Tractive effort:** 10,810kg (23,840lb)
**Total weight:** 83.5t (184,117lb) (engine only)

## CLASS AD60 4-8-4+4-8-4 NEW SOUTH WALES GOVERNMENT RAILWAY AUSTRALIA 1952

Promoted misleadingly as 'the most powerful locomotive in the southern hemisphere', this was the largest and heaviest steam locomotive to run in Australia, and the first Garratt type bought by the NSGWR, whose lines, standard gauge, had generous loading gauge limits which suited this type of locomotive. Though the engine was of large dimensions, its maximum axle loading did not exceed 16.2t (16 tons), enabling it to work over most of the system, including branch lines if they generated heavy freight traffic. This could be 1524t (1500-ton) trainloads of wheat hoppers just as much as coal, and the class also operated on general city-to-city goods trains. In the west of the state, beyond Dubbo, they ran on lightweight 27kg (60lb) rails, and reached such remote parts on the southern division as Captain's Flat, Temora and Narrandera. Originally intended to be a class of 60, the order placed with Beyer Peacock of Manchester was reduced to 50, and in the end only 42 were assembled, the last entering service in January 1957. Three were cancelled and five delivered in pieces as 'spare parts'. Handsome and imposing engines, they had curved-front water tank similar to those of post-war African Garratts. The boiler was supported on a one-piece 'Commonwealth' cast steel frame with integral cylinders, and all axles and the main crank pins had roller bearings.

Diesel-electric traction was also being developed on the NSWGR at this time, and one writer witnessed an occasion when a double-headed diesel freight failed on the 1 in 55 Wingello bank. An AD60 was sent to the rescue and took the train and its engines, 1443t (1420 tons) in all, up the hill 'in no uncertain manner, without wheel slip.' In service a number of modifications were made to the original design. On some engines the tender unit was built up, increasing their coal capacity from 14.2t (14 tons) to 18.3t (18 tons); and 29 also had their cylinder diameter increased, which boosted their tractive effort to 28,570kg (63,000lb). In addition, 30 were fitted with dual controls, enabling them to be easily driven in either direction, a useful facility on branch lines where the terminal depot might not have a turntable of the necessary great length.

The AD60 was an effective engine, though its overall power in relation to its great weight has been criticised as less than it could have been. At 85 per cent of maximum boiler pressure, its tractive effort was calculated as 28,843kg (63,600lb), compared to the South African GL Garratt with 40,421kg (89,130lb) but which weighed only 214t (471,780lb). A number of other African Garratts also outclassed it in this respect. Nevertheless, the boiler and firebox were of exceptionally favourable dimensions: the boiler had an outer dimension of 2208mm (87in) and the mechanically-stoked firebox was 2944mm (116in) long. Twenty-five of the class had two thermic syphons fitted in the firebox, plus two arch tubes; the others had two arch tubes only. The class worked until the 1970s, apart from one early withdrawal, No 6012, and one damaged beyond repair in a 1963 accident, No 6003. In fact, one, No 6042, was assembled from the available parts as late as 1969, replacing the original 6042, which needed major repair. Their last years were spent working north of Sydney, stabled at Broadmeadow shed, Newcastle, often in a poor state of maintenance, and mostly hauling coal trains from the Newstan and Newdell collieries to the docks at Port Waratah. No 6042, withdrawn on 18 March 1973, was the last steam locomotive in regular government service in Australia, working the short branch from the Awaba colliery to Wangi power station. It remains in working order, and another three of the class have also been preserved.

**In the summer of 1968, No 6006 halts by a signal at Campbelltown, NSW, before moving on with a trainload of Glenlee coal to the docks at Rozelle.**

**The AD60 was one of the most successful of standard-gauge Garratts. Four have been preserved.**

**Boiler pressure:** 14kg/cm² (200psi)
**Cylinders:** 488.5x660mm (19.25 x26in)
**Driving wheels:** 1396mm (55in)
**Grate area:** 5.8m² (63.3sq ft)
**Heating surface:** 282m² (3041sq ft)
**Superheater:** 69.5m² (748sq ft)
**Tractive effort:** 29,456kg (59,650lb)
**Total weight:** 264t (582,400lb)

## CLASS LV 2-10-2 SOVIET RAILWAYS RUSSIA 1952

This was really an adapted version of the highly successful Class L of 1945, intended to have a greater facility for running tender-first, and to have a bigger boiler. A feedwater heater was also incorporated. The prototype came from the Voroshilovgrad works, and series production began in 1954. Several hundred were built until the sudden decision to abandon stream traction was taken in 1956. Most of them operated on routes in Siberia, including the 'Gulag peninsula' line of grim reputation. The plans for this type were passed on to China, and production continued there of a very similar engine, the QJ class, from 1956. The Lv reproduced the lofty appearance of the L class, with a wide space between the frames and the boiler. On the boiler top, a casing ran from the chimney to the dome. A number are preserved, including examples at the railway museums of St Petersburg and Tashkent.

**Boiler pressure:** 14kg/cm² (199psi)
**Cylinders:** 650x799mm (25.6x31.5in)
**Driving wheels:** 1497mm (59in)
**Grate area:** 45m² (669.5sq ft.)
**Heating surface:** 256.6m² (2762.6sq ft)
**Superheater:** 149m² (1605sq ft)
**Tractive effort:** 26,750kg (59,000lb)
**Total weight:** 123.4t (272,160lb) (engine only)

## CLASS P36 4-8-4 SOVIET RAILWAYS RUSSIA 1952

**Two preserved P 36 locomotives, in immaculate condition, No 0064 in the lead, pose for the camera. Among other details can be noted the klaxon horn attached to the inner smoke deflector plate.**

**Boiler pressure:** 15kg/cm² (213psi)
**Cylinders:** 574x799mm (22.6x31.5in)
**Driving wheels:** 1846mm (72.75in)
**Grate area:** 6.7m² (72.6sq ft)
**Heating surface:** m²)
**Superheater:** 132m² (1420sq ft)
**Tractive effort:** 18,160kg (40,040lb)
**Total weight:** 149.3t (302,400lb) (engine only)

Passenger traffic in Russia was the poor relation of freight throughout the period from 1920 to 1960: it was not until 1953 that a modern express locomotive went into production. Designed by I.S. Lebedyanskii at the Kolomna Works, its prototype, P36.001, appeared in March 1950. It was the first 4-8-4 to be built in Russia, and the first Russian locomotive to have roller bearings on all axles.

Between 1954 and 1956, Kolomna built 250, and the last one, P36.0251, was also the last main-line steam locomotive constructed for the Soviet Railways. This was an effective design which, if government decree had not put a sudden stop to steam construction, would undoubtedly have been produced in far greater numbers.

It was, typically, a two-cylinder simple, built on conventional lines but with the upper part of the cab backward-slanted, and large smoke deflectors extending from the buffer beam back alongside the smoke box. As with some North American locomotives, a heat exchanger for feedwater heating was situated transversely on the smoke-box top, in front of the chimney, and the main steam pipe was carried from the dome to just behind the chimney in an insulated 'skyline' casing which was continued back to the cab. A few were painted blue, but most were painted light green, with red wheel centres and white rims.

**Another preserved pair, Nos 0218 and 0050, in full cry on a demonstration run with a heavy train near Toporisher, Ukraine, on 26 February 1994.**

## CLASS 2MT 2-6-0 BRITISH RAILWAYS (BR) GREAT BRITAIN 1953

Among the British Standard types of the early 1950s were three variants on the 2-6-0 theme, their different power classifications and axle loadings related to the intended work and the nature of the lines traversed.

Essentially, the 2MT class were to be used on longer secondary routes like the Shrewsbury–Aberystwyth line across Wales, and the cross-country lines from the English Midlands into East Anglia, and in southwest Scotland.

Despite the mixed-traffic denotation, most of the 2MTs' work was on lighter passenger services.

**British Railways No 78000, first of the class, heads a freight near Kings Sutton, just south of Banbury, in 1957. The lamp code denotes an express freight not fitted with continuous brakes. Few British freight trains were 'fully fitted' with these kinds of brakes at this time.**

**Boiler pressure:** 14kg/cm$^2$ (200psi)
**Cylinders:** 419x609mm (16.5x24in)
**Driving wheels:** 1294mm (51in)
**Grate area:** 1.6m$^2$ (17.5sq ft)
**Heating surface:** 95.2m$^2$ (1025sq ft)
**Superheater:** 11.5m$^2$ (124sq ft)
**Tractive effort:** 8396kg (18,513lb)
**Total weight:** 50t (110,320lb) (engine only)

## CLASS MA 2-10-2 HELLENIC STATE RAILWAYS (SEK) GREECE 1953

Greece tended to buy German and Austrian locomotives, but this late and very large steam design came from Ansaldo of Sampierdarena, Italy. Twenty were delivered between 1953 and 154, but it was an unsuccessful design, the plate frame too lightweight to support the huge boiler, and the firebox too small to generate enough steam for the two big cylinders. Despite many modifications, they remained unreliable, and between 1957 and 1961 several Austrian 2-10-0s were borrowed to supplement them. They were scrapped in the late 1960s. The reason for the Italian construction was as part of war reparations to be paid to Greece. It is possible that some of the deficiencies in the design were a result of the pressures on costing. By 1953, Italy was no longer building large steam locomotives on its own account, though many were being repaired and rebuilt around that time and later.

**Boiler pressure:** 18kg/cm$^2$ (256.5psi)
**Cylinders:** 660x750mm (26x29.5in)
**Driving wheels:** 1600mm (63in)
**Grate area:** 5.6m$^2$ (60.3sq ft)
**Heating surface:** not known
**Superheater:** not known
**Tractive effort:** 31,290kg (69,000lb)
**Total weight:** 135t (297,675lb) (engine only)

## CLASS TY 51 2-10-0 POLISH STATE RAILWAYS (PKP) — POLAND 1953

These were the last new steam locomotives built for PKP, though some rebuilding of older types continued. Between 1953 and 1957, the Cegielski works in Poznan built 232.

Closely based on the American-built Ty 246 of 1947, the TY51s had slightly bigger fireboxes, Laird crossheads working on a single slide-bar, smoke deflectors fitted alongside the chimney, Polish-style cabs, and a new, less box-like type of eight-wheel tender. Mechanical stokers were fitted. One engine is preserved.

**The imposing Class Ty 51. No 57 heads a main-line mixed freight at Modlin, Poland, on 12 October 1972.**

**Boiler pressure:** 16kg/cm$^2$ (228psi)
**Cylinders:** 630x700mm (24.8x27.6in)
**Driving wheels:** 1450mm (57in)
**Grate area:** 6.3m$^2$ (67.8sq ft)
**Heating surface:** 242m$^2$ (2605sq ft)
**Superheater:** 85.6m$^2$ (921.6sq ft)
**Tractive effort:** 26,175kg (57,715lb)
**Total weight:** 112t (246,960lb) (engine only)

## CLASS 25 4-8-4 SOUTH AFRICAN RAILWAYS (SAR) — SOUTH AFRICA 1953

**The original appearance of the Class 25, with condensing tender, is shown in this drawing. It is startling to remember that this massive locomotive ran on the 1065mm (3ft 6in) gauge.**

The tenders of the Class 25s were longer than the locomotives, though most of their space was occupied by condensing apparatus. South Africa and the Soviet Union were the two countries to make most use of this equipment, whose technical development was done by Henschel in Germany from 1933 onwards. The condenser had the dual effect of water conservation, valuable in arid country, and of re-cycling the exhaust steam which is otherwise lost through the chimney and other vents. Having passed through the cylinders, the steam was transferred via a flexible pipe to the tender, in which a grease separator and turbine fans were mounted. The latter were used to cool the steam back to water, assisted by air-vents in the tender sides, and the water was then reused to make steam. The exhaust steam also drove a smaller turbine fan which provided draught in the smoke box to draw heat through the boiler tubes. With no blast up the chimney, these engines did not 'puff'; instead the whine of the fan was heard.

An effective condenser system offered a 90 per cent saving on water use, and around 10 per cent on fuel. For working the SAR Cape Town–Johannesburg trunk line, which crosses the arid Karoo Desert, this was an attractive proposition, and after a successful single-engine experiment carried out with Henschel in 1948, the Class 25 was developed. Between 1953 and 1955, 89 more were built by North British Locomotive Co,

Glasgow, though Henschel built the tenders. Most were stationed at Beaufort West, between Cape Town and De Aar. An expert observer noted that the condensing locomotives 'were not an unqualified success.' From 1974, they were rebuilt with conventional tenders. In addition, 50 non-condensing engines were built, Class 25NC, of which 10 were from NBL and 40 from Henschel.

**Against a background of colliery slag-heaps, a Class 25 gets a long train of coal hoppers moving. The country's plentiful coal, and lack of oil, helps explain the SAR's long retention of steam power.**

**Boiler pressure:** 15.5$kg/cm^2$ (220psi)
**Cylinders:** 610x711mm (24x28in)
**Driving wheels:** 1524mm (60in)
**Grate area:** 6.4$m^2$ (68.9sq ft)
**Heating surface:** 284.1$m^2$ (3059sq ft)
**Superheater:** 58.5$m^2$ (630sq ft)
**Tractive effort:** 23,353kg (51,492lb)
**Total weight:** 238t (525,000lb)

## CLASS 141F 2-8-2 SPANISH NATIONAL RAILWAYS (RENFE) SPAIN 1953

On its formation in 1943, RENFE inherited a huge range of locomotive types, most of which continued to work until steam was being phased out in the late 1960s and the 1970s. But a few new large classes were designed, including this express mixed-traffic 'Mikado', of which 241 were built between 1953 and 1960, mostly at Spanish works, Euskalduña, Babcock & Wilcox, Maquinista

**Fast freight was the most common duty of the Class 141F 2-8-2s. This engine was photographed on just such a service in October 1968.**

and Macosa, but with the first 25 coming from the North British Locomotive Company in Glasgow. All were 2-cylinder simples, with varying types of feedwater heaters; the final 116 were oil burning, with double chimneys. Walschaerts valve gear was fitted.

RENFE operated the Spanish sectors of international expresses to Portugal and France. The 'Lusitania Express' ran between Madrid and Lisbon from 1943, while the 'Sud Express' from Paris had been running since 1887. Until electrification of the trunk routes, the 2-8-2s took their turn on these prestige trains as well as on internal services between Madrid and major Spanish cities. Long single-track sections and steep grades meant that Spain was not a country of high speeds, and a limit of 110kph (68mph) was imposed.

**Boiler pressure:** 15kg/cm² (214psi)
**Cylinders:** 570x710mm (22.4x28in)
**Driving wheels:** 1560mm (61.5in)
**Grate area:** 4.8m² (51.5sq ft)
**Heating surface:** 239m² (2578sq ft)
**Superheater:** 74.5m² (802sq ft)
**Tractive effort:** 20,520kg (41,553lb)
**Total weight:** 166.5t (367,132lb)

**On the open road, in typical bare and rocky Spanish terrain, No 2112 hurries an express freight along near Biurrun, on 22 January 1971.**

## CLASS 498.1 4-8-2 CZECHOSLOVAK STATE RAILWAYS (CSD) CZECHOSLOVAKIA 1954

**Boiler pressure:** 16kg/cm² (228psi)
**Cylinders:** 500x680mm (19.75x26.75in)
**Driving wheels:** 1830mm (72in)
**Grate area:** 4.9m² (52sq ft)
**Heating surface:** 228m² (2454sq ft)
**Superheater:** 74m² (797sq ft)
**Tractive effort:** 19,018kg (41,920lb)
**Total weight:** 194t (428,500lb)

Among the last steam locomotives designed and built by Skoda was this impressive simple-expansion express passenger type, which improved on the 1947 class 498.0. Typical of modern three-cylinder Czech steam locomotives, the valve gear for the inside cylinder was operated by a long rod off a return crank from the crank-pin of the third coupled axle on the left side. Like most post-war Czech engines its styling was German, though its internal arrangements owed much to Chapelon's work in France. The firebox, of welded construction, had a combustion chamber, a thermic syphon and two tubular arches. Roller bearings were fitted to all axles, including those of the big type-935.2 five-axled tender.

Anticipating eventual displacement from main line services, there was a provision for adjusting the axle load between coupled and supporting wheels, to enable it to run on secondary lines.

The class ran long-distance expresses on routes such as Prerov–Kosice. As electrification of the network advanced, the CSD required its express engines to run certain routes, like that from Prague to Kolín, to schedules devised for electric traction. The two 498 classes rose magnificently to this demand. No 498.106, on a test run on 27 August 1964, achieved the maximum speed on Czechoslovakian rails, of 162kph (100.6mph). This engine, and one other of the class, are preserved.

**Under the electric catenary, and running to an electric schedule, 4-8-2 No 498.016 powers an express through Wranov, on 14 May 1967.**

# CLASS 9F 2-10-0 BRITISH RAILWAYS (BR) GREAT BRITAIN 1954

**Boiler pressure:** 15.8kg/cm$^2$ (225psi)
**Cylinders:** 508x711mm (20x28in)
**Driving wheels:** 1525mm (60in)
**Grate area:** 3.73m$^2$ (40.2sq ft)
**Heating surface:** 181m$^2$ (1950sq ft)
**Superheater:** 49.3m$^2$ (530.6sq ft)
**Tractive effort:** 18,140kg (40,000lb)
**Total weight:** 88.4 tonnes (194,880lb) (engine only)

A 2-8-2 had been considered for the post-war British standard heavy freight locomotive, but the success of the wartime 'Austerity' 2-10-0 was decisive in making this the adopted wheel arrangement. Once again, it was designated 'mixed traffic' and in this case the claim was true – in passenger service it could be remarkably fast. The boiler was similar to that of the 'Britannia' 4-6-2 class, but 533mm (21in) shorter, and set high, in orderto provide the widest possible space for the ashpan. The resultant space between boiler and frame earned the class the nickname of 'spaceships'. Nevertheless, the compromise necessary between a wide, deep ashpan and 1525mm (60in) wheels was perhaps the weakest point in a generally excellent design. As in the 'Austerity' engines, the central drivers had no flanges, in order to improve turning. Many of the class were provided with a concrete arch in the firebox instead of the conventional brick arch. The provision of smoke deflectors, unusual in a freight engine, may have been in anticipation of a low-pressure exhaust that would not rise clear of the boiler. The British Railways designers were reluctant to use double blast-pipe chimneys, partly because they believed these were best employed at full power

**Above and left: The preserved *Evening Star* near Stocksfield, on the Newcastle–Carlisle line in northern England, 9 March 1985.**

**The last of the class to be built, at the former works at Swindon, was the only one to be named, in GWR's traditional lettering style.**

output, not a common occurrence. However, later engines of this class were so equipped, and one was experimentally fitted with a Giesl ejector. Three were also fitted with mechanical stokers in 1958.

The '9F' class numbered 251, employed chiefly on vacuum-brake fitted mineral trains. They were allocated to the larger locomotive sheds responsible for bulk freight motive power, like Wellingborough, Motherwell, Newport, and Saltley (Birmingham). Although not fitted with train heating apparatus, they did run passenger trains on occasions. One of these was to deputize on the 'Flying Scotsman' from Grantham to Kings Cross, done at an average 93kph (58mph) start to stop, and including a maximum of 145kph (90mph). At least one other authenticated maximum this fast was recorded, and the operating authorities later placed a maximum of 96.5kph (60mph) on the class.

In 1955, Crewe works built 10 engines of this class with the Franco–Crosti boiler. Developed in Italy, its purpose was to pre-heat water before it entered the boiler. This had been thought desirable since the early days of steam locomotives, and feedwater heaters were a normal sight on American, French and German locomotives, among others, but had never been widespread in Britain. The British distaste for external fittings may have played a part in this. This was by far their most serious attempt to provide such an aid to efficient steam generation, in which exhaust steam is channelled back through a pre-heater fitted beneath the main boiler. The injectors fed water into the pre-heater, from which it passed through top-mounted clack valves into the boiler. Unlike Italian Crosti-boilered engines, the 2-10-0 retained its front chimney in addition to the exhaust vent fitted on the right-hand side of the boiler, though it was used only for lighting-up. Sulphur dioxide corrosion of the tubes was a problem, and the Crosti variation was not particularly successful.

This was the last steam locomotive designed for British railways, and No 92220, named *Evening Star* and built at Swindon in 1960, was the last steam locomotive built for regular service in Britain.

**No 92250, the BR 2-10-0 fitted with a Giesl ejector and its accompanying oblong chimney, at Oxley locomotive depot, Wolverhampton, in the English West Midlands, on 30 January 1966.**

## CLASS P-38 2-8-8-4 SOVIET RAILWAYS — RUSSIA 1954

In 1954, steam power still seemed to have a vigorous future; Kaganovich, the Commissar of Transport announced: 'I am for the steam locomotive and against those who imagine we will not have any steam locomotives in the future.' With such encouragement, a large steam locomotive type was designed, and two prototypes were built. In order to haul freight trains of 3556t (3500 tons), it needed to have an adhesive weight of 16.25t (160 tons) to stay within the maximum axle load. This required eight coupled axles, so the Mallet type, with simple expansion, was chosen. The two P-38s emerged from Kolomna Works in December 1954 and January 1955. Although lighter than the Ya-01 Beyer Garratt of 1932, these were the biggest engines actually built in Russia. On test, P-38.001 pulled a 3556t (3500-ton) train at 24kph (15mph) up an incline of 1 in 110. The new engines were tried out in southern Siberia on lines between Krasnoyarsk and Ulan Ude. Details of their performance were not published, but it was later stated that they had not functioned well in conditions of extreme cold. After a brief working life, both were withdrawn. Meanwhile, by 1957, Kaganovich was disgraced, part of the case against him being that: '. . . he stubbornly insisted on developing steam traction, though it is well known that steam traction is uneconomic and out of date.' It was a dismal end to the great Russian steam tradition.

**Boiler pressure:** 15kg/cm$^2$ (213psi)
**Cylinders:** 574x799mm (22.6x31.5in)
**Driving wheels:** 1497mm (59in)
**Grate area:** 10.7m$^2$ (115sq ft)
**Heating surface:** 396.3m$^2$ (4266.8sq ft)
**Superheater:** 236.7m$^2$ (2548.4sq ft)
**Tractive effort:** N/A
**Total weight:** 218.3t (481,376lb)

## CLASS GMA 4-8-2+2-8-4 SOUTH AFRICAN RAILWAYS (SAR) — SOUTH AFRICA 1954

The history of steam locomotion in southern Africa in the mid-twentieth century is in stark contrast to the picture of almost universal decline in South America. On the African lines, steam power was not only vibrant but fully up to date in technology. It was here that the Garratt type reached its peak of effectiveness, and the SAR had more of them than any other railway. The SAR's first Garratts for the 1065mm (3ft 6in) gauge, Class GA, were delivered in 1919, already giants for their time; and a variety of Garratts and other articulated types followed, some of them highly efficient and others less so. In the late 1920s, the original Garratt patents expired, and though Beyer Peacock of Manchester patented new features, the way was open for other manufacturers to use the principle. The Germans were foremost in this, and Hanomag, Maffei, Krupp and Henschel feature among the Garratt suppliers from 1927, as well as Beyer Peacock. The North British Locomotive Company of Glasgow also contributed from 1924, though its 'Modified Fairlies' were not true Garratts. In the mountainous districts of South Africa, Garratts were an established part of the railway scene, and hauled all kinds of traffic.

In 1954, no less than three new classes were introduced, GMA, GMAM and GO. The first two were identical in their main dimensions and power rating, the difference being that GMAM carried 14.2t (14 tons) of coal and 2160gals (2594 US gals) of water, and GMA 11.8t (11.6 tons) and 1650gals (1980 US gals). The

**Class GMAM Garratt No 4122 at Witbank loco shed, east of Pretoria, on 27 July 1986. At this time, the engine was being kept only for special workings and was not in regular service.**

maximum axle load was the same, 15.2t (15 tons), enabling them to work on lightweight 27kg (60lb) rails, but GMAM weighed an extra 13.3t (13.1 tons). Both had a water-cart tender in addition to the front-end tank, and the latter had had the curved-front, round-edged streamlined style of most post-war Garratts. It was treated as a reserve supply, the engine normally taking its water from the detachable tender, and this helped to maintain the locomotive's total adhesive weight. The 'Commonwealth' cast steel bed-frames were made in the USA. Welding was extensively used in the boiler and firebox, and all axles had roller bearings, with Franklin spring-loaded wedge horns fitted in the horn-blocks. All were equipped with a mechanical stoker, and mechanically rocked firebars in the grate. Some GMAs were altered to GMAM, and vice versa; the combined total number built between 1953 and 1958 was 120, making it by some way the most numerous Garratt class ever built. Henschel, Beyer Peacock, and North British were the builders. These were not the most powerful South African Garratts. That distinction belonged to the remarkable Class GL, also a 4-8-2+2-8-4, built by Beyer Peacock in 1929, which had a

**Black smoke spreads as a Class GMAM toils with a lengthy freight. Behind the engine is a supplementary water tank truck.**

**With the Cape Mountains in the background, Class GMAM No 4137 stands with a freight train at Worcester, junction for the Port Elizabeth line.**

nominal tractive effort of 35,675kg (78,650lb) at 75 per cent of maximum boiler pressure. Despite the possession of so much up-to-date steam power, and a high-technology development programme, the SAR was also pushing ahead with electrification and dieselization plans, and the Garratts were moved around the country as the tide of modernization caught up with them. Their last great stronghold was in Natal, when for a time more than half of the GMA/Ms were stabled at Pietermaritzburg. Increasingly, their use was freight only, often working double-headed on coal trains loading up to 914t (900 tons) on lines like the long Franklin and Greytown branches, where the ruling gradient was 1 in 30. Although GMA/Ms were still in use in the late 1970s, some had been put into storage, and the SAR was able to hire 21 to the National Railways of Zimbabwe in 1979; others were hired out to Mozambique. Combined steam and diesel operations went on until the mid-1990s, when the GMA/Ms were finally phased out.

**A moment of repose at George, Cape Province, for the Port Elizabeth-Cape Town express. The lower plate on the cab side of Class GMAM No 4103 shows it was one of the Henschel-built locomotives.**

Specifications are for class GMA.

**Boiler pressure:** 14kg/cm$^2$ (200psi)
**Cylinders:** 520x660mm (20.5x26in)
**Driving wheels:** 1370mm (54in)
**Grate area:** 5.9m$^2$ (63.5sq ft)
**Heating surface:** 298.6m$^2$ (3215sq ft)
**Superheater:** 69.4m$^2$ (747sq ft)
**Tractive effort:** 27,528kg (60.700lb)
**Total weight:** 190.3t (419,776lb)

## Class 464.2 4-8-4T CZECHOSLOVAK STATE RAILWAYS (CSD) CZECHOSLOVAKIA 1955

Skoda built this last class of steam locomotives to be ordered by the Czechoslovakian State Railways. It numbered only two. Lighter but more powerful than the 477.0 of 1951, it too was modelled on the very successful 2-cylinder class 475.1 4-8-2 of 1947. They were intended for short-haul fast passenger service, but the decision to speed up electrification meant that no more were built. Like the 476.1 class, they had small water tanks fitted to the sides, with the main supply at the back. With their very high running plates, wing-type smoke deflectors and an overall height of 4650mm (15ft 3in), they were imposing machines. Political separation from western Europe made it difficult for the qualities and performance of Czech locomotives to be appreciated.

**Boiler pressure:** 18kg/cm$^2$ (256psi)
**Cylinders:** 500x720mm (19.7x28.4in)
**Driving wheels:** 1624mm (64in)
**Grate area:** 3.8m$^2$ (41sq ft)
**Heating surface:** 166m$^2$ (1787.2sq ft)
**Superheater:** 67.1m$^2$ (399.4sq ft)
**Tractive effort:** 16,990kg (37,470lb)
**Total weight:** 112t (246,960lb)

## CLASS 83$^{10}$ 2-8-4T GERMAN STATE RAILWAYS (DR) GERMANY 1955

In 1955, both the DB and the DR, in West and East Germany respectively, introduced their last new tank types. The DB's was a 2-6-4T, class 66; the DR's a larger 2-8-4T, of which 27 were built by *Lokomotivbau* 'Karl Marx' at Babelsberg. It was a slightly smaller version of the class 65$^{10}$, built in the previous year. Water was carried in side tanks and beneath the bunker. Two cylinders, operated by outside Heusinger valve gear, drove the third set of coupled wheels via long connecting rods. The boilers and fireboxes were of all-welded construction. Even in this late model, there were problems with the prototype, and alterations were made, including the repositioning of a sandbox from running plate to boiler top, and a second regulator in the superheater header was removed, leaving a single regulator in the dome. Feedwater pumps and heater were installed, as was an electric turbo-generator.

Heavy local services were the function of the class, with a brief to haul a 1000t (984-ton) passenger train at 60kph (37mph) on level track, and a 1500t (1476-ton) goods train at 45kph (28mph) The advent of diesel traction in the form of railbuses and the V60 and V100 locomotives curtailed both the production and the working lives of the class 83$^{10}$ tanks. Mostly stationed at Saalfeld and Haldensleben, they began to be withdrawn from 1970, and by 1973 all had been scrapped at the Brandenburg steelworks.

**Boiler pressure:** 14kg/cm$^2$ (199psi)
**Cylinders:** 500x660mm (19.7x26in)
**Driving wheels:** 1250mm (49.25in)
**Grate area:** 2.5m$^2$ (26.9sq ft)
**Heating surface:** 106.6m$^2$ (1147.7sq ft)
**Superheater:** 39.25m$^2$ (422.6sq ft)
**Tractive effort:** 15,716kg (34,655lb)
**Total weight:** 99.7t (219,838lb)

## CLASS 30 2-8-4 EAST AFRICAN RAILWAYS (EAR) KENYA 1955

The heavier of two 2-8-4 classes introduced throughout 1955–56, the 25 engines of class 30 were built by the famous North British Locomotive Co, in Glasgow, Scotland.

The 4-wheel bogie, with outside frame, gave more support to the Belpaire firebox than the class 29 2-8-2, with the same boiler, had offered. Some adhesive weight was lost as a result, but the bogie was not booster-fitted.

A large-capacity twelve-wheel tender with 7000gals (8400 US gals) of water and 1950gals (2340 US gals) of oil was supplied to allow the engines to work over long distances where water supplies were uncertain in isolated areas of the country.

Double-blast Giesl ejectors were fitted in place of the original chimneys during the 1960s.

**Boiler pressure:** 14kg/cm$^2$ (200psi)
**Cylinders:** 457x660mm (18x26in)
**Driving wheels:** 1218mm (48in)
**Grate area:** 3.5m$^2$ (38sq ft)
**Heating surface:** 169.6m$^2$ (1826sq ft)
**Superheater:** 41.4m$^2$ (446sq ft)
**Tractive effort:** 13,531kg (29,835lb)
**Total weight:** 85.9t (189,588lb)

## '59TH' CLASS 4-8-2+2-8-4 EAST AFRICAN RAILWAYS (EAR) KENYA 1955

These were the most powerful locomotive ever to run on metre-gauge (39.4in) tracks anywhere in the world, and, when the American 'Big Boys' were retired from the Union Pacific Railroad in the late 1950s, they became the largest steam locomotives in regular service, their 2284mm (7ft 6in) boilers being more than twice the width of the rail gauge. The line from Mombasa on the coast to the Kenyan capital, Nairobi, climbed from sea level to 1705m (5600ft) over a distance of 531km (330 miles), at a ruling gradient of 1 in 66. The summit level of the East African Railway, 853km (530 miles) inland, was at 2740m (9000ft). A long-distance line of this kind – single track with crossing loops – was normally worked by infrequent though very heavy trains, but in the late 1940s, traffic was increasing and congestion creating serious delays. The EAR had a stock of heavy rigid-frame engines, the most recent being 2-8-2s supplied in 1951, but since 1926, it had also made good use of Garrat-type locomotives; with their articulated frames and low axle loading they were ideal for the slow, heavy hauling the EAR required, and engine crews and depot fitters had developed an expertise in handling

**No 5918 Mount Gelai in the locomotive sheds at Mombasa, on the Kenya coast, on 19 December 1970. After Nairobi, this was the largest locomotive depot in the country.**

them. But the need for engines to haul greater loads at greater speeds was clear. The 59th class was ordered in 1950, with detailed design entrusted to the manufacturers, Beyer Peacock of Manchester. The original order was for nine, increased to 34 before deliveries began in 1955; all were in service by the end of 1956.

Some technical uncertainties hung over the railway at this time. Oil was the fuel of preference, but coal might become cheaper; the metre gauge might be widened to 1065mm (3ft 6in), compatible with the South African and Rhodesian systems, which meant building new engines whose axles could be readily widened. In the '59th' class, this meant providing for the installation of a mechanical stoker if necessary, though these were never used. Pumps for both vacuum and air braking were fitted on the left-hand side of the smoke box. Some 34 of the class were ordered. They were simple-expansion types, the four cylinders operated by piston valves actuated by outside Walschaerts valve gear.

**The number plates of the '59s' gave the heights of the mountains whose names they carried.**

Long connecting rods, tapering towards the crosshead, drove the third sets of coupled wheels. Roller bearings were fitted to all axles and to the big ends of the connecting rods. The maximum axle loading, at 21.3t (21t) was not light, reflecting improvements to the track and strengthening of embankments and bridges.

With this class, the haulage power available took a great leap forward. The schedules between Mombasa and Nairobi were improved by up to a third. Unaided, the '59ths' could take a 1219t (1200 ton) train up gradients of 1.5 per cent at 22.5kph (14mph) and round curves, and the driver could sometimes see the tail end of his train running parallel to him in the opposite direction. The 'caboose' system was used, by which a relief crew slept in the wagon and took over its shift at one of the crossing loops. Development continued after delivery and the class was fitted with Giesl ejectors in the early 1960s. Pride in the engines was reflected by the policy of naming them, after the great East African mountains. Further enlargements of the Garratt design were drawn up in the late 1950s, including one with a condensing tender, but none were built. When diesel-electric locomotives took over the mail trains, the Garratts continued to haul freights and mixed trains on some long branches. Withdrawals began in 1973, and by 1980 all were out of service.

**Fighting up the curving grades of the Mombasa–Nairobi line – one of the '59s' at work, with over 1000t of loaded boxcars behind it.**

**Boiler pressure:** 15.7kg/cm$^2$ (225psi)
**Cylinders:** 521x711mm (20.5x28in)
**Driving wheels:** 1372mm (54in)
**Grate area:** 69.4m$^2$ (72sq ft)
**Heating surface:** 331m$^2$ (3560sq ft)
**Superheater:** 69.4m$^2$ (747sq ft)
**Tractive effort:** 38,034kg (83,350lb)
**Total weight:** 256t (564,000lb)

## 500 CLASS 4-8-2 SUDAN RAILWAYS SUDAN 1955

Sudan was formerly a British Protectorate and its railway system was developed by the British; it followed that the locomotives were made in Britain. Built to the 1065mm (3ft 6in) gauge, 42 of the 500 class were shipped in fully erected condition from Glasgow to Port Sudan. They were oil burners, with a light axle-load of 15.2t (15 tons) maximum, intended to run both passenger and freight services on the Sudan Government's sparse but long-distance network, with its central depot at Atbara. Steam in independent Sudan was phased out in the 1970s but revived for a time in the 1980s, using reconditioned 2-8-2s.

**At one time, Sudan had an efficient system, using oil-fired steam locomotives, as this blue-liveried Class 500 4-8-0 shows. After the country's political disasters, steam was revived to run famine-relief trains to the south.**

**Boiler pressure:** 13kg/cm² (190psi)
**Cylinders:** 546x660mm (21.5x26in)
**Driving wheels:** 1370mm (54in)
**Grate area:** 3.7m² (40sq ft)
**Heating surface:** 207m² (2230sq ft)
**Superheater:** 50.3m² (542sq ft)
**Tractive effort:** 16,299kg (35,940lb)
**Total weight:** 96.3t (212,280lb)

## CLASS QJ 2-10-2 RAILWAYS OF THE PEOPLE'S REPUBLIC CHINA 1956

In the standardization scheme developed by the Chinese railways since 1948, this was the largest freight type, and also the most numerous. QJ, 'Qian Jing' means 'March Forward'. More than 4500 were built from 1957 until the late 1980s, mostly at the giant Datong works but also at five other locomotive works in China, and they were to be seen in almost every part of the country. The basis of the type was the Russian Lv class, whose specifications and detailed drawings had been sold or given to the Chinese, but subsequent modifications included the provision of a combustion chamber with a shorter boiler. The degree of finish of these

**Two QJs get the drag on a long freight, leaving the busy Harbin marshalling yards for the main line southbound through Manchuria to Changchun.**

locomotives would have distressed an engineer from Doncaster, England, or Roanoake, Virginia, but in response to an insatiable demand for more motive power, they were being built at maximum speed, with intensive use of fabricated parts and wholly welded boilers. Vibration, 'hunting' and self-detaching fittings were common problems, and considerable maintenance was needed, but in the basics it was a solidly built class, capable of handling 3000t (2953-ton) trains. On grades, they were double-headed or banked. Mechanical stokers and feed water heaters were among the ancillary equipment fitted. The standard tender was an eight-wheeler, with capacity for 14.5t (14.2 tons) of coal and 8700gals (10,450 US gals) of water, but engines operating in the drier provinces were provided with twelve-wheel tenders of greater water capacity.

**Boiler pressure:** 15kg/cm$^2$ (214psi)
**Cylinders:** 650x799mm (25.6x31.5in)
**Driving wheels:** 1497mm (59in)
**Grate area:** 6.4m$^2$ (69.5sq ft)
**Heating surface:** 265.6m$^2$ (2859.6sq ft)
**Superheater:** 141.2m$^2$ (1520.2sq ft)
**Tractive effort:** 28,725kg (63,340lb)
**Total weight:** 123.4t (272,160lb) (engine only)

**On the long viaduct above the dunes, at Singing Sands, Shawan, a QJ is still at work in November 2001, hauling a coal train for the Shen Mu Coal Corporation.**

**Few Chinese locomotives had names, but Class QJ No. 2470 honoured Zhou De, the Red Army marshal who led the revolutionary troops from 1927 to 1949.**

## CLASS 10 4-6-2 GERMAN FEDERAL RAILWAYS (DB) GERMANY 1956

**Boiler pressure:** 18kg/cm$^2$ (256psi)
**Cylinders:** 480x720mm (19x28in)
**Driving wheels:** 2000mm (79in)
**Grate area:** 3.96m$^2$ (42.6sq ft)
**Heating surface:** 205.3 m$^2$ (2211sq ft)
**Superheater:** 105.6m$^2$ (1137sq ft)
**Tractive effort:** 16,797kg (37,037lb)
**Total weight:** 119.5t (263,424lb) (engine only)

Nos 10.001 and 002 of the DB were the last high-speed express steam locomotives to be built, by Krupps of Essen, long associated with iron and steam. Both were three-cylinder simple expansion types, with the inside cylinder driving the leading coupled axle, and the outside cylinders driving the second. Three sets of Walschaerts valve gear operated long-travel piston valves. Double blast-pipes and double chimneys were fitted. All axles and main bearings were of the roller type. Their front look-out windows had revolving clear-vision screens (as fitted to torpedo boats); they had air-assisted reversers, dual-pressure air brakes and a range of instrumentation that would have amazed drivers of an earlier generation. Below boiler level, they were partially streamlined, with a deep valance covering the cylinders, partly obscuring the wheels and motion, and terminating in a rounded casing covering the front end between smoke box and buffer-beam, with inset electric headlights.

The main difference was that 001 began as a coal burner, with a coal oil supply available as a supplement on long grades or with heavy loads; 002 burned oil only, and 001 was converted to this form also. These were steam engines designed to compete with diesels on the diesels' terms, with comparable economies of maintenance and similar levels of availability, capable of an average monthly running of 20,000km (12,435 miles) and a fuel consumption of around 11t per 1000km (620 miles). 'The finest riding and most responsive steam locomotive on which I have ever travelled', was the comment of one British expert after a 515km (320-mile) footplate journey. But only two were built.

**Comparable in efficiency with the last American express steam locomotives, the Class 10 was a worthy finalé of the great German steam tradition.**

## 4-8-4 SPANISH NATIONAL RAILWAYS (RENFE) SPAIN 1956

**Much of the RENFE network was single-track, with frequent use of crossing loops on the busier lines. Here 242.2004 runs with a passenger express through the cutting near Selgua, on 26 October 1968.**

Ten of these engines were built, at Maquinista Terrestre y Maritima, Barcelona; a fitting climax to the Spanish steam tradition. Though not the last Spanish steam locomotives to be built – 2-8-2 mixed-traffic engines were built up to 1960 – this was the most advanced design. Spain had a long history of using eight-coupled engines, which suited both the hilly terrain and the often lightly laid tracks. The 4-8-4s, a stretched and enlarged form of the RENFE 4-8-2s, and built to the Spanish 1674mm (5ft 6in) gauge, were used to haul international expresses to and from France on the not-yet electrified main line section between Avila and Miranda del Ebro. These sleeping car trains could weigh in excess of 762t (750 tons), but this was well within the compass of the 4-8-4s.

Spain had formerly been a compounding country, but these, like all its post-1943 locomotives were simple expansion, two-cylinder types. The ubiquitous Walschaerts motion was used, but the valves themselves were Lentz-type poppet valves, actuated by oscillating camshafts. All had double blast pipes and Kylchap double chimneys. Auxiliary equipment included a water treatment system to reduce boiler scale, feed water heater and pump, and a turbo generator which provided train lighting. Roller bearings were fitted on all axles. The engines were oil-fired. One of the class has been preserved.

**Boiler pressure:** 16kg/cm$^2$ (228psi)
**Cylinders:** 640x710mm (25.25x28in)
**Driving wheels:** 1900mm (74.75in)
**Grate area:** 5.3m$^2$ (57sq ft)
**Heating surface:** 293m$^2$ (3161sq ft)
**Superheater:** 104.5m$^2$ (1125sq ft)
**Tractive effort:** 21,000kg (46,305lb)
**Total weight:** 213t (469,500lb)

**Judging from the amount of smoke, this 4-8-4 is making something of a performance out of backing to the water column.**

## TURF BURNER 0-6-6-0T IRISH RAILWAYS COMPANY (CIE) IRELAND 1957

Peat was the country's main fuel reserve, so CIE tried burning it in dried form. In 1952, the old 2-6-0 engine No 256 had been converted to powdered peat fuel, and in 1957, with Oliver Bulleid as consulting engineer, a locomotive was built at Inchicore works to continue the tests. In many ways a smaller version of the designer's 'Leader' in England, it had two cylinders driving each of two six-wheeled chain-drive power bogies. Two mechanical stokers fed crushed peat to the firebox. Many problems meant it was mainly confined to short freight transfer trips between Kingsbridge and North Wall, in Dublin. In 1965, it was withdrawn.

**Looking like an armoured engine, Bulleid's prototype stands outside Inchicore Locomotive Works, Dublin, in 1957.**

**Boiler pressure:** 17.5kg/cm² (250psi)
**Cylinders:** 304.5x355mm (12x14in)
**Driving wheels:** 1091mm (43in)
**Grate area:** not known
**Heating surface:** not known
**Superheater:** not known
**Tractive effort:** not known
**Total weight:** 130.5t (287,920lb)

## RM CLASS 4-6-2 RAILWAYS OF THE PEOPLE'S REPUBLIC CHINA 1958

These tall engines (4873mm/16ft) were made to look even taller by the built-up front ends, with fairings to each side of the chimney, a feed water heater cylinder in front of it, and a Russian-style casing above the boiler, enclosing the main steam pipe on its way from dome to cylinders.

Originally built at the Szufang (Tsingtao) works, about 250 of the class were constructed between 1958 and 1964. Diesel and electric services replaced them after the 1980s, though some have been preserved, in addition to a streamliner of the preceding SL class of 4-6-2.

**Boiler pressure:** 15kg/cm² (213psi)
**Cylinders:** 570x660mm (22.5x26in)
**Driving wheels:** 1750mm (69in)
**Grate area:** 5.75m² (62sq ft)
**Heating surface:** 210m² (2260sq ft)
**Superheater:** 65m² (700sq ft)
**Tractive effort:** 15,698kg (34,597lb)
**Total weight:** 174t (380,349lb)

**No 1228 stands at Changchun locomotive depot. The somewhat makeshift guard-railing emphasizes the height of the running plate on these large and powerful 'Pacifics'.**

## CLASS WT 2-8-4T INDIAN RAILWAYS (IR) INDIA 1959

American at the front end, British at the bunker end, and intended for heavy suburban services, this powerful tank class was designed to use standard parts. The boiler was that of the WL 'Pacific', and it shared cylinders and wheels with the WP class. Thirty were built at Chittaranjan Works between 1959 and 1965. Electrification displaced them to cross-country services, but they remained in action until the final end of scheduled steam services on the IR system, in 1995.

**A Class WT 2-8-4 has its left-side water tank topped up. In latter years, the 'facilities' for servicing and refuelling were often poor.**

**Boiler pressure:** 14.7kg/cm² (210psi)
**Cylinders:** 514x710.6mm (20.25x28in)
**Driving wheels:** 1700mm (67in)
**Grate area:** 3.5m² (38sq ft)
**Heating surface:** 121.9m² (1613sq ft)
**Superheater:** 41.8m² (450sq ft)
**Tractive effort:** 14,520kg (32,000lb)
**Total weight:** 136t (300,120lb)

## SERIES 282 2-8-2+2-8-2 SPANISH NATIONAL RAILWAYS (RENFE) SPAIN 1961

**No 0428 standing at Algimia, a station on the hilly line between Sagunto, on the Mediterranean coast, and the inland city of Teruel, on 15 April 1966.**

Europe's last new main-line steam locomotives were these 10 oil-burning Garratts, built under licence by Babcock & Wilcox's Bilbao works. Spain had used Garratts since 1930 for passenger and freight work on the Central Aragón Railway from Valencia through Teruel to Calatayud; and the new ones were employed on the same section, hauling heavy freight. They were effectively a re-order of the 282 freight class supplied by the same builders in 1930, with minimal differences in dimensions and appearance despite a 31-year gap.

**Boiler pressure:** 15kg/cm² (213psi)
**Cylinders:** 440x610mm (17.3x24in)
**Driving wheels:** 1200mm (47.2in)
**Grate area:** 4.2m² (45.2sq ft)
**Heating surface:** 197m² (2121sq ft)
**Superheater:** 69.4m² (747sq ft)
**Tractive effort:** 22,226kg (49,000lb)
**Total weight:** 170.25t (375,401lb)

**No 0430 in profile, on 24 October 1968. The brakeman's perch on the leading van stands out clearly.**

## SERIES 2 2-10-2 RIO TURBIO INDUSTRIAL RAILWAY (RFIRT) ARGENTINA 1963

The world's most southerly railway, this 750mm (29.5in) gauge line, 255km (158 miles) long, completed in 1951 and linking a coal mine to the Atlantic coast, was the unlikely scene of a new leap in steam technology. In 1957, L.D. Porta became manager, and applied his own gas producer firebox and exhaust system to three out of 10 2-10-2 Mitsubishi locomotives supplied in 1956. He left the RFIRT in 1960, but the remaining engines plus 10 new ones from Mitsubishi in 1963 were fitted with his improvements. The nominal tractive effort was increased by 30 per cent, fuel consumption was greatly reduced, and reliability greatly increased. Porta's work was to be fundamental to the improved Class 25 of the South African Railways in 1981. Fifteen of the 2-10-2s were still in service in 1992.

**Boiler pressure:** 15.7kg/cm$^2$ (224psi)
**Cylinders:** 420x440mm (16.5x17.3in)
**Driving wheels:** 850mm (33.5in)
**Grate area:** 2.4m$^2$ (25.8sq ft)
**Heating surface:** 91.9m$^2$ (989.4sq ft)
**Superheater:** 30.3m$^2$ (326.2sq ft)
**Tractive effort:** 12,441kg (27,433lb)
**Total weight:** 48.5t (106,942lb) (engine only)

## CLASS SY 'AIM HIGH' 2-8-2 RAILWAYS OF THE PEOPLE'S REPUBLIC OF CHINA 1969

Constructed at the Tangshan workshops, this was the last of the standard Chinese steam classes to enter production. A light freight type, its design appears to derive from the JF6 2-8-2 introduced in Japanese-occupied Manchuria in 1934. The railed bogie tender with its sloping back suggests shunting or backwards-running work. The SY class was extensively used on industrial lines and was an unusual sight on main lines. The total number produced is not known, but was more than 1000.

This class, as modified, reached the peak of non-articulated traction on the African metre gauge.

**Class SY No 1719, on 6 January 1994. Moving slag trains and ladle trucks in steelworks, and hauling ore and coal from mine-heads, were the main tasks of this class, replacing British built Class ET 0-8-0s of 1936–50. Locomotives of this type are still at work on industrial services.**

**Boiler pressure:** 14kg/cm$^2$ (199psi)
**Cylinders:** 530x710mm (20.8x28in)
**Driving wheels:** 1370mm (54in)
**Grate area:** 4.57m$^2$ (49.2sq ft)
**Heating surface:** 171.9m$^2$ (1850.7sq ft)
**Superheater:** 42.8m$^2$ (460.8sq ft)
**Tractive effort:** 17,209kg (37,945lb)
**Total weight:** 88.2t (194,481lb) (engine only)

## CLASS 26 'RED DEVIL' 4-8-4 SOUTH AFRICAN RAILWAYS (SAR) SOUTH AFRICA 1981

Following André Chapelon's principles and practice, an eminent Argentinian engineer, L.D. Porta, a specialist in thermodynamics who had also qualified as a locomotive driver, pursued further improvements in steam locomotive technology. In the 1950s, his workshops in Buenos Aires transformed the performance of many elderly steam locomotives of the Argentinian State Railways. Porta developed a new method for coal-burning, the Gas Producer Combustion System. It required a thick but relatively cool bed of burning coal, with the greatest heat, around 1400°C (2552°F), generated above it. Air inlets and steam jets into the firebox had been used before, as long ago as the 1850s, but this was the first scientifically worked-out method. Exhaust steam was piped to the ashpan and mixed with air, keeping the temperature down and preventing the formation of clinker. Live steam jets and air intakes from above helped in the gasification process by creating a controlled turbulence that kept coal particles in suspension rather than blasting them almost instantaneously through the tubes and out of the chimney. Reduction of coal and water consumption was the main aim, but it also meant that less soot and smoke were produced. Porta also made great improvements in locomotive draughting and lubrication systems. During four years as engineer of the Rio Turbio coal-carrying railway in southern Patagonia, he demonstrated the practical value of his ideas, fitting the gas-producer system to the line's Mitsubishi-built 2-10-2s. Dramatic improvements in performance and fuel efficiency resulted.

Porta's ideas were taken up in South Africa by David Wardale, an Assistant Mechanical Engineer (Steam) on the SAR system. In 1979, he successfully modified a class 19D 4-8-2, built in 1938, which had been a notoriously poor steamer. In 1981, he was allowed to tackle a non-condensing class 25 4-8-4 dating from 1953, No 3450. At this time, the Class 25 was still considered an epitome of steam design, with virtually every modern feature from Timken roller bearings to a self-cleaning smokebox. In the course of the work, at the SAR Salt River workshops in Cape Town, 34 significant modifications were implemented. Among the most important were the fitting of a Porta gas producer firebox, a Lempor (Lemaître-Porta) double-exhaust system, a longer and internally aerodynamic smokebox, and an enlarged superheater with a superheat booster, achieving temperatures of around 440°C (824°F). New steam pipes, an enlarged steam chest, and a feedwater heating system (this last previously unknown on SAR locomotives) were fitted, the cylinders were insulated, and many improvements were made to the valves and pistons. Wardale seized the opportunity to show what a modern technological approach to steam power design could achieve. He named the engine *L.D. Porta*, after his mentor, but its bright red paint coat earned it the nickname of 'Red Devil'. Tests of the engine in service revealed a 28 per cent reduction in coal consumption and a 30 per cent drop in water consumption, compared to the Class 25s. But in addition, the maximum recorded power output of No 3450 was 2823kW (3785hp) at 74kph (46mph), remarkable for what Wardale described as 'a 2-cylinder simple expansion locomotive with moderate boiler pressure burning mediocre coal,' and showing a 43 per cent improvement on the Class 25. The transformation was such that the locomotive was reclassed 26. Like all prototypes, it had weaknesses and problems, including difficulty in managing the GPC fire with a mechanical stoker, and a definite proneness to slipping; but such technically resolvable items were minor compared with the levels of economy and performance promised. But SAR policy was already firmly committed to the phasing-out of steam. Wardale, discouraged by apathy or hostility among the organization's senior engineers, and realizing that his achievement was not going to result in the hoped-for programme of 'second-generation steam', left his job in 1983. The 'Red Devil', though remaining in service, suffered from the effects of unspecialized maintenance. In 1992, steam locomotives were finally taken off main line work in South Africa. But fortunately, No 3450 was saved from scrap and restored to running order.

**The rebuild in its final form, 1983, with large smoke deflectors. During this year, it made many test runs between Pretoria and Witbank, sometimes double-headed with Garratts or 4-8-4s, as here.**

**The rebuild of the Class 26 'Red Devil' as it first looked, with distinctive wing-type smoke deflectors, undergoes steam tests at Capital Park, Pretoria, on 31 July 1981.**

**Boiler pressure:** 15.5kg/cm² (220psi)
**Cylinders:** 610x711mm (24x28in)
**Driving wheels:** 1524mm (60in)
**Grate area:** 6.4m² (68.9sq ft)
**Heating surface:** 288.3m² (3104sq ft)
**Superheater:** 171.2m² (1843.2sq ft)
**Tractive effort:** 22,914kg (50,526lb)
**Total weight:** 136.1t (300,120lb)

PART TWO

# DIESEL LOCOMOTIVES AND TRAINS

The development of diesel power on the railways was slow compared to the rapid way in which the basics of steam locomotion were established. In 1896, a small locomotive built by Hornsby & Sons of Grantham, England, was first to use a pump injection system to force fuel oil into the combustion space at a relatively low compression rate. It was based on a patent design by Herbert Akroyd-Stuart. Dr Rudolf Diesel was subsidized by the mighty German engineering firm of Krupps to work on his 'rational heat motor'. In 1897, after some 15 years of experimentation, Diesel demonstrated the first practical high-compression-ignition engine at the MAN works in Augsburg. The diesel engine, like the steam engine, has pistons working in cylinders, but there the resemblance ends. Combustion takes place inside the cylinders, where intake air is compressed until its temperature rises to 1000°F (540°C) and it ignites injected fuel oil. The resultant expanding gas forces the piston down the cylinder.

**Left: British Rail Class 47 Co-Co diesel-electric No. 47703 *The Queen Mother* passes Pirbright with a London Waterloo–Exeter service on 20 April 1993.**

**Above: Purchased from America, this diesel-electric locomotive was used by the Royal State Railway in Thailand from the late 1960s.**

The pioneering diesel engines were low-powered, with heavy ancillary machinery. By this time, steam locomotives were hauling freight trains of up to 1016 tonnes (1000 tons) and passenger expresses were reaching speeds of 128kph (80mph) in regular service. Against this sort of performance, the internal combustion engine seemed a very modest rival, for all its success on the roads. But engineers were attracted by its potential efficiency and economy – if only the various technical problems could be resolved.

Chief among these was how to transmit power from the engine to the wheels. As the internal combustion engine cannot start under load, a transmission system was essential. From an early stage, it was plain that one effective way was to use the diesel engine to operate a generator. This then supplied direct current electric power to traction motors, which drove the wheels. The technology of the electric locomotive was becoming established by the end of the 19th century, and engineers could make use of proven experience when designing traction motors.

For two and a half decades, the diesel-engined locomotive remained a minor and obscure aspect of railway traction. But it was never dropped. Its trump card, compared to electric locomotives, was that it needed no power lines, and it was a self-mover in a way that the electric locomotive could not be. Compared to steam locomotives, it was more thermally efficient, produced a better tractive effort when starting in relation to its potential full power, offered a better driving position, gave no risk of lineside fires and required less in the way of ancillary equipment such as turntables. And one man could drive three linked-up diesels, whereas six would have been needed for steam. Especially in North America, where railway tracks often ran in city streets, municipalities were beginning to legislate against steam locomotives within their boundaries. The diesel had a bright future, if the problems could be overcome. In 1912, an oil-electric railcar was built by Atlas and ASEA of Stockholm, and worked on the Swedish Södermanland Mainland Railway. This was the first commercial application of diesel power on the rails.

## By the late 1930s, General Motors was ready to mount a full-scale challenge to the dominance of steam on the railway lines. The plan was to do this with engine designs that had been exhaustively tested and a special demonstration train.

**A pair of single-ended diesel units at the yard in Krasnodar, southern Russia, in 1992.**

It was not until 1924 that further progress was made, and appropriately it took place in the land where the diesel-electric would triumph on a vast scale, with construction of a prototype Bo-Bo 'oil electric' switching engine by Alco in the United States, using electrical components from Ingersoll-Rand and GEC. Baldwins built a larger 746kW (1000hp) road engine in 1925, with controls arranged to allow for multiple-unit working and Westinghouse electric motors. Although the cost of these locomotives (around $100,000) was more than twice that of a steam switching engine, they were cheaper to run and capable of far more intensive usage. Still, there was to be no instant revolution. Diesels were seen chiefly as low-speed switching engines, fulfilling a task at which steam locomotives were at their least efficient. But even so, by 1936, only about 190 of them had been sold to US railways, mostly for specialized tasks. Another precursor was to appear on the Canadian National in 1928, the first diesel road engine. This was a 303-tonne (668,000lb) double unit of 1985kW (2660hp), powered by Beardmore V12 engines driving four traction motors, and built by the Canadian Locomotive Company.

A few years later, the advent of high-speed railcars altered the perception of diesels. Germany's 'Fliegende

Hamburger', France's Bugatti railcar, the United States's 'Burlington Zephyr', Britain's GWR Birmingham-Cardiff railcar – all showed that diesel or petrol services could match or beat the fastest steam schedules. Just prior to these, in 1934, the Union Pacific Railroad had launched a General Motors-built streamliner; however, its spark-ignition distillate engine was not to be the way forward. General Motors, already a major business, had embarked on a research project aimed at reducing the weight and increasing the power of a big diesel engine. Using new alloys, by 1935, it had produced a 672kW (900hp), 12-cylinder engine, known as the 201-A. General Motors had had nothing to do with railways before, and this challenge from outside the industry was responded to by Alco, which developed a unit of similar power, but with six cylinders and turbo-charging. General Motors set up its Electromotive Division (EMD) at La Grange, Illinois.

By the late 1930s, General Motors was ready to mount a full-scale challenge to steam, with engine designs that had been exhaustively tested, a demonstration train showing a sleek new look that owed as much to the company's automobile-building background as to the railway tradition and a team of eager salesmen. The campaign was backed up by a fully developed after-sales and spare parts service.

The demands of warfare between 1939 and 1945 produced further improvements in diesel technology. American railways were firmly focused on the diesel-electric, but, in Germany, the hydraulic transmission system also found favour, and it was developed to successful use on high-speed express locomotives. Railroads in America were now converting to diesel as fast as they could. And from the early 1950s, the same process was beginning to take place in most other countries. Lightweight railcars had been operating on many secondary lines since the 1930s, but now large-scale dieselization of suburban and main-line services went ahead. It meant a huge culture change in railway operation, in which almost everyone from designers to fitters, drivers, timetablers and controllers had to re-learn their trades. The physical appearance of depots and works was transformed, as were the tooling and equipment inside.

Like the national railway companies and systems, the locomotive building industry was in a state of turmoil and change. Some of the most famous companies, such as Baldwins, Lima, North British and Beyer Peacock, would fail to survive in the new power era. Others would merge and re-merge. The Société Alsacienne and Thomson-Houston became Alsthom. ASEA and Brown-Boveri became ABB. Henschel became part of Thyssen-Krupp. Even more than their predecessors, these international conglomerates were dependent on a worldwide scale of business. From 1960 onwards, however, the main basis of that business was the diesel engine and the diesel locomotive.

**A pair of Chicago & North-Western GP50s, at Wood Street Yard, Chicago, on 21 December 1982.**

## GAS ELECTRIC MOTOR CARS VARIOUS RAILROADS USA 1906

Beginning about 1906, American railroads started to acquire self-propelled gas-electric railcars for use on light branch lines and secondary passenger services where steam-powered trains were not cost effective. These gas-electrics, which were commonly known as 'Doodlebugs', were built to many different plans by dozens of different manufacturers. In the early days, General Electric was one of the largest producers of gas-electric cars. In the 1920s, the Electro-Motive Corporation established its reputation as the producer of gas-electric cars and ultimately became one of America's foremost diesel-electric builders. Some gas-electrics were powerful enough to pull a trailer or a few freight cars, and were used in mixed train services. By the 1960s, the era of the gas-electric had passed. Some gas-electrics were converted to Sperry rail-defect detection cars.

**Type:** Gas-electric
**Power and output:** Various
**Tractive effort:** Various
**Max. operating speed:** Various
**Weight:** Various
**Overall length:** Various
**Gauge:** Various

**Pennsylvania's East Broad Top was a three-foot gauge railway. Its sole gas-electric, M-1, was built in 1926 at the company shops from a kit from the J.G. Brill company. M-1 is preserved on the line, which now operates as a seasonal tourist railway.**

## ATLAS-ASEA RAILCAR SÖDERMANLAND MAINLAND RAILWAY SWEDEN 1912

The Atlas and ASEA engineering works in Sweden were the original pioneers of diesel-electric transmission locomotives. Their Atlas-ASEA model was the first diesel-powered railcar in the world. It ran on eight wheels, all fixed to the frame, with the traction motors applied to the two inner axles.

The Södermanland line ran through well-populated countryside southeast of Stockholm, and the railcar operated a regular service, with capacity for 51 passengers. Later models had more powerful engines fitted and could haul up to four four-wheel trailer cars for passenger services.

This can truly claim to be the predecessor of all diesel-electric railcars and indeed of the 'power car' with one or more non-powered vehicles attached. However, there was no direct international follow-up to the pioneering Swedish models. The rigid frame offered limited flexibility, and it was soon abandoned for anything other than the more versatile short four-wheel car. It was only with the development of the powered bogie that the railcar really came into its own internationally.

**Type:** Diesel-electric railcar
**Power:** Six-cylinder diesel engine developing 55.9kW (75hp) at 55rpm, coupled to a DC generator supplying current to two axle-hung traction motors
**Tractive effort:** Not known
**Maximum operating speed:** Not known
**Total weight:** Not known
**Maximum axle load:** 10 tonnes (22,050lb)
**Overall length:** Not known
**Gauge:** Not known

## BENZOL-ELECTRIC RAILCAR EGYPTIAN GOVERNMENT RAILWAYS (EGR) EGYPT 1913

Petrol engines, which were already in large-scale production for the motor industry, offered a tempting method of traction to rail designers. Built by Metropolitan Carriage & Wagon Co of Britain, the power car of this particular two-car unit resembled a standard clerestory-roofed railway carriage, with a long bonnet grafted to the front, covering the prime mover engine, and a wide vertical exhaust pipe separating the two front windows. The motor bogie had an outside frame. Westinghouse air brakes were fitted, and toilet accommodation was provided in each car. This up-to-date set, with its first-, second- and third-class seats, worked between Cairo and Alexandria, supplementing steam services. Its appearance in Egypt, where the railways were British-run, was an indication that the 'colonial' railways were quite as modern in their ideas as the 'home' ones. The Egyptian Government Railways' chief mechanical engineer, Mr Peckett, had incidentally taken over just a year before from Francis Trevithick, grandson of the builder of the very first steam locomotive.

**Type:** Two-car petrol passenger set
**Power:** AEG 74.6kW (100hp) petrol engine linked to dynamo of 350V and excitator of 100V, driving two bogie-mounted motors, one on each car
**Tractive effort:** Not known
**Maximum operating speed:** Not known
**Total weight:** Not known
**Maximum axle load:** Not known
**Overall length:** 19.2m (63ft)
**Gauge:** Not known

## 2-B-2 ROYAL PRUSSIAN RAILWAYS (KPEV) GERMANY 1913

Borsig constructed this early experimental diesel locomotive before the outbreak of World War I for Königlich Preussische Eisenbahn (KPEV). It was powered by a four-cylinder two-stroke Diesel Klose Sulzer V configuration engine for traction, with a second 184kW (246hp) engine for auxiliary equipment. It used direct drive (i.e. there was no transmission) – the engine output was coupled to the wheels by jackshaft and side rods. The transverse engine was installed so that the crankshaft lay at the same height as the driving wheel axles, simplifying the mechanical layout. Test running started in autumn 1912 and revealed several shortcomings, and a number of revisions were made before tests restarted in spring 1913. A year or so later, the power unit itself suffered mechanical damage and further development was aborted by the outbreak of war.

**Type:** 2-B-2 experimental prototype diesel
**Power:** 883kW (1184hp) from Sulzer engine
**Tractive effort:** 100kN (22680lbf)
**Max. operating speed:** 100km/h (62.1mph)
**Weight:** 95 tonnes (209,475lb)
**Overall length:** 16.6m (54ft 5in)
**Gauge:** 1435mm (4ft 8.5in)

## 1E1 SOVIET STATE RAILWAYS RUSSIA 1924

Soviet traction engineers were world pioneers in instigating a number of prototypes. Through the 1920s, three experimental designs of around 746kW (1000hp) engines appeared, two with electric transmission and one with mechanical drive. The 1E1 diesel-electric from Esslingen (under Lomonosov design Yue-002 – later Eel-2) with a MAN 883kW (1200hp) submarine engine was reasonably successful, lasting until 1954. Regrettably Eel-2 has not been preserved, but Ge-1 (later Yue-002, then Shch-El-1) was actually the first to work in the Soviet Union and exists today. Developed by Gakkel, it was powered by a 746kW (1000hp) Vickers engine (also from a submarine design) which ran ten 100kW (134hp) traction motors. Both the engine and electrics proved unreliable, and Shch-El-1 was withdrawn from traffic in 1927 after running 40,000km (25,000 miles), from then on serving as a mobile generator. This ungainly 1CoDoCo1 machine was 22.76m (74ft 7in) long.

**Type:** 1-Eo-1 experimental prototype diesel electric
**Power:** 883kW (1200hp) from MAN six-cylinder engine
**Tractive effort:** 220kN (49500lbf)
**Max. operating speed:** 50km/h (31.3mph)
**Weight:** 124.8 tonnes (275,142lb); 98.2 tonnes (216,492lb) adhesive
**Overall length:** 13.822m (45ft 4in)
**Gauge:** 1524mm (5ft)

## CNJ-1000 CENTRAL RAILROAD OF NEW JERSEY USA 1925

By the mid-1920s, a market had developed for diesel-powered switchers in large cities where anti-smoke legislation discouraged the use of steam locomotives. Ingersoll-Rand teamed up with locomotive producers Alco and GE, and built a prototype diesel, which they demonstrated in 1924. Several railroads were interested in the slow-speed, low-output switchers. In 1925, Central Railroad of New Jersey bought the first of these, which was built as a 'stock' locomotive at the end of 1924. It was numbered 1000 and assigned to CNJ's isolated waterfront trackage in The Bronx, New York City. After more than 30 years of regular service, CNJ 1000 was retired and preserved at the Baltimore & Ohio Museum in Baltimore, Maryland.

**Type:** Bo-Bo, diesel-electric
**Power and output:** Ingersoll-Rand 6-cyl engine producing 300 hp/229 kW
**Tractive effort:** 133kN (30,000lbf) starting TE
**Max. operating speed:** N/A
**Weight:** 60 tonnes (120,000lb)
**Overall length:** 9.956m (32ft 8in)
**Gauge:** 1435mm (4ft. 8.5in)

**Many early box-cab diesels shared a common appearance with straight electrics of the same period. CNJ 1000 was the first commercially successful diesel-electric locomotive in the United States.**

**Compared with modern diesel engines, the prime mover in CNJ 1000 was heavy and ponderous. Later locomotives used compact high-output diesels originally designed for marine applications.**

## Class 2090 Bo AUSTRIAN FEDERAL RAILWAYS (ÖBB) AUSTRIA 1927

This one-off small locomotive built at the Floridsdorf works in Vienna operates on one of the narrow-gauge systems operated by Austrian Federal Railways (*Österreichische Bundersbahnen*, or ÖBB). Despite its age, the class 2090 Bo is in operational stock, rather than being preserved, and it is used on shunting work at Waidhofen an der Ybbs. Other elderly small shunting locootives of classes 2190 (Bo of 1934), 2091 (1Bo1 of 1936) and 2093 (Bo-Bo of 1930) still operate on the same 760mm (2ft 6in) gauge network. In fact, Austria has proved something of a 'safe' home for several of this type of veteran.

**Austrian narrow-gauge railways provide havens for other veterans, including the sole member of the Class 2190 diesel-powered Bo at Obergrafendorf and the remaining four of class 2091 1Bo1 (built in 1936). Two specimens remain of the C six-wheeler class 2092, built in 1943 for the Heeresfeld Bahn.**

**Type:** Four-wheel narrow-gauge petrol-electric
**Power:** 88kW (118hp) from Saurer BXD series engine
**Tractive effort:** 102kN (22950lbf)
**Max. operating speed:** 40km/h (25mph)
**Weight:** 12 tonnes (26,460lb)
**Overall Length:** 5.62mm (18ft 4in)
**Gauge:** 760mm (2ft 6in)

## Class V3201 2-C-2 GERMAN STATE RAILWAYS (DRG) GERMANY 1927

Esslingen in Germany was an early diesel traction pioneer, building prototypes (for Soviet Russia as well as Germany) with MAN submarine engines. Several parallel experiments took place in this period. including direct and indirect mechanical drive systems, electric or hydraulic transmissions. and different thermodynamic cycle engines. Completed in 1929 and launched with much publicity at a world power convention in Berlin, V32 01 was a development design using compressed hot gases. This modified air-diesel cycle was followed up in several countries before being abandoned as impractical. Essentially, V32 01 used compressed gases at a temperature of 350°C to expand in steam locomotive–style horizontal cylinders, driving the three coupled axles through side rods. Like several unsuccessful ideas of this era, there were several changes to its design before it was scrapped.

**Type:** 2-C-2 prototype compressed air diesel
**Power:** 883kW (1200hp) from MAN engine
**Tractive effort:** 148kN (33250lbf)
**Max. operating speed:** 45km/h (28mph)
**Weight:** 96 tonnes (211,680lb)
**Overall length:** 13.5m (44ft)
**Gauge:** 1435mm (4ft 8.5in)

## CLASS ABMOT HUNGARIAN STATE RAILWAYS (MÁV) HUNGARY 1927

A total of 128 two- and three-axle railcars were built by Ganz from 1927 to serve both branch and secondary lines in Hungary. These small, rigid wheelbase railcars not only proved to be cheaper than steam trains, but also enabled faster speeds to be run. The first examples appeared with petrol engines; however, these were replaced by Ganz diesel engines from 1934. The radiators were set vertically above the driving cabs. The railcars could haul four-wheeled trailers, and eventually covered 55 per cent of the MÁV network. Fortunately, at least one of these antique machines is preserved in working order as part of Hungary's well-established national collection of locomotives and rolling stock.

**The two-axle diesel railcar type ABMOT was once a regular sight on branch and secondary lines throughout Hungary. A prominent and unusual feature of this particular railcar is the radiator for diesel engine cooling water, which is carried on the roof. In fact, at the time, these railcars would have been considered to quite innovative.**

**Type:** Local and branch passenger diesel railcar
**Power:** 110kW (147bhp)
**Tractive effort:** N/A
**Diesel engine (one per car):** Ganz VIJaR 135 underfloor diesel
**Gearbox:** Four-speed mechanical
**Max. operating speed:** 60kph (37mph)
**Weight:** 18 tonnes (39,530lb)
**Overall length:** 12.02m (39ft 5in)
**Gauge:** 1435mm (4ft 8.5in)

## BO-BO HALMSTAD–NÄSSJÖ RAILWAY SWEDEN 1928

Running through forest country, this line carried much timber, and so perhaps it was fire risk from engine sparks that prompted the railway's pioneering experiments with diesel traction. The Atlas-ASEA combine in Stockholm was to build several locomotives and railcars for it. This was No. 5. In its box-cab form, it foreshadowed the general shape of Swedish diesel and electric locomotives to come; however, its eight wheels, with outside roller bearings, were not mounted on bogies. At this time, the most effective form of transmission was by no means clear. The electric-drive option was not as obvious as it might seem – it was both an expensive and a complicated option. In other countries, designers and builders were still experimenting using a process of trial and error which, although far more sophisticated in its procedures and tests, was not unlike that undertaken by the steam engineers of the 1830s. In the mid-1920s, MAN of Germany was experimenting with a diesel-pneumatic drive on a 2-C-2 locomotive with outside cylinders and valve gear, which was driven by compressed air. In 1924, the eminent Russian professor of locomotive engineering, Georgi Lomonosov, had built experimental diesel types for the Soviet Railways, trying out both electrical and mechanical transmissions at the Krupps works in Essen. The work was carried out in conjunction with the *Deutsche Reichsbahn*. A design with pneumatic transmission was a failure, while one using hydraulic transmission was not completed: this form had not yet been sufficiently developed to attempt road testing.

**Type:** Diesel-electric freight locomotive
**Power:** Eight-cylinder 149.25kW (200hp) engine working at 500rpm, driving two electric motors geared to the driving axles
**Tractive effort:** Not known
**Maximum operating speed:** Not known
**Total weight:** Not known
**Maximum axle load:** Not known
**Overall length:** Not known
**Gauge:** Not known

## NO. 9000 2-DO-1 CANADIAN NATIONAL RAILWAY CANADA 1929

In 1928, the newly formed Canadian National Railway made a bold experiment with emerging diesel-electric technology that many consider to be the first successful road diesel. The two-unit machine was the brainchild of Henry W. Thornton and built by the Canadian Locomotive Company with Canadian-Westinghouse electrical components. The two units initially carried the number 9000 and worked together as a single 2-Do-1+1-Do-2 locomotive producing 1984kW (2660hp). Each unit used a William Beardmore V-12 diesel engine working at 800rpm. The locomotive was designed for freight and passenger service. Later, the two units were split up and one numbered 9001. This later machine survived until 1947. The 9000 was never duplicated, but did prove the capabilities of diesel-electric power.

**Type:** 2-Do-1, diesel-electric
**Power and output:** Beardmore diesel producing 992kW (1330hp)
**Tractive effort:** 222kN (50,000lbf)
**Max. operating speed:** 120km/h (75mph)
**Weight:** 170 tonnes (374,080lb)
**Overall Length:** 14.34m (47ft 1in)
**Gauge:** 1435mm (4ft 8.5in)

## CLASS 100 BO GERMAN STATE RAILWAYS (DRB) GERMANY 1929

In 1930, the Deutsche Reichsbahn received 14 prototype *Kleinloko-motiven*, i.e. small shunting tractors designed for work in sidings away from running lines. V6004–V6006 were built by Berliner Maschinebau (BMAG) with 31kW (42hp) Kamper engines; V6007–V6009 from BMAG with 29kW (40hp) Deutz; V6010–V6012 from Deutz with same engine; V6013–V6015 from Rheiner Maschinfabrik Windhoff with 35kW (48hp) Hanseatischen engines; and V6016–V6017 from Fuerst Stollberg Huette with 26kW (36hp) engines. In 1931, these were renumbered 4000–4011 and 0001–0002, numbers to 3999 indicating under 40hp, above that power from 4000. The two power ranges were established as Leitstungsgruppen I and II, using unified production of type I by Humbolt-Deutz, Gmeinder and Windhoff, and type II by BMAG, Deutz, Jung, Krauss-Maffei and Orenstein & Koppel. Higher power requirements gave way to new 87/94kW (118/128hp) designs by 1934.

**Type:** Four-wheel light shunting tractor
**Power:** Type I to 29kW (40hp); type II from 29kW (40hp)
**Tractive effort:** Various
**Max. operating speed:** Up to 30km/h (19mph)
**Weight:** 10 to 16 tonnes (22,050 to 35,280lb)
**Overall length:** 6.45m (21ft)
**Gauge:** 1435mm (4ft 8.5in)

## FIVE-AXLE RAILCAR '*MICHELINE*' EASTERN RAILWAY (EST) FRANCE 1931

**In coachbuilding and style, the railcars of the 1930s owed much more to the recently developed motor bus than to established railway designs.**

Railway engineers and designers in the 1930s were happy to borrow from other technologies as they explored the possibilities of the internal combustion engine. The steam railcar, which had been revived around 1905, had been a slow vehicle, intended for light branch-line work. The purpose of the lightweight petrol-engined railcar was quite different. It was meant for high-speed intercity work, carrying a small number of passengers who were willing to pay premium fares for a fast and prestigious service. But this model

also had a distinctive feature. The Michelin brothers were tyre makers who, in the late 1920s, began to take an interest in producing pneumatic tyres with special profiles for rail use. In 1929, their first prototype was built and tried out on a test track at their factory in Clermont-Ferrand. Two more were built before No. 4, the first to be fitted with passenger seats. In January 1931, the Michelin railcar, fitted with a Hispano-Suiza engine, and with its inspired name of *Micheline*, was introduced to the public. In a demonstration run in September of that year, on the Paris-Deauville line, with ten passengers on board, it maintained an average speed of 107km/h (66.5mph).

The *Micheline* was built on the lines of a contemporary road vehicle, with the engine placed beneath an extended bonnet in front of the cab and the leading wheels on either side of it. Two more axles behind the cab helped to bear the weight both of the traction unit and part of the car body, which was articulated to the traction unit. Two further axles supported the rear of the car. Five axles were required because the pneumatic tyres could not support an axle-load in excess of 14,000kg (12.6 tons).

Production began in 1932, using a Panhard engine, rather than the Hispano-Suiza. The first purchaser was the French Eastern Railway, and the example of the *Est* was followed by the *Nord*. The railcars captured passengers' imagination and became both fashionable and popular. Railway companies elsewhere took note. The LMS in Great Britain experimented with one in 1932. The SJ in Sweden did likewise. The Pennsylvania Railroad, always keen to be at the cutting edge of progress, tested one. Other motor manufacturers produced their own models, so that

**An experimental *Micheline* seen here at work in Britain passing Bentley Heath Crossing, near Birmingham, in 1933. The board announces: 'Running on Michelin Pneumatic Tyres.'**

France in particular had a range including Renault vehicles and the high-speed Bugatti cars, although the others all ran on conventional steel-tyred wheels.

It was to be in France, and in French colonies and dependencies, that the fast petrol railcar would establish itself most firmly. All railcars were withdrawn during World War II when petrol and other fuel rationing was introduced, but reinstated after 1945. The *Michelines* had a high petrol consumption, and the consequent running costs made it difficult to operate them economically. By 1953, the last of the type were being withdrawn. But their impact was hard to efface, and the name lived on, attached by both railways and the public to single or double-unit railcars with neither petrol engines nor pneumatic tyres.

The rubber tyres were not to be forgotten, either. In the mid-1950s, the *Est* was running steam-hauled expresses between Paris and Strasbourg, with locomotives of the 230 K-class hauling rolling stock fitted with rubber tyres. The concept was revived once again on the rebuilding of Line 1 of the Paris Métro, around 1960, when its trains were fitted with pneumatic tyres, running on flat concrete tracks, with vertical guide-rails and horizontal guide-wheels.

This method harked back to very early days of French railways, on the Paris-Sceaux line, in 1846, when the engineer Claude Arnoux devised a system in which the carrying wheels were free to move laterally, and guiding wheels, set at 75° to the vertical and pressing against the guide-rails, steered the locomotive round the curves.

The last *Michelines* to run were on the metre-gauge Madagascar Railways, into the early 1960s, and they were described as 'quite comfortable and fast, so long as none of the tyres had a puncture' by the railway explorer C.S. Small. One of these examples was brought back to France for restoration.

**Type:** Articulated railcar
**Power:** Panhard motor engine
**Tractive effort:** Not known
**Maximum operating speed:** 100km/h (62mph)
**Weight:** 72 tonnes (158,760lb)
**Maximum axle load:** 14 tonnes (30,864lb)
**Overall length:** 12.4m (40ft 7in)
**Gauge:** Not known

## IRISH DIESEL RAIL CAR COUNTY DONEGAL RAILWAYS IRELAND 1931

**This railcar is seen standing at Stranorlar station, in County Donegal, Ireland. The County Donegal Railways Joint Committee (CDRJC) was actually the first to utilize diesel engines in the British Isles.**

Ireland's County Donegal Railways Joint Committee (CDRJC) operated a network of narrow-gauge lines connecting Strabane, Letterkenny, Stranorlar, Donegal (town), Ballyshannon, and Killybegs, among other small towns in the northwest of the country. Today, CDRJC is remembered for its scenic routes and its pioneering use of internal combustion–powered rail cars. Its first railcar, acquired in 1906, was a small four-wheel, 10-seat railbus powered by a 7.46kW (10hp) petrol engine. This primitive machine inspired further use of self-propelled railcars in the 1920s and 1930s. Railcars cost about one-third the price of steam trains, offering considerable savings for the lightly travelled railway. Perhaps the most significant cars were Nos. 7 and 8, built in 1931. These represented the first use of diesel engines in the British Isles. They were built by Doherty of Strabane and the Great Northern Railways (GNR) shops at Dundalk, and were powered by a Gardner 6L2 diesel operating at 1300rpm that drove a power bogie. Each car carried 32 passengers, and they were capable of operating together. CDRJC gradually assembled a small fleet of railcars. While some of these later cars have been preserved, the original diesel cars were scrapped.

**Type:** Diesel mechanical railcar
**Power and output:** Gardner 6L2 diesel producing 55kW (74hp)
**Tractive Effort:** N/A
**Max. Operating Speed:** 64kph (40mph)
**Weight:** 7 tonnes (15,680lb)
**Overall Length:** 8.534m (28ft)
**Gauge:** 914mm (36in)

## 2-Do-2 551 CLASS ROYAL SIAMESE RAILWAYS (RSR) THAILAND 1931

The fact that the chief officer of the RSR, H.A.K. Zachariae, was a Dane may explain the placing of an order for seven new large diesel-electric locomotives for the metre-gauge with Frichs of Aarhus, in Denmark. But Frichs, with much experience in marine diesel engines, was among the world leaders in diesel-electric technology, and the RSR took a pioneer interest in developing diesel traction because of the low thermal efficiency of the wood burned by its steam locomotives. At an output of 746kW (1000hp), the 2-Do-2s were powerful engines, and they were employed on main-line long-distance trains, including the International Express along the Thai-Malayan peninsula from Bangkok via Kuala Lumpur to Singapore.

A double version was supplied as a one-off in 1932, a 2-Do+Do-2, effectively two 551s back-to-back, and this was used on heavy freight work as an alternative to the RSR Garratt locomotives. The 551s were not wholly successful; their design had not taken the heat, dust and track conditions of Thailand into account, and there were problems with corrosion and effective lubrication. The fixed driving wheels lacked the flexibility on the track of the A1A bogies of the RSR's Sulzer-built 335.8kW (450hp) diesel electrics (six of which had also been supplied in 1931). The less powerful bogie engines proved to be the more durable, with some still in service in the 1970s, while the 551 class was withdrawn in the mid-1950s. No. 556 is preserved, and the 2-Do+Do-2 also remains, in semi-derelict condition.

**Type:** Heavy express diesel-electric locomotive
**Power:** Two Frichs 6285CL six-cylinder four-stroke engines each delivering 373.1kW (500hp) at 600rpm, driving four axle-mounted traction motors
**Tractive effort:** 64.5kN (14,500lbf)
**Maximum operating speed:** 60km/h (37mph)
**Total weight:** 86.1t (189,850lb)
**Maximum axle load:** 10.9t (24,034lb)
**Overall length:** 15.38m (50ft 6in)

## SVT 877 '*FLIEGENDE HAMBURGER*' GERMAN STATE RAILWAYS (DRB) GERMANY 1932

Although steam traction in Germany was limited to a maximum speed of 100km/h (62mph) until 1933, engineers of the *Reichsbahn* had been experimenting for some time before that with some very high-speed vehicles using the internal combustion engine. One of these, the Kruckenberg four-wheel unit, powered by an aircraft engine and with a large four-bladed propeller mounted on the nose, reached a world record rail speed of 230km/h (143mph) on a 10km (6.2-mile) track between Karstadt and Dergenthin. In another example of interlinked technologies, the streamlining of the new trains was developed in the wind tunnel set up by the Zeppelin works at Friedrichshafen.

On test in 1932, the first two-car SVT, or *Schnellverkehrsverbrennungtriebwagen* ('fast traffic internal combustion railcar'), reached a speed of 198.5km/h (124mph). The aim was to provide high-speed rail links between Berlin and major provincial cities. Comfort rather than luxury was provided, and all 68 seats were second-class. In May 1933, the first service began to operate between Berlin and Hamburg. The

**When it first entered service in 1932, the SVT caused something of a sensation because of the high speeds of which it was capable, a characteristic on which the railcar built its reputation.**

two cars were articulated, sharing a central bogie. The engines were mounted on the bogies at each end, each supplying current to traction motors on the near axles of the central bogie. The total weight of the two-car unit was less than that of all but the smallest of steam locomotives, which had to expend power on moving their own substantial weight as well as that of their trains.

The route covered 286.6km (178.1 miles), and the timing from Berlin was 138 minutes; from Hamburg, 140 minutes. At both ends, there were speed restrictions, and another through Wittenberg, where a maximum of 60km/h (37mph) was allowed. Otherwise the maximum permitted speed was 160km/h (100mph). The cars were painted in a special brown and cream colour scheme. The new service caused a sensation in railway circles. In 1934, a further 13 two-car sets were ordered and, in the course of 1935, went into operation between Berlin and Frankfurt (the 'Flying Frankfurter'), Berlin–Cologne, Berlin–Munich, and Cologne–Hamburg. Among these were the world's first services to be scheduled at more than 128.7km/h (80mph) from terminus to terminus. A three-car articulated train was introduced in 1936, with exhaust turbo-pressure chargers fitted to the engines, resulting in a power uprating to 448kW (600hp). Two of the three-car sets were given Voith hydraulic transmissions, with a 10-tonne (9.8-ton) weight saving over electric transmission.

Until 1930, Germany had more of such high-speed services than any other country. During World War II oil fuel shortages, the railcars were not used. Brought out of store after the war, they were found to be of little use on the truncated and divided German railway system, with its single access route to Berlin from West Germany via Helmstedt. Until the German economy was rebuilt, and the rail network of the *Bundesbahn* developed, there was little opportunity or need for prestige services. Some of the power cars were adapted to hydraulic transmission, but by 1959 all were taken out of service. An original set has been re-created using a car body and a power bogie from the first train.

**Type:** Two-car articulated diesel-electric train
**Power:** Two Maybach 12-cylinder 305kW (410hp) engines supplying DC traction motors on the axles of the middle bogie
**Tractive effort:** Not known
**Maximum operating speed:** 161km/h (100mph)
**Total weight:** 78 tonnes (171,990lb)
**Maximum axle load:** 16.4 tonnes (36,150lb)
**Overall length:** 41.906m (137ft 6in)
**Gauge:** Not known

## A-A SCHIENENBUS (RAILBUS) BREMEN–THEDINGHAUSEN RAILWAY GERMANY 1932

The four-wheel railbus was a popular vehicle on rural German light railways, and a number of factories specialized in its manufacture, including the Uerdingen works. Most made diesel-powered vehicles, but the Wismar 'bus' was petrol-driven.

From 1932 to 1941, *Wagenfabrik Wismar* built four-wheel petrol-engined railbuses for light railways, on a variety of gauges from 750mm (29.6in) to standard. With an engine bonnet at each end, these railbuses were known as *Schweineschnäutzchen* ('pig-noses'). A roof-rack was provided for luggage, and they could pack in up to 40 passengers. Only one of the two Ford motors was operated at a time, controlled like a car with a mechanical gearbox, but with a notched control handle instead of an accelerator.

The Wismar bus T2BTh ran for 32 years between Bremen and Thedinghausen (1936 to 1968) and is now preserved. Another ran on the causeway line to the island of Borkum into the 1970s.

**Type:** Petrol railbus
**Power:** Two Ford motor engines, driving via manual gearbox
**Tractive effort:** Not known
**Maximum operating speed:** 60km/h (37mph)
**Total weight:** Not known
**Maximum axle load:** Not known
**Overall length:** Not known
**Gauge:** Not known

## BUGATTI RAILCAR STATE RAILWAY (ETAT) FRANCE 1933

Although Ettore Bugatti's car factory was on the territory of the *Est* railway, in Alsace, it was the *Etat* system, serving the country northwest of Paris, that enlisted his collaboration both as a designer and an engine-builder.

New thinking showed itself in the resulting railcar in various ways. The two-way driving position was from a raised central cabin. Although accommodating this required a low height for the passenger compartments – only 2.692m (8ft 10in) – it enhanced the long, low, speedy look. Bugatti's wedge-shaped ends, tested in a wind tunnel and similar to the front of the British A4 'Pacific', and the circular windows of the toilet compartments, also helped to give the whole unit something of a marine, or even submarine,

**The advent of the railcar, and its association with the glamour and modernity of motor racing, boosted traffic; however, the limited accommodation provided confined it to secondary but not unimportant routes.**

appearance. Four Bugatti 'Royale' engines were placed centrally, driving the two middle axles on each eight-wheel bogie by means of cardan shafts, which were hydraulically coupled to the engine, with no gearbox. The bogies had inside frames and bearings, with each axle suspended independently and able to move laterally to accommodate to curves.

The interior was divided into two saloons each with 24 seats, by the engine and driving compartments. A simple mechanism reversed the position of seats and seat backs to allow passengers to sit facing the oncoming scene. This came on at considerable speed. On test, the car ran at 172km/h (107mph), although the service speed was at first restricted to the French Railways' maximum of 120km/h (75mph). Later, this was raised for the railcars to 140km/h (87mph). The Bugatti cars first went into service on the line from Paris to the fashionable Normandy seaside resorts of Deauville-Trouville. The last Bugatti was withdrawn in 1958; however, one, restored to original condition, is preserved at Mulhouse.

**Type:** Petrol-mechanical railcar
**Power:** Four 150kW (200hp) benzol-alcohol engines driving two axles on each four-wheel bogie via hydraulic couplings and cardan shafts
**Tractive effort:**
**Maximum operating speed:** 140km/h (87mph)
**Total weight:** 32 tonnes (70,530lb)
**Maximum axle load:** 4 tonnes (8820lb)
**Overall length:** 22,300mm (73ft 2in)

## AEC DIESEL RAILCARS GREAT WESTERN RAILWAY — GREAT BRITAIN 1933

In December 1933, the Great Western Railway accepted the first AEC diesel railcar, streamlined No. 1. In total, 38 railcars were to be built, two of them solely for parcels transport. The last of these ran until 1962.

Each diesel railcar had two AEC vertically mounted engines (No. 1 had just one) on outrigger frames suspended from the underframes. Each engine drove through a Wilson four- or five-speed epicyclic gearbox, cardan shafts and reversing gearbox at the outer end of one axle. The axle was joined to its neighbour in the same bogie by a further shaft and gearbox. (On Nos 2 to 8, the second engine did not use a gearbox, but rather had a direct drive to one axle.)

Nos 18 upwards could haul conventional rail vehicles. These had a more angular appearance than the preceding railcars. The last four railcars, Nos 35 to 38, were single-ended and formed as three-car sets with standard carriages as intermediate trailers.

**GWR diesel bogie railcar No. 7, one of the streamlined examples of these pioneer British vehicles, stands at Coleford station in 1947. The livery was brown and cream.**

**Type:** Express and local passenger (36), parcels (2)
**Power:** AEC 90/97kW (120/130bhp) six-cylinder
**Tractive effort:** N/A
**Gearbox:** Wilson epicyclic, four/five-speed
**Max. operating speed:** 130kph (80mph)
**Weight:** 24 to 38 tonnes (53,760 to 84,225lb)
**Overall length:** 19.406m to 20.015m (63ft 8in to 65ft 8in)
**Gauge:** 1435mm (4ft 8.5in)

**Single diesel railcar No. 22 demonstrates the more angular body construction of the later GWR vehicles. No. 22 is preserved at the Great Western Railway Society depot at Didcot in England.**

## 1-B-1 GAS TURBINE LOCOMOTIVE HALMSTAD–NÄSSJÖ RAILWAY SWEDEN 1933

The brothers Birger and Frederik Ljungstrøm set up a company in 1908 to exploit the double-action rotating steam turbine, developed by Birger. They worked on the development of the steam turbine, but their engines were commercial failures, and they finally withdrew from the business. This first turbo-diesel was a relatively simple and small locomotive, with mechanical drive from the turbine shaft. A free-piston diesel compressor supplied the power gas. A reverse gear was fitted, but there was no change of speed gearing. Later turbo-diesel locomotives would use axial-flow compressors and electric transmission, but this one was the pioneer. Among the main advantages of the gas turbine were its lack of reciprocating parts and its use of low-grade fuel; it also had better torque than the diesel-electric and required no water as coolant. However the disadvantages, including high fuel consumption, the drawing-off of power output by the compressor, diminishing efficiency at increasing altitude, and turbine noise, were sufficient to place serious limitations on its development.

**Type:** Turbo-diesel locomotive
**Power:** 485kW (650hp) diesel engine driving gas turbine. Drive to wheels via reduction gearing, jack shaft and side rods
**Tractive effort:** 60kN (13,500lbf)
**Max. operating speed:** 72km/h (45mph)
**Total weight:** 104 tonnes (229,320lb)
**Maximum axle load:** 15.5 tonnes (34,162lb)
**Overall length:** Not known
**Gauge:** Not known

## CLASS 323 BO GERMAN STATE RAILWAYS (DRB) GERMANY 1934

**Enclosed full-width cabs were features of the later built Kof II type as shown here, while all tractors share the low height overall height, barely twice the buffer height and narrow engine housing.**

More than a thousand of these small, low-profile two-axle light tractors were constructed in long production runs from 1934 until 1966. The final development of the pre-war Kof II prototypes, they used similar layout and dimensions, and 850mm (33.5in) wheels, but with hydraulic transmission and power significantly increased above the original 29kW (40hp) specification to 87/94kW (118/128hp). They were built by Deutz, Jung, BMAG, Krauss-Maffei and Krupp, with KHD or Kaeble engines. Traffic changes, cessation of freight wagon load traffic, and increased passenger multiple-unit operation caused the withdrawal of these tractors through the 1990s. A number were passed on to industry for further use, in addition to many supplied directly. Under the DB computer system, Kof II were numbered 321001 to 321626, 322001 to 322663, 323001 to 323999 and 324001 to 324060.

**Type:** B diesel-hydraulic light shunting tractor
**Power:** 87 or 94kW (118 or 128hp)
**Tractive effort:** 47kN (10575lbf )
**Max. operating speed:** 30 or 45km/h (18.8 or 17.5mph)
**Weight:** 15-17 tonnes (33,075-37,485lb)
**Overall length:** 6450mm (21ft)
**Gauge:** 1435mm (4ft 8.5in)

## ÁRPÁD DIESEL RAILCARS HUNGARIAN STATE RAILWAYS (MAV) HUNGARY 1934

Between the two 20th-century wars, central Europe was relatively backward when compared with some western European countries, and this was demonstrated in part by slow speeds on the main railways. At a time when Great Britain, Germany and France were operating heavy express passenger trains at running speeds of more than 130kph (80mph) daily, many central and eastern European railways could barely muster speeds above 100kph (62mph).

There was nonetheless a demand for fast travel by businessmen and other senior figures in the establishment. In several countries, this need was met by the introduction of lightweight trains hauled by streamlined steam locomotives, or by diesel railcars like Germany's 'Flying Hamburger'. Hungary had a pair of services worked by streamlined tank engines, one of which is preserved in working order. MÁV, however, was keen to explore what could be done with diesel traction. The Ganz company was in the forefront of diesel railway developments at that time, and it was able to design a lightweight railcar vehicle that contained a powerful enough engine to accelerate well and to reach a useful maximum speed.

Seven 'Árpád' fast-speed, streamlined diesel railcars were put into service from 1934. They were named as a group after the ninth-century leader of one of the last invading hordes from the east to occupy the territory now known as Hungary. With good acceleration performance and a top speed of 110kph (69mph), the railcars were used for fast intercity-type services. A large diesel engine was mounted on one bogie and drove both axles of that bogie through a five-speed mechanical gearbox and propeller shafts. A capacious radiator for cooling water was fitted under the vehicle body behind the driven bogie. The other bogie was not driven. Each railcar contained 64 seats as well as eight folding seats in the entrance vestibules. There was a toilet compartment and a wash room in the centre of the car, and a luggage compartment next to the cab at the non-powered end. Each railcar was named after a famous Hungarian historical personality. The railcars were not intended to haul trailers, and thus they had only small side buffers and a drawhook below each cab front.

The 'Árpád' railcars operated fast services between Hungary's capital, Budapest, and principal cities. When they were applied to the international Budapest to Wien (Vienna) service, 'Árpád' diesel railcars achieved a city-to-city timing of 2 hours 58 minutes, a record timing that was not achieved again following World War II until several years after the end of communism, indeed not until the end of the 20th century.

Even today's electric-hauled EuroCity trains need 2 hours 40 minuutes for the journey, although a two-hour timing is targeted for when the current infrastructure upgrades are complete. Thus the passengers of 1934 had very good reason to be extremely pleased with the performance of the 'Árpád' diesel railcars, which achieved everything their designers and operators had required.

MÁV 'Árpád' railcar No. 23, named *Tas*, is preserved in working order and appears in public at special events. It is worth adding that a similar railcar was supplied by Ganz to the Ulster Transport Authority in the United Kingdom around 1950. The 'Árpád' railcars were smaller than most continental gauge vehicles, and so were actually quite close to the Irish loading gauge. UTA diesel railcar No. 5 was based at Belfast York Road and worked local services in Northern Ireland, but unfortunately has not been preserved.

**Type:** Express passenger diesel railcar
**Power:** Ganz VIJaR 170, 160kW (215bhp), bogie frame mounted
**Tractive effort:** N/A
**Gearbox:** Five-speed mechanical, driving two axles on one bogie
**Max. operating speed:** 110kph (68mph)
**Weight:** 33 tonnes (72,470lb)
**Overall length:** 22.00m (72ft 2in)
**Gauge:** 1435 (4ft 8.5in)

## M-10000 UNION PACIFIC — USA 1934

In the early 1930s, the Electro-Motive Corporation, a gas-electric motorcar producer that had recently been acquired by automotive giant General Motors, set about to change the face of American railroading.

The Great Depression combined with the advent of private automobiles and airline travel resulted in a precipitous decline in railroad passenger traffic. Two lines, Union Pacific and Burlington, set out to reverse this negative trend with the introduction of new fast passenger trains. Union Pacific worked with passenger car manufacturer Pullman to construct a three-car aluminium articulated streamlined train. Completed in early 1934, this train was powered by a Winton distillate engine with electric transmission. (A distillate engine required a spark plug for ignition and is not a diesel.) Numbered the M-10000, and originally known as the *Streamliner,* the train was painted in a flashy mustard and brown colour scheme and sent on a nationwide publicity tour by Union Pacific. It was America's first streamlined passenger train and helped to spur a national interest in railway streamliners.

Later, Union Pacific assigned the M-10000 to service as its *City of Salina* (Kansas). The train was too small for long-haul service; however, Union Pacific was to order a fleet of similarly styled, streamlined diesel trains for its long distance services.

**Type:** Distillate-electric powered streamlined articulated high speed train
**Power:** Not known
**Tractive effort:** N/A
**Max. operating speed:** 178km/h (111mph)
**Weight:** 77 tonnes (170,000lb)
**Overall length:** 62.331m (204ft 6in)
**Gauge:** 1435mm (4ft 8.5in)

## BURLINGTON'S *ZEPHYR* BURLINGTON RAILROAD — USA 1934

**Type:** Diesel-electric powered streamlined articulated high speed train
**Power and output:** Winton 201E diesel producing 44kW (600hp)
**Tractive effort:** N/A
**Max. operating speed:** 186km/h (116mph)
**Weight:** 79 tonnes (175,000lb)
**Overall length:** 59.741m (196ft)
**Gauge:** 1435mm (4ft 8.5in)

Burlington's shining *Zephyr* emerged from the depths of the Great Depression, dazzled the American public and forever changed both passenger travel and the state of motive-power on US railways. In the 1920s, railroad passenger services had been hit hard by highway transport and air travel. The Depression aggravated the situation, and many railways saw passenger numbers plummet. In order to reverse this trend, two large Western railroads, Union Pacific, and the Chicago, Burlington & Quincy, decided to introduce flashy new services using all-new lightweight trains. In April 1934, Burlington debuted the sleek, streamlined, stainless-steel *Zephyr,* a lightweight three-car articulated passenger train powered by a state-of-the-art Winton diesel engine with electric traction motors. The *Zephyr* was the result of pairing modern vehicular construction techniques with recently developed high-output diesel engines. In 1930, automotive manufacturer General Motors had purchased both Winton Engine and one of its largest customers, rail car manufacturer Electro-Motive. In 1932, the German *Flying Hamburger* trains set an important precedent, demonstrating that a streamlined diesel-powered railcar could offer fast service and attract passengers. Working with Electro-Motive and Pullman, Union Pacific brought out its aluminium-bodied *Streamliner* two months ahead of the *Zephyr.* Although similar to the *Zephyr*, the *Streamliner* was powered by a petrol engine that burned a fuel known as distillate and required spark plugs for ignition. By contrast, *Zephyr* was powered by a diesel engine and is credited as America's first diesel-powered passenger train. A diesel engine uses compression for combustion and does not require a spark plug. More importantly, diesel fuel is a lower grade of petroleum and costs less to manufacture than distillate or gasoline. The *Zephyr* was capable of speeds well in excess of 160kph (100mph) and

**The *Zephyr's* shovel-nose design proved hazardous in the event of a head-on collision and was discontinued on later diesel-electric trains.**

## ELECTRO-MOTIVE EA BALTIMORE & OHIO RAILROAD USA 1936

Electro-Motive's initial success with diesel-powered articulated streamlined trains put it in a position to develop a passenger diesel independent of an articulated set. The control cab was elevated with a strengthened nose section placed in front, while the locomotive's body was designed as structurally integral framework using an attractive modern streamlined design, and the intake vents were located to the sides behind the cab. The first of the new and much improved locomotives was Model EA, Baltimore & Ohio No. 51, delivered in 1937.

**Type:** A1A-A1A, passenger diesel-electric
**Power and output:** A pair of Winton 12-cylinder 201-A diesels producing 1343kW (1800hp)
**Tractive effort:** 216kN (48,600lbs) starting TE
**Max. operating speed:** N/A
**Weight:** 129 tonnes (285,000lbs)
**Overall length:** N/A
**Gauge:** 1435mm (4ft 8.5in)

**Baltimore & Ohio's EA featured a smoother streamlined treatment than later E-units. This locomotive was powered by a Winton 201A diesel engine, while later models used the more successful 567 engine.**

**The preserved shell of B&O EA No. 51 can be seen at the Baltimore & Ohio Railroad Museum in Baltimore, Maryland.**

## 2-Co-2+2-Co-2 262 BD1 PARIS-LYONS-MEDITERRANEAN RAILWAY (PLM) FRANCE 1937

Two experimental locomotives of this 2-Co-2+2-Co-2 type were built in 1937–38. They were the BD1 with MAN, and AD1 with Sulzer engines, both developing 3060kW (4100hp). They were intended to be capable of similar performance to steam express engines, but with a higher availability, set at an annual rate of 275,000km (171,000 miles). These air-smoothed engines were not articulated, but had a semi-permanent corridor link. Mothballed during World War II, they were returned to service in 1945 and ran until 1955.

**Type:** Twin unit express diesel-electric locomotive
**Power:** Four 765kW (1025hp) MAN six-cylinder four-stroke diesel engines each driving a generator mounted on the main frame and supplying power to six traction motors via a Kleinow quill drive
**Tractive effort:** 314kN (70,500lb)
**Max. operating speed:** 130km/h (81mph)
**Total weight:** 224 tonnes (493,700lb)
**Maximum axle load:** 18 tonnes (39,670lb)
**Overall length:** Not known
**Gauge:** Not known

## 3-CAR ARTICULATED RAILCAR SET LONDON MIDLAND AND SCOTTISH RAILWAY GB 1938

If there were ever a case of a good railway design coming along at the wrong time, then it is the LMS/Leyland three-car articulated, streamlined diesel set. This was built at Derby in 1938 under the supervision of William Stanier. All three cars had two 93.25 kW (125hp) Leyland engines with all but the two outermost axles being powered. Many forward-looking features were incorporated, including guard-controlled, air-operated sliding doors and Skefco roller bearing axleboxes. It was finished in an attractive livery of red and cream with a silver roof, and black lining bands at the cantrail and waist.

The unit ran between Cambridge and Oxford in the autumn of 1938, then from March 1939 worked regular stopping train services between St Pancras and Nottingham on the Midland main line. It was stored during the war and withdrawn in February 1945, its underframe and bogies being donated to help construct a departmental vehicle for overhead electric work – a sad end for such an advanced concept train.

**Despite its streamlined design and outstanding features for the time, the three-car articulated train set did not have the success it deserved.**

**Type:** Lightweight diesel unit for stopping services
**Power:** Six Leyland diesel engines each developing 93.25kW (125hp) at 2200rpm
**Max. operating speed:** 120.675km/h (75mph)
**Weight:** 74 tonnes (163,520lb)
**Overall length:** 56.24m (184ft 6in)
**Gauge:** 1435mm (4ft 8.5in)

**London Midland and Scottish Railway's advanced concept railcar set suffered as a result of poor timing. Brought out just before the outbreak of World War II, it was mothballed during the conflict, only to be dismantled at the war's end so that some of its components could be utilized elsewhere.**

## ELECTRO-MOTIVE SW1 VARIOUS RAILROADS USA 1939

Electro-Motive's model SW1 was one of the builder's more popular early switcher types. Powered by a six-cylinder 567 engine, the SW1 was designed for slow-speed assignments in freight and passenger yards. In Electro-Motive's original parlance, the initials SW indicated 'six hundred horsepower, welded frame'; however, the SW designation obviously had connotations of 'Switcher', and later, more powerful switchers retained the SW prefix in their model designations.

The SW1 was built between 1939 and 1953, and it operated on many lines. A few can still be found working on American short lines. The SW1 can be quickly identified from other EMD switchers by its single, narrow exhaust stack, the large platform behind the cab, and the exterior sandbox which is located below the radiator on the long hood end of the locomotive.

**Burlington Northern inherited numerous switcher types from its predecessor lines. The Electro-Motive SW1 No. 102 and NW-2 No. 475 are seen at Portland, Oregon, on 8 May 1982.**

**Type:** Diesel-electric
**Power and output:** Six-cylinder 567 engine producing 450kW (600hp)
**Tractive effort:** 107kN (24,000lbf) at 16km/h (10mph)
**Max. operating speed:** 50mph (80km/h)
**Weight:** 90.8 tonnes (200,000lb)
**Overall length:** 13.538m (44ft 5in)
**Gauge:** 1435mm (4ft 8.5in)

**Electro-Motive's 600 hp SW1 was a common type used in passenger train coach yards. Chicago, Rock Island & Pacific No. 4801 is seen a Chicago's La Salle Street Station in November 1977.**

# ELECTRO-MOTIVE FT FOUR UNIT SET VARIOUS RAILROADS USA 1939

**Santa Fe's F units lead the *Super Chief* at Chicago in 1952. The success of the FT model led Electro-Motive to improve its F unit line by boosting output and improving reliability. The FT can be distinguished from other models by a row of four 'porthole' windows on the locomotive's side. Later models such as these seen here only used two or three windows. Santa Fe operated the largest fleet of FTs. Unfortunately, color photos of them are very rare, as many photographers were concentrating on capturing steam locomotives rather than diesels.**

By 1939, Electro-Motive had mastered the American passenger diesel and diesel switcher trade. The next market for it to tackle was the heavy freight locomotive business. It was in this area that the most amount of money could be made, as American railroads earned most of their money hauling freight and were looking for means to reduce their costs. Electro-Motive's FT freight diesel was the machine that railroads had waited for. A four-unit 5400hp demonstrator toured the United States in 1939 and 1940, proving that a diesel-electric could move heavy tonnage in demanding circumstances. In the following months and years, several major railroads jumped at the opportunity to buy FT freight diesels. Most FT diesels comprised two semi-permanently coupled A-B units designed to form an A-B-B-A set. The 'A' units featured an engineer's (driver's) cab, the 'B' unit was a cabless booster. Initially the entire four-unit set was treated as a single locomotive because of concerns that labour unions would insist on putting a driver on each 'unit' if they were treated as individual locomotives. With later F unit types, the semi-permanently coupled arrangement was discontinued and normal couplers became standard.

**Type:** Four unit diesel-electric in 'A-B-B-A' configuration, all units using Bo-Bo wheel arrangement
**Power and output:** Each unit powered by an EMC 16-567 diesel rated at 1007kW (1350hp), for a total output of 4023kW (5400hp)
**Tractive effort:** 978kN (220,000lbf) starting TE
**Max. operating speed:** N/A
**Weight:** 400 tonnes (900,000lb)
**Overall length:** 58.826m (193ft)
**Gauge:** 1435mm (4ft 8.5in)

## ALCO DL109 V VARIOUS RAILROADS USA 1940

Steam builder Alco had been building diesels since the 1920s as a sideline to its locomotive business. On the eve of US involvement in World War II, it introduced a high-speed road diesel to compete with the Electro-Motive E. Known by their specification numbers, these locomotives were designated DL103b to DL110, with the most numerous being the DL109 (69 built). The various DL locomotives had only minor differences between them. They were powered by a pair of turbocharged six-cylinder inline diesels with 317.5 x 330.2mm (12.5 x 13in) bore and stroke operating at 740 rpm. Otto Kuhler styled the carbodies, giving them a futuristic Art Deco image that contrasted with the cleaner image of EMD's E-unit.

**Alco hired Otto Kuhler, one of the best known earlier industrial designers, to style the streamlined carbody of its first road diesel. These locomotives were known by their specification numbers, DL103b to DL109. Ironically, the paint livery which was applied to these Alco's was actually designed for Santa Fe by the Electro-Motive Corporation.**

**Type:** A1A-A1A, diesel-electric
**Power and output:** A pair of Alco 6-539T diesels producing 1492kW (2000hp)
**Tractive effort:** 136kN (30,500lbf) continuous TE at 32.2 km/h (20mph); 250kN (56,250lbf) starting TE
**Max. operating speed:** 192km/h (120mph) with 58:20 gear ratio
**Weight:** 153 tonnes (337,365lb)
**Overall length:** 22.758m (74ft 6in)
**Gauge:** 1435mm (4ft 8.5in)

## ALCO S-2 VARIOUS RAILROADS USA 1940

In the decade between 1940 and 1950, Alco built more than 1500 746kW (1000 hp) model S-2 switching locomotives for service in North America. In 1950, the S-2 was superseded by the S-4 model, while its 448kW (600 hp) S-1 was superseded by the S-3. Alco's S model switchers were a ubiquitous workhorse in yards and on short local freights. They were powered by Alco's successful 539 engine, and many had long careers. Like all Alco diesels of the period, they employed General Electric electrical components. The generator was a GE GT-533, while traction motors were GE-731-D. Both the S-1 and S-2 models used the unusual Blunt trucks, while S-3, S-4 and later switcher models used variations of the more common Association of American Railroad truck design.

**Type:** Diesel-electric
**Power:** Alco six-cylinder 539 diesel producing 746kW (1000hp)
**Tractive effort:** 151kN (34,000lbf) at 12.9km/h (8mph) continuous TE; 307kN (69,000lbf) starting TE
**Max. operating speed:** N/A
**Weight:** 104 tonnes (230,000lb)
**Overall length:** 13.862m (45ft 6in)
**Gauge:** 1435mm (4ft 8.5in)

**A Canadian Pacific railway Alco S-2 switcher is seen here with a caboose, known as a 'van' on CPR, near Toronto in Ontario.**

**The Alameda Belt Line was a switching line on the California island of Alameda in San Francisco Bay. The S-2 featured the Blunt truck and a large front-end radiator. American switchers designated the long hood as the front.**

## GENERAL ELECTRIC 44-TON VARIOUS RAILROADS USA 1940

**Type:** Bo-Bo, diesel-electric
**Power and output:** A pair of Caterpillar D17000 eight-cylinder diesels rated between 207kW (350hp) and 305kW (410hp)
**Tractive effort:** 99 kW (22,280 lbf) starting TE
**Max. operating speed:** 56kph (35mph)
**Weight:** 40 tonnes (89,112lb)
**Overall length:** N/A
**Gauge:** 1435mm (4ft 8.5in)

In the early years of the transfer to diesel, railroads and locomotive manufacturers needed to overcome strong resistance from railway labour. Railwaymen knew that diesels would drastically cut employment. The 44-ton switcher came about because of laws that guaranteed the firemen's position on all locomotives weighing more than 90,000 lb (which equals 45 US tons, a US ton being made up of 2000lb). GE was one of several manufacturers to offer lightweight center-cab diesel-electric switchers, and the GE 44-tonner was among the most popular models. Purchased by many large railroads for light branch line work, they were also popular with shortlines and industrial lines. More than 350 were built for domestic lines over a 16-year period and were powered by a pair of small diesel engines, one at each end of the locomotive.

**The 44-ton was one of several General Electric center-cab switchers built in the 1940s and 1950. This Housatonic Railroad GE center-cab is seen at Canaan, Connecticut, on the tracks of the former Central New England line.**

## SLM Am4/6 SWISS FEDERAL RAILWAYS (SBB) SWITZERLAND 1941

SLM Am4/6 of 1941 may be considered the world's first successful gas turbine electric. Although only of moderate power, it ably demonstrated the practicalities of locomotive turbines. The Brown Boveri seven-stage axial flow 5800rpm turbine and 18-stage compressor drove (through reduction gearing stepping down to 876 rpm) a generator which in turn powered four traction motors. Eleven running notches corresponded with turbine speed from 3529 to 5257 rpm. With an air intake temperature of 20°C (68°F), turbine efficiency was reckoned at 17.7 per cent at 1620kW (2200hp) shaft output. An auxiliary diesel engine assisted turbine starting and for limited shunting of the locomotive only. The 18-tonne (39,690lb) maximum axle load made the engine suitable for branch-line routes where electrification could not be justified, and testing found it to be generally sound. Taken into SBB stock, 1101 was tested in France in 1946, and in Germany in 1950.

**Type:** 1ABoA1 gas turbine electric prototype
**Power:** 1620kW (2200hp) from Brown Boveri industrial turbine
**Tractive effort:** Not known
**Max. operating speed:** 110km/h (68.8mph)
**Weight:** 92 tonnes [34,170lbs]
**Overall length:** 16.34m (53ft 4in)
**Gauge:** 1435mm (4ft 8.5in)

## ALCO RS-1 ROCK ISLAND RAILROAD USA 1941

The basic configuration of Alco's model RS-1 makes it the granddaddy of all modern American freight diesels. It was one of the most influential designs. First built in 1941 for the Rock Island, the RS-1 was the first road switcher designed to work equally well as a road diesel or yard switcher. Previous diesel models were designed for more specific service. Over a nearly 20-year span, more than 400 RS-1s were built for North American service. More significant than the number of RS-1s built was the effect on future development. Versatility was key to the success of the road switcher type. By 1949, all the major builders were offering road switcher types, and by the 1950s the road switcher had become the dominant type bought by American railroads. Today nearly all freight diesels are variations on the road switcher. The RS-1 had another significant influence. A variation of the type known as an RSD-1 used a Co-Co arrangement. During World War II, Alco provided a fleet of RSD-1 to the Russians. Russian diesel development was a direct outgrowth of the RS-1; thousands of Russian diesels were built based on RS-1 era technology.

**Above: A Green Mountain Railroad RS-1 leads the company's excursion train towards Chester, Vermont, in October 2001.**

**Green Mountain Railroad Alco RS-1 405 photographed crossing the Connecticut River main line at Bellows Falls, Vermont, in October 2001.**

**Type:** Bo-Bo, diesel-electric
**Power and output:** Alco 6-539 diesel producing 746kW (1000hp)
**Tractive effort:** 151kN (34,000lbf) continuous TE at 12.9km/h (8mph); 264kN (59,500lbf) starting TE.
**Max. operating speed:** 96.6km/h (60mph) with 75:16 gear ratio
**Weight:** 108 tonnes (238,000lb)
**Overall length:** N/A
**Gauge:** 1435mm (4ft 8.5in)

## FAIRBANKS-MORSE H10-44 VARIOUS RAILROADS USA 1944

By the 1940s, Fairbanks-Morse had been a well-known American railroad equipment supplier for some decades. Their business was diversified, and it included the manufacture of various types of petrol engines. During World War II, Fairbanks-Morse opposed piston diesel engines were well regarded in marine applications, especially in US Navy submarines. As the war drew to a close, Fairbanks-Morse decided to enter the heavy locomotive business in order to expand the market for its O-P engines. The company's first mass-produced type was the H10-44, a 746kW (1000hp) switcher, which was in fact very similar to Baldwin's successful VO1000. Fairbanks-Morse hired industrial designer Raymond Loewy to style the H10-44, giving the other wise utilitarian machine a bit of flair. Nearly 200 were built in the period up until 1950, when the more powerful H12-44 was introduced.

**Type:** Bo-Bo, diesel-electric
**Power and output:** Fairbanks-Morse six-cylinder opposed piston diesel producing 746kW (1000hp)
**Tractive effort:** 275kN (61,775lbf)
**Max. operating speed:** N/A
**Weight:** 112 tonnes (247,100lb)
**Overall length:** N/A
**Gauge:** 1435mm (4ft 8.5in)

## FAIRBANKS-MORSE *'ERIE BUILT'* MILWAUKEE RAILROAD USA 1945

When Fairbanks-Morse entered the locomotive business toward the end of World War II, it did not yet have suitable facilities for building large road locomotives, so it contracted with General Electric to assemble its large A1A-A1A cab types. These were built at GE's Erie, Pennsylvania, facilities. With 1492kW (2000hp) per locomotive, these streamlined diesels were intended to compete with EMD's latest E-units, as well as models by Alco and Baldwin. Only a few railroads operated them, largely for passenger services.

**Type:** A1A-A1A, diesel-electric
**Power and output:** Fairbanks-Morse model 38D81/8 (eight-cylinder opposed piston diesel) producing 1492kW (2000hp)
**Tractive effort:** 117kN (26,400lbf) continuous TE at 38.6km/h (24mph); 265kN (59,600lbf) starting TE
**Max. operating speed:** N/A
**Weight:** 155 tonnes (341,500lb)
**Overall length:** 19.761m (64ft 10in)
**Gauge:** 1435mm(4 ft 8.5in)

## *'CENTIPEDE'* MODEL DR-12-8-1500/2 PENNSYLVANIA RAILROAD USA 1945

During World War II, Baldwin set out to built a multi-engine high-speed diesel based largely on electric locomotive practice. This 4470kW (6000hp) machine was intended for speeds up to 187kph (117mph), but never entered production. Baldwin did build a scaled-back diesel with two engines that produced 2235kW (3000hp) per unit using an articulated frame with a 2-Do+Do-2 wheel arrangement. It was known as a *'Centipede'* because of its many wheels and baby-faced cab. Seaboard Air Line was the first to order the type; Pennsylvania Railroad (PRR) and National Railways of Mexico (NdeM) also bought them. PRR had the largest fleet, used initially in passenger service.

**Intended for high-speed passenger work, Pennsylvania Railroad's Baldwin *'Centipedes'* worked their last days as freight helpers, such as these two seen shoving a freight around the Horseshoe Curve near Altoona, Pennsylvania.**

**Type:** 2-Do+Do-2, diesel-electric
**Power and output:** A pair of Baldwin eight-cylinder 608SC engines producing 2235kW (3000hp)
**Tractive effort:** 235kN (52,800lbf) continuous TE at 28.7km/h (17.8mph); 454kN (102,205lbf) starting TE
**Max. operating speed:** 150kph (93.5mph) with 21:58 gear ratio
**Weight:** 269 tonnes (593,700lb)
**Overall length:** 27.889m (91ft 6in)
**Gauge:** 1435mm (4ft 8.5in)

## ALCO FA/FB VARIOUS RAILROADS USA 1946

The FA/FB, intended for heavy road freight service, had an Alco/GE standard cab unit and the same basic configuration as the more common EMD F-unit. It had similar streamlining to the PA passenger diesel, but was shorter and featured a Bo-Bo wheel arrangement. The FA was intended to operate in and sets of three or four, and was often run in multiple with other Alco types, especially RS-2 and RS-3 road switchers. The FA/FB type was produced between 1946 and 1956.

**Type:** Bo-Bo, diesel-electric
**Power and output:** Alco 12-cylinder 244 diesel producing 1119 to 1194kW (1500 to 1600hp)
**Tractive effort:** 167kN (37,500lbf) continuous TE at 20.1km/h (12.5 mph); 256kN (57,500lbf) starting TE (depending on weight)
**Max. operating speed:** 105km/h (65mph) with 74:18 gear ratio
**Weight:** 104 tonnes (230,000lb)
**Overall length:** 15.697m (51ft 6in)
**Gauge:** 1435mm (4ft 8.5in)

## EMD F-UNITS, MODEL F7 VARIOUS RAILROADS USA 1946

**Burlington Northern displays its 'Executive F-units' at Galesburg, Illinois, in June 1996. Burlington Northern used these two F-units on its deluxe business train.**

The success of the FT in the World War II period set up EMD as the leading builder of road diesel-electric locomotives. After the war ended and the restrictions on implementing new designs were lifted, EMD improved its F-unit line and introduced the F3 (an interim model, designated F2, was built for a short period). The F3 was slightly more powerful than the FT, with each of its units rated at 1119kW (1500 p), instead of 1007kW (1350hp).

**Chicago & North Western was one of many American railroads that used F-units for both freight and passenger services.**

Other mechanical improvements enhanced the F3's performance and reliability. In 1949, the F7 superseded the F3, although output remained the same. Then, in 1954, the F9 superseded the F7. The F9 was rated at 1306kW (1750hp). EMD's streamlined F-units were a ubiquitous symbol of American dieselization and used by nearly all of the railroads.

**Type:** Bo-Bo, diesel-electric
**Power and output:** EMD 16-567B producing 1119kW (1500hp)
**Tractive effort:** Various
**Max. operating speed:** Various
**Weight:** Various
**Overall length:** 15.443m (50ft 8in) (A-unit)
**Gauge:** 1435m (4ft 8.5in)

**Facing page: Although once the most common locomotive in America, the day of the F-unit has come and gone. Boston & Maine 4266 is one of many preserved F7s and is occasional operated at North Conway, New Hampshire.**

4266
4266
4266
BOSTON and MAINE
RAILROAD

## ALCO RS-2/RS-3 VARIOUS RAILROADS USA 1946

After World War II, American railroads set out to transfer to diesel as quickly as possible. Alco introduced several new models that proved popular with railroads. In the late 1940s, its 1119kW (1500hp) semi-streamlined RS-2 road switcher was one of its better selling designs. The versatility offered by the road-switcher type allowed railroads to assign them to a variety of different services. New York Central, for example, used RS-2s in suburban and local passenger service, on local freights that needed to switch en route, on branch-line freights, and in multiple on heavy road freights. In 1950,

**Left: Delaware & Hudson dieselized its operations with Alco road switchers. In April 1952, a pair of Alco road switchers leads a 4-8-4 at Schenectady, New York.**

**Below: RS-3 engine No. 8223 in Dewitt, New York, awaits servicing and repairs while working on a shortline route.**

Alco boosted the output of its 12-244 engine to 1194kW (1600hp). Some RS-2s were built with the higher rating, but, by mid-1950, the RS-3 superseded the RS-2. With more than 1350 RS-3s built for North American service, it became one of the most common Alco designs.

In 1956, Alco's RS-11, powered by the newer 251 diesel, superseded the RS-3. Despite greater reliability, fewer RS-11s were sold, as by that time most railroads had largely finished their transfer to diesel. The RS-11 had a taller hood and more boxy appearance than the RS-2/RS-3 models. A few RS-3s had very long service lives; some survived on shortlines past the year 2000.

**Type:** Bo-Bo, diesel-electric
**Power and output:** 12-cylinder Alco 244 producing 1119kW (1500hp)
**Tractive effort:** 271kN (61,000lbf) starting TE
**Max. operating speed:** 105kph (65mph) with 74:18 gear ratio
**Weight:** 111 tonnes (244,000lb)
**Overall length:** 16.91m (55ft 6in)
**Gauge:** 1435mm (4ft 8.5in)

**An Alco RS-3 parked in the sidings at Eagle Bridge, New York. The RS-3 was built with a larger engine capacity than the RS-2, and some RS-3s were still in service 40 years later.**

## EMD E-Units; Model E7 VARIOUS RAILROADS USA 1946

The Electro-Motive E-units were designed in response to railroad requests for a practical streamline diesel-electric locomotive with conventional couplers that was not integrated in a fixed train set. Baltimore & Ohio and Santa Fe were the first railroads to use the streamlined Es.

Both lines had experience with Electro-Motive's early box-cab types which preceded the E. All E-units used a pair of high-output two-cycle diesel-engines in a streamlined body riding on A1A trucks. The earliest Es (models EA & EB, E1 and E2), those built in 1937 and early 1938, were powered by Winton 201 diesels. However, from mid-1938 onwards, the Es were powered by the highly successful Electro-Motive 567 diesel in 12-cylinder configurations. The 'E-unit' designation reportedly stems from the locomotive's initial output of 'eighteen-hundred' (1800hp/1343kW) per unit. With the introduction of the 12-567 engine, the per unit output was boosted to 2000hp (1492kW), but the 'E' designation continued.

The earliest Es, those built for B&O, Santa Fe, and Union Pacific, featured more flamboyant and varied streamlined styling, with each railroad's locomotives treated differently. With the E3, the styling became more standardized, although the paint liveries were still tailored to individual railroad's image. Electro-Motive artists often designed the liveries, which were then adopted by the railroads. Models E3 to E6, built from 1938 until 1942, featured a steeper sloping nose than the postwar E7, E8 and E9s, which used the standard 'Bulldog' nose that debuted on the FT freight diesel in 1939. The E5 was a model only built for Burlington, and featured stainless-steel styling to match its

**This photograph features a Wisconsin and Southern E9. With the more powerful 1790kW (2400hp) engine, the E9 remained in production until 1963.**

*Zephyr* consists. The A1A truck was a three-axle design, with the two outside axles powered and the center axle used to help distribute the locomotive weight.

The two most numerous E-unit models were the E7 and E8, which were built from 1946 to 1949, and 1949 to 1953, respectively. The last E-unit type was the 1790kW (2400hp) E9, which remained in production until 1963. By then, American passenger operations were in serious decline; there was almost no market for new passenger locomotives. E-units were built in both 'A' and 'B' configurations, the later type being a cabless 'booster' type. Most railroads ran E-units in multiples to haul long-distance passenger trains. Among America's best-known trains hauled by Electro-Motive E's were: New York Central's *Twentieth Century Limited*, Pennsylvania's *Broadway Limited*; Southern Pacific's *Daylight* trains; Southern Railway's *Crescent* and Illinois Central's *City of New Orleans*. Amtrak inherited a sizeable fleet of E-units, some of which it operated until the mid-1980s. As passenger services declined in the 1960s, a few lines, such as Erie-Lackawanna, assigned Es to freight services, often using them on priority intermodal trains. In more recent times, American freight haulers such as Illinois Central, and Conrail, used E-units for company 'executive trains' – deluxe passenger consists reserved for officers inspection trips and customer relations jaunts. The last large fleet of E-units in regular service was Burlington Northern's used to haul its 'Dinkys' – Chicago area suburban trains which operated from Union Station to Aurora over its triple-track main line.

**Wisconsin & Southern E8A 801 at Horicon, Wisconsin in 1995.**

A B&O postwar E7 was 4547mm (14ft 11in) tall and 21,673mm (71ft 1.25 in) long. It used a pair of GM Model D-4 generators, and four GM Model D-7 traction motors. With a 55:22 gear ratio, B&O permitted the E7 158km/h (98mph). By contrast, Burlington's E7s used a 57:20 gear ratio and were capable of speeds up to 187km/h (117mph).

**In the livery of the Gulf, Mobile and Ohio Railroad, a pair of EMD E7s leaves Chicago with a southbound train in 1952.**

**Type:** A1A-A1A, passenger diesel-electric
**Power and output:** A pair of EMD 12-567-A diesel producing 2681kW (2000hp)
**Tractive effort:** 84kN (18,800lbf) continuous TE at 53.1kph (33 mph); 236kN (53,075lbf) starting TE
**Max. operating speed:** 157.7kph (98mph) with 55:22 gear ratio
**Weight:** 143 tonnes (315,000lb)
**Overall length:** 21.673m (71ft 1in)
**Gauge:** 1435mm (4ft 8.5in)

## ALCO PA/PB VARIOUS RAILROADS USA 1947

The handsome streamlined carbody with its long, pronounced nose section and throaty 244 diesel made Alco's PA one of the most popular American diesels among railway enthusiasts. This machine was Alco/GE's competition for EMD's E-units and designed for premier passenger services. The cab units were known as 'PA's' while the cabless 'B' units were called 'PBs'. This designation system was actually adopted after the locomotives were already in production, as the early PA/PBs were originally known by their specification numbers. Santa Fe and Southern Pacific had some of largest fleets of PA/PB diesels.

The best remembered are four former Santa Fe PAs which were operated by Delaware & Hudson through the late 1970s. They later went to Mexico and have since been preserved.

**A pair of Nickel Plate Road Alco PA diesels is seen at right leading a Buffalo-bound passenger train at Dunkirk, New York, in March 1952.**

**Type:** A1A-A1A, passenger diesel-electric
**Power and output:** 16-cylinder Alco 244 diesel engine producing 1492kW (2000hp); boosted to 1676kW (2250hp) on PA-2/PB-2 models
**Tractive effort:** 227kN (51,000lb) for PA-1/PB-1
**Max. operating speed:** Various
**Weight:** 139 tonnes (306,000lb)
**Overall length:** 20.015m (65ft 8in) (PA only)
**Gauge:** 1435mm (4ft 8.5in)

## BALDWIN '*SHARK NOSE*' VARIOUS RAILROADS — UNITED STATES 1947

In the postwar race to dieselize American railroads, Baldwin looked to distinguish its road diesels from those of EMD. Its early road units had a carbody style that looked remarkably similar to the EMD, so it hired a industrial design firm to give its locomotives a distinctive look. The result was the so-called 'shark nose' body style. This name was not formally used by Baldwin, and several different locomotives used this style, including DR-6-4-20 A1A-A1A high-speed passenger diesels built for the Pennsylvania Railroad (PRR). Other DR-6-4-20s did not use the sharknose body, but instead had a 'Babyface' body style. Likewise, only some Baldwin DR-4-4-15s, a Bo-Bo freight diesel, used sharknose bodies, while others used a Babyface design. These locomotives were built between 1947 and 1950. The most numerous type of Sharks were 1192kw (1600hp) RF-16s built in the early 1950s. These were bought by the PRR, New York Central, and Baltimore & Ohio. The RF-16 was essentially an upgraded DR-4-4-15. The Baldwin engine was good for low-speed heavy freight service, and many sharks worked in coal and iron ore service. The last sharks in service were a pair of former New York Central RF-16s that worked for Monongahela, then Delaware & Hudson, and later shortlines in Michigan.

**The Pennsylvania Railroad was the only railroad to order passenger locomotives with the 'shark nose' body style. A pair of DR-6-4-20s is seen in 1963, toward the end of their active service.**

**Type:** Bo-Bo, diesel-electric
**Power:** Baldwin eight-cylinder 608A producing 1194kW (1600hp)
**Tractive effort:** 328kN (73,750lbf)
**Max. operating Speed:** 112km/h (70mph)
**Weight:** 113 tonnes (248,000lb)
**Overall length:** 16.739 m (54ft 11in)
**Gauge:** 1435mm (4ft 8.5in)

# 10000 AND 10001 LONDON MIDLAND & SCOTTISH RAILWAY (LMS/BR) GREAT BRITAIN 1948

**With a deep roar from their two big diesel engines supplemented by the whistle from their turbo-chargers, British pioneer Co-Co diesel electrics Nos 10000 and 10001 leave London's Euston Station with the *Royal Scot* train to Glasgow early in 1948.**

The London Midland & Scottish Railway was determined to get its first main-line diesel-electric locomotive into service before British Railways was formed. No. 10000 actually emerged from Derby works in December 1947, just in time legitimately to carry the initials 'LMS' on its bodysides. No. 10001, which was completed in 1948, first entered service with no ownership branding. This first essay into serious use of diesel power on main-line express trains used the expertise of the English Electric Company by providing for each locomotive a 16-cylinder, V-form, supercharged, low-speed diesel engine coupled to a large EE823A DC generator. The engine cylinders were 254mm (10in) bore and 305mm (12in) stroke. This supplied power for six EE519 traction motors, one coupled to each axle and suspended directly on it through a nose suspension bearing. Each locomotive was carried on two three-axle bogies in

**No. 10001 on a West Coast main-line express in the early days of BR passes over water troughs for topping up steam locomotive tenders, soon to be made redundant.**

Co-Co formation. The engine also drove an EE909A auxiliary generator providing power for battery charging, control circuits, lighting, drives to compressors and vacuum exhausters.

At 1194kW (1600hp), the diesel power was about that obtainable from a good class 5 or 6 steam locomotive, but the diesel locomotive's tractive effort, that is the force it could exert on the rails, was equivalent to a much larger class 8P steam locomotive. The six powered axles enabled this tractive effort to be produced by a diesel locomotive without wheel slip. Thus the starting and initial acceleration performance of these new locomotives was outstanding for that time. The locomotives needed no sanding apparatus because of this inherent better adhesion factor.

These two locomotives were initially used singly on express trains on the Midland main line. Later they were run in multiple on 'The Royal Scot' over the difficult West Coast main line between London and Glasgow, the total of 2387kW (3200bhp) producing unprecedented performances. The locomotives had been designed for multiple working, with the ability to be driven as a pair from the controls in the leading cab of the leading locomotive. There were flush doors in the nose fronts of each locomotive that could be opened to release a concertina corridor connection so that train crew could move about between the locomotives, for example, to attend to the train heating steam boiler.

In 1953, the two locomotives were transferred to operate on the Southern Region. Here they worked singly on intensive diagrams on the London Waterloo to Bournemouth and Weymouth routes, effectively linking two steam locomotive workings in one day. They also worked some Salisbury and Exeter trains. The workings were shared with the SR's own trio of diesel locomotives, Nos 10201 to 10203, until 1955, when all five locomotives were transferred for their final years to work on the LM Region.

When new, the two locomotives were outshopped in overall gloss black livery offset by silver-grey roofs and bogies, and with stainless steel bodyside decorative metal stripe and large numerals. BR lion-over-wheel symbols were added in 1948/49. Nos 10000 and 10001 were repainted in the late 1950s in BR Brunswick green, with GWR-style black-and-orange lining painted over the stainless steel bodyside band. The later BR emblem with a lion holding a rail wheel was applied at this time.

**When painted in BR Brunswick green, Nos. 10000 and 10001 did not look so smart as in the original black. This is 10001 in the works yard at Derby after repainting in the late 1950s.**

**This official photograph taken for the London, Midland & Scottish Railway shows the diesel-electric No. 10000 as built, with the initials LMS emblazoned on its sides.**

Nos 10000 and 10001 ran their last years on the West Coast main line on freight and passenger trains. No. 10001 was withdrawn from service in 1963, and No. 10000 was out of action also about that time, although it was not officially withdrawn until three years later; regrettably neither has been preserved.

**Type:** Mixed-traffic main-line diesel-electric
**Wheel arrangement:** Co-Co
**Power unit:** English Electric 16SVT 16-cylinder V-form diesel, 1194kW (1600bhp); DC generator; six axle-hung DC traction motors
**Tractive effort:** 184kN (41,400lbf)
**Max. operating speed:** 145km/h (90mph)
**Weight:** 124 tonnes (272,160lb)
**Overall length:** 18.644m (61ft 2in)
**Gauge:** Not known

## CP CLASS 1500 PORTUGUESE STATE RAILWAYS — PORTUGAL 1948

Painted in Portuguese Railways' overall orange livery, in their later years these typical American 'heavy switcher' locomotives proved reliable and competent on mixed-traffic duties anywhere in the country.

Portugal's oldest main-line diesel locomotives survived, just, into the 21st century. Delivered from Alco, USA, these 'hood units' worked on main-line passenger and freight trains throughout the country, ending up in the south on overnight passenger trains between Barreiro and Faro, and in the Barreiro suburban area. CP re-engined them in the 1970s to raise their power from 1230kW (1650bhp) to 1600kW (2150bhp).

**Type:** Mixed-traffic main-line diesel-electric
**Wheel arrangement:** A1A-A1A
**Power unit:** Alco 244 12-cylinder V-form diesel, 1230kW (1650bhp), changed to Alco 251-C 12-cylinder V-form diesel, 1600kW (2150bhp); General Electric DC generator; four axle-hung DC traction motors
**Tractive effort:** 153kN (37,400lbf)
**Max. operating speed:** 120km/h (75mph)
**Weight:** 111 to 114 tonnes (243,765 to 250,355lb)
**Overall length:** 16.99m (55ft 9in)
**Gauge:** 1668mm (5ft 6in)

## GENERAL ELECTRIC GAS TURBINES UNION PACIFIC RAILROAD — USA 1948

In 1948, General Electric built an experimental double-ended gas-turbine electric that offered an alternative to the diesel-electric locomotive. The gas turbine turned a generator that powered DC traction motors. The advantage of the turbine was that it produced very high output and burned a very low grade fuel oil that was much cheaper than diesel. On the downside, the turbine locomotive had significantly higher fuel consumption because the turbine operated at a constant high rate of speed, even when the locomotive was travelling at relatively slow speeds. Union Pacific was the only railroad to buy a fleet of turbines, and in the 1950s ordered three varieties. The first were 3357kW (4500hp) machines that used a Bo-Bo+Bo-Bo wheel arrangement. Later turbines rode on Co-Co trucks and delivered 6341kW (8500hp). (Statistics below based on Union Pacific Nos. 51-60.)

**General Electric's gas turbines were taken up by Union Pacific Railroad, and in fact the line was to utilize three varieties of the experimental double-ended units on its routes.**

**Type:** Gas-turbine electric
**Power:** 3357kW (4500hp)
**Tractive effort:** 467kN (105,000lbf)
**Max. operating speed:** 104km/h (65mph)
**Weight:** 250 tonnes (551,000lb)
**Overall length:** 25.45m (83ft 6in)
**Gauge:** 1435mm (4ft 8.5in)

## CLASS 350 BO-BO SOUTH AUSTRALIAN RAILWAYS — AUSTRALIA 1949

Class 350 Bo-Bos were the first Australian-built diesels with electric transmission. Built by SARA, the two machines were deployed on shunting (switching) work in the Adelaide area for their entire working lives until the late 1970s. Both 350 and 351 are preserved, the first still in full working order. The UK English Electric company supplied diesel engine and traction equipment, establishing a long association. In time English Electric set up its own plant at Rocklea for local construction.

SARA class 350 were four-axle Bo-Bo machines, the EE 6KT engine driving an EE801 traction generator and four EE506 traction motors. In many respects, the design was similar to the range of standard rigid wheelbase 0-6-0 (or C) layout designs in the United Kingdom, but adapted to an Australian bogie layout that was not used in Britain for shunting.

**Type:** Bo-Bo diesel-electric shunting
**Power:** EE 6KT series engine producing 250kW (335hp)
**Tractive effort:** 39kN (8775lbf) at 28km/h (17.5mph)
**Max. operating speed:** 40km/h (25mph)
**Weight:** 50 tonnes (110,250lb)
**Overall length:** 5.44m (17ft 7in)
**Gauge:** 1600mm (5ft 3in)

# No 18000 GREAT WESTERN RAILWAY GREAT BRITAIN 1949

**Buzzing along the West of England main line with former Great Western Railway carriages in tow, No. 18000 was a frequent sight on express trains.**

The Great Western Railway ordered a pioneer gas turbine electric locomotive from Brown Boveri of Switzerland, delivered to BR Western Region in 1949. It used a gas turbine engine coupled to a DC generator. Four traction motors drove the outer axles on two three-axle bogies. The motors drove through spring drives to reduce the unsprung weight on each driving axle. WR used 18000 intermittently on premier express trains between London, Bristol and the southwest until 1960. It is now preserved.

**Type:** Main-line gas turbine electric
**Wheel arrangement:** A1A-A1A
**Power unit:** Brown Boveri gas turbine 1865kW (2500bhp); DC generator; four DC traction motors
**Tractive effort:** 267kN (60,000lbf)
**Max. operating speed:** 145kph (90mph)
**Weight:** 117 tonnes (257,600lb)
**Overall length:** 19.22m (63ft 1in)
**Gauge:** 1435mm (4ft 8.5in)

**The No. 18000 locomotive is now preserved in its original external condition. In BR black with the large emblem high on the bodyside, and with silver roof and bogies, it was exhibited at Willesden in 1994.**

# EMD GP7/GP9 VARIOUS US AND CANADIAN RAILROADS USA/CANADA 1949

**Type:** Bo-Bo, diesel-electric
**Power and output (based on GP9):** EMD 16-567C producing 1306kW (1750hp)
**Tractive effort:** 196kN (44,000lbf) at 19.3km/h (12mph)
**Max. operating speed:** 104km/h (65mph)
**Weight (based on Burlington Northern GP9):** 115 tonnes (254,000lb)
**Overall length:** 17.12m (56ft 2in)
**Gauge:** 1435mm (4ft 8.5in)

By the time EMD introduced a proper road switcher model in 1949, all the other major diesel locomotive builders were offering the type. Until introduction of the GP7 (GP standing for 'General Purpose' in EMD lexicon), EMD had primarily focused on the building of small switch engines, F-units for road freight and passenger duties, and its E-units for passenger service.

Prior to the GP7, EMD had dabbled in the road switcher with its BL2 'Branch Line' locomotive without a great deal of success, and it had also constructed a few hybrid switcher types such as the NW3 and NW5.

**Internally, the GP7 was effectively the same as EMD's successful F7, but without all the streamlining. It used a 16-cylinder 567 engine and was rated at 1119kW (1500 hp).**

In 1954, EMD upgraded its locomotive line, introducing a host of small improvements that resulted in substantially better performance and reliability.

Its improved road switcher model was the GP9, which used the 16-567C engine rated at 1306kW (1750hp). This basic locomotive became a ubiquitous symbol of modern American railroading and one of EMD's bestselling locomotive models. More than 4000 were sold to railroads in the United States and Canada.

**This photograph shows a well-restored EMD GP9 standing on a bridge in Illinois. Although a basic locomotive, the GP9 was so widely used it became a ubiquitous symbol of the American railroad in the 1950s, outselling all of its rivals.**

# EMD SD7/SD9 SOUTHERN PACIFIC RAILROAD USA 1949

Above: **The SD7s and SD9s were excellent engines for utilizing on difficult terrain.**

**Above: An SD9 engine, No. 4372, waits in the sidings for repairs and servicing. Units were often stored if business was slack.**

**Type:** Co-Co, diesel-electric
**Power:** EMD 15-567C (on SD9) producing 1303kW (1750hp)
**Tractive effort:** continuous TE 67, 300kN (500lbf) at 12.8km/h (8mph)
**Max. operating speed:** 105km/h (65mph)
**Weight:** 147 tonnes (324,000lb)
**Overall length:** 18,491mm (60ft 8in)
**Gauge:** 1435mm (4ft 8.5in)

In EMD parlance, SD stood for 'Special Duty'. When EMD brought out its first six-motor road switcher, the SD7, in 1952, there was only minimal demand for such a locomotive. Greater tractive effort with lower axle-loading was the primary attraction of the SD7 type, which was basically a six-motor variation of the GP7 'General Purpose' diesel. In 1954, EMD increased the power output of its 16-567 engine, resulting in new model types. At this time, the SD9 replaced SD7.

With its heavily graded profile, Southern Pacific was the largest user of these early SDs. Southern Pacific operated many of its SD7s and SD9s for more than 40 years, extending their lives by rebuilding them at its Sacramento (California) shops. On Southern Pacific, they were known as 'Cadillacs'.

**Below: This SD7 was used by Southern Pacific for more than 30 years throughout California.**

# BUDD RAIL DIESEL CAR (RDC) VARIOUS RAILROADS USA 1949

**Chicago & North Western Budd RDCs are seen in a Chicago coach yard in 1952.**

**Type:** Self-propelled diesel-hyraulic passenger rail car
**Power and output:** A pair of GM 6-110 diesel engines producing 205kW (275hp) to 224kw (300hp)
**Tractive effort:** N/A
**Max. operating speed:** 136km/h (85mph)
**Weight:** 58 tonnes (126,730lb)
**Overall length:** 25.908m (85ft)
**Gauge:** 1435mm (4ft 8.5in)

Edward Budd, the founder of the Budd company, had previously worked for the McKeen Company, which produced self-propelled gasoline-engine railcars in the early 1900s. The Philadelphia-based Budd Company, however, was to enter the limelight with the introduction of Burlington's famous *Zephyr*, which used Budd's lightweight, stylish streamlined stainless steel cars.

By the late 1930s, Budd was producing streamlined passenger cars for many of the American railroads. The company's fluted stainless steel cars were assigned to some of America's best known trains, including Santa Fe's famous *Super Chief*.

Although Edward Budd died in 1946, his company went on to design a successful diesel-powered railcar. The first Budd Rail Diesel Car (commonly known as an RDC) was built in 1949. Like Budd's passenger cars, the RDC used lightweight stainless-steel construction and featured fluted sides. RDCs were designed to operate singly or in multiples.

In the 1950s, hundreds of Budd Cars were ordered by North American railways for use on secondary passenger services. While some RDCs were relegated to branch-line or suburban services, others were equipped for long-distance runs. There were several standard types of cars. The RDC-1 was a basic coach, while the RDC-2 had a baggage compartment, and the RDC-3 had baggage and Railway Post Office sections, in addition to its coach seats.

**The Budd Rail Diesel Car was well suited to secondary passenger services. In 1983, Metro-North assigned RDCs to its Waterbury branch in Connecticut. A single car is pictured below near Derby, Connecticut.**

## X-3800 DIESEL RAILCARS FRENCH RAILWAYS (SNCF) FRANCE 1950

**Characteristic of the 'Picasso' diesel railcar was the driving cab projecting above the passenger saloon's roof, giving both the passengers and driver a clear view of the railway forward or aft.**

French engineers have often produced quirky designs. Such is the case of the SNCF 'Picasso' diesel railcars. Designed as single railcars that could haul trailers at times of extra traffic, oddly, their driver's cab projected above the low roof of the vehicle. Thus, although the carriage was relatively low slung, the driver had a good view in either direction. The class X-3800 railcars were also unusual in that they had passenger access doors at two levels, one suitable for high platforms and one for low ones. More than 100 were built by four manufacturers: ANF, de Dietrich, Renault and Saurer.

The 'Picassos' operated on secondary routes and branch lines in most areas of France. The whole class had gone by the end of the 1980s. A few are preserved.

**Type:** Diesel mechanical railcar for local and branch-line services
**Power:** Renault 517G or 575 or Saurer BZDS of 250 to 265kW (335 to 355bhp); mechanical transmission
**Tractive effort:** N/A
**Max. operating speed:** 120kph (75mph)
**Weight:** 33 tonnes (71,680lb)
**Overall length:** 21.85m (71ft 8in)
**Gauge:** 1435mm (4ft 8.5in)

## CLASS TM$^{II}$ SWISS FEDERAL RAILWAYS (SBB) SWITZERLAND 1950

These small four-wheeled shunting tractors have additional uses. Some are equipped to carry snowploughs for line clearance. All have a large cab able to accommodate four personnel and a long flat platform for carrying tools and materials. In addition to acting as shunting locomotives in local stations or freight yards, they can be used to take small teams to mailine work sites.

**This Tm$^{II}$ has a covered load platform, but many are open. This one is working a short train carrying packages.**

**Type:** Diesel mechanical shunting tractor
**Wheel arrangement:** B (0-4-0)
**Power unit:** Saurer C615D diesel, 70kW (94hp); mechanical transmission driving axles through cardan shafts and bevel gears
**Tractive effort:** N/A
**Max. operating speed:** 45km/h (28mph)
**Weight:** 10 tonnes (21,960lb)
**Overall length:** 5.24m (17ft 2in)
**Gauge**: 1435mm (4ft 8.5in)

## FAIRBANKS-MORSE C-LINER VARIOUS RAILROADS USA 1950

Fairbanks-Morse Consolidated Line was introduced in 1950 and offered customers a variety of options and different outputs housed in a standard streamlined carbody. Six different models of C-Liner 'A-units' were produced over a six-year period. The most common variety was the CFA-16-4 which used an eight-cylinder F-M opposed piston engine to produce 1194kW (1600hp). The C-liner carbody shared styling with F-M's Erie-builts of the 1940s, but featured a shorter nose section and had a more conservative, refined appearance than the brutish Eries. C-Liners came as both 'A' unit and 'B' unit (cabless boosters), and could be ordered with either a Bo-Bo or a Bo-A1A wheel arrangement.

**Type:** Diesel-electric
**Power and output:** Various
**Tractive effort:** Various
**Max. operating speed:** Various
**Weight:** Various
**Overall length:** Various
**Gauge:** 1435mm (4ft 8.5in)

## CLASS 40 A1A-A1A NEW SOUTH WALES GOVERNMENT RAILWAYS AUSTRALIA 1951

The New South Wales Government Railway class 40 were the first main-line diesel locomotives to be used on the Australian continent. Supplied by the US Alco company, the 20 machines were of RSC3 model of A1A-A1A layout to keep the overall weight down. Alco was later to supply many locomotives to various Australian railway systems through licensing arrangements and local construction by Goodwin competing in the market against their rivals, EMD and Clyde, GE and Gonian, and English Electric Rocklea.

The wheel layout was found to be a problem locally, with the class experiencing a high incidence of heavy wheel wear throughout their working lives.

First used on main-line freight duties, the class 40s were later extended to conventional passenger work. The class 40 was retired from traffic between 1968 and 1971. All the models were broken up except for number 4001, which has been preserved.

**Type:** A1A-A1A diesel electric
**Power:** 1305kW (1750hp) from Alco 12-244 series engine
**Tractive effort:** 205kN (46,125lbf) at 18km/h (11.3mph)
**Max. operating speed:** 120km/h (75mph)
**Weight:** 113 tonnes (249,165lb)
**Overall length:** 17.26m (56ft 4in)
**Gauge:** 1435mm (4ft 8.5in)

## FIVE-CAR DIESEL TRAIN EGYPTIAN STATE RAILWAYS (ESR) EGYPT 1951

Although built in Britain, the modernistic, air-smoothed lines of this five-car articulated were more reminiscent of American styling. With two power coaches and three trailers, it provided high-speed transport on the level Nile Valley routes north and south of Cairo. Sixty first-class and 112 second-class passengers were carried, in air-conditioned saloons. It was intended to be a self-contained unit, and the ends had buffers but no coupling gear. A very similar two-car unit was supplied by the same manufacturers to the Argentine Central Railway.

**Type:** Articulated diesel-electric train
**Power:** Two English-Electric 4 SRKT engines developing 298.5kW (400hp), driving two power bogies via electric transmission
**Tractive effort:** 80kN (18,000lbf)
**Max. operating speed:** 120km/h (75mph)
**Total weight:** 154.4 tonnes (340,452lb)
**Max. axle load:** 11 tonnes (24,255lb)
**Overall length:** 83.14m (255ft 3in) Electric
**Gauge:** Not known

## 10201 TO 10203 SOUTHERN RAILWAY GREAT BRITAIN 1951

**Type:** Main-line diesel-electric
**Wheel arrangement:** 1Co-Co1
**Power:** English Electric 16SVT 16-cylinder V-form diesel, 1194kW (1600bhp)/ 1492kW (2000bhp)*; DC generator; six axle-hung DC traction motors
**Tractive effort:** 214kN (48,000lbf)/ 222kN (50,000lbf)*
**Max. operating speed:** 145km/h (90mph)
**Weight:** 138 tonnes (302,400lb)/ 136 tonnes (279,920lb)*
**Overall length:** 19.43m (63ft 9in)
**Gauge:** 1435mm (4ft 8.5in)

* Details for 10203

**The smart outline of the Southern Railway diesel-electric 1Co-Co1 No. 10203, seen here standing in the locomotive works yard at Eastleigh, reveals the vast bulk of this design. This type was the progenitor of BR's later class 40 locomotives.**

The Southern Railway encouraged the use of modern traction with its extensive electrification and by introducing technically advanced locomotives. Its first large main-line diesel was No. 10201, which was built in Ashford, Kent, and entered traffic early in 1951.After display at the Festival of Britain exhibition, it joined its sister locomotive No. 10202 on fast trains from London Waterloo to Bournemouth/ Weymouth and Exeter. As with the 10000 and 10001 models, the engine used was the EE16SVT, upgraded to 1305kW (1750hp). The unusual bogie design had no centre pivot. The locomotive body rested on lubricated segmental side bearers, a feature (like most of the locomotive design) that reappeared in the BR class 40 locomotives. In 1954, Brighton Works produced a 1492kW (2000hp) version, No. 10203. In 1955, all three went to work on the LM Region until their end in 1963.

## RS-3 ESTRADA DE FERRO CENTRAL DO BRAZIL (EFCB) BRAZIL 1952

**Type:** Bo-Bo diesel-electric freight
**Power:** 1193kW (1620hp) from Alco 244 or 251 series engine
**Tractive effort:** 245kN (55,000lbf)
**Max. operating speed:** 100km/h (62.1mph)
**Weight:** 109 tonnes (240,345lb)
**Overall length:** 16.988m (55ft 5in)
**Gauge:** 1600mm (5ft 3in)

Estrada de Ferro Central do Brazil (EFCB) took 58 Alco RS3 locomotives, mainly for freight until cascaded to lighter duties by newer types. Several survive today, as both Sao Paulo and Rio de Janeiro suburban train operators utilize refurbished RS-3s as works trains. In Rio de Janeiro, some FLUMITRENS machines now have GE 7FDL-12 engines, while others retain the original Alco 244. CPTM units in Sao Paulo have similar GE engines recovered from U20C locomotives.

**Some of RS-3s bought from Alco by Brazil's EFCB are still in use today as works trains on suburban lines in Sao Paulo and Brazil.**

## DB CLASS V80 B-B GERMAN FEDERAL RAILWAYS (DB) GERMANY 1952

Ten prototype diesel-hydraulic B-Bs were produced from 1952 by Krauss Maffei and MaK. Each locomotive had one medium-speed engine driving through a hydraulic transmission to all axles through cardan shafts and right-angle gearboxes. The layout was asymmetric, the main engine compartment being much longer than the equipment compartment behind the cab. Smoothly styled, the design led to the standard classes in Deutsche Bundesbahn's (DB) dieselization programme.

**The V80 design was notable for its compact form, a single-engined diesel-hydraulic on a B-B chassis packing 820kW (1100bhp) power output, a revolution at the time.**

**Type:** Mixed-raffic diesel-hydraulic
**Wheel arrangement:** B-B
**Power:** Medium speed 12-cylinder 821kW (1100bhp) diesel; hydraulic transmission
**Tractive effort:** 180kN (40,000lbf)
**Max. operating speed:** 100km/h (62mph)
**Weight:** 58 tonnes (127,370lb)
**Overall length:** 12.8m (42ft)
**Gauge:** 1435mm (4ft 8.5in)

## DB CLASS VT95 DIESEL RAILBUSES GERMAN FEDERAL RAILWAYS (DB) GERMANY 1952

The large fleet of four-wheeled railbuses supplied by Uerdingen for DB was intended for rural branch lines, to reduce costs. Each railcar had two automotive diesel engines underneath, each with mechanical transmission driving one axle. The vehicle interior was open with a clear view forward for passengers. Bench seats were trimmed in wipeable, leather-like material. The ride was uncomfortable because these were the days before long-link suspensions were invented to give a better lateral ride and also before hydraulic damping became the norm. Often each railbus hauled a non-powered trailer of similar design. Trains of up to four vehicles were possible.

**A single railbus arriving at a wayside halt epitomizes the nature of services for which these Uerdingen railbuses were designed. Their four-wheeled chassis gave a hard and definitely uncomfortable ride, but at least passengers could console themselves with the good viewing conditions throughout their journey.**

**Type:** Secondary and branch-line passenger
**Power:** 112kW (150bhp) six-cylinder, two per power car
**Tractive effort:** N/A
**Transmission:** Mechanical
**Max. operating speed:** 90km/h (56mph)
**Weight:** 27 tonnes (59,295lb)
**Overall length:** 13.95m (45ft 9in)
**Gauge:** 1435mm (4ft 8.5in)

## CLASS 04 DIESEL SHUNTING LOCOMOTIVE BRITISH RAILWAYS GREAT BRITAIN 1952

**Not so many of the class 04s actually survived long enough to be repainted in BR blue livery as seen here: most retained the earlier Brunswick green throughout their short lives.**

For shunting wagons in small goods yards, the Drewry Car Company built its standard C (0-6-0) diesel mechanical shunting locomotive for BR. Using a mechanical gearbox in a shunting locomotive caused snatching of wagon couplings and crashing of buffers, which compared poorly with diesel-electric and hydraulic shunting locomotives with a continuous torque curve. The 133 class 04s and their 192 BR-built '03' sisters succumbed to the closures of local goods yards and were scrapped from the late 1960s onwards. Many examples are preserved today.

**Type:** C (0-6-0) diesel mechanical shunting
**Power:** Gardner 8L3 eight-cylinder diesel engine, 150kW (204hp); four-speed epicyclic gearbox, cardan and jack shafts and external coupling rods
**Tractive effort:** 75kN (16,850lbf)
**Max. operating speed:** 32km/h (20mph)
**Weight:** 30 tonnes (66,640lb)
**Overall length:** 7.93m (26ft 2in)
**Gauge:** 1435mm (4ft 8.5in)

# CLASS TE3 CO-CO SOVIET STATE RAILWAYS RUSSIA 1952

**A TE3 twin unit showing the later cab styling applied to the majority of TE3 construction. The bogie can be seen to be copied directly from a 1940s US imported type.**

The TE3 '*troiyak*' could be a contender for the diesel locomotive built in the greatest numbers. TE3s started construction in 1953 and were heavily mass produced from 1956 until 1973. Actual units are: TE3 001 to 598 built at Kharkov, TE3 1001 to 1406 at Kolomna, and TE3 2001 to 7805 at Lugansk, plus 7807 to 7809 created in 1983 from spare parts. To these must be added triple units 3TE3 001 to 073 built up to 1962 and the higher geared TE7 001 to 113 built 1956 to 1964.

Under the Soviet numbering system, a multi-section unit is considered a single entity with both cab units of a twin suffixed 'A' and 'B'. The middle section of a triple unit was suffixed 'V', and the second middle in a four unit 'G'. The Soviet numbering system was complicated by single and twin units having no prefix, but triple units always being prefixed '3' and quads '4'. Later this was revised, with twin units prefixed '2', but this change did not affect TE3s.

Production of main-line diesels started at the Kharkov factory from 1948 onwards with TE1 and TE2 designs. Under the postwar lend lease scheme, 100 engines – 30 from Baldwin (Soviet railways class Db) and 70 from Alco (Da) – were imported. Class Da units were modified RS1s, which were then copied by Soviet engineers to produce the 1947 TE1 Co-Co. Twin unit Bo-Bo TE2s followed – with 78-tonne (171,990lb) axle load – giving much wider route availability over the lighter Soviet track. In all, 527 TE2 units were built from 1950–55, with 746kW (1000hp) engines in each unit. The Co-Co TE3 was the next step.

Keeping to a ruling 20-tonne (44,100lb) axle load, power was doubled to 1492kW (2000hp). Engines were two stroke opposed piston 2D100s copied from the Fairbanks-Morse 38D1/8 marine engine with identical 210mm (8.25in) bore and 254mm (10in) stroke. The TE3 bogie was also copied from the imported Da units. Early TE3s from Karkhov used the TE2 cab design, changing to a revised design first introduced on the TE7 as production progressed. The 3TE3 variant appeared during the period when Soviet engineers were looking ahead to 4416kW (6000hp) twin units. The 3TE3 had a cabless middle section between two cab units not initially intended for production, but a small series were built as delays to the TE10 created an urgent need for 4416kW (6000hp) units. The TE3 was essentially a freight design geared for 100km/h (62.1mph), but it was also used for passenger services. The TE7 was simply a TE3 modified for passenger use by altering the traction motor gear ratio – increasing service speed from 120 to 140km/h (75 to 87.5mph) at the expense of tractive effort. Top-line passenger work for the TE7 included principal expresses between Moscow and Leningrad (today St Petersburg) until the early 1960s, and Moscow to Minsk and Kiev.

By the beginning of the 1990s the TE3 fleet had diminished by around one-third, and by 2000 use had all but ceased, although many could be found as active spare units at depots and in strategic reserve dumps. The Chinese DF is a TE3 copy following a 1958 prototype 'Ju Long' (great dragon). Between 1964 and 1974, 706 DFs and 226 DF3s were built. They were slightly lower powered at 1325kW (1800hp) than the T3 and also heavier at 126 tonnes (277,830lb).

**Each TE3 comprises two identical single-cab units coupled back to back designated 'A' and 'B' units by Soviet and Russian railways; however, both would be 'A' units under North American terminology.**

**Type:** Co-Co diesel electric freight twin unit
**Power:** 1492kW (2000hp) from Kolomna 2D100 series engine
**Tractive effort:** 198kN (44,550lbf) at 21km/h (13.1mph)
**Max. operating speed:** 100km/h (62.1mph)
**Weight:** 120.6 tonnes (265,923lb)
**Overall length:** 16.974m (55ft 5in)
**Gauge:** 1524mm (5ft)

## DB CLASS V200 B-B GERMAN FEDERAL RAILWAYS (DB) GERMANY 1953

**So proud was *Deutsche Bundesbahn* of the streamlined appearance of its 'flagship' V200 diesel-hydraulics that a series of publicity paintings showed them in their striking red-and-black livery lined in stainless steel.**

If any locomotive can be said to epitomize postwar Germany in its appearance, it must be the class V200. Introduced as five prototypes in 1953, and extended in series in 1955 to a grand total of 86 locomotives, these machines were envied by many outsiders because 1640kW (2200hp) with a capability for shifting trains as heavy as 600 tonnes (1,322,760,lb) was packed into a locomotive weighing no more than 80 tonnes (176,368lb) on four axles. How was this done?

Even though two were used in each locomotive, the engines were all medium speed, rotating under maximum load at around 1500rpm, and so were much smaller and lighter than the well-tried but cumbersome marine-based diesel electric engines used elsewhere, which thump along at around 750rpm. The engines in the V200s were coupled to hydraulic converter units, each of which in turn transmitted its drive to the wheelsets of the adjacent bogie through cardan shafts and permanently engaged bevel gears.

There was more innovation in the locomotive body design and construction. The body was built as a box, all members contributing to carrying the load and the traction, buffing and braking forces. Even the steel sheeting that covered the sides was stressed. And there was yet more innovation in the way *Deutsche Bundesbahn* persuaded the manufacturers to adapt their engines and transmissions so that different designs could be fitted on to the same mountings and couplings. Thus a Maybach engine could be interchanged with a MTU or MAN engine, and a Voith transmission became interchangeable with a Mekydro.

The bogie design was also unusual in that the wheelsets had inside bearings – that is, the axleboxes were behind the wheels, and the bogie frames were strong structures, not riveted plate constructions as had previously been normal.

The V200s looked good in their red livery with black roof and body base lines, set off by stainless steel lining, stainless steel number plates and stainless raised lettering which read 'DEUTSCHE BUNDESBAHN' on the bodysides. As the pride of the non-electrified railway, which in the early 1950s was most of it north of Heidelberg, the V200s held their place for years. They performed reliably on heavy passenger express trains as far north as Hamburg to as far south as Munich. They were equally at home on freight, to which they drifted more in later years.

A further batch of 50 similar locomotives began entering service in 1960. These were the V200.1s, later reclassified 221 (by which time the earlier locomotives were class 220). These later locomotives had 1000kW (1350bhp) diesel engines in pairs which put 2000kW (2700bhp) on one B-B chassis.

As electrification spread across Germany, the V200 locomotives' duties changed to secondary passenger and freight work, with the class being finally withdrawn from Germany in the 1980s.

This was not to be their end, however. Many were exported to countries such as Greece and Albania, particularly the more powerful class 221 variety. Later, sold-off examples ended up in Switzerland and Italy on infrastructure trains. In the 21st century, we are now seeing some of these expatriates returning to Germany for possible use by open access railway operators. And, of course, several are preserved in working order and see occasional use on special trains.

The V200 design was adapted by BR Western Region and the North British Locomotive Company for their diesel-hydraulic 'Warship' class locomotives, described later in this book.

**Type:** Mixed-traffic main-line diesel hydraulic
**Wheel arrangement:** B-B
**Power:** Maybach, MAN, MTU 745, 820 and 1000kW (1000, 1100 and 1350bhp)
**Tractive effort:** 220kN (50,000lbf)
**Max. operating speed:** 120 and 140km/h (75 and 87mph)
**Weight:** 79 tonnes (173,490lb)
**Overall length:** 18.53m (60ft 10in)
**Gauge:** 1435mm (4ft 8.5in)

**Despite their high power-weight ratio, the V200 locomotives were quite compact for such a large locomotive. The symmetrical layout can be seen if one studies the bodyside windows and grilles.**

## CLASS 08 DIESEL SHUNTING LOCOMOTIVE BRITISH RAILWAYS GREAT BRITAIN 1953

Like many did with diesel electric shunting locomotives built for the pre-nationalization railways, British Railways adopted the standard English Electric type for further construction, the first of which appeared in 1953. The design had outside frames with adequate width for the two traction motors. These drove through double reduction gears to the front and rear wheelsets, connected externally by coupling rods on fly cranks. The EE6KT naturally aspirated in-line engine had six 254mm (10in) by 305mm (12in) cylinders. In all, 1010 class 08s were built, and more than 300 survive today.

**The class 08s were extremely sturdy locomotives that were well able to shift heavy loads, despite only having a low power unit of just 260kW (350bhp). These diesel-electric locomotives were the most prolific of all the British Railways diesel types and were mainly utilized in freight yards.**

**Type:** C (0-6-0) diesel-electric shunting
**Power unit:** EE6KT diesel engine, 260kW (350bhp), DC generator, two axle-hung traction motors, double-reduction gears
**Tractive effort:** 156kN (35,000lbf)
**Max. operating speed:** 32km/h (20mph)
**Weight:** 50 tonnes (109,760lb)
**Overall length:** 8.92m (29ft 3in)
**Gauge:** 1435mm (4ft 8.5in)

## CLASS CC200 Co-2-Co INDONESIAN STATE RAILWAYS (PNKA) INDONESIA 1953

Although US manufacturers had not supplied many steam locomotives to Indonesian State Railways, with diesels it was another matter. Twenty-seven of these road engines were supplied by General Electric, Indonesia's first main-line diesels and precursors of many more. They went into service on the 1650mm (3ft 6in) gauge main lines in Java, running with passenger trains from Jakarta to Bandung, Solo and Surabaya, but, despite being designed with the heat and humidity of Indonesia in mind, they were not very successful. The Co-2-Co wheel arrangement was unusual, caused by the requirement for a maximum axle loading not to exceed 12.2 tonnes (26,896lb). The carrying wheels were set in a truck which could be detached from the locomotive frame, converting it into a Co-Co type, if the axle-weight restrictions were relaxed. The format was not repeated in further orders, which were all for Co-Co locomotives. By the 1960s, several of the class were out of service, being cannibalized for spare parts to keep others going. One was completely rebuilt into a switching engine. By the end of the 20th century, three remained in store, and in 2001 No. 200 15 was selected for repair and restoration.

**Type:** Diesel-electric mixed-traffic locomotive
**Power:** Alco 12-cylinder 244E engine developing 888kW (1190hp) at 1000rpm
**Tractive effort:** 211kN (47,500lb)
**Max. operating speed:** 100km/h (62mph)
**Total weight:** 96 tonnes (234,420lb)
**Maximum axle load:** 12 tonnes (26,455lb)
**Overall length:** 13.147m (43ft 2in) (wheelbase)
**Gauge:** Not known

## DEII DIESEL MULTIPLE UNITS DUTCH RAILWAYS (NS) THE NETHERLANDS 1953

**In the yellow livery used by NS from the 1960s to the present day, this two-car articulated diesel train shows how up to date was the concept of these DMUs with sliding doors, articulation and hydraulically damped suspension.**

From 1953 to 1954, the Dutch firm of Allan supplied *Nederlandse Spoorwegen* (NS) with 23 two-car articulated diesel units with sliding doors for passenger access. The units were smart in appearance, with semi-streamlined cab fronts, even though intended for secondary services on non-electrified routes. Each outer bogie was motored with two axle-mounted DC motors. The articulated bogie was not motored, but carried the weight of the inner ends of the two carriage bodies. Each car had one diesel engine. On the unconventional bogies, the axleboxes were carried on two long links hinged to the bogie frame near the centre. Primary coil springs located at the outer ends of the bogie were damped by vertical hydraulic dampers angled at about 40º. The DEII units, later classified Plan X-v in NS's standard system, have all been withdrawn from NS, but several are now working for Holland's new private operators on routes near the German border.

**Type:** Local passenger diesel-electric two-car multiple unit
**Power:** Cummins NT895R2 180kW (240bhp) six-cylinder, under each car
**Power train:** Dc generator; two traction motors on each outer bogie
**Tractive effort:**
**Max. operating speed:** 120km/h (75mph)
**Weight:** 45 tonnes (98,824lb) per half-unit
**Overall length:** 22.7m (74ft 6in) per half-unit
**Gauge:** 1435mm (4ft 8.5in)

## H-24-66 'TRAIN MASTER' VARIOUS RAILROADS USA 1953

In 1953, Fairbanks-Morse brought out the most powerful of its road switcher types, the 1790kW (2400hp) six-axle, six-motor model H-24-66, advertised as the 'Train Master'. These were powered by a 12-cylinder Fairbanks-Morse opposed piston engine. In its time, the 'Train Master' was by far the most powerful single engine road switcher on the market. It proved versatile in its applications. The Virginian used its H-24-66 in heavy coal service, while Southern Pacific employed its fleet on weekday San Francisco–San Jose suburban services and on weekends for heavy freight work. Despite its promise and versatility, 'Train Master' production totalled just 127 locomotives, tiny compared to the number of EMD road switchers built in the same period.

**Against the backdrop of the Manhattan skyline, Central Railroad of New Jersey F-M Train Master 2413 leads a five-car suburban train west from CNJ's Jersey City terminal in May 1964.**

**Type:** Co-Co, diesel-electric
**Power and output:** 12-cylinder Fairbanks-Morse opposed piston diesel producing 1790kW (2400hp)
**Tractive effort:** 500kN (112,500lbf)
**Max. operating speed:** Various depending on gear ratio
**Weight:** 170 tonnes (375,850lb)
**Overall length:** 20.117 m (66ft)
**Gauge:** 1435mm (4ft 8.5in)

## 2-Do-2 Type WESTERN AUSTRALIA GOVERNMENT RAILWAYS AUSTRALIA 1954

Western Australia Government Railways class X resulted from a demanding specification for 10-ton axle loadings. Metropolitan Vickers built the 32 unconventional units with Crossley two-stroke engines. Excessive vibration, aluminium pistons, cracked heads, smoky exhaust, ring scuffing and oil-flow problems beset the class. XA were multiple unit fitted from new, while XB were X so fitted in 1963. They were withdrawn in the 1980s, having been used for light rail passenger and freight.

**Type:** 2-Do-2 light axle diesel-electric
**Power:** 825kW (1105hp) from Crossley HSTV8 series engine
**Tractive effort:** 116kN (26,100lbf) maximum; 53kN at 39km/h (11,925lbf at 24.4mph) continuous
**Max. operating speed:** 89km/h (55.6mph)
**Weight:** 80 tonnes (176,400lb)
**Overall length:** 14.63m (47ft 9in)
**Gauge:** 1067mm (3ft 6in)

**The unique cab style of these unconventional British-built units makes the X series unmistakable. The locomotive is probably not under power, as the diesel engines produced notoriously oily black emissions when working.**

## EMD 16 Co-Co VARIOUS RAILWAYS CHILE /URUGUAY 1954

In the mid-1950s, General Electric of America supplied the railways of Latin America with numerous different diesel-electric designs. Among the most distinctive are the single ended 'shovelnose' body units, of which several built for both Chile and Uruguay remain in service today on some passenger services.

Seventeen units were supplied to Chile in two batches, with D7001 to D7012 delivered in 1954 and D7013 to D7017 a few years later over 1956–57. Ferrocarril del Pacifico SA (FEPASA) continues to operate five today as its class D1600 on freight traffic from La Paz.

Forty-seven less powerful engines were built for Uruguay railways, again in two batches with 20 units (1501 to 1520) being delivered in 1952 and 27 units (1521 to 1547) two years later in 1954. About 10 of these units survive today, perhaps remarkably so, as these are still used on regular passenger services.

Class 1500 operates four daily commuter services between Montevideo and 25 de Agosto.

**Type:** Co-Co diesel-electric
**Power:** Chile 1288kW (1750hp); Uruguay 1030kW (1400hp) from Alco 12-244 series engine
**Tractive effort:** 245kN (55000lbf)
**Max. operating speed:** 120km/h (75mph)
**Weight:** 106 to 112 tonnes (233,730lb to 246960lb)
**Overall length:** 17m (55ft 6in)
**Gauge:** Chile 1676mm (5ft 6in); Uruguay 1435mm (4ft 8.5in)

## Class 2400 DUTCH RAILWAYS (NS) THE NETHERLANDS 1954

**The two class 2400 Bo-Bos pictured here at Utrecht represent a large class of general-purpose Alsthom diesels that spent most of their long lives on freight work.**

The 130 Bo-Bo hood units of class 2400 were a typical Alsthom product of the 1950s. Designed for short-distance freight and heavy shunting duties, these locomotives were used all over Holland, including on heavy freights in multiples of up to four locomotives under control of one driver. They were withdrawn by the end of the 1990s.

**Type:** Freight main-line diesel-electric
**Wheel arrangement:** Bo-Bo
**Power unit:** SACM V12 SHR 12-cylinder V-form diesel, 625kW (840bhp); DC generator; four axle-hung DC traction motors
**Tractive effort:** 161kN (36,195lbf)
**Max. operating speed:** 80km/h (50mph)
**Weight:** 134 tonnes (293,440lb)
**Overall length:** 18.64m (61ft 2in)
**Gauge:** 1435mm (4ft 8.5in)

## DF CLASS 2CO-CO2 NEW ZEALAND RAILWAYS (NZR) NEW ZEALAND 1954

**Long bodysides, large porthole-type windows and long cab noses make up the unmistakable shape of the class DF. With weight spread over 10 axles, DF units were able to operate on the lightly laid track once common in New Zealand.**

The New Zealand Railways class DF built by English Electric were the first main-line diesels for NZR. The original NZR order was for 31, but it was amended to 10, with the balance converted to 42 smaller DG locomotives. Class DF units were not noted for their reliability in their early days. English Electric installed the same Mk II engine version that British Railways used in class 40. Although the 16SVT engine was to evolve into a reliable robust power unit over time, the early versions were beset with problems and numerous modifications were required. DF entered traffic on the North Island, mostly freight. Later deliveries of newer diesels cascaded class DF on to secondary work where the relatively light axle load compared to newer types remained useful over light track. Partly due to the small quantity and partly due to low availability, DF suffered premature withdrawal between 1972 and 1975.

**Type:** 2Co-Co2 diesel-electric
**Power:** 1119kW (1500hp) from EE 16SVT series engine
**Tractive effort:** 180kN (40,500lbf)
**Max. operating speed:** 96km/h (60mph)
**Weight:** 110 tonnes (242,550lb)
**Overall length:** 18.7m (61ft)
**Gauge:** 1067mm (3ft 6in)

## CLASS M2 A1A-A1A CEYLON RAILWAYS SRI LANKA 1954

Sri Lanka, formerly Ceylon, moved towards diesels in the 1950s, with two contrasting main-line A1A-A1A classes: M1 supplied by Brush Bagnall (UK) with Mirrlees engines; and M2 which was an EMD model G12 export version. The G12 was more commonly produced in Bo-Bo form, but the A1A-A1A version was specified by Ceylon for the light track found there. It had a distinctive livery of silver, light blue and dark blue, with red buffers and cowcatchers. In fact, it is this colour scheme which makes it stick in most people's minds. They were built in several small batches at London, Ontario, from 1954 onwards, leading to the first one being named 'Ontario'. The majority are still in service today, unlike class M1, which was withdrawn from service a few years ago.

**Type:** A1A-A1A or Bo-Bo diesel electric
**Power:** 1065kW (1425hp) from EMD 12-567 series engine
**Tractive effort:** 201kN (45000lbf)
**Max. operating speed:** 80km/h (50mph)
**Weight:** 90 tonnes (198,450lb)
**Overall length:** 14.507m (47ft 4in)
**Gauge:** 1676mm (5ft 6in)

## CLASSES 202 TO 204 BELGIAN RAILWAYS (SNCB) BELGIUM 1955

For Belgian political reasons, approximately equal numbers of early diesel locomotives were ordered from builders in the Flemish and Walloon parts of the country. Anglo-Franco-Belge was licensed to build Nohab/General Motors diesel locomotives, with the first of these appearing in 1955. The 39 Co-Co locomotives had American-style streamlining, heavy GM two-stroke diesel engines, DC generators and six axle-hung traction motors. In the 1970s, these locomotives became classes 52 to 54.

The class number differences were to reflect that the class 53 locomotives had no train heating boilers, while class 54 had no rheostatic braking. Changes in use have since resulted in locomotives being transferred both ways between classes 52 and 53. Later survivors were rebuilt with new cabs to improve driver comfort.

The locomotives were used on mixed-traffic duties, including multiple pairs on heavy block freight trains through the Ardennes. Their last duties are on infrastructure trains and mixed-freight workings.

**Type:** Mixed-traffic main-line diesel-electric
**Wheel arrangement:** Co-Co
**Power unit:** GM 16-567C 16-cylinder V-form two-stroke diesel, 1265kW (1700bhp); DC generator; six axle-hung DC traction motors
**Tractive effort:** 245kN (55,080lbf)
**Max. operating speed:** 120km/h (75mph)
**Weight:** 108 tonnes (237,176lb)
**Overall length:** 18,850mm (61ft 10in)
**Gauge:** 1435mm (4ft 8.5in)

## DY CLASS INDIAN RAILWAYS — INDIA 1955

Designed and built by the North British Locomotive Company (NBL) in Glasgow, Scotland, class YDM1 was the first metre-gauge diesel locomotive for Indian Railways, originally designated class DY. They were specifically built for use on freight traffic over the section between Kandhla and Palanpur of the Ahmedabad to Delhi main line, where there was difficulty in maintaining adequate water supplies for steam locomotives. Subsequently moved away from these duties, class YDM1 was rebuilt by CLW in the mid-1970s with the original Paxman 12RPHXL 12-cylinder V-type engine replaced by the simpler MaK 6M282 series 515kW (700hp) in-line six-cylinder unit. The Voith hydraulic transmission remained unchanged. Unlike the majority of NBL diesel products, this type was persisted with by Indian Railways; a few are still in service today, still valued for their relatively light weight.

**Type:** B-B diesel-hydraulic lightweight
**Power:** 460kW (625hp) from Paxman 12RPH
**Tractive effort:** 80kN (18,000lbf) at 12km/h (7.45mph)
**Max. operating speed:** 96km/h (60mph)
**Weight:** 44 tonnes (97,020lb)
**Overall length:** 16.63m (54ft 3in)
**Gauge:** 1000mm (3ft 3in)

## DA CLASS NEW ZEALAND RAILWAYS (NZR) — NEW ZEALAND 1955

**Type:** A1A-A1A diesel-electric
**Power:** 1060kW (1425hp) from EMD 12-567 series engine
**Tractive effort:** continuous 140kN (31500lbf)
**Max. operating speed:** 100km/h (62.1mph)
**Weight:** 81 tonnes (178,605lb) (GMD and EMD built); 79 tonnes (174,195lb) (Clyde)
**Overall length:** GM-built 14.1m (46ft); Clyde-built 14.6m (47ft 8in)
**Gauge:** 1067mm (3ft 6in)

**The curved cab tops will usually identify the EMD export designs typified here in this six-axle G12 example. The middle axle on each of the two bogies is unpowered on this particular type.**

Supplied in eight batches to New Zealand Railways from 1955 until 1967, classes DA and DAA were EMD model G12. In total, 146 were supplied, imported from the US EMD, La Grange plant; GMD, Canada; and from the Australian licensee Clyde Engineering. As A1A-A1A units, the weight was spread over six axles for the lighter axle load North island routes, although most were deployed on main-line passenger and freight work. The first 30 were soon restricted after delivery to freight work due to excessive rolling on curves; later deliveries were fitted with revised bogie and suspension arrangements to overcome this. In 1970, five class DAs were modified with slow speed hump shunting controls and designated class DAA. Clyde rebuilt 80 units to class DC between 1977 and 1983.

## DG/DH CLASS NEW ZEALAND RAILWAYS (NZR) — NEW ZEALAND 1955

Class DG and DH were converted from 21 larger DF engines originally ordered from English Electric, making each DG/DH effectively a half-power DF, although EE had proposed a larger 736kW (1000hp) 8SVT engine. Thirty-one DGs and eleven DHs were built, all 42 weighing 70 tonnes (154,350lb), but the DH had a greater load over the powered axles of the A1A-A1A arrangement as a result of alterations to the suspension. North Island locos operated around Auckland and Wellington on secondary traffic, with migration of the whole class to the South Island taking place slowly between 1962 and 1976. All DHs were converted to DGs in 1968, while other modifications included new driving cabs for 10 and a further 10 modified as slaves to operate with the rebuilt units. The DG was extinct from revenue earning service in 1983; however, four are preserved, two in full working order.

**Type:** A1A-A1A diesel-electric
**Power:** 560kW (750hp) from EE 6SRKT series engine
**Tractive effort:** DG: 114kN (25,650lbf) DH: 130kN (29,250lbf )
**Max. operating speed:** 96km/h (60mph)
**Weight:** 70 tonnes (154,350lb)
**Overall length:** 14.7m (48ft)
**Gauge:** 1067mm (3ft 6in)

## CLASS M44 SWITCHER HUNGARIAN STATE RAILWAYS (MAV) — HUNGARY 1956

The M44 was in production for a relatively long period from 1956 until 1971, made by Ganz-MAVAG for MAV. The design was also delivered to Hungarian industry (class A25) and to GySEV, with the production totalling well over two hundred. M44 may be found distributed throughout Hungary on shunting, station pilot and light freight trip and transfer duties. M44.5 is a 1524mm (5ft) gauge subclass used on exchange traffic on the border with Ukraine. Starting in 2002, MAV is replacing the original Ganz Jendrassik engines with Caterpillar series 3508 power units at the same 440kW (598hp) rating. Designated class M44.4, around 50 or so are expected to see service to beyond 2010. GySEV has acquired several second-hand M44s and A25s to supplement its original five, and it also has a re-engining programme, but with Deutz 626kW (850hp) engines. Ganz-Mavag exported versions of the type between 1958 and 1982 to the former Soviet Union, Bulgaria, Poland, Yugoslavia and China (ND1).

**A Hungarian M44 working in a typical former Eastern bloc scene – shunting (switching) freight cars amid old-style semaphore signals.**

**Type:** Bo-Bo diesel-electric shunter
**Power:** 440kW (598hp) – Ganz-Jessendrik 16JV17/24 series engine
**Tractive effort:** 97kN (21825lbf) at 10.7km/h (6.9mph)
**Max. operating speed:** 80km/h (50mph)
**Weight:** 66 tonnes (145,530lb)
**Overall Length:** 11.24m (36ft 8in)
**Gauge:** 1435mm (4ft 8.5in) or 1524mm (5ft)

## CLASS DL500 SOUTHERN RAILWAY OF PERU — PERU 1956

The British-financed Southern Railway of Peru, Ferrocarrile del Sur, took Alco 'World Series' DL500 units for mountain work. This line is actually the 'highest' in the world, running as it does through the Andes.

Derated from the standard power setting to take account of oxygen starvation in high-altitude mountain operation, the DL500Bs usually worked as back to back pairs with dynamic braking. Full power was later permitted at low altitudes by barometric governors. Surviving into the 1990s, all class DL500s were gradually stopped by 2000.

**Type:** Bo-Bo diesel-electric
**Power:** 1324kW (1800hp) from Alco 251 series engine
**Tractive effort:** 273kN (61,380lbf)
**Max. operating speed:** 96km/h (60mph)
**Weight:** 104 tonnes (229,320lb)
**Overall length:** 17.958m (58ft 7in)
**Gauge:** 1435mm (4ft 8.5in)

## ALCO RS-11 VARIOUS RAILROADS — USA 1956

**A former Central Vermont Railway RS-11, lettered for Genesee Valley (a locomotive leasing company), is seen here on the Rochester & Southern at Brooks Avenue Yard in Rochester, New York.**

Alco's post–World War II road locomotives were powered by its 244-series diesel engine. Flaws in this design unfortunately resulted in greater maintenance costs and poorer-than-hoped-for sales by Alco. To rectify this situation, Alco developed a better engine design, its 251-series, which was first used in six-cylinder configuration on the S-5 and S-6 switcher models built in 1954 and 1955.

In 1956, Alco introduced the 1341kW (1800 hp) RS-11 road switcher powered by a 12-cylinder 251B engine. This locomotive featured a taller hood and a more boxy appearance than Alco's earlier RS-2/RS-3 road switcher types. More than 425 RS-11s were built over the next five years for North American service. The RS-11s were to be brought into service by many lines, including the Central Vermont, the Delaware & Hudson, the Lehigh Valley, and the Pennsylvania Railroad.

**Type:** Bo-Bo, diesel-electric
**Power and output:** Alco 12-cylinder 251B engine producing 1341kW (1800hp)
**Tractive effort:** N/A
**Max. operating speed:** N/A
**Weight:** N/A
**Overall length:** N/A
**Gauge:** 1435mm (4ft 8.5in)

# EMD FL9 NEW HAVEN RAILROAD USA 1956

The EMD FL9 was a specialized hybrid locomotive developed especially for the New Haven Railroad. An unusual adaptation of the diesel-electric locomotive, it was equipped with third-rail shoes that allowed it to run as an electric locomotive in electrified territory. This allowed New Haven to run the FL9s directly into New York's Grand Central Terminal and Penn Station, both of which required long journeys through tunnels where diesel engine emissions were prohibited. By using these dual-mode locomotives, the New Haven Railroad was able to run through passenger trains from Boston to New York without changing locomotives.

**Amtrak regularly assigned its small fleet of former New Haven FL9s to Empire Corridor trains between Albany–Rensselaer and New York City; FL9 484 is seen at the former station in October 1993.**

**Type:** B-A1A diesel-electric/electric
**Power and output:** EMD 16-567C producing 1305kW (1750hp) and powered by a 660 volt DC third rail.
**Tractive effort:** 258kN (58,000lbf)
**Max. operating speed:** 145km/h (90mph)
**Weight:** 130 tonnes (286,614 lb)
**Overall length:** 17.882m (58 ft 8in)
**Gauge:** 1435mm (4ft 8.5in)

# MLW RS-18 VARIOUS RAILROADS CANADA 1956

Alco's Montreal Locomotive Works affiliate produced the RS-18 from 1956 to 1968. In most respects, this model was the same as Alco's RS-11 (specification No. 701), but featured a slightly higher hood style. Rated at 1341kW (1800hp), the RS-18 was comparable to EMD's GP9 road switcher type and used in a variety of services. Canadian Pacific (CPR) and Canadian National were the primary users of the RS-18 type and they were common on lines in eastern Canada. CPR chopped the nose off most of its RS-18s to improve visibility, and the RS-18 was among the last types of MLW power in service on CPR, with some locomotives surviving in regular service until the late 1990s.

**On 11 January 1993, a Canadian Pacific RS-18 works at St Martins Junction, north of Montreal, Quebec. Originally the RS-18 featured a high short-hood.**

**Type:** Bo-Bo, diesel-electric
**Power and output:** Alco 12-cylinder 251B engine producing 1341kW (1800hp)
**Tractive Effort:**
**Max. operating speed:** 120 km/h (75mph)
**Weight:** N/A
**Overall length:**
**Gauge:** 1435mm (4ft 8.5in)

## CLASS 31 BRITISH RAIL GREAT BRITAIN 1957

The 263 Brush Type 2 locomotives were medium-powered diesel electrics with Mirrlees engines. The diesel engines developed early fatigue cracks, so they were replaced by more powerful English Electric engines using the original Brush electrical equipment. The locomotives worked on the Eastern Region, and later the WR and LMR. Most of them were scrapped in the 1980s and 1990s. A small number work for Fragonset, and several are preserved.

**Type:** Mixed-traffic main-line diesel-electric
**Wheel arrangement:** A1A-A1A
**Power:** Mirrlees JVS12T 933kW (1250bhp), then EE12SVT 12-cylinder 1095kW (1470bhp); Brush DC generator, four axle-hung traction motors
**Tractive effort:** 176 to 190kN (39,500 to 42,800lbf)
**Max. operating speed:** 120 to 145km/h (75 to 90mph)
**Weight:** 106 tonnes (232,960lb)
**Overall length:** 17.3m (56ft 9in)
**Gauge:** 1435mm (4ft 8.5in)

**The Brush Type 2s, later classified 31, were equally at home on passenger or freight trains, although if the latter were heavy they were usually worked in multiple pairs.**

## 'TRANS EUROP EXPRESS' DUTCH RAILWAYS/SWISS NATIONAL RAILWAYS (NS/SBB) 1957

As Europe's railways recovered from the deprivations of war, and continental businesses once again began to prosper, there was a perceived need for some luxury international business trains to attract businessmen from other forms of travel, including the developing motorway and airline networks. International rail travel at that time consisted generally of long-distance trains of locomotive hauled stock, often mixed from several countries, that suffered delays at borders while locomotives were changed and at staging points where carriages were shunted on and off for different destinations. Very often customs and passport examinations were held at border stations while the trains stopped for anything up to half an hour. This even happened between France and Belgium, a fact we have since all but forgotten in the European Union. Many international trains were hauled by steam locomotives for parts of their journeys. Someone travelling in those days from Amsterdam to Milan would usually opt to stay overnight *en route* in, say, Munich, and catch a further train or trains the next day. So international rail travel in the 1950s was perceived as slow and not suitable for fast connections between capital cities and major business centres across borders. The railways of five nations decided to launch an attack on the business market by what were then seen as innovative means.

The Dutch-Swiss 'Trans Europ Express' (TEE) sets introduced in 1957 were part of this cooperative attempt to promote high-quality international business railway travel. Germany, Switzerland, France, Italy and the Netherlands each contributed trains. and destinations ranged from Hamburg, Brussels, Paris and Amsterdam in the north to Munich, Zürich, Bern and Milan in the south. NS and the Swiss National Railways (SBB)

**Probably the most successful of all the diesel unit TEE trains were the *Deutsche Bundesbahn*'s eight-car units because they were long enough to carry an economic loading (and also because they looked so impressive!).**

cooperated in producing some luxury sets that were idiosyncratic and jointly owned by the two railways. Unusually, one vehicle in each four-car set was totally given over to power equipment and services. In effect, there was one locomotive and just three carriages. The power cars were designed by Werkspoor in the Netherlands; the cab fronts, as with the driving trailer cars at the other end of the units, were distinctly Dutch with their rounded noses, giving the trains a somewhat heavy appearance.

Traction equipment on the Dutch-Swiss sets was diesel-electric, designed for high performance. Diesel traction was chosen for all the original TEE trains; electric technology could not then reliably enable electric trains to operate under four different traction voltages and systems. For example, the Netherlands used 1500V DC, Belgium was 3000V DC, France in the northeast used 25,000V AC 50Hz, and DB and SBB were at the voltage of 15,000V AC 16.67Hz. In any case, there were still long stretches of European main lines that were not electrified.

The TEE passenger carriages raised the standard of European first-class travel to new heights. All vehicles were first class only. They were fully air-conditioned, the first general use of saloon cooling and air filtering in standard railway trains in Europe. The layout ensured that all seats had ample space and legroom, and tables at which meals and refreshments could be served. Considerable effort was made to insulate the carriages, including double-glazed windows, so that temperatures were steady and sound levels reduced substantially. These trains were deservedly popular, although, like other DMU TEE sets, their short length together with their business success sealed their eventual fate. Because the trains did not need to change locomotives, and passport and customs checks were usually undertaken on the trains, journey times were substantially reduced, aided by the higher performance possible with dedicated, fixed-formation unit trains.

With the exception of Germany, other TEE sets were based on existing DMU designs. France adapted its two-car RGP diesel-hydraulic design for TEE use by including air-conditioning equipment and improving the interior to luxury standard. Italy also provided two-car diesel units of a smart appearance. These also had the common TEE standards of air-conditioned interiors with high comfort. But two coaches were just not enough, and all the French and Italian units, as well as the Dutch-Swiss sets, succumbed to the need to expand train lengths.

The West German TEE trains were eight-car fixed-formation units with power cars at each end that had a small seating section in each. These were diesel-hydraulics using similar, proven equipment to that used in the V200 B-B locomotives, 820kW (1100bhp) in each power car. They were particularly prominent because of their bulbous front ends and strikingly streamlined appearance. Their longer train length enabled them to cope much better than other countries' designs with the expanding need for TEE-type travel. When the TEE concept was eventually abandoned in favour of international trains such as the Eurocity brand, these units took over some internal DB InterCity services.

East Germany also tried to emulate the West German TEE sets by producing similar eight-car diesel-hydraulic trains, which it put into service between Berlin and Vienna. Some services also penetrated into Scandinavia. The streamlined ends of the DR units were somewhat less rounded than the DB version, but were no doubt copies of the original in concept.

All original TEE trains ran in a common livery of red and cream. France had to abandon use of DMUs on TEE trains quite quickly because the demand outstripped the supply of seats. SNCF therefore introduced stainless steel clad air-conditioned locomotive-hauled stock on TEE routes such as Paris to Brussels. The RGP railcars reverted to internal French express duties. The Swiss introduced five-car EMUs on the 'Cisalpin' service between Milan and Paris, letting Italian State Railways (FS) off the hook. Locomotive haulage also became the order of the day between Milan and Munich. The TEE brand later became outmoded during the 1970s and 1980s when the concept of regular-interval InterCity and Eurocity trains spread across the continent. These longer locomotive-hauled formations had separate restaurant cars and accommodated both first- and second-class passengers.

The Dutch-Swiss TEE sets were sold to the Ontario Northland Railway in Canada where they provided services around Toronto, with standard diesel locomotives replacing the Werkspoor power cars.

**Type:** 'Trans Europ Express', first class only diesel-electric units
**Power:** Werkspoor 16-cylinder diesels (two per power car), each of 746kW (1000hp)
**Transmission:** Electric DC generator and four traction motors, two per three-axle bogie
**Max. operating speed:** 140km/h (87mph)
**Weight per four-car set:** 253 tonnes (555,610lb)
**Overall length:** 96.926m (318ft)
**Gauge:** 1435mm (4ft 8.5in)

**The 'Trans Europ Express' was an attempt to overcome the perceived 'inconvenience' of intercountry rail travel in Europe, aimed at luring travelling businesspeople away from the burgeoning motorway and air networks.**

## CLASS V100 GERMAN FEDERAL RAILWAYS (DB) GERMANY 1958

As a replacement for smaller steam locomotives, DB ordered the V100 class. The V100 is in effect half a V200 in power. Once there were over 700 of these locomotives and the later, more powerful class 212 derivatives in service. These compact B-B hydraulics were used all over western Germany until electrification, new multiple units and freight rationalization ensured withdrawal. Very few are left today.

**Type:** Mixed traffic secondary service diesel-hydraulic
**Wheel arrangement:** B-B
**Power:** Medium speed MTU 12-cylinder 820kW (1100hp) diesel; Voith L216rs hydraulic transmission
Tractive effort: 183kN (41,140lbf)
**Max. operating speed:** 100km/h (62.1mph)
**Weight:** 62 tonnes (136,160lb)
**Overall length:** 12.1m (39ft 8in)
**Gauge:** 1435mm (4ft 8.5in)

## TYPE 2 CO-BO BRITISH RAILWAYS GREAT BRITAIN 1958

Two features were unusual in the 20 Type 2 locomotives which came from Metropolitan Vickers. One bogie had two axles, the other three. The diesel engine was a Crossley two-stroke that used the patented 'exhaust pulse pressure charging' system. In theory, contact with the high-pressure exhaust gases pushed the intake air pressure up. The fleet operated from Barrow-on-Furness for most of its life, but was not a technical success, and all were withdrawn by 1968. D5705 is preserved.

**Type:** Mixed-traffic main-line diesel-electric
**Wheel arrangement:** Co-Bo
**Power:** Crossley HSTV8 two-stroke V-form diesel 895kW (1200bhp); Metro-Vick DC generator and five axle-hung traction motors
**Tractive effort:** 220kN (50,000lbf)
**Max. operating speed:** 120km/h (75mph)
**Weight:** 97tonnes (213,020lb)
**Overall length:** 17.27m (56ft 8in)
**Gauge:** 1435mm (4ft 8.5in)

**It was not the asymmetrical wheel-arrangement of Co-Bo, but the technical behaviour of the Crossley two-stroke diesel engine that caused the premature scrapping of the Metropolitan-Vickers Type 2s.**

## CLASS 40 BRITISH RAILWAYS GREAT BRITAIN 1958

**Type:** Mixed-traffic main-line diesel-electric
**Wheel arrangement:** 1Co-Co1
**Power:** English Electric 16SVT 16-cylinder 1490kW (2000bhp); DC generator; six DC axle-hung traction motors
**Tractive effort:** 230kN (52,000lbf)
**Max. operating speed:** 145km/h (90mph)
**Weight:** 136 tonnes (297,920lb)
**Overall length:** 21.19m (69ft 6in)
**Gauge:** 1435mm (4ft 8.5in)

In all, there were 200 Type 4 class 40 locomotives built by English Electric and Robert Stephenson & Hawthorns. Mechanical and electrical design followed closely that of the Southern Region diesel No. 10203: bogies, power unit and traction equipment were virtually identical. The main difference was in body styling, which was straight-sided and had the cabs set back behind nose compartments that contained auxiliary equipment.

**'Handsome is as handsome does,' so goes the saying, and the EE Type 4s were certainly good-looking locomotives of their day. They performed well on express passenger and heavy freight services. This photograph shows an example in BR Brunswick green locomotive.**

With a top speed of a fast 145km/h (90mph), the class 40s performed well and reliably, although their heavy weight limited their fast running capability on express lines. Initially allocated to BR's Eastern, North Eastern and London Midland regions, they hauled named expresses such as 'The Royal Scot' and 'The Flying Scotsman', 'The Norfolkman', 'The Master Cutler' and the 'Queen of Scots' Pullman train. In later years, the class 40 locomotives drifted to lesser duties and freight workings on minor lines.

The first loco D322, was withdrawn in September 1967 after receiving collision damage, and cut up at Crewe in November of the same year. The first 'proper' withdrawals began in January 1976. The advent of the British Rail high-speed trains caused them finally to be displaced, and all were withdrawn by 1984.

## CLASS TE10 TWIN CO-CO SOVIET STATE RAILWAYS LATVIA 1958

The TE10 designation covers a range of subtype classes indicative of Soviet engineers predilection of extending successful models to meet production targets. TE10 exists in single, double, triple and quadruple unit form and with two distinct body shells.

Prototype TE10 001 was completed at the Lugansk factory in November 1958. It was the first Soviet 2208kW (3000hp) unit design, specified to supplant the 1492kW (2000hp) TE3 with minimal weight increase. Key was the development of new engines, initially using the 9D100 based on the 2D100 opposed piston two stroke, but with 12 cylinders.

However, the 9D100 gave way to the 10D100, achieving the same power from its 10 cylinders as the 2D100 by increasing boost pressure. Initial limited numbers of single-unit TE10L were quickly replaced by the mass production 2TE10L, running to more than 3000 twin units from 1961. These locomotives were of the original Kharkov cab design similar to that used on the later export M62.

From 1974, the 2TE10V version featured a new body and increased axle load. The shell had a negative rake cab front window layout similar to the 2TE116 also in contemporary production. Bogies of TE116 type replaced the original design copied from the Alco DA imports of the 1940s. The TE10 'V' suffix denotes 'Voroshilogradskii', the then name of the Lugansk factory, with units built up to 2TE10V 5090, and one 3TE10V of 1978.

Next came the double- and triple-unit TE10M modernized ('M' for 'modernizirovannyi') built as 3TE10M 0002-0200, 2TE10M 0201-1000, 3TE10M 1001-1440 and 2TE10M 2001-3664.

Designed for use on the Baikalo Amurskaya magistrale route, 25 quadruple units with suffix 'S' for 'severnyi' (north) operation were built (4TE10S 0001-0025) by 1983. Two further production versions were introduced in 1989–90: 2TE10U 0001-0549 and 3TE10U 0001-0079 'universalnyi' and 2TE10UT 0001-0099, the latter with electropneumatic train braking for passenger work and 120km/h (75mph) maximum speed and power.

The basic TE10L performance characteristics per single unit are: maximum tractive effort 375kN (84375lbf), continuous 248kN at 23.3km/h (55800lbf at 14.6mph) increasing to 399kN (89775lbf ) maximum and 248kN at 23.4km/h (55800lbf at 14.6mph in the TE10V version, remaining at similar values in the main TE10S and TE10U models.

One interesting diversion was the experimental 2TE10G of 1988 for dual fuelling on diesel and natural gas. Although classed as 2TE10G, both units were triple section with a middle unpowered cryogenic tender carrying liquified gas at minus 162°C. Like many Soviet locomotive developments little was heard of this after trial running and initial publicity.

Another limited production version was 2TE10MK locomotive, from 1981, with the same Kolomna 5D49 engine as installed in the 2TE116. The passenger version was originally to have been model TE11, but was altered to TEP10. It was first built at Kharkov from 1960 and later also at Lugansk.

**Type:** Co-Co diesel electric freight
**Power:** 2208kW (3000hp) per unit from Kolomna 10D100 series engine
**Tractive effort:** Various
**Max. operating speed:** 100km/h (62.1mph)
**Weight:** TE10L 130 tonnes (286,650lb); TE10V 138tonnes (304,290lb)
**Overall length:** 16.969m (55ft 5in)
**Gauge:** 1524mm (5ft)

## SEVEN-CAR TRAIN MOROCCAN RAILWAYS (CFM) MOROCCO 1958

Passenger numbers on the CFM were falling during the 1950s, and this air-conditioned high-speed seven-car diesel-electric set, built in France, was intended to attract custom back to the railways. It had two power cars, with engines mounted in the car frames. Two auxiliary diesel generators for train lighting, air conditioning etc meant that the engines' full power could be applied to traction. There were driving positions at each end, and it accommodated 288 passengers.

**Type:** Seven-car diesel-electric multiple-unit train
**Power:** Two MGO engines with an output of 746kW (1000hp) at 1500rpm, driving two power bogies via Alsthom electric transmission
**Tractive effort:** Not known
**Maximum operating speed:** 121km/h (75mph)
**Total weight:** 251.2 tonnes (553,896lb)
**Maximum axle load:** 12 tonnes (26,460lb)
**Overall length:** Not known
**Gauge:** Not known

## EMD SD24 VARIOUS RAILROADS USA 1958

The SD24 was EMD's first turbocharged high-horsepower six-motor diesel. Introduced in 1958, and built until 1963, this 1788kW (2400 hp) machine was a preview of the type of motive power that would become the standard on most American freight railroads. Externally, the SD24 was similar to EMD's SD9, although the SD24 could easily be identified by the circular bulge located behind the cab on the long hood that housed the turbocharger. Santa Fe and Union Pacific both ordered SD24s with the low nose option that was just becoming popular and, by the late 1960s, would be a standard option, while Burlington and Southern had high-hood SD24s. Santa Fe rebuilt its SD24 fleet with EMD 16-645 engines to boost output and improve reliability, these were re-designated as SD26s.

**Type:** Co-Co, diesel-electric
**Power:** EMD 16-567D3 producing 1788kW (2400hp)
**Tractive effort:** 425kN (95,700lbf)
**Max. operating speed:** N/A
**Weight:** 174 tonnes (382,800lb)
**Overall length:** N/A
**Gauge:** 1435mm (4ft 8.5in)

## CLASS V 0-4-0 D/H VICTORIAN RAILWAYS AUSTRALIA 1959

This was a small, one-off design of four-wheel diesel-hydraulic shunting locomotive and one of the smallest ever to operate for any main line Australian railway. V56 was constructed by Victorian Railways, and was used for passenger car shunting.

**Type:** 0-4-0 diesel-hydraulic light shunter
**Power:** 30kW (40hp) from Fordson Major engine
**Tractive effort:** 48kN (10800lbf)
**Max. operating speed:** 16km/h (10mph)
**Weight:** 22 tonnes (48510lb)
**Overall Length:** 6.32m (20ft 7in)
**Gauge:** 1600mm (5ft 3in)

## CLASS 48 NEW SOUTH WALES GOVERNMENT RAILWAYS AUSTRALIA 1959

New South Wales class 48, built from 1959 to 1970, was one of the more numerous in Australian service. The first 45 had all GE electrical parts, the next 40 GE generators but British-designed AEI motors, and the last 80 were all AEI. The switch from GE to AEI was due to GE competing directly against Alco, whereas previously the two had cooperated. By 2002, more than 100 remained operational, deployed largely on New South Wales grain and coal routes, as well as most branch freight traffic. Some have been refurbished, and three of these are used on Austrac's freight services. They were also employed at one time on Sydney–Melbourne routes.

**No 4827 exemplifies a typical road switcher configuration with off-centre cab and full-height bonnet, which also shows off its relatively short body length for a six-axle freight unit of this power range.**

**Type:** Co-Co freight
**Power:** 780kW (1050hp) from Alco 6-251 series engine
**Tractive effort:** (serials 4801-4885): 151kN (33975lbf) at 10km/h (6.2mph)
**Max. operating speed:** 120km/h (75mph)
**Weight:** 75 tonnes (165,375lb)
**Overall length:** 14.76m (48ft 2in)
**Gauge:** 1435mm (4ft 8.5in)

## CLASS 44 BRITISH RAILWAYS GREAT BRITAIN 1959

It is surprising that British Railways' own design of Type 4 diesel electric should mirror so closely the Southern Region '10201' series, thus being very similar to the English Electric type. Yet at the least the 1Co bogie design was clearly derived from the SR machine. The power unit had a more powerful Sulzer twin-bank engine, the 12LDA28 type, coupled to robust Crompton Parkinson electric traction equipment. Ten class 44s were built, and they were the prototypes for the 183 classes 45 and 46 locomotives that followed. The '44s' began on main-line passenger work, particularly on the Midland division of the LM Region, but graduated to freight work as the 45s and 46s became more numerous. Known as the 'Peak' class, and named after eight English and two Welsh mountains, the 44s ended their days working on heavy freight trains from Toton depot in the East Midlands.

**Type:** Mixed-traffic main-line diesel-electric
**Wheel arrangement:** 1Co-Co1
**Power:** Sulzer 12LDA28 12-cylinder twin-bank diesel 1715kW (2300bhp); Crompton Parkinson DC generator and six DC axle-hung traction motors
**Tractive effort:** 310kN (70,000lbf)
**Max. operating speed:** 145km/h (90mph)
**Weight:** 141 tonnes (309,345lb)
**Overall length:** 20.7m (67ft 11in)
**Gauge:** 1435mm (4ft 8.5in)

**The class 44 No. D4, photographed at an exhibition after its preservation, was named Great Gable.**

## CLASS 060-DA ROMANIAN RAILWAYS (CFR) ROMANIA 1959

Romania has tended to buy in technical designs, mainly from Western European countries. Its choice for a main-line diesel locomotive rested on Switzerland, which offered a compact Brown Boveri (BBC) Co-Co with a powerful Sulzer diesel engine and BBC electric traction equipment. In all, 1407 class 060-DA locomotives (later reclassified '60' to '62') were built for CFR, the majority in the Electroputere workshops in the southern Romanian city of Craiova. They are extremely successful locomotives, being suitable for heavy passenger and freight trains. Electroputere has also supplied many examples for the railways of Poland and Bulgaria.

CFR has recently refurbished several locomotives for further service. Two have been updated with Caterpillar engines and more advanced electrical equipment. The type still operates in Romania and Poland; however, many surplus locomotives have been sold to private operators in Germany, Italy and elsewhere.

**One of the excellent Co-Cos of CFR heads a typical passenger train. Most of the 1407 locomotives were built in Romania.**

**Type:** Mixed-traffic main-line diesel-electric
**Wheel arrangement:** Co-Co
**Power:** Sulzer 12LDA28 12-cylinder twin-bank diesel 1544kW (2070hp); Brown Boveri DC generator and six axle-hung traction motors
**Tractive effort:** 314kN (70,590lbf)
**Max. operating speed:** 120km/h (75mph)
**Weight:** 118 tonnes (259,840lb)
**Overall length:** 17m (55ft 9in)
**Gauge**: 1435mm (4ft 8.5in)

## EMD GP20 VARIOUS RAILROADS USA 1959

**Type:** Bo-Bo, diesel-electric
**Power and output:** EMD 16-567D2 producing 1492kW (2000hp)
**Tractive effort:** 200kN (45,000 lbf) at 22.4 km/h (14 mph)
**Max. operating speed:** 104 km/h (65mph)
**Weight:** 116 tonnes (256,000 lbs)
**Overall length:** 17.12m (56ft 2in)
**Gauge:** 1435m (4ft 8.5in)

One of the strengths of Electro-Motive early diesel locomotives was the powerful, compact and extraordinarily reliable 567 engine. Thousands of Fs, GPs, Es and switcher types were powered by variations of the 567 diesel. The 567 was traditionally supercharged using a Roots scavenger blower.

In the late 1950s, Union Pacific modified some of its EMD GP9s with turbochargers to obtain greater output. EMD followed suit by introducing its own turbo-charged 567 diesel, the 1492kW (2000hp) GP20. This model was also one of the first that was offered with either a traditional high short-hood (nose section) or a low short-hood for better forward visibility. The GP20 was well suited to fast intermodal services, and the model set an important technological precedent; however, it was relatively short lived and was only in production from 1959 until 1962.

**Several railroads, including Santa Fe, originally assigned GP20s to fast freight service. Later, they were often used on local freights.**

## CLASS MX DANISH STATE RAILWAYS (DSB) DENMARK 1960

**Looking smart in DSB's corporate black-and-red livery, the class MX is similar to locomotives that operated in Belgium, Luxembourg, Hungary, Norway and Sweden.**

Otherwise very similar to the SNCB class 202, the Danish class MX and the subsequent class MY were of A1A-A1A wheel arrangement in which the outer wheelsets of each bogie only were motored. These mixed-traffic machines were used on passenger trains all over the country, initially on the top express and international trains. They later downgraded to secondary working when more powerful diesels arrived. The 'MXs' continued on heavy freight and infrastructure trains until withdrawn by DSB at the end of the 1990s. Built by Nohab of Sweden, they were American in concept and had General Motors engines and electrical equipment, a very reliable combination.

When built, they were painted wine red with the 'flying wheel' symbol splashed across their streamlined noses. Later they appeared in the brighter DSB corporate red that is still the company's standard. After withdrawal, several locomotives were sold to private operators in Denmark and elsewhere, and to infrastructure maintainers.

**Type:** Mixed-traffic main-line diesel-electric
**Wheel arrangement:** A1A-A1A
**Power:** GM 12-567C 12-cylinder V-form diesel, 1050kW (1405bhp), DC generator, four traction motors
**Tractive effort:** 176kN (395,665lbf)
**Max. operating speed:** 133km/h (83mph)
**Weight:** 89 tonnes (195,450lb)
**Overall length:** 18.3m (60ft)
**Gauge:** 1435mm (4ft 8.5in)

## 'BLUE PULLMAN' BRITISH RAILWAYS GREAT BRITAIN 1960

The 'Blue Pullmans' were the first air-conditioned trains in the United Kingdom and introduced much higher standards of sound insulation for a quiet passenger environment. They were fixed formation, diesel-electric units, conceptually similar to 'Trans Europ Express' units. For the Midland main-line Manchester to London service, the six-car formations were all first class. The Birmingham to London Paddington route received eight-car trains with

**One of the Western Region's eight-car diesel Pullman sets in the original blue-and-white livery leaves Newport in South Wales for London Paddington.**

first-and second-class seats. Each of the two streamlined power cars contained a MAN 12-cylinder engine with a GEC generator. Two traction motors were under the rear bogie of the power car and two on the leading bogie of the adjacent trailer coach. Later, all sets went to the Western Region and worked on the Bristol to London and Swansea to London peak business services. They ran until 1973.

**Type:** Pullman diesel unit
**Power (each of two power cars):** MAN L12V18/21S 12-cylinder V-form diesel, 746kW (1000bhp); GEC DC generator; four fully suspended DC traction motors
**Max. operating speed:** 145km/h (90mph)
**Weight:** 305 tonnes (669,760lb) six-car sets; 371 tonnes (815,360lb) eight-car sets
**Overall length:** 20.9m (68ft 7in) power cars; 20.725m (68ft) trailer cars
**Gauge:** 1435mm (4ft 8.5in)

## CLASS 02 DIESEL-HYDRAULIC SHUNTING LOCOMOTIVES BRITISH RAIL GB 1960

BR introduced a variety of small B (0-4-0) diesel shunting locomotive for use in locations with tight curves and light loads. One such was a class of 20 locomotives that came from the Yorkshire Engine Company. This type used a Rolls-Royce high-speed diesel engine coupled to a three-stage hydraulic torque converter.

**Type:** B (0-4-0) diesel-hydraulic shunting
**Power:** Rolls-Royce C6NFL diesel 125kW (170hp); RR series 10,000 three-stage torque converter; YEC final drive to one axle, outside coupling rods
**Tractive effort:** 67kN (15,000lbf)
**Max. operating speed:** 32km/h (20mph)
**Weight:** 29 tonnes (62,720lb)
**Overall length:** 6.7m (22ft) approx.
**Gauge:** 1435mm (4ft 8.5in)

## CLASS 37 BRITISH RAILWAYS GREAT BRITAIN 1960

**Type:** Mixed-traffic main-line diesel-electric
**Wheel arrangement:** Co-Co
**Power:** English Electric 12CSVT 12-cylinder V-form diesel, 1305kW (1750bhp); DC generator; six axle-hung DC traction motors
**Tractive effort:** 245kN (55,500lbf) to 280kN (62,680lbf)
**Max. operating speed:** 130km/h (80mph)
**Weight:** 104 tonnes (228,480lb) to 122 tonnes (268,880lb)
**Overall length:** 18.745m (61ft 6in)
**Gauge:** 1435mm (4ft 8.5in)

**The class 37/4 has been modified with a train heating alternator to provide electric train supply for passenger trains in remote areas such as the Scottish Highlands.**

The first BR diesel class to emerge that did not have its origin in the 1955 Modernisation Plan prototypes was the English Electric Type 3, later class 37. Initially delivered to the Eastern Region, this mixed-traffic type was used on express trains to East Anglia before being distributed more widely and settling down mainly on heavy freight duties. These were conventional and extremely reliable Co-Co diesel electric locomotives. In the 1970s, pairs of '37s' were drafted to work Britain's heaviest freight trains, the 2140-tonne iron ore trains from Immingham Docks to Scunthorpe steelworks. Others were later modified with train heat alternators and used on secondary passenger work on the remotest railways. The class is reducing quickly. A few have been sold to private freight operators and some work for the nuclear industry. They have proved useful in France and Spain in handling heavy construction trains for high-speed railways.

## CLASS 124 'TRANS-PENNINE' BRITISH RAILWAYS GREAT BRITAIN 1960

The challenge of operating fast passenger trains across the Pennine hills was met by construction of powerful six-car DMUs formed of four power cars and two trailers, and known as class 124.

Five carriages of the train were second class, and the buffet car had first-class compartments. Later the buffet cars were removed. The class 124s worked from Hull to Liverpool via Leeds and Manchester. 'Sprinter' DMUs replaced them in the early 1980s.

**The 124s started life as six-car sets for the Hull-Leeds-Manchester-Liverpool run. Reduced patronage resulted in them later being reduced to five-car formations and latterly to four cars.**

**Type:** Express diesel multiple-unit six-car (later five-car) set
**Power:** Leyland Albion horizontal six-cylinder diesel (two per power car), 170kW (230bhp); fluid flywheel; four-speed epicyclic gearbox; cardan shaft to reversing gearbox on nearest axle
**Max. operating speed:** 110km/h (70mph)
**Weight:** 41 tonnes (89,600lb) power cars; 33 tonnes (71,680lb) trailers
**Overall length:** 19.66m (64ft 6in)
**Gauge:** 1435mm (4ft 8.5in)

## TEM2 SOVIET STATE RAILWAYS RUSSIA 1960

The Soviet railway model TEM2 six-axle heavy shunter and transfer locomotive is another example of a mass-produced, long production run design. In parallel with the domestic-built TEM2, SZD was also importing the ChME3 design of similar layout and power from Czechoslovakia. Both TEM2 and ChME3 were deployed on similar duties across the entire Russian railway and successor networks. Several improved and revised versions of TEM2 appeared, while others have been exported. TEM2 can be seen to be descended directly from the DA units imported from the United States under lend lease, these being Alco RS1 units. The 746kW (1000hp) TEM1 model produced between 1958 and 1968 followed from the DA being the first Soviet switcher design, with nearly 2000 built in a serious attempt at ending steam shunting. TEM stands for '*teplovoz elecktroperedachei manevrovyi*', literally diesel-electric shunter, while the '1' simply represents the first type. TEM2 is an uprated version with 883kW (1200hp) power unit and same maximum tractive effort, but increased line service speed from 90 to 100km/h (62.1mph) and reduced weight. The first three prototypes appeared from the Bryansk factory in 1960. There were several pilot batches, then it went into mass production from 1967 to 1987 from both Bryansk and Lugansk works. The basic TEM2 has spawned a number of different subtypes with suffix letters including M (*modernizirovannyi*), U (*uluchshchennyi*) and T (*tormozhenie*), indicating modernized, improved and electric dynamic braking, respectively. TEM2 is widely associated with the BAM line (*Baikalo Amurskaya magistrale*), the extensive construction project of the second trans-Siberia route. TEM2 provided the works locomotives for the entire new works route that opened for through trains in the late 1990s after decades of slow progress, and even now there are several kilometres of temporary works. Model TEM2U dating from the 1978 prototype and 1984 production features a revised body design of more angular styling as well as technical revisions over the TEM2, while TEM2UT and TEM2T are electric braking versions of both. TEM2M was a trial fitting with a Kolomna 6D49 V8 configuration power unit in place of the standard in-line Penza six-cylinder engine, while TEM2US were experiments with electromagnetic adhesion equipment. TEM2UM appeared in prototype form in 1988, entering series building the following year with 994kW (1350hp) engines. Both standard and broad-gauge versions were supplied to Poland are found on Polish railways, the wide gauge machines on border transfer duties as well as for shunting and works trains on the LHS 'Iron and Sulphur' line extending to Katowice area. A large number are also operated on the Silesian sand railway, an extensive industrial system around Katowice to move sand to infill old mining works. Cuba also still operates this locomotive.

**Like many Soviet examples, the diesel-electric heavy shunter TEM2 had a long production run and can still be seen in use today. Both Polish and Cuban railways still utilize the TEM2.**

**Type:** Co-Co diesel-electric heavy shunter
**Power:** 883kW (1200hp) from Penza PD1 series engine
**Tractive effort:** 206kN (46,350lbf) at 11km/h (6.9mph)
**Max. operating speed:** 100km/h (62.1mph)
**Weight:** 120 tonnes (264,600lb)
**Overall length:** 16.97m (55ft 4in)
**Gauge:** 1524mm (5ft)

## TEP-60 Co-Co SOVIET STATE RAILWAYS RUSSIA 1960

Prior to the introduction of class TEP-60, Soviet diesel locomotives for passenger service were derived from mass-produced freight types, such as the higher geared TE7 variant of the TE3, and TEP10 based on TE10.

More than 1200 TEP-60s were series built until 1985, with many surviving today in some areas, although in other regions they are held in reserve or stored out of use. Two twin-unit version 2TEP60 prototypes appeared in 1964, with production from 1966 to 1987 totalling 116, along with some rebuilds from pairs of single units.

All class TEP-60 locomotives were built at the Kolomna works, and they were all powered by Kolomna's own 11D45 two-stroke V16 engines, which were reputed to be the most fuel-efficient in the Soviet Union.

Despite being dedicated passenger units, as was the convention in Russia, no provision was made for any train heating supply. Coaches were self-heated, usually from coal-fired stoves or boilers.

**Type:** Co-Co diesel electric passenger
**Power:** 2208kW (3000hp) from Kolomna 11D45 series engine
**Tractive effort:** 124kN (27,900lbf) at 47km/h (29.4mph)
**Max. operating speed:** 160km/h (100mph)
**Weight:** 129 tonnes (284,445lb)
**Overall Length:** 19.25m (62ft 10in)
**Gauge:** 1524mm (5ft)

## GE U25B VARIOUS RAILROADS USA 1960

General Electric had long been a producer of straight electric locomotives, a supplier of electrical components for diesel-electric locomotives, and a builder of small diesel locomotives for switching and industrial service. Until 1960, however, when it debuted its U25B road switcher, it had not directly competed in the American market for heavy freight locomotives. General Electric's Universal line began with the U25B, a four-motor heavy freight locomotive. It was powered by 7FDL-16 diesel engine, a design GE licensed from Cooper-Bessemer. With the U25B, GE established its place in the American market and in 1963 it introduced a six-motor road diesel, the U25C. One of the largest proponents of the GE's U25B was Southern Pacific, which had been looking for more powerful diesel locomotives.

**In the early 1980s, Maine Central acquired a small fleet of General Electric U25Bs from the defunct Rock Island.**

**Type:** Bo-Bo, diesel-electric
**Power and output:** General Electric 7FDL-16 producing 1863kW (2500hp)
**Tractive effort:** Various
**Max. operating speed:** Various
**Weight:** 118 tonnes (260,000lb)
**Overall length:** 18.339m (60ft 2in)
**Gauge:** 1435mm (4ft 8.5in)

## Class 212 BELGIAN RAILWAYS (SNCB) BELGIUM 1961

So useful were Belgium's class 212 diesels (later class 62) that a total of 231 were built. These conventional Bo-Bo diesel electrics had General Motors two-stroke diesel engines, intended for mid-range mixed-traffic duties. They were built by Brugeoise et Nivelles, and were used in multiples on heavy freight trains – singly on lighter freight and local passenger trains including push-pull workings from Antwerpen and Charleroi. In the 1980s, some were employed on passenger services between Liège and Luxembourg, and were fitted for electric train heating. Now being withdrawn, several have been sold to private operators in Holland and elsewhere. These include the prototype 212.001 (later 6391), retired in April 1999 after working from five separate motive power depots: Brussels (Schaerbeek), Kinkempois, Ronet, Alst and Merelbeke. The longevity of the class 212s, despite intensive usage, reflects the improvements in diesel technology from earlier years.

**Type:** Mixed-traffic main-line diesel-electric
**Wheel arrangement:** Bo-Bo
**Power:** GM 12-567C 12-cylinder V-form diesel, 1050kW (1405bhp), DC generator, four traction motors
**Tractive effort:** 212kN (47,660lbf)
**Max. operating speed:** 120km/h (75mph)
**Weight:** 79 tonnes (172,610lb)
**Overall length:** 16.79m (55ft 1in)
**Gauge:** Not known

## KRAUSS-MAFFEI DIESEL HYDRAULICS SOUTHERN PACIFIC — USA 1961

**Southern Pacific's first six Krauss-Maffei locomotives were traditional carbody units, such as 9000 pictured here. Later hydraulics were built as road switchers.**

In the early 1960s, Southern Pacific was looking for diesel locomotives with significantly greater output than available from domestic locomotive builders at that time. Southern Pacific was a heavy freight hauler facing rugged mountain grades on most of its principal routes. One solution to its power problem appeared to be diesel-hydraulic technology, so, in 1961, Southern Pacific and mountainous western carrier Denver & Rio Grande Western each imported three diesel-hydraulic locomotives from German manufacturer Krause-Maffei. These had an engine output of 2984kW (4000hp), with 2570kW (3450hp) available for traction. Two years later, SP imported a second batch of d-h locomotives, these in a road switcher configuration instead of the earlier carbody design. It also bought some experimental d-h units from Alco. By the late 1960s, SP gave up on d-h technology and turned to the latest high output diesel-electric designs.

**Type:** Co-Co, diesel-hydraulic
**Power and output:** A pair of Maybach 16-cylinder MD870 engines producing 2570kW (3450hp)
**Tractive effort:** 400kN (90,000lbf)
**Max. operating speed:** 112km/h (70mph)
**Weight:** 150 tonnes (330,600lb)
**Overall length:** 20.1m (66ft)
**Gauge:** 1435mm (4ft 8.5in)

## CLASS 55 'DELTIC' BRITISH RAILWAYS — GREAT BRITAIN 1961

The 22 'Deltic' Type 5 locomotives were British Railways' first diesel locomotives that were designed to operate at 160km/h (100mph). They replaced 55 Pacific steam locomotives on the East Coast main-line express passenger trains and became immediately popular among railway enthusiasts because of their lofty, streamlined noses and even more so because of their deep exhaust roar when accelerating. At 2460kW (3300bhp), the 'Deltics' were BR's most powerful diesels, not being outclassed in power throughout the life of BR and only equalled more than 20 years later

**In 1955, before ordering the production 'Deltics', the English Electric Company produced and demonstrated its prototype locomotive, often on regular passenger trains.**

by the classes 58 and 59 freight diesel locomotives.

Technically, the Napier 'Deltic' diesel engine, of which each locomotive had two, was a complex device, designed to produce high power from a compact size and low specific weight. In concept, the engine had three crankshafts arranged in triangular formation, which gave rise to the 'Deltic' nickname. Between each pair of crankshafts were six pairs of opposed pistons operating in six cylinders, 18 in all. They were two-stroke engines, originally designed for high-speed marine applications such as motor torpedo boats. Otherwise the locomotives were entirely conventional Co-Cos with six axle-hung traction motors on two three-axle bogies with compensation beams in their primary suspensions. Indeed, they shared their bogie design and traction motors with the class 37 locomotives, which were also designed by English Electric. Initially able to work only vacuum braked trains, the fleet was modified to operate both air and vacuum braked trains in the 1970s, ready for the allocation of air-braked Mark 2 passenger coaches to the East Coast main-line trains. At about the same time, the locomotives were fitted with generators to deliver electric train heat (ETH) supply. An odd feature of this equipment was that ETH was only delivered to the train when the diesel engines were idling, or when at full power; at intermediate speeds the voltage regulator cut off the ETH. This caused a number of problems with the carriage air-conditioning equipment cutting out when a train was not in a high-speed area.

**Not yet carrying its nameplates, this production 'Deltic' is forging northwards at Hadley Wood in April 1963 on an East Coast main line express.**

All the 'Deltics' were named, those on the Eastern Region after racehorses, the North Eastern and Scottish Region locomotives after army regiments. The locomotives originally appeared in Brunswick green livery with a lighter green strip along the base of the body. When brass nameplates were added, the centrally placed BR insignia was replaced by duplicate ones on the cab sides. Yellow warning panels followed from the early 1960s. The complete change to BR corporate blue with yellow nose ends came from 1965, a style which made the locomotives appear heavy. In fact, at 100 tonnes (22.057lb), they were lightweight mechanical race horses compared with other contemporary British diesel-electric classes.

Throughout their whole lives, they performed magnificently on the fastest trains between London and Newcastle, Edinburgh and Aberdeen and to Leeds and Hull. They were the only power rostered regularly for 'The Flying Scotsman' from their introduction in 1961 until the High Speed Trains took over from them in 1979. When the end came there were emotional scenes at London's King's Cross station. As the last 'Deltic'-hauled express reached the buffer stops, it was said that grown men cried and that some would never watch trains again.

A number of 55s have been preserved privately, and one is in the national collection; three preserved 'Deltics' are permitted to operate on Railtrack routes and thus appear on special trains from time to time, with running up to 150km/h (90mph) allowed.

**Type:** Express passenger main-line diesel-electric
**Wheel arrangement:** Co-Co
**Power:** Two Napier 'Deltic' D18.25 diesels with DC generators, totalling 2462kW (3300hp); six EE DC axle-hung traction motors
**Tractive effort:** 225kN (50,000lbf)
**Max. operating speed:** 160km/h (100mph)
**Weight:** 100 tonnes (221,760lb)
**Overall length:** 21.185m (69ft 6in)
**Gauge:** 1435mm (4ft 8.5in)

## EXPERIMENTAL GAS TURBINE GT3 BRITISH RAILWAYS — GREAT BRITAIN 1961

In its unusual brown livery, the 4-6-0 gas turbine locomotive No GT3 stands ready for service at the English Electric works.

A really unexpected concept for a modern gas turbine experimental locomotive was for GT3 to emerge on what looked like steam locomotive frames. English Electric was determined to demonstrate to BR the potential for this form of power to be coupled to mechanical drive for simplicity's sake. GT3 had a top speed of 145km/h (90mph) and was a powerful performer during trials over Shap incline. However, BR had opted for electrification and dieselization, and there was no place for turbines on UK railways.

**Type:** Experimental mixed-traffic gas turbine
**Wheel arrangement:** 2-C (4-6-0)
**Power:** EE EM27L 2014kW (2700hp) gas turbine; mechanical drive
**Coupled wheel diameter:** 1752mm (5ft 9in)
**Tractive effort:** 160kN (36,000lbf)
**Max. operating speed:** 145km/h (90mph)
**Weight:** 126 tonnes (276,640lb)
**Overall length:** 20.74m (68ft 1in)
**Gauge:** 1435mm (4ft 8.5in)

## 'HYMEK' CLASS 35 BRITISH RAILWAYS — GREAT BRITAIN 1961

**Type:** Mixed-traffic main-line diesel-hydraulic
**Wheel arrangement:** B-B
**Power:** Bristol-Siddeley/Maybach MD870 16-cylinder V-form diesel, 1270kW (1700bhp), Mekydro K184U torque converter and gearbox unit
**Tractive effort:** 205kN (46,600lbf)
**Max. operating speed:** 145km/h (90mph)
**Weight:** 75 tonnes (165,760lb)
**Overall length:** 15.76m (51ft 9in)
**Gauge:** 1435mm (4ft 8.5in)

Attractive styling brought the Beyer Peacock 'Hymek' (hydro-mechanical) Type 3 design of B-B locomotive to the attention of an admiring public. These 101 competent yet relatively small locomotives delivered 1270kW (1700bhp) from Maybach diesel engines to such effect that they coped manfully with working up to 13 coaches on London to South Wales expresses, their light weight enabling a greater load to be hauled. Initially liveried in standard

**A medium-sized locomotive that packed a bigger locomotive's punch, the Hymek had Maybach 1270kW (1700bhp) diesel engines and performed outstandingly on heavy South Wales expresses.**

Brunswick green with a light green lower bodyside band, and with off-white cab window surrounds, they looked less attractive when painted overall rail blue with yellow ends from 1965. Always allocated to the Western Region, which alone on BR promoted the use of diesel-hydraulic main-line traction, they lasted until the mid-1970s. By then the collapse of much of the freight railway made available surplus diesel-electrics such as classes 31 and 37. Being non-standard, the 'Hymeks' were withdrawn prematurely. A small number is preserved.

**This official photograph of No. D7000 illustrates well the attention to design detail by the BR Board's design panel, particularly the shape around the front ends and the driving cabs.**

## CLASS 52 BRITISH RAILWAYS — GREAT BRITAIN 1961

**Type:** Mixed-traffic main-line diesel-hydraulic
**Wheel arrangement:** C-C
**Power units (2):** Maybach MD655 V-form medium speed diesel 1005kW (1350hp); Voith L630rU three stage hydraulic torque converter; cardan shafts to adjacent bogie and between all wheelsets on bogie
**Tractive effort:** 310kN (70,000lbf)
**Max. operating speed:** 145km/h (90mph)
**Weight:** 110 tonnes (241,920lb)
**Overall length:** 20.725m (68ft)
**Gauge:** 1435mm (4ft 8.5in)

Building on the success of the 'Warship' classes 42 and 43 that had in turn been developed from the DB class V200, BR decided to invest in 74 more powerful diesel-hydraulics for top-line express passenger duties. Unlike the DB solution that put bigger engines in

**One of the seven privately restored 'Westerns' hauls a tourist train on a British preserved railway. This one is painted in BR's final livery (for this class) of rail blue with yellow ends.**

the same-sized locomotives, the 'Westerns' were stretched to C-C wheel arrangement. They had the same size power units as the DB class 221s, developing the same combined power of 2015kW (2700hp). With their maximum speed of 145km/h (90mph) and very high tractive effort, they were equally at home on express passenger and heavy freight services. Originally in BR Brunswick green livery, although there were some experimental colours, all were subsequently repainted maroon, before ultimately ending up in corporate BR blue with yellow ends. The last member was withdrawn by BR 1977, but seven are preserved.

## CLASS 121 BO-BO IRISH RAIL — IRELAND 1961

entered service in 1961 and have been used in main-line services for more than 40 years. In modern times a single 121 has been assigned to the Limerick-Limerick Junction push-pull shuttle. Others are used in freight services, including cement trains and seasonal sugar beet trains.

**Type:** Bo-Bo, diesel-electric
**Power and output:** EMD 8-567CR producing 652kW (875hp) for traction
**Tractive effort:** 156kN (35,000lbf) starting TE; 135kN (30,400lbf) continuous TE at 12.8km/h (8mph)
**Max. operating speed:** 123km/h (77mph)
**Weight:** 65 tonnes (143,325lbs)
**Overall length:** 12.141m (39ft 10in)
**Gauge:** 1600mm (5ft 3in)

**The class 121 Bo-Bo can still be seen in Ireland today, typically in freight services such as hauling cement or sugar beet trains.**

In 1960, Córas Iompair Éireann (Irish Transport Company) ordered its Class 121 Bo-Bo locomotives from US diesel builder Electro-Motive Division. In many respects the 121s were simply an adaptation of a standard American switcher design and in fact were closely based on EMD's SW9 switcher type. Among the differences with the 121 was a low-profile cab to accommodate the lower clearances in Ireland than in America, and a different bogie type. Fifteen 121s

**These locomotives have provided long and steady service in Ireland, particular on main-line services throughout the country.**

## C CLASS D235 ITALIAN STATE RAILWAYS (FS) — ITALY 1961

The 'C' wheel formation, equivalent to the steam-powered 0-6-0, was the standard for diesel-engined yard shunters on virtually all European railways. In Italy, in 1961, the bulk of shunting in non-electrified yards was still carried out by steam tank engines, but these were being withdrawn as new diesel types came into service. The FS introduced two 'C' diesel classes in this year, both with hydraulic transmission, supplied in the case of D235 by Voith of Heidenheim, Germany, with a single torque converter and two fluid couplers. The final reduction gearing provided two possible ratios, to be engaged while the locomotive was stationary: a lower one for shunting and a higher one for road work. D235, though with a lower power rating than D234, had lower gearing, smaller coupled wheels – 1070mm (42.2in) compared to 1310mm (51.5 in) – and a consequently higher tractive effort. The D234 could manage a higher speed on open track, with a maximum of 60km/h (37mph). These apparently minor differences were significant in operation, depending on requirements and conditions in the large freight yards. Trip workings between yards were more effective with the D234.

**Type:** Diesel-hydraulic shunting locomotive
**Power:** Diesel engine rated at 261.2kN (350hp) driving all axles via hydraulic transmission and coupling rods.
**Tractive effort:** 143.2kN (32,200lbf)
**Maximum operating speed:** 55km/h (34mph)
**Total weight:** 39 tonnes (85,995lb)
**Maximum axle load:** 13 tonnes (28,665lb)
**Overall length:** 9.54m (31ft 4in)
**Gauge:** Not known

# CP CLASS 1200 PORTUGUESE RAILWAYS PORTUGAL 1961

**Type:** Mixed-traffic main-line diesel-electric
**Wheel arrangement:** Bo-Bo
**Power unit:** MGO V 12ASHR 12-cylinder V-form diesel, 615kW (825bhp), DC generator, four traction motors
**Tractive effort:** 157kN (35,200lbf)
**Max. operating speed:** 80km/h (50mph)
**Weight:** 61tonnes (134,180lb)
**Overall length:** 14.68m (48ft 2in)
**Gauge:** 1668mm (5ft 6in)

Holidaymakers in the Algarve were very familiar with the 25 class 1200 Bo-Bo diesel electrics that worked most trains along the coastal railway. These French-designed hood units also worked local trains north to Beja, and passenger and trip workings around Porto, and from Barreiro south of the River Tejo (Tagus). Now displaced by the more powerful English Electric locomotives and diesel railcars, the '1200s' are scattered throughout Portugal on shunting duties. These low-powered machines were standard Brissonneau et Lotz locomotives, of which over 800 were built for French Railways (SNCF). In Portugal, they haul vacuum-braked stock, but cannot work in multiple. Liveried in blue when delivered, they spent most of their lives in the standard CP orange with white diagonal stripes across the ends. Now they are receiving the CP shunting locomotives' yellow style.

**Above: Seen here in its original dark blue livery, a 615kW (825bhp) Bo-Bo of class 1200 trundles a train of four-wheeled passenger cars near the western Portuguese coast.**

**Later, the CP orange livery was applied. This Bo-Bo waits a turn of duty at Tunes on the Algarve.**

## CLASS 17 'CLAYTON' BRITISH RAILWAYS GREAT BRITAIN 1962

**Type:** Mixed-traffic main-line diesel-electric
**Wheel arrangement:** Bo-Bo
**Power units (2):** Paxman 6ZHXL diesel, 670kW (900bhp), DC generator, four traction motors
**Tractive effort:** 178kN (40,000lbf)
**Max. operating speed:** 95km/h (60mph)
**Weight:** 69tonnes (152,320lb)
**Overall length:** 15.24m (50ft 7in)
**Gauge:** 1435mm (4ft 8.5in)

British Railway's preference for small locomotives continued into the 1960s. The Scottish and North Eastern Regions acquired 117 centre-cab Bo-Bo Type 1s, mainly for freight workings in coalfield areas. The 'Claytons' had two diesel engine–driven generator sets under low bonnets at each end of the locomotive. Electrical equipment was from Clayton (88 locomotives) and Crompton Parkinson. The central cab had two driving positions facing either possible direction of travel. These locomotives gained a reputation for unreliability. They were all withdrawn by 1971 after very short lives. One is preserved.

**The low bonnets of the Clayton Bo-Bos gave the drivers clear vision in either direction, but necessitated the Paxman diesel engines being fitted horizontally, an unusual arrangement in a main-line diesel locomotive.**

## CLASS 47 BRITISH RAILWAYS GREAT BRITAIN 1962

**Type:** Mixed-traffic main-line diesel-electric
**Wheel arrangement:** Co-Co
**Power unit:** Sulzer 12LDA28C 12-cylinder twin-bank diesel, 2050kW (2750bhp) reduced to 1925kW (2580bhp); Brush DC generator and six axle-hung DC traction motors
**Tractive effort:** 265kN (60,000lbf)
**Max. operating speed:** 150 to 160km/h (95 to 100mph)
**Weight:** 111 to 125 tonnes (243,765 to 274,510lb)
**Overall length:** 19.355m (63ft 6in)
**Gauge:** 1435mm (4ft 8.5in)

There has never been a more widely useful and adaptable locomotive type in the United Kingdom than the Brush class 47 Co-Co diesel electrics. Equally at home on 145km/h (90mph) express trains as on heavy oil tank trains, the class 47 could be seen anywhere between Penzance and Aberdeen, and Ramsgate and Holyhead or Glasgow. Their success justified construction of 512 locomotives, by far the largest class numerically of non-steam main-line locomotives ever operated in the United Kingdom. Introduced in 1962, the class 47s were among the more powerful diesels on BR. Their Brush traction equipment enabled them to exert high tractive effort, thus improving the acceleration performance of express trains, as well as enabling the haulage of acceptably heavy freights. They took over the top link passenger work on the Western Region (shared with class 52), on the BR cross-country routes and in Scotland. On the East Coast main line, they backed up the 'Deltic' fleet, and they performed reliably on overnight sleeping car trains between London King's Cross, Edinburgh and Aberdeen. Other 47s worked coal trains, for which

**Here, a class 47 no. 47738 pulls into Oxford station. The class 47s were the most numerous diesel locomotives to ever operate in the United Kingdom.**

many were modified with slow speed control for automated loading and unloading of 'merry-go-round' wagons. They were the staple power for the growing oil train network across the United Kingdom. They also became the regular traction for container trains, part of the burgeoning network of Freightliner Limited.

Inside a class 47 was the familiar Sulzer twin-crankshaft 12-cylinder diesel engine driving Brush main and auxiliary generators, a steam heating boiler and a copious radiator bank. The six traction motors were axle-hung, nose-suspended. Five locomotives were delivered in the mid-1960s with Sulzer V-form engines of type 12LVA24 engines of 1975kW (2650hp). These non-standard diesel engines were subsequently replaced by standard ones.

The maximum speed of 150km/h (95mph) was exceeded only when 16 locomotives were equipped for the Scottish Region InterCity push-pull services between Glasgow, Edinburgh, Aberdeen and Inverness. These 47/7s were uplifted for 160km/h (100mph) running. Many locomotives on InterCity Cross-Country services received larger fuel tanks, thus extending their operating range. This modification utilized the redundant steam heating water tanks.

In recent times, the class has dwindled in the face of newer forms of passenger train and the influx of new, specially built freight diesel locomotives from General Motors of Canada. The last principal class 47 passenger workings were among the First Great Western and Virgin CrossCountry services. There are now very few regular passenger duties for them, other than in emergencies.

When built, the locomotives were liveried in overall Brunswick green with a pleasant mid-green band around the centre of the bodysides. They later received the standard rail blue. In the 1980s and 1990s, the different BR businesses painted them in their own colours, but it is in the privatized Virgin red with white stripes that many will prefer to remember them. A small fleet of locomotives is operated now by Fragonset Limited on a spot hire basis. These are black with smart maroon lining edged in gold Withdrawals of 47s are proceeding apace; a few are being re-engined with General Motors engines and Brush alternators extracted from withdrawn class 56s, being reclassified class 57 and extending their lives by up to 15 years. They work Freightliner trains; others are high-speed train rescue units.

**Two class 47s owned by EWS are the pride of the modern fleet – 47 798 and 47 799 are the official Royal engines, named 'Prince William' and 'Prince Henry', respectively.**

**Much modified during their long and very useful lives, several class 47s were fitted with larger fuel tanks for InterCity passenger work. The 47 829 seen here is on a Virgin train.**

## WDM-2 INDIAN RAILWAYS — INDIA 1962

**Type:** Co-Co diesel-electric
**Power:** 1914kW (2600hp) from Alco 16-251 series engine
**Tractive effort:** 241kN (54,120lbf) at 18km/h (11.3mph)
**Max. operating speed:** 120km/h (75mph)
**Weight:** 113 tonnes (249,165lb)
**Overall length:** 17.120m (55ft 10in)
**Gauge:** 1676mm (5ft 6in)

Indian Railways began the large-scale acquisition of diesels with 100 class WDM1 imports from Alco in 1958–59. Introduced to India Railways in 1962, class WDM2 units were first imported as complete locomotives from Alco, with production taken over locally later. The Diesel Locomotive Works (DLW) at Varanasi was established in 1961, producing the first-class WDM2 in early 1964. After the first few Alco model RSD29 units to specification DL560C arrived complete, a further 12 were supplied to DLW in completely knocked-down kit form for local assembly. Following the kit, DLW went on to produce WDM2 until the total reached around 2700.

DLW has produced a number of different versions for Indian railways as well as export units. Earlier units have 298kW (405hp) GE 752 traction motors – later locally supplied motors of 320kW

**A Northern Railway of India WDM2 clearly showing off its North American Alco heritage with its squared-off driving cab lines and three-axle bogies (trucks) equipped with substantial equalization beams, but looking quite un-American with round side buffers and centre coupling hook.**

**A WDM2 at work in typical setting on a passenger train passing semaphore signals indicating the substantial British railway heritage in India.**

(435hp). Road numbers are not in numerical order of construction, but the first machine imported from Alco was 18040 and the first to be built by DLW was 18233. Class WDM2A were modified with air train braking equipment after entry into service while class WDM2B had this from new. WDM2C was a modification carried out by DCW Patiala with a GE turbocharger, Woodward governor, and roller bearing suspension, the last-mentioned change to overcome one of the weakest points of the design.

Under a recent new locomotive classification system new WDM2C conversions are now WDM3A. (Confusingly, there is another series of WDM2C which are newly built with 2281kW (3100hp) engines. These are numbered in the 14000 series.) DCW Patiala is also modifying some units with alternating current traction alternators replacing the direct current main generator. Class WDM2s modified for push-pull passenger work are described as class WDM2D. A number of class WDM2s constructed in the late 1970s have a different body style, with the short hood of full width. These are in the high 17000 number range and are known to train crew as 'Jumbo'. Another variation, a local modification, is a cab repositioned right forward at one end involving relocating items of equipment such as the dynamic brake resistor grid behind the new cab. Aside from these alterations, the majority of class WDM2s feature both short and long high hood sections either side of the driving cab in traditional early North American road switcher styling.

Class WDM7 is a lighter, lower power version designed for branch-line operation and is numbered in the 11000 series. Only 15 were built in the late 1980s and are 1492kW (2000hp) with the 12-cylinder Alco 12-251 rather than the 16-cylinder 1914kW (2600hp) 16-251 of class WDM2, and 100km/h (62.5mph) maximum speed instead of 120km/h (75mph). The last five WDM7s were built new with traction alternators with 105km/h (65.6mph) maximum speed, and all class WDM7 are now generally used on shunting duties. Quite simply with such a large quantity built and in service, class WDM2s may be found throughout the subcontinent as the default motive power for freight, with many passenger workings. The DLW factory and India railways depots seem likely to continue to improve, modify and alter the basic type.

## C-C TYPE TG400 SOVIET STATE RAILWAYS — RUSSIA 1962

Despite the Cold War, Soviet railways took two high-power hydraulic transmission prototypes from Germany. TG400 from Henschel was the larger and more powerful, with two Maybach MD870 engines. TG400-01 can be considered as technically equivalent to the Krauss Maffei units delivered to the United States for Southern Pacific and Denver & Rio Grande.

**Type:** C-C diesel-hydraulic prototype
**Power:** 2944kW (4000hp)
**Tractive effort:** 303kN (68,200lbf) at 20kmh
**Max. operating speed:** 160kmh (100mph)
**Weight:** 112 tonnes (246,960lb)
**Overall length:** 22.98m (75ft)
**Gauge:** 1524mm (5ft)

## C-C TYPE (TG300) SOVIET STATE RAILWAYS — RUSSIA 1962

The second German prototype, the TG300, was built by MaK to a design by Deutz. Lighter and less powerful, the TG300-01 had two Maybach MD655 12-cylinder engines, compared to 16 cylinders in TG400, and Voith transmissions. TG300 was technically similar to the six-axle V200 derivations exported to Spain.

**Type:** C-C diesel-hydraulic prototype
**Power:** 2208kW (3000hp) from two Maybach MD655 series engines
**Tractive effort:** 187kN (42,020lbf) at 22.8km/h (14.3mph)
**Max. operating speed:** 140km/h (87mph)
**Weight:** 109 tonnes (24,030lb)
**Overall length:** 22060mm (72ft 0in)
**Gauge:** 1524mm (5ft 0in)

## CLASS 352 B-B SPANISH RAILWAYS (RENFE) — SPAIN 1962

The Spanish Railways RENFE class 352 locomotives are a special design for Talgo haulage. Developed in Spain, Tren Articuldao Ligero Goicoechea Oriol (Talgo) were lightweight articulated passenger cars, developed by Goicoechea and backed by Oriol from as early as 1942.

Known as 2000T trains, class 352 used German know-how in a lightweight, single-cab, low-profile machine matching the passengers cars.

Built in two batches by Krauss Maffei of Germany and Babcock & Wilcox in Spain, the 10 locomotives have Maybach engines and Mekydro transmissions. The contemporary 2000T cars are each 11.1m (36ft 3in) long, operated in 10- or 15-car sets.

Initial services were between Madrid and Irun/Hendaye, Barcelona, Bilbao and Seville. Services further expanded in 1968, joined by T3000 sets and double-ended class 353s, which had 1650kW (2242hp) engines and were capable of 180km/h (112.5mph). Electrification and high-speed (AVE) routes gradually eroded the need for Talgo diesels and had been expected to eliminate them altogether by 2001. Into 2002, however, three 352s and two 353s were in use on daily services from Madrid.

**The semi streamlined cab of the class 352 and exceptionally low profile matching the rakes of rolling stock of the special Talgo hauling units are unmistakable and unique to Spanish Railways.**

**Type:** B-B diesel-hydraulic Talgo
**Power:** 2200kW (2990hp) from two Maybach MD655 engines
**Tractive effort:** 173kN (39,000lbf)
**Max. operating speed:** 140kmh (87mph)
**Weight:** 74 tonnes (163,170lb)
**Overall length:** 17.45m (56ft 11in)
**Gauge:** 1676mm (5ft 6in)

## EMD GP30 VARIOUS RAILROADS USA 1962

In the late 1950s and 1960s, North American locomotive manufacturers kept upping the horsepower output of their top performing diesels in what has been commonly described as a horsepower race. In 1959, the 1492kW (2000hp) GP20 superseded the 1306kW (1750hp) GP9, then, in 1961, the 1679kW (2250hp) GP30 superseded the GP20. The GP30 was in production for just two years when it was replaced by the 1865kW (2500hp) GP35.

The EMD GP30's distinctive appearance set it apart from other road switchers. It featured a semi-streamlined cab with a hood extension reaching over the top. GP30s were ordered in both high-nose and low-nose variations, as well as a cabless, GP30B type which was used by Union Pacific.

Although they were built for fast freight use, in later years, many GP30s were assigned to local freight service.

**Type:** Bo-Bo, diesel-electric
**Power and output:** EMD 16-567D3 producing 1676kW (2250hp)
**Tractive effort:** 227 kN (51,000 lbf) at 19.2km/h (12 mph)
**Max. operation speed:** 105km/h (65mph)
**Weight:** 118 tonnes (260,000 lb)
**Overall length:** 17.12m (56ft 2in)
**Gauge:** 1435mm (4ft 8.5in)

**A pair of Rio Grande GP30s switch at Denver's North Yard in September 1998. The GP30 is characterized by the hood extension over the top of the cab.**

## CLASS 04 BO-BO BULGARIAN STATE RAILWAYS (BDZ) BULGARIA 1963

Bulgarian state railways (BDZ) class 04 is a twin-engined diesel-hydraulic type imported from Austria. Based on the one-off prototype of 1959, 50 units were delivered to Bulgaria from 1963. The prototype was ÖBB number 2020.01 – preserved today outside Wien Sud station in Vienna after withdrawal in 1980.

The BDZ units were the first main-line diesels in service, and they were used throughout the Bulgarian system on freight and passenger services, but were gradually withdrawn throughout the 1990s.

**Type:** B-B diesel-hydraulic
**Power:** 1620kW (2200hp) from two SGP T12 series engines
**Tractive effort:** 187kN (42,000lbf)
**Max. operating speed:** 120kmh (75mph)
**Weight:** 82 or 83.5 tonnes (180,810lb or 184,118lb)
**Overall length:** 18.24m (59ft 6in)
**Gauge:** 1435mm (4ft 8.5in)

## CLASSES 68000 AND 68500 FRENCH NATIONAL RAILWAYS (SNCF) FRANCE 1963

**The classes 68000 and 68500 were given heavily stylized exteriors with flashy treatment of the ventilation grilles and white lining bands. The body colour was pale green.**

For many decades, the railways of France have given priority to main-line electrification schemes. The earlier main-line diesels that were bought by SNCF were mainly to permit electric-hauled freight and passenger trains to be shunted off the main lines, to be handled in non-wired marshalling yards or to be worked along secondary or minor branch lines at slower speeds. For these duties, low-powered Bo-Bo diesel electrics were acquired in the 1950s. These were unsuitable for true main-line work such as long express passenger trains at 75mph (120km/h) or more, or freight in heavy volumes. On non-electrified main and secondary lines, SNCF's fleet of powerful and relatively advanced steam locomotives were still up to the principal haulage jobs, although proving unpopular and expensive to maintain. It was only when the eventual size of the electrified network became clear, and the need to dispose of steam locomotive operation became pressing, that batches of larger main-line diesels were contemplated. The purchase of anything like large numbers of main-line diesel locomotives only came about in the early 1960s.

Among the largest diesel locomotives at that time were the class 68000 and the very similar 68500 series. Over 100 were supplied, more than 80 of these being the Sulzer-engined '68000s', the more powerful '68500s' having AGO engines; otherwise the two classes are identical. They were built by five different manufacturers: CAFL, CEM, Sulzer, SACM and Fives-Lille-Cail. Unlike later French diesel-electrics (which are of the *monomoteur* type with one traction motor on each bogie), these locomotives have traction motors on the outer axles on each bogie producing the A1A-A1A wheel arrangement. The locomotives were originally fitted with train heating boilers and intended for mixed-traffic duties. More recently, the spread of electrification and electric train heating has rendered this equipment redundant, and it has been removed. The locomotives are thus now restricted to heavy freight work. Their area of operation extends from Normandy and Brittany to central France on the Rouen – Le Mans – Tours route and across the eastern part of the country between Paris, Troyes and Belfort, with some duties in the Vosges mountains. On these routes their presence has been threatened by incursions of the larger CC72000 locomotives, which have been displaced by the electrification of the main line through the Massif Central, and withdrawals are proceeding.

In appearance, the classes 68000 and 68500 are heavily stylized at the front ends and with a large arrow formation surrounding the bodyside equipment room grilles. Lining out is with two white lines at one end and one at the other, which gives the end views different aspects when seen approaching. The French diesel locomotive fleet has remained relatively stable since the 1960s construction phase. Nothing new has appeared since 1975, and so the fleet generally is ageing fast. Replacement is now on SNCF's agenda, but the final choice of replacements is as yet unknown.

**Type:** Mixed-traffic main-line diesel-electric
**Wheel arrangement:** A1A-A1A
**Power:** Sulzer 12LVA24 12-cylinder V-form diesel, 1950kW (2615bhp) class 68000, AGO 12DSHR 12-cylinder V-form diesel, 1985kW (2660bhp) class 68500; DC generator; four DC traction motors
**Tractive effort:** 298kN (66,995lbf)
**Max. operating speed:** 130km/h (80mph)
**Weight:** 102 to 104 tonnes (224,000 to 228,400lb)
**Overall length:** 17.91m (58ft 9in)
**Gauge:** 1435mm (4ft 8.5in)

## CLASS X4300 FRENCH NATIONAL RAILWAYS (SNCF) FRANCE 1963

These conventional diesel multiple units became France's standard trains for local services on non-electrified routes. Each power car has one underfloor diesel engine driving a six-speed mechanical gearbox linked to the axles on one bogie. The time that is necessary for each gear change, particularly while in the lower gears, makes for

**A two-car set of the lumbering but nonetheless popular standard diesel railcars of SNCF. This large fleet is now beginning to be withdrawn from service, displaced by modern railcars capable of much higher performance.**

slow acceleration. Nonetheless, nearly 900 of these units and later derivatives were built, a testimony to their general usefulness. They work almost all over France, except in the southwest. Most were originally liveried in the standard SNCF railcar colour scheme of red and cream, but several have since received the colours of local authorities who give financial support to local rail services.

**Type:** Diesel multiple unit 2-car set
**Power:** Poyaud or Saurer horizontal diesel engine, 320kW (430hp); fluid flywheel; six-speed epicyclic gearbox; cardan shaft to gearbox on axle
**Max. operating speed:** 120km/h (75mph)
**Weight:** 35 to 36 tonnes (76,850 to 79,060lb) power cars; 23 tonnes (50,510lb) trailers
**Overall length:** 21.24m (69ft 8in)
**Gauge:** 1435mm (4ft 8.5in)

## CLASS M61 HUNGARIAN STATE RAILWAYS (MÁV) HUNGARY 1963

When Hungarian industry could not respond to the need for main-line diesel locomotives, MÁV ordered 20 Co-Cos from Nohab in Sweden. These were an uprated version of the type described in this book as SNCB class 202. They worked express trains to the south out of Budapest Deli station. With increasing electrification, they are spending their last years based at Tapolca depot working passenger trains in the area to the west of Lake Balaton.

**Painted in MÁV's bright red livery reserved for diesels, the class M61 Co-Cos looked impressive with their streamlined outline.**

**Type:** Mixed-traffic main-line diesel-electric
**Wheel arrangement:** Co-Co
**Power:** GM 16-567D1 16-cylinder V-form two-stroke diesel, 1435kW (1925bhp); DC generator; six axle-hung DC traction motors
**Tractive effort:** 198kN (44,510lbf)
**Max. operating speed:** 105km/h (65mph)
**Weight:** 106 tonnes (232,785lb)
**Overall length:** 18.9m (62ft)
**Gauge:** 1435mm (4ft 8.5in)

## ALCO C-420 VARIOUS RAILROADS USA 1963

In the early 1960s, Alco brought out its new Century line in an effort to compete more effectively with new locomotives offered by EMD and GE. The C-420 was a road switcher designed for freight or passenger service, similar to the 1492kW (2000hp) RS-32 that it effectively replaced. A longer low hood than other Century types quickly identifies most C-420s. Long Island Rail Road had a fleet of high-nose C-420s, which closely resembled Alco RS-11save for minor styling attributes and air intake placement.

**Type:** Co-Co, diesel-electric
**Power and output:** Alco 12-cylinder 251C producing 1492kW (2000hp)
**Tractive effort:** N/A
**Max. operating speed:** N/A
**Weight:** N/A
**Overall Length:** N/A
**Gauge:** 1435mm (4ft 8.5in)

**Long Island bought C-420s for passenger service. One of the Long Island Rail Road's unusual high-hood C-420s seen in work train service on Metro-North at Waterbury, Connecticut.**

## GE U50C UNION PACIFIC — USA 1963

Union Pacific, well known for its extraordinarily large and powerful locomotives, experimented with very large double-diesels in the 1960s. General Electric supplied two varieties.

The first were U50s (sometimes described as U50Ds), which rode on four sets of Bo trucks in a Bo-Bo+Bo-Bo arrangement like that of Union Pacific's early gas-electric turbines. These were built between 1963 and 1965. The later locomotives used a more common Co-Co wheel arrangement and were built between 1969 and 1971.

Both the U50 and the U50C delivered 3730kW (5000hp); however, while the earlier locomotives used a pair of 7FDL-16 diesels, the U50Cs used smaller 7FDL-12 engines.

All of these big GEs possessed unusually tall cabs with almost no nose section, marking them as especially odd in the annals of American dieseldom.

**Type:** Co-Co, diesel-electric
**Power and output:** A pair of 7FDL-12 diesel engines producing 3730kW (5000hp)
**Tractive effort:** N/A
**Max. operating speed:** N/A
**Weight:** N/A
**Overall length:** 24.079m (79 ft)
**Gauge:** 1435mm (4ft 8.5in)

## CLASS 2043 AND 2143 AUSTRIAN STATE RAILWAYS (ÖBB) — AUSTRIA 1964

**Type:** Mixed-traffic main-line diesel-hydraulic
**Wheel arrangement:** B-B
**Power:** Jenbach LM1500 (class 2043) or SGP T12c (2143) V-form diesel, 1100kW (1475bhp); Voith L830 rU2 torque converter; cardan shafts to gearboxes on axles
**Tractive effort:** 197kN (44,285lbf)
**Max. operating speed:** 100 to 110km/h (63 to 69 mph)
**Weight:** 68 tonnes (149,335lb)
**Overall length:** 14.76 to 15.8m (48ft 5in to 51ft 10in)
**Gauge:** 1435mm (4ft 8.5in)

About 160 of these useful if modestly sized mixed traffic locomotives are employed on non-electrified secondary routes. They are single-engined diesel hydraulics, and, until the current deliveries of class 2016, they were the most powerful diesels in Austria. The two classes were built by Jenbach (class 2043) and SGP ('2143'). In configuration, they are full-body-width twin-cab locomotives. They are liveried in the standard ÖBB red with cream band around the base of the bodysides and ends, and with dark grey surrounds to the cab windows. They used to undertake one international duty, namely the route from Innsbruck via Brennero to San Candido and Lienz, entailing a section of travel in Italy. Four class 2043s were modified with magnetic track brakes for the now closed Leoben to Hieflau route.

**Smart and compact, this class 2043 Bo-Bo heads a regional service of low-profile carriages, typical of lighter mixed traffic work units.**

## CLASS 749 BO-BO CZECH RAILWAYS (CD) — CZECH REPUBLIC 1964

Following 1964 prototypes, production from 1967 of these Bo-Bo mixed-traffic units ran to a total of 312 by 1970. T478 1001 and 1002 (751001 and 751002, retained as operational museum items) were built by CKD using its 310mm (12.13in) bore six-cylinder in-line four-stroke engine.

Specified to equal class 475.1 and 477.0 steam locomotives, the simple design was successful. Originally T478.1s were steam heated for mixed-traffic work and T478.2 without heat for freight. The series has become muddled in recent years. 296 units were operating with CSD computer numbers 751 and 752, Czech Railways taking 145 and 81, and Slovak 43 and 27. ZSR machines are unaltered, but CD equipped 60 from 1992 with electric train heating with modified 751s and 752s becoming 749s. On both systems, the type is outliving newer 753s, as the latter are less reliable.

**Type:** Bo-Bo diesel-electric
**Power:** 1102kW (1500hp) from CKD K6S310DR series engine
**Tractive effort:** 185kN (41,624lbf)
**Max. operating speed:** 100km/h (62.1mph)
**Weight:** 75 tonnes (165,375lb)
**Overall length:** 16.5m (54ft 2in)
**Gauge:** 1435mm (4ft 8.5in)

## Co-Co DJIBOUTI-ADDIS ABABA RAILWAY (CFE) ETHIOPIA 1964

The CFE's first postwar diesel locomotives had been 12 twin-unit A1A-A1A types from SLM in 1951, acquired to supplement its stock of around 65 steam locomotives. By the time these two Alsthom Co-Cos were delivered in 1964 and 65, diesel power monopolized the services and the remaining steam locomotives were in store. Of the CFE's 25 main-line diesels, these were the most powerful to run on this metre-gauge line, their services required by a steady increase in freight traffic. When fully loaded with fuel, they stretched the line's maximum axle loading to the limit.

The CFE posed difficulties for diesel operation, rising to 2470m (8105ft) at Addis Ababa from sea level at Djibouti, through a possible temperature range from 0°C to 43°C, and from a maximum humidity of 96 per cent on the coast to the aridity and dust storms of the interior. Alsthom had considerable experience of building locomotives for hot conditions, having supplied 1864kW (2500hp) CC diesels for Mauritania with special anti-sandstorm protection and built Bo-Bo and Bo-Bo-Bo types for Burma. On the CFE engines this showed itself in such external details as the inwards-sloping anti-glare windscreens.

Politics and warfare made operations very difficult in the last decade of the 20th century, and the railway, which is currently being refurbished with French aid, has only 13 locomotives.

**Type:** Diesel-electric freight locomotive
**Power:** 16-cylinder PA 4 Chantiers de l'Atlantique diesel engine, rated at 1343.3kW (1800hp) and delivering 189.3kN (42,560lb) at 17km/h (10.6mph)
**Tractive effort:** 259kN (58,240lb)
**Maximum operating speed:** 70km/h (43mph)
**Total weight:** 86.3 tonnes (190,320lb)
**Maximum axle load:** 14.4 tonnes (31,752lb)
**Overall length:** 17.398m (56ft 9in)
**Builder:** Alsthom, France
**Gauge:** Not known

## Dv12 FINNISH STATE RAILWAYS (VR) FINLAND 1964

**Here, a Finnish State Railways Dv12 shunts empty cargo wagons in Oulu, Finland.**

Dv12s are very versatile. They have two gear ratios and are used in both freight and passenger service. It is common practice to run them in multiple sets of two or three locomotives.

**Type:** Mixed-traffic diesel-hydraulic
**Power and output:** Tampella-MGO V16 BSHR producing 1000kW (1360hp)
**Tractive effort:** N/A
**Max. Operating speed:** 85km/h (53mph) in freight service; 125km/h (78mph) in passenger service
**Weight:** 60.8 tonnes (134,064lb)
**Overall length:** 14m (45ft 11in)
**Gauge:** 1524mm (5 ft)

(Statistics based on 2501 series)

The most numerous type of diesel on Finnish State Railways (VR) are the Dv12 types. These were built over a 20-year span beginning in 1964. The production was split between two different companies, with some locomotives built by Lokomo and others by Valmet. There are three different series: 2501–2568; 2601–2664; and 2701–2760, with minor differences between them. All use a Tempella 16-cylinder diesel engine (a French design built in Finland under licence) and a Voith L216rs hydraulic transmission.

Originally known as Sv12, the locomotive model designation was changed to Dv12 in 1976. The

**With their distinctive box-shaped noses and redand-white livery, the Dv12 harks back to the golden age of diesel.**

## CLASS 290 FEDERAL GERMAN RAILWAYS (DB) GERMANY 1964

These class 290 powerful diesel-hydraulic shunting locomotives in their smart red livery can be seen at freight yards all over Germany, particularly in the western part of the country.

German freight trains still include many that require remarshalling at key points on the network. Large marshalling yards with humps for splitting up arriving trains use heavy class 290 diesel hydraulics to propel the trains slowly over the humps, from where the wagons are distributed among the sidings to form trains for different destinations. The class 290 uses a similar layout to the class V80 described earlier in this book.

**Type:** Diesel-hydraulic shunting locomotive
**Wheel arrangement:** B-B
**Power:** MTU MB 16V 6652 TA 10, 16-cylinder V-form medium speed, 820kW (1100hp); Voith L206rs hydraulic transmission
**Tractive effort:** 241kN (54,180lbf)
**Max. operating speed:** 70 to 80km/h (45 to 50 mph)
**Weight:** 77 to 79 tonnes (169,100 to 173,050lb)
**Overall length:** 14 to 14.32m (45ft 11in to 47ft)
**Gauge:** 1435mm (4ft 8.5in)

## CLASS 14 BRITISH RAILWAYS GREAT BRITAIN 1964

**Type:** Freight main-line diesel-hydraulic
**Wheel arrangement:** C (0-6-0)
**Power:** Paxman Ventura 6YJX six-cylinder diesel 485kW (650bhp), Voith L217U torque converter, jackshaft, external coupling rods
**Tractive effort:** 137kN (30,910lbf)
**Max. operating speed:** 65km/h (40mph)
**Weight:** 51 tonnes (112,000lb)
**Overall length:** approx. 11m (36ft)
**Gauge:** 1435mm (4ft 8.5in)

From 1964, Swindon workshops surprisingly produced 57 Type 1 C (0-6-0) freight diesel-hydraulics. At that time shunting and transfer work was shrinking. The rigid-framed diesels were similar to the DB class V60 shunting locomotives. Numbered only in the D9500 series, the short-lived class had disappeared from BR by 1971.

The shortest-lived of all the BR main-line diesel classes were the Swindon-built C (0-6-0) diesel-hydraulics. They were withdrawn before any could have their new class 14 numbers applied.

## CHME3 SOVIET STATE RAILWAYS RUSSIA 1964

Built by Ceskemoravkse Kolben Danek (CKD) in Praha for Soviet railways, the ChME3 is the world's most numerous single-unit diesel: 7454 units were built before the break-up of the Soviet Union. The three T669.0 prototypes were CSD T669.001 (preserved by CD) and SZD ChME3 001 and 002, the first preserved in St Petersburg. The engine was the robust CKD 310mm (12.2in) bore six-cylinder of the same 993kW (1200hp) rating as the Bryansk-built TEM2 model produced in parallel. The Czech engine is more reliable than Soviet ones and has been used to repower some TEM1 units. ChME3 subtypes include the updated ChME3T with electric braking and the ChME3E as ChME3T without electric brake. ChME3B is a switcher-slug set with the slug's rebuilt TE10 frames for slow-speed shunting. More recently twin ChME3 switcher sets have been created.

**Type:** Co-Co diesel-electric heavy shunter
**Power:** 993kW (1350hp) from CKD K6S310DR series engine
**Tractive effort:** 226kN (50850lbf) at 11.4kmh (7.1mph)
**Max. operating speed:** 95kmh (59.4mph)
**Weight:** 123 tonnes (271,215lb)
**Overall length:** 17.22m (56ft 2in)
**Gauge:** 1524mm (5ft)

# CLASS 73 BRITISH RAILWAYS GREAT BRITAIN 1965

**This pair of class 73 electro-diesels is in BR's InterCity livery. Several of this class were dedicated to the push-pull Gatwick Express airport service.**

How do you run electric-hauled freight trains into goods yards that, for safety, cannot have overhead wires or third rails in them? Answer: use electro-diesels. The concept is simple. BR Southern Region designed a DC electric locomotive with components common to EMUs and included in it a modest diesel power unit like that in their DEMUs. A class 73 electro-diesel locomotive could operate in a yard as a low-speed diesel-electric locomotive and, when it reached the main line, it could switch off the diesel and become a more powerful straight electric locomotive. In total, 49 were built: 6 prototypes and the rest as a production batch for the Bournemouth electrification scheme and to eliminate steam from the SR. The details are for the production batch.

**Another duty of the class 73s was to power the Weymouth/Channel Islands boat trains between London Waterloo and Bournemouth, such as this one in full Network SouthEast livery.**

**Type:** Mixed-traffic main-line electro-diesel
**Wheel arrangement:** Bo-Bo
**Power:** English Electric 750V DC camshaft control electric traction equipment, four traction motors, 1195kW (1600hp); 4SRKT four-cylinder in-line vertical diesel engine, 450kW (600bhp); DC generator
**Tractive effort:** 180kN (40,000lbf) electric mode; 160kN (36,000lbf) diesel mode
**Max. operating speed:** 145km/h (90mph); some reduced since to 95km/h (60mph)
**Weight:** 77 tonnes (170,240lb)
**Overall length:** 16.36m (53ft 8in)
**Gauge:** 1435mm (4ft 8.5in)

## CLASS M62 CO-CO HUNGARIAN STATE RAILWAYS (MÁV) HUNGARY 1965

Known variously as 'Sergei', 'Gagarin', 'Iwan', 'Taiga trommel', 'Wummen' or 'Mashka', well over 2000 M62s were exported from Soviet Russia to eastern Europe. Into 2002, few remain at work. After the break-up of the Iron Curtain and the decline in freight traffic that followed, the M62s (high on fuel and lubricating oil consumption) were early targets for withdrawal. German railways (DB) ended Class 220 work in 1994, but by 2000 there were more than 50 other M62s in service with private operators. Hungary (MÁV) retains the highest number, although declining – a life extension programme will see many survive past 2010. Activity in the Czech Republic (CD) has all but ceased while Slovakia (ZSR) retains them only as snowploughs. Poland has fewer than 100 operable, with activity expected to cease in 2002.

In the region of the former Soviet Union, M62s are in normal traffic, being of more recent construction than the export units. Even today, the Ukraine factory still offers new M62s, most recently for Iran. All are built in Lugansk, known at the beginning of M62 production as *'Luganskii Teplovozostroitel'nyi Zavod imeni Oktyabr'skoi Revolyutsii'* or 'October Revolution Locomotive works'. Two 1962 prototypes numbered M62-01 and M62-02 were designated M62S in SZD stock, and M62-01 survives today in the St Petersburg museum collection. The Kolomna 14D40 engine is a two-stroke 12-cylinder V type of 230mm (9in) bore 300mm (11.8in) driving a DC generator supplying six permanent parallel motors. Control is by 15 notches increasing engine speed from 400rpm idle to 750rpm in even steps. Outside temperature operating range is –30° to +35°C.

Deliveries through the 1960s and 1970s targeted steam traction, and, as heavy freight units capable of heavy loads, M62s went to the more industrialized regions, cascading as electrification progressed. Early production was without silencing, the noise produced giving rise to the nickname *'taiga trommel'*, meaning 'drum of the taiga (northern steppe)'. Standard-gauge M62s are fitted with European screw couplings and side buffers. Russian-gauge are fitted with Soviet SA3 centre couplers. None is fitted with train heating. A total of 2479 M62s were exported between 1965 and 1979: Hungary 288 for MAV (270 standard gauge, 18 broad gauge) and GySEV six; Czechoslovakia CSD 601 (574 standard 25 broad) and two for industry; Poland PKP 1182 (1114 standard and 68 broad) and industry nine; GDR 378 and 18 for industry.

Low axle weight relative to other Soviet domestic types made the M62 design attractive for SZD's own use for secondary routes with a lighter permanent way, carrying ever increasing freight traffic. An updated M62U series was devised to extend working ranges with bigger fuel tanks and increased sand supplies. Temperature operating ranges were extended to –50° to +45°C to meet the extremes of Soviet conditions.

Production for SZD was at least 723 M62s, 1261 2M62s, 389 2M62Us and 104 3M62Us, totals being complicated by industrial batches. Military locomotives include 41 M62UPs and nine 3M62UPs. M62UP was the motive power for rail launched SS-24 'Scalpel' intercontinental ballistic missiles deployed from 1989. The 3M62UP is used for hauling the Russian space shuttle starting towers at the Baikonur space port (in today's Kazakhstan). M62s also went to other countries under Soviet influence, including North Korea, Mongolia and Cuba.

**Type:** Co-Co diesel-electric freight
**Power:** 1492kW (2000hp) from Kolomna 14D40 series engine
**Tractive effort:** 196kN (44100lbf) at 20.0kmh (12.5mph)
**Max. operating speed:** 100kmh (62.1mph)
**Weight:** 118 to 126 tonnes (260,190lb to 277830lb)
**Overall Length:** 17.56m (57ft 4in)
**Gauge:** 1435mm (4ft 8.5in) or 1524mm (5ft)

**The M62 series for the eastern bloc railways was devised for heavy freight traffic, but Hungarian state railways (MAV) deployed many on passenger trains as seen here. Immediately behind the locomotive is a train heating generator (hotel power) vehicle.**

## EMD SD45 VARIOUS RAILROADS USA 1965

With 2686kW (3600hp) produced by a single turbocharged 20-cylinder engine, the SD45 quickly became the shining star of many American railroads. By the 1960s, fast freight was the story of the day, and the SD45 locomotive the one to move it. Western railroads such as the Southern Pacific and Santa Fe were especially keen on the SD45 and subsequent 20-cylinder types, and they ordered hundreds of them. Although enthusiasm for the 20-cylinder engine faded because of its higher maintenance costs and greater fuel consumption when compared with the 16-cylinder 645E, some railroads continued to operate SD45s down to 2002. From the mid-1980s, the type was popular among regional railroads looking for second-hand 'bargain' power.

**Type:** Co-Co, diesel-electric
**Power:** EMD 20-645E producing 2686kW (3600hp)
**Tractive effort:** 330kN (74,200 lbf) at 14.4km/h (9 mph) continuous TE
**Max. operating speed:** 125km/h (77mph)
**Weight:** 185 tonnes (407,000 lb)
**Overall length:** 20.053m (65ft 9.5in) or 20.015m (65ft 8in)
**Gauge:** 1435m (4ft 8.5in)

**New York, Susquehanna & Western acquired a fleet of second-hand SD45s in the 1980s. NYSW SD45 3620 leads an eastbound Delaware & Hudson freight at Dixons east of Attica, New York, in March 1989.**

## ALCO C-630 VARIOUS RAILROADS USA 1965

**Here, Alco C-630 locomotive number 2032 moves some trucks in the McMillan freight depot in Toronto, in July 1981. Most C-630s ended working on Canadian lines.**

Alco's Century-630, or C-630, was its six-motor, 2238kW (3000hp) diesel, built to compete with EMD's SD40 and GE's U30C. While by far the most stylish of these three models, it had the worst reputation in service. Fewer than 100 were built for American railroads, although slightly more than 50 were constructed in Canada by MLW for Canadian lines. American C-630s were built for just two years, starting in 1965, and are noted as the first North American locomotives to employ an AC-DC transmission system, a type soon adopted by EMD and GE as well.

**Type:** Co-Co, diesel-electric
**Power:** Alco 16-cylinder 251E diesel producing 2238kW (3000hp)
**Tractive effort:** 458 kN (103,000lbf) starting TE
**Max. operating speed:** 105km/h (65mph)
**Weight:** N/A
**Overall length:** 21.184m (69ft 6in)
**Gauge:** 1435mm (4ft 8.5in)

## K CLASS CO-CO WESTERN AUSTRALIAN GOVERNMENT RAILWAYS (WAGR) AUSTRALIA 1966

WAGR classes K and R were built by the English Electric Rocklea plant, and both were powered by the EE 12CSVT engine. Perhaps if the North American hood unit style had been adopted in the United Kingdom, then British Railways class 37 may have looked like these. Introduced in 1966, the 10 K class 201-210s were built for standard-gauge operation, and the five R class 1901-1905 for narrow-gauge work. K and R class engines were set at 1455kW (1950hp), but the second narrow-gauge batch of 13 class RAs were lower rated at 1339kW (1795hp). Class KA appeared in 1974 being three regauged former class RAs.

Class K was used first used for construction works on the standard-gauge route between Perth and Kalgoorlie, then grain and passenger work. Iron ore from Koolyanobbing mines also featured four class Ks in multiple.

**English Electric designed, but a very un-English hood-styled road switcher. Built by the Australian EE subsidiary at Rocklea. Inside the long equipment hood lies a noisy V12 cylinder engine.**

Several class Ks were passed on into industrial use or small users for shunting work. Class Rs were used on bauxite, salt, grain and general freight in the south and west of Western Australia.

**Type:** Co-Co diesel-electric
**Power:** K/R 1455kW (1950hp) KA/RA1340kW (1795hp) from EE 12CSVT series engine
**Tractive effort:** 225 to 264kN (50,625 to 59,400lbf) at 18/19kmh (11.3/11.9mph)
**Max. operating speed:** K/KA: 128kmh (80mph); R/RA 96kmh (60mph)
**Weight:** (K) 110 tonnes (242,550lb)
**Overall length:** 15.24 to 16.76m (49ft 7in to 54ft 8in)
**Gauge:** K/KA 1435mm (4ft 8.5in); R/RA 1067mm (3ft 6in)

## CLASS 120 EAST GERMAN RAILWAYS (DR) GERMANY 1966

Supplied by the Soviet Union in large numbers from Voroshilovgrad for mixed-traffic work in East Germany, this class's low maximum speed was little hindrance in a regime that gave passenger travel a lower priority than freight.

Although they were heavy in fuel consumption, thousands were built for use across the Soviet Union, as well as in Hungary, Poland and Czechoslovakia. All the DR class 120s have been withdrawn, although some are returning to Germany as open access operators buy them up.

**A DR class 120 moves though signals outside Frankfurt railway station in June 2001.**

**Type:** Mixed-traffic main-line diesel-electric
**Wheel arrangement:** Co-Co
**Power:** Kolomna V-form diesel, 1470kW (1970hp); DC generator; six axle-hung DC traction motors
**Tractive effort:** 373kN (83,855lbf)
**Max. operating speed:** 100km/h (62mph)
**Weight:** 116 tonnes (254,745lb)
**Overall length:** 17.55m (57ft 7in)
**Gauge:** Not known

## Class DE10 Japanese Railways (JR) — Japan 1966

Japan class DE10 locomotives are a rather unusual, asymmetric five-axle diesel-hydraulic design developed in the 1960s for light-weight main-line work. The 475 class DE10s that were built were largely responsible for eliminating steam locomotives from secondary routes, but they were also used for heavy shunting and trip and transfer work at freight marshalling yards.

Class DE15 is a DE10 equipped for winter snowplough operation. Many DE10s were made redundant in the 1970s and 1980s due to a drastic decline in freight carried by Japanese state railways through restructuring. But JR Freight, the new cargo operator resulting from the division of JNR into business units, continues to operate around 150 of these locomotives. JR East uses a fleet of around eight class DE10s and DE15s, while JR Central, JR West, JR Hokkaido, JR Kyushu and JR Shikoku each retain a few.

**Type:** AAA-B diesel-hydraulic lightweight
**Power:** 1000kW (1359hp) from DML6ZB series engine
**Tractive effort:** 191kN (42,900lbf)
**Max. operating speed:** 85km/h (53.1mph)
**Weight:** 65 tonnes (143,325lb)
**Overall length:** 14. 15m (46ft 2in)
**Gauge:** 1067mm (3ft 6in)

**The most numerous Japanese railways diesel type showing its asymmetric wheel layout and off-centre cab configuration. Low-height equipment bonnets are essential to aid all-round visibility when shunting (switching) in yards and terminals.**

## Class 3100 Bo-Bo Korean National Railways (KNR) — South Korea 1966

In 1966, Korean National Railways received 49 Alco/MLW model RS8s of 746kW (1000hp). Class 3100s were mainly utilized on freight traffic, usually in the northern region of the country. KNR has repowered the machines, replacing the original Alco 251 series engine with EMD 645 units and renumbering the locomotives as class 3200, but not in order of the original class. Such procedures highlight the difficulties often experienced by observers in establishing the correct identity and life history of a locomotive or type. However, the original Schenectady build can still be identified, as the hood shape of the Class 3100 had to be altered to accommodate the EMD power unit, and the long, raised section in the roof, as well as as the difference in sound, clearly identifies the re-engined examples. All engines in the class are painted in the KNR's orange and black freight livery.

**Type:** Bo-Bo diesel-electric freight
**Power:** 709kW (950hp) from EMD 8-645 series engine
**Tractive effort:** 160 kN (36,000lbf)
**Max. operating speed:** 105km/h (65.6mph)
**Weight:** 72 tonnes (158,760lb)
**Overall length:** 14.65m (47ft 10in)
**Gauge:** 1435mm (4ft 8.5in)

# EMD GP38 VARIOUS RAILROADS USA 1966

The American locomotive market in the 1960s was dominated by new turbocharged high-horsepower models such as the SD45. But there was still a large demand for more moderately powered machines. The GP38 was among the new 645 diesel models that EMD introduced in the mid-1960s and was effectively an improved version of the popular 'General Purpose' models that had dominated EMD's locomotive production through the 1950s. It used a normally aspirated 16-cylinder 645 diesel to produce 1492kW (2000hp). The GP38 and its successor GP38-2 were standard workhorse locomotives that handled a variety of freight services from local switching work to heavy unit coal trains. They were ordered by most American railroads and were a typical example of new freight power in the 1970s.

**Type:** Bo-Bo, diesel-electric
**Power:** EMD 16-645E producing 1492kW (2000hp)
**Tractive effort:** 245kW (55,000lbf) at 17.2 kmh (10.7 mph)
**Max. operating speed:** 104 km/h (65mph)
**Weight:** 119 tonnes (262,000lb)
**Overall length:** 18.034m (59ft 2in)
**Gauge:** 1435mm (4ft 8.5in)

**A trio of New England Central GP38s leads southbound freight 608 through Stafford Springs, Connecticut. New England Central operates the former Central Vermont main line.**

**A single New England Central GP38 is seen here leading the Great Train Escapes autumn tour train across a wooden trestle at New London, Connecticut, in September 1998.**

# EMD GP40 VARIOUS RAILROADS USA 1966

EMD's GP40 was introduced along with other new models that shared the 645 engine in 1965. This engine was basically an expansion of the successful 567 design. The new 645-powered locomotives also featured improved electrical components and an AC/DC transmission system (yet still used conventional direct current traction motors). The GP40 was a high-output four-motor locomotive designed for fast freight service. Its 16-645 engine delivered 2235kW (3000hp). New York Central was first to order GP40s, and the type became popular with other railroads that had ordered EMD's earlier high-output four-motor types. Variations of the GP40, such as the GP40P, were designed for passenger service. In 1972, the model was succeeded by the GP40-2, which had most of the same characteristics and looked basically the same.

**A Guilford Rail System GP40 leads a consist of four EMDs hauling a freight bound for Portland, Maine, at Dover, New Hampshire, in March 2002.**

**Baltimore & Ohio GP40 3684 has been preserved and is displayed at the Baltimore & Ohio Railroad Museum in Baltimore, Maryland.**

**Type:** Bo-Bo, diesel-electric
**Power:** EMD 16-645E3 producing 2235kW (3000hp)
**Tractive effort:** 213kN (48,000lbf) at 21km/h (13mph)
**Max. operating speed:** 104km/h (65mph) to 123km/h (77mph)
**Weight:** 126 tonnes (277,500 lbs) (based on CSX units)
**Overall length:** 18,034m (59ft 2in)
**Gauge:** 1435mm (4ft 8.5in)

# EMD SD40 VARIOUS RAILROADS

USA 1966

**Conrail SD40-2s used the older Flexicoil truck (bogie) rather than the more advanced HTC truck used by most SD40-2 models. Former Conrail SD40-2s work in rear-end helper service on Norfolk Southern at Lilly, Pennsylvania, in May 2002.**

Introduced in 1966, the SD40 quickly became a standard model on many American railroads for heavy freight services. The winning combination of high horsepower, reliability and versatility made the SD40 the first choice for many main-line services. The locomotive used a 16-cylinder version of the new 645E3 engine. With a 60:17 gear ratio, the SD40 could operate at a maximum speed of 113kmh (70mph), which was the absolute maximum allowable speed for freight operations by most American railroads. The SD40 used a AR10 main generator and D77 traction motors. In 1972, the type was improved with the introduction of EMD's Dash-2 line; the subsequent SD40-2 became one of the bestselling American diesel-electric models, with more than 4000 built for North American service.

**Union Pacific assembled one of the largest fleets of SD40 and SD40-2 locomotives, altogether consisting of more than 800 units. Here, five Union Pacific SD40-2s lead an eastbound freight at Echo, Utah.**

**Type:** Co-Co, diesel-electric
**Power:** 16-cylinder 645 producing 2235kW (3000hp)
**Tractive effort:** Depends on gear ratio
**Max. operating speed:** 104–141km/h (65–88 mph) depending on gear ratio
**Weight:** 173 tonnes (382,000 lb)
**Overall Length:** 20.015m (65ft 8in) – based on earlier models
**Gauge:** 1435mm (4ft 8.5in)

# EMD SW1500 VARIOUS RAILROADS

USA 1966

Electro-Motive Division's SW1500 was a switcher model built from 1966 to 1974 using a 12-cylinder 645 engine. With the introduction of the 645 engine, the SW1500 effectively suplanted the older SW1200 model.

While many American lines did indeed buy SW1500s, by the mid-1960s, the demand for new switching diesels had declined dramatically in the United States. Some lines used SW1500s in road freight service, lashing them up together in pairs, or in combination with other diesels.

Southern Pacific possessed one of the largest fleets of SW1500s and used them to switch yards and industrial parks around its vast system. Other switcher types using the 645 engine were the eight-cylinder SW1000 and SW1001, the latter type featuring a low-profile cab to allow it to serve places with low clearances.

**Type:** Bo-Bo, diesel-electric
**Power:** EMD 12-645 producing 1118kW (1500hp)
**Tractive effort:** 200kW (45,000lbf) at 19.3kmh (12 mph)
**Max. operating speed:** 104km/h (65mph)
**Weight:** 118 tonnes (260,000lb)
**Overall length:** 13.614m (44ft 8in)
**Gauge:** 1435mm (4ft 8.5in)

**Southern Pacific was one of the last of the large American railroads to buy a large fleet of switchers. SP SW1500 2680 is seen at South San Francisco, California, in 1992.**

## GMD GP40TC AMTRAK USA 1966

The precipitous decline of North American passenger services in the late 1950s and 1960s resulted in a huge decline in the need for new passenger diesels. In the mid-1960s, Toronto's suburban passenger operator, Government of Ontario (GO Transit), ordered eight specialized GP40 diesels from General Motors Diesel. The GP40TC is an adaptation of the GP40 freight locomotive. Its frame is 1.981m (6ft 6in) longer than a conventional GP40, and it had greater distance between the truck (bogie) centres. The greater length is needed to accommodate an auxiliary head end power generator used for passenger car heating and lighting in place of a conventional steam generator. Although GO Transit was the only operator to order GP40TCs new, it sold its fleet to Amtrak in the late 1980s.

**Type:** Bo-Bo, diesel-electric
**Power:** EMD 16-643E3 producing 2235kW (3000hp)
**Tractive effort:** N/A
**Max. operating speed:** N/A
**Weight:** N/A
**Overall length:** 20.015m (65ft 8in)
**Gauge:** 1435mm (4ft 8.5in)

**In the 1960s, the Government of Ontario's GO Transit ordered GP40TCs from General Motor's Canadian locomotive subsidiary, General Motors Diesel.**

## GE U30B VARIOUS RAILROADS USA 1966

**Pennsylvania short-line freight hauler, Reading, Blue Mountain & Northern former Conrail U30Bs lead a freight at Solomon Gap in October 1997.**

kKeeping pace with new models introduced by its competition in the mid-1960s, General Electric boosted the output of its Bo-Bo Universal Line road switcher models. In 1966, it introduced the U28B, which was more powerful than GE's pioneering U25B. In late 1966, GE introduced its U30B, which remained in production for the better part of the next decade. Intended to compete with EMD's GP40/GP40-2, GE's U30B did not enjoy the same robust sales. Both high-nose and low-nose U30Bs were built to customer specifications. Burlington, New York Central, and Western Pacific were among the lines to order new U30Bs.

**Type:** Bo-Bo, diesel-electric
**Power:** GE 7FDL-16 producing 2235kW (3000hp)
**Tractive effort:** 229kN (51,500lbf) continuous TE at 20.8km/h (13mph)
**Max. operating speed:** 127km/h (79mph)
**Weight:** 123.5 tonnes (272,000 lbs)
**Overall length:** 18.339m (60ft 2in)
**Gauge:** 1435mm (4ft 8.5in)

## CLASS L CO-CO WESTERN AUSTRALIAN GOVERNMENT RAILWAYS (WAGR) AUSTRALIA 1967

WAGR class L were the highest-powered and first turbocharged diesels in Australia aside from the privately operated iron ore railways. Twenty-five were supplied by Clyde – effectively a US domestic SD40 of reduced loading gauge. Initially used on Koolyanobbing iron ore, displacing class K, the design was later replaced on this work by class Q. In the 1990s, several passed to Australian Transport Network (ATN Access) for export grain flows in New South Wales and Victoria.

**Four WAGR class L Co-Cos have been resuscitated for use on construction trains on the Darwin to Alice Springs line.**

**Type:** Co-Co diesel-electric
**Power:** 2460kW (3300hp) from EMD 16-645 series engine
**Tractive effort:** 298kN (67050lbf) at 21kmh (13.1mph)
**Max. operating speed:** 134kmh (83.8mph)
**Weight:** 137 tonnes (302,085lb)
**Overall length:** 19.36m (63ft 2in)
**Gauge:** 1435mm (4ft 8.5in)

## CLASS CC72000 FRENCH NATIONAL RAILWAYS (SNCF) FRANCE 1967

France's most powerful diesel locomotives, built by Alsthom, are mainly used on express passenger trains on non-electrified routes, including the Paris–Basle line and at the extremities of Brittany. They worked heavy trains on the main line through the Massif Central via Clermont Ferrand until electrification displaced them to the Amiens–Calais and Paris–Trouville lines.

**Large and impressive, the class CC72000 C-C locomotives have *monomoteur* bogies. A small batch was exported to Morocco for the Tangier branch.**

**Type:** Mixed-traffic main-line diesel-electric
**Wheel arrangement:** C-C
**Power:** SACM 16-cylinder V-form diesel, 2648kW (3550hp); DC generator; two *monomoteur* frame mounted DC traction motors
**Tractive effort:** 189kN (42,490lbf) passenger; 362kN (81,380lbf) freight
**Max. operating speed:** 140 to 160km/h (88 to 100mph)
**Weight:** 114 tonnes (250,355lb)
**Overall length:** 20.19m (66ft 3in)
**Gauge:** 1435mm (4ft 8.5in)

## CLASS 50 BRITISH RAILWAYS GREAT BRITAIN 1967

**Type:** Mixed-traffic main-line diesel-electric
**Wheel arrangement:** Co-Co
**Power:** English Electric 16CSVT 16-cylinder V-form diesel, 2014kW (2700hp); DC generator; six axle-hung DC traction motors
**Tractive effort:** 215kN (48,500lbf)
**Max. operating speed:** 160km/h (100mph)
**Weight:** 117 tonnes (256,940lb)
**Overall length:** 20.88m (68ft 6in)
**Gauge:** 1435mm (4ft 8.5in)

**This class 50 is working a London Waterloo to Exeter train and passes under the up Bournemouth line flyover at Worting Junction near Basingstoke. For this service, a group of class 50s received Network SouthEast livery.**

The 'Hoovers' (so nicknamed because of their noisy fans) were generally a conventional diesel-electric design; however, BR had insisted on the use of 'modern' electronics in the power circuits, and these became unreliable. Their first duties included working in pairs between Crewe and Glasgow, in order to speed up the Glasgow service after electrification from London to Crewe.

Later, electrification from Crewe to Glasgow displaced the Class 50s to the Western Region. WR engineers simplified their control systems to improve reliability. The 50s and the high-speed trains displaced the hydraulics from the main lines to Bristol, South Wales and the West Country. A few examples are preserved.

## GE U30C VARIOUS RAILROADS USA 1967

**Type:** Co-Co, diesel-electric
**Power:** GE 7FDL-16 producing 2235kW (3000hp)
**Tractive effort:** 329kN (74,000lbf) at 18.3km/h (11.4mph) (varied - these figures based on some Burlington Northern U30Cs)
**Max. operating speed:** 113kmh (70mph)
**Weight:** 176 tonnes (388,000 lbs)
**Overall length:** 20.498m (67ft 3in)
**Gauge:** 1435mm (4ft 8.5in)

**Above: A GE U30C, No. 1582 of Family Lines, at Dalton, Illinois, on 26 February 1983. Lines in the CSX system were among the main users of the 'U-boats'.**

In the 1960s, General Electric ascended to the position of America's no. 2 diesel-electric manufacturer with the development of its Universal line, pushing one-time partner Alco into a distant third position. By the end of the decade, Alco exited the American market. The biggest seller of GE's 'U-boats', as the Universal line locomotives came to be known, was its six-motor U30C, which competed directly with EMD's SD40/SD40-2 as a heavy freight locomotive. In a 10-year span starting in 1967, EMD sold nearly 600 U30Cs in the United States. It also offered the more powerful U33C and the U36-C. All three locomotives used the same 7FDL-16 diesel-engine. In 1977, GE's improved DASH-7 line superseded the Universal line, and the C30-7 replaced the U30C, proving even more successful.

**Right: The U33C, seen here near Charlemont, Massachusetts, on 2 January 1986, extracted a further 224kw (300hp) from the FDL-16 power unit. In total, 375 were built, in the same time span as the U30C.**

## CLASS 753 AND 754 CO-CO CZECHOSLOVAKIAN RAILWAYS (CSD) CZECHOSLOVAKIA 1968

**Type:** Bo-Bo diesel-electric general purpose
**Power:** (753) 1325kW (1800hp); (754) 1492kW (2000hp) from CKD K12V230DR series engines
**Tractive effort:** 185kN (41,625lbf)
**Max. operating speed:** 100kmh (62.1mph)
**Weight:** 753 - 76.8 tonnes (169,344lb); 754 - 74.4 tonnes (164,052lb)
**Overall length:** 16.5m (53ft 10in)
**Gauge:** 1435mm (4ft 8.5in)

An unusual cab window styling gives this design the nickname '*brejlovec*' ('goggles'). Despite appearances, the CSD class 753s and754s are quite conventional. A total of 408 class T478.3 (later 753) were built to 1977. Class 753 has train steam heating, while T478.4s (class 754s) have electric supply only. Prototypes were built in 1975 and 84 in full production from 1978 to 1980. Class 750 from 1989 are converted 753s with electric heating. At the division of Czechoslovakia into the Czech Republic and Slovakia in 1993, the two railway systems acquired 41 and 18 class 750s, 275 and 53 class 753s and 60 and 26 class 754s, respectively. Class 750 conversions eventually reached 117 and 45, respectively. ZSR machines haul regional trains on a number of scenic mountain routes, while the CD machines are widespread.

These locomotives are being rapidly withdrawn due to the low reliability of the engines and a high fuel consumption. Surplus Czech machines are being rebuilt with reused 6K310DR (752.5) or new CAT (753.7) engines for further use in Italy.

**The unique cab window styling projecting forwards easily lends itself to the nickname 'goggles'. Inside, this is a conventional diesel-electric locomotive, one of the most heavily silenced of any diesel.**

## CLASS 218 FEDERAL GERMAN RAILWAYS (DB) GERMANY 1968

Over 400 '218s' were supplied to DB, and they operate all over western Germany. They work express passenger trains off the electrified routes, and are equally at home on general freight workings as on local push-pull trains. Their large, higher speed diesel engines enable a single-engined B-B to exceed the power output of the earlier twin-engined V200.

**No. 218 162 stands between duties and wears DB's *Neuesrot* ('new red') livery, slightly paler than the current standard 'traffic red'.**

**Type:** Mixed-traffic main-line diesel-hydraulic
**Power:** MTU MA 12V 956 TB 10, 12-cylinder V-form diesel, 1840kW (2465hp), or MTU MA 12V 956 TB 11 or Pielstick 16 PA 4V 200, 2060kW (2760hp); Voith L820rs hydraulic transmission
**Tractive effort:** 245kN (55,080lbf)
**Max. operating speed:** 140km/h (87mph)
**Weight:** 76.5 to 78.5 tonnes (168,000 to 172,390lb)
**Overall length:** 16.4m (53ft 10in)
**Gauge:** 1435mm (4ft 8.5in)

## DJ Bo-Bo-Bo NEW ZEALAND RAILWAYS (NZR) NEW ZEALAND 1968

New Zealand Railways eliminated steam in the South Island with these 64 class DJs, largely deployed on freight traffic. Low axle loading demanded the six-axle three-bogie layout of these Mitsubishi-supplied machines. The all-adhesive Bo-Bo-Bo wheel arrangement is found on several types of electric locomotive around the world, but (other than units supplied to various African countries by Alsthom) is relatively unusual on diesels. Class DJs were also among some of the earliest in the world with a traction alternator producing alternating current rectified for direct current traction motors. Unfortunately these features were offset by technical difficulties and the overrated, unreliable engines of the original 773kW (1050hp) were later modified to 671kW (900hp). Withdrawal from service started as early as 1986 despite the down-rating. The last DJ was taken out of service by NZR in 1991.

**Type:** Bo-Bo-Bo diesel-electric
**Power:** 671kW (900hp) from Caterpillar D398 V12 series engine
**Tractive effort:** 128kN (28,800lbf)
**Max. operating speed:** 96km/h (60mph)
**Weight:** 64 tonnes (141,120lb)
**Overall length:** 14.1m (46ft)
**Gauge:** 1067mm (3ft 6in)

**Three bogies can be seen carrying what is otherwise a conventional road switcher of intermediate power designed for mixed traffic.**

## EMD FP45 SANTA FE RAILROAD USA 1968

In 1967, Santa Fe needed new passenger locomotives for its highly acclaimed streamlined stainless steel passenger trains, including the *Super Chief*. The company ordered semi-streamlined diesels from both EMD and GE. Unlike early streamlined diesels such as the EMD F-units where the outer carbody was integral to the locomotive structure, these second-generation passenger locomotives used road-switcher platforms with a non-structural metal ‘cowl’ covering. Initially, Santa Fe

**Santa Fe was the first railroad to order ‘cowl’ locomotives. The FP45 was intended for dual freight and passenger service, but the more common F45 was strictly a freight locomotive. At left is a detailed view of Santa Fe F45 5972, clearly showing the locomotive’s full-width cab.**

ordered nine FP45s which used the 20-645E3 engine. These contained a large steam generator to provide steam heat for passenger cars. Later it ordered a freight-only version which was designated F45. These were similar to the FP45, but did not feature the large steam generator and were several feet shorter. Burlington Northern and Milwaukee Road also ordered F45s.

**Santa Fe–painted F45 5972 leads a freight on the Wisconsin Central near Fond du Lac, Wisconsin, in March 1995.**

**Type:** Co-Co, diesel-electric
**Power and output:** Not known
**Tractive effort:** 316kN (171,000lbf) at 21km/h (13.2mph)
**Max. operating speed:** 123km/h (77mph)
**Weight:** 175 tonnes (386,000 lb)
**Overall length:** 20.561m (67ft 5.5in)
**Gauge:** 1435mm (4ft 8.5in)

## EMD SD39 VARIOUS RAILWAYS — USA 1968

Although only built from 1968 to 1970, EMD's SD39 filled a gap for a medium output six-motor road switcher. Externally, the SD39 closely resembled the more powerful SD40. The primary difference was the smaller, less powerful engine – a 12-cylinder 645. Milwaukee Road was the only line to buy the SDL39, ordering 10.

**Type:** Co-Co, diesel-electric
**Power:** EMD 12-645E3 at 1714kW (2300hp)
**Tractive effort:** 365kN (82,200lbf) at 12.9km/h (8mph)
**Max. operating speed:** 115km/h (71mph)
**Weight:** 161 tonnes (356,000 lb)
**Overall length:** 20.1m (65ft 10in)
**Gauge:** 1435mm (4ft 8.5in)

## AB CLASS CO-CO WESTRAIL — AUSTRALIA 1969

Westrail class AB was one of three designed for freight traffic. Classes A, AA and AB were built by Clyde and were made up of 14 EMD 567-engined class As (model G12), and the 645 powered classes, six each, of AA and AB (G22 model) from 1967 and 1969. The A, AA nor AB are not now in use in mainland Australia.

**Type:** Co-Co diesel-electric
**Power:** 1231kW (1650hp)
**Tractive effort:** 226kN (50,850lbf) at 14kmh (8.8mph)
**Max. operating speed:** 100km/h (62.1mph)
**Weight:** 99 tonnes (218,295lb)
**Overall length:** 15.04 to 15.49m (49ft to 50ft 5in)
**Gauge:** 1067mm (3ft 6in)

## 422 CLASS CO-CO AUSTRALIA SOUTHERN RAILROAD — AUSTRALIA 1969

Class 422s are a box-like external design produced by Clyde. They were originally deployed in the Melbourne region, where work included some passenger duties to Sydney, but were withdrawn in the late 1990s. Sixteen machines passed to the Australia Southern Railroad and are being progressively returned to operational service. Two others are operated by Interail and three by Freightcorp.

**Type:** Co-Co diesel-electric
**Power:** 1641kW (2200hp) from EMD 16-645 series engine
**Tractive effort:** 271kN (60,975lbf) at 12km/h (7.5mph)
**Max. operating speed:** 124km/h (77.5mph)
**Weight:** 110 tonnes (242,550lb)
**Overall length:** 18.44m (60ft 2in)
**Gauge:** 1435mm (4ft 8.5in)

**On this class 422 co-co style engine, the substantial box carbody design leading to the nickname of the 'flying brick' can clearly be seen.**

## MLU-14 Co-Co BANGLADESH RAILWAYS — BANGLADESH 1969

Bangladesh railways had bought broad-gauge Alco units since 1965 and four years later bought some model DL535s for the metre-gauge network. MLW supplied 24 (numbers 2301 to 2324) in 1969 and a further 12 (2401 to 2412) in 1978, forming class MLU14. This design is found on freight and passenger services across the whole of the Bangladesh 1000mm (3ft 3.4in) gauge system.

**The very square-lined cab and bevelled hood line identify this Alco heritage India-built DL535 model in Bangladesh service.**

**Type:** Co-Co narrow-gauge
**Power:** 1030kW (1400hp) from Alco 6-251 series engine
**Tractive effort:** 178kN (40,000lbf) at 11.6kmh (7.3mph)
**Max. operating speed:** 96km/h (60mph)
**Weight:** 70.5 tonnes (155,453lb)
**Overall length:** 13.818m (45ft 1in)
**Gauge:** 1000mm (3ft 3.4in)

## MLW M-630 CANADIAN PACIFIC RAILROAD — CANADA 1969

Alco's Canadian affiliate, Montreal Locomotive Works, continued to build locomotives based largely on its Century-series for several years after Alco ceased American locomotive production. MLW's primary six-motor designs were the M-630 and M-636, models that closely resembled the C-630 and C-636, respectively.

The M-630 was a 2238kW (3000hp) locomotive that used a 16-cylinder Alco 251 diesel. It employed a different style of bogie (truck) from that of the C-630 and also had a slightly different hood configuration.

Canadian Pacific was the largest buyer of the M-630 type. Fewer than 70 were built for service in North America in the three-year production run that began in 1969. Some of the M-630s were to remain in service on CPR into the late 1990s.

**Type:** Co-Co, diesel-electric
**Power:** Alco 16-cylinder 251E diesel producing 2238kW (3000hp) for traction
**Tractive effort:** 329kN (74,000lbf) continuous TE
**Max. operating speed:** 120km/h (75mph)
**Weight:** 177 tonnes (390,000 lb)
**Overall length:** 21.184m (69ft 6in)
**Gauge:** 1435mm (4ft 8.5in)

**Canadian National regional spin-off, Cape Breton & Central Nova Scotia, was among the last lines to operate the M-630s in heavy main-line service. Three MLW M-630s and an RS-18 lead an eastbound freight in 1997.**

**The size and powerful looks of the M-630 are displayed by No. 724 of the British Columbia Railways, seen here on the fuelling road at North Vancouver Depot, on 29 May 1983.**

## DF4 Co-Co CHINESE STATE RAILWAYS CHINA 1969

**Type:** Co-Co diesel-electric
**Power:** 2430kW to 2940kW (3295 or 3995hp) from 16V240ZJ series engines
**Tractive effort:** 215 to 302kN (48,375 to 67,950lbf) continuous; 303kN to 440kN (68,175 to 99,000lbf) maximum
**Max. operating speed:** 100 or 120km/h (62.1 or 75mph)
**Weight:** 138 tonnes (304,290lb)
**Overall length:** 20.5m (66ft 11in)
**Gauge:** 1435mm (4ft 8.5in)

**Steam locomotives gave way to diesels such as the DF4 in the 1990s. Here two such units are coupled at the head of a mixed-freight consist commonly found throughout the region.**

Class DF4 comes in several variations, geared for passenger or freight traffic, and these are the most numerous diesel locomotives in China. Class DF4 120kmh (75mph) passenger units first appeared from the Dalian locomotive works in 1969 and 100kmh (62.1mph) freight from 1974 with 2430kW (3302hp) engines. Up to 1984 390 class DF4 and 360 class DF4A units appeared when production switched to the uprated class DF4B, with the freight units featuring significantly increased tractive effort capability. In all, 4250 units were built from four factories – Dalian, Datong, Sifang and Ziyang. Class DF4Cs were also introduced a year later with 2650kW (3600hp) engines, but lower performance; 920 of these were built. Further class DF4 designations appearing through the 1990s include high-speed 132kmh (82.5mph) freight, higher powered 2940kW (3995hp) passenger, asynchronous motor versions and single cab hood–styled units used for switching.

## EMD DDA40X UNION PACIFIC USA 1969

The largest and last of Union Pacific's 'double-diesels' were the 47 massive DDA40Xs built by EMD. These locomotives were effectively two GP40s on one frame. Interestingly, the DDA40X used a 'wide nose' cowl-style cab, as first introduced on Santa Fe's FP45 in 1967. This cab style predated the now common North American Safety Cab by more than two decades. Each DDA40X was powered by a pair of turbocharged 16-645E engines. The DDA40Xs are the world's largest diesel locomotives – known as 'Centennials' and numbered in the 6900 series because they were introduced in 1969, which was the 100th anniversary of the completion of the first transcontinental railroad. By 1985, most were out of service, but one locomotive, number 6936, remains in Union Pacific's heritage fleet.

**Type:** Do-Do, diesel-electric
**Power:** Two 16-645E3 diesel engines producing 4923kW (6600hp)
**Tractive effort:** 596kN (133,766 lbf) starting TE
**Max. operating speed:** N/A
**Weight:** 247 tonnes (545,400lb)
**Overall length:** 30m (98ft 5in)
**Gauge:** 1435m (4ft 8.5in)

**Union Pacific retains one DDA40X in its historic fleet, and this locomotive is variously used on passenger excursions and occasionally in freight service.**

## CLASS CL AUSTRALIAN SOUTHERN RAILROAD AUSTRALIA 1970

**With lines reminiscent of classic North American E- and F-units, the CLFs and CLPs are still hard at work today, despite the external design apparently dating them from the 1940s US streamliner era.**

Clyde built EMD units for the Broken Hill to Port Pirie freight service, but they were also used on Leigh Creek coal and Broken Hill ore workings. In 1992–93, they were rebuilt by Morrison Knudsen into seven class freight CLFs and 10 passenger class CLPs, with a maximum speed of 130 and 140kmh (80.7 and 87mph). Class CLP was subsequently cascaded on to freight duties – class CLF remains on similar freight work as that performed by the original design. Both are operated by Australian Southern Railroad, the successors as freight operator to Australian National in South Australia.

**Type:** Co-Co diesel-electric
**Power:** 2460kW (3300hp) from EMD 16-645 series engine
**Tractive effort:** 270kN (60,750lb) at 24km/h (15mph)
**Max. operating speed:** 155km/h (97mph)
**Weight:** 129 tonnes (284,445lb)
**Overall length:** 19.58m (63ft 10in)
**Gauge:** 1435mm (4ft 8.5in)

## CF7 SANTA FE RAILROAD USA 1970

**Type:** Re-manufactured Bo-Bo diesel-electric
**Power:** EMD 16-567BC producing 1119kW (1500hp)
**Tractive effort:** N/A
**Max. operating speed:** N/A
**Weight:** N/A
**Overall length:** 17.043m (55ft 11in)
**Gauge:** 1435mm (4ft 8.5in)

**Louisiana & Delta, one of the Genesee & Wyoming family of short lines, operates former Southern Pacific branch lines with a fleet of former Santa Fe CF7s. L&D CF7 1503 is seen at the L&D shops in New Iberia, Louisiana.**

Throughout the 1960s and 1970s, many American railroads traded in their 1940s and early 1950s era EMD F-units for new locomotives. The Santa Fe railroad took a different approach and, between 1970 and 1978, converted more than 230 of its F7s into home-built road switchers which were designated CF7. As the F-unit used a supporting carbody, Santa Fe needed to manufacture a frame, hood and cab for the CF7. The primary mechanical and electrical components from the F7 were retained and incorporated in the 'new' CF7. Early CF7s featured a contoured cab that matched the profile of the F7 carbody, while the later CF7s were to feature a taller, boxy cab.

In the early 1980s, Santa Fe began selling off its CF7 fleet, and many were bought by short lines. Amtrak acquired a few in exchange for its SDP40Fs and assigned them to maintenance trains.

**Still in Santa Fe livery, CF7 No. 2318 stands in the yard at Corwith, Chicago, on 6 July 1983. In all, 233 conversions were built, in what was to be one of the largest programmes of its kind.**

## MLW M-640 CPR 4744 CANADIAN PACIFIC (CPR) CANADA 1971

The most powerful single-engine Alco diesel locomotive was a single Montreal Locomotive Works M-640 built in 1971. This was Canadian Pacific (CPR) 4744, which was powered by an 18-cylinder Alco 251 diesel engine.

Although similar in appearance to the M-630 and M-636, the locomotive had large 'bat-wing' radiators at the rear of the unit. At the time, 4744 was significantly more powerful than production single-engine diesel-electrics, which topped out at 2686kW (3600hp). In America, EMD also built very high horsepower experimental diesels.

For 15 years, Canadian Pacific 4744 worked in the railroad's road freight fleet and was assigned to trains with Canadian Pacific's other large MLW diesel locomotives. In 1985, the locomotive was substantially rebuilt and remodelled as a test-bed for alternating current traction.

**Type:** Co-Co, diesel-electric
**Power:** Alco 18-cylinder 251 diesel, producing 2984kW (4000hp)
**Tractive effort:** 354kN (79,590lbf) continuous TE
**Max. operating speed:** N/A
**Weight:** 177 tonnes (390,000lb)
**Overall length:** 21.298m (69ft 11in)
**Gauge:** 1435mm (4ft 8.5in)

## CLASS BJ CHINESE STATE RAILWAYS — CHINA 1971

Series production of China State Railways class BJ started in 1975 after 1971 prototypes. Intended originally for passenger work, but cascaded by class DF4 to freight or withdrawn, 340 were built.

A freight version had 1840kW (2500hp) engines geared for 90kmh (145mph). A single-ended version for working back to back in pairs also appeared in small numbers. A few run 1524mm (5ft) wheelsets in border exchange sidings areas.

**Type:** B-B diesel-hydraulic passenger and freight
**Power:** 1990kW (2700hp) from 12V240ZJ series engine
**Tractive effort:** 163kN (36,675lbf) continuous; 227kN (51,075lbf) maximum
**Max. operating speed:** 120km/h (75mph)
**Weight:** 92 tonnes (202,860lb)
**Overall length:** 16.505m (53ft 10in)
**Gauge:** 1435mm (4ft 8.5in)

**Externally there is nothing to distinguish a diesel-hydraulic from a diesel-electric. The BJ is the only mass-produced diesel with a hydraulic transmission to be found in China.**

## M41 RATTLER HUNGARIAN STATE RAILWAYS (MÁV) — HUNGARY 1971

**Type:** B-B diesel-hydraulic mixed-traffic
**Power:** 1325kW (1800hp) from Pielstick 12PA4-185 series engine
**Tractive effort:** 151kN (34,000lbf)
**Max. operating speed:** 100kmh (62.1mph)
**Weight:** 66 tonnes (145,530lb)
**Overall length:** 15.5m (50ft 7in)
**Gauge:** 1435mm (4ft 8.5in)

In total, 107 general-purpose machines were built for MAV and seven for GySEV. Two 1967 prototypes, M41-2001 and 2002, were of different appearance, being centre-cab units. They were later renumbered M42 001 and 002, but are now no longer in existence. Production M41 units had a two-cab layout of simple but not unattractive box design. M41 2001–2207 were built new for MAV use, while 2208–2214 were originally GySEV, but have since transferred to MAV. M41 is equipped for electric train heating, allowing MAV to dispense with the separate heating cars previously used. These locomotives are distributed throughout Hungary and are found on passenger work on the majority of non-electrified secondary routes. Recent intercity work has allowed removal of M62 from these duties. MAV intends keeping up to 100 beyond 2010 and is evaluating new engines. In 2001–02, M41 2207 (now M41 2301) was rebuilt with a MTU 16V4000 engine and M41 2115 (now M41 2302) with CAT 3516. Only the engine was replaced; the transmission remained unchanged.

**Simple lines round off what is otherwise the plain M41 box. The electric train heating (hotel power) connections may be found below the buffer line, essential for these mixed-traffic units found all over the MÁV system.**

## CLASS 92 1-CO-CO-1 KENYA RAILWAYS — KENYA 1971

**Type:** 1Co-Co1 diesel-electric
**Power:** 1876kW (2550hp) from Alco 12-251 series engine
**Tractive effort:** 193kN (43,500lbf) at 26.4km/h (16.5mph)
**Max. operating speed:** 72km/h (45mph)
**Weight:** 118 tonnes (260,190lb)
**Overall length:** 18.015m (58ft 9in)
**Gauge:** 1000mm (3ft 3.4in)

Fifteen Class 92s were delivered to East African Railways by MLW in 1971, and all today are operated by Kenya railways following the break-up of EAR into separate Kenya, Tanzania and Uganda systems in 1976. The Montreal Locomotive Works MX636 model number rather belies the design when it comes to the machine's

**The MLW 'Africa Cab' with its low nose can be clearly seen here and gives members of this family unmistakable lines unlikely to be confused with anything else.**

wheel configuration of 1Co-Co1 four axle bogies with unpowered outer axles. To reduce axle loading on the lighter permanent way, it follows the layout adopted by English Electric on several export models. Similar machines were supplied to Nigeria railways – a batch of 54 MLW MX615s. The Kenyan locomotives have a so-called 'Africa cab' with full-width low nose styling not used on other MLW exports. Similar smaller Co-Co units with Alco 8-251 series 1120kW (1522hp) engines were also supplied to Malawi in 1980.

## Z Class Co-Co TRANZRAIL — AUSTRALIA 1972

These were two small batches of locomotives delivered to Tasmania from GEC of Australia, successors to English Electric Rocklea. Class Zs were based on WAGR classes K and R, while ZAs were similar to QR class 2350, but with revised body and low noses in place of the high short-nose hoods of the original design. Class Zs have 12CSVT engines rated at 1510kW (2052hp) and the five class ZAs at 1900kW (2852hp). Both batches were built for a new traffic flow of logs and woodchips on the northern section of the main Tasmania line and on the Bell Bat, Fingal and Western routes. Class Z and ZA operate side by side and may be found on other parts of the network. Interestingly, the 16 second-class ZB introduced in 1973 are the QR units class ZA was derived from; these were displaced by electrification in Queensland and sold to Tasmania, arriving in 1987–88.

**Type:** Co-Co diesel-electric freight
**Power:** Z - 1502kW (2025hp); ZA - 1900kW (2580hp)
**Tractive effort:** Z - 221kN (49750 lbf); ZA - 289kN (65000lbf)
**Max. operating speed:** 37.3km/h (60mph)
**Weight:** 96 tonnes (211,642lb)
**Overall length:** 16.31m (53ft 3in)
**Gauge:** 1067mm (3ft 6in)

## SNCF RTG FRENCH NATIONAL RAILWAYS (SNCF) — FRANCE 1972

Almost alone in the world, SNCF purchased 41 sets of gas-turbine trains for important passenger services off the electrified main lines. The orange-liveried RTGs work express trains out of Cherbourg, as well as being used on cross-country services out of Lyon to Strasbourg and Bordeaux, and from Caen to Tours. Each unit has two turbine engines, each of which drives wheelsets through a hydro-dynamic transmission.

**Type:** Express passenger gas-turbine electric five-car unit
**Gas turbine engine:** Turboméca Turmo XII 1200kW (1610hp) at one end of unit; Turmo IIIF1 820kW (1100hp) at other end; hydraulic transmission
**Max. operating speed:** 160km/h (100mph)
**Weight:** Power cars (2) 54 tonnes (118,590lb); trailers (3) 37 to 42 tonnes (81,255 to 92,235lb)
**Overall length:** Power cars 26.22m (86ft); trailers 25.5m (83ft 8in)

**SNCF was alone in Europe in operating gas-turbine trains in intercity-type services. This pair, coupled in multiple, is ready to leave Cherbourg for Paris in 1978, before electrification.**

## Dx Class Co-Co NEW ZEALAND RAILWAYS (NZR) — NEW ZEALAND 1972

General Electric built these 49 freight units with a relatively heavy axle load, restricting class DX initially to North Island coal traffic until electrification released some to the South Island in the 1980s. Modifications to 15 units in 1997 led to the end of electric working through the Otira tunnel, with 'tunnel motor' conversions featuring redirected air intake ducts and the tunnel itself equipped with a ventilation system. Two DX models were substantially rebuilt as DXR, one with a new cab and one retaining the original layout.

**This is one of the class DX 'tunnel motor' rebuilds – the additional air ducting can clearly be seen on the side of the engine compartment hood. This was necessary to draw clean air for the engine from low level away from exhaust fumes in a non-ventilated tunnel.**

**Type:** Co-Co diesel-electric
**Power:** 2050kW (2750hp) from GE 7FDL12 series engine
**Tractive effort:** 207kN (46,575lb)
**Max. operating speed:** 120km/h (75mph)
**Weight:** 97.5 tonnes (214,988lb)
**Overall length:** 17.9m (58ft 5in)
**Gauge:** 1067mm (3ft 6in)

## A1A-2+2-Bo Class RM 'Silver Fern' NEW ZEALAND RAILWAYS NEW ZEALAND 1972

**The substantial weight of the 'Silver Fern' units can be inferred from their solidly built appearance; this solidity has substantially helped to prolong their operating lives.**

The silver fern, New Zealand's national emblem, was borrowed to name the diesel-electric two-car sets of this unusual configuration. Three were built by Nissho-Iwai, the first diesel-electric railcars to run in New Zealand. They were also the most comfortable cars that the NZR had built, with air conditioning and aircraft-style seating for 96 passengers.

Apart from some special excursion services, for which they were ferried across to the South Island, the 'Silver Ferns' worked only in the North Island. Although each car was powered on the end bogie, and each end had a driving compartment, the main driving car was the A1A-2 vehicle, which also housed the main engine. They replaced the older British-built Drewery-Fiat powered 'Blue Streak' units on the Auckland–Wellington services and were widely used for specials. From December 1991, they inaugurated a 'Geyserland Express' twice-daily between Auckland and Rotorua, replacing locomotive-hauled trains, and also the Auckland–Tauranga 'Kaimai Express'. These services lasted until 1999. After that they were considered for service on the main South Island Christchurch–Dunedin–Invercargill route, but this option was not pursued. In the current uncertain and rundown state of New Zealand rail passenger services, the 'Silver Ferns' have no definite role, but are still used for special tours.

**Type:** Two-car diesel-electric express set
**Power:** 670kW (898hp) Caterpillar D398TA engine, V12, bore 159mm (6.25in), stroke 203mm (8in) driving four traction motors. Auxiliary Caterpillar D330T generator engine
**Tractive effort:** Not known
**Maximum operating speed:** 120km/h (75mph)
**Total weight:** 107 tonnes (235,935lb)
**Maximum axle load:** Not known
**Overall length:** 47.2m (155ft)
**Builder:** Nissho-Iwai, Japan
**Gauge:** Not known

## EMD SD45T-2 SOUTHERN PACIFIC RAILROAD USA 1972

The SD45T-2 was developed in response to Southern Pacific's need to get better performance on its high-altitude California Sierra crossing. On the line over Donner Pass, high-horsepower EMD diesels suffered from the effects of numerous long tunnels, snow sheds and lower oxygen levels which caused engine overheating and lower productivity. To correct this, EMD altered the air flow pattern on the SD45T-2, lowering the air intakes from the top of the hood to a location along the running boards (footwalks), allowing the locomotive to take in cooler air in tunnels. The changes were implemented along with new Dash-2 components introduced in 1972. Southern Pacific and its Cotton Belt subsidiary took delivery of all 247 SD45T-2s between 1972 and 1975.

**Former SP SD45-T2s, leased by CEFX to the Toledo, Peoria & Western, is seen here at Remington, Indiana.**

**Type:** Co-Co, diesel-electric
**Power:** 20-cylinder 645 producing 2686kW (3600hp)
**Tractive effort:** 408.9 kN (92,000 lbf)
**Max. operating speed:** 114km/h (70.8mph)
**Weight:** 176 tonnes (388,000 lb)
**Overall length:** 21.539m (70ft 8in)
**Gauge:** 1435mm (4ft 8.5in)

## GMD GP40-2L CANADIAN NATIONAL CANADA 1973

In the 1970s, Electro-Motive's Canadian subsidiary, General Motors Diesel, built a variation of the GP40-2 for Canadian National and Toronto's GO Transit that used a full-width nose section and a four-piece windshield. Sources vary, and this model is sometimes described as GP40-2W, GP40-2L or just as a GP40-2 with no suffix to distinguish it from models with the standard cab. Canadian National routinely operated its wide-nose GP40-2s with the conventional cab variety, as well as other diesels. In addition to operating in Canada, some were cleared for international service and were regularly assigned to service on Central Vermont and other American subsidiaries.

**Type:** Bo-Bo, diesel-electric
**Power:** EMD 16-643E3 producing 2235kW (3000hp)
**Tractive effort:** N/A
**Max. operating speed:** N/A
**Weight:** N/A
**Overall length:** 20.015m (65ft 8in)
**Gauge:** 1435mm (4ft 8.5in)

**The GP40-2L, a model sometimes designated GP40W, was built new for both Canadian National and GO Transit. GO Transit 710 is seen at Eglinton station in suburban Toronto.**

## CLASS 810 CZECHOSLOVAKIAN RAILWAYS (CD) CZECHOSLOVAKIA 1973

Possibly the best example of a lightweight four-wheel railbus, this one is found on rural lines throughout the Czech Republic, Slovakia and Hungary. Several international border crossing routes between those countries and into Austria and Germany are worked by members of class 810, notwithstanding the spartan 2+3 bench seating.

The 680 class 810 were supplied by Vagonka Studenka. Today, Czechoslovakian Railways (CD) operates around 530 and the Slovakian ZSR 130. In addition, large numbers of Baafx (class 010) trailers are at work as railbuses. The relatively low 80kmh (50mph) speed is not a problem on many lines, which have a 40kmh (25mph) speed limit. ZSR has rebuilt some Baafx to class 811 and 812 diesel-electric railbuses with revised cab designs. CD is rebuilding its 810s as a new class 812 for work with class 912 driving trailers. Hungary took 205 class Bzmot railbuses of the same type, also now rebuilding with various Raba MAN and Volvo engines and hydraulic transmissions. Some have revised 2+2 seating and air conditioning for intercity feeder services marketed as '*inter picy*' ('inter tiny').

**Type:** four-wheel diesel railbus
**Power:** 155kW (208hp)
**Tractive effort:** N/A
**Max. operating speed:** 80km/h (50mph)
**Weight:** 20 tonnes (40,500lb)
**Overall length:** 13.97m (45ft 6in)
**Gauge:** 1435mm (4ft 8.5in)

## CLASSES 130 TO 132 EAST GERMAN RAILWAYS (DR) EAST GERMANY 1973

Later known as DB class 230 to 232, more than 700 of this group of large locomotives was supplied to DR from Voroshilovgrad in Russia. Since reunification, these locomotives have proved popular in western Germany and penetrate as far west as Aachen and Rotterdam. The class differences relate to the provision of electric train heat supply and different maximum speeds. The type also works in Bulgaria and in some former Soviet countries. The details below refer to class 232.

**This Soviet-built Co-Co diesel-electric heads a passenger train on the former *Deutsche Reichsbahn* in East Germany (DDR). The class has proved popular in western Germany since reunification. Others work in Bulgaria and some of the countries which formerly made up the Soviet Union.**

**Type:** Mixed-traffic main-line diesel-electric
**Wheel arrangement:** Co-Co
**Power:** Kolumna V-form diesel, 2200kW (2950hp); DC generator; six axle-hung DC traction motors
**Tractive effort:** 340kN (76,435lbf)
**Max. operating speed:** 120km/h (75mph)
**Weight:** 123 tonnes (270,120lb)
**Overall length:** 20.62m (67ft 8in)
**Gauge:** 1435mm (4ft 8.5in)

# 'INTERCITY 125' HIGH SPEED TRAINS BRITISH RAIL GREAT BRITAIN 1976

**A First Great Western HST heading for Plymouth passes a harbour on the Exe estuary in Devon. This train is in First Great Western's first livery of dark green and beige.**

If ever a train design rescued the future of a major national railway, the high-speed trains (HST) did so for BR. Coming at a time when the future was seen by some to favour tilting trains (one of which, the Advance Passenger Train – APT – was being developed in the United Kingdom), there were voices against the decision in 1972 to build a prototype for a conventional train that could achieve a new top speed for Britain of 200km/h (125mph). Yet the wisdom of having a prototype was proven. Two power cars that were basically simple, single-ended, streamlined, light-weight Bo-Bo diesel-electric locomotives were positioned at each end of a rake of what BR called their Mark 3 coaches. These used a new design of air-sprung bogie with a swing bolster, carrying carriage bodies of longer length than had previously been used in the United Kingdom – 23m (75ft). Earlier BR coaches had usually been of 20m (65ft 6in) length. The extra length did not increase the vehicle weights because of the intelligent design of the steel body structures. Indeed, at 37 tonnes (82,570lb) they are models of engineering efficiency. To enable the power cars to be lightweight, a high-speed Paxman Valenta engine was installed, coupled to a brushless alternator to feed four fully suspended DC traction motors. High speed was assured with the combined power of the two engines totalling 3357kW (4500hp).

The carriages were fully air-conditioned and used standard body layouts for both first and standard classes. Inside, the carriages had airline-type seat rails on the floors and bodysides that enabled different seating layouts to be fitted easily without disturbing the wall-to-wall carpets.

After extensive prototype running, 98 HST production sets were built, some as seven-car sets for the Western Region services, others as eight-car sets for the East Coast main line (ECML). The WR sets worked fast services between London Paddington and Swansea,

**The original livery style for the HSTs when built by BR was a striking adaptation of the railway's rail blue-and-grey colours, with plenty of yellow being used to decorate the power cars. The trains were nstantly popular.**

Bristol and the West Country. Later a train to Cheltenham was added. The ER and ScR sets covered the ECML services from London King's Cross to Leeds, York, Newcastle, Edinburgh and Aberdeen.

An unusual change was made to a small number of power cars to assist in the introduction of fast electric push-pull trains when the ECML was being electrified. In the absence of driving trailer cars, eight HST power cars were equipped with side buffers at the streamlined cab ends and used as powered driving trailers for the class 91 electric locomotives working temporarily rakes of mark 3 stock taken from HSTs that would soon be moved elsewhere. After the IC225 mark 4 carriages and driving trailers arrived, the HST sets were reformed and sent to work on cross-country services. The side buffers remain an anomaly on the few cars that have them.

In the years that followed, several more changes took place, particularly after electrification pushed many HSTs off the ECML. The cross-country fleet was established, and HSTs began working the Midland main line from London St Pancras to Nottingham and Sheffield. The establishment by BR of the InterCity business resulted in a new livery for the HSTs. This used dark grey across the window band, with light beige below the side windows and a dark grey roof. Each coach was lined out in white and red just below the window line. The overall effect was very smart, and boosted the image of BR. The BR double-arrow symbol was, bravely, omitted and replaced by a swallow motif and the legend '*INTERCITY*' in specially designed script.

The HST was designed for long stretches of running at up to 200km/h (125mph). The Midland main line and cross-country services introduced them to more stop–start working in which trains ran fast between towns no more than 20 to 40 minutes apart. The Paxman Valenta engines were stressed more by what some commentators have called 'on-off' or 'binary' driving. In warm weather, the heat of an engine that has been running hard to accelerate from a stop has to be dissipated even when the engine is shut down to idling speed when the train slows down and calls at the next stop. The radiator system on the HSTs is not quite man enough for this treatment unless it is in absolutely tiptop condition with no coolant leaks and no build-up of sludge or scale inside. Such constant attention is not always possible. As the engines became in need of more mechanical attention, Paxman supplied for trial five of their VP185s, a more modern engine rated at the same output and with the same 'footprint', but with stronger components, better wear rates and a more capacious cooling system. Indeed, this successful engine is now the standard replacement for the HST power cars as the older Valenta engines wear out. The VP185s' reliability is good, and they need overhauling only after running at least twice the engine hours of the older engines.

Privatization of BR brought many changes to the trains, particularly in liveries. The ECML sets went to the Great North Eastern Railway (GNER), which painted them dark blue with a red stripe. These were for services that ran beyond Leeds and Edinburgh to Bradford, Aberdeen and Inverness. The Midland Mainline (MML) company painted its eight-coach sets green with tangerine stripes, and set up a fast service using DMUs to call at the intermediate stations, connecting into half-hourly HSTs at Leicester; MML carryings have since risen by more than 60 per cent. Virgin operates HSTs on the cross-country sections, but is replacing most of them with 'Voyager' DEMUs. This will help the Great North Eastern Railway (GNER) get extra coaches to extend their HSTs to nine cars to cope with traffic growth. First Great Western's (FGW) HST fleet is deservedly popular with its customers in view of the excellent interior layout and furnishings, and much the same can be said for the GNER ones. So much traffic has been earned by these trains that FGW is timetabling a half-hourly service to both Bristol and Cardiff, with extra trains in the morning and evening peaks; Swindon has a 15-minute interval HST service to London Paddington in the morning rush period!

Even though they are now more than 25 years old, the HST fleet is still very popular with passengers, and their presence on the railways of Great Britain is assured for many years yet. GNER, MML and FGW all have yet to announce any plans completely to replace their HST fleets, even though MML has placed an order for fast DMUs to supplement them and FGW is putting its 'Adelante' high-speed DMUs into service. Virgin Trains did announce such a plan, but hastily amended it because of the growth in passenger carryings real and expected. Around a dozen are being rebuilt as upgraded five-car sets for services that include the main line into London Paddington. These sets will have extensive engineering improvements, as well as a much smarter interior and new livery to match Virgin Trains' new high-speed fleets.

**For cross-country services, a number of seven-car trains were transferred from WR services and subsequently taken over by the privatized Virgin Trains company.**

Details below are for the production power cars (two per train):

**Type:** 'InterCity 125', diesel-electric power cars
**Wheel arrangement:** Bo-Bo
**Power equipment:** Paxman Valenta 12RP200L, high speed V-form diesel, 1680kW (2250bhp); Brush alternator with rotating diodes; four Brush or GEC traction motors, fully suspended with flexible drives to each axle
**Max. operating speed:** 200km/h (125mph)
**Weight:** 70 tonnes (153,725lb)
**Overall length:** 17.805m (58ft 5in)
**Gauge:** 1435mm (4ft 8.5in)

## CLASS 56 BRITISH RAIL — GREAT BRITAIN 1976

Needing more locomotives for coal trains, BR contracted Brush to supply 120 large diesels. Brush subcontracted the first 30 to Electroputere of Romania, the remainder being shared between BREL Crewe and Doncaster works. The bogie design was based on the CFR class 060-DA, while the body was based on the BR class 47. Ruston supplied a development of the EE 16-cylinder diesel engine. The locomotives have slow speed control for automatic loading and unloading of wagons. Some are now withdrawn.

**Type:** Freight main-line diesel-electric
**Wheel arrangement:** Co-Co
**Power:** Ruston 16RK3CT 16-cylinder V-form diesel, 2425kW (3250hp); Brush alternator; six axle-hung DC traction motors
**Tractive effort:** 275kN (61,800lbf)
**Max. operating speed:** 130km/h (80mph)
**Weight:** 126 tonnes (276,705lb)
**Overall length:** 19.355m (63ft 6in)
**Gauge:** 1435mm (4ft 8.5in)

**This class 56 in BR Railfreight's two-tone grey livery sports a decal with black diamonds to show that it is part of the coal traffic fleet. It heads a train of coal hoppers.**

## CLASS 071, CO-CO IRISH TRANSPORT COMPANY (CIE) — IRELAND 1976

**In August 1998, Irish Rail Class 071 No. 084 pauses at Balbriggan on the former Great Northern line with a suburban passenger train travelling uproad to Dublin.**

In 1976, Córas Iompair Éireann (Irish Transport Company), known by its initials, CIE, took delivery of 18 six-axle JT22CW locomotives from EMD, class 071 (Nos 071 to 088). When new, the 071s were known as the 'big engines' because at 100.5 tonnes (221,606lb), more than 17.3m (56.8ft) long and generating 1844kW (2475hp) with a 12-cylinder 645E3 prime mover (1679kW (2250hp) available for traction), they were simply the largest and most powerful locomotives ever to operate in Ireland. However, the class 201s delivered in 1994–95 are now larger and heavier. The class 071s work intercity passenger trains and through freights, and they are preferred power on the Dublin–Rosslare Europort and Dublin–Sligo runs where 201s are presently prohibited because of weight restrictions on these lines.

**Type:** Co-Co, diesel-electric
**Power:** EMD 12-645 producing 1679kW (2250hp) for traction
**Tractive effort:** 209kN (48,850lbf) continuous TE at 24.2km/h (15.1mph)
**Max. operating speed:** 144km/h (90mph)
**Weight:** 100.5 tonnes (221,606lb)
**Overall length:** See text
**Gauge:** 1600mm (5ft 3in)

## EMD F40PH AMTRAK

USA 1976

The F40PH was introduced in 1976 and quickly became the standard Amercian passenger locomotive. It is essentially a 'cowl' version of the GP40 road-switcher type. Amtrak, the nationally run passenger operator which had assumed most intercity passenger operations from the private railroads in 1971, was the largest operator of the F40PH. Amtrak assigned F40PHs to passenger services networkwide. On the unelectrified section of the Northeast Corridor between Boston, Massachusetts and New Haven, Connecticut, F40PHs were permitted to operate at their highest speeds. By 2002, Amtrak had retired most of its F40PHs, largely replacing them with General Electric GENESIS types. F40PHs are still operated by commuter agencies and Canada's VIA Rail, while a few have been modified for freight service.

**Type:** Diesel-electric
**Power:** 16-cylinder 645 engine producing 2235kW (3000hp).
**Tractive effort:** 304kN (68,440lbf)
**Max. operating speed:** 103km/h (64mph)
**Weight:** 117 tonnes (257,985 lbs.)
**Overall length:** 17.12m (56ft 2in)
**Gauge:** 1435mm (4ft 8.5in)

**A pair of Amtrak F40PHs leads Amtrak's *Vermonter* at CP83 in Palmer, Massachusetts, in October 2000. To the right, a pair of new CSX AC6000s wait to head west with a long freight bound for Selkirk, New York.**

## GE C30-7 VARIOUS RAILROADS

USA 1976

**A former Norfolk & Western C30-7 and an EMD, both wearing the colours of Norfolk Southern, lead a double-stack container train.**

General Electric built more than 1100 C30-7s for North American service between 1976 and 1986, making it one of GE's most successful models prior to the DASH-8 line. It was offered with three gear ratios: 83:20 for 43.5km/h (70mph) service; 81:22 for 49km/h (79mph); and 79:24 for 52km/h (84mph).

North American railroads primarily acquired C30-7s for heavy freight work, such as coal services, so the 83:20 ratio best represents the typical C30-7. The standard C30-7 used GE's turbocharged 7FDL-16 engine, while the variation designated C30-7A used a GE 7FDL-12 for better fuel economy.

**Type:** Co-Co, diesel-electric
**Power:** GE 7FDL-16 producing 2238kW (3000hp)
**Tractive effort:** 402kN (90,500lb) at 13.6km/h (8.5mph)
**Max. operating speed:** 112km/h (70mph) with 83:20 gear ratio
**Weight:** 189 tonnes (420,000lb)
**Overall length:** 20.5m (67ft 3in)
**Gauge:** 1435mm (4ft 8.5in)

## GE B23-7 VARIOUS RAILROADS USA 1977

**Conrail B23-7 1933 was semi-permanently assigned to haul the company's track geometry train. It is seen here climbing around the Horseshoe Curve, west of Altoona, Pennsylvania, in August 1987.**

General Electric's U23B moderate horsepower Bo-Bo road-switcher was replaced with the B23-7 when the Dash-7 line supplanted GE's older Universal line in 1977. Using a 12-cylinder 7FDL diesel engine operating at 1050rpm to produce 1676kW (2250hp), the B23-7 was well suited for moderately heavy freight service, switching and branch-line work, making it comparable to EMD's GP38-2. Conrail, CSX, NS, Santa Fe, and Union Pacific were among large railroads that employed fleets of B23-7s. Conrail was the first line to order B23-7s, and it used them in a variety of secondary freight services. On its New England Division, it used them to switch yards and work local freights, as well as running them in sets of five or more to haul heavy ballast trains.

**Type:** Bo-Bo, diesel-electric
**Power and output:** GE FDL-12 producing 1676kW (2250hp)
**Tractive effort:** 271kN (61,000lbf) at 6.2kmh (10mph) with 83:20 gear ratio
**Max. operating speed:** 112km/h (70mph)
**Weight:** 127 tonnes (280,000lb)
**Overall Length:** 18.948m (62ft 2in)
**Gauge:** 1435mm (4ft 8.5in)

## GE C36-7 VARIOUS RAILROADS USA 1978

General Electric's high-horsepower C36-7 was introduced in 1978 and succeeded its earlier 3600hp six-motor U36-C. As with other DASH-7 models, the C36-7 featured a number of small improvements over earlier designs which were aimed at improving locomotive reliability. Early C36-7s were nearly identical to GE's 2237kW (3000hp) C30-7, and the primary difference between the two was a change in the output of the 7FDL-16 diesel-engine.

From 1983, GE supplied an improved C36-7 that incorporated some of the microprocessor controls featured on the DASH-8 types and also a new adhesion system. The last of the type featured a slightly higher output and had a pronounced hump behind the cab that housed dynamic brake grids. In 2002, a fleet of former Union Pacific C36-7s were rebuilt by General Electric and shipped to the Estonian Railways.

**Type:** Co-Co, diesel-electric
**Power and output:** GE 7FDL-16 producing 2686kW (3600hp)
**Tractive effort:** 431kN (96,900lbf) at 17.6km/h (11mph) with 83:20 gear ratio
**Max. operating speed:** 112km/h (70mph)
**Weight:** 189 tonnes (420,000lb)
**Overall length:** 20.5m (67ft 3in)
**Gauge:** 1435mm (4ft 8.5in)

**Conrail's twenty-five C36-7s were built in 1985. In 1997, a Conrail C36-7 leads a westbound freight at Tyrone, Pennsylvania.**

## U20C Co-Co JORDANIAN AQABA RAILWAY JORDAN 1980

**The Jordanian Aqaba Railway dedicated its fleet of GE model U20C machines to hauling phosphates traffic from El Abyad and El Hasa to the Red Sea port of Aqaba.**

The railways of Jordan use an unusual 1050mm (3ft 5in) gauge lying between the more common 'narrow' metre gauge (3ft 3in) and 'colonial' 1067mm (3ft 6in) gauge. The Jordanian Aqaba Railway bought 18 GE model U20C machines built in Brasil in 1980. Eleven units were operational in 2002. The U20C is a standard catalogue model which is produced by General Electric for export and supplied to several countries with many detailed variations and options available.

The basic U20C is a single-cab road switcher type hood unit powered by General Electric's own 12-cylinder 7FDL series engine, normally rated in this model at 1583kW (2150hp). Standard options on the design included weights ranging from 90 to 120 tonnes (19,841 to 26,455lb), 1000 to 1676mm (3ft 3in to 5ft 6in) gauge and 914 (3ft) or 1016mm (3ft 4in) driving wheel diameter.

**Type:** Co-Co diesel-electric
**Power:** 1583kW (2150hp) from GE 7FDL12 series engine
**Tractive effort:** 251kN (55,000lbf)
**Max. operating speed:** 100kmh (62.1mph)
**Weight:** 112 tonnes (246,960lb)
**Overall length:** 17.2m (56ft 1in)
**Gauge:** 1050mm (3ft 4in)

## Class Di4 NORWEGIAN STATE RAILWAYS (NSB) NORWAY 1980

Back in the late 1950s, NSB purchased the standard Nohab/GM Co-Co design of streamlined diesel locomotive for its main-line services on non-electrified routes. These were very similar to the Danish class MX and MY (A1A-A1As) and the Co-Cos purchased around the same time by the Belgian and Luxembourg railways, and later by Hungary. After 25 years of successful operation of the Nohab/GM class Di3 locomotives, NSB decided to stick to General Motors for its next main-line diesel purchase. They needed five locomotives for the non-electrified routes radiating out of Trondheim on the west coast, in particular the long line to Bodø in the north and the mountainous Røros route towards Oslo. These large locomotives were supplied by Henschel of Germany. Together with the forward-thrusting snowplough below the buffers and couplings, the pointed cab front design is said to be intended to sweep large drifts of snow aside should any be encountered at speed.

**NSB needed these large class Di4 Co-Cos to enable older locomotives to be displaced and also to raise freight loads on the mountainous railways out of Trondheim on the Norwegian west coast.**

**Type:** Mixed-traffic main-line diesel-electric
**Wheel arrangement:** Co-Co
**Power:** General Motors 16-645E3B 2451kW (3285hp); NEBB electric traction equipment
**Tractive effort:** 360kN (80,930lbf)
**Max. operating speed:** 140km/h (87.5mph)
**Weight:** 114 tonnes (249,475lb)
**Overall length:** 20.8m (68ft 3in)
**Gauge:** 1435mm (4ft 8.5in)

## 040 DL/DO TUNISIAN NATIONAL RAILWAYS (SNCFT) TUNISIA 1980

Société Nationale de Chemins de Fer Tunisiens (SNCFT) took delivery from Ganz-Mavag of Hungary of these two similar designs of four-axle Pielstick-engined diesel-hydraulic locomotives. Classes 040 DL and 040 DO were similar to the Hungarian class M41, the DL being of the same 1325kW (1800hp) power rating, while the later DO was 1764kW (2400hp).

The 040 DLs 231 to 240 were built in 1980 and the 040 DOs 281 to 285 and 040 DOs 321 to 335 in 1984. Both types have proved unreliable, however.

The remaining operational DLs appear to be occupied only in the Tunis area on empty passenger stock trains, while Dos work between Tunis and Monastir. Class DLs were all built and remain metre-gauge units, but the class DL unitss are alterable with SNCFT exchanging bogies and repositioning buffers as necessary. On both the narrow- and standard-gauge lines both classes may be found hauling air-conditioned passenger sets (formerly DMU)

**Unfortunately for SNCFT, both the 040 DL and 040 DOs proved unreliable in service and are being withdrawn early.**

**Type:** B-B diesel-hydraulic
**Power:** DL 1325kW (1800hp); DO 1764kW (2400hp) from Pielstick PA4-185 series engines
**Tractive effort:** 143kN (33,000lbf)
**Max. operating speed:** DL – 110km/h (68.3mph); DO – 130km/h (81.3mph)
**Weight:** DL – 62 tonnes (136,710lb); DO – 64 tonnes (141,120lb)
**Overall length:** 15.5m (50ft 7in)
**Gauge:** DL – 1000mm (3ft 3in); DO – 1000 or 1435mm (3ft 3in or 4ft 8.5in)

# EMD GP50 VARIOUS RAILROADS USA 1980

**Type:** Bo-Bo diesel-electric
**Power:** 2611kW (3500hp)
**Tractive effort:** 285kN (64,200 lbf) based on 70:17 gear ratio
**Max. operating speed:** 112km/h (70mph)
**Weight:** 117.9 tonnes (260,000lb)
**Overall length:** 18.211m (59 ft 9in)
**Gauge:** 1435mm (4ft 8.5in)

In the late 1970s, EMD pushed the limits of its 645 engine design, building experimental GP40X prototype locomotives. In 1980, it introduced the GP50, a more powerful successor to the popular GP40-2 model. The GP50, like its Co-Co counterpart the SD50, was powered by a 16-645F engine. Among the features on the GP50 was EMD's new Super-Series wheel slip control that used micro-processor control and ground speed radar inputs to improve tractive effort. The GP50's first purchaser was Chicago & North Western. Southern Railway ordered high-hood GP50s.

Reported flaws in the 645F engine hampered GP50 reliability, and a general sag in the railroad industry limited sales. In 1985, EMD's new GP60 succeeded the GP50 model.

**The GP50, like other high-horsepower Bo-Bo locomotives, was intended for fast intermodal container services and Chicago & North Western and Southern Railway were among the lines to purchase this locomotive.**

# GE B36-7 VARIOUS RAILROADS USA 1980

**Type:** Bo-Bo, diesel-electric
**Power:** GE FDL-12 producing 2686kW (3600hp)
**Tractive effort:** 287kN (64,600lbf) with 83:20 gear ratio
**Max. operating speed:** 113km/h (70mph)
**Weight:** 127 tonnes (280,000lb)
**Overall length:** 18.948m (62ft 2in)
**Gauge:** 1435mm (4ft 8.5in)

General Electric's B36-7 was a high-horsepower four-motor (Bo-Bo wheel arrangement) locomotive intended for fast freight service and typically used in multiples on priority intermodal trains. Externally, the B36-7 closely resembled lower output Dash-7 four-motor GE diesel electrics. The B36-7s were normally equipped with GE's FB-style bogie, a type often known as the floating bolster truck. Santa Fe, Seaboard System (a component of CSX), Southern Pacific, and Conrail were primary users of the B36-7 type. Conrail typically used B36-7s in sets of three (or mixed with GP40-2s) on its fast 'Trail-Van' intermodal trains which regularly operated at speeds up to 113km/h (70mph). Likewise, Southern Pacific often assigned its B30-7s and B36-7s to intermodal trains operating on its Sunset Route.

**Demoted from priority intermodel service, CSX B36-7 5834 and an EMD GP40-2 lead a westbound local freight on the old Boston & Albany at CP 83 in Palmer, Massachusetts, in December 2000.**

## CLASS ME DANISH RAILWAYS (DSB) DENMARK 1981

**With General Motors engines and alternating-current traction motors, the class ME Co-Cos were state-of-the-art machines when delivered to DSB. They work intercity and regional passenger trains.**

The last of the main-line diesel locomotives purchased by Danish Railways were principally for express passenger trains on the island of Zeeland. Initially, all the 'MEs' were painted in DSB corporate red livery. Class ME introduced DSB to the use of alternating current traction equipment in a diesel-electric design, with particularly lightweight traction motors.

**Type:** Mixed-traffic main-line diesel-electric
**Wheel arrangement:** Co-Co
**Power unit:** General Motors 16-645E3B 16-cylinder V-form two-stroke diesel, 2450kW (3285hp); alternator; six axle-hung AC traction motors
**Tractive effort:** N/A
**Max. operating speed:** 175km/h (110mph)
**Weight:** 115 tonnes (252,550lb)
**Overall length:** 21m (68ft 11in)
**Gauge:** 1435mm (4ft 8.5in)

## CLASS 2180 AUSTRIAN STATE RAILWAYS (ÖBB) AUSTRIA 1982

Beilhack is a prominent producer of rail-mounted snow-clearing machines, not just to European continental railways where snow is a frequent hazard to reliable train operation, but also to less snowy countries such as Great Britain. The machines are simple, self-propelled, two-axle vehicles with a full-width cab at the rear. At the front each machine has an array of rotating blades and screws for breaking up and slicing loose or packed snow, and for propelling it through directed shutes to the lineside. Purchased in 1982, the class 2180 machine has three 370kW (495hp) diesel engines, one for forward movement and two for working the snow clearing blades and screws. It is a development of a similar but smaller machine bought by ÖBB in 1975. In the UK a similar machine is based at Inverness in the highlands of Scotland, and one is in the southeast of England.

**Type:** Rail-mounted snow-clearing machine
**Wheel arrangement:** B
**Power unit:** Three 370kW (495bhp) diesel engines, one for traction and two for snow-clearing equipment
**Max. operating speed:** 80km/h (50mph)
**Weight:** 43 tonnes (94,430lb)
**Overall length:** 12.35m (40ft 6in)
**Gauge:** 1435mm (4ft 8.5in)

## MLW LRC VIA RAIL CANADA 1982

**Type:** Bo-Bo, diesel-electric
**Power and output:** 16-cylinder 251 producing 2760kW (3700hp)
**Tractive effort:** N/A
**Max. operating speed:** 200km/h (125mph)
**Weight:** 113.4 tonnes (250,000 lb)
**Overall length:** 19.406m (63ft 8in)
**Gauge:** 1435mm (4ft 8.5in)

**In May 1985, a VIA Rail LRC locomotive leads a westbound train of five non-tilting passenger cars in Toronto, Ontario. These uniquely styled diesel-electric locomotives are unlikely to be mistaken with other types.**

In the early 1980s, Canadian long-distance passenger operator VIA Rail sought to replace United Aircraft TurboTrains in high-speed service, primarily on the important Montreal–Toronto route. Bombardier designed a modern lightweight tilting train system dubbed LRC (for 'Light, Rapid, Comfortable') which used an active tilting system to provide great passenger comfort rounding curves by reducing the effects of centrifugal forces. To haul the trains, Bombardier built high-speed diesels with wedge-shaped low-profile carbodies powered by 16-cylinder Alco 251 diesels. The LRC locomotives were numbered in the 6900 series. Although often used to haul the LRC tilting trains, the 6900 series locomotives were also used to haul traditional non-tilting ones. By 2002, the LRC locomotives had been replaced with new GE GENESIS types.

## A CLASS CO-CO FREIGHT AUSTRALIA AUSTRALIA 1983

**A Class, a classic. Still hard at work 50 years from first entry into service. Two are captured here heading a fast passenger train, a sight still to be found into the 21st century.**

Rebuilt from class B, the 11 class As were originally for express passenger services, but are now used on freight. Twenty-six class Bs were built in 1952 by Clyde with 1178kW (1600hp) 16-cylinder 567 series engines and were the first main-line diesels in Victoria on both freight and passenger until the 1980s before scrapping or rebuild with 12-cylinder 645 power engines. V/Line still uses four class As, despite the class being 50 years old, while Freight Australia operates seven.

**Type:** Co-Co diesel-electric
**Power:** 1846kW (2475hp) from EMD 12-645 series engine
**Tractive effort:** 212kN (47700lbf) at 24km/h (15mph) continuous
**Max. operating speed:** 133km/h (83mph)
**Weight:** 118 tonnes (260,190lb)
**Overall length:** 18.542m (60ft 6in)
**Gauge:** 1435mm and 1600mm (4ft 8.5in and 5ft 3in)

## CLASS 58 BRITISH RAIL GREAT BRITAIN 1983

Similar to the standard GM-built locomotives in Ireland in layout, the British Rail class 58 diesel-electric was a simple if unusual in looks, freight diesel locomotive with a full-width cab at each end, but a narrow body between.

In all, 50 class 58s were built. Each had a modern Ruston engine developed from the much older English Electric type in the class 37 fleet. The engine drove an alternator, current from which was rectified and fed to six axle-mounted DC traction motors.

In service, the class 58 fleet operated coal trains in the English Midlands and later gravitated towards general freight, finishing their work in the south of England. All are now withdrawn from service in the United Kingdom, having been displaced by the GM class 66 fleet which has much higher tractive effort. At the time of writing, the present owners of these locomotives, English, Welsh & Scottish Railway (EWS), is negotiating a possible sale of some class 58s to ACTS of Holland.

**Type:** Freight main-line diesel-electric
**Wheel arrangement:** Co-Co
**Power unit:** Ruston 12RK3ACT 12-cylinder V-form diesel, 2462kW (3300hp); Brush alternator; six axle-hung DC traction motors
**Tractive effort:** 275kN (61,800lbf)
**Max. operating speed:** 130km/h (80mph)
**Weight:** 130 tonnes (285,490lb)
**Overall length:** 19.140m (62ft 9in)
**Gauge:** 1435mm (4ft 8.5in)

**This is 58 050, named Toton Traction Depot, in EWS maroon-and-gold livery, hauling a track maintenance train at Didcot. This class has been withdrawn from UK service.**

## CLASS 141 BRITISH RAIL — GREAT BRITAIN 1984

At a time when British Rail wanted to replace older diesel multiple units with something of lower cost, a small series of prototype two-axle diesel mechanical railcars was developed using road bus–style bodies on what in effect was a modern wagon underframe. The class 141 was the first series production group of two-car sets in this format, each car having one underfloor diesel engine driving through a hydraulic transmission to one axle. The 20 '141' units were never popular and were withdrawn after only 15 years service. Classes 142 to 144 live on.

**In West Yorkshire Passenger Transport Executive maroon livery, this class 141 has carriage bodies narrower than the railway standard as a result of road bus components being used in the construction.**

**Type:** Local passenger diesel multiple unit
**Diesel engine (per car):** Leyland TL11 149kW (200hp) six-cylinder
**Transmission:** Voith T211r hydraulic
**Max. operating speed:** 120km/h (75mph)
**Weight:** 25+26 tonnes (54,880+56,000lb)
**Overall length:** 15.25m (50ft)
**Gauge:** 1435mm (4ft 8.5in)

## CLASS 150 SPRINTER BRITISH RAIL — GREAT BRITAIN 1984

The now familiar Class 150 Sprinter heralded the arrival of a new generation of diesel mechanical multiple units and also marked the end of locomotive haulage on many of the United Kingdom's secondary passenger services.

A contract for two prototype three-car diesel multiple units was placed with British Rail Engineering Limited (BREL) in 1983. The first to be built was powered by a Cummins NT855R5 engine rated at 213kW (285hp) at 2100rpm, driving a Voith 211 hydraulic transmission via a cardan shaft. The second unit originally featured a Rolls-Royce Eagle C6280HR engine. This drove a R500 fully automatic gearbox via a cardan shaft. Subsequent builds were fitted with Cummins/Voith power equipment. Maximum speed for the prototype units was 120km/h (75mph). The prototypes ran extensive trials on regular passenger services on the Derby -Matlock branch, clipping up to10 minutes off the normal journey time.

So impressive were these prototypes that an order was placed in November 1984, with BREL, York, for further two-car Sprinter sets, Nos 150 010–150 150 (some three-car sets operate with Class 150/2 centre cars). The subsequent Class150/2 two-car sets from BREL York (Nos150 201–150 285) appeared with cab end corridor connections making them more attractive than their predecessors and operationally more flexible when working in multiples.

**This is one of the two-car formations of the original Class 150 Sprinter design, in British Rail's original Provincial Railways livery of pale blue and beige.**

**Type:** General-purpose passenger diesel multiple unit
**Power:** 1 x Cummins NT855R5 of 213kW (285hp)
**Tractive effort:** N/A
**Max. operating speed:** 121km/h (75mph)
**Weight:** 38.45 tonnes (84,782lb)
**Overall length (average vehicle):** 19.964m (65ft 6in)
**Gauge:** 1435mm (4ft 8.5in)

# GE B39-8 'DASH 8' VARIOUS RAILROADS USA 1984

**A trio of GE's LMX leasing B39-8s leads a long freight on the former Burlington (later Burlington Northern, now BNSF) Chicago to Aurora, Illinois, triple-track main line.**

**Type:** Bo-Bo, diesel-electric
**Power:** GE 7FDL-16 producing 2909kW (3900hp)
**Tractive effort:** 303kN (68,100 lbf) continuous TE at 29.3km/h (18.3 mph) with the 112km/h (70mph) gear option
**Max. operating speed:** 112km/h (70mph); 120km/h (75mph) using optional gearing
**Weight:** 127 tonnes (280,000 lbs)
**Overall Length:** 20.218m (66ft 4in)
**Gauge:** 1435mm (4ft 8.5in)

General Electric pioneered microprocessor control systems designed to improve the performance and efficiency of diesel-electric locomotives. Its microprocessor controlled locomotives appeared in the early 1980s as its DASH 8 line. Prior to regular production of DASH 8 locomotives, GE built several fleets of 'pre-production' DASH 8s for service on North American railways. Santa Fe operated three B39-8s numbered 7400 to 7402. These locomotives produced 2909kW (3900hp) and, like other high-horsepower Bo-Bo types, were primarily used on fast intermodal trains. Later, GE built production B39-8s (designated B39-8E by some sources) for Southern Pacific and LMX, the latter being a lease fleet originally assigned to Burlington Northern. The B39-8 was superseded by the DASH 8-40B in the late 1980s.

# 'CASTLE' CLASS NORTHERN IRELAND RAILWAYS (NIR) GREAT BRITAIN 1985

In the 1980s, Northern Ireland Railways needed to replace older DEMUs with a low-cost solution. BREL in England supplied a three-car design that used underframes from withdrawn BR mark 1 carriages – new bogies, new bodies like the BR class 455 suburban EMUs and existing but redundant NIR power units and electric traction equipment. Nine such half-price units were shipped to Northern Ireland. They operate over the whole NIR system.

**One of the NIR Castle class DEMUs passes the cliffs and beach at Downhill on the line to Londonderry. Unlike the driving trailer, the cab end of the power car is non-gangwayed.**

**Type:** Passenger DEMU
**Power:** English Electric 4SRKT 410kW (550bhp) four-cylinder upright diesel (one per three-car unit); EE DC generator; two EE DC traction motors on power car's inner bogie
**Max. operating speed:** 120km/h (75mph)
**Weight:** 62.0+30.4+32.4 tonnes (138,880+68,095+72,575lb)
**Overall length:** 20.28m (66ft 6in) end cars; 20.38m (66ft 10in) centre cars
**Gauge:** 1600mm (5ft 3in)

## DE 11000 TURKISH STATE RAILWAYS (TCDD) TURKEY 1985

The TCDD made extensive use of diesel railcars, mostly power cars with trailers for branch-line use, but including long-distance express units running such trains as the Bogaziçi Express between Haydarpasa (Istanbul) and Ankara. They were mostly German-built. The product of a joint venture between Krauss-Maffei of Munich and the Tülomsas works of Turkey, 85 of these diesel-electric railcars were built in Turkey between 1985 and1990 for use on branch lines.

**Railcars were extremely suitable for Turkish branch lines, but competition from minibus-type road transport in recent years has severely reduced the number of passenger-carrying branches.**

**Type:** Diesel-electric railcar
**Power:** 780kW (1045.2hp)
**Tractive effort:** 225kN (50,593lbf)
**Max. operating speed:** 80km/h (50mph)
**Total weight:** Not known
**Overall length:** 13.25m (43ft 6in)
**Gauge:** Not known

## CLASS 59 FOSTER YEOMAN MENDIP RAIL GREAT BRITAIN 1986

The first privately owned main-line diesel locomotives for operation on BR tracks were the Foster Yeoman class 59 General Motors Co-Cos. For hauling stone trains of up to 3000 tonnes (2953 tons) with one locomotive, class 59s have electronic wheel creep control enabling the wheels to slip very slightly when starting heavy loads, maximizing wheel/rail adhesion. ARC and Northern Power also purchased small numbers of these locomotives.

**A very heavy train (for British conditions) of stone hoppers snakes its way towards Greater London from a Somerset quarry with a class 59 at its head.**

**Type:** Freight main-line diesel-electric
**Wheel arrangement:** Co-Co
**Power unit:** GM 16-645E3C 16-cylinder V-form two-stroke diesel, 2460kW (3300bhp); GM alternator; six axle-hung DC traction motors
**Tractive effort:** 542kN (122,000lbf)
**Max. operating speed:** 95 to 120km/h (60 to 75mph)
**Weight:** 126 tonnes (276,705lb)
**Overall length:** 21.35m (70ft 1in)
**Gauge:** 1435mm (4ft 8.5in)

# CLASS 5047 DMUS AUSTRIAN STATE RAILWAYS (ÖBB) AUSTRIA 1987

Austrian railways include a number of secondary lines that meander up narrow valleys among the mountains, as well as some quite long secondary routes that offer limited traffic. Built by Jenbacher Werke, class 5047 was designed to meet this requirement, and it does so well. It is a conventional single car design with cab at each end and swing plug entrance doors at each end of each bodyside. The driving cabs have a hatch through which the driver can walk to inspect tickets, and he has a passenger communication microphone in the cab for travel information.

These vehicles are particularly used in the lowlands and hills in a radius of about 200km (120 miles) around Vienna, and they also cross into Hungary at Sopron and further south. The joint Austro-Hungarian GySEV railway company has also taken delivery of some of this class. ÖBB has more than 30. Following the success of class 5047, some trailer cars have also been purchased.

**Type:** Secondary and branch-line passenger diesel multiple unit
**Power:** Daimler Benz OM 444A 420kW (560bhp) six-cylinder diesel (one car only)
**Transmission:** Hydraulic
**Max. operating speed:** 120km/h (75mph)
**Weight:** Not known
**Overall length each car:** 25.42m (83ft 5in)
**Gauge:** 1435mm (4ft 8.5in)

**One of ÖBB's excellent class 5047 diesel railcars arriving at a main-line station, having worked a branch-line service. These cars have comfortable accommodation suitable for medium distances.**

# CLASS 628.2 FEDERAL GERMAN RAILWAYS (DB) GERMANY 1987

To replace its old Uerdingen diesel railbuses and its battery electric railcars that worked local and branch-line passenger services, *Deutsche Bundesbahn* took delivery of 460 two-car diesel multiple units split between classes 628.2 (150) and 628.4 (with more powerful engines). The layout of these vehicles follows from the success of a small fleet of prototypes that entered service from 1974. Underneath one car of each two-car unit is a horizontally mounted diesel engine driving through an hydraulic torque converter gearbox and cardan shafts to the wheels of one bogie. There are three passenger entrance doors on each side, two located at the bodyside ends behind the cabs, and one door at the inner end of one vehicle. The units are designed for one-man operation.

**A familiar sight at most German railway stations, here a class 628 diesel unit is ready to leave a branch terminus.**

**Type:** Secondary and branch line passenger diesel multiple unit
**Power:** Daimler Benz OM 444A 410kW (550bhp) 6-cylinder diesel (one car only)
**Transmission:** Voith T320rz hydraulic
**Max. operating speed:** 120km/h (75mph)
**Weight:** 40+28tonnes (87,845+61,490lb)
**Overall length each car:** 23.2m (76ft 1in)
**Gauge:** 1435mm (4ft 8.5in)

## GE DASH 8-40B VARIOUS RAILROADS USA 1987

The DASH 8-40B was General Electric's production DASH-8 high-horsepower four-motor model, which effectively superseded the B39-8. The DASH-8 line was characterized by its use of microprocessor controls for better performance and reliability. Like other GE high-horsepower four-motor models, the DASH 8-40B (often listed as a B40-8 to keep in accordance with GE's earlier nomenclature) was designed for high-horsepower applications such as fast intermodal work. The principal intermodal carriers (Conrail, Southern Pacific and Santa Fe) were the primary customers.

**One of Susquehanna's second order of DASH 8-40Bs at Buffalo, New York, in 1989. Most of Susquehanna's DASH 8-40Bs became part of the CSX fleet in the early 1990s.**

New York, Susquehanna & Western (a regional railroad competing with Conrail for intermodal traffic) also operated a fleet of DASH 8-40Bs. Standard DASH 8-40B have a boxier cab than early DASH-8 types. Santa Fe ordered DASH 8-40BWs featuring North American Safety Cabs.

**Type:** Bo-Bo, diesel-electric
**Power:** GE 7FDL-16 producing 2984kW (4000hp)
**Tractive effort:** N/A
**Max. operating speed:** N/A
**Weight:** 130.1 tonnes (287,000lb)
**Overall Length:** 20.218m (66ft 4in)
**Gauge:** 1435mm (4ft 8.5in)

## GE DASH 8-40C VARIOUS RAILROADS USA 1987

**Type:** Co-Co, diesel-electric
**Power:** GE 7FDL-16 producing 2984kW (4000hp)
**Tractive effort:** N/A
**Max. operating speed:** N/A
**Weight:** 176.6 tonnes (389,500lb)
**Overall length:** 21.539m (70ft 8in)
**Gauge:** 1435mm (4ft 8.5in)

General Electric's DASH-8 line introduced microprocessor controls to obtain greater locomotive performance and reliability. The DASH 8-40C was a six-motor model introduced in 1987. This was among GE's most successful products and helped the company to become America's foremost locomotive builder. With 2984kW (4000hp), the DASH 8-40C is a powerful machine designed for heavy freight service, with the '40' in the designation indicating horsepower and the 'C' six-motors.

The production DASH-8s such as the DASH 8-40C featured more boxy cabs than those used by early pre-production models such as the C32-8. Union Pacific was the first to order the DASH 8-40C and amassed a roster of 256 numbered in the 9100-9300 series. It acquired more DASH 8-40Cs (which Union Pacific designates C40-8) with the purchase of Chicago & North Western in 1995.

**A quartet of GE DASH 8-40Cs leads a westbound autorack train down Archer Hill near Burns, Wyoming, in September 1989. Each locomotive develops 2984kW (4000hp), giving this consist has a combined output of 11,931kW (16,000hp), more than five EMD SD40-2s.**

## CLASS 6400 NETHERLANDS RAILWAYS (NS) NETHERLANDS 1988

**Type:** Freight main line diesel-electric
**Wheel arrangement:** Bo-Bo
**Power:** MTU 12V396 TC 13 12-cylinder V-form diesel, 1180kW (1580hp); Brown Boveri alternator; four axle-hung AC traction motors
**Tractive effort:** 290kN (65,195lbf)
**Max. operating speed:** 120km/h (75mph)
**Weight:** 80 tonnes (175,685lb)
**Overall length:** 14.4m (47ft 3in)
**Gauge:** 1435mm (4ft 8.5in)

To replace the class 2200 and 2400 diesels, *Nederlandse Spoorwegen* ordered 120 Bo-Bo diesel 'hood units' for freight haulage and shunting. These MaK-built locomotives work in multiples of one, two or three as required by the weight of trains and have three-phase AC traction. A few are equipped to work into Germany or into Belgium. The 120 '6400s' began life in NS grey-and-yellow livery, but are now being repainted in NS Cargo (Railion) red.

**NS purchased 120 of these modern mixed-traffic Bo-Bos, used on freight and heavy shunting. Heavy freights use multiple groups of up to three locomotives.**

## CLASS IC3 DANISH RAILWAYS (DSB) DENMARK 1989

**Type:** Express three-car articulated diesel multiple unit
**Power:** Four Deutz BF8L eight-cylinder diesel engines, each of 294kW (395hp); hydraulic drive
**Tractive effort:** N/A
**Max. operating speed:** 180km/h (112mph)
**Weight per unit:** 97tonnes (213,020lb)
**Overall length per unit:** 58.8m (192ft 11in)
**Gauge:** 1435mm (4ft 8.5in)

Faced with a need to upgrade its intercity services, DSB decided on a radical approach that resulted in these unusual but highly successful trains. The 92 DSB 'IC3s' are three-car articulated DMUs designed to couple in multiples of up to 12 vehicles.

Externally, the class IC3s have white-painted ribbed bodysides in a curved profile. The sound insulation is very good, even outside the trains, as the running of the diesel engine under each car is not obtrusive even at enclosed stations such as Copenhagen. The cab fronts have a novel style of gangway end. The driver sits in a central position with a wide view windscreen. Surrounding the vehicle front is a deep and flexible rubber-type ring. When units are coupled together the driver's cab swings inwards into the side of the vehicle interior to reveal a gangway, and the rubber rings compress to seal the join between the adjacent carriages.

Unusually, the IC3s are regularly worked in multiple with the later class IR4 electric multiple units, which are constructed to a similarly innovative design.

**Danish State Railways has 92 of these unusual units in its fleet, all of which are used on intercity routes out of Copenhagen. Other units of this design were exported to Sweden and to Israel.**

## CLASS 240 FEDERAL GERMAN RAILWAYS (DB) GERMANY 1989

In the late 1980s DB needed some large diesel locomotives capable of hauling InterCity express passenger trains and heavy freights. Three powerful prototypes emerged from Krupp, with three-phase electric traction equipment. After testing, they worked on express trains running north from Hamburg. German reunification brought the East German DR class 232 series locomotives to the DB, and the need for the class 240 evaporated. DB has sold them to a Dutch company called Short Lines who use them on freights from Rotterdam.

**Type:** Mixed traffic main line diesel-electric
**Wheel arrangement:** Co-Co
**Power:** MaK 12M282 12-cylinder V-form diesel, 2650kW (3550hp); alternator; six AC traction motors
**Tractive effort:** 400kN (89,925lbf)
**Max. operating speed:** 160km/h (100mph)
**Weight:** 120 tonnes (263,530lb)
**Overall length:** 20.96m (68ft 9in)
**Gauge:** 1435mm (4ft 8.5in)

## CLASS 60 BRITISH RAIL GREAT BRITAIN 1989

**Type:** Freight main-line diesel-electric
**Wheel arrangement:** Co-Co
**Power:** Mirrlees 8MB275T eight-cylinder diesel, 2313kW (3100hp); Brush alternator; six axle-hung DC traction motors
**Tractive effort:** 475kN (106,500lbf)
**Max. operating speed:** 100km/h (62mph)
**Weight:** 129 tonnes (283,295lb)
**Overall length:** 21.335m (70ft)
**Gauge:** 1435mm (4ft 8.5in)

In the late 1980s, British Rail required some more heavy haul diesel locomotives. The successful bidder was the Brush company, which delivered a fleet of 100 locomotives, designated class 60. These used separately excited traction motors for high adhesion, and they were put to work on coal, oil, steel and aggregate trains as well as general freight. BR's Railfreight business painted the locomotives in three shades of grey with decals for particular product groups.

**This class 60 is heading a train of aggregate stone hopper wagons. Other class 60 duties include coal traffic, heavy steel trains, and long trains of 100 tonne oil tank cars from refineries such as at Immingham on the Humber estuary.**

## CLASS 158 BRITISH RAIL — GREAT BRITAIN 1989

**Type:** Express passenger diesel multiple unit
**Power:** Cummins NTA855R 260 to 300kW (350 to 400bhp) or Perkins 2006-TWH 260kW (350bhp) horizontal diesel (one per car)
**Transmission:** Hydraulic
**Max. operating speed:** 145km/h (90mph)
**Weight:** 38 to 39 tonnes (84,670 to 86,240lb)
**Overall length each car:** 22.57m (74ft 1in)
**Gauge:** Not known

British Rail's ultimate development of the class 150 Sprinter range of DMUs was an express design with full air-conditioning, double-glazed and carpeted throughout, and with a top speed of 145km/h (90mph). The 158s are formed as 17 three-car sets and 155 twins. They work cross-country routes between major provincial centres including the trans-Pennine axis and between East Anglia, the Midlands, Wales and the southwest. The three-car class 159s at South West Trains (derived from the 150s) have set even higher standards of comfort for DMU passengers.

**The class 158 diesel multiple units work cross-country routes in Britain and provide passengers with the benefits of air conditioning and double glazing to cut down noise.**

## CLASS 601/651 HELLENIC RAILWAYS ORGANIZATION — GREECE 1989

To operate comfortable long-distance services on its relatively slow main lines, Greek Railways uses a group of well-appointed diesel-electric trains. Twelve are four-car sets built in 1989, and a further eight five-car units were delivered from LEW in Germany from 1995. The two power cars, one at each end of a unit, each employ a 1343kW (1800hp) diesel power unit supplying current for the electric traction motors. The units have comfortable, spacious seating, air conditioning and buffet facilities. They are used on the trunk main line that links Athens with Greece's second city, Thessaloniki, and also on the long, straggly, single-track main line that links the Bulgarian and Turkish borders with Thessaloniki. The units are able to operate in multiple as eight, nine or ten-car trains, and they have a top speed of 160km/h (100mph) which will be achieved when the upgrading of the trunk main line is further advanced. After electrification of the main line, these units are expected to be used primarily on trains from Athens that branch off the main line to serve coastal and interior cities.

**Type:** InterCity express diesel-electric four-car (class 601) and five-car (651) multiple units
**Power:** 1343kW (1800hp) diesels (2), electric transmission to bogie mounted traction motors
**Tractive effort:** N/A
**Max. operating speed:** 161km/h (100mph)
**Weight:** Not known
**Overall length:** Not known
**Gauge:** 1435mm (4ft 8.5in)

## EMD SD60M VARIOUS RAILROADS — USA 1989

**Type:** Diesel-electric
**Power:** 16-cylinder 710G producing 2831kW (3800hp)
**Tractive effort:** 445kN (100,000lbf) continuous TE; 664kN (149,500lbf) starting TE with 70:17 gear ratio and 25 per cent adhesion
**Max. operating speed:** N/A
**Weight:** N/A
**Overall length:** 21.819m (71ft 7in)
**Gauge:** 1435mm (4ft 8.5in)

In 1984, Electro-Motive introduced the SD60 model which used its new 710G engine, a power plant that replaced the troubled 645F engine in EMD's domestic locomotive line.

Rated at 2831kW (3800hp), the SD60 was nominally more powerful than the SD50 model, yet it was substantially more reliable. In 1989, the Union Pacific railroad received the first SD60Ms, which were significant because of their first use of the

**The EMD SD60M was the first American type to use the modern North American Safety Cab, a style that has become predominant with new freight locomotives. In this photograph, a former Conrail SD60M leads a westbound at Mexico, PA, in November 2001.**

North American Safety Cab, the so-called 'wide-nose' cab. This particular cab has since become the predominant crew accommodation on new American locomotives. The 'M' prefix used in EMD's designation indicates the Safety Cab option.

Some later locomotives were equipped with an 'Isolated Cab' (with considerably better sound proofing), and these locomotives are designated SD60I. Union Pacific, Conrail, Burlington Northern and Soo Line were among SD60M operators.

## GE DASH 8-40CW VARIOUS RAILROADS USA 1989

One of the most significant changes in the appearance of freight diesels in the United States was to come with the adoption in the late 1980s and early 1990s of the North American Safety Cab, the so-called 'wide-nose cab'. Union Pacific bought the first GE wide-nose cabs in 1990, with an order of DASH 8-40CWs. The 'W' in GE's model designation signifies the locomotive uses the North American Safety Cab.

Other than the cab, which adds a few thousand pounds to the locomotive weight, the DASH 8-40CW is mechanically the same as the DASH 8-40C. By the mid-1990s, nearly all new freight locomotives were being built with wide-nose cabs. Conrail, CSX, and Santa Fe also bought DASH 8-40CWs, assigning them to general road freight service.

**Type:** Co-Co, diesel-electric
**Power:** GE 7FDL-16 producing 2984kW (4000hp)
**Tractive effort:** N/A
**Max. operating speed:** N/A
**Weight:** 180 tonnes (398,000lb)
**Overall length:** 21.539m (70ft 8in)
**Gauge:** 1435mm (4ft 8.5in)

**The former Pennsylvania Railroad main line across its namesake state is one of the busiest freight corridors in North America, as evidenced here with three freight trains on the move simultaneously. Leading a RoadRailer on the centre track is a GE DASH 8-40CW.**

## CLASS EL CO-CO AUSTRALIAN NATIONAL RAILWAYS AUSTRALIA 1990

The 14 members of Australian National class EL are General Electric model C30-8 built by the Australian GE licensee Gonian. Despite being relatively new and with more than 10 years in service, all were taken out of traffic on privatization of Australian National. As mileage and engine hours were low, further use was expected of them and all but one has been sold to Chicago Freight Car Leasing for contract leasing to other operators within Australia. All may be found today working on the eastern side of Australia with companies such as Freight Australia, Austrac, and Lachlan Valley Railfreight.

**Type:** Co-Co diesel-electric
**Power:** 2462kW (3300hp) from GE 7FDL-12 series engine
**Tractive effort:** 197kN (44,325lbf) at 34km/h (21.3mph)
**Max. operating speed:** 140km/h (87mph)
**Weight:** 114 tonnes (251,370lb)
**Overall length:** 19.6m (64ft)
**Gauge:** 1435mm (4ft 8.5in)

**Distinctive raked back but flat cabs combined with rather angular overall styling identify this pair of class EL units coupled back to back working in multiple-unit operation on heavy freight duty.**

## EMD GP60M SANTA FE RAILROAD USA 1990

**In the early 1990s, Santa Fe's GP60Ms were among the line's star performers in transcontinental intermodal service. Several lines, including Santa Fe, ordered GP60s with conventional cabs.**

It was the Santa Fe railroad that led the development of the North American Safety Cab in the late 1980s, in order to provide its crews with a better and safer working environment. Based in part on the Cowl locomotives of the 1960s, and also the Canadian Cab used since the early 1970s, the North American Safety Cab was designed to provide a better forward view and greater crew protection in a collision.

The first Santa Fe locomotives to use the new cab were its EMD GP60Ms delivered in 1990. These were also the first new locomotives since the 1960s to be delivered in the railroad's famous 'Warbonnet' livery. Designated as Super Series machines, the GP60Ms were primarily assigned to priority intermodal freight. Santa Fe was the only line to order them.

**Type:** Diesel-electric
**Power and output:** EMD 16-710G producing 2835kW (3800hp)
**Tractive effort:** N/A
**Max. operating speed:** N/A
**Weight:** 118 tonnes (260,000lb)
**Overall length:** 18.212m (59ft 9in)
**Gauge:** 1435mm (4ft 8.5in)

## EMD F40PHM-2 METRA — USA 1991

**Type:** Bo-Bo passenger diesel-electric
**Power:** EMD 16-645E producing 2384kW (3200hp)
**Tractive effort:** N/A
**Max. operating speed:** N/A
**Weight:** N/A
**Overall length:** 17.2m (56ft 2in)
**Gauge:** 1435mm (4ft 8.5in)

The F40PHM-2 is a model produced by EMD between 1991 and 1992 for Chicago's METRA suburban passenger railway. In most respects, the F40PHM-2 is the same as late model EMD F40PH-2s – the primary difference is a modified cab style. The roof line of the F40PHM was extended forward and, instead of a traditional nose, the windshield dropped down at an angle to join the front of the locomotive. This cab style was first used on EMD's experimental F69PH-AC – a model which was used in the late 1990s to forward AC traction technology and assigned to Amtrak.

As with METRA F40PH models, the F40PHM-2 has two sets of headlights, the top headlights being of the oscillating variety. The F40PHM-2s were largely used to replace ageing Burlington Northern E9s on the Chicago Union Station to Aurora route.

**The F40PHM-2 was a type peculiar to Chicago's Metra commuter rail operator. They are known as 'Winnebagos' because their appearance resembles the popular highway camper.**

## CLASS 165 BRITISH RAIL — GREAT BRITAIN 1992

For an outer suburban train, the class 165 three-car units set new standards of comfort for their passengers. Wider than standard, by taking advantage of the former Great Western Railway's bigger structure gauge, the Networker Turbos provide comfortable seating with a quiet ambience that is not typical of earlier suburban DMUs. Internal sliding doors keep down the draughts when the bodyside sliding doors are open to the platforms. These vehicles operate services from London Paddington to Oxford, Stratford and Hereford, as well as from London Marylebone to Aylesbury.

**The class 165s were delivered in two-car (as seen here) and three-car formations, and they serve suburban routes out of London Paddington and Marylebone stations. The example seen in this photograph is decked out in the Network SouthEast colours, as delivered new.**

**Type:** Outer suburban diesel multiple unit
**Power:** Perkins 2006-TWH 260kW (350bhp) horizontal (one per car)
**Tractive effort:** N/A
**Transmission:** Hydraulic
**Max. operating speed:** 145km/h (90mph)
**Weight:** 38 tonnes (82,880lb)
**Overall length each car:** 23m (77ft 1in)
**Gauge:** 1435mm (4ft 8.5in)

## CLASS DK5600 TURKISH STATE RAILWAYS (TCDD) TURKEY 1992

Ten units of this class were built, with bodies by the Turkish Tüvasas works and the mechanical parts provided by the Budapest-based British–Hungarian joint venture of Ganz-Hunslet.

Diesel-hydraulic railcars were certainly not new to the TCDD, which had been operating MAN-engined express units with Voith transmission since the 1960s. Holding 68 passengers, these are relatively high-speed units which are intended to operate between major centres on main lines.

**Type:** Diesel-hydraulic railcar
**Power:** 300kW (402hp)
**Tractive effort:** Not known
**Max. operating speed:** 120km/h (75mph)
**Total weight:** Not known
**Maximum axle load:** Not known
**Overall length:** Not known
**Gauge:** Not known

## EMD SD70MAC BURLINGTON NORTHERN RAILROAD USA 1993

Up until the SD70MAC, all commercial mass-produced diesel-electrics used conventional direct-current traction motors. In the late 1980s and early 1990s, EMD worked with Siemens to develop a practical alternating current traction system for heavy North American service. The advantages of AC traction include significantly greater tractive effort through superior motor control, more effective dynamic braking (especially slow speeds) and longer motor life.

Burlington Northern supported the development of the SD70MAC by ordering hundreds of the type for use on its Powder River Coal trains. BN could use three SD70MACs in place of five SD40-2s in coal service as a result of the significantly higher tractive effort produced by AC traction. CSX and Conrail also ordered small fleets of SD70MACs for heavy service.

**Shortly before Conrail was divided by CSX and Norfolk Southern, it received 15 SD70MACs from EMD built to CSX specifications. A pair of SD70MACs is seen at Lock 10, near Hoffmanns, New York.**

**Type:** Co-Co, AC traction, diesel-electric
**Power:** EMD 16-710G3C-T1 producing 2980kW (4000hp)
**Tractive effort:** 609kN (137,000lbf) continuous TE; 778kN (175,000lbf) starting TE with 85:16 gear ratio and 33 per cent adhesion.
**Max. operating speed:** N/A
**Weight:** N/A
**Overall length:** 22.555m (74 ft)
**Gauge:** 1435mm (4ft 8.5in)

# GE DASH-9-44CW VARIOUS RAILROADS USA 1993

**Burlington Northern Santa Fe has settled on GE's DASH 9-44CW as its standard locomotive for intermodal and general freight work. These GE DASH 9-44CW's wear the BNSF 'Heritage II' livery.**

In 1993, General Electric was to introduce its 'DASH 9' line to reflect important technological modifications in its domestic locomotive line – improvements that resulted in better fuel efficiency, tighter emission control and better adhesion. Externally one of the most obvious differences between the DASH 9 line and DASH 8 models is the use of a new bogie design known as GE's 'Hi-AD' truck. The DASH 9 line became GE's standard direct current traction model line. The DASH 9-44CW should not be confused with the outwardly similar AC traction AC4400CW.

Initially, the DASH 9 line consisted of just the DASH 9-44CW, which was ordered by Chicago & North Western, Southern Pacific and Santa Fe among other carriers. Later other models were ordered, such as the DASH 9-40C which was taken up by Norfolk Southern.

**One of the features of the GE DASH 9-44CW is the Hi-AD truck. This style of truck, or bogie, was also utilized on some AC4400CWs, a model built concurrently with the DASH 9.**

**Type:** Co-Co, diesel-electric
**Power:** GE 7FDL-16 producing 3278kW (4400hp)
**Tractive effort:** Varies with options
**Max. operating speed:** Not known
**Weight:** Varies with options; 181.6 tonnes (400,000lb)
**Overall length:** 22.403m (73ft 6in)
**Gauge:** 1435mm (4ft 8.5in)

## GE GENESIS, MODEL DASH-8-40BP AMTRAK USA 1993

By the early 1990s, Amtrak's fleet of EMD F40PHs, the mainstay of its long-distance passenger fleet for almost two decades, was showing its age. Amtrak worked with General Electric to design an all-new locomotive specifically for passenger service. Specification for the new locomotive was AMD-103 (which is what the locomotives were often called in their early years), but they are also known as model DASH 8-40BP, called P40s by Amtrak and the GENESIS type by GE. The locomotive used a newly designed monocoque body, where the shell is integral to the structure of the locomotive. The first GENESIS locomotives were built in 1993 and numbered in the 800 series. There are now three types of GENESIS, including a dual-mode AC traction model.

**Type:** Bo-Bo, passenger diesel-electric
**Power:** GE 7FDL-16 producing 2984kW (4000hp)
**Tractive effort:** 171kN (38,500lbf) at 53km/h (33mph) with 74:20 gear ratio
**Max. operating speed:** 165km/h (103mph)
**Weight:** 121.8 tonnes (268,240lb)
**Overall length:** 21.031m (69 ft)
**Gauge:** 1435mm (4ft 8.5in)

**A pair of GENESIS and a pair of EMD F40PHs lead Amtrak's *Southwest Chief* over the former Santa Fe. Today the GENESIS type is the most common long-distance passenger locomotive used by Amtrak.**

## CLASS 201 CO-CO IRISH RAIL (CIE) IRELAND 1994

By 1994, when Irish Rail took delivery of the first of its 201 Class locomotives (model JT42HCW), it had more than 30 years experience with Electro-Motive products. The first locomotive, No. 201, was delivered by an Antonov 124 aircraft. The 201s feature a cab at either end and are equipped with head end power for use on the Dublin–Belfast *Enterprise* service. Two of the 201s are owned by NI Railways. As of 2002, five of the 35 Class 201s were painted for the *Enterprise* service, the remainder were in Irish Rail orange, black and yellow livery. The 201s are the primary type of main-line locomotive on most Irish Rail routes.

**Type:** Co-Co, diesel-electric
**Power:** EMD 12-710G3B producing 2253kW (3000hp) for traction.
**Tractive effort:** 194kN (43,611lbf) continuous TE
**Max. operating speed:** 161km/h (100mph)
**Weight:** 112 tonnes (230,000 lbs)
**Overall length:** 20.949m (68ft 9in)
**Gauge:** 1600mm (5ft 3in)

**On 4 March 2000, an Irish Rail Class 201 leads a suburban consist downroad across the causeway near Donebate. The first of these EMD-built locomotives was delivered by airplane in 1994.**

## MK5000C SOUTHERN PACIFIC RAILROAD USA 1994

Since 1970, American road diesel production has been dominated by General Motors' Electro-Motive Division and General Electric. However, in the mid-1990s, locomotive re-manufacturer and railroad equipment supplier MK Rail made an effort to penetrate the highly competitive road diesel market.

For heavy freight service, MK Rail brought out its MK5000C, a locomotive which was designed to rival similar products offered by EMD and GE. The MK5000C was powered by a turbocharged 12-cylinder Caterpillar 3612 diesel engine, and it used electrical components supplied by KATO Engineering.

For a short time, this locomotive was the most powerful diesel-electric available in the United States. Three prototypes were painted for Southern Pacific, where they operated for a few years. Despite its promise, the MK5000C did not progress much beyond the prototype phase, and it remains an obscure type.

**Type:** Co-Co diesel-electric
**Power:** 3612 Caterpillar diesel producing 3725kW (5000hp)
**Tractive effort:** 506kN (113,800lbf) with 83:20 gear ratio
**Max. operating speed:** 112km/h (70mph)
**Weight:** 177 to 190 tonnes (390,000 to 420,000lb) depending on options
**Overall length:** 22.352m (73ft 4in)
**Gauge:** 1435mm (4ft 8.5in)

## EMD F59PHI VARIOUS RAILROADS USA 1994

In 1994, EMD brought out its new passenger locomotive. Designated as F59PHI, it featured a streamlined design with a distinctive rounded cab. EMD promotional literature described the new image as 'Swoopy', but the similarity between the F59PHIs and the popular General Motors Chevy minivan resulted in many railroaders nick-naming them '*Luminas*'. Amtrak was the first customer and assigns its F59PHIs for medium-distance trains on the West Coast. Some suburban passenger operators, such as Los Angeles' Metrolink, also acquired small fleets of F59PHIs. Perhaps the most unusual owner of the type was cigarette manufacturer Marlboro, which acquired two for use on a deluxe passenger train as part of a promotional scheme; however, the scheme was scrapped before the locomotives

**Type:** Bo-Bo, passenger diesel-electric
**Power:** EMD 12-710G producing 2387kW (3200hp)
**Tractive effort:** N/A
**Max. operating speed:** 176km/h (110mph)
**Weight:** 115.6 tonnes (254,900lb)
**Overall length:** 17.856m (58ft 7in)
**Gauge:** 1435mm (4ft 8.5in)

**An Amtrak F59PHI leads a Sacramento to San Jose *Capitols* across the Yolo Bypass near Davis, California. The F59PHI shares most internal components with the Irish Rail class 201 pictured on the opposite page.**

## WDG2 INDIAN STATE RAILWAYS INDIA 1995

The newly built class WDG2 is a development of the basic class WDM2 workhorse design. Power-increased from 1914kW (2600hp) using the same Alco engine, but with a GE or ABB turbocharger. The engine drives an alternator in place of a generator. It runs on the same type of high-adhesion bogie design as the electric locomotives of class WCAM3 and WAG7. Class WDG2 can be identified by its cab, which is set further back giving a longer hood than a class WDM2.

**Type:** Co-Co diesel-electric freight
**Power:** 2282kW (3100hp) from Alco 16-251 series engine
**Tractive effort:** 258kN (58,080lbf) at 19km/h (11.9mph)
**Max. operating speed:** 100km/h (62.1mph)
**Weight:** 123 tonnes (271,215lb)
**Overall Length:** 17.12m (55ft 10in)
**Gauge:** 1676mm (5ft 6in)

## EMD SD70I CANADIAN NATIONAL USA 1995

EMD's modern direct-current alternative to its successful SD70MAC was the SD70, which like the SD70MAC used a 16-710G3 prime mover to generate 2980kW (4000 hp). The basic SD70 locomotive was built in several variations depending on the crew cab specifications desired by the purchasing railroad. The SD70I uses a wide-nose safety cab that appears similar to that found on other modern EMD locomotives. The difference is that the SD70I employs what EMD calls a 'WhisperCab' that is physically isolated from the rest of the locomotive in order to provide a significantly quieter and more comfortable ride for crews. This arrangement can be identified by the vertical breaks on the cab-nose of the locomotive. Canadian National has been the only purchaser of the SD70I model.

**Canadian railways were the pioneers of 'safety cabs'. Here CN No. 5690 takes a line of tank wagons off a siding at Lee, Illinois.**

**Type:** Co-Co, diesel-electric
**Power:** EMD 16-710G3C-T1 producing 2980kW (4000hp)
**Tractive effort:** 484kN (109,000lbf) continuous TE; 707kN (159,000lbf) starting TE
**Max. operating speed:** N/A
**Weight:** N/A
**Overall length:** 22.047m (72ft 4in)
**Gauge:** 1435mm (4ft 8.5in)

## EMD SD80MAC CONRAIL USA 1995

One of the more unusual modern American AC traction diesel-electrics were Conrail's 30 EMD SD80MACs built in 1995. Externally these locomotives were very similar to the SD90MAC, but used a 20-cylinder 710G engine to develop 3730kW (5000hp) for traction. This made the SD80MAC the most powerful single-engine diesel-electric until the first 4476kW (6000hp) locomotives were ready for service in the late 1990s. Initially Conrail bought 28, numbering them in the 4100 series. It later bought two SD80MAC demonstrators. All the SD80MACs were painted in an attractive blue and white livery to distinguish them from Conrail's DC fleet. In 1999, the SD80MAC was split between Norfolk Southern and CSX when the two railroads divided Conrail operations between them. These locomotives were provided with a new design of power bogie, the HTCR-11, which acted to steer the long frame into curves and also minimized adverse impact on the rails. They were also operated by CP Rail. Their rugged looks make the SD80 MACs popular with locomotive modellers.

**Type:** Co-Co, AC traction diesel-electric
**Power:** EMD 20-710G3B producing 3730kW (5000hp)
**Tractive effort:** 653kN (147,000lbf) continuous TE ; 822kN (185,000lbf) starting TE with 83:16 gear ratio and 35 per cent adhesion
**Max. operating speed:** 120km/h (75mph)
**Weight:** 192.7 tonnes (425,000lb)
**Overall length:** 24.435m (80ft 2in)
**Gauge:** 1435mm (4ft 8.5in)

**A pair of EMD SD80MAC grinds upgrade at the 'Twin Ledges' west of Middlefield, Massachusetts, with a heavily laden train of ballast in tow.**

# EMD SD90MAC-H UNION PACIFIC RAILROAD USA 1995

The most powerful modern diesel in EMD's catalog is the 4476kW (6000hp) SD90MAC-H, an AC traction model powered by the new GM16V256H engine. This new 'H' engine was a radical departure from previous EMD engines, as it uses a four-cycle instead of a two-cycle design. The SD90MAC-H has led to some confusion because, before the new engine was ready for production, EMD delivered a large number of locomotives with the SD90MAC platform, but powered by a 16-cylinder 710G engine rated at just 3208kW (4300hp) with the intention of installing the H engine when it was ready. Some sources designate these locomotives as SD9043AC; others use the SD90MAC designation (no 'H'). Union Pacific was the first and largest user of the SD90MAC and subsequent SD90MAC-H.

**Although anticipated as the power of the future, EMD's SD90MAC-H has faded into relative obscurity as 2983–3281kW (4000–4400hp) locomotives now do most of the work. Union Pacific and Canadian Pacific were the only North American lines to order the big locomotives.**

**Type:** Co-Co, AC traction diesel-electric
**Power:** GM16V256H producing 4476kW (6000hp)
**Tractive effort:** 755kN (170,000 lbf) continuous TE; 889kN (200,000 lbf) starting TE with 83:16 gear ratio
**Max. operating speed:** 120km/h (75mph)
**Weight:** 192.7 tonnes (425,000 b)
**Overall length:** 24.435 m (80ft 2in)
**Gauge:** 1435mm (4ft 8.5in)

## GE AC4400CW VARIOUS RAILROADS USA AND CANADA 1995

The AC4400CW is General Electric's first commercial alternating traction diesel and has proven to be one of the bestselling and best-performing modern diesel-electric locomotives since it was first introduced in 1994.

These modern microprocessor-controlled locomotives use General Electric's single inverter per axle system of AC motor control. While similar in appearance to other modern General Electric 'wide-nose cab' diesels, the AC4400CW can be distinguished from its DC traction counterparts by the large inverter cabinets behind the cab on the left-hand or 'fireman's' side of the locomotive. The AC4400CW is typically used in very heavy freight services, and it would be a standard locomotive assigned to coal trains.

The Union Pacific, Canadian Pacific and CSX railroads were all operating large fleets of AC4400CWs by the late 1990s.

**Type:** Co-Co, AC traction diesel-electric
**Power:** GE 7FDL-16 rated at 3267kW (4380hp)
**Tractive effort:** Various
**Max. operating speed:** 120km/h (75mph)
**Weight:** 188 tonnes (415,000lb) – varied with options
**Overall length:** 22.301m (73ft 2in)
**Gauge:** 1435mm (4ft 8.5in)

**A pair of Southern Pacific AC4400CWs works as a radio-controlled remote helper on the back of an empty coal train ascending the Colorado Front Range in March 1997.**

## GE AC6000CW UNION PACIFIC RAILROAD USA 1995

A single 4476kW (6000hp) locomotive was appealing because it would allow for a two-for-one replacement of older 2238kW (3000hp) locomotives. A single-engine Co-Co delivering 4476kW (6000hp) for traction was made practical with the successful development of three-phase AC traction and the development of new diesel engines. Instead of the standard Cooper-Bessemer–inspired 7FDL diesel, the AC6000CW uses the new 7HDL engine. As the new engine was not ready at the time that Union Pacific (one of two American AC6000CW users) needed them, some locomotives were delivered with 7FDL engines and temporarily rated at 3282kW (4400hp). General Electric's AC6000CW is almost a metre (3ft) longer than conventional AC4400CWs and features a large radiator section at the rear of the locomotive. AC6000CW uses GE 5GEB13 AC traction motors.

**Type:** Co-Co, diesel-electric, AC traction
**Power:** GE 7HDL-16 producing 4476kW (6000hp)
**Tractive effort:** 738kN (166,000lbf) at 18.8km/h (11.6mph)
**Max. operating speed:** 120km/h (75mph)
**Weight:** 192.7 tonnes (425,000lb)
**Overall length:** 23.165m (76ft)
**Gauge:** 1435mm (4ft 8.5in)

**In May 2002, a pair of CSX AC6000CWs leads an eastbound intermodal train east of Palmer, Massachusetts, at CP79. Pairs of these big GEs are standard power on the old Boston & Albany route.**

## DE2550 EGYPTIAN RAILWAYS EGYPT 1996

The former Henschel factory of ABB Thyssen supplied 45 single cab freight units to Egypt in 1996 for phosphates traffic over a newly constructed line between Abu Tartour to the Red Sea port of Safarga. The route was inaugurated in 1996.

A further batch of 23 double-cab locomotives followed for general traffic in the Nile Delat region. Both batches are designated DE2550 by the makers or JT22CW by EMD.

**Type:** Co-Co diesel-electric
**Power:** 1877kW (2550hp) from EMD 12-645 series engine
**Tractive effort:** 282kN (63,500lbf)
**Max. operating speed:** 80 or 160kmh (50 or 100mph)
**Weight:** 126 tonnes (277,830lb)
**Overall length:** Not known
**Gauge:** 1435mm (4ft 8.5in)

## CLASS 670 FEDERAL GERMAN RAILWAYS (DB) GERMANY 1996

There was considerable excitement when five single-unit double-deck four-wheeled diesel railcars appeared as part of DB's call for DMU prototypes to be demonstrated. Railway history is littered with attempts to produce small, cheap diesel railcars to eke out the finances of minor railway routes. The British Railways two-axle railbuses of the later 1950s are classic examples of the situation where the fare box never contains enough cash to cover running costs, let alone a return on the capital invested in new railcars. Scepticism was therefore all the more rife when the German double-deck railbuses appeared. Attractive-looking in their red livery, the class 670s have not been widely utilized. Of the five, only one still operates in 2002, on abranch line from Stendal to Tangermünde.

**Type:** Two-axle double-deck diesel railcar
**Power:** 250kW (335bhp) underfloor diesel engine
**Tractive effort:** Not known
**Max. operating speed:** 100km/h (63mph)
**Weight per vehicle:** Not known
**Overall length:** Not known
**Gauge:** Not known

## CLASS DI8 NORWEGIAN STATE RAILWAYS (NSB) NORWAY 1996

Norwegian State Railways has had a difficult period in its quest for new diesel locomotives with which to replace the ageing Nohab/GM class Di3s, used for so many years throughout the Norwegian rail system.

The first locomotives to begin the process were the five Di4s described earlier in this book, but more locomotives were needed, and they came in the form of class Di6 Co-Cos of similar outline to the Di4s.

The Di6 locomotives had so many 'teething problems' that NSB returned them to their manufacturers (who have since overhauled them and are leasing them on spot hire elsewhere). Instead NSB opted for a smaller, lighter locomotive after trying out some Dutch class 6400 Bo-Bos in order to see if a three-phase design could meet their requirements. The 20 new class Di8 Bo-Bos in operation are hood units from Krupp/Siemens, and they are performing satisfactorily on freight duties.

**Type:** Freight main line diesel-electric
**Wheel arrangement:** Bo-Bo
**Power:** 1570kW (2105hp) diesel; Siemens alternator; four axle-hung three-phase AC traction motors
**Tractive effort:** 270kN (60,700lbf)
**Max. operating speed:** 120km/h (75mph)
**Weight:** 82 tonnes (180,080lb)
**Overall length:** 17.380m (57ft 3in)
**Gauge:** Not known

## CARGO SPRINTER/MULTI-PURPOSE VEHICLES VARIOUS OPERATORS GERMANY/GB 1997

Traditional freight operation used to involve freight wagons being picked up at thousands of loading points around the country, being tripped by small locomotives to concentration yards to be marshalled into longer trains, which in turn were remarshalled several times en route in major marshalling yards; then the process was reversed, and the wagons eventually tripped to distant sidings or small yards for unloading. This was very intensive of labour and equipment, so the railways, including DB in Germany, favoured running block trains of one product from a loading point direct to the unloading point. Instead of being loaded into wagons, smaller consignments were placed in containers, taken by road lorry to large container handling depots at strategic points and lifted there onto flat wagons for onward transit either in block container trains or in general freight trains (the latter still needing marshalling).

All this tripping and remarshalling needs locomotives and men for each stage, as well as shunting staff for coupling and uncoupling wagons. DB was interested in an idea for a freight multiple-unit train. This developed experimentally with a pair of 'multi-purpose vehicles' (MPVs), each with a cab at one end, a flat topped underframe suitable for carrying containers, and a diesel engine and transmission under the underframe driving the wheels of an adjacent bogie. Between each pair of MPVs a number of container-carrying wagons would be coupled semi-permanently. These wagons had through piping and wiring to enable the MPVs to operate as linked power cars.

The project envisaged that short freight multiple unit trains would load at small yards and set off to couple with similar trains from other yards to form a long train for the trunk haul, then split up again to reach their various destinations. In practice, the general freight market is rarely as rigid as this, needing collection and delivery of containers from different places in varying quantities. Where more regular flows of containers are possible, the current use of block container trains with lorry tripping at source and destination serves the market well. In Germany, the freight DMU operated for a couple of seasons in 1998–2000, but was deemed not to have a strong market and was summarily withdrawn.

In the United Kingdom, on the other hand, the MPV concept is proving very useful in infrastructure maintenance and renewal. MPVs can carry small equipment containers or 'modules'. The UK Network Rail uses Windhoff MPVs for weed spraying in the spring and summer. These carry modules that consist of tanks and pumps for the chemicals used. In autumn and winter, the weed killer tanks are replaced by de-icing fluid tanks and grit solution tanks together with their associated pumps, so that the MPVs can prevent electric conductor rails from icing up and can also lay a film of adhesion-enhancing substance on the running rails at places of low adhesion. In addition there are also two MPV powered trains in the United Kingdom for installing and renewing overhead electrification wiring and a train for conveying and erecting lineside masts. The details below are for a Windhoff multi-purpose single-cab vehicle.

**Type:** General-purpose diesel freight vehicle
**Wheel arrangement:** 1A-A1
**Power:** Two Volvo horizontal diesels 265kW (355bhp)
**Tractive effort:** Not known
**Max. operating speed:** 95 and 120km/h (60 and 75mph)
**Maximum gross laden weight:** 78 tonnes (171,295lb)
**Overall length:** 20.5m (67ft 3in)
**Gauge:** Not known

## WDP-4 BO1-1BO INDIAN STATE RAILWAYS INDIA 1997

In 1995, Electro-Motive Division (EMD) and India's Diesel Locomotive Works (DLW) at Varanasi signed a transfer of technology agreement for initial import then local production of asynchronous motor locomotives and 710 series engines. India Railways freight class WDG4 is EMD model GT46MAC and the passenger version class WDP4 corresponds to model GT46PAC.

The first 13 WDG4 units were completed in the United States from 1997, with the next eight delivered as completely knocked kits in late 1998. Components for the next 80 for local build by DLW were ready, with the first 10 expected in 2002.

While the freight units had conventional Co-Co wheel arrangement, the class WDP4 units have a very unusual Bo11Bo configuration by simple omission of one traction motor from the inner end of each bogie. Otherwise the same design of high adhesion truck is used on both.

The first 10 class WDP4s were built by EMD in 2001, with DLW also set to series build in the future. Class WDP4s are numbered in the 20000 series and are so far based at Hubli alongside class WDG4s which carry 12000 series numbers.

**Type:** WDG4 Co-Co heavy freight; WDP4 Bo11Bo passenger
**Power:** 2944kW (4000hp) from EMD 16-710 series engine
**Tractive effort:** WDG4 539kN (121,220lbf); WDP4 269kN (60,500lbf)
**Max. operating Sspeed:** WDG4 120km/h (75mph); WDP4 160km/h (100mph)
**Weight:** WDG4 - 126 tonnes (277,830lb); WDP4 - 119 tonnes (262,395lb)
**Overall length:** Not known
**Gauge:** 1676mm (5ft 6in)

## CLASS ALN DAP STATE RAILWAYS (FS) ITALY 1997

This is a specialized unit for the transportation of prisoners and therefore lacks the usual amenities of a passenger vehicle. The interior is divided into benched cells and 'passengers' are locked in for the journey's duration. Five DAP units were built. They are based on the class Aln 663 introduced in 1983 and itself a development of class Aln 668. Over 400 of Aln diesel cars are in operation on the FS.

**Type:** Diesel-mechanical special unit
**Power:** 340kW (455.6hp)
**Tractive effort:** Not known
**Max. operating speed:** 120km/h (75mph)
**Total weight:** Not known
**Overall length:** Not known
**Gauge:** Not known

## TEM18 Co-Co RUSSIAN RAILWAYS RUSSIA 1997

The Russian-built TEM18 is the latest of the shunting locomotives descended from the class TEM1 model. Produced by Bryansk (BMZ) in the city of the same name in central Russia, the TEM18 is available in various weight, power, gauge and environmental options. Approximately 150 have been built, all of them for Russian railways and industry. A gas-powered TEM18G is availables.

**Type:** Co-Co diesel-electric heavy shunter
**Power:** 757 to 993kW (1030 to 1350hp) from PD4A series engine
**Tractive effort:** Up to 283kN (63675lbf) maximum
**Max. operating speed:** 100k/mh (62.1mph)
**Weight:** 108 to 124 tonnes (238,140 to 273,420lb)
**Overall length:** 16.9m (55ft 2in)
**Gauge:** Adaptable 1435 to 1676mm (4ft 8.5in to 5ft 6in)

## EMD DE30AC LONG ISLAND RAIL ROAD (LIRR) USA 1997

New York's Long Island Rail Road (LIRR) is one of the most intensive suburban railways to be found in North America. Its lines crisscross all over New York State's Long Island, bringing passengers to and from New York City.

Until the 1950s, the LIRR was a subsidiary of the Pennsylvania Railroad, which began electrifying its lines. Today, most LIRR routes are electrified with a third rail. To provide through services on non-electrified lines, LIRR operates one of the most unusual locomotive types in the United States: the dual mode DE30AC. Assembled by Super Steel Products, these units use an EMD 12-710G3B engine housed in a monocoque body with stainless steel sides.

Like EMD's FL9, the DE30AC can operate from the third rail in electrified territory. The LIRR also operates a straight diesel-electric designated DM30AC.

**Type:** Diesel-electric/electric
**Power:** Dual mode-EMD 12-710G3B producing 2235kW (3000hp); and third-rail electric pick-up
**Tractive effort:** N/A
**Max. operating speed:** N/A
**Weight:** N/A
**Overall length:** 22.86m (75 ft)
**Gauge:** 1435mm (4ft 8.5in)

## AC6000CW Co-Co BHP AUSTRALIA 1998

The world record for both the heaviest and longest train is held by Australian ore-carrying railway BHP. The train was hauled by US-built General Electric model AC6000CW units.

All eight locomotives of the BHP fleet, under the control of a single driver, were used to work the record-breaking train. They were distributed to work as three pairs and two solo, all linked by the GE Locotrol radio remote control system. On 21 June 2001, the 7300m (23,950ft) long 682-wagon train weighing 99734 tonnes (98,158 tons) worked over the 275km (172 miles) between Yandi and Port Hedland on the BHP Mount Newman line.

BHP Iron Ore (Port Hedland) mines ore in the Pilbara region, a rather inaccessible, inhospitable area of northwestern Australia. BHP ranks alongside Hamersley Iron, also mining from the Pilbara region, in the heavy haul rail league. There are several such railways across the world dedicated to the movement of bulk iron ore – in Sweden, Mauritania, Brazil and South Africa.

Mount Newman began mining in 1969 with its BHP railway and is now carrying an estimated 65,000 million tonnes (63,973 million tons) of ore each year. BHP runs more than 600km (375 miles) of track and over 50 locomotives.

The AC6000CWs were acquired to permit a reduction in both total quantity of locomotives and number of units per train. The 6070 to 6077 are currently the most powerful traction units to be found operating in Australia, with AC6000CW being the most powerful model offered by General Electric – reputed to be the highest power production freight design in the world.

The rival EMD SD90MAC-H unit is also rated at and lays claim to this title. The GE model was released in 1995. Power of the order of 4476kW (6000hp) was beyond the ability of the previous GE rail traction engine. This was the model 7FDL that had been in production for more than 40 years.

General Electric partnered the German concern Deutz MWM for the new engine model 7HDL with 15.7-litre cylinders. Electric transmission in the AC6000CW is provided by alternating current asynchronous traction motors, each with its own inverter which allows maximum tractive effort independent of wheel diameter variation.

Just over 200 AC6000CWs are operated worldwide, with the US company CSX having 117, Union Pacific 79, and BHP the remainder. BHP's machines are lighter than the 216 tonnes (476,280lb) of the US specification. Union Pacific uses standard GE 'HiAd' trucks, CSX has first version steerable trucks, while BHP utilizes the more complex second version.

**Type:** Co-Co diesel-electric
**Power:** 4660kW (6250hp) from GE 7HDL-16 series engine
**Tractive effort:** 753kN (169,425lbf) at 19km/h (11.9mph) continuous; 890kN (792,100lbf ) maximum
**Max. operating speed:** 120km/h (75mph)
**Weight:** 198 tonnes (436,590lb)
**Overall length:** 23.165m (75ft 7in)
**Gauge:** 1435mm (4ft 8.5in)

## Class 66 ENGLISH, WELSH & SCOTTISH RAILWAY (EWS) GREAT BRITAIN 1998

**Type:** Freight main-line diesel-electric
**Wheel arrangement:** Co-Co
**Power:** GM 12N-710G3B-EC 12-cylinder V-form two-stroke diesel, 2385kW (3200hp); GM alternator; six axle-hung DC traction motors
**Tractive effort:** 409kN (91,945lbf)
**Max. operating speed:** 120km/h (75mph)
**Weight:** 126 tonnes (276,705lb)
**Overall length:** 21.35m (70ft 1in)
**Gauge:** 1435mm (4ft 8.5in)

**Here, an EWS class 66 locomotive number 66165 restarts a train of bogie stone empty trucks from the down through road at Newbury station, Berkshire, 11 November 2001.**

After railway privatization in the United Kingdom, English, Welsh & Scottish Railway (EWS) opted to purchase 250 large diesels from North America to replace older and less reliable freight classes. In some ways, the class 66 was a development of the General Motors heavy haul class 59, but designed as a general freight machine. In service, 66s are reliable and competent, and work all over the British railway system. Inspired by the success of the EWS machines, two other British freight operators have purchased the same design. Freightliner Limited, the container haulage company, now has a fleet of 77 class 66s, of which six are geared for heavy freight haulage. GB Rail Freight (GBRf) has a new fleet of 12 class 66s. Around 30 more are now in use on the European continent, mainly in the Netherlands, Germany and Scandinavia, having proved popular among smaller 'open access' freight companies there.

**No. 66 079 is one of the 250 ordered by EWS for general freight in the United Kingdom. The majority were delivered from a GM factory in Canada less than a year after each batch was ordered.**

## Class 170 'Turbostar' Various Operators — Great Britain 1998

**This Turbostar is on a Midland Mainline semi-fast service between London and Nottingham or Derby. MML is to replace these units with more up-market, higher speed units from 2004.**

After privatization, British train operating companies wanted to buy modern trains 'off the shelf' to manufacturers' standard designs. Adtranz (later purchased by Bombardier) developed a modular vehicle body for its 'Turbostar' range of DMUs. Engineered as two- or three-car sets, they employ more powerful underfloor engines driving through hydraulic transmissions, are fully air-conditioned, but retain the suburban layout of two pairs of double-leaf doors in the bodysides. They have proved popular where operators have specified comfortable, more spacious interiors, such Anglia (London–Norwich) and ScotRail for its express services. Central Trains uses them on cross-country work.

**Type:** Express and local passenger two-car and three-car diesel multiple unit
**Power:** MTU 6R183TD13H six-cylinder horizontal diesel, 315kW (422bhp)
**Transmission:** Voith T211rzze hydraulic torque converter/gearbox
**Max. operating speed:** 160km/h (100mph)
**Weight:** 45 tonnes (98,825lb)
**Overall length:** 23.62m (77ft 6in)
**Gauge:** 1435mm (4ft 8.5in)

## CLASS DE2000 HELLENIC RAILWAYS ORGANIZATION GREECE 1998

OSE class A471 locomotives are twin-engine diesel-electrics built by ADtranz in Switzerland and specified for future conversion to electric locomotives.

Limited in its present form to 160km/h (100mph), the AEG electric traction package will permit 5500kW (7473hp), while the bogies are designed for 200kmh (125mph).

A471s are medium-term traction for the Athens–Thessaloniki route, which is in the course of major upgrading and new realignment. Delivery started a cascade, resulting in complete or near elimination of several other classes including A551, A301, A321 and A351.

**Seen leaving Drama on an overnight train from Athens to the Bulgarian border, No A.487 is one of a group that have enabled Greece's OSE seriously to reduce their traction variety.**

**Type:** Diesel-electric express passenger
**Power:** 2100kW (2853hp) from two MTU 12V386 series engines
**Tractive effort:** 202kN (45,360lbf)
**Max. operating speed:** 160kmh (100mph)
**Weight:** 90 tonnes (198,450lb)
**Overall length:** 18.5m (60ft 4in)
**Gauge:** 1435mm (4ft 8.5in)

## CLASS 67 ENGLISH, WELSH & SCOTTISH RAILWAY (EWS) GREAT BRITAIN 1999

The idea that postal trains should operate at 200km/h (125mph) in the United Kingdom is a novel one. No UK rail vans are equipped to operate above 200km/h (125mph) at present, although second-hand BT10 bogies could be fitted if necessary. Against that scene, EWS ordered 30 Bo-Bo diesel-electrics from General Motors with a 200km/h (125mph) capability; Royal Mail and parcels trains are their principal duties. They were built by Alstom at Valencia, Spain.

**Type:** Mixed-traffic main-line diesel-electric
**Wheel arrangement:** Bo-Bo
**Power:** GM 12N-710G3B-EC 12-cylinder V-form two-stroke diesel, 2385kW (3200hp); GM alternator; four frame mounted DC traction motors
**Tractive effort:** 141kN (31,750lbf)
**Max. operating speed:** 200km/h (125mph)
**Weight:** 90 tonnes (197,645lb)
**Overall length:** 19.69m (64ft 8in)
**Gauge:** 1435mm (4ft 8.5in)

**The EWS class 67s are Britain's fastest diesel locomotives. They bear a strong family resemblance to new locomotives recently exported by Alstom to Iran and Israel.**

## CLASS 643/644 'TALENT' FEDERAL GERMAN RAILWAYS (DB) GERMANY 2000

After a pause of about 15 years, *Deutsche Bundesbahn* (DB) ordered more diesel railcars for local and suburban working. Talbot (later Bombardier) built two classes of 'Talent' DMUs, class 643 and class 644. They are streamlined, articulated three-car units with a low floor section between the outer bogies. Some have hydraulic transmission.

Most of the diesel-hydraulic version are employed on regional and secondary line services, many of which have been reorganized on a regular-interval basis. However, the units on the Köln (Cologne) S-Bahn services are diesel-electrics with more passenger access doors.

Some private operators also use 'Talent' railcars. Among these is the *Ostmecklenburgische Eisenbahn* in eastern Germany, which fitted out its units with higher quality seats and also provides catering on board for its passengers. An electric version version of the 'Talent' units is being delivered to both Austria and Slovenia as well.

The details given in the table are for the diesel versions of the class 643/644s.

**Type:** Local and suburban passenger diesel-hydraulic (electric) multiple units
**Power:** Two 315kW (420hp) or 550kW (735hp) diesels
**Tractive effort:** N/A
**Transmission:** Hydraulic torque converter; or alternator, four traction motors
**Max. operating speed:** 120km/h (75mph)
**Weight:** Not known
**Overall length:** Not known
**Gauge:** 1435mm (4ft 8.5in)

## MAK G2000BB VARIOUS OPERATORS GERMANY 2000

Vossloh launched model G2000BB at the Berlin Innotrans 2000 exhibition. A diesel-hydraulic with Voith transmission, it follows a long line of German hydraulic designs. The innovative asymmetric front-end layout combines near full-width cabs with platforms for shunting personnel on one side at each end. This feature is aimed at open access operators where train locomotives handling contract flows shunt their own payloads. Options offered are radio and remote control, long-range fuel tanks, alternative power units up to 2500kW (2297hp) and maximum speed from 100 to 140kmh (60 to 87.5mph). Ten machines were ordered by Locomotion Capital, jointly owned by Vossloh and Angel, while a further 10 were speculatively built by Vossloh ahead of real orders.

**Type:** B-B diesel-hydraulic freight
**Power:** 2240kW (3043hp) from Caterpillar 3516 series engine
**Tractive effort:** 283kN (63675lbf )
**Max. operating speed:** 120km/h (75mph)
**Weight:** 87.3 tonnes (192,497lb)
**Overall length:** Not known
**Gauge:** 1435mm (4ft 8.5in)

## CLASS 175 NORTH WEST TRAINS GREAT BRITAIN 2000

Train operator North West Trains required quality DMUs for cross-country services. Alstom's Birmingham factory delivered 11 two-car sets and 16 three-car 'Coradia' units. The units are air-conditioned, have sliding plug doors at the ends of each bodyside and are painted in First Group's blue livery with pink and white lining.

**Type:** Express diesel-hydraulic multiple units
**Power:** 335kW (450bhp) Cummins N14 underfloor horizontal diesel (one per car)
**Transmission (one per car):** Voith T211rzze hydraulic torque converter gearbox, cardan shafts to wheelsets on one bogie
**Max. operating speed:** 161km/h (100mph)
**Weight:** 51 tonnes (112,000lb) driving cars; 48 tonnes (104,315lb) intermediate cars
**Overall length:** 23.71m (77ft 9in) driving cars; 23.03m (75ft 7in) intermediate cars
**Gauge:** 1435mm (4ft 8.5in)

**The 175s are used on express services linking major cities such as Birmingham and Manchester with Chester and North Wales.**

## 'VOYAGER' CLASSES 220/221 VIRGIN TRAINS GREAT BRITAIN 2000

Wishing to replace its locomotive-hauled trains and High-Speed Trains (HSTs) on cross-country services, Virgin Trains ordered 34 four-car non-tilting (220) and 44 five-car tilting (221) diesel trains with a 200km/h (125mph) top speed. These operate in multiple on heavily trafficked routes, and singly elsewhere, at much improved frequencies. Bombardier delivered these trains on time from its factories at Brugge in Belgium and Wakefield in the United Kingdom, and they were placed in service with very few development problems.

The class 220 bogie has, unusually for a UK design, an inside frame layout. The 221 bogie

is more normal, with an outside frame giving the width and strength needed to support the body tilting mechanism. Both trains have the same body and interior, with air conditioning, comfortable seating (albeit at somewhat close spacing) and a buffet incorporating a shop.

**The 'Voyagers' have a striking external appearance with backward-raked, streamlined fronts and silver-and-red livery. Entrance doors have diagonal stripes to aid the visually impaired.**

**Type:** High-speed diesel-electric four-car (220) and five-car (221) multiple units
**Power:** One per car – 560kW (750bhp) Cummins underfloor horizontal diesel; Alstom ONIX three phase control; rheostatic braking; underframe mounted traction motors; cardan shafts to nearest axle on each bogie
**Max. operating speed:** 200km/h (125mph)
**Average vehicle weight:** 46 tonnes (101,020lb) class 220; 54 tonnes (118,590lb) class 221
**Overall length:** 23.85m (78ft 3in) driving cars; 22.82m (74ft 10in) intermediate cars
**Gauge:** 1435mm (4ft 8.5in)

## CLASS M9 CO-CO SRI LANKA RAILWAYS — SRI LANKA 2000

The Sri Lanka Railways order for 10 AD32C diesel-electric locomotives from Alstom form part of the modular 'Prima' range. In this case, the locomotives are six-axle units with the 12-cylinder RK215 engine. Thirty similar machines but of higher power are being built for Syria. The first class M9 for Sri Lanka was delivered in 2000.

**Type:** Co-Co diesel-electric
**Power:** 1350kW (1834hp) from Ruston 12RK215 series engine
**Tractive effort:** 240kN (54000lbf)
**Max. operating speed:** 110kmh (68.3mph)
**Weight:** 108 tonnes (238,140lb)
**Overall length:** Not known
**Gauge:** 1676mm (5ft 6in)

## CLASS 2070 AUSTRIAN STATE RAILWAYS (ÖBB) — AUSTRIA 2001

**Type:** Mixed-traffic light diesel-hydraulic
**Wheel arrangement:** B-B
**Power:** Medium-speed diesel, 500kW (670hp); hydraulic transmission with cardan shaft drives
**Tractive effort:** 233kN (52,380lbf) freight gearing; 151kN (33,945lbf) passenger gearing
**Max. operating speed:** 45km/h (28mph) freight gearing; 100km/h (62mph) passenger gearing
**Weight:** 80 tonnes (176,368lb)
**Overall length:**Not known
**Gauge:** 1435mm (4ft 8.5in)

**These neat B-B diesel-hydraulic locomotives are spreading across Austria. They are mainly used on short-distance freight and heavy shunting duties.**

After a long period of stagnation in its diesel locomotive fleet, Austrian State Railways (ÖBB)

ordered 60 medium-range freight locomotives from Vossloh/ Siemens, with an option to obtain a further 90. These engines replaced the second-hand ex-DB class V100 B-Bs, as well as enabling the removal of all rod drive shunting locomotives and several earlier diesel types from ÖBB's fleet.

The class 2070s locomotives are hood units with off-centre cabs. They are of interest because they have two-speed gearing, to be used for either freight or light passenger use.

## CLASS 605 FEDERAL GERMAN RAILWAYS (DB) GERMANY 2001

**Viewed from the side, the sleek streamlining of the later ICE series trains, including the class 605s, is impressive. The interior of the diesel version is basically the same as the electric ICEs.**

Encouraged by the success of its InterCity Express (ICE) high-speed electric trains, DB went on to purchase some four-car diesel ICE trains for important journeys on non-electrified routes. Many of these sections were not originally laid out as high-speed railways, and so curves restrict maximum speeds attainable. DB thus decided to incorporate carriage body tilting into the diesel ICE design.

The principle of tilting trains was developed in the 1970s and early 1980s in the United Kingdom and France, but not pursued further in either country at the time. Swedish and Italian train builders took up the idea in the 1980s, and most later designs of tilting train derive from this work. The principle is that passengers in a train rounding a curve at speed experience discomfort from centrifugal forces at a much lower speed than the theoretical safe maximum curving speed. By tilting the carriage body around its centre of gravity as a train rounds a curve in the track, passengers feel much less of the outward force and do not experience lateral discomfort, even though the actual curving speed is up to 30 per cent higher. The tilting is triggered on the approach to a curve by a combination of accelerometers and gyroscopes on the leading bogie of a vehicle (or even from those on the vehicle in front). The gyroscope indicates when the train meets a change in the superelevation of the track, and the accelerometer measures the lateral acceleration due to the curvature. These inputs are computed in the tilt mechanism to determine the amount of body tilt required and the rate at which the angle of the body must change. Tilting is normally achieved by hydraulic or electric rams acting on a swing cradle or similar structure between the body underframe and the bogie frame. The maximum tilt is usually 6° to 8° from the vertical. This permits the train to run through a curve at a maximum speed 20 to 30 per cent faster than conventional trains without passengers being flung to the side. The degree of tilting in modern trains (unlike Britain's Advanced Passenger Train of the early 1980s) does not compensate for all lateral forces: engineers discovered that the average traveller on a train going round a curve expects to experience some lateral movement; if this is fully compensated, passengers have been known to experience travel sickness, whereas partial compensation virtually eliminates this problem.

One disadvantage of tilting trains is that, because the body tilts about its centre of gravity, the upper corners would foul the loading gauge if the train were built to normal dimensions. Therefore tilting trains have bodies that slope in more sharply towards the roof line. This leaves less room inside for useful luggage racks, and headroom can be restrictive. Also, some passengers may find the interior more claustrophobic, though this depends on the quality of the interior design. Another disadvantage is the increase in lateral forces on the track caused by the train running faster round curves. The use of multiple-unit trains replacing heavy locomotives mitigates this problem.

The DB tilting ICE is a streamlined, fully air-conditioned, sound-insulated and comfortable train in which travellers are well cosseted from both external noises and external forces. The trains are painted in the standard ICE white livery with red band running along the bodyside below the carriage windows. The diesel tilting ICEs operate on cross-country routes from Nürnberg to Leipzig and Dresden, and Munich to Hamburg via Leipzig.

**Type:** InterCity Express diesel-electric tilting four-car multiple units
**Power units (four):** 425kW (570hp) diesel, AC alternator, body-mounted traction motors with cardan shafts to bogie wheelsets
**Tractive effort:** N/A
**Max. operating speed:** 200km/h (125mph)
**Weight:** 220 tonnes
**Overall length:** 105m (345ft)
**Gauge:** 1435mm (4ft 8.5in)

## CLASS M62.3 CO-CO HUNGARIAN RAILWAYS (MÁV) HUNGARY 2001

The MÁV subclass M62.3 is a refurbished M62 freight locomotive. MÁV plans to retain about 40, with life expectancy past 2010. In parallel with similar re-engining of the M41, both MTU and CAT engines are fitted, selected for compliance with future EU emissions regulations. The original DC generator is replaced by an alternator.

**Type:** Co-Co diesel-electric freight
**Power:** 1500kW (2038hp) from MTU 12V4000 or CAT 3512 series engine
**Tractive effort:** 196kN (441,00lbf) at 20km/h (12.5mph)
**Max. operating speed:** 100km/h (62.1mph)
**Weight:** 120 tonnes (264,600lb)
**Overall length:** 17.56m (57ft 4in)
**Gauge:** 1435mm (4ft 8.5in)

## AD43C IRANIAN ISLAMIC REPUBLIC RAILWAYS (RAI) IRAN 2001

After a gap of several years, GEC Alsthom Diesels Ruston (as it then was) won three orders for its new Ruston RK215 series 'Prima' locomotives for Iran, Syria and Sri Lanka. Introduced in 1991, the RK215 has a 215mm (8.42in) bore, 275mm (10.77in) stroke four-stroke engine and is the first Ruston design with an underslung crankshaft. Ruston engines of earlier English Electric design were of bedplate design. No longer part of Alsthom, Ruston is now owned by the MAN group. The AD43C locomotives ordered for Iranian Islamic Republic Railways (RAI) has 16-cylinder engines of 3160kW (4240hp) driving a traction alternator and three-phase asynchronous traction motors through Alsthom's Onix IGBT system. The order specified the first 20 locomotives be contructed by Alsthom, with five kits for assembly in Iran and the remainder built in Iran. The first Belfort-built model appeared in 2002 with delivery of the whole order to be completed in 2003. Designed for 150kmh (93.8mph) passenger and 110kmh (68.9mph) freight operation, 30 models for passenger services numbered 200–229 are named after Iranian provinces; the unnamed freight locos are 230–299.

**Type:** Co-Co diesel-electric
**Power:** 3160kW (4240hp) from Ruston 16RK215 series engine
**Tractive effort:** 542kN (121,950lbf) unballasted to 662kN (148,950lbf) ballasted
**Max. operating speed:** 150km/h (93.8mph)
**Weight:** 123 tonnes (271205lb) - ballasted up to 150 tonnes (330,750lb)
**Overall length:** 22.33m (64ft 3in)
**Gauge:** 1435mm (4ft 8.5in)

## TER 2N NG DMU LUXEMBOURG RAILWAYS (CFL) LUXEMBOURG 2001

These two- or three-car double-deck NG ('new generation') units operate on the regional service from Gouvy (Belgium) through Luxembourg to Metz in eastern France. The CFL has 12 piggy-backing its order, as often before, with a larger one of 72 units from the SNCF, on which system they form class Z23500.

**Type:** Diesel-electric multiple-unit train.
**Power:** 1500kW (2010hp)
**Tractive effort:** Not known
**Maximum operating speed:** 161kmh (100mph)
**Total weight:** Not known
**Maximum axle load:** Not known
**Overall length:** 52.5m (172ft 4in)
**Builder:** Alstom-Bombardier
**Gauge:** Not known

## SIEMENS HERCULES AUSTRIAN STATE RAILWAYS (ÖBB) AUSTRIA 2002

Austrian state railways ÖBB first started receiving these advanced diesel-electrics from Siemens in 2001. They were intended to replace classes 2050 2043 and 2143. Originally 70 firm and 80 options were ordered, with so far 30 options being taken up. Class 2016 is of modular construction and is also longer than ÖBB required, as Siemens allowed for larger engine options and a 22.5-tonne (22.1-ton) axle loading for other potential clients.

The ÖBB 'Hercules' has 1000kW (1341hp) electric braking power available. Class 2106 is fitted with full multiple unit and push-pull capability for ÖBB's existing passenger train sets, as well as signalling and safety systems for operations into the neighbouring countries of Slovenia and Germany. Complementing its 'Eurosprinter' electric locomotive, Siemens markets the diesel as 'RegioRunner'.

**Type:** Bo-Bo diesel-electric universal
**Power:** 2000kW (2717hp) from MTU 16V4000 series engine
**Tractive effort:** 235kN (61,875lbf)
**Max. operating speed:** 140km/h (88.5mph)
**Weight:** 80 tonnes (176,400lb)
**Overall length:** 19.275m (62ft 10in)
**Gauge:** 1435mm (4ft 8.5in)

DB
140 363-3

PART THREE

# ELECTRIC LOCOMOTIVES AND TRAINS

Electricity as a source of motive power attracted the attention of railway engineers from an early stage. In 1835, the Dutch inventors Strattingh and Becker made an attempt to build a battery-powered two-axled vehicle. In 1837, Thomas Davenport operated an electric locomotive on a short miniature-gauge track in Vermont in the United States, and, in 1842, Robert Davidson tried out a standard-gauge battery-powered engine on the Edinburgh & Glasgow Railway in Scotland. What these early electrical pioneers lacked was adequate power, something that only became available with the invention of the dynamo by the Italian Antonio Pacinotti in the 1860s.

Until the advent of big internal combustion engines, however, a locomotive could not generate or conserve enough electricity to do other than very limited light shunting work. The answer was to bring power to the engine by means of an external supply delivered via a third rail or an overhead wire, thus making room for powerful electric motors. In 1879, the German engineer Werner von Siemens was to build the small two-axle 2.2kW (3hp) electric locomotive which, still preserved in Munich, is the direct ancestor of the modern electric train.

**Left: No. 140.363 of the *Deutsche Bundesbahn*. This class was a staple of the West German system, with more than 800 being built between 1957 and 1974.**

**Above: Class Re 6/6 Bo-Bo-Bo of the Swiss Federal Railways. Thirteen of this heavy-traction class were built in 1972. Their maximum operating speed was 140km/h (87mph).**

**Amtrak Metroliner 88 is seen here on 'Northeast Corridor' service passing Harrison, New Jersey, en route for New York, on 26 September 1982. The six-car consist includes club and café cars.**

Electric traction was clean, efficient and quiet, but electric locomotives were very expensive to build and required a source of power, either from an overhead wire or a third rail. This brought an additional capital expense, one which many railway companies and even national systems could not afford. The first electric trains were therefore specialized ones, for use in long tunnels or on very steep gradients. They were particularly suited to 'underground' railways, the first electric one being the City & South London line of 1890, with third-rail power supply, followed by the Baltimore & Ohio's overhead-powered lines of 1894–5. The electric locomotive's combination of powerful traction and rapid acceleration also made it appealing to railways operating busy suburban networks. Although the first manifestation of this was the electric tram-car, which killed off many suburban railway services altogether, it led to the current virtual monopoly of electric traction on urban rapid-transit lines. Electricity could be delivered in various forms, and, though direct current was first to be used, alternating current was introduced from 1899 on the Burgdorf–Thun mountain line in Switzerland. At first this was three-phase, requiring two or three contact wires (where two wires were used, the running rails served as third conductor). It might be cumbersome to pick up, but nevertheless experimental German Siemens-AEG railcars achieved speeds of more than 200km/h (124mph) in 1903. A significant step forward was made with single-phase AC, developed by the Swiss Oerlikon company and first used in 1905, requiring only one overhead wire.

By 1918, numerous electrified lines were working in Europe and the United States, including longer distance routes such as New York–New Haven and the first stage of the 'iron ore' line of northern Sweden. A variety of voltages and frequencies were employed, which from 1918 became more standardized, if only on a national basis. France, Great Britain and the Netherlands used 1500V DC (although the extensive British third-rail supply was at 600V). Germany and the Scandinavian countries used single-phase 15,000V AC at a frequency of 16.667Hz. Belgium, Italy, Russia and Spain chose 3000V DC. Supplies came chiefly from dedicated power stations. In the 1920s, the Hungarian engineer Kalmán Kandó was working on a supply system of single-phase alternating current at a frequency of 50Hz. This was standard industrial supply current and required no special generating equipment or transforming stations. By the 1970s, this had become the standard form of supply in Britain, France, Turkey and India, and on many Japanese lines. Other countries, however, notably Germany and Sweden, use lower frequency 15,000V AC at 16.667Hz, and Italy continues to use 3000V DC. The consequence has been the development of electric locomotives and multiple-unit trains which can draw power under three or even four different supply systems.

> A great surge in electric traction took place in the 50 years after 1945, driven by the need to restore war-damaged systems and by the wish to use home-generated power, whether hydro-electric, nuclear or fossil fueled.

A great surge in electric traction took place in the half-century after 1945, driven in countries such as the Netherlands by the need to restore war-damaged systems and in others by the wish to use home-generated power, whether hydro-electric, nuclear or fossil fuel in origin. Much of the development was in multiple-unit passenger trains, with a consequent steep drop in the number of passenger locomotives required. Many locomotives are used in push-pull formats with driving trailer carriages at the opposite end, as in Swiss and German *Pendelzüge* and British intercity services. Because it was necessary to mount heavy equipment such as transformers, usually under the floor, the design of electric multiple-unit trains was a challenge to combine power, passenger space, quietness of operation, structural strength and operating speed. A modern power coach has as much power output and tractive effort as a medium-sized locomotive, while the combined output of the two power cars of a 10-car 'high-speed' set is of the order of 6300kW (8450hp), quite enough to run the 400-tonne (393.7-ton) train at 300km/h (186mph). The special qualities of electric traction, first shown to startling effect in 1903 and further revealed in the Italian and French record-breaking runs of the 1930s and 1950s, make such performance possible and have led to a regeneration of railway services on many routes where the city-centre to city-centre timing compares with, or beats, that of air travel. And only electric trains could operate in the undersea tunnels linking Honshu and Hokkaido in Japan, and between France and England. As this section shows, work is already advanced on magnetic-levitation technology that does away with wheel-on-rail altogether, but it is also clear that the potential of electric traction is by no means yet fully exploited.

**Austrian Federal Railways class 1018 1-Do-1 is seen here. Dating from 1940, the class began life as German *Reichsbahn* class E18.2.**

## VOLK'S ELECTRIC RAILWAY RAILCAR BRIGHTON SEAFRONT GREAT BRITAIN 1884

The first electric line in Britain – and one of the first in the world – was a modest light railway system which was built along the seafront at Brighton, Sussex. This railway was the brainchild of Magnus Volk, a local inventor. His original 610mm (2ft) gauge line was officially opened on 4 August 1882, with Volk himself driving a diminutive four-wheeled car.

This original line was extended to 1280m (1400yd), the track was re-gauged and an impressive new car was provided for the opening ceremony on 4 April 1884. There was seating for 16 within the central saloon, with additional seating provided on the platforms at either end. A similar second car was subsequently introduced. With solid mahogany bodies, these two railcars survived into the 1940s, until being cut up at the Lewes Road trolleybus depot.

**A pair of more modern cars is seen on the seafront Volk's Electric Railway, which claims to be the oldest electric railway in the world.**

**Type:** Seaside passenger tramcar
**Power:** 160V two-rail, 4.5kW (6hp) Siemens D2 wound motor with transmission by belt drive via a counter-shaft to the axles
**Tractive effort:** N/A
**Max. operating speed:** 16.09km/h (10mph)
**Max. axle-load:** N/A
**Overall length:** 5.791m (19ft)
**Gauge:** 1435mm (4ft 8.5in)

## BO CITY & SOUTH LONDON RAILWAY GREAT BRITAIN 1890

The City & South London Railway was London's first deep-level tube and the world's first underground electric railway. The railway's four-wheeled electric locomotives were ordered from Mather & Platt of Salford, with parts supplied by Beyer, Peacock of Gorton, Manchester. Fourteen locomotives were ordered in a batch in 1889 for delivery the next year for the opening of the 8km (5-mile) line from King William Street in the City to Stockwell, South London.

One of these electric locomotives, No. 13, survives in preservation and is owned by the Science Museum, but loaned to London's Transport Museum and based at its Acton depot. It was in service until 1907. The City & South London used locomotive-hauled trains until it was rebuilt in 1924 to the same diameter as other routes.

**Type:** Underground suburban services
**Power:** Not known
**Max. operating speed:** 40.225km/h (25mph)
**Max. axle load:** Not known
**Weight:** 10.3 tonnes (227,115lb)
**Gauge:** 762mm (2ft 6in)

## BO-BO B&O, MT ROYAL ELECTRICS USA 1896

In the mid-1890s, Baltimore & Ohio pioneered mainline electrification to pacify opposition to its proposed Baltimore Belt Line, an improved route that involved a long tunnel underneath residential areas. The electrification section was very short and used an unusual form of rigid overhead. The initial electric locomotives were short articulated machines built by General Electric and used gearless motors. These were used to tow steam-powered trains through the tunnels (steam locomotive and all). After the turn of the 20th century, the overhead system was scrapped in favour of an electric third rail. By 1912, the original locomotives had been supplanted by more modern ones. Although only a few miles long, B&O's electrification demonstrated the practicality of electrifying heavy railroad operations.

**Type:** Bo-Bo, electric
**Power:** Not known
**Tractive effort:** 200kN (45,000lbf)
**Max. operating speed:** 96km/h (60mph)
**Weight:** 87 tonnes (192,000lb)
**Overall length:** 8.268m (27 ft 2 in)
**Max. axle load:** 22 tonnes (48,488lb)
**Gauge:** 1435mm (4ft 8.5in)

**Baltimore & Ohio was the first mainline steam railroad to embrace electrification when, in 1896, it electrified its new Baltimore Belt Line.**

## B GOODS ENGINE BURGDORF-THUN RAILWAY (BTE) SWITZERLAND 1899

Three-phase alternating current electrification was used for the first time in the world on this line, 45km (28 miles) long, with gradients up to 1 in 40. Despite its need for a double set of overhead wires, the three-phase current, at 750V, did away with the need for substations and allowed for lighter weight motors and regeneration of current on the downhill sections. Railcars were used for passenger services; the two four-wheel locomotives were used for freight, drawing trains of up to 100 tonnes (98 tons) and with a maximum speed of 32km/h (20mph). Drivers stood at the control positions, behind an open front platform. Square-framed current collectors were fitted at each end. Both axles were driven by rods from a central jackshaft. Designers of electric locomotives at the time turned naturally to rod drive, following the steam model, and at low speeds it was effective. The wheel diameter of 1230mm (48.5in) was very like that of a steam locomotive of similar power and function. Two gear ratios, of 1:1.88 and 1:3.72, allowed for slow uphill traction. Only one of the 'B' locomotives is preserved.

**The preserved 'B' locomotive, first in the world to be powered by three-phase alternating current.**

**Type:** Branch freight locomotive
**Power:** Two 112kW (150hp) motors, supplied by three-phase AC at 750V via overhead collectors
**Tractive effort:** Not known
**Max. operating speed:** 32km/h (20mph)
**Total weight:** 30 tonnes (66,150lb)
**Max. axle load:** 15 tonnes (33,075lb)
**Overall length:** 7.8m (25ft 7in)
**Builder:** Brown-Boveri, Zürich

## A1A-A1A TEST VEHICLES 'A' AND 'S' (STES) GERMANY 1901

StES was a consortium formed in 1899 by the two electrical companies Siemens & Halske and AEG, with the Prussian government and certain banks as interested parties. Its sole purpose was to explore the practicability of high-speed electric traction, and it was allowed to use 23km (14.5 miles) of military railway between Zossen and Marienfeld, to the southwest of Berlin, to carry out its experiments, which went on between 1901 and 1903. Three vehicles were built: railcars 'A' by AEG and 'S' by Siemens, and also a Bo-Bo steeple-cab locomotive from Siemens. The railcars were genuine ones, not merely power units, with seating for about 50 passengers in two compartments. The StES brief set out a range of technical requirements, including the attainment of what was then a super-high operating speed of between 200 and 250km/h (125 and 155mph). The maximum axle load was set at 16 tonnes (15.75 tons), and the cars had to be capable of pulling up to three trailer coaches.

A complex power supply system was set up. Direct current supply, as fitted to Werner von Siemens' pioneer locomotive of 1879, was rejected in favour of alternating current, provided by a three-wire catenary hung from poles alongside rather than above the track. Car A had three separate bow-type pantographs at each end of the vehicle to collect current from the wires, strung at different levels. Car B also had three current collectors at each end, but they were mounted together on single poles. Both systems required modification during the tests. The current used could be varied between 10,000 and 14,000V, three-phase AC at 38-48Hz, transformed on the railcars to 435V on car A and 1150V on Car S. The vehicles themselves resembled interurban cars of slightly later date, with wooden bodies built on a steel framework, separate first- and second-class compartments, and driving cabs at each end. Clerestory roofs provided ventilation and additional light. Air ducts in the roofs also provided cooling for the transformers. The electrical systems were assembled in two self-contained parts so that failure of one would not affect the other. All high-voltage equipment was mounted either beneath the floor or in the roof space, and the switchgear was operated pneumatically. In the Siemens car, the motors were axle-mounted; in the AEG vehicle, they were placed on hollow shafts around the axles and vertically sprung, with power transmission by spring drive from the hollow shafts to the wheels.

No one before had worked with this combination of high voltage and high speed. Matters such as braking distances, air resistance and brake pressures had to be established, as well as the effect of very high speed on working parts, brakes and the track itself. The original track was much too lightly laid and one of the cars derailed at 160km/h (100mph). It was rebuilt and the track relaid and realigned, with heavier rails and deep ballast; and tests resumed. Braking tests were carried out in September–November 1903, and, in the course of these, both railcars exceeded 200km/h (124mph) – sensational for the time. On 28 October, car A reached 210.2km/h (130.6mph), a world record speed not broken until the Kruckenberg propeller vehicle of 1931 and not attained again by an electric train until the SNCF Co-Co 7121 reached 239.8km/h (149mph) in 1953. It was found that hauling a trailer made little difference to speed or air resistance, although a Prussian 12-wheel sleeping car came off the rails behind one of the test cars at 174km/h (108mph). Tests ended in November 1903. The cars performed to very similar standards, and Reichel believed that they could have attained 230km/h (143mph). Valuable data was gathered from the experiments, but they did not lead to a sudden increase in electrification schemes. Quite apart from the capital costs of building electric railways, there were still many practical and operational problems to be solved. They did, however, conclusively establish that electric traction was not just suitable for low speeds and specialized routes such as urban networks, long tunnels and mountain sections, but also could be adapted to very high mainline speeds.

Specifications are for the AEG car:

**Type:** Experimental high-speed railcar
**Power:** Four gearless synchronous motors supplied with 10,000V three-phase AC at 50Hz collected from triple overhead wire and developing from 186 to 560kW (250 to 750hp)
**Tractive effort:** Not known
**Max. operating speed:** 210km/h (130.85mph)
**Total weight:** 60 tonnes (132,250lb)
**Max. axle load:** 10 tonnes (22,050lb)
**Overall length:** 22,100mm (72ft 6in)
**Builder:** Van der Zypen Charlier, Cologne; electrical equipment by AEG

## ELECTRIC MULTIPLE UNITS LANCASHIRE & YORKSHIRE RAILWAY (L&YR) GREAT BRITAIN 1904

**The L&YR introduced more modern stock from 1916 for the Manchester to Bury electrification. This is one of the later sets in BR days at Bury Bolton Street. These lasted until 1962.**

The Lancashire & Yorkshire Railway introduced electric multiple units as early as 1904 to work between Liverpool Exchange and Southport. These used 1200V direct current (DC) third rail collection, initially with a fourth rail bonded to the running rails for return current, although the fourth rail was later abandoned. These five-car sets were extended to seven cars at peak times. At 3050mm (10ft) wide, they were the widest railway coaches ever to operate in the United Kingdom. All had been withdrawn by 1942.

**Type:** Suburban electric five car electric multiple units
**Power:** 1200V DC conductor rail collection, four 112kW (150hp) DC traction motors on three power cars
**Max. operating speed:**
**Max. axle load:** Not known
**Overall length:** 18,290mm (60ft)
**Gauge:** 1435mm (4ft 8.5in)

## S-MOTOR NEW YORK CENTRAL USA 1904

New York Central was considering the electrification of its exceptionally heavily travelled Park Avenue line in Manhattan, New York City, when a disastrous collision between two packed passenger trains in January 1902 forced the issue. The disaster was caused as a result of a train overrunning a stop signal obscured by dense locomotive smoke in the Park Avenue tunnel and ramming the train ahead of it. Excessive locomotive smoke was the problem and New York passed laws prohibiting the use of steam locomotives in New York City. New York Central responded by pioneering heavy electric railway traction, a project undertaken in conjunction with the construction of an all-new and greatly expanded terminal, the world famous Grand Central Terminal. To develop practical electrification, New York Central assembled a team of some of the foremost engineers. A prototype electric locomotive was built in 1904 by General Electric at Schenectady, New York. In its original configuration, this locomotive employed a 1-Do-1 wheel arrangement and was known as T-Motor. It drew 660V DC from a third rail. A fleet of similar electric locomotives was built following the success of the prototype. After a derailment in 1907 that killed many passengers, the locomotives were rebuilt with a 2-Do-2 wheel arrangement and reclassed as S-motors. In later years, the S-motors were largely relegated to switching duties. A few served until the early 1980s, and several have been preserved, including the pioneering S-1 electric.

**Type:** 1-Do-1 (later modified to 2-Do-2) third-rail passenger electric
**Power:** 660V DC at 1640kW (2200hp)
**Tractive effort:** 145kN (32,000lbf)
**Max. operating speed:** 128km/h (80mph)
**Weight:** 90.9 tonnes (200,500lb)
**Overall length:** 11,278mm (37ft)
**Max. axle load:** 16 tonnes (35,500lb)
**Gauge:** 1435mm (4ft 8.5in)

**New York Central S-2 electric at Mott Haven Yard in The Bronx, New York, in 1961. Later, these pioneering electrics were used in switching service.**

## E69 LOKALBAHN AG (MÜNCHEN) GERMANY 1905

The E69 designation covers a group of five individual electric locomotives dating from 1905 to 1930. Built for the Lokalbahn AG (München) route between Murnau and Oberammergau in southern Bavaria, the line was first powered at 5500V 16Hz AC in 1904 and later altered to 5000V 16.2/3Hz AC. LAG 1 to 5 became DB E69.01 to E69.05, later class 169. In 1954, the locomotives were adapted to standard DB 15kV, and E69.02 and E69.03 were redeployed on shunting work at Heidelberg. They were near identical in external appearance, while E69.01 and E69.05 are variations of the same single centre steeple cab design layout. E69.04 originally featured a cab at one end, but was rebuilt in similar steeple cab style in 1934. All five machines survive, with 169002 and 169003 as operational museum locomotives used in 2002 on special working days with new DB computer numbers 188691 and 188692.

**Type:** Bo local passenger and freight
**Power:** E69.01 160kW (214hp); E69.02/03 306kW (410hp); E69.04 237kW (318hp); E69.05 565kW (758hp)
**Tractive effort:** E69.01 24kN (5400lbf); E69.02/03 33kN (7500lbf); E69.04 30kN (6850lbf); E69.05 54kN (12300lbf)
**Max. operating speed:** E69.01 40km/h (25mph); E69.02-05 50km/h (31.3mph)
**Weight:** 23.5 to 32 tonnes (51,818 to 70,560lb)
**Max. axle load:** 11.8 to 16 tonnes (26,019 to 35,280lb)
**Overall length:** 7.35 to 8.7m (24ft to 28ft 4in)
**Gauge:** 1435mm (4ft 8.5in)

## BO-BO METROPOLITAN RAILWAY — GREAT BRITAIN 1905

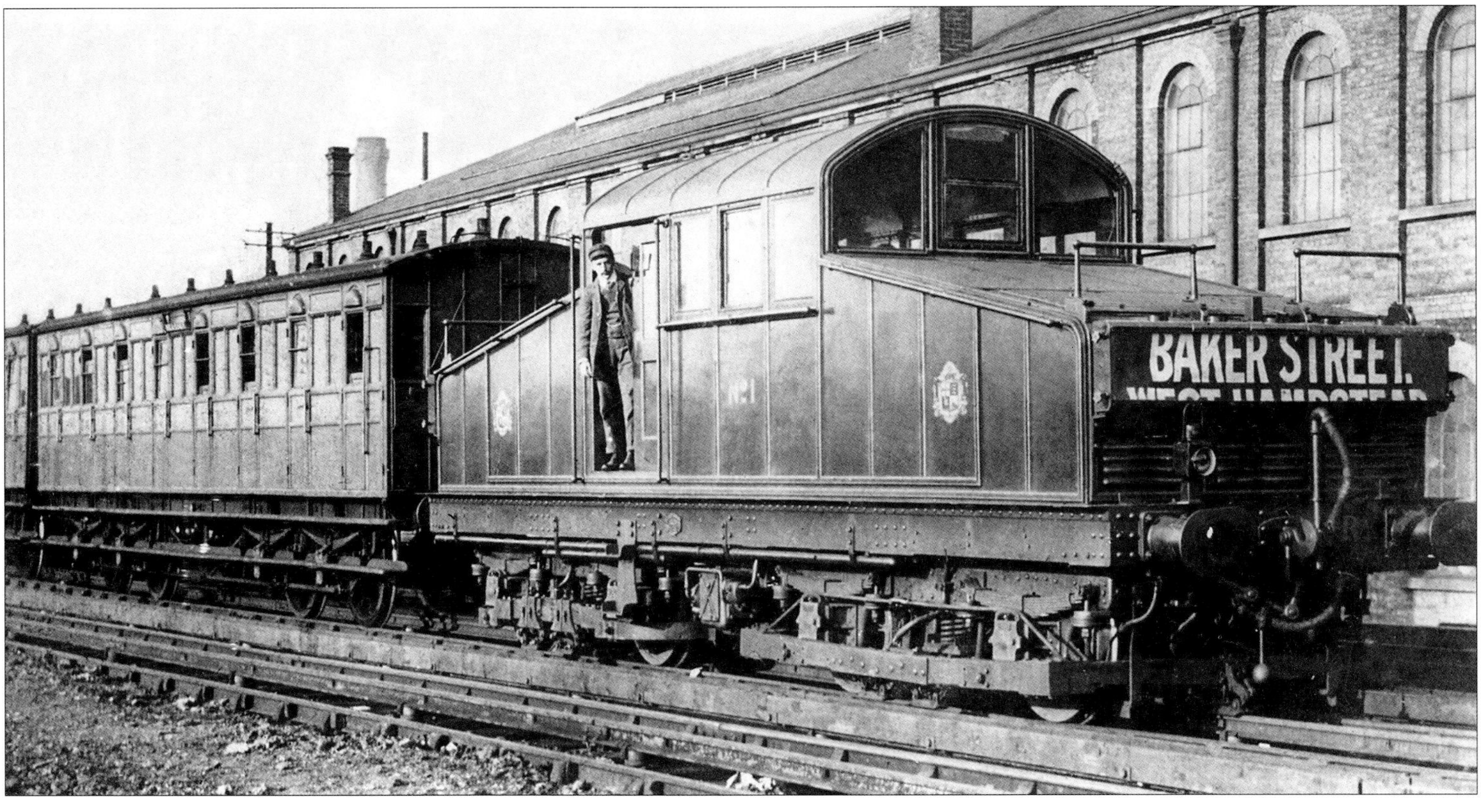


**Here, a Metropolitan Railway Bo-Bo locomotive on the world's first underground line pulls a passenger train outside Baker Street station in London in 1907. The Westinghouse loco was nicknamed the 'Camelback', because of its distinctive shape.**

The Metropolitan Railway was the world's first underground railway and commenced running on 10 January 1863. Steam locomotives equipped with condensers provided the motive power until 1906, when electrification was introduced. Electric locomotives in the shape of 10 British Westinghouse locos – called 'Camelbacks' because of their shape with centre cabs and sloping bonnets – made their debut on the Metropolitan in 1906. Numbered 1–10, they originally ran from the City or Baker Street to Wembley Park before changing over to a steam locomotive. When electrification continued, locomotive changeovers switched to Harrow-on-the-Hill from 1908.

Supplied by Westinghouse, these locomotives were actually built by the Metropolitan Amalgamated Railway Carriage and Wagon Company of Saltley. The electrics were originally fitted with enormous roller destination blinds, which were replaced by more modest-sized ones about 1911. The Westinghouse locomotives were followed in 1907 by a further 10 Bo-Bo locomotives, numbered 11–20, from the same builder, but to a totally different design. These were equipped throughout with British Thomson-Houston electrical equipment, were some three tons lighter than their predecessors and looked very different with end cabs.

In 1913, electrical equipment was standardized when 11–20 were relieved of their bogies plus BT-H motors and given new bogies fitted with Westinghouse 86M traction motors. The locomotives were judged inadequate for the Metropolitan's increasing traffic, leading to their role in the 'rebuilds' of the line's 895.2kW (1200hp) locomotives.

**Type:** Suburban electric locomotives
**Power:** 600V DC, four British Westinghouse Type 86M nose-suspended traction motors, 596.8kW (800hp)
**Tractive effort:** Not known
**Max. operating speed:** Not known
**Weight:** 50.8 tonnes (112,000lb)
**Max. axle load:** Not known
**Gauge:** 1435mm (4ft 8.5in)

## CLASS E550 STATE RAILWAYS (FS) — ITALY 1908

Italy's State Railways (FS) was unique in Europe, with its three-phase electrification peaking at 1900km (around 1200 miles) in northwest Italy before the outbreak of World War II interrupted further expansion. The development of electrification was an 1897 government-financed initiative with Societa Italiana delle Strade Ferrate Meridionali Esercente la Rete Adriatica electrifying its Valtellina line. Ganz of Hungary built the double-contact wire system from Lecco to Sondrio, and the government made that the standard in 1906.

The American company Westinghouse built a locomotive factory near Genoa, inviting the engineer Kandó from Ganz. First route was the Giovi incline between the Italian mainland and Genoa harbour, with class E550 'cinquanta' 0-10-0 designed for this work with cascade parallel control. A total of 186 was built to 1921 in four series, with two body-mounted motors driving through jackshaft and yoke. Despite its slow continuous speed of 50km/h (31.3mph), the E550 survived almost to the end of the three-phase era. Slowly converted to DC, AC operation lasted around Acqui until 1976. E550.025 was donated to the United States (now in St Louis), while E550.030 survives in Milan.

**Type:** 0-10-0 three-phase electric freight
**Power:** 1500kW (2011hp) from two body-mounted motors
**Supply:** 3300V 16.2/3Hz AC from two-wire three-phase
**Tractive effort:** 139kN (30,800lbf) at 43.2km/h (27mph)
**Max. operating speed:** 50km/h (31.3mph)
**Weight:** 60.1 to 64.0 tonnes (132,521lb to 141,120lb)
**Max. axle load:** 15 tonnes (33,075lb)
**Overall length:** 9520mm (31ft)
**Gauge:** 1435mm (4ft 8.5in)

## CLASS 1099 C-C MARIAZELLERBAHN AUSTRIA 1910

Although class 1099s as existing today date from 1910, they were heavily rebuilt from 1959 with new bodywork. Built by Krauss with Siemens electrical equipment for the Mariazellerbahn from St Polten to Mariazell and Gusswerk, these narrow-gauge machines are likely to see a century of regular traffic. The 91km (56.9-mile) line was constructed in sections between 1898 and 1907, with the severe gradient making it an early candidate for electrification. It was the first important electrified line in Austria and today the only remaining narrow-gauge one. Each of the two 1099 bogies has one traction motor each driving three axles by jackshaft and coupling rod transmission. Class 1099s dominated traffic on the line until a handful of 4090 railcar vehicles arrived in 1994. Despite introduction of these units, insufficient numbers are available to cover all traffic and 1099s continue in regular traffic today with no signs of imminent replacement. Only one machine has so far been withdrawn.

**Type:** C-C light branch narrow-gauge
**Power:** 420kW (563hp)
**Supply:** 6600V AC 25Hz
**Tractive effort:** 45kN (10125lbf) at 29km/h (18.1mph)
**Max. operating speed:** 50km/h (31.3mph)
**Weight:** 50 tonnes (110250lb)
**Max. axle load:** 8.3 tonnes (18,302lb)
**Overall weight:** 11,020mm (36ft 2in)
**Gauge:** 760mm (2ft 6in)

**ÖBB No. 005.9 is pictured here standing in the bay platform at St Polten, the junction with the Vienna–Linz main line, ready for the southward trek into the mountains to Mariazell.**

## DD1 PENNSYLVANIA RAILROAD (PRR) USA 1910

**Pennsylvania Railroad and its Long Island Rail Road subsidiary used DD1 third rail electrics to move trains to New York's Pennsylvania Station.**

Certainly one of the Pennsylvania Railroad's greatest undertakings was the construction of its New York Pennsylvania Station and tunnels beneath the Hudson and East rivers. To operate its trains underground through these long tunnels, Pennsylvania Railroad chose a 600V DC electrification system and designed a fleet of powerful siderod electrics.

These machines were semi-permanently coupled pair of locomotives based on the 4-4-0 steam locomotive arrangement. In Pennsylvania Railroad parlance, a 4-4-0 was designated as Class D, therefore these 'double D' electrics were designated DD1s and used a 2-Bo-Bo-2 (or, in steam terms, a 4-4-0+0-4-4) wheel arrangement.

Using Westinghouse electrical equipment, Pennsylvania Railroad built 33 DD1 pairs at its famous Juniata Shops in Altoona, Pennsylvania in 1910 and 1911. In later years, a few DD1s were retained for wire train service.

**Type:** 2-Bo-Bo-2, passenger electric
**Power:** 600V DC from third rail
**Output:** 1587kW (2130hp)
**Tractive effort:** 220kW (49,400lbf)
**Max. operating speed:** 128km/h (80mph)
**Weight:** 144 tonnes (313,000lb)
**Overall length:** 19.787m (64ft 11in)
**Max. axle load:** 23 tonnes (50,750lb)
**Gauge:** 1435mm (4ft 8.5in)

**Until the Pennsylvania Railroad had completed its overhead electrification from New York to Washington DC in the 1930s, it used DD1 siderod electrics to haul trains from Pennsylvania Station under the Hudson River to Manhattan Transfer in the New Jersey Meadows, where they were exchanged for steam power.**

## C+2Z EC 40 JAPANESE GOVERNMENT RAILWAYS (JNR) JAPAN 1911

Japan's first electric railway was opened in 1906, a short line from Nakano to Ochanumizo (12.5km (7.6 miles)); the next was the rack section of the Shinetsu line over the Usui Pass in 1912. This section, from Usui to Toge, was originally electrified at 600V DC using a third-rail supply. Twelve locomotives were delivered in 1911, and a further 14, slightly heavier, were built in JNR workshops in 1919. All were replaced by more powerful Hitachi-built engines from 1934.

**Type:** Rack-and-adhesion passenger locomotive
**Power:** 470.1kW (630hp)
**Max. operating speed:** 20km/h (12.4mph)
**Total weight:** 46 tonnes (101,430lb)
**Max. axle load:** 15.3 tonnes (33,736lb)
**Overall length:** 9.746m (32ft)
**Builder:** Esslingen, Germany; electrical equipment by AEG

## Class Be 5/7 1-E-1 BERNE-LÖTSCHBERG-SIMPLON RAILWAY (BLS) SWITZERLAND 1911

**Type:** Mixed-traffic locomotive.
**Power:** Two 933kW (1250hp) motors fed by single-phase current at 15,000V 16.67Hz via overhead catenary, with jackshaft drive via connecting rod
**Tractive effort:** 176kN (39,670lbf)
**Max. operating speed:** 75km/h (47mph)
**Total weight:** 91.4 tonnes (201,537lb)
**Max. axle load:** 16.6 tonnes (36,586lb)
**Overall length:** 15.228m (50ft)
**Builder:** Oerlikon, Brown-Boveri

**A transitional design, the BLS class Be 5/7 shows the form of the modern electric locomotive beginning to develop from the steam-based fame and wheel arrangement.**

Twelve of these locomotives were constructed for the new BLS railway, opened in 1912: the most powerful electric locomotives yet built. The two traction motors transmitted their drive via jackshafts on either side of the central coupled wheel, with heavy steel castings in the form of inverted triangles providing the link. The class remained in service into the mid-1950s. One is preserved.

## E Series E.50 STATE RAILWAYS (FS) ITALY 1912

The FS's predecessors had built special steam locomotives for the steep Giovi Pass lines between Genoa and Turin; now electrification was decided on, on the pattern of the system installed by Ganz of Budapest on the Valtellina line in 1902 – three-phase 3000/3300V AC 15/16.7Hz. This locomotive was for goods haulage, a compact, rugged-looking steeple-cab machine which was reminiscent of Kandó's Ganz-built designs for the Valtellina line.

**Type:** Heavy goods locomotive
**Power:** Two 746kW (1000hp) motors, driving five axles via jackshafts and triangular connecting rod
**Tractive effort:** 131.4kN (29,547lbf)
**Max. operating speed:** 44km/h (27mph)
**Total weight:** 60.2 tonnes (132,741lb)
**Max. axle load:** 12 tonnes (26,460lb)
**Overall length:** 9.5m (31ft 2in)

## Bo-Bo NORTH EASTERN RAILWAY GREAT BRITAIN 1914

**Type: Bo-Bo**
**Power:** 1500V DC overhead, four Siemens traction motors, each axle driven by a geared motor, 820.6kW (1100hp)
**Tractive effort:** 125kW (28,000lbf)
**Max. operating speed:** 72.4km/h (45mph)
**Weight:** 75.7 tonnes (166,656lb)
**Max. axle load:** Not known
**Overall length:** 11.99m (39ft 4in)
**Gauge:** 1435mm (4ft 8.5in)

The 29km (18-mile) Shildon to Newport line was electrified by the North Eastern Railway in 1915. It was an experiment to see whether electric traction was suitable for hauling heavy coal trains, and one that proved successful. For this scheme, 10 centre-cab overhead electric locomotives were built at Darlington, numbered 3 to 12, fitted with twin pantographs to the cab roof. On 1 July 1915, No. 3 hauled the first train along the route. The cost of maintaining the overhead equipment – and the 1930s recession – led to the abandonment of the electric workings in 1935 by the London & North Eastern Railway. The locomotives were stored at Darlington works for 12 years, then moved to South Gosforth car sheds in 1947. Except for No. 11, the other locomotives saw no further service and were withdrawn on 21 August 1950 and sent for cutting up.

No. 11 went to Doncaster Works in 1942 for rebuilding for potential use as a banker on the Worsborough incline on the electrified Woodhead route. After rebuilding, its tractive effort was increased to 167kN (37,600lb). The Woodhead scheme was put on hold due to the war, and it was returned to store. It was transferred to Ilford car sheds and renumbered as Departmental Locomotive 100 in 1959. It became redundant in 1960 and was withdrawn in April 1964, being cut up at Doncaster works that year.

**No. 10 was one of the centre-cab electric locomotives, numbered 3 to 12, which was built for hauling heavy coal trains on the North Eastern Railway's Shildon to Newport line.**

## SERIES E.91 B+B+B ROYAL PRUSSIAN RAILWAYS (KPEV) GERMANY 1914

This was one of several locomotives built for the electrified line through the Silesian mountains between Berlin and Breslau, and a vital stage in German electric locomotive design. Twelve were built between 1915 and 1921 to handle heavy goods traffic: one of the first big electric engines to dispense with carrying wheels and use all its weight for adhesion. The body was in three sections, with transformers and switchgear equipment in the front and rear parts, while the central one had a parcels compartment as well as two driving cabs.

**Type:** Articulated heavy freight locomotive
**Power:** Three motors with an hourly output of 873kW (1170hp), supplied by 15kV single-phase AC via overhead catenary
**Tractive effort:** Not known
**Max. operating speed:** 50km/h (31mph)
**Total weight:** 101.7 tonnes (224,248lb)
**Max. axle load:** 16.9 tonnes (37,374lb)
**Overall length:** 17.2m (56ft 6in)
**Builder:** Linke-Hoffman Werke, Breslau; electrical equipment by Siemens

## BOXCAB CLASS EF-1 MILWAUKEE ROAD USA 1914

Milwaukee Road's first electric locomotives were massive EF-1 boxcabs, each consisting of two units semi-permanently coupled with a 2-Bo-Bo+Bo-Bo-2 wheel arrangement. Used to haul freight up mountain grades as steep as 2.2 per cent, they featured regenerative braking (which turned traction motors into generators).

**Type:** 2-Bo-Bo+Bo-Bo-2, freight electric
**Power:** 3000V DC from overhead wire
**Output:** 2235kW (3000hp)
**Tractive effort:** 501kN (112,750lbf)
**Max. operating speed:** N/A
**Weight:** 261 tonnes (576,000lb)
**Max. axle load:** 26 tonnes (56,250lb)
**Overall length:** 34.138m (112ft)
**Gauge:** 1435mm (4ft 8.5in)

## MP54 EMU PENNSYLVANIA RAILROAD (PRR) USA 1914

**Type:** Suburban passenger electric EMU
**Power:** 11,500V at 25Hz alternating current
**Output:** 298 kW (400hp) per car
**Max. operating speed:** 104km/h (65mph) with some cars 128km/h (80mph)
**Weight:** 59 tonnes (130,000lb) - varied among different classes
**Overall length:** 19.653m (64ft 6in)
**Max. axle load:** N/A
**Gauge:** 1435mm (4ft 8.5in)

In 1915, PRR began electrifying its intensive Philadelphia area suburban services using a 11kV AC overhead system. The first route under wire was the famous Main Line from Broad Street to Paoli. To provide service on the electric lines, PRR's Altoona shops rebuilt steel P54 passenger cars into MP54 electric multiple units using Westinghouse electrical components. Each car used a single pantograph and one powered bogie with two AC traction motors. The ends of the cars were equipped with running controls and a pair of porthole-style windows, giving the MP54s a characteristic 'owl-eyed' look. Hundreds of MP54s were built and, after the electrification of the New York–Washington DC route, were a common sight on PRR's electrified lines.

**A three-car set of Pennsylvania MP54s heads towards Newark, New Jersey, on the PRR high line in 1961. This type of electric multiple unit worked PRR rails for more than five decades.**

## CLASS BE 4/6 1-B-B-1 SWISS FEDERAL RAILWAYS (SBB) SWITZERLAND 1918

**Type:** Express passenger locomotive
**Power:** Four 380kW (510hp) motors, in pairs, supplied by single-phase current at 15,000V 16.67Hz via overhead catenary, each pair driving a four-wheel bogie via jackshafts
**Tractive effort:** 196kN (44,080lbf)
**Max. operating speed:** 75km/h (47mph)
**Total weight:** 106.5 tonnes (234,730lb)
**Max. axle load:** 19.25 tonnes (42,427lb)
**Overall length:** 16.5m (54ft 1in)
**Builder:** SLM, Brown-Boveri

With 46km (28.6 miles) of tunnels out of a total route of 219km (136 miles), the Gotthard line through the Alps from Lucerne to Chiasso in Italy was an obvious case for electrification following the Berne-Lötschberg-Simplon scheme's success. Designed in anticipation of the line's completion date (May 1921), this locomotive triumphed over two competing designs to be the passenger engine of choice, and 40 were built between 1918 and 1922. They were articulated engines, with the body mounted on two power bogies, each with two coupled axles driven by jackshafts. Maximum power output per hour was 1641kW (2200hp) at 60km/h (37mph). Buffers and drawgear were fitted to the bogies and not to the body frame. Substantial and solidly built, the excellent Be 4/6s worked passenger and express freight trains for more than 50 years.

**The class Be 4/6 could take 230-tonne (227-ton) trains up the Gotthard grades at a steady 60km/h (37mph).**

## 'BI-POLAR', TYPE EP-2 MILWAUKEE ROAD USA 1919

Milwaukee Road's westernmost electrification crossed the Washington Cascades. For passenger traffic, Milwaukee turned to General Electric, and, in 1919, it built five massive three-piece articulated electrics using a 1-Bo-Do-Do-Bo-1 wheel arrangement. These were powered using state-of-the-art gearless two-pole, or 'Bi-Polar', motors whereby the armatures were mounted on the driving axles.

The EP-2 types featured a distinctive exterior design with a centre-cab arrangement and rounded hood sections at both ends. These 12-motor machines were extraordinarily powerful for the period, and Milwaukee Road demonstrated this power by staging a well-publicized 'tug of war' between a Bi-Polar electric and a pair of steam locomotives – the electric won.

The 'Bi-Polars' were withdrawn in the 1950s, and Milwaukee's Washington electrification

**General Electric built five massive Bi-Polar electrics for Milwaukee Road's Pacific electrification. Although the locomotives were withdrawn in the 1950s, one has been preserved for display in St Louis.**

**Type:** 1-Bo-Do-Do-Bo-1 passenger electric
**Power:** 3000V DC from overhead
**Tractive effort:** 187kN (42,000lbf) at 43km/h (27mph)
**Max. operating speed:** 112km/h (70mph)
**Weight:** 240.4 tonnes (530,000lb)
**Overall length:** 23.164m (76ft)
**Max. axle load:** 17.5 tonnes (38,500lb)
**Gauge:** 1435mm (4ft 8.5in)

## BO-BO METROPOLITAN RAILWAY GREAT BRITAIN 1922

**Metropolitan Railway's No. 12 'Sarah Siddons' is one of two survivors of the Bo-Bo electric locomotives built from 1922. Still in operational condition, No. 12 is a popular visitor at works and depot open days.**

This class of 20 electric locomotives was the backbone of Metropolitan Railway's mainline services for almost four decades. Sometimes confusingly classified as rebuilds, 18 of these locomotives were actually brand new. Pilot conversions of the Metropolitan's 598.6kW (800hp) electrics Nos 6 and 17 proved it would be easier to start from scratch. Vickers of Barrow-in-Furness produced the new locomotives on Metropolitan Vickers' behalf, the first of which was delivered in 1922. Fifteen of the locomotives were refurbished in the 1950s, when the Metrovick controllers and electrical equipment were replaced by BT-H control equipment.

The changeover point from electric to steam motive power changed from Harrow-on-the-Hill to Rickmansworth in January 1925, an arrangement which continued until the end of locomotive haulage and the switch to multiple units on 9 September 1961. Some locomotives survived in departmental use and for shunting work.

Numbered 1–20, each member of the class was given a name honouring a famous person within the Metropolitan Railway area. Two of the locomotives survive in preservation: No. 5 'John Hampden' (London Transport Museum) and No. 12 'Sarah Siddons'.

**Type:** Suburban passenger locomotive
**Power:** 600V DC, four Metropolitan Vickers MV 339 self-ventilated traction motors, one per axle, 895.2 kW (1200hp)
**Tractive effort:** 100kN (22,600lbf)
**Max. operating speed:** 104.5km/h (65mph)
**Weight:** 62.18 tonnes (137,087lb)
**Overall length:** 12.04m (39ft 6in)
**Gauge:** 1435mm (4ft 8.5in)

## 2-CO-2 NORTH EASTERN RAILWAY — GREAT BRITAIN 1922

**Power:** 1500V DC overhead, six Metropolitan-Vickers traction motors, 1343kW (1800hp)
**Tractive effort:** 125kN (28,000lbf)
**Max. operating speed:** 145km/h (90mph)
**Weight:** 104 tonnes (228,480lb)
**Overall length:** 16.307m (53ft 6in)
**Gauge:** 1435mm (4ft 8.5in)

**Raven's prototype high-speed locomotive No .13 was built for use on NER's proposed electrified York to Newcastle main line.**

In 1922, the then Chief Mechanical Engineer of the North Eastern Railway, Sir Vincent Raven, had a powerful-looking high-speed electric locomotive constructed. Numbered 13, it was intended for experimental work on the proposed York to Newcastle mainline electrification project. This never materialized under the NER.

Built at Darlington works, the experimental locomotive had a centre cab and six large driving wheels. No. 13 only ever worked on test under its own power on the Shildon to Newport electrified line. It was then stored at Darlington, only seeing the light of day for annual test trips and exhibitions. The locomotive was towed in the parade for the Stockton and Darlington Railway celebrations on 2 July 1925.

It was withdrawn on 21 August 1950, still retaining its LNER green livery, and sent to the scrap yard.

## CLASS E330 1-C-1 STATE RAILWAYS (FS) — ITALY 1922

Known as '*trenta*', Italian railways class E330 1-C-1 appeared in 1914 for 100km/h (62.1mph) passenger work. Built by Breda Westinghouse, the 16 machines – numbered E330 001 to 016 – had an enormous 51 tonnes (112,455lb) adhesive weight on the three coupled driving axles.

Running from the Italian three-phase system, synchronous speeds at 16.2/3Hz were 37.5, 50, 75 and 100, with corresponding outputs of 750, 700, 2000 and 1600kW (1019 951 2717 2174hp).

**No. 330.003 spreads its collecting arms wide to gather the three-phase current. The class e330's bodywork is very distinctive, cut away over the wheels. Sanding-pipes are attached on the outside of the engine.**

**Type:** 1-C-1 three-phase electric
**Power:** 2000kW (2717hp)
**Supply:** 3300V 16.2/3Hz AC two-wire three-phase
**Tractive effort:** 93kN (20900lbf) at 104km.h (65mph)
**Max. operating speed:** 100km/h (62.1mph)
**Weight:** 74 tonnes (163,170lb)
**Max. axle load:** 17 tonnes (37,485lb)
**Overall length:** 11.008m (35ft 11in)
**Gauge:** 1435mm (4ft 8.5in)

## BO-BO CLASS EO NEW ZEALAND RAILWAYS (NZR) — NEW ZEALAND 1923

**Type:** Heavy-duty mixed-traffic locomotive
**Power:** Four motors with a one-hour rating of 133.6kW (179hp) at 750V, supplied by 1500V DC via overhead catenary
**Tractive effort:** 63kN (14,166lb)
**Max. operating speed:** 58km/h (36mph)
**Total weight:** 55.3 tonnes (121,936lb)
**Max. axle load:** 13.8 tonnes (30,429lb)
**Overall length:** 11.7m (38ft 4in)
**Builder:** English Electric, Great Britain

English Electric supplied the five members of this class, New Zealand's first electric locomotives. The machines were put to work immediately on the sector for which they had been planned: the newly electrified summit section between Arthur's Pass and Otira, on the steeply graded 1065mm (3ft 6in) gauge South Island Christchurch–Greymouth line. With a maximum gradient of 1 in 33, and an unventilated single-track 8.5km (5.3-mile) tunnel at a height of 737m (2420ft), this line had always been a difficult one for steam working.

The electrics were limited to train weights of 127 tonnes (125 tons) going uphill and had three forms of brake, Westinghouse automatic and air brakes, and a locomotive handbrake. A big headlight was mounted on the cab roof. Drawgear, with central buffer-coupler in the usual New Zealand Railways style, was mounted on the bogies, not on the frame, as was frequently the case with locomotives which ran on sharply curving track. From 1942, they were deployed as a multiple-unit set of three, with one acting as stand-by and another undergoing servicing. At that time, they were partially rebuilt, with a driving cab at one end only. The three-in-one could take 381-tonne (375-ton) trains over the summit section in a shuttle service, and they did this regularly until they were finally displaced by the Toshiba-built EA class in 1968.

Four EOs were broken up at Christchurch, New Zealand, in 1969. No. E.03 is preserved in running order, having outlived the electrified line, the catenary of which was dismantled in 1998.

**At Otira station, on the west side of Arthur's Pass, a triple set of class Eo, led by No. 2, passes with a freight train against a mountain background. In June 1957, these electric locomotives still had 11 years' service ahead of them.**

## CLASS 1080/1180 AUSTRIAN FEDERAL RAILWAYS (ÖBB) AUSTRIA 1924

**The 'diamond' form of pantograph was by now standard. It was usual for a locomotive to draw current via its rear pantograph, as here. On some trains, however, when goods susceptible to sparks were carried, the forward pantograph was raised instead.**

Prompted by an energy shortage after World War I caused by reparation payments and suspension of coal supplies by Czechoslovakia, the Austrian government legislated for electrification of principal routes in 1920. The initial project was in the Vorarlberg, and electrification of the *Arlbergbahn* began between 1925 and 1927, using local hydro-electric power for the Innsbruck – Bludenz – Bregenz to Buchen, St Margrethen and Lindau route. Several designs of electric locomotive evolved, with the locally designed classes 1080 and 1180 for freight, 1089 and 1189 (developed from Swiss designs) for mountain work, and 1570 and 1670 for duties over flatter sections. Class 1080 dates from 1924/25 and the increased power output 1180 from 1926/27, all supplied by Krauss with Siemens electrical equipment in a heavy, rigid five-axle layout based on steam locomotive designs.

Members of this venerable class survived into the early 1990s on pilot and transfer work until they were displaced by the modern asynchronous motored class 1063.

**Type:** E, freight
**Power:** 1080 – 1020kW (1386hp); 1180 – 1300kW (1766kW)
**Supply:** 15kV 16.2/3Hz AC
**Tractive effort:** 1080 – 189kN (42,525lbf); 1180 – 197kN (44,325lbf)
**Max. operating speed:** 50km/h (31.3mph)
**Weight:** 1080 – 77 tonnes (169,785lb); 1180 – 80.5 tonnes (177,503lb)
**Max. axle load:** 20 tonnes (44,100lb)
**Overall length:** 12.75m (41ft 7in)
**Gauge:** 1435mm (4ft 8.5in)

**A class 1180 on yard shunting duty. These slow but steady locomotives had a freight-hauling career of some 70 years on the ÖBB, outlasting many swifter types.**

## EP5 (BAYER EP5, E52) GERMAN STATE RAILWAYS (DRB) GERMANY 1924

The class EP5 electric locomotive was introduced in 1924 by the *Deutsche Reichsbahn* for Bavarian electrified routes.

The class featured four body-mounted traction motors in pairs driving jackshaft, enabling smaller, lighter motors to be used in comparison with the larger single machines which were to be found in contemporary locomotives. A full-length body with cabs located at the extreme ends featured above the massive 1400mm (55in) diameter driving wheels.

Constructed by Maffei and WASSEG (a cooperation between Siemens-Schukert and AEG), the 35 locomotives were delivered as EP 5 21 501 to 535, becoming E52 01 to 35 in 1927. Twenty-eight examples survived post–World War II to become DB class 152.

The designation class 152 has subsequently been reused for the DB Cargo Eurosprinter which is currently in traffic.

**Type:** 2B-B2 heavy passenger
**Power:** 1660kW (2255hp)
**Supply:** 15kV 16.2/3Hz AC
**Tractive effort:** 78kN (17600lbf)
**Max. operating speed:** 90km/h (56.3mph)
**Weight:** 140 tonnes (308,700lb)
**Max. axle load:** 19.6 tonnes (43,218lb)
**Overall length:** 17.21m (56ft 2in)
**Gauge:** 1435mm (4ft 8.5in)

## CLASS AE3/6 ELECTRIC LOCOMOTIVES SWISS FEDERAL RAILWAYS (SBB) SWITZERLAND 1924

For use on middle-range passenger services, Swiss railways decided to purchase a group of class Ae3/6 locomotives. These locomotives had rigid-framed bodies, riding on three coupled axles with a bogie at one end and a pony truck at the other. The traction motors were locomotive body mounted. All 114 'Ae3/6s' have been withdrawn, but one or two are preserved. The larger 'Ae4/7' 2-Do-1s were a development of the Ae3/6s with an extra motor and pair of driving wheels.

**Type:** Mainline mixed-traffic electric locomotive
**Wheel arrangement:** 2-Co-1
**Power:** 15,000V 16.67Hz AC overhead line collection; 1560kW (2090hp); three body-mounted single-phase AC traction motors with Büchli flexible drives
**Tractive effort:** 147kN (33,045lbf)
**Max. operating speed:** 110km/h (69mph)
**Weight:** 94 and 96 tonnes (205,990 and 213,920lb)
**Max. axle load:** Not known
**Overall length:** 14.7m (48ft 3in)

**A class Ae3/6 electric locomotive, showing the separate motor drives to the individual axles. The motors were AC with slip rings.**

## 1-C-C-1 CHILEAN TRANSANDINE RAILWAY (FCCT) CHILE 1925

The South American Andes offered an even greater challenge to railway engineers than did either the Alps and the Rockies. The Chilean *Transandino* was built to the metre gauge, a 254km (159-mile) line connecting Mendoza in Argentina through the Uspallata Pass below Mt Aconcagua to Los Andes in Chile. The summit tunnel of La Cumbre is at a height of 3186m (10,450ft), with gradients of 1 in 12.5 on either side, where the rails are fitted with an Abt triple-rack system. Between 1927 and 1942, 76km (47 miles) of this extremely steep central section were electrified. The voltage was 3000V DC.

Three locomotives were ordered, Nos 101–103, one from SLM and two from Brown-Boveri. They were in effect a pair of 1-Cs joined back-to-back, rather than the articulated-bogie type, but very similar to other Swiss-built locomotives in style and appearance. Each unit had three traction motors, one in each case for the rack wheels. With these engaged, tractive effort was 220kN (49,500lb).

Trainloads of up to 150 tonnes (147 tons) were taken up the rack section at a speed of 15km/h (9.5mph). The line was susceptible to landslide, floods and snow, with no economic resources to invest in protective works.

Between 1934 and 1944, a long section was closed following a huge glacial washout. Brown-Boveri supplied a further two locomotives in 1961, of higher power rating, which could take trains at 30km/h (18.6mph) over the rack section. Services were suspended in 1978, and the line was closed in 1982, but a renovation project was proposed in 2001.

**Type:** Rack-and-adhesion mixed-traffic locomotive
**Power:** Four 239kW (320hp) motors supplied by 3000V DC via overhead catenary, driving the coupled wheels through jackshafts; plus two 403kW (540hp) motors driving the rack wheels
**Tractive effort:** 98kN (22,000lbf)
**Max. operating speed:** 40km/h (25mph)
**Total weight:** 85.5 tonnes (188,450lb)
**Max. axle load:** 12 tonnes (26,450lb)
**Overall length:** 16.12m (52ft 11in)

## CLASS 161.BE 1-A-B+B-A-1 PARIS-LYONS-MEDITERRANEAN RAILWAY (PLM) FRANCE 1925

The busy international line which linked Milan and Turin in northern Italy with the French city of Lyons via Modane and Chambéry had many steep gradients, and the Paris-Lyons-Mediterranean Railway looked to heavy electrical power to take trains of 800 tonnes (787 tons) over the route.

At this time, French railways were still very much committed to working on a supply system of 1500V DC, even though Kandó's pioneering work using industrial-strength power was already well in hand in Hungary and also on the Höllenthal Railway in Germany.

Although the PLM locomotives developed 1791kW (2400hp), they were superseded by the AE.2 class 2-Co-Co-2 locomotives of 1930, which had an output of 2985kW (4000hp) per hour and worked 800-tonne (787-ton) trains uphill at 85km/h (53mph).

**Type:** Heavy freight twin locomotive
**Power:** Two 1791kW (2400hp) motors driving nose-suspended motors on three axles in each part
**Tractive effort:** Not known
**Max. operating speed:** 80km/h (50mph)
**Total weight:** 122 tonnes (269,010lb)
**Max. axle load:** Not known
**Overall length:** 20.58m (67ft 6in)
**Builder:** MTE, Paris; Thomson-Houston, Belfort; Schneider, Le Creusot

## 2-CO-1 CLASS EA-1 GREAT INDIAN PENINSULA RAILWAY (GIPR) INDIA 1925

Electrification of parts of this 1675mm (5ft 6in) gauge system began in 1922, initially on the intensively used Bombay (Mumbai) suburban tracks, but later extending to the Bombay–Poona–Manmad main line. The supply system chosen was 1500V DC, from overhead wires.

It was for service on the main line that the 22 locomotives of this class were ordered, to specifications laid down by the Great Indian Peninsula Railway's consulting engineers, Merz & Maclellan. A single prototype was supplied in 1928.

A central corridor through the body linked the ends of the box cab, and the main body was divided into three sections. Over the single carrying wheel was housed auxiliary equipment such as vacuum pumps, air reservoirs, blowers for the motors and braking gear. Control gear was placed in the middle part, on either side of the corridor, and the section over the bogie held resistances, unit switches and some other items of control equipment.

Reduction gearing transmitted the power from the six motors paired above each axle to hollow shafts surrounding the axles. The couplings between shaft and axle were designed to absorb movement of the wheels as they met bumps and irregularities in the tracks. The motors could be run as all six in series, or as two parallel groups of three in series, or three parallel groups of two in series. There were three field strengths available for selection, giving in all a total of nine possible economic speeds without incurring circuit resistances.

The driving wheels were large, of 1599mm (63in) diameter, with prominent sand-boxes to supply air-pumped sand to the wheels. Two driving axles were fixed in the frame, and the third was linked in a form of Krauss-Helmholtz bogie with the single front truck. All wheels had inside bearings.

They were well-proportioned engines and painted in the Great Indian Peninsula Railway black livery with red trim, with gently rounded ends and visors set above the windscreens, as handsome as a box-body could be. Their arrival revolutionized long-distance services, inaugurating what was referred to as a 'high-speed' era in India. In road tests, the EA-1s comfortably maintained an average speed of 96km/h (60mph), with trainloads around the 365-tonne (360-ton) mark. Although capable of running at 137km/h (85mph), their maximum operating speed was restricted to 112km/h (70mph). The 'Punjab Mail', which travelled from Bombay to Peshawar, a journey of 2496km (1551 miles), was considerably speeded up at the southern end.

In June 1930, the EA-1–hauled 'Deccan Queen' express was introduced, running the 192km (119.3 miles) between Bombay and Poona in 2hrs 45mins – not an exceptional speed, but the fastest yet achieved on a section that included the 1 in 37 Bhore Ghats gradient, on the long climb from the coast on to the Deccan plateau.

With their freight-hauling companions of class EF-1, the class EA-1s provided an excellent advertisement for electric traction. Despite this, there was little further electrification in India until the post-1945 years. The Great Indian Peninsula Railway was to later become the Central Railway of Indian Railways, and the class EA became class WCM/1. These locomotives had a long career, but with the conversion of the Deccan line to 25kV AC supply in 2000, all were finally withdrawn from service in 1999. Two are preserved, one at the National Rail Museum, Delhi, the other at the Nehru Science Centre, Mumbai.

**Type:** Express passenger locomotive
**Power:** Six 268.6kW (360hp) motors wound for 750V DC supplied from 1500V DC current via overhead catenary, with a continuous effort of 77.8kN (17,500lbf) at 63km/h (39mph).
**Tractive effort:** 149.4kN (33,600lbf)
**Max. operating speed:** 120km/h (75mph)
**Total weight:** 110.6 tonnes (244,000lb)
**Max. axle load:** 20 tonnes (44,100lb)
**Overall length:** 16.294mm (53ft 6in)
**Builder:** Metropolitan-Vickers, Great Britain

## 1-C-1 Class D STATE RAILWAYS (SJ) SWEDEN 1925

Drive by jackshaft and connecting rod was favoured by the SJ for a long time after most electric locomotive users had abandoned it for a drive mode direct to axles or wheels. It was not, however, a high-speed system. Variations on the basic 1-C-1 mixed-traffic theme were made for more than 25 years. The original examples had beautifully carpentered, varnished wooden bodies mounted on metal frames. As on steam locomotive cabs, the wooden skin was intended to provide insulation against the winter cold. This class was the most familiar sight on the SJ system, on passenger and local freight services, with 417 being built, and many of the later-built variants still remain in service. Specifications refer to Class Dg.

**Type:** Mixed-traffic locomotive
**Power:** Two 930kW (1250hp) motors supplied by single-phase current at 15,000V 16.67Hz via overhead catenary, driving the wheels via gearing, jackshaft and connecting rods
**Tractive effort:** 154kN (34,600lb)
**Max. operating speed:** 100km/h (62mph)
**Total weight:** 75 tonnes (165,300lb)
**Max. axle load:** 17 tonnes (37,468lb)
**Overall length:** 13m (42ft 6in)
**Builder:** ASJ Linköping; Motala Verkstad; NOHAB, Trollhättan

**The wooden-bodied No. 244 stands at the country junction of Borås in southern Sweden. This was the first of several D classes to be built over a period of 27 years. Other countries were already moving away from using rod drive, but the SJ used it right up to the 1970s.**

## RhB class Ge6/6 RHÄTISCHE BAHN SWITZERLAND 1925

**Type:** Mainline mixed-traffic electric locomotive
**Wheel arrangement:** C-C
**Power:** 11,000V 16.7Hz AC overhead line collection; 794kW (1065hp); one single phase AC traction motor on each bogie driving through jackshaft and side coupling rods
**Tractive effort:** 172kN (38,665lbf)
**Max. operating speed:** 55km/h (34mph)
**Weight:** 66 tonnes (144,940lb)
**Max. axle load:** Not known
**Overall length:** 13.3m (43ft 8in)
**Gauge:** 1000mm (3ft 3in)

The class Ge6/6 'baby crocodiles' were once a happy feature of a splendid metre-gauge railway system in the southeast corner of Switzerland. The *Rhätische Bahn* is a lifeline to the towns and villages in the mountains high above the Rhine valley floor on which nestle the larger towns of Chur and Landquart.

The railway consists of the main line from Chur up into the Alps, climbing via the Albula Pass and tunnel to the well-known skiing resort of St Moritz; the loop from Chur via Landquart round to Klosters, Davos and Filisur; the westbound line to Disentis (where there is an end-on junction with the Furka Oberalp Bahn); and the railway along the lovely Engadin valley to Scuol Tarasp. Most places on this system have populations that speak the local language of Romansche, Switzerland's fourth and least known tongue.

The *Rhätische Bahn* main line in its upper reaches swings wildly across the valley through loops and spirals, and across numerous viaducts in order to gain height. The railway does not use a rack, so powerful locomotives are necessary to haul the heavy trains.

Train services nowadays consist of express trains of up to 13 bogie carriages, a few local trains in the lower reaches that are formed by EMUs, and freight trains that in winter (until very recently) have been the only reliable way of getting goods to the Engadin and to St Moritz. There is a mixed-gauge section (standard and metre) southwest from Chur that occupies a few kilometres of one of the two tracks on the Chur–Reichenau Tamins section in the Rhine valley. Beyond the end of the standard-gauge part of this track, the metre gauge continues, and the *Rhätische Bahn* carries standard-gauge wagons on narrow-gauge transporters to reach more distant freight sidings.

A new base tunnel now links the Landquart to Filisur loop line with the Engadin valley, through which operates a shuttle service of trains carrying road vehicles. Thus the character and traffic distribution of the railway has changed significantly. Slower moving rod drive locomotives have little part to play on this modern railway.

At one time there were as many as 15 'baby crocodile' articulated electric locomotives working on the *Rhätische Bahn* narrow-gauge system. Five of these class Ge6/6s locomotives survived into more recent years. Delivered from 1925, these locomotives were designed for mixed-traffic duties. In the last years of their scheduled operation, they worked pick-up freight trains between Chur and Samedan. They are very popular among tourists and railway enthusiasts, and one or two are still maintained for such special work.

The class Ge6/6 locomotive design is articulated. There is a central equipment section with cabs facing front and back. On the roof are two box-type pantographs. Each end of this central section rests on a powered bogie, and each bogie is a six-coupled unit carrying a large traction motor under a nose section. The locomotive's motor drives a jackshaft which in turn drives the wheels through side coupling rods. Centre couplings for hauling trains are carried at the outer ends of the bogies.

The locomotives are liveried in brown with stainless raised numerals and the letters 'RhB'.

**The *Rhätische Bahn* Ge6/6 'baby crocodile' electric locomotives were an ideal early solution to the problem of hauling heavy loads through steep, mountainous terrain. Two large motors drove through jackshafts and side rods.**

## EL-3A Boxcab VIRGINIAN RAILWAY — USA 1925

The Virginian Railway was an Applachian coal hauler, known for operating some of the largest and heaviest steam locomotives in the world. In the mid-1920s, the railway electrified 216km (134 miles) of mountainous mainline between Mullens and Roanoke, Virginia, with an 11kV AC overhead system provided by Westinghouse. It bought 12 mammoth three-unit siderod class EL-3A electrics from Baldwin-Westinghouse. Huge traction motors powered the drive wheels through jackshafts and siderods. Virginian operated these giant machines until the 1950s, when they were supplanted by more modern ignitron rectifier electrics.

**Type:** 1-B-B-1+1-B-B-1+1-B-B-1, siderod electric
**Power:** 11kV AC at 25Hz from overhead
**Output:** 1 hour output at 44km/h (28.4mph) 5315kW (7125hp)
**Tractive effort:** 420kN (94,500lbf) at 45km/h (28.3mph) continuous TE; 1233kN (277,500lbf) starting TE
**Max. operating speed:** 61km/h (38mph)
**Weight:** 583 tonnes (1,285,160lb)
**Overall length:** 46.406m (152ft 3in)
**Gauge:** 1435mm (4ft 8.5in)

## E.401 2-B-B-2 PARIS–ORLEANS RAILWAY (PO) FRANCE 1926

At this time, partly under the historic influence of steam design, and partly because of unresolved technical problems with direct drive to the axles, the lower parts of most electric locomotives still resembled those of steam-powered engines. Carrying wheels or bogies preceded and followed large-diameter coupled wheels, driven by connecting and coupling rods from a jackshaft turned by the traction motor. The rod arrangements were usually quite straightforward, with connecting rod to a driving crank, and coupling rods spreading the drive to the other big wheels. Even when a form of spring drive was fitted, as in the British North Eastern Railway 2-Co-2 of 1922, the driving wheels were 2032mm (6ft 8in) in diameter, equivalent to those of a 'Pacific' express type.

Under the leadership of Kálmán Kandó, the Ganz locomotive works in Budapest had taken a prime part in the development of electric traction, laying its own special test track and catenary in 1922. When, in 1923, the Paris-Orleans Railway set out to electrify 204km (127 miles) of track between Paris and Vierzon, it also began to assess the potential of electric motive power. Up until this time, electrification had been mostly associated with mountain lines and short, densely worked urban and industrial lines, but this was a long crosscountry express route. Ganz supplied two out of three prototype locomotives tested by the Paris-Orleans Railway. The electrical supply was direct current at 1500V, not what Kandó was most accustomed to working with. He was a pioneer of three-phase and later of alternating current supply.

The E.401 was an engine of striking appearance, enhanced by silver-grey paintwork. Its running plate was raised from buffer-beam level to clear the jackshafts. The cab was mounted centrally, with two-way driving positions and a pronounced V-shape extending over the hoods, which had rounded and tapered ends. Each hood had a pantograph mounted on it. The carrying bogies, with inside frames and bearings, carried supports for third-rail pick-up shoes. These were for use in tunnels within the Paris metropolitan area, where clearances did not allow for the overhead catenary. The traction motors were adapted to use the third rail's 600V at a reduced power output. Perhaps the most remarkable aspect of the locomotive, however, was the complicated system of connecting rods. Two motors drove each set of four-coupled wheels, which were mounted in the main frame. The Kandó rod arrangement drove the outer coupled wheels from the jackshafts; however, a series of subsidiary couplings and connections made for an intricate dance of metal parts when the engine was in motion. These supplementary couplings were needed in order to allow for movement of the big 1751mm (69in) driving wheels on their laminated under-set springs. Though admired for its appearance, and known to the Paris-Orleans staff as *'La Belle Hongroise'* ('the Hungarian Beauty'), the locomotive was not reliable in service. Failures were frequent, and, though its power rating was 3580kW (4800hp), ample for high-speed express work, they were transferred from the intended passenger services to freight work and were withdrawn in 1942.

**Type:** Express passenger locomotive
**Power:** Four 895kW (1200hp) motors in the main frame, supplied by 1500V DC via overhead catenary or 600V via rail shoes, driving two sets of two coupled axles via connecting rods
**Tractive effort:** 176kN (39,670lb)
**Max. operating speed:** 120km/h (75mph)
**Total weight:** 131.7 tonnes (290,330lb)
**Max. axle load:** 18 tonnes (39,670lb)
**Overall length:** 16.04m (52ft 7in)
**Builder:** Ganz, Budapest

## CLASS 1045 BO-BO AUSTRIAN FEDERAL RAILWAYS (ÖBB) AUSTRIA 1926

**The compact form of the Class 1045 is seen in this shot. In latter years, their use was largely restricted to yard shunting, and they could still be found in action on some quite heavy freight work using triple headers.**

These were a series of general-purpose, four-axle, all-adhesion electric locomotives developing through time with successive builds of ever-increasing capability. The three basic classes were introduced by the pre-war Austrian railway administration *Österreichische Bundesbahnen* (ÖBB) as classes 1170.0, 1170.1 and 1170.2, which under German wartime occupation from 1938 became *Deutsche Reichsbahn* (DRB) E45.0, E45.1 and E.45.2. The postwar *Österreichische Bundesbahnen* (ÖBB) classed them as 1045, 1145 and 1245. The successive increases in output power and maximum speed were matched by proportional increases in weight. The three types lasted through the late 1980s and into the mid-1990s – the last class, 1245, was displaced by delivery of class 1163 from 1993–95.

**Type:** Bo-Bo mixed-traffic
**Power:** 1140kW (1549hp)
**Supply:** 15kV 16.7Hz AC
**Tractive effort:** Up to 196kN (44,100lbf)
**Max. operating speed:** 60km/h (37.5mph)
**Weight:** 61 tonnes (134,505lb)
**Max. axle load:** 21 tonnes (46,305lb)
**Overall length:** 12.89m (42ft)
**Gauge:** 1435mm (4ft 8.5in)

## CLASS AE 4/7 SWISS FEDERAL RAILWAYS (SBB) SWITZERLAND 1926

**The 2-Do-1 wheel formation of Class Ae 4/7 was unusual; most electric types were symmetric. The uneven weight distribution of the machinery is responsible for this particular characteristic.**

This long-lived class is a rigid-frame design with four body-mounted Brown Boveri or SAAS single-phase commutator traction motors powering the four driving axles. The Büchli drive system has an asymmetric layout, giving a different appearance to the two sides of the locomotive. In all, 127 Ae4/7 and 114 similar Ae3/6Is were built– the latter, with one less motored axle, were confined to flatter areas. Until displacement by newer all-adhesion locomotives of type Re4/4, the 127-strong Ae4/7 fleet was responsible for working the majority of frontline passenger services up to the 1960s. Cascaded on to secondary duties and parcels and mail work, Ae4/7 continued to operate throughout Switzerland except for mountain routes such as the St Gotthard. Bern depot was deploying multiples on heavy freight from the Lausanne yard until 1995. Deliveries of new class 460s were responsible for eliminating the Ae4/7s from service. The last Ae4/7 was taken out of traffic in autumn 1996, having achieved more than eight million kilometres (five million miles) of revenue earning service.

**Type:** 2-Do-1 passenger
**Power:** 2294kW (3075hp)
**Supply:** 15kV 16.7Hz
**Tractive effort:** 196kN (44,100lbf)
**Max. operating speed:** 100km/h (62.1mph)
**Weight:** 118 or 123 tonnes (260,190lb or 271,215lb)
**Max. axle load:** 18 tonnes (39,690lb)
**Overall length:** 16.76m or 17.1m (54ft 8in to 55ft 9in)
**Gauge:** 1435mm (4ft 8.5in)

## 1-DO-1 CLASS E466 CZECHOSLOVAK STATE RAILWAYS (CSD) CZECHOSLOVAKIA 1928

Electrification was installed on lines from Prague's main station in 1928, and some passenger engines were needed to haul express trains to the meeting point with steam traction. Three of class E466 were built by Skoda, and two of the same 1-Do-1 formation were built by CKD in conjunction with Czech engineer F. Krizik and Brown-Boveri. E466s were sturdy locomotives with paired motors driving gear wheels fixed to hollow shafts around the driving axles, with universal link couplings to the wheels.

**Type:** Express passenger locomotive
**Power:** Single-phase 15kV AC at 16.67Hz
**Tractive effort:** Not known
**Max. operating speed:** 110km/h (68mph)
**Total weight:** 86 tonnes (189,630lb)
**Max. axle load:** 17.5 tonnes (38,587lb)
**Overall length:** 14.5m (47ft 6in)
**Builder:** Skoda, Plzen

## C-C CLASS EF-1 GREAT INDIAN PENINSULA RAILWAY (GIPR) INDIA 1928

SLM at Winterthur built the first of these 1675mm (5ft 6in) gauge engines, India's first heavy freight electric locomotives, closely modelled on the famous Ce 6/8 '*Krokodil*' class for the SBB Gotthard line from 1918, and the Ge 6/6 type built by the same workshops for the Rhaetian Railway. In India, however, they were known as '*Khekda*', or 'Crabs'. They proved extremely reliable and durable, although the external rodding needed frequent lubrication.

Later examples of the class – which totalled 41 – were built by the Vulcan Foundry of Manchester, England, with electrical equipment by Metropolitan-Vickers. The design was articulated, with the central body section, containing the main transformer, pivoted on two power bogies. The bogies contained the motor units, wound for full line voltage of 1500V. The bonnets of the bogie units were joined by concertina links to the closely fitted main body section. The electro-pneumatic control equipment gave nine running positions, and a regenerative braking system, by Newport-Shildon of Great Britain, was provided.

Heavy freight trains on the lines running inland from Bombay were the prime task, undertaken by the EF-1s for more than three decades. Reclassed as WCG-1 under Indian Railways, they worked mostly as banking engines on the steep gradient between Karjat and Lonavla; some were still on these duties in 1992, although withdrawals had begun in the mid-1970s.

**Type:** Heavy freight locomotive
**Power:** Four 485kW (650hp) motors in pairs driving two three-axle bogies through twin helical gears and jackshaft, supplied by 1500V DC via overhead catenary
**Tractive effort:** 135.5kN (30,480lb)
**Max. operating speed:** 80km/h (50mph)
**Total weight:** 138.3 tonnes (305,000lb)
**Max. axle load:** 23 tonnes (50,825lb)
**Builder:** SLM, Winterthur, and Vulcan Foundry, Manchester

## EA1/WCP1 INDIAN STATE RAILWAYS — INDIA 1928

Class WCP1 (originally class EA1) were India's first operational electric locomotives, built for passenger work between Bombay and Poona and Manmad. Each of the two rigidly mounted driving axles and one articulated axle was powered by two traction motors. Retired many years ago, they were built by SLM and Metropolitan Vickers.

**Type:** 2-Bo-A-1
**Power:** 1656kW (2250hp)
**Supply:** 1500V DC
**Tractive effort:** 95kN (21,500lbf) at 59.2km/h (37mph)
**Max. operating speed:** 136km/h (85mph)
**Weight:** 100 tonnes (220,460lb)
**Max. axle load:** 20 tonnes (44,100lb)
**Overall length:** 17.214m (56ft 2in)
**Gauge:** 1676mm (5ft 6in)

## CLASS E432 1-D-1 STATE RAILWAYS (FS) — ITALY 1928

Constructed by Breda, the 40 members of the E432 class (which were numbered 001 to 040) operated over the 3300V three-phase AC network favoured by Italian railways with its 1900km (1200-mile) network in northwest Italy. With a liquid rheostatic control system, class E432 had 18 tonnes (39,690lb) over each of the four driving axles and four speeds up to 100km/h (62.1mph).

**Type:** 1-D-1 three phase electric
**Power:** 2200kW (2989hp)
**Supply:** 3300V 16.7Hz AC two-wire three-phase
**Tractive effort:** 161kN (36,225lbf)
**Max. operating speed:** 100km/h (62.1mph)
**Weight:** 94 tonnes (207,270lb)
**Max. axle load:** 18 tonnes (39,690lb)
**Overall length:** 13.910m (45ft 4in)
**Gauge:** 1435mm (4ft 8.5in)

**No. E432.029 stands near the water tower at Alessandria locomotive shed on 18 September 1947.**

## CLASS EC NEW ZEALAND RAILWAYS (NZR) — NEW ZEALAND 1929

The six members of NZR class EC were built by English Electric's Dick Kerr in 1929 for the electrification from Christchurch to Lyttelton. This project aimed to reduce smoke problems in the Heathcote Tunnel. EC7 to EC12 were used exclusively on this section, which was turned over to diesel operation in 1970.

**Type:** Bo-Bo
**Power:** 885kW (1188hp)
**Supply:** 1500V DC
**Tractive effort:** 112kN (25000lbf)
**Max. operating speed:** 85km/h (53.1mph)
**Weight:** 50.8 tonnes (112,000lb)
**Max. axle load:** 12.5 tonnes (27,563lb)
**Overall length:** 12m (39ft 2in)
**Gauge:** 1067mm (3ft 6in)

## BVZ CLASS HGE4/4 SWISS FEDERAL RAILWAYS (SBB) — SWITZERLAND 1929

The rack-and-adhesion railway that links Brig and Visp in the Rhône valley with Zermatt near the Matterhorn mountain purchased six electric locomotives as far back as 1929, and these still survive in occasional and peak period service.

At first glance, the HGe4/4s look similar to the *Rhätische Bahn* 'crocodiles'; however they are actually of Bo-Bo arrangement. There is a large centre section with cabs, and two pronounced noses at each end.

**Type:** Mixed-traffic rack-and-adhesion electric locomotive
**Wheel arrangement:** Bo-Bo
**Power:** 11,000V 16.7Hz AC overhead line collection; 735kW (985hp); single-phase AC traction motors
**Tractive effort:** Not known
**Max. operating speed:** 45km/h (69mph) off rack, 25km/h (16mph) on rack
**Weight:** 47 tonnes (102,775lb)
**Max. axle load:** Not known
**Overall length:** Not known
**Gauge:** 1000mm (3ft 3in)

## P5 PENNSYLVANIA RAILROAD (PRR) USA 1930

In the 1920s, the Pennsylvania Railroad (PRR) set out to electrify its busy multiple-track New York to Washington DC main line. The PRR was known for its home-built locomotive designs and set out to build a fleet of electrics for service on this route. The P5 Class was a boxcab that used a 2-Co-2 wheel arrangement, making it effectively an electric version of the K4s Pacific type. Although intended for fast passenger service, the P5 was plagued by lateral swaying and cracked axles, so PRR relegated the P5s to freight service.

**Type:** 2-Co-2, mixed-traffic electric
**Power:** 11,500 V at 25Hz AC from overhead
**Output:** 2794kW (3750hp)
**Tractive effort:** 254kN (57,250lbf) starting TE
**Max. operating speed:** Originally intended for 144km/h (90mph); later limited to 112km/h (70mph)
**Weight:** 178 tonnes (392,000lb)
**Overall length:** 19.101m (62ft 8in)
**Max. axle load:** 35 tonnes (77,000lb)
**Gauge:** 1435mm (4ft 8.5in)

## 1-E-1 SERIES 1082 AUSTRIAN FEDERAL RAILWAYS (ÖBB) AUSTRIA 1931

Of all electric locomotives, this was perhaps the one that looked most like a steam tank engine, with pantographs instead of boiler fittings. A leading locomotive historian described it as ‘probably the most interesting electric locomotive then existing in Europe’. Like many other interesting designs, it remained a one-off, although it ran successfully for 10 years. Its most notable piece of equipment was a rotary converter. The rotary equipment was housed in a great cylindrical drum of boiler size, with the alternator in the place of the firebox and a driving cab behind it. Coupling rods linked the five driving axles, though, as with inside cylinders, the actual drive mode was hidden. Three axle-hung nose-suspended motors drove the three centre sets of wheels, as in the Series 1080 ‘E’ goods engines. For its electrified lines, the ÖBB had settled on single-phase AC, at 15kV and 16.7HZ. The 1082 locomotive reduced the tension through a transformer, then altered it to three-phase AC in the rotary converter. This was again changed into DC, which was fed to the three DC traction motors. The motors could be worked in series or in parallel. Although the locomotive was reported to have performed well during thorough testing, in 1941 it was removed from service and broken up.

**Type:** Heavy-duty freight locomotive
**Power:** Three axle-hung motors, rated at 507.3kW (680hp) and supplied with single-phase current at 15kV, 16.7Hz, via overhead catenary
**Tractive effort:** Not known
**Max. operating speed:** 50km/h (31mph)
**Total weight:** Not known
**Max. axle load:** Not known
**Overall length:** Not known
**Builder:** Wiener Lokomotivfabrik; Siemens-Schuckert

## CLASS V40 HUNGARIAN STATE RAILWAYS (MÁV) HUNGARY 1931

**Type:** Mainline passenger electric locomotive
**Wheel arrangement:** 1-D-1
**Power:** 16,000V 50Hz AC overhead line collection; 1620kW (2170hp); one body mounted three-phase AC traction motor with Kandó rod drive to side coupling rods
**Tractive effort:** 166kN (37,350lbf)
**Max. operating speed:** 100km/h (62.1mph)
**Weight:** 94 tonnes (207,270lb)
**Max. axle load:** 18.5 tonnes (40,793lb)
**Overall length:** 13.83m (42ft 2in)
**Gauge:** 1435mm (4ft 8.5in)

Innovation comes easily to Hungarian engineers. In the early 1930s, MÁV was electrifying at the industrial voltage and frequency of 16,000V 50Hz, a frequency not used again on railways until the French mastered it (at 25kV) in the 1950s. Engineer Kandó developed a rotating phase converter that transformed the input voltage and current into 1000V three-phase AC. By switching the motor poles in different combinations, the locomotive speed could be locked into the electricity frequency at 25, 50, 75 and 100km/h (40, 80, 121 and 161mph). The motor was fixed in the locomotive body and drove a jackshaft with crank pins at the ends. These drove connecting rods which were linked with the side coupling rods through a Kandó-patented triangular device that allowed for the vertical movement of the springs. The system worked, and 29 locomotives were used on the Budapest–Hegyeshalom route. MÁV is now electrified at 25kV.

**One of MÁV’s class V40, engine number V41.529, is seen here standing at the station in the town of Miskolc, Hungary, in 1956.**

## EP-3 NEW HAVEN RAILROAD USA 1931

General Electric built 10 box-cab electrics for the New Haven Railroad in 1931 which used a 2-Co-Co-2 wheel arrangement. Designated EP-3, these electrics were regularly used to haul long-distance and suburban passenger trains over the railroad’s four-track electrified mainline between New Haven, Connecticut, and its two New York terminals, Grand Central and Penn Station. The latter was reached by the line over New York’s Hell Gate Bridge. They would also be used on electrified branches, such as the line to Danbury, Connecticut. In 1938, GE built six EP-4 electrics that were mechanically similar, but featured

**A New Haven EP-3 electric rolls through Mott Haven Yard over the New York Central route from Grand Central Terminal. These electrics operated off both third-rail and overhead electrification.**

a double-ended streamlined carbody. During World War II, GE and Westinghouse divided an order for 10 additional streamlined freight electrics, designated EF-3. Most were displaced in the late 1950s by new EMD FL9s.

**A Milwaukee Road 'Little Joe' and box-cab electric are seen here wearing the railroad's maroon and orange livery. This particular livery was also featured on Milwaukee Road diesel electrics in the 1950s.**

**Type:** 2-Co-Co-2, passenger electric
**Power:** 11kV alternating current at 25Hz from overhead, or 660V DC from third rail
**Tractive effort:** 304kN (68,500lbf) starting TE
**Max. operating speed:** 128km/h (80mph) - one unit modified for 192km/h (120mph) running in tests
**Weight:** Approx. 183 tonnes (404,000lb)
**Overall length:** N/A
**Max. axle load:** 21 tonnes (46,000lb)
**Gauge:** 1435mm (4ft 8.5in)

## 5BEL PULLMAN ELECTRIC MULTIPLE UNITS SOUTHERN RAILWAY (SR) GREAT BRITAIN 1932

**Type:** Five-car electric multiple-unit Pullman trains
**Power:** 660V DC conductor rail collection, two power cars, each with four BTH 168kW (225hp) axle-mounted traction motors, resistance control
**Tractive effort:** Not known
**Max. operating speed:** 120km/h (75mph)
**Weight:** 40 to 63 tonnes (87,360 to 138,880lb) per vehicle
**Max. axle load:** Not known
**Overall length:** 20.115m (66ft) per vehicle
**Gauge:** 1435mm (4ft 8.5in)

England's Southern Railway (SR) was progressive in its development of third rail DC electrification across the south coast and in the South London suburban areas. The railway's first key mainline electrification was from London Victoria and London Bridge stations to Brighton, which was followed by extensions to Eastbourne, Hastings, Littlehampton, Bognor and Portsmouth via the south coast. For these lines, the SR built a fleet of comfortable, corridor electric multiple units in its own workshops at Lancing and Eastleigh (some were also built by contractors). The top link sets were six-car units for the hourly Brighton express services ('On the hour every hour'). These had a motor coach at each end, each with four powerful motors permitting the track speed of 120km/h (75mph) to be maintained on the significant gradients on that route. Each peak-hour train had two of these sets in multiple, making a 12-coach train. One set had a pantry car which served snacks. The other had a Pullman car for the more affluent passengers who wanted breakfast on the way to the capital and high tea on the way home.

Metropolitan Cammell received an order for three five-car all-Pullman electric multiple units to replace the former steam-hauled morning and evening Pullman trains called the 'Southern Belle'. Two of these would form the morning up train, a return working to Brighton during the day, and the evening peak train back to Brighton. The third unit was held in reserve and formed cover for maintenance and works overhauls.

In 1934, the train was named the 'Brighton Belle'. The cars were a mixture of first- and third-class Pullmans for which the Pullman supplement was payable above the normal fares, and meals and snacks were served at all seats. First class was lavish – with individual seats, one each side of the central gangway – whereas the third-class seats were in 2 + 1 formation.

As with the hourly trains on the Brighton main line, the 5BEL sets had a motor coach at each end, each with two power bogies carrying two axle-mounted 168kW (225hp) traction motors. Control of acceleration was provided through resistances brought into use via cams on the driver's controller energizing relays: as acceleration continued, the resistances were cut out one by one until the full line voltage was available to the traction motors.

The livery of these trains was at first that of the Pullman Car Company, a separate company with its own depot and workshops at Preston Park in the railway triangle just outside Brighton. The carriages were umber brown with cream window panels lined out lavishly in gold leaf, with the Pullman crest displayed below the cab windows and at each end of each bodyside.

When the 1932 mainline fleet was replaced by British Railways' new 4CIG and 4BIG units from 1963, the 5BEL units continued to operate. The popularity of the Pullman train was championed by local dignitaries and media folk, and BR had little choice but to continue it. In 1969, BR was to overhaul and repaint the trains in blue-and-grey with white lining, which only served to make them look out of date when compared with the modern stock covering all other services on the Brighton line. In 1972, it was easier just to withdraw the 5BELs and lose the Pullman service for good.

**The Brighton Belle train heads for the coast. It is in the umber-and-cream livery of the Pullman Car Company, with the wider crest used in its last years before the BR blue-and-grey era.**

## C-C VL-19 SERIES SOVIET RAILWAYS — RUSSIA 1932

Although Russia had been an early participant in the field of electric design, the pioneer Lomonosov left the country for the US railway industry in 1926, and the Soviet Railways were slow to take up electric traction in a big way. During the interwar years, political interference and lack of production capacity inhibited progress. In fact, it was 1947 before a specialist electric locomotive works was set up. The first mainline electric scheme was begun in 1928 and completed in 1932, over the Suram Pass on the Trans-Caucasus line, with gradients as steep as 1 in 34.

In anticipation of completion, eight electric locomotives were ordered from General Electric in the United States (Type S) and seven from Brown-Boveri in Switzerland (Type Si), and the Dinamo Works in Moscow began production of electric motors based on the GE design, known as Type Ss. All the locomotives were of the C-C configuration.

The Suram Pass electrification was a success, and the VL (Vladimir Lenin) 19 series was intended to become a standard class. Its 19-tonne (18.7-on) axle load was considered to be the maximum possible without having to upgrade the tracks as well as build a power supply system. The first was completed at the Dinamo Works in November 1932. About 145 more were built between 1933 and 1938, when the larger VL-22 type was introduced. Rated at an hourly 2071kW (2775 hp), they were fitted with rheostatic brakes, rather than the regenerative brakes of the GE and Italian locomotives, which had produced problems. Drawgear was fitted to the bogie, not the frame, and railed platforms fronted the cab ends.

The VL-19s went into service on the newly electrified Donetz line from 1935, hauling trains of up to 2540 tonnes (2500 tons) at speeds between 50 and 60km/h (31 and 37mph). The work of six of the electric locomotives was stated to have replaced that of between 35 and 40 steam engines of the E-class, although this claim may well owe something to propaganda. VL19.01, the first Soviet-built electric locomotive, is preserved at Khashuri.

**Type:** Mixed-traffic locomotive
**Power:** Six 340kW (455.6hp) traction motors, based on GE design, supplied with 3000V DC via overhead catenary.
**Tractive effort:** 245kN (55,116lbf)
**Max. operating speed:** 75km/h (47mph)
**Total weight:** 120 tonnes (264,600lb)
**Max. axle load:** 19 tonnes (41,895lb)
**Overall length:** Not known
**Builder:** Dinamo Works, Moscow

## CLASS EE3/3 SWISS FEDERAL RAILWAYS (SBB) SWITZERLAND 1932

**Once ubiquitous all over the network, more than 100 Ee3/3 shunters still operate on Swiss Federal Railways, produced at different times and with various speed and power ratings.**

These electric shunters (switchers) were once found throughout the SBB network. The design originated in 1928. They were all adhesion machines with the three axles connected by coupling rod by jackshaft to a single commutator motor. Earlier designs featured end cabs and shunting personnel platforms, but the later series described here has a single centre cab. Production ran from 1932 until 1966, hence the variations over time in weight and performance.

**Type:** C shunter
**Power:** 428 to 502kW (581 to 682hp)
**Supply:** 15kV 16.2/3Hz AC
**Tractive effort:** 88 to 118kN (19800 to 26550lbf)
**Max. operating speed:** 40 to 50km/h (25 to 31.3mph)
**Weight:** 39 to 45 tonnes (85,995 to 99,225lb)
**Max. axle load:** 13 to 15 tonnes (28,665 to 33,075lb)
**Overall length:** 9.51 to 9.75m (31ft to 31ft 10in)
**Gauge:** 1435mm (4ft 8.5in)

## CLASS 2D2 5500 STATE RAILWAY (ETAT) FRANCE 1933

**Type:** 2-D-2 heavy passenger
**Power:** 2888kW (3924hp)
**Supply:** 1500V DC
**Tractive effort:** 127kN (28600lbf) at 49.6km/h (31mph)
**Max. operating speed:** 120km/h (75mph)
**Weight:** 141 tonnes (310,905lb)
**Max. axle load:** 18 tonnes (39,690lb)
**Overall length:** 17.8m (58ft)
**Gauge:** 1435mm (4ft 8.5in)

The 'pig's nose' class 2D2 5500s proved themselves the most reliable of several French 2-D-2 designs. Introduced by the Paris Orleans Railway (PO) in 1933 following two prototypes, the production series E503–E537 (later SNCF 2D2 5503–5537) was constructed by Fives-Lille ultilizing both BBC and CEM electrical equipment. They were deployed initially on express passenger work on the PO 1500V DC network.

Two further series with differing styling (PO E538–545 and SNCF 2D2 5546–5550) were to appear before World War II intervened. Postwar development saw the 2-D-2 9100, which adopted the

**In September 1959, Class 2D2 No. 5505 stands over an inspection pit at the electric depot built beside the old steam roundhouse at Tours, western France.**

same overall mechanical design and wheel arrangement. These 2-D-2 5500s were to operate in service for nearly 50 years – other 2-D-2 machines were less robust, lasting 20 years or less.

They were concentrated at the Toulouse depot from 1960 on more menial duties such as parcels and freight traffic, with withdrawals taking place from 1977. The last ones survived to the end of 1980. The 2-D-2 5518 is in the Mulhouse national railway museum, while 5525 is privately preserved.

**Tours station is the scene in this photograph, as 5545, with remodelled ends providing a degree of air-smoothing, stands ready to depart with a Paris express on 1 October 1960.**

## CLASS E04 1-CO-1 GERMAN STATE RAILWAYS (DRB) GERMANY 1933

E04 was developed by AEG for the flatter land of Saxony in 1933 and had three powered axles. The first eight E04 had a maximum speed of 110km/h (68.3mph), but altered gearing in the next 15 increased this to 130km/h (81.3mph), trading off speed against decreased tractive effort. The final two locomotives, E04 22 and 23, were equipped with an early push-pull system for propelling passenger trains.

**Type:** 1-Co-1 fast passenger
**Power:** 2010kW (2731hp)
**Supply:** 15kV 16.7Hz AC
**Tractive effort:** 83 or 63kN (18,590 or 14,190lbf)
**Max. operating speed:** 110 or 130km/h (68.7 or 81.2mph)
**Weight:** 92 tonnes (202,860lb)
**Max. axle load:** 20.5 tonnes (45,203lb)
**Overall length:** 15.12m (49ft 4in)
**Gauge:** 1435mm (4ft 8.5in)

## CLASS E428 2-BO-BO-2 STATE RAILWAYS (FS) ITALY 1934

**Type:** 2-Bo-Bo-2 fast passenger
**Power:** 2800kW (3804hp)
**Supply:** 3000V DC
**Tractive effort:** 93 to 113kN (20,925 to 25,425lbf)
**Max. operating speed:** 100km/h (62.1mph)
**Weight:** E428 001-096 - 131 tonnes (288,855lb); E428 097-241 - 135 tonnes (297,675lb)
**Max. axle load:** 18 tonnes (39,690lb)
**Overall length:** 19m (62ft)
**Gauge:** 1435mm (4ft 8.5in)

Breda, Ansaldo, TIBB, Fiat and Reggiane supplied these 241 express passenger locomotives for the rapidly expanding Italian railways 3000V DC system from the 1930s. The articulated underframe was in two sections, supporting a rigid body. There were several different external styling variants within the class. Up to E428 096, the locomotives had a boxy structure with small, squared-off noses, while later machines had various rakeback or curved, semi-streamlined designs. Eight DC frame-mounted motors in pairs drove the four main wheels. Three gear ratios were available, giving tractive effort ranges from 113kN at 72km/h (25,400lbf at 45mph) from the lowest through 103kN at 78km/h (23,100lbf at 48.8mph) to 93kN at 88km/h (20,900lbf at 55mph) at the highest. Availability of different gear ratios was a feature of Italian electric locomotive development of that era, with higher traction pull traded off against speed, depending on the duties required. The original highest 150km/h (93.8mph) maximum speed of some members of the class was later reduced to 100km/h (62.1mph).

**A veritable box-on-wheels, the preserved E428.014, still roadworthy, is seen standing at Pistoia locomotive depot in Italy on 7 May 2001.**

## GG1 PENNSYLVANIA RAILROAD (PRR) USA 1934

**Detailed view of Pennsylvania Railroad GG1 4800, showing the railroad's trademark keystone, also the Commonwealth of Pennsylvania's symbol.**

The high-profile service, long life and classic lines of Pennsylvania Railroad's GG1 made it one of the best-known American locomotives. PRR was among the pioneers of electric traction in the United States. Construction of its New York Pennsylvania Station resulted in a third-rail 600V DC electrification through tunnels underneath the Hudson and East rivers. PRR also electrified its Philadelphia suburban services, but instead of third rail chose a high-voltage overhead system using 11,000V AC at 25Hz. The PRR decided that this latter electrification was the way forward and, in 1928, revealed ambitious plans to electrify its entire New York, Philadelphia, Washington DC mainline operations. At the time this was one of the most heavily travelled mainlines in North America, with exceptionally heavy freight and passenger traffic.

In conjunction with this electrification scheme, the PRR developed several series of boxcab electric locomotives that were based upon its most successful steam locomotive types. Its P5 electric used a 2-Co-2 arrangement patterned after the famous K4s Pacific type and was intended for heavy passenger trains. The 2-Bo-2 O1 class was designed for light passenger work, while the 1-Do-1 L6 types patterned after PRR's 2-8-2 L1 Mikado were to be the primary freight electrics. PRR's locomotive plans were disrupted when serious problems developed with the P5 class, making the type unsuitable for fast passenger work. Among the problems were serious lateral swaying and axle cracks, but PRR also found the P5s were underpowered, which meant that they would have to be run in pairs on the heaviest passenger trains. A collision that crushed the front cab of a P5 persuaded PRR to move the cab position further back.

Before building a replacement fleet of electrics, PRR experimented with different wheel arrangements to select the best possible combination for high-speed service. It borrowed a New Haven EP-3 electric that used a 2-Co-Co-2 arrangement and, in 1934, built two prototype machines, both of

**In the 1950s, PRR introduced a simplified paint livery on its GG1s that featured a single broad stripe instead of the five stripe 'cat's whiskers' that had been designed by Raymond Loewy.**

which used a streamlined centre-cab design. One used a 2-Do-2 arrangement patterned from the 4-8-4 type steam locomotive and was classed R1, the other mimicked the New Haven EP-3 and was classed GG1. After extensive testing, PRR decided upon the GG1 type and, over the following decade, amassed a fleet of 139. To improve the appearance

**GG1 4800, now on display at Strasburg, Pennsylvania, is the prototype, while XG1 4910 (opposite page) reflects styling changes implemented by Loewy.**

**PRR GG1 4800 was the first of the type and used a riveted skin instead of the welded skin of the production locomotives, hence its nickname of 'Old Rivets'.**

of its premier electric, PRR hired industrial designer Raymond Loewy, who cleaned up the lines of the locomotive, developed the famous 'cats whiskers' five-stripe livery and, most importantly, suggested a welded carbody instead of a traditional riveted design. From the 1930s until the 1950s, the standard GG1 livery was PRR's 'Brunswick Green' (a very dark colour that often appeared black in photographs) with gold pin stripes and a crimson keystone, PRR's corporate logo. The GG1s were variously built by PRR's Altoona, Pennsylvania shops, Baldwin, and General Electric. Initially, the GG1s were primarily passenger service locomotives. They had a 24:77 gear ratio and 1448mm (57in) wheels for 161km/h (100mph) operation, and could easily accelerate an 18-car passenger train to top speed. Power was delivered by 12 287kW (385hp) traction motors, two on each powered axle, giving the locomotive a continuous 3447kW (4620hp). The GG1 could generate much more power for short periods of rapid acceleration. In later years, some GG1s were re-geared for freight services.

The GG1 fleet continued as the mainstay of the passenger electric fleet after the Pennsylvania–New York Central merger of 1968. The New Haven Railroad was absorbed into Penn-Central in 1969. The subsequent financial collapse of Penn-Central led to the creation of Amtrak as the national passenger operator. Amtrak acquired a sizeable fleet of former PRR GG1s for its Northeast Corridor services. The last GG1s were operated by New Jersey Transit and made their final runs in October 1983.

**Type:** Mixed-traffic high-speed electric
**Power:** 11,500V at 25Hz AC
**Output:** 3442kW (4620hp) to 3680kW (4930hp)
**Tractive effort:** 314kN (70,700lbf) to 333kN (75,000lbf) – varied depending on weight – starting TE with 24:77 gear ratio
**Max. operating speed:** 161km/h (100mph)
**Weight:** 208.6 tonnes (460,000lb) to 216.3 tonnes (477,000lb)
**Overall length:** 24.232m (79ft 6in)
**Max. axle load:** 22.9 tonnes (50,500lb)
**Gauge:** 1435mm (4ft 8.5in)

## CLASS E18 1-DO-1 GERMAN STATE RAILWAYS (DRB) GERMANY 1935

**Class E18.050 at Frankfurt am Main *Hauptbahnhof*, in May 1969. The air-streamed front makes a contrast to the almost contemporary Italian E428. The class won a gold medal at the Paris World Exposition of 1937.**

By the early 1930s, Germany had three similar but separate 15kV systems in Bavaria and southern Germany around Munich and Stuttgart, in Saxony around Leipzig and Halle, and Silesia around Breslau (today Wroclaw in Poland). In 1933, it was planned to connect the Bavarian and Saxon systems with through-electric operation between Munich and Leipzig. A speed of 150km/h (93.8mph) was specified and based on tests which showed class E04 performing satisfactorily at this speed. Similar motors, transmissions and driving wheels would be used in an otherwise new class E18. Prototypes were ordered, and, in May 1935, the first was delivered from AEG. It was put on high-speed testing the following month. E18 01 met all specified parameters between Munich and Stuttgart and attained 165km.h (103.1mph) between Munich and Augsburg. DRB ordered the design into production, with up to E18 053 under construction before war production took priority.

The first series locomotives delivered in 1936 were operated between Munich and Stuttgart, Nürnberg and Regensburg. Eight others were used on the Breslau–Görlitz route. November 1942 saw completion of electrification works allowing through working between Munich and Leipzig, although not without difficulty due to different contact wire and pantograph arrangements between the Bavarian and Saxon networks. The Saxon lines used a ±500mm (19.5in) wire zigzag and 2100mm (82.7in) pantograph head, but only ±400mm (15.7in) zigzag and 1950mm (76.8in) head on E18 based in Bavaria. This latter head arose from the 1938 annexation of Austria by Germany and take over of BBÖ by DRG. Austria used a narrower pantograph head, and, for inter-working, the Bavarian machines had been reduced from the original width. Under war conditions, standardization was slow. In 1945, of the total of 53 class E18 in existence before 1939, six were completely destroyed by enemy action, six remained in the Russian occupied zone, two in Austria and 41 in Allied-occupied western Germany. Around half the latter were in a seriously damaged condition, demanding major attention to return them to service.

Two new E18s were built in 1954–55 by AEG and Krupp out of existing parts from machines cancelled at the outbreak of war. In 1977, main works overhauls were ceased on the class, which was reduced to 33 in DB traffic, being finally withdrawn in XXX. In the eastern zone, five locomotives were transported by the Soviets as war booty for use on a projected 15kV line at the northern polar circle, Workuta. This never materialized, and the machines were returned to East Germany in 1952. Using parts recovered from scrap E17s, the DR rebuilt two E18s for work after restarting electric train working in 1955. In 1967, DR investigated 180km/h (112.5mph) operation and altered the gear ratio, fitting new wheels and hollow drive shafts. E18 19 and E18 31 remained operational at Leipzig until XXXX, with E18 31 set aside early as a museum locomotive. The two machines in Austria became ÖBB class 1118, along with eight locally assembled class 1018 machines. These outlived those in Germany by several years.

**Type:** 1-Do-1 express passenger
**Power:** 2840kW (3859hp)
**Supply:** 15kV 16.7Hz AC
**Tractive effort:** 84kN (18,800lbf)
**Max. operating speed:** 150km/h (93.8mph)
**Weight:** 108.5 tonnes (239,243lb)
**Max. axle load:** 19.6 tonnes (43,218lb)
**Overall length:** 16.92m (55ft 2in)
**Gauge:** 1435mm (4ft 8.5in)

## CLASS E19 01/02 1-DO-1 GERMAN STATE RAILWAYS (DRB) GERMANY 1935

The E19 was essentially a higher speed version of the E18 of similar layout. E19.01 and E19.02 were built by AEG in 1939, with four single armature motors and 20-step control. E19.11 and E19.12 were from Siemens, with four double armature motors and 15-step control system.One E19 is preserved at Nürnberg complete with swastikas.

**Type:** 1-Do-1 express passenger
**Power:** 3720kW (5054hp)
**Supply:** 15kV 16.7Hz AC
**Tractive effort:** 77kN (17270lbf
**Max. operating speed:** 180km/h (112.5mph)
**Weight:** 113 tonnes (249,165lb)
**Max. axle load:** 20.2 tonnes (44,541lb)
**Overall length:** 16.92m (55ft 2in)
**Gauge:** 1435mm (4ft 8.5in)

## RAE 2/4 RAILCAR 'ROTE PFEIL' SWISS FEDERAL RAILWAYS (SBB) SWITZERLAND 1935

**Type:** Single railcar
**Power:** Two 200kW (268hp) motors driving the outer axles, supplied with current at 15kV, 16.7Hz, via overhead catenary
**Tractive effort:** 25kN (5621lbf)
**Max. operating speed:** 125km/h (78mph)
**Total weight:** Not known
**Max. axle load:** Not known
**Overall length:** Not known
**Builder:** Not known

**Something of a streamliner in its time, the preserved *Rote Pfeil* car, with its buffers and upright, squared-front screens, looks quite rugged against coaching stock of a later day.**

*Rote Pfeil*, ('Red Arrow') was a single-unit bogie railcar, looking more like a diesel than an electric, with a bulbous bonnet protruding before the driving cab at each end. Six were built, plus two others which were rebuilds of class RCm 2/4 cars. Passenger capacity was 60, in one-class accommodation. To maximize speed, they were built as lightweight units, with tubular steel seat frames and wide-view windows. Other up-to-date features included automatic doors. When new, they were the fastest machines running on the SBB and also the first on that system to provide the driver with a chair rather than have him standing at a control pedestal. These units were built to compete with car or coach traffic on standard-gauge lines leading to mountain and lake resorts, and as such they were very successful. Indeed, their main problem was that they were too small to accommodate the number of people wishing to use them and did not have the power to pull a trailer car. This led to the building of an extended fast railcar, the Rce 2/4, in 1936. After World War II, the 'Red Arrows' were mostly used for hire and for special services, rather than on scheduled services. One is preserved in the Lucerne *Verkehrshaus* museum.

## CLASS 5400 2-DO-2 STATE RAILWAY (ETAT) FRANCE 1937

Of the 105 2-Do-2s built for French railways (soon to be the SNCF), the most successful were the 22 locomotives of this class. They were fitted with the Büchli drive developed by Brown-Boveri in Switzerland. Intended for individual axle drive, their tension bars and universal joints allow a wheel to move horizontally and vertically without inhibiting the transmission of drive from the motor. Developing 3694kW (4950hp) at 96.5km/h (60mph), they gave many years of heavy express duty. In fact, locomotives of this class were still doing express work on the Le Mans–Paris route in the 1960s.

**The Paris Orleans Railway had pioneered the 2-Do-2 in France, and the Etat locomotives were closely modelled on the Paris Orleans design of 1932; both were absorbed into the SNCF from 1938 and classed as 5400.**

**Type:** Express passenger locomotive
**Power:** 3780kW (5065hp) 1500V DC from overhead catenary
**Tractive effort:** 225.5kN (50,700lbf)
**Max. operating speed:** 130km/h (81mph)
**Total weight:** 130 tonnes (286,650lb)
**Max. axle load:** 18t (39,690lb)
**Overall length:** 17,780mm (58ft 4in)
**Builder:** Fives-Lille-Cail; electrical equipment Cie. Electro-Mécanique

## SR 4COR SOUTHERN RAILWAY (SR) GREAT BRITAIN 1937

For the 1937 electrification of the London Waterloo to Portsmouth line the Southern Railway ordered a fleet of four-car express EMUs with gangways throughout including the cab ends. A total of 87 was built and which also covered services from London Victoria to Littlehampton and Bognor. They were liveried in Southern green, later in BR blue, and were withdrawn by 1972.

**Type:** Four-car electric multiple-unit express trains
**Power:** 660V DC conductor rail collection, two power cars, each with two English Electric 168kW (225hp) axle-mounted DC traction motors, resistance control
**Tractive effort:** Not known
**Max. operating speed:** 120km/h (75mph)
**Weight:** 33 to 47 tonnes (72,350 to 104,160lb) per vehicle
**Max. axle load:** Not known
**Overall length:** 19.355m (63ft 6in)

**A 12-car formation of 4COR+4RES+4COR units heads for the south coast. Because of the visual effect of a single cab window to one side, these units were nicknamed 'Nelsons'.**

## CLASS 1018 1-DO-1 AUSTRIAN FEDERAL RAILWAYS (ÖBB) AUSTRIA 1939

Class 1018 were constructed as DRG E18 201–208 while Austria was under German occupation. The eight were built at Floridsdorf, being returned to Austria at the end of hostilities and used by ÖBB on express passenger working on long-distance duties, including towards Germany, balancing DB use of E18s. Modified cabs were fitted in the 1970s, in common with the two 1118s running in traffic until the early 1990s, operating from Linz.

**With new-style cab, Class 1018 002.4 stands at Linz with a train from Vienna.**

**Type:** 1-Do-1 express passenger
**Power:** 2840kW (3859hp)
**Supply:** 15kV 16.7Hz AC
**Tractive effort:** 196kN (44,100lbf)
**Max. operating speed:** 130km/h (81.2mph)
**Weight:** 110 tonnes (242,550lb)
**Max. axle load:** 19.6 tonnes (43,218lb)
**Overall length:** 16.92m (55ft 2in)
**Gauge:** 1435mm (4ft 8.5in)

## ETR-200 STATE RAILWAYS (FS) ITALY 1939

In 1913, Italy's State Railways (FS) began to build a new route through the mountainous backbone of Italy between Florence and Bologna, to replace the original tortuous line via Pistoia with its 24km (15 miles) at 1 in 45. As this was part of Italy's prime trunk line, linking Milan to Rome, speeding it up was essential to cope with the growing rate of traffic. Although the distance was only 80km (50 miles) from the junction at Prato, north of Florence, the line was not completed until 1934. The works required were very substantial, including the 18.5km (11.5-mile) Appennine Tunnel and 27 other tunnels, some of them of considerable length, plus many viaducts, cuttings and embankments, and the average gradient was reduced to a much more manageable 1 in 106.

Known as the *direttissima* (most direct), it nevertheless has some fairly sharp curves, of 600–800m (660–880yd) radius on both sides of the summit. The line was electrified from the first, and, encouraged by the government of the time, the FS set out to provide a luxury high-speed train that would fully exploit its possibilities. The ETR ('*elettrotreno*') 200 was an articulated three-car set designed for rapid intercity travel. Its streamlining was developed in the wind tunnel of the Turin Polytechnic. All three cars were powered, driving both axles of the front bogie of the front and rear cars, and the outer axles of the inner bogies. Early on, the steel tyres fitted to the wheels proved incapable of coping with the stress created at high speed, and a fatal accident was caused before they were replaced. At speeds of more than 130km/h (80mph), the behaviour of the pantograph (the one on the rear was always raised in Italian practice) also caused concern, and, in addition to the two drivers positioned at the front, a third driver was stationed in the rear compartment to observe and operate it. The Italian practice of using DC line at 3000V enabled the designers to dispense with the heavy transformers needed to convert AC, and it was this that was directly responsible for the light weight and consequent high speed of the train.

On 20 July 1939, a special run was arranged for the ETR-200, from Florence to Milan. The train covered the distance of 315km (195.8 miles) in the remarkable time of 115.2 minutes – an average speed of 163.8km/h (101.8mph). The train entered the Appennine Tunnel at 159.3km/h (99mph) and accelerated on the final climb to 175.4km/h (109mph); on the curving descent towards Bologna, speed never fell below 144.8km/h (90mph), and a maximum of 189.9km/h (118mph) was reached. After Bologna, speeds in excess of 161km/h (100mph) were maintained virtually all the way to Milan, except for a few restricted sections. On the racing stretch just before Piacenza, the train reached a maximum speed of 202.8km/h (126mph). Apart from the train's performance, two factors made this an exceptional working: most normal speed restrictions were raised for it, and the voltage over the line was increased from 3000V to 4000V, making a considerable amount of extra power available to the motors. No train in the world had ever gone so far, so fast, and the record remained unbroken until 1964. It was a final gesture of bravado at the end of the 1930s, a decade that had seen speed records made and broken on numerous occasions. Only a month later, the outbreak of World War II turned the attention of railway staff in Europe to more serious and sombre business.

After the war ended, the ETR 200 reinaugurated a high-speed Milan–Florence service (in August 1946). Between 1960 and 1966, ETR 200 sets were converted by the addition of a fourth car and other alterations and refurbishments, and redesignated as ETR 220.

**Type:** Three-car express train set
**Power:** Six axle-hung motors of Type 62 (derived from FS class E624) with hourly rated power output of 1100kW (1474hp), supplied by current at 3000V DC via overhead catenary
**Tractive effort:** Not known
**Max. operating speed:** 210km/h (130mph)
**Total weight:** 103 tonnes (227,115lb)
**Max. axle load:** 10 tonnes (22,050lb)
**Overall length:** 62.8m (206ft 2in)
**Builder:** Breda, Milan

## AE8/14 1-BO-1-BO-1 SWISS FEDERAL RAILWAYS (SBB) SWITZERLAND 1939

This unique SBB class Ae8/14 machine was effectively two Ae4/7 locomotives permanently coupled back to back, although the wheel configuration is altered from the asymmetric 2-Do-1 to a symmetrical 1-AA-1-AA-1 in each half. The Ae8/14 class was the result of investigations by SBB into high-power locomotives for mountain routes, notably the St Gotthard line. Three prototype designs were

**The preserved Ae8/14 double-unit locomotive, temporarily moved outside from its normal position at the Transport Museum at Lucerne.**

evaluated; however, operational experience demonstrated smaller locomotives were more effective.

Although it never went into series production, Ae8/14 11801 remains today as an operational museum locomotive at the SBB Erstfeld depot at the base of the northern ramp of the St Gotthard. Similar Büchli drive machines Ae3/6 10664 and Ae4/7 10976 survive as museum locomotives, and all are occasionally on special traffic, often marking local anniversaries and events.

**Type:** 1-AA-1-AA-1+1-AA-1-AA-1 heavy freight double unit
**Power:** 4650kW (6320hp)
**Supply:** 15kV 16.7Hz AC
**Tractive effort:** 490kN (110,250lbf)
**Max. operating speed:** 100km/h (62.1mph)
**Weight:** 240 tonnes (529,200lb)
**Max. axle load:** 19.5 tonnes (42,998lb)
**Overall length:** 34m (110ft 11in)
**Gauge:** 1435mm (4ft 8.5in)

**One of Swiss Federal Railways' unique class Ae8/14 pulls a long freight train near Lagorvo, Switzerland, in 1966.**

## CLASS 1020 CO+CO AUSTRIAN FEDERAL RAILWAYS (ÖBB) AUSTRIA 1940

The ÖBB class 1020 originated from the wartime occupation of Austria by Germany. At the end of hostilities, 44 German class E94s remained in Austria and were adopted as class 1020, followed by three further units built in Vienna. Class E94, produced from 1940 to 1944, was designed to meet the need for a higher powered freight locomotive derived from the earlier class E93. The graded Geislinger Steige section between Ulm and Stuttgart was electrified in 1933, with class E93 specified for freight on this line and rated continuously at 2214kW (3008hp) at 62km/h (38.8mph). The 18 units appear to be of simple design, but the two connect a bridge structure containing transformer cabs and control equipment, with batteries compressor and auxiliary gear carried in low housings over the bogies. Class E94 followed this layout, but increased power output.

The first 11 class E94s were converted from orders for E93, and, on annexation of Austria in 1938, 87 more were ordered for service there. Further orders through to 1941 took the planned total to 285 units. Delivery started in 1940 with the first six going to Austria at Innsbruck depot, the next 10 to Pressig Rothenkirchen in Franconia and the next group to the Schlesien area (today Silesia in Poland), where coal traffic

**This class 1020 locomotive was still in ÖBB service when photographed in 1991. The central frame structure can clearly be seen. No. 1020.044 has been restored to original condition.**

important for the German war effort was handled by 15 machines based at Waldenburg, Dittersbach and Schlauroth. By 1943, class E94 could be found working over every electrified graded route in Germany (Franconia, Geislinger Stteige, Thüringer and Schlesien) and Austria (Arlberg, Brenner and Tauern). Simultaneously, both bomb damage and materials shortages were affecting the class.

E94 026 entered service with aluminium windings on three traction motors, while damaged E94 053 was rebuilt with main transformer aluminium windings, both resulting from copper shortages. Other machines such as E94 083 were destroyed even before entering service. At the ceasefire in May 1945, 76 were found in the western zone of occupation, 51 in Austria and 23 in the Soviet zone. Fifty-three were war damaged. Seized as war booty in 1946, 25 class E94s were taken east, with around 20 made operational between 1948 and 1951 as class TEL ('*trofeija*', or trophy, electric locomotive) between Koshwa (Koyza) and Workuta (Vorkuta), electrified at 15kV. In 1952 ,these were returned to the GDR in bad condition, remaining unused until the Dessau works started returning them to service from 1956 as DR class 254 (running in traffic until 1990). In West Germany, DB gradually returned its fleet to service (largely for freight traffic) in southern Germany, adding 16 newly built units E94 189–196 and 278–285 in 1954. In 1970, a 100km/h (62.1mph) version of class 194 (as they had become) was created with subclass 194.5 194 541–542 and 194 562–585. Class 194 continued in freight in southern Germany until around 1988. Class 1020 was refurbished between 1967 and 1980 with new cabs and 675kW (917hp) electric brakes. No fewer than 36 are still in existence, with 15 in Germany and 19 in Austria. Many are restored as museum items, but interestingly two E94s were restored in 2002 (ex-DR E94 052 and DB E94 051) for revenue-earning freight service by private operator PEG.

**Type:** Co+Co heavy freight
**Power:** 3000kW (4076hp)
**Supply:** 15kV 16.7Hz AC
**Tractive effort:** 314kN (70,650lbf)
**Max. operating speed:** 90km/h (56.3mph)
**Weight:** 118.5 tonnes (261,293lb)
**Max. axle load:** 20 tonnes (44,100lb)
**Overall length:** 18.6m (60ft 8in)
**Gauge:** 1435mm (4ft 8.5in)

**Villach, on the mountainous Tauern route to Klagenfurt, was the last operational base of the class 1020, and these particular locomotives worked from the depot here until 1995.**

## CLASS E636 STATE RAILWAYS (FS) ITALY 1940

**Type:** Bo-Bo-Bo mixed-traffic
**Power:** 2100kW (2853hp)
**Supply:** 3000V DC
**Tractive effort:** Low gear 113kN at 54km/h (25400lbf at 33.8mph); high gear 84kN at 45km/h (19000lbf at 45mph)
**Max. operating speed:** Low gear 105km/h (65.6mph) or high gear 120km/h (75mph)
**Weight:** 101 tonnes (222,705lb)
**Max. axle load:** 17 tonnes (37,485lb)
**Overall length:** 18.25m (59ft 6in)
**Gauge:** 1435mm (4ft 8.5in)

Nearly 500 of these articulated machines were supplied to Italian State Railways. The design of three four-axle bogies was carried over from the earlier E626 series, while the two-piece articulated body was to set the standard for the following E646/645 and E656 designs. Class E636 was in production over a relatively long period, first 1940 to 1942 until disrupted by World War II, resuming in 1952 until 1963. Most had frame-mounted flexible quill drive motors for 120km/h (75mph) work, but 49 are geared for 105km/h (65.6mph) with axle-hung nose-suspended motors. Into 2002, the 300 still in service were largely employed by the cargo business; however, until the late 1990s, they were regularly used on passenger work, including heavy international expresses over mountain routes. In addition to the 469 for FS, 50 similar locomotives were delivered to Yugoslavian Railways from 1960 as JZ class 362; however, these were adapted for 120km/h (75mph) operation, with rheostatic braking, 2640kW (3587hp) continuous power and 18-tonne (39,690lb) axle load. FS is slowly reducing numbers of E636s, while at the same time carrying out improvements, such as equipping some with air conditioned cabs for train crew comfort.

**Here, a Class E636 pulls into Milan station. In 2002, 3000 of these engines were still in service, mainly in the cargo business.**

**Here, Class E636 no. 070 pulls a heavy freight train through the town of Guincano in northern Italy. Many E636 locos were delivered to the former Yugoslavia from the early 1960s onwards.**

## CLASS CC SOUTHERN RAILWAY (SR) GREAT BRITAIN 1941

**Type:** Co-Co mixed-traffic mainline electric locomotive
**Power:** 660V DC conductor rail collection; 1095kW (1470hp); motor-generator control; six axle-hung DC traction motors
**Tractive effort:** 178 and 200kN* (40,000 and 45,000lbf*)
**Max. operating speed:** 120km/h (75mph)
**Weight:** 102 and 107 tonnes* (223,440 and 234,640lb*)
**Max axle load:**
**Overall length:** 17,295mm (56ft 9in)
**Gauge:** 1435mm (4ft 8.5in)
* Second figure for 20003

Two Southern Railway Co-Co electric locomotives were built at Ashford works, the first emerging in 1941. They were numbered CC1 and CC2 (later BR Nos 20001 and 20002). A third, No. 20003, came from Brighton works in 1949. These locomotives used a motor-generator set (with a flywheel to maintain smooth output) to convert the 660V DC conductor rail current into the lower voltages required at the traction motors in the acceleration phase. The flywheel had a secondary advantage in that it kept the motor-generator set spinning as the locomotive traversed gaps in the third rail. The class CCs were painted malachite green under Southern Railway ownership, then BR black with silver-grey details, and finally No. 20001 appeared in BR blue with yellow ends. The last survivor was withdrawn in 1968.

**Bulleid/Raworth Co-Co electric locomotive No. 20002 awaits departure from London Victoria with a boat train for Newhaven Harbour, a journey that was one of the class's regular duties.**

## NORTH SHORE 'ELECTRO-LINER' CHICAGO, NORTH SHORE & MILWAUKEE RAILROAD USA 1941

The Chicago, North Shore & Milwaukee was an interurban electric railway connecting its namesake cities on a direct route that ran parallel to Chicago & North Western, Milwaukee Road steam railroad lines. The North Shore line tied into Chicago's famous 'Loop', a third rail electrified rapid transit line operated in later years by the Chicago Transit authority. Competition on the 145km (90-mile) run was intense. In an effort to stay in business, the company had two four-piece streamlined articulated trains built by St Louis Car Company using Westinghouse electrical components. These were named the *Electro-Liners* and painted in a distinctive aqua and salmon livery. They made multiple round trips daily over the North Shore route, supplementing the line's intensive Chicago-Milwaukee service. North Shore was one of the last interurban lines abandoned (in 1963); the *Electro-Liners* were sold to Philadelphia's Red Arrow Lines where they were known as *Liberty-Liners*.

**Type:** High-speed articulated four-car electric train
**Power:** 650V DC via trolley wire or third rail
**Tractive effort:** N/A
**Max. operating speed:** 136 km/h (85mph)
**Weight:** 95.5 tonnes (210,500lb)
**Overall length:** 47.346m (155ft 4in)
**Max. axle load:** 9.7 tonnes (21,380lb)
**Gauge:** 1435mm (4ft 8.5in)

## CLASS 2000/2050 SOROCABANA RAILWAY BRAZIL 1943

**Type:** 1-Co-Co-1 freight and passenger
**Power:** 1350kW (1840hp)
**Supply:** 3000V DC
**Tractive effort:** 137kN (30800lbf)
**Max. operating speed:** 90km/h (56.3mph)
**Weight:** 130 tonnes (286,720lb); 108.7 tonnes (239,680lb)adhesive
**Max. axle load:** 18.29 tonnes (40,320lb)
**Overall length:** 18.59m (61ft)
**Gauge:** 1000mm (3ft 3in)

Electrification of the metre-gauge Estrada de Ferro Sorocabana was interrupted by the war effort in the United States – deliveries of the 46 locomotives were delayed from 1943 until 1948. Originally numbered from 2001 to 2046, there were differences between the 25 nominally GE-built (2001–2025) and the 21 Westinghouse machines (2051–2071). Heavily constructed 1-Co+Co-1 interconnected bogies ran on 1117mm (44in) drivers and 838mm (33in) idlers. Deployed solo on passenger services and with up to three in multiples at the head of freight trains, they dominated traffic from São Paulo and Sorocaba, and westwards. In 1968, they were joined by GE Brazil-built Bo-Bo class 2100s of similar power. A few class 2000 were taken out of traffic in 1995, but the end came suddenly in 2000 when private operator Ferroban took over from state-controlled FEPASA and ceased electric operation. A few 2000s are retained on works trains in the inner São Paulo suburban area.

## CLASS AE4/4 BO-BO BERN LOTSCHBERG SIMPLON (BLS) SWITZERLAND 1944

**An Ae 4/4 catches the autumn sunlight as it pauses at Brig with a long northbound train of international stock on 19 September 1990.**

The Lotschberg tunnel opened in 1906 and the through route in 1913 with electric traction at 15kV AC. Single-phase AC commutator motors, body mounted with mechanical jackshaft or Büchli drives, were conventional Swiss electric designs until 1944. The Bern Lotschberg Simplon (BLS) Ae4/4 is a milestone design as the world's first with 1000hp (736kW) on each axle. Built by SLM and Brown Boveri, it broke with previous Swiss electric designs, using an all-adhesion bogie layout with fully suspended spring-borne traction motors and flexible drive system. Eight were built from 1944–55 numbered 251 to 258. In 1959, the twin unit Ae8/8 of two Ae4/4 units permanently coupled back to back entered service. Three Ae8/8 271–273 were built new in 1959–63, with 274/275 created 1965–66. Ae8/8s were used for heavy freight traffic between Bern, Brig and Domodossola, but were also used on the heaviest international overnight sleeping car trains. Ae4/4s were used on a wide range of duties, but both types were redundant with BLS class 465 by the late 1990s. Ae4/4 and Ae8/8 were stored from 1995 onwards, and two Ae8/8s were destroyed in a fire. No. 275 is kept on as a reserve locomotive. The Ae4/4's last regular duties were on car-carrying tunnel shuttle trains.

**The solid frame of the Ae4/4 helped to contribute to its longevity in heavy-duty service, as well as to its 80-tonne (176.400lb) weight.**

**Type:** Bo-Bo heavy passenger and freight
**Power:** 3238kW (4400hp)
**Supply:** 15kV 16.7Hz AC
**Tractive effort:** 235kN (52,875lbf)
**Max. operating speed:** 125km/h (78.1mph)
**Weight:** 80 tonnes (176,400lb)
**Max. axle load:** 20 tonnes (44,100lb)
**Overall length:** 15.6m (50ft 11in)
**Gauge:** 1435mm (4ft 8.5in)

## CLASS 1001 1-DO-1 STATE RAILWAYS (SS) — NETHERLANDS 1948

Faced with a rundown, depleted and damaged system after 1945, the Dutch railways opted for a locomotive type of unusual versatility, capable of heavy, high-speed freight haulage and also of express passenger work. Having turned to Sweden for new steam power, they went to Switzerland for electric development in this case (other new classes showed French and American influence), and this class of 10 locomotives owed much to the SBB Ae4/6 and 8/14 classes. Eight traction motors were the key to its adaptability, with SLM individual axle drive. These could be operated in series-parallel grouping at low speed or in parallel grouping at speeds in excess of 100km/h (62mph). The engines had driving wheels of 1550mm (61in) diameter, and the pantographs were mounted on an unusual clerestory-style roofline. In service, they lived up to the universality that had been designed into them, hauling 2000-tonne (1968-ton) coal trains at 60km/h (37mph), mixed freight of 850 tonnes (836 tons) at 80km/h (50mph) and 250-tonne (246-ton) passenger expresses at 161km/h (100mph) – although schedules at the time rarely required the latter speed. If this might seem like the answer to a traffic manager's dream, the disadvantage was expense in construction and maintenance, and the fact that the South Limburg mineral lines were some distance from the termini of fast express services. Nevertheless, they played a useful part in restoring postwar services.

**Type:** Universal locomotive
**Power:** Eight traction motors developing a maximum of 3343kW (4480hp) hourly, or 2836kW (3800hp) continuous, supplied by 1500V DC via overhead catenary
**Tractive effort:** 176.5kN (39,690lb)
**Max. operating speed:** 161km/h (100mph)
**Total weight:** 99.6 tonnes (219,618lb)
**Max. axle load:** 20 tonnes (44,100lb)
**Overall length:** 16.22m (53ft 3in

## CLASS 101 BELGIAN NATIONAL RAILWAYS (SNCB) — BELGIUM 1949

After World War II, Belgium needed time to recover from the extreme damage done to its railways. Nonetheless, SNC was able to embark on an intensive electrification scheme, for which the company ordered 20 Bo+Bo electric locomotives. Intended for the SNCB standard 3000V DC overhead line system, class 101s were simple machines with four traction motors, acceleration being achieved by diverting traction current through body mounted resistances. These were mixed-traffic machines, well able to cope with fast passenger services or moderately heavy freight. Larger, more modern locomotives were supplied to Belgium from 1953, and the class 101s were diverted almost wholly to freight work.

Belgium was unusual in that its locomotive numbering changed in the 1970s from a 'class + serial' number scheme to a much more straightforward four-digit scheme, under which No. 101.001 became 2901. One class 29 locomotive is preserved today.

**Type:** Bo+Bo mixed-traffic electric locomotive
**Power:** 3000V DC overhead line collection; 1620kW (2170hp); resistance control; four axle-hung DC traction motors
**Tractive effort:** Not known
**Max. operating speed:** 100km/h (62mph)
**Weight:** 81 tonnes (17,790lb)
**Max. axle load:** Not known
**Overall length:** Not known
**Gauge:** 1435mm (4ft 8.5in)

## GE 'LITTLE JOE' VARIOUS RAILROADS — USA 1949

In 1948, General Electric constructed 20 very powerful modern streamlined electrics for Russia. Cold War hostilities between the United States and the Soviet Union, however, prevented the locomotives from reaching their intended buyer, and General Electric sought other customers for the machines which became known as 'Little Joes' in reference to the Soviet premier of the time, 'Big Joe' Stalin.

Milwaukee Road took 12 of the 'Little Joes' for use on the eastern electrified segment of its Pacific Extension between Harlowton, Montana, and Avery, Idaho (Milwaukee Road operated two disconnected segments of electrification, and the western segment was in Washington State). Chicago-area interurban electric line Chicago, South Shore & South Bend took three 'Little Joes', while Brazil's Paulista Railway was to buy the remaining five. As the Russian standard gauge is 1524mm (5ft), the locomotives needed new wheel sets to accommodate the American 1435mm (4ft 8.5in) gauge.

**Type:** 2-Do-Do-2, electric
**Power:** 3000V DC on Milwaukee/1500V DC on South Shore
**Tractive effort:** 492kN (110,750lbf)
**Max. operating speed:** 112km/h (70mph)
**Weight:** 243 tonnes (535,572lb)
**Overall length:** 27.076m (88ft 10in)
**Max. axle load:** 25 tonnes (55,100lb)
**Gauge:** 1435mm (4ft 8.5in) – originally built for 1524mm (5ft)

**Right: Milwaukee Road received 12 of the 20 Little Joe electrics originally built for Russia. These were used on Milwaukee's Rocky Mountain electrification. Some remained in service until 1974.**

**Below: Interurban electric railway Chicago, South Shore & South Bend operated three Little Joes in freight service until the early 1980s. Its freights are now diesel powered.**

## CLASS 2D2-9100 FRENCH NATIONAL RAILWAYS (SNCF) FRANCE 1950

The last of a long line of 2-Do-2 designs that worked on the 1500V DC railways in France, the 35 class 2D2-9100 locomotives were impressive in appearance and reliable in performance. They were built for the postwar electrification of the Paris-Lyon-Méditerranée (PLM) main line with its heavy loads and long inclines, now part of the French National Railways system. Liveried in pale green, they lasted in service for more than 30 years, and were still in use on Paris-Lyon-Méditerranée route freights in the early 1980s.

**At the inauguration of electric services on the Paris–Lyon–Méditerranée main line, a class 2D2-9200 locomotive arrives with a *rapide* at Paris Gare de Lyon.**

**Type:** 2-Do-2 mixed-traffic mainline electric locomotive
**Power:** 1500V DC overhead line collection; 3690kW (4950hp); resistance control; four body frame mounted, axle-hung DC traction motors; four carrying axles
**Tractive effort:**
**Max. operating speed:** 140km/h (87mph)
**Weight:** 144 tonnes (316,235lb)
**Max. axle load:** 89.4 tonnes (197,120lb)
**Overall length:** 18.08m (59ft 4in)
**Gauge:** 1435mm (4ft 8.5in)

## SERIES E10 GERMAN FEDERAL RAILWAYS (DB) GERMANY 1950

**Type:** Bo-Bo express passenger electric locomotive
**Power:** 15,000V 16.7Hz AC overhead line collection; 3620kW (4855hp); mechanical notching-up control; rheostatic brakes; four frame mounted DC traction motors
**Tractive effort:** 275kN (61,820lbf)
**Max. operating speed:** 150km/h (93mph)
**Weight:** 85 tonnes (185,790lb)
**Overall length:** 16,490mm (54ft 1in)
**Gauge:** 1435mm (4ft 8.5in)

**A class E10 Bo-Bo locomotive of the later, more streamlined series is pictured here. Note the neat arrangement of ventilation grilles on the bodyside.**

After 1945, fewer than a quarter of Germany's pre-war stock of 880 electric locomotives were in a usable state. In a process similar to that which took place with the *Deutsche Reichsbahn* in the 1920s, the postwar *Bundesbahn* began to develop a new range of standard types, steam, diesel, and electric. Initially, five Bo-Bo prototypes were produced, with various forms

**Built for express passenger trains, the E10s are used nowadays mostly on regional and local services which they can operate in push-pull mode.**

of drive as well as certain other differences, although in many dimensions they were very similar.

By this time, it was clear that rod drive was not a viable option for a fast mainline electric locomotive. The alternatives were all forms of wheel- or axle-drive: Alsthom universal link drive in 001, Siemens rubber ring transmission on 002, and two forms of disc drive, Brown-Boveri's on 002 and Sécheron's on Nos 004 and 005. Another of the aims was to ensure that the ultimate production runs would share as many standard parts as possible. The manufacturers Henschel, Krauss-Maffei and Krupp participated, with the electrical companies Brown-Boveri, Siemens-Schuckert, and AEG. The chief aim was to produce a locomotive that would be versatile and reliable in service.

After extensive comparative trials, the first production run of 200 E10 locomotives was ordered, with the Siemens rubber ring transmission, four nose-suspended motors and twin transformers for HT regulation. The wheel diameter was 1250mm (49in).

The work on class E10, though it drew on extensive German, Swiss and French experience, was actually fundamental to the further development of German electric motive power, with both increased traffic demands and technical progress leading towards ever-greater power and ever-better power:weight ratios.

## Class V55 Bo-Co HUNGARIAN STATE RAILWAYS (MÁV) HUNGARY 1950

Although MÁV class V55 were the first postwar electric locomotives for Hungary, they still employed synchronous motors with phase converters and fluid resistor control. Hungarian engineers produced the relatively unusual asymmetric five-axle layout of one three- and one two-axle bogie in attempting to achieve all adhesion with the very heavy phase splitting equipment. Ten production examples of class V55 were built; however, low quality construction and materials produced an unreliable type, which meant that the bulk of electric traffic remained with class V40.

Five synchronous speeds were possible in the prototypes; however, the later 10 production examples had a blanket upper speed limit of 100km/h (62.1mph).

V55 014 survives today and is preserved in the official national railway museum in Budapest, which is found in the northern part of the city at the former Eszaki roundhouse and opened to the public in 2000.

**Type:** Bo-Co synchronous electric
**Power:** 2354kW (3198hp)
**Supply:** 16kV 50Hz AC
**Tractive effort:** 208kN (46800lbf)
**Max. operating speed:** 125km/h (78.1mph)
**Weight:** 92.5 tonnes (203,963lb)
**Max. axle load:** 18.5 tonnes (40,793lb)
**Overall length:** 14.6m (47ft 8in)
**Gauge:** 1435mm (4ft 8.5in)

## Class 1200 NETHERLANDS RAILWAYS (NS) NETHERLANDS 1950

In recovering after World War II, the Netherlands had to rebuild its railways almost from scratch. The urgent need for new locomotives was met by spreading the purchase among a number of different countries including Holland, France and the United States. The 35 class 1200 locomotives were intended for freight haulage and were supplied with Dutch-built electrical equipment, bogies with prominent compensating beams for the primary springing from Baldwin in the United States, and final assembly by Werkspoor in the Netherlands. With their prominent cab front noses, these locomotives were impressive to see in action and became popular for passenger work, as well as for freight. Initially in blue livery, in which they looked smart, the class received the later standard NS grey-and-yellow style in the late 1970s. They lasted until the late 1990s on NS. A small number are now operated by the private company ACTS.

**Netherlands Railways Co-Co electric locomotive No. 1204 shows off its rugged American lines. Some of these locomotives survive today, working freight trains for ACTS.**

**Type:** Co-Coo mixed-traffic electric locomotive
**Power:** 1500V DC overhead line collection; 2360kW (3165hp); resistance control; six axle-hung DC traction motors
**Tractive effort:** 194kN (43,615lbf)
**Max. operating speed:** 135km/h (85mph)
**Weight:** 108 tonnes (237,175lb)
**Max axle load:** Not known
**Overall length:** 18.085m (59ft 4in)
**Gauge:** 1435m (4ft 8.5in)

## CLASS CC7100 FRENCH NATIONAL RAILWAYS (SNCF) FRANCE 1952

**The CC7100 class was SNCF's foray into the modern layout of double-bogie electric locomotive that is now standard throughout the world.**

Following hard on the heels of the heavy and rigid-framed class 2D2-9100 locomotives after only two years, the class CC7100 was seen as revolutionary when it appeared on the Paris-Lyon-Méditerranée mainline express trains, although in reality two prototypes, Nos CC7001 and 7002, had been running since 1949. The 58 class CC7100 locomotives were France's first express electric locomotives, with all axles motored (a development that some would comment was long overdue – recall the British class EM1 Bo+Bo prototype of 1941 that became BR No. 26000 *Tommy*). They were competent machines predominantly of Alsthom design and supplied by that company with the support of CEM and Fives-Lille.

In layout, they would now be regarded as highly conventional. They had two three-axle bogies, each with three DC traction motors driving the axles individually. Current collection was from overhead wires through a box pantograph, a typical design of the period. DC series wound traction motors were, for a century, considered ideal for railway traction. It is characteristic that such motors have a high starting torque, the torque dropping off as speed increases, levelling out to a level sufficient to sustain the train's designed maximum speed. This characteristic is natural to the motor and needs no additional controls, other than some means, usually resistance banks, for holding the initial starting voltage at the armature below line voltage.

The body design was neat, with slightly raked back cab fronts and a row of four 'port holes' as windows in the bodyside to illuminate the equipment compartment. More modern locomotives eventually displaced them from Paris-Lyon-Méditerranée expresses, and they gravitated to heavy freight work, as well as duties in the southwest of France. The class CC7100s last work in the year 2000 saw them on freights on the line between Marseilles and Toulouse, and towards the Spanish frontier.

When new, they were liveried in the standard SNCF pale turquoise, in two tones separated by an pair of stainless metal lines with blue in between. This livery has been sustained right to the end of their lives. In 1955, No. CC7107 was selected to undertake trials of high-speed current collection on the southwest main line through the flat area known as the Landes. New Bo-Bo No. BB9004 also took part and gained the world speed record of 331km/h (206mph) for electric locomotives, which it still holds. No. CC7107 was also credited with reaching this speed in the trials and came close, but in fact did not equal it. Both of these locomotives are displayed at the French national railway museum at Mulhouse.

This class of locomotive caught the eye of railways elsewhere in Europe. A group of more than 130 locomotives of this type was supplied to RENFE Spain from 1956 as its class 276, modified to that railway's 1674mm (5ft 6in) gauge and designed to operate under 3000V DC overhead supply. In the Netherlands, the class 1300 Co-Co design is basically the same as the SNCF CC7100 class. It was introduced there in 1952, and these locomotives also ended their years on heavy freight work. They were all withdrawn by the end of 2001.

**Type:** Co-Co mixed-traffic mainline electric locomotive
**Power:** 1500V DC overhead line collection; 3240 and 3490kW (4350 and 4690hp); six bogie frame mounted DC traction motors
**Tractive effort:** 225kN (50,580lbf)
**Max. operating speed:** 140km/h (87mph)
**Weight:** 107 tonnes (234,980lb)
**Max. axle load:** Not known
**Overall length:** 18.922m (62ft 1in)
**Gauge:** 1435mm (4ft 8.5in)

**A class 7100 Co-Co takes a long and heavy express train through the lush Savoy countryside.**

## CLASS EW BO-BO-BO NEW ZEALAND RAILWAYS (NZR) NEW ZEALAND 1952

**Type:** Bo-Bo-Bo
**Power:** 1340kW (1800hp)
**Supply:** 1500V DC
**Tractive effort:** 187kN (42075lbf)
**Max. operating speed:** 96km/h (60mph)
**Weight:** 76 tonnes (167,580lb)
**Max. axle load:** 13 tonnes (28,665lb)
**Overall length:** 18900mm (61ft 8in)
**Gauge:** 1067mm (3ft 6in)

These locomotives had articulated bodies with Bo-Bo-Bo wheel arrangement and were introduced for passenger and freight on the 1500V Wellington area system.

After tunnel floor lowering between Wellington and Paekakariki in 1967 allowed diesels to work this section, the class EWs gradually found less work.

**Left: English Electric and Robert Stephenson & Hawthorn were the builders of the EW class. One is kept in preservation.**

**Below: Hardly the duty for which it was built – EW 142 comes down into Wellington with a four-coach local service on 21 October 1982.**

## CLASS 277 CO-CO SPANISH RAILWAYS (RENFE) SPAIN 1952

Spanish Railways (RENFE) class 277 were built by English Electric, making an interesting parallel order with the French Alsthom-built class 276. The 75 class 277 were for work in the Cantabrian mountain area of northern Spain. They were withdrawn from service in the 1990s, although several are preserved. Similar machines both electrically and in appearance were delivered to India and Brazil.

**Type:** Co-Co heavy passenger and freight
**Power:** 2208kW (2960hp)
**Supply:** 3000V DC
**Tractive effort:** 136kN (30500lbf) at 58km/h (36.3mph)
**Max. operating speed:** 110km/h (68.8mph)
**Weight:** 120 tonnes (264,600lb)
**Max. axle load:** 20 tonne (44,100lb)
**Overall length:** 20.657m (67ft 5in)
**Gauge:** 1676mm (5ft 6in)

**This long-lived class ended up looking rather old-fashioned, especially with its V-shaped speed stripe. Its performance, however, was strong to the end.**

## CLASS AE6/6 SWISS FEDERAL RAILWAYS (SBB) SWITZERLAND 1952

The Ae6/6s are a 120-strong all-adhesion class from SLM, Brown Boveri and Oerlikon for heavier traffic over the SBB Gotthard and Simplon alpine routes. Specification called for 650 tonnes on 2.6 per cent grades at 75km/h (46.9mph). The prototypes of 1952/3 were followed by slightly heavier production machines with improved tractive effort between 1955 and 1966. The bogie design featured advanced weight transfer and equalization, with 11401–11414 coupling between the bogies transmitting vertical and transverse forces, but from 11415 altered to transverse only. Power equipment is similar to BLS Ae4/4 with a 27-notch high tension tap changer and permanent parallel connected motors. Fifty were allocated to Erstfeld and 70 to Bellinzona (ie north and south of the St Gotthard pass), displacing Ae4/7s from passenger services and Ce6/8 1C+C1s from freight. The Ae6/6s were later cascaded onto freight, hauling loads up to 1600 tonnes (1626 tons). Switzerland is notable for the longevity of electric locomotives, with still 93 daily duties and only one withdrawn so far with accident damage. They have been designated class 610 by the new computer numbering system.

**Type:** Co-Co heavy passenger and freight
**Power:** 4300kW (6437hp)
**Supply:** 15kV 16.7Hz AC
**Tractive effort:** 11403-11520 - 392kN (88200lbf)
**Max. operating speed:** 125km/h (78.1mph)
**Weight:** (11403-11520) 128 tonnes (282,240lb)
**Max. axle load:** 21.5 tonnes (47,408lb)
**Overall length:** 18.4m (60ft)
**Gauge:** 1435mm (4ft 8.5in)

**A class Ae6/6 with freight train is seen here at Sisikon. The all-welded body reduced weight as well as giving a smooth effect. All members of this class were named after Swiss cantons and towns.**

## CLASS 122 BELGIAN NATIONAL RAILWAYS (SNCB) BELGIUM 1953

**Among the oldest electric locomotives still operating in Europe, the SNCB class 22s still operate suburban passenger trains, as well as heavy freight.**

Later known as class 22, this compact design was the first of Belgium's more modern electric locomotives and proved successful. They have been used all over the SNCB system, on heavy freights and initially on mainline passenger trains. The class 122s were painted dark green in their first decade or so, and they later appeared in the lighter mid-blue/green. Even though almost 50 years old, the class is still in use, although its potential replacements in the form of the new class 13 locomotives are already in position.

**Type:** Bo-Bo mixed-traffic mainline electric locomotive
**Power:** 3000V DC overhead line collection; 1880kW (2520hp); four axle-hung DC traction motors
**Tractive effort:** 196kN (44,060lbf)
**Max. operating speed:** 130km/h (80mph)
**Weight:** 87 tonnes (191,060lb)
**Max. axle load:** Not known
**Overall length:** 18m (59ft 1in)
**Gauge:** 1435mm (4ft 8.5in)

## CLASS BB12000 FRENCH NATIONAL RAILWAYS (SNCF) FRANCE 1953

For the Valenciennes–Thionville 25kV AC electrification scheme, SNCF purchased 150 centre-cab Bo-Bos. In those early days of high-voltage AC electrification, various kinds of current rectification were tried. Two other classes, class BB13000 and the heavier class CC14000, were also ordered for this initial mainline electrification. The BB12000s were mixed-traffic locomotives. They were later retained almost totally for freight work as other classes displaced them. All have been withdrawn.

**Type:** Bo-Bo mixed-traffic mainline electric locomotive
**Power:** 25,000V 50Hz AC overhead line collection; 2477kW (3320hp); four axle-hung DC traction motors
**Tractive effort:** 353kN (39,360lbf)
**Max. operating speed:** 120km/h (75mph)
**Weight:** 82 to 86 tonnes (180,080 to 190,060lb)
**Max. axle load:** Not known
**Overall length:** 15.2m (49ft 10in)
**Gauge:** 1435mm (4ft 8.5in)

**The pioneering French class 12000 Bo-Bo design was Europe's first use on a busy mainline railway of a fleet of 25kV 50Hz locomotives. Here a BB12003 locomotive stands in the sidings at Longuyon, France, in 1955.**

## CLASS EM2 BRITISH RAIL — GREAT BRITAIN 1953

BR built seven class EM2 Co-Cos at its Gorton works in Manchester to work the hourly passenger trains between Manchester and Sheffield, many of which went forward to London Marylebone via the former Great Central route. These were more than sufficient for what was basically an hourly service, though later there were additional trains with extra stops, and the one daily 'boat train' that linked Liverpool and Manchester with (eventually) Harwich Parkestone Quay. The Brunswick green EM2s hauled standard BR vacuum-braked carriages and fed them with steam for heating from steam boilers on the locomotives. The EM2s actually had quite short lives on British Rail because the passenger trains were found not to lose much time if they were hauled by the 95km/h (60mph) EM1s, which were becoming available as freight carryings diminished.

The EM2 locomotives were sold to Nederlandse Spoorwegen (Netherlands Railways), which used six of them on intercity trains between Amsterdam and Heerlen, Maastricht and Venlo for more than two decades. Three examples are preserved.

**The doyen class EM2 locomotive No. 27000, later to be named *Electra*, is seen at Manchester London Road after working a train from Sheffield.**

**Type:** Co-Co mainline passenger electric locomotive
**Power:** 1500V DC overhead line collection; 1716kW (2300hp); six axle-hung DC traction motors; regenerative braking
**Tractive effort:** 200kN (45,000lbf)
**Max. operating speed:** 145km/h (90mph)
**Weight:** 104 tonnes (228,480lb)
**Max. axle load:** Not known
**Overall length:** 17.985m (59ft)
**Gauge:** 1435mm (4ft 8.5in)

## ETR-300 'SETTEBELLO' STATE RAILWAYS (FS) — ITALY 1953

*Settebello*, 'beautiful seven', is a lucky hand in cards, and a seven-card motif was used for the logo of this seven-car set, composed of two articulated end units and a central three-car articulated set. It was Europe's first postwar luxury train, with all first-class accommodation, at first for only 160 – later 190 – passengers, all of whom paid first-class fare plus a large premium. The driving positions were in raised cupolas towards the rear of each of the end cars, allowing for observation lounges – hence the slightly disconcerting 'frilly-curtained' look of the end window. The three-car central set was entirely formed of service

**In a famous shot, the '*Settebello*' set comes sweeping round a curve. In 1953, it epitomized the speed and luxury of the new, postwar European express trains.**

vehicles, with separate restaurant-bar car, kitchen, baggage and mail compartments and quite spacious crew quarters. The design, in green and grey livery, was a streamlined one, though the somewhat bulbous 'dodgem-car' ends did not share the refined appearance of the rest of the train. Some features such as streamlined fairings between the articulated units showed the way forward for the high-speed intercity trains of the later 20th century, although these would not match its ratio of more than two tonnes (4410lb) of train-weight per passenger. The interiors were divided into 10-seater compartments, and the train was sound-proofed, double-glazed and air-conditioned. Among the amenities were shower compartments, a shop and a radio/telephone office.

Pantographs were fitted to the second car of each end-unit, and the six bogies of these were all motored, with a traction unit for each axle. The four-wheeled bogies were supported on laminated springs, supplemented by hydraulic shock-absorbers, with rubber pads between the bogie frame and the centre pivot and also at the side bearers. The riding quality of the bogies was first-class. A crew of three qualified drivers worked the train, two in the front cupola-cab and a third in the rear, whose job it was to watch over the auxiliary equipment. The two driving cabs were linked by telephone.

The *Settebello* ran on the Milan–Bologna–Florence–Rome route, (633.25km (393.5 miles)), reaching a maximum height of 325m (1058 ft) in the Appennine Tunnel on the section between Prato and Bologna. Until the completion of the first section of the Rome–Florence *direttissima* ('most direct') line in 1977, the speed was limited to a 112km/h (70mph) maximum for the first 145km (90 miles) because of the severe curvature of the old main line. Nevertheless, a 5hrs 55mins timing was achieved, extended to 6hrs 5mins from 1958. The 314km (195.1-mile) section from Rome to Florence, where the train reversed direction in the terminal station, was the longest nonstop run on the FS system. Speeds of 161km/h (100mph) were regularly achieved on the more open stretches of track between Arezzo and Florence, and in the Lombardy plain.

The *Settebello* was allowed 72 minutes for the 146.8km (91.2-mile) stretch between Bologna and Piacenza, and it was recorded in 1958 as beating this by 3.5 minutes, despite twice being slowed to almost walking pace by permanent-way repairs: a mean speed of 135.5km/h (84.2mph) from start to stop.

Later alterations to the three *Settebello* train sets (one being required as a reserve) included the fitting of more powerful motor units, giving an increase in rated output of 28 per cent. Rheostatic or regenerative braking, in addition to the original air brakes, was also installed, and cab signalling was fitted. In 1968, the *Settebello* was incorporated into the Trans-Europ Express (TEE) network, first as TEE 68, then as 76. In 1976, it was renamed as *Colosseum* and ran under this name until 1987, when the train was discontinued as a special service.

**Type:** Articulated electric express train
**Power:** Twelve 187kW (250hp) motors fed by overhead catenary at 3000V, driving twelve axles via gearing and hollow-axle flexible drive
**Tractive effort:**
**Max. operating speed:** 161km/h (100mph)
**Total weight:** 325 tonnes (716,300lb)
**Max. axle load:** 17 tonnes (37,468lb)
**Overall length:** 165.202m (542ft)
**Builder:** Ernesto Breda, Milan

## CLASS DA STATE RAILWAYS (SJ) SWEDEN 1953

For a postwar light mixed-traffic electric locomotive, the Swedish class Da was surprisingly old-fashioned in its rigid-frame layout. Yet these locomotives worked reliably all over Sweden on all types of traffic. When Sweden's state railways (SJ) purchased more powerful locomotives, the Da class was eventually downgraded to secondary duties, short passenger trains and branchline and short-distance freights. Examples lasted into the 1980s, and one or two survive today with privatized infra-structure support companies.

**Last of the Swedish D-types, the basic design of which went back to the 1920s, 90 of the class Da were built between 1953 and 1957. Intended for mixed-traffic use, they served the Swedish state railways well for three decades.**

**Type:** 1-C-1 mixed-traffic light electric locomotive
**Power:** 15,000V 16.67Hz AC overhead line collection; 1840kW (2500hp); one large body mounted AC traction motor driving the wheels through a jackshaft and side coupling rods
**Tractive effort:** 205kN (46,085lbf)
**Max. operating speed:** 100km/h (62mph)
**Weight:** 75 tonnes (164,705lb)
**Max. axle load:** Not known
**Overall length:** 13m (42ft 8in)
**Gauge:** 1435mm (4ft 8.5in)

## BO-BO TURKISH STATE RAILWAYS (TCDD) TURKEY 1953

Electrification in Turkey began in 1953, on the suburban line from Istanbul's west-side terminus, Sirkeçi, running along the Marmara coast to Halkali, and the scheme was completed in 1955. This was also the route by which the Orient Express and other long-distance trains came and went, and three Bo-Bo locomotives were provided to haul heavy passenger and freight trains over the 27km (16.8-mile) electrified section. The supply was single-phase 25kV AC, at 50Hz – soon to become the international standard. It was the first time a system of this voltage and frequency had been installed on what was almost wholly a suburban operation. The catenary and infrastructure were relatively cheap to install, with little need for substations and drawing power at the same frequency as other industry. The SNCF had adopted this system in 1945, and French influence on the electrified TCDD line was strong, with the suburban multiple-unit stock as well as the locomotives being built by Alsthom to French design, and with transformers and gradation equipment from Matériel de Traction Electrique (MTE) of Paris. Unsurprisingly, the locomotives had a distinctly SNCF look. For more than 10 years, they remained the TCDD's only electric locomotives, until electrification of the Istanbul-Ankara main line. They were withdrawn from service during the late 1960s.

**Type:** Mixed-traffic locomotive
**Power:** Four 300V (500hp) traction motors of 14-pole commutator type, supplied by 25kV AC at 50Hz via overhead catenary
**Tractive effort:** 156.8kN (35,280lbf)
**Max. operating speed:** 90km/h (56mph)
**Total weight:** 77.5 tonnes (170,887lb)
**Max. axle load:** 19.4 tonnes (42,722lb)
**Overall length:** 16.138m (53ft)
**Builder:** Alsthom, France

## ETA515 BATTERY CAR FEDERAL GERMAN RAILWAYS (DB) GERMANY 1954

The wartime development of large batteries for U-boats proved useful for the development of railcars. DB class 515 numbered more than 200. Only lead acid accumulators were suitable, but made up one-third of the vehicle weight, with 11 battery troughs of 20 cells, each suspended from the ETA car underframe. The 86-seat Class 515 vehicles operated with class 815 trailers. ETAs entered service from 1954 in Munich (München Ost depot), and in the following year began operation from Basel, Buchloe, Hameln, Limburg, Ludwigshafen, Oberlahnstein and Recklinghausen, spreading through the entire system. Even international cross-border services such as Aachen to Maastricht were worked by class 515. Their last regular work (in the Ruhr metropolitan area) ended in 1995.

**Type:** Single battery railcar
**Power:** 200kW (268hp)
**Tractive effort:** N/A
**Max. operating speed:** 100km/h (62mph)
**Weight:** Up to 56 tonnes (123,480hp)
**Max. axle load:** 14 tonnes (30,870lb)
**Overall length:** 23.5m (76ft 8in)
**Gauge:** 1435mm (4ft 8.5in)

## CLASS WCM1 INDIA RAILWAYS INDIA 1954

India Railways class WCM1 and class WCM2 were two very similar types built by English Electric Vulcan Foundry. The seven larger class WCM1 of 1954 were 1500V DC for use in the Bombay area, while the 12 smaller class WCM2 of 1957 were originally 3000V DC for the Calcutta area. Later class WCM2s were modified for 1500V operation on conversion of the Calcutta electrified lines to 25 kV AC. Both types were used on passenger work throughout most of their working lives, with class WCM1 continuing on fast express work into the 1990s. Last allocated to Kalyan shed, no class WCM1 is in service; however, two class WCM2s remain operational into 2002 (also based at Kalyan).

**The resemblance between the WCM1 and the Spanish Class 277 of 1952 is no coincidence: in all significant respects they are the same English Electric/Vulcan Foundry design.**

**Type:** Co-Co electric mixed-traffic
**Power:** 2365kW (3170hp)
**Supply:** WCM1 1500 V DC
**Tractive effort:** 306kN (68860lbf)
**Max. operating speed:** 120km/h (75mph)
**Weight:** 124 tonnes (251,100lb)
**Max. axle load:** 21 tonnes (46,305lb)
**Gauge:** 1676mm (5ft 6in)

## CLASS 4E 1-CO-CO-1 SOUTH AFRICAN RAILWAYS (SAR) SOUTH AFRICA 1954

**Type:** 1-Co-Co-1
**Power:** 1878kW (2518hp)
**Supply:** 3000V DC
**Tractive effort:** 141kN (31,725lbf)
**Max. operating speed:** 96km/h (60mph)
**Weight:** 157.49 tonnes (347,200lb)
**Max. axle load:** 22 tonnes (48,510lb)
**Overall length:** 21.844m (71ft 3in)
**Gauge:** 1067mm (3ft 6in)

Metropolitan Vickers (later AEI) supplied many electric locomotives to South African Railways, but the class 4E broke this pattern, being contracted to the British General Electric Company and assembled by the North British Locomotive Company using GEC electrical parts. Forty units were supplied – designed with bogie articulation like the previous class 3E. The design was in many ways similar to the 1000mm (3ft 3in) gauge units supplied by American GE to the Brazilian Sorocabana railway, although there is no connection between the coincidentally named US GE and UK GEC. Later SAR orders were for a much improved design of Bo-Bo class 5E.

**Seen here on level track near East London, the Class 4E was intended primarily to work trains up the long gradients of the Hex River Pass between Worcester and Touws River, in Cape Province.**

## CLASS 1010 AUSTRIAN FEDERAL RAILWAYS (ÖBB) AUSTRIA 1955

For the completion of electrification of the spinal main line between Vienna, Salzburg, Innsbruck and Bregenz, ÖBB purchased 20 modern mixed traffic electric locomotives, principally for express passenger trains. The 1010 class (and the class 1110 variant for heavier freight, of which there were 30) began life in ÖBB's standard dark green livery. They lasted 45 years in service. Their last duties concentrated them on road lorry trains that brought heavy trucks across the Alps without blocking or wearing out Austria's road network. In the Austrian class numbering system, the first digit indicates the locomotive type ('1' is electric locomotive), the second digit is a variant within the general class ('0' being the first version), and the third and fourth digits represent the general class number (in this case '10'). The locomotive number within the class follows afterwards (e.g. 1010.015).

**A class 1010 Co-Co electric locomotive in the later ÖBB red livery. This type was built for the arduous mountainous main line over the Arlberg route and to take heavy trains on to Vienna.**

**Type:** Co-Co mixed-traffic mainline electric locomotive
**Power:** 15,000V 16.67Hz AC overhead line collection; 4000kW (5360hp); six axle-hung SC traction motors
**Tractive effort:** 275kN (61,820lbf)
**Max. operating speed:** 130km/h (80mph)
**Weight:** 106 tonnes (232,785lb)
**Max. axle load:** Not known
**Overall length:** 17.86m (58ft 7in)
**Gauge:** 1435mm (4ft 8.5in)

**A class 1010 electric locomotive in modern times is pictured here on a local passenger train, having been displaced from heavier trains by the class 1044 Bo-Bo locomotives.**

## CLASS 5E SOUTH AFRICAN RAILWAYS (SAR) SOUTH AFRICA 1955

**Type:** Bo-Bo universal
**Power:** 5E 1300kW (1743hp)
**Supply:** 3000V DC
**Tractive effort:** 122kN (27400lbf) at 43km/h (26.9mph)
**Max. operating speed:** 96km/h (60mph)
**Weight:** 86 tonnes (189,630lb)
**Max. axle load:** 21.5 tonnes (47,408lb)
**Overall length:** 15.495m (50ft 10in)
**Gauge:** 1067mm (3ft 6in)

SAR awarded English Electric the 5E contract in 1955, specifying Bo-Bo machines for all foreseeable needs, with heavier traffic to be worked by up to six in multiple. All 160 class 5Es were built in the United Kingdom with Belgian-supplied cast bogies transmitting tractive effort at axle level, minimizing weight transfer through a spring loaded link between the bogies. This connection did not take drawbar load, as does articulation, but reduced horizontal forces on curves. The 5Es are conventional series parallel resistance control machines with regenerative braking. Class 5E1 was first built with AEI electrical parts (from 1959 by Metropolitan Cammell, one of relatively few locomotive designs built by this firm, more commonly associated with London underground trains), and 135 locomotives were assembled before production moved to South Africa, taken over by Union Carriage & Wagon.

**Class 5E marked SAR's decision to use only Bo-Bo type electric locomotives. With tractive effort less than the 4E, multiple-unit working was intended when needed.**

**Paired engines of Class 5E/1, Nos. 764 and 1078, seen here at Newcastle, Natal, with the 'Durban Mail' on 6 February 1978. The consist runs to 15 coaches and two mail vans.**

## E8000 EMU TURKISH STATE RAILWAYS (TCDD) TURKEY 1955

Twenty-eight three-car EMUs were delivered by French industry to Turkey in 1955. Among the earliest for 25kV operation, they used the then conventional transformer and camshaft-driven tap changer. TCDD class E8000 units had a second locally built intermediate trailer added, running in this form for several years, but since removed.

**Type:** EMU three-car
**Power:** 1100kW (1495hp) per unit
**Supply:** 25kV 50Hz AC
**Tractive effort:** N/A
**Max. operating speed:** 90km/h (56.3mph)
**Weight:** 120 tonnes (264,600lb)
**Max. axle load:** 17.5 tonnes (38,588lb)
**Overall length:** 68m (221ft 10in) per unit
**Gauge:** 1435mm (4ft 8.5in)
**Builder:** Alsthom, Jeumont and De Dietrich

## EP-5 NEW HAVEN RAILROAD USA 1955

**Type:** Co-Co, passenger electric
**Power:** 11kV AC at 25Hz from overhead
**Output:** 2980kW (4000hp) at 70km/h (44mph)
**Tractive effort:** 387kN (87,000lbf) starting TE; 151kN (34,000lbf) continuous TE
**Max. operating speed:** N/A
**Weight:** 157 tonnes (348,000lb)
**Overall length:** N/A
**Max. axle load:** 30 tonnes (65,000lb)
**Gauge:** 1435mm (4ft 8.5in)

New Haven Railroad's last new straight electrics were 10 double-ended streamlined EP-5s built by General Electric in 1955–6. These used then state-of-the-art ignitron rectifier technology to convert 11,000V AC from New Haven's overhead catenary to low-voltage DC traction motors. Ignitron rectifier tubes were a variation of mercury arc technology. The EP-5s featured a cab style very similar to those used by Alco-GE built FA diesel-electrics.

**A New Haven EP-5 is pictured here leading a Boston-bound passenger train near Woodlawn in The Bronx in the summer of 1961.**

## CLASS 276 CO-CO SPANISH RAILWAYS (RENFE) SPAIN 1956

Spanish Railways (RENFE) class 276 totalled 136 locomotives, and they were essentially broad-gauge 3000V variants of the standard-gauge 1500V SNCF class CC7100.

Class 276 locomotives were supplied for the electrification of the Catalan region in the 1950s. Although Alsthom built the first 20 machines in 1952, they did not actually enter traffic until 1956. Further locomotives were licence-built in Spain until 1965.

Withdrawals of 276s began in the 1990s, and the class was virtually eliminated, except for special duties.

**The French parentage of the Class 276 is apparent in this shot. This is one of two painted in the livery of the 'Talgo' express train, used to switch the stock at Madrid Perta de Atocha.**

**Type:** Co-Co heavy passenger and freight
**Power:** 2355kW (3155hp)
**Supply:** 3000V DC
**Tractive effort:** 162kN (36,400lbf) at 49.5km/h (31mph)
**Max. operating speed:** 110km/h (68.3mph)
**Weight:** 120 tonnes (264,600lb)
**Max. axle load:** 20 tonnes (44,100lb)
**Overall length:** 18.83m (61ft 9in)
**Gauge:** 1676mm (5ft 6in)

## EL-C/EF-4 Rectifier Electrics VIRGINIAN RAILWAY USA 1956

In 1955, Virginian Railway ordered 12 state-of-the-art ignitron rectifier electrics from General Electric for use in heavy coal service between Mullens and Roanoke, Virginia. Virginian's competitor, Norfolk & Western, acquired the line in the early 1960s and discontinued its electrified operations by 1963. New Haven Railroad picked up the Virginian rectifiers in 1964 and classed them as EF-4.

**Type:** Co-Co, heavy freight electric
**Power:** 11kV AC at 25Hz from overhead
**Output:** 2459kW (3300hp)
**Tractive effort:** 353kN (79,500lbf) continuous TE at 25.35km/h (15.75mph)
**Max. operating speed:** 104km/h (65mph)
**Weight:** 177 tonnes (389,760lb)
**Max. axle load:** 29 tonnes (64,960lb)
**Overall length:** 21.184m (69ft 6in)
**Gauge:** 1435mm (4ft 8.5in)

## Class E40 FEDERAL GERMAN RAILWAYS (DB) GERMANY 1957

Mixed-traffic clones of the class E10, the E40s were outwardly distinguished by their dark green livery. Later class 140, these mixed-traffic Bo-Bos totalled nearly 900 and were a mixed-traffic version of class 110 with lower maximum speed. They are still widespread across Germany, mainly the western part, and carry out heavy freight haulage in pairs and also carriage shunting at termini.

**Type:** Bo-Bo mixed-traffic mainline electric locomotive
**Power:** 15,000V 16.67Hz AC overhead line collection; 3620kW (4855hp); mechanical notching up control; rheostatic brakes; four DC traction motors
**Tractive effort:** 275kN (61,820lbf)
**Max. operating speed:** 110km/h (69mph)
**Weight:** 83 tonnes (182,275lb)
**Overall length:** 16.49m (54ft 1in)
**Gauge:** 1435mm (4ft 8.5in)

**The Bo-Bo class E40s can still be found in service on DB's lines throughout Germany, usually hauling heavy freight, but they are also put to use carrying out quite mundane tasks such as carriage shunting.**

## CLASS BB16000 FRENCH NATIONAL RAILWAYS (SNCF) FRANCE 1958

**The class 16000 was also a pioneer class for SNCF, being the first high-powered 25kV locomotive for 160km/h (100mph) on a simple Bo-Bo chassis. This one is at Paris Gare du Nord.**

This class was the French pioneer modern express passenger AC electric locomotive. Extremely successful, the class still operates, although some have been modified for outer suburban push-pull trains. Most work north of Paris. There is also a 1500V DC version known as class BB9200. Their early duties included the fastest passenger trains between Paris and Lille, Aulnoye (the Belgian frontier station) and to Amiens on the route to Boulogne and Calais, until they were displaced by more modern locomotives and TGVs.

**Type:** Bo-Bo passenger mainline electric locomotive
**Power:** 25,000V 50Hz AC overhead line collection; 4130kW (5538hp); four DC traction motors
**Tractive effort:** 309kN (69,465lbf)
**Max. operating speed:** 160km/h (100mph)
**Weight:** 88 tonnes (193,250lb)
**Max. axle load:** Not known
**Overall length:** 16.68m (54ft 9in)
**Gauge:** 1435mm (4ft 8.5in)

## CLASS BB16500 FRENCH NATIONAL RAILWAYS (SNCF) FRANCE 1958

**Type:** B-B mixed-traffic mainline electric locomotive
**Power:** 25,000V 50 Hz AC overhead line collection; 2580kW (3460hp); two frame mounted DC traction motors; alternate gears for passenger or freight work
**Tractive effort:** (passenger or freight ratios) 192 or 324kN (43,165 or 72,840lbf)
**Max. operating speed:** 140km/h (87mph) or 100km/h (62mph)
**Weight:** 71 to 81 tonnes (155,920 to 177,880lb)
**Max axle load:**
**Overall length:** 14.4m (47ft 3in)
**Gauge:** 1435mm (4ft 8.5in)

Built by Alsthom, this class initiated a subsequently common French locomotive practice. Each bogie carried only one traction motor, hence the term *monomoteur* was used to describe this generic type. Each motor was geared for two speeds, passenger and freight, and these can only be changed when the locomotive is stopped. Nearly 300 of these locomotives are used all over France.

**On a typical working of a local passenger train, the versatile class 16500 *monomoteur* B-Bs are equally at home hauling heavy freights in multiple pairs.**

**In a more modern SNCF livery, this class 16500 locomotive heads up a double-deck suburban train.**

## CLASS 4CEP BRITISH RAIL GREAT BRITAIN 1958

For the electrification of the Kent Coast main lines, BR Southern Region ordered a fleet of modern express EMUs. These had corridors throughout and internally were decorated in more modern style than the BR mark I hauled stock on which they were based. Replacing steam traction, the 102 '4CEP' units and the 20 buffet-fitted '4BEPs' speeded up and improved services to such an extent that passenger carryings rose by more than 30 per cent.

**Type:** Four-car electric multiple unit express trains
**Power:** 750V DC conductor rail collection, two power cars, each with two English Electric 187kW (250hp) axle-hung DC traction motors, resistance control
**Tractive effort:** Not known
**Max. operating speed:** 145km/h (90mph)
**Weight:** 33 to 42 tonnes (71,680 to 91,840lb) per vehicle
**Overall length:** 19.66m (64ft 6in)
**Gauge:** 1435mm (4ft 8.5in)

**Some class 4CEP units, later BR class 411, worked for over 45 years in express service in the Southern Region third rail area. Here some children wave to a 4CEP as it pulls a passenger train in Faversham, Kent, in 1959.**

## CLASS WCM-3 AND WCM-4 INDIAN STATE RAILWAYS INDIA 1958

497kW (675hp) axle-hung nose-suspended motors. The WCM3 had lower rated 442kW (600hp) motors. Both types ended their days on freight traffic, but class WCM4 was originally used on express and fast passenger duties. Of similar external body design, these were the last with end noses.

**Type:** Co-Co
**Power:** WCM3 1835kW (2460hp); WCM4 2454kW (3290hp)
**Supply:** 3000 V DC later 1500 V DC
**Tractive effort:** WCM3 - 276kN (62040lbf); WCM4 - 306kN (68860lbf)
**Max. operating speed:** 120km/h (75mph)
**Weight:** WCM3 - 113 tonnes (249,165lb); WCM4 - 125 tonnes (275,625lb)
**Max. axle load:** Up to 21 tonnes (46,305lb)
**Overall length:** Not known
**Gauge:** 1676mm (5ft 6in)

Classes WCM3 and WCM4 were two similar-looking designs built by Hitachi, originally for the Calcutta area 3000V DC system. As with British-supplied class WCM2, the three WCM3s of 1958 and seven WCM4s of 1960 were modified to accept 1500V DC on conversion of the Calcutta DC system to 25kV AC. Both the Japanese-supplied machines used conventional three series and parallel traction motor combinations and weak fielding. Class WCM4 had six Hitachi

**Above: Even with no steam in sight, Indian State Railways certainly did not lack 'atmosphere'. Here a somewhat unkempt WCM5 Co-Co heads the Bombay–Hyderabad Express. All WCM types are now gone.**

**Right: The seven Hitachi-built WCM-4s were the last bonnet-nosed electric locomotive to be imported by India. This particular example was photographed on 17 January 1978.**

## 'KODAMA' TRAIN JAPANESE NATIONAL RAILWAYS (JNR) JAPAN 1958

**Type:** Electric passenger train.
**Power:** Sixteen 100kW (134hp) motors supplied by 1500V DC via overhead catenary, geared to axles of two power cars and of the two adjacent inner cars
**Tractive effort:** 48.9kN (11,000lbf)
**Max. operating speed:** 125km/h (75mph)
**Total weight:** 276.3 tonnes (609,242lb)
**Max. axle load:** 9.6 tonnes (21,168lb)
**Overall length:** 166.42m (546ft)
**Builder:** Kawasaki, Kinki Sharyo, Kisha Seizo Kaisha; electrical equipment supplied by Toshiba

This train formed the model for the development of Japan's celebrated 'bullet trains'. In 1958, its average of 80km/h (50mph) on the newly electrified 1065mm (3ft 6in) gauge between Tokyo and Osaka was remarkable enough. The 553km (344-mile) route was covered in 6hrs 50mins. The *Kodama* ('Echo') trains were made up of eight air-conditioned cars, with a cupola-style raised driving position in each end car. The motors, with an hourly-rated output of 1550kW (2077hp), were fitted in the second and seventh cars, which had dynamic and clasp brakes; the trailer cars had disc brakes.

The trains were capable of carrying 425 passengers, and they were an instant success with the Japanese public.

**When viewed from above, the *Kodama*'s raised driving position can be clearly seen. The roof fittings on the cars hold air-cooling equipment. Demand for the service was such that the original eight-car sets were soon extended to 12. *Kodama* sets were later classified as class 481.**

## CLASS CHS2 CO-CO SOVIET STATE RAILWAYS RUSSIA 1958

Soviet State Railways took electric freight locomotives from domestic suppliers, but passenger designs were supplied by Czechoslovakia's Skoda. The 1958 prototypes of the ChS2 were not very powerful at only 3516kW (4715hp), until motors capable of a 700kW (938hp) increase proved satisfactory for production. Between 1964 and 1973, a total of 942 ChS2s with the improved motors were built.

**Type:** Co-Co electric passenger
**Power:** 4200kW (5632hp)
**Supply:** 3000V DC
**Tractive effort:** 162kN (36,450lbf) at 91.5km/h (57.2mph)
**Max. operating speed:** 140km/h (87.5mph)
**Weight:** 125 tonnes (275,625lb)
**Max. axle load:** 21 tonnes (46,305lb)
**Overall length:** 18.92m (61ft 9in)
**Gauge:** 1524mm (5ft)

## CLASS AL1 BRITISH RAIL (BR) GREAT BRITAIN 1959

**This class 81 locomotive is in British Rail's corporate rail blue livery and has been modified to operate air-braked trains in addition to vacuum-braked, as with previous models.**

When British Railways decided to electrify its West Coast main line from London Euston to Manchester, Liverpool and Birmingham at 25,000V AC, there was minimal experience of high-voltage railway electrification in the United Kingdom and indeed not a great deal elsewhere outside France. For the first group of 100 locomotives, all of which were specified to be 2240kW (3000hp) Bo-Bos, the order was split between five different British manufacturers. The intention was to gain experience of several types, so that when more locomotives were required the preferred design could be selected for larger volume production. The class AL1 locomotives were built by the Birmingham Railway Carriage & Wagon company with electric equipment by Associated Electrical Industries (AEI). Other classes came from Beyer Peacock/Metropolitan Vickers, English Electric, the North British Locomotive Company/GEC, and British Railways/AEI. They were classified from AL1 to AL5 (AL indicating an AC electric locomotive) and were later reclassified from 81 to 85 as BR adopted a more logical numbering system in the 1970s. Twenty-five class AL1 locomotives were built, two of them being geared as mixed-traffic locomotives with a reduced top speed of 130km/h (80mph).

Initially, the rectification of AC to DC for the traction equipment was by means of mercury arc rectifiers. These employed three phase cathodes to strike arcs to the liquid mercury that was sloshing about in the bottom of the tank. One stands amazed that it worked as well as it did, but in the 1950s there was little else that could have been done. Later, the advances in solid state rectification enabled the relatively unreliable mercury arc rectifiers to be replaced with silicon rectifiers. Traction motor voltage was adjusted by means of mechanical tap changers which were tapped into different stages of the transformer windings. When built, the locomotives had two pantographs; however, one was removed. The pantographs were of the Faiveley single arm type.

Because these were 160km/h (100mph) locomotives, to keep track stresses low, the traction motors were not axle-hung, but were fully suspended in the bogie frames. Drives to the axles were by means of spring drives that could take up the vertical movement of the wheelsets. Such complexity was not always totally reliable, but the design was not changed in the life of these locomotives. As BR developed its passenger and freight services, these locomotives were modified to handle air-braked stock in addition to the earlier vacuum-braked vehicles which they had hauled since new. The class 81s, as the 'AL1s' had become, were downgraded in 1986 to 130km/h (80mph) and ended up on parcels and freight trains and trip workings of empty stock into and out of terminus stations.

**Type:** Bo-Bo passenger mainline electric locomotive (two mixed-traffic locomotives)
**Power:** 25,000V 50Hz AC overhead line collection; 2385kW (3200hp); mercury arc rectification with tap changer control; four DC traction motors
**Tractive effort:** 222kN (50,000lbf)
**Max. operating speed:** 160km/h (100mph); two locomotives 130km/h (80mph)
**Weight:** 81 tonnes (178,305lb)
**Max axle load:** not known
**Overall length:** 17.22m (56ft 6in)
**Gauge:** 1435mm (4ft 8.5in)

## CLASS WAG1 INDIAN RAILWAYS — INDIA 1959

India Railways class WAG1 was designed by the European 50Hz consortium, and these were actually the first 25kV industrial frequency AC locomotives to work on the subcontinent.

Mechanical and electrical parts came from several members of the consortium, with the two Belgian companies, La Brugeoise et Nivelles and Société des Forges et Ateliers, assembling 30 of the WAG1s in Europe and the remaining 92 being built by the Chittaranjan Locomotive Works (CLW) in India from 1963–6.

The traction motors were of Siemens origin, with a power output of 2900kW (3940hp), and were fitted in Alsthom-designed monomotor bogies. Control was by transformer tap changing through ignitron rectifiers with traction motors connected in permanent parallel. They were also equipped for regenerative braking and multiple-unit working.

**Type:** B-B freight
**Power:** 2900kW (3940hp)
**Supply:** 25kV 50Hz AC
**Tractive effort:** 293kN (66,000lbf)
**Max. operating speed:** 80km/h (50mph)
**Weight:** 85 tonnes (187,425lb)
**Max. axle load:** 21.3 tonnes (46,967lb)
**Overall length:** 20.66m (67ft 5in)
**Gauge:** 1676mm (5ft 6in)

## CLASS 165 JAPANESE NATIONAL RAILWAYS (JNR) — JAPAN 1959

Between 1959 and 1971, a large variety of EMUs were built for local and suburban traffic, with all the large Japanese builders sharing in the work, including Nippon Sharyo Seizo, Kinki Nihon Sharyo, and Hitachi, with Mitsubishi and Tokyo Shibaura Electric Co. contributing electrical equipment. Equipment had to be rugged and reliable to keep the system on the move. Class 165 was a three-car set with two power cars, but configurations went up to 10-car sets.

**Type:** Three-car electric suburban train
**Power:** Eight traction motors supplied by 1500V DC via overhead catenary, driving all axles of two power cars
**Tractive effort:** 31.3kN (7050lbf)
**Max. operating speed:** 110km/h (68mph)
**Total weight:** 108 tonnes (238,140lb)
**Max. axle load:** 9 tonnes (19,845lb)
**Overall length:** 59.923m (196ft 9in)
**Builder:** Nippon Sharyo, Kawasaki, Kisha Seizo Kaisha

**The 165s, like other sets, were used in multiple during peak periods. Japan had probably the most intensive and heavily used suburban networks in the world, often with a two-minute headway between trains.**

## CLASS E.321 AND E.322 STATE RAILWAYS (FS) — ITALY 1960

**Here, an 0-6-0 locomotive no. E321.007 is employed shunting some coaches in Rome station, June 1978. The driver's son appears to be having an enjoyable afternoon in the cabin.**

Class E.321 are simple electric shunting locomotives with rod drives. A single traction motor under the low bonnet drives a jackshaft to supply torque to the coupling rods that drive the three coupled axles.

Current collection is via a box pantograph on the cab roof. FS uses single locomotives for lighter duties such as at passenger terminals. For heavier loads, as in marshalling yards, some of these locomotives are coupled in multiple with slave units of class E.322. These are basically the same locomotive as the master E.321, except for the absence of a cab. The slave units receive their control and traction current from the E.321.

Some E.321s can be in multiple with two class E.322 slaves to maximize tractive effort.

**Type:** Shunting electric locomotive (class E.321) and slave unit (class E.322)
**Wheel arrangement:** C+C (0-6-0 + 0-6-0) when in multiple with one slave
**Power per unit:** 3000V DC overhead line collection; 190kW (255bhp); one body-mounted DC traction motor, jackshaft drive to side coupling rods
**Tractive effort:** Not known
**Max. operating speed:** 50km/h (31mph)
**Weight per unit:** 36 tonnes (79,060lb)
**Overall length:** 9.28m (30ft 5in) per unit
**Gauge:** 1435mm (4ft 8.5in)

## CLASS V41 BO-BO HUNGARIAN STATE RAILWAYS (MÁV) HUNGARY 1961

MÁV class V41 used Ward Leonard control using rotating machines to feed a synchronous motor which drove two DC generators, which in turn powered the traction motors. Complicated and heavy, it permitted dual-voltage 15kV and 25kV input by switching main transformer primary winding. All have now been withdrawn.

**Type:** Bo-Bo light duty and shunting
**Power:** 1214kW (1649hp)
**Supply:** 16 or 25kV 50Hz AC
**Tractive effort:** 152kN (34,200lbf)
**Max. operating speed:** 80km/h (50mph)
**Weight:** 74 tonnes (163,170lb)
**Max. axle load:** 18.5 tonnes (40,793lb)
**Overall length:** 12.29m (40ft 1in)
**Gauge:** 1435mm (4ft 8.5in)

## CO-CO SOVIET RAILWAYS (SZD) RUSSIA 1961

Krupp of Germany supplied 20 class Ks to Soviet Railways (SZD) at a period when the communist system urgently needed high-power traction, but domestic industry was failing to produce high-power 25kV units. Class K were required to move heavy loads in the extreme temperatures ranges found in typical Russian working environments. Class K stayed in traffic until the late 1970s.

**Type:** Co-Co
**Power:** 4965kW (6734hp)
**Supply:** 25kV 50Hz AC
**Tractive effort:** 357kN (80,300lbf) at 48.4km/h (30.2mph)
**Max. operating speed:** 100km/h (62.1mph)
**Weight:** 138 tonnes (304,290lb)
**Max. axle load:** 24 tonnes (52,920lb)
**Overall length:** 21.02m (68ft 7in)
**Gauge:** 1524mm (5ft)

## CLASS AM9 BRITISH RAILWAYS GREAT BRITAIN 1962

For the electrification to Clacton and Walton-on-the-Naze, BR's fleet of 19 four-car and four two-car express units was gangwayed throughout and rode on Commonwealth bogies. These were geared for 160km/h (100mph), and were the only UK express EMUs on the 25kV routes. Their status was rewarded by being painted in the lined maroon livery carried by express locomotive hauled stock.

**Type:** Four-car electric multiple unit express trains (also two-car)
**Power:** 25,000V 50Hz AC overhead line collection, one power car, four GEC 210kW (280hp) axle-mounted DC traction motors, tap changer control
**Max. operating speed:** 160km/h (100mph)
**Weight per vehicle:** 35 to 60 tonnes (78,400 to 134,400lb)
**Max axle load:** Not known
**Overall length:** 19.76m (64ft 10in) outer cars; 19.66m (64ft 6in) inner cars

**The class AM9 EMUs, later known as class 309, were Britain's fastest electric multiple units until the arrival of the class 442s in 1988. A class AM9 engine number 601 stands at Colchester North Station in September 1962.**

## CLASS V43 HUNGARIAN STATE RAILWAYS (MÁV) HUNGARY 1963

**A new V43, No. 1081, stands in Budapest Keleti station in 1963, its crisp lines contrasting with the 19th-century station building. The red star testifies to the still-prevailing communist rule.**

Designed by the 50Hz Group, the first seven of these locomotives were built by Krupp in Germany with French monomotor bogies. while the remainder were built in Hungary by Ganz MAVAG – eventually totalling 379.

V43s may be found everywhere as the default motive power for all but the heaviest passenger and freight traffic on the Heygeshalom route. Class V43s also operate for GySEV with 15 locomotives all acquired from MÁV. From 1999 onwards, a modification programme created class V43.2 for push-pull suburban work.

**Type:** Bo-Bo multipurpose
**Power:** 2290kW (3111hp)
**Supply:** 25kV 50Hz AC
**Tractive effort:** 265kN (59,625lbf)
**Max. operating speed:** 130km/h (81.3mph)
**Weight:** 80 tonnes (176,400lb)
**Max. axle load:** 20 tonnes (44,100lb)
**Overall length:** 15.7m (51ft 2in)
**Gauge:** 1435mm (4ft 8.5in)

## CLASS VL80 BO-BO+BO-BO SOVIET RAILWAYS RUSSIA 1963

Soviet railways class VL80 was the first mass-produced twin-unit AC rectifier design for 25kV operation and was of similar external design to the six-axle class VL60. Well over 4000 were built at the Novocherkassk factory in several versions, with production continuing into the 1990s. The basic class VL80 (25 built) had mercury arc rectifiers, but the bulk of production were class VL80K with silicon rectifiers, and class VL80T with electric resistance braking (of which 718 and 1073, respectively, were constructed). Following were 373 VL80Rs with electric regenerative braking. Series building of type VL80S started in 1980, equipped for multiple unit operation – around 3000 constructed. Several other experimental versions appeared over time. The various main versions (VL80K, VL80T, VL80R, VL80S) remain in freight service throughout the AC electrified network of RZD.

**Nearly 40 years on from inception of the class, VL80T No. 2040 awaits duty at Kolosovka yard in Omsk province, on 22 April 2002.**

**Type:** Bo-Bo+Bo-Bo twin unit freight
**Power:** 3160kW (4293hp)
**Supply:** 25kV 50Hz AC
**Tractive effort:** 220kN (49,500lbf) at 52km/h (32.5mph)
**Max. operating speed:** 110km/h (68.3mph)
**Weight:** 92 tonnes (202,860lb)
**Max. axle load:** 23 tonnes (50,715lb)
**Overall length:** 16.42m (53ft 7in)
**Gauge:** 1524mm (5ft)

## CLASS DM3 SWEDISH RAILWAYS (SJ) SWEDEN 1963

**A class Dm3 1D+D+D1 takes a heavy 52-wagon iron ore train away from Kiruna in northern Sweden.**

Across the far north of Sweden and penetrating a few miles into Norway is the Kiruna–Narvik iron ore railway. The railway also carries heavy ore traffic eastwards from Kiruna to Luleå on the Gulf of Bothnia. Trains of 52-bogie iron ore hopper wagons totalling 5200 tonnes (5118 tons) gross operate on both single-track routes several times a day. To move these heavy loads, SJ purchased a fleet of 16 enormous triple-unit electric locomotives. (NSB in Norway provided three pairs of powerful Co-Cos as its share of the operation.) The Swedish class Dm3 locomotive is based on three semi-permanently coupled units each powered by a large body-mounted AC motor driving eight wheels through a jackshaft and coupling rods. The Dm3s are now owned by mining company LKAB, through its subsidiary MTAB.

**Type:** Heavy freight triple-unit electric locomotive
**Power:** 15,000V 16.67Hz AC overhead line collection; 7200kW (9600hp); body-mounted AC traction motor on each unit driving jackshaft and eight coupled wheelsets
**Wheel arrangement:** 1D+D+D1
**Tractive effort:** 940kN (211,320lbf)
**Max. operating speed:** 75km/h (47mph)
**Weight:** 270 tonnes (592,940lb)
**Max axle load:** Not known
**Overall length:** 35.25m (105ft 10in)
Gauge: 1435mm (4ft 8.5in)

**The Swedish Railways Dm3s are coupled in semi-permanent groups of three units, with each unit capable of 7200Kw (9600bhp) output.**

**This class Dm3 combination is coupled head of a Norwegian class El15 Co-Co. The ore trains normally load to 5200 tonnes (5118 tons).**

## CLASS CC40100 FRENCH NATIONAL RAILWAYS (SNCF) FRANCE 1964

**One of SNCF's smart quadri-voltage class 40100 C-Cs awaits departure from Paris Gare du Nord with a special train. Belgian Railways also had six locomotives of this type, its class 18.**

A big problem that faces attempts to operate international express passenger trains around Europe is the many different systems and voltages of overhead electrification. France alone has two, 1500V DC and 25,000V AC at 50Hz; Belgium has 3000V DC; Luxembourg is also 25,000V AC; the Netherlands use 1500V DC; and the German railways use 15,000V AC at 16.67Hz.

The ten locomotives of class CC40100 were designed to operate under all these current collection voltages. They thus had four pantographs to meet the design differences of each country, and they were *monomoteur* locomotives, although not intended for freight work.

Externally, the CC40100s were striking in appearance with sharply raked cab windows and ribbed stainless steel bodywork. The demise of this class of locomotive came when the Thalys network of jointly owned TGVs serving Paris, Brussels, Amsterdam and Köln came into service.

**Type:** C-C quadri-voltage mainline passenger electric locomotive
**Power:** 25,000V 50Hz AC, 1500V DC, 3000V DC and 15,000V AC 16.67Hz overhead line collection; 3710kW (4985bhp) first four locomotives and 4480kW (6020bhp) last six locomotives; two DC frame-mounted traction motors
**Tractive effort:** 196kN (44,060lbf)
**Max. operating speed:** 160km/h (100mph)
**Weight:** 109 tonnes (239,375lb)
**Max axle load: Not known**
**Overall length:** 22.03m (72ft 3in)
**Gauge:** 1435mm (4ft 8.5in)

## SHINKANSEN 16 CAR SETS JAPANESE NATIONAL RAILWAYS (JNR) JAPAN 1964

**A Series 100 train blasts through Shizuoka on the New Tokaido Shinkansen on its run from Tokyo to Osaka, Japan, in April 1997.**

In 1964, Japan brought out the world's first high-speed railway, in conjunction with the 1964 World's Fair in Tokyo. This all-new line was designed from scratch specifically for high-speed passenger services. Unlike the rest of the Japanese National Railways (JR) network, which used 1067mm (3ft 6in) gauge tracks on traditional alignments, the new line, called the Shinkansen, used 1435mm (4ft 8.5in) gauge line on a completely grade-separated alignment.

The initial route connected Japan's two largest cities, Tokyo and Osaka, traversing one of Japan's densest areas of population. There were just 10 intermediate stations. A simplified standard track layout made for straightforward operations. The trains were specially engineered to operate on the new line, which

**The low-profile Series 300 trains introduced in 1992 are much faster and more efficient than early Japanese trains. The one seen here is pictured at Tokyo.**

featured relatively steep gradients. In some places, grades of 2 per cent (a climb of 1 in 50) were used on the old main line. By contrast, the Shinkansen route was as tangent as possible and rode on long sections of elevated viaducts, to allow for continuous, fast running. The Tokyo–Osaka Shinkansen route is 200 km (320 miles) long and runs roughly parallel to the existing 1067mm (3ft 6in) gauge Tokaido line (which was one of Japan's most heavily used lines prior to the opening of the Shinkansen). As a result, the first Shinkansen route is known as the New Tokaido line.

Initially, 12-car double-ended Shinkansen electric multiple-unit trains were used on this route. Their high-speed operation and characteristic streamlined front ends earned these Shinkansen trains the nickname 'Bullet Trains' by visiting westerners. In JR parlance, these trains are known as Series 0 to distinguish them from later ones. The coach-class cars featured 3-2 seating – comfortable, but simple. First-class cars, known in Japan as 'Green Cars', featured larger, more comfortable seats in a 2-2 arrangement.

Each intermediate Series 0 car measures 24.5m (80ft 5in) long, 3.38m (11ft 1in) wide, and 3.98m (13ft 1in) tall. The fronts of the trains have a characteristic nose section with a pair of lights on either side. These display white at the front and red at the rear, which makes identifying the direction of the train simple. In operation, many Shinkansen runs regularly averaged 160km/h (100mph) or more between terminals, which made them by far the fastest regularly scheduled trains in the world for the better part of two decades. Although some trains had been operated at faster speeds in specialized test runs, maximum running speed for the Series 0 trains was set at 208km/h (130mph). Stopping trains are designated Kodama, while express services are known as Hikari.

The Shinkansen was very successful, and passenger traffic grew rapidly. Eventually the 12-car trains were expanded to 16-car configurations. As each car had its own traction motor, expansion did not present a power problem. More than 3200 Series 0 cars were produced over a 23-year period from 1963 to 1986. These were typically painted in a blue and white livery. This first Shinkansen route has become the most heavily travelled high-speed railway in the world – there are often 10 or more trains per hour in each direction over the line between the cities of Tokyo and Osaka.

With the success of the initial Tokyo–Osaka route, JR set out to expand its Shinkansen network. First the original line was extended southeast, and later a separate network of Shinkansen lines was built north and west of Tokyo. Later lines were engineered to an even higher standard than the original New Tokaido route to allow for faster operations. The lines south and east of Osaka traversed very mountainous terrain, which required many very long tunnels. On the lines north and west of Tokyo, the electrification standard is different as a result of differences in Japan's national electric grid. Instead of 25kV at 60Hz, which is used by the original lines, and those to the south and west, the lines north and west use 25kV at 50Hz. This electrification change is often cited as one of the reasons why the two Shinkansen networks do not offer a through service. All Tokyo-bound trains terminate there, despite the fact that the Shinkansen terminal platforms are adjacent to one another at Tokyo Central Station.

To accommodate these new lines, new Shinkansen trains were developed. These new trains have embraced new technologies and are designed for significantly faster speeds. Unlike the Series 0 trains, which used a traditional propulsion system that powered every axle on the train using DC traction motors, advanced propulsion systems employed by later trains resulted in fewer power axles and gave greater efficiency. In 1982, Series 200 trains were built for service north and west of Tokyo. The earliest of these train sets appear similar to the traditional Series 0 trains, but carry a green and cream livery and are equipped with snowploughs. Internally, they are more advanced than the older trains. Bodies are made of aluminium, and motors use thyristor controls. Top speed for the earlier Series 200 trains was designated at 240km/h (149mph). Later 200 series trains share styling with the 100 Series trains, and some are capable of 275km/h

**The oldest and most famous of all Japanese high-speed trains is the original Series 0 'Bullet train' introduced in 1964. Today, few of these trains remain, as more modern sets ply the Shinkansen.**

**This profile represents the second generation of Japanese streamlining and is more refined than the 1964 'bullet train' look that made the Shinkansen famous.**

(170 mph). The 100 Series entered service in 1985, and they were designed for service south and west of Tokyo. They have sharper, more angular styling than the Series 0 trains. After privatization of JR in 1987, three different companies assumed operations of Shinkansen routes, and a host of new trains have appeared. The Series 300 train is a futuristic modern train with a sleek wedge-like front end. It has a lower profile than the earlier trains and is designed for 269km/h (168mph) in regular service on lines south and west of Tokyo, with its fastest regular running on lines south of Osaka. The Series 300 train is capable of speeds up to 296km/h (185mph). This train was among the first high-speed trains in the world to employ a modern three-phase AC traction system that uses asynchronous motors with forced air ventilation. For services north and west of Tokyo, six-car Series 400 and various 'E Series' trains made their debuts in the 1990s. Of these, the E1 and E4 trains used a double-deck design to increase capacity. The E1 uses just 12 cars, while the E4 features 8-car sets, but is designed to run in multiple to allow for a 16-car train.

The fastest of all the Shinkansen are JR West's Series 500 trains, which were introduced in 1997. Initially these operated in exclusive *Nozomi 500* service between Osaka and the southern city of Hagata. Designed for a top speed of 300km/h (186mph), these trains were advertised as having the world's fastest station to station times. Despite the introduction of all these new trains, JR's original Series 0 train remains one of the most readily recognized high-speed trains in the world. Thousands of photographs have been published of it since its introduction almost 40 years ago. Its familiar profile is still used in Japanese promotional literature. The last of these trains were to be withdrawn from high-speed services on the New Tokaido route at the end of 1999. While some of these trains were supposed to survive in other services for a few more years, they are now museum pieces for the most part. Portions of Series 0 trains are displayed at museums in Tokyo and Osaka, and also at the National Railway Museum in York, England.

**Type:** 'Series-0' high-speed electric passenger train
**Power:** 25kV 60Hz via overhead
**Output:** 11,846kW (15,900hp)
**Tractive effort:** N/A
**Max. operating speed:** 208km/h (130mph) in regular operation
**Weight:** N/A
**Overall length:** Intermediate cars 24.5m (80ft 5in)
**Max. axle load:** 16 tonnes (35,280lb)
**Gauge:** 1435mm (4ft 8.5in)

**A Series 200 train races towards its station stop at Fukushima. Early series 200 trains shared streamlining characteristics with the original Series 0 sets, but were used on the Shinkansen routes north and east of Tokyo.**

## MAT '64 NETHERLANDS RAILWAYS (NS)

NETHERLANDS 1964

In all, 214 two-car and 32 four-car electric multiple units were supplied to NS both for stopping services and for selected intercity routes, the four-car units being known as 'ELD4' sets. They are the successors to the formerly well-known 'dog nose' EMUs. The nickname originated from the shape of the nose end that protruded under the driver's cab windscreens. The 1964 sets had such a nose, but it was less pronounced. The units carried heavy Scharfenberg automatic couplers to facilitate joining and splitting operations, which were carried out efficiently. Internally, the trains were basic, even spartan, by modern standards, but enough for the stopping train duties to which all of them have since been relegated.

**Type:** Two-car and four-car electric multiple-unit stopping trains
**Power:** 1500V DC overhead line collection, two power cars per unit, four GEC 210kW (280hp) axle-mounted DC traction motors (eight on four-car sets)
**Max. operating speed:** 140km/h (87mph)
**Weight per vehicle:** 35 to 47 tonnes (76,860 to 103,215lb)
**Max axle load:** Not known
**Overall length:** Outer cars - 26.07m;inner cars - 24.93m (85ft 6in and 81ft 9in)
**Gauge:** 1435mm (4ft 8.5in)

**This Mat '64 unit on suburban service carries diagonal advertising panels across the windows.**

## CLASS EU07 POLISH STATE RAILWAYS (PKP)

POLAND 1964

**An EU07 leads a long-distance PKP passenger train at Sulechów. Polish infrastructure suffers from underinvestment, and many lines are a shadow of former glory.**

The Polish railway system had relied on British electrification technology since the 1930s, and in the early 1960s Polish State Railways (PKP) went to England for the construction of a class of modern electric locomotives. Between 1961 and 1965, PKP placed 20 Class EU06 electrics in service. These machines were derived from British Rail class 83 and built by English Electric at its Vulcan Foundry Works. In the mid-1960s, Poland's Pafawag licensed the type and built a fleet of additional electrics to the same basic pattern at its Wroclaw facilities. These Polish-built machines were known as class EU07 and usually assigned to passenger services. In most respects, they are the same as the EU06 Class. Pafawag built 240 EU07s over 10 years from 1964.

**Type:** Bo-Bo, electric
**Power:** 3000V DC from overhead wire
**Output:** 2000kW (2685hp)
**Tractive effort:** N/A
**Max. operating speed:** 125km/h (78mph)
**Weight:** 83.5 tonnes (184,123lb)
**Overall length:** N/A
**Max. axle load:** N/A
**Gauge:** 1435mm (4ft 8.5in)

**PKP electrics catch the afternoon sun near Kraków in April 2002. Polish electrics such as these are based on British designs and bear a resemblance to British electrics of the same period.**

## CLASS 060-EA ROMANIAN RAILWAYS (CFR) ROMANIA 1964

**This class 41 loco has been decorated by its crew with additional lining and even curtains in the cab windows.**

**Type:** Co-Co mixed-traffic mainline electric locomotive
**Power:** 27,000V 50Hz AC overhead line collection; 5100kW (6835hp); six DC traction motors
**Tractive effort:** 412kN (92,620lbf)
**Max. operating speed:** Class 40 120km/h (75mph); class 41 160km/h (100mph)
**Weight:** Approx. 120 tonnes (263,530lb)
**Max axle load:** Not known
**Overall length:** 19.8m (65ft)
**Gauge:** 1435 (4ft 8.5in)

When electrifying its main lines CFR needed a Co-Co general-purpose heavy electric locomotive. ASEA of Sweden already had the popular Rc2 and was able to offer a larger Co-Co based on this design. More than 900 were built at the Electroputere works at Craiova in southern Romania. They were later reclassified class 40. There is a variant geared for passenger operation, class 060-EA1 (class 41).

Liveried in the standard CFR grey with metallic stripes, these locomotives are seen all over the country where there are electrified tracks. Class 41s haul international and internal passenger trains. The class 40s, sometimes in tandem, work heavy freight trains. The class 41s are often decorated by their depots or crews.

This type has also been exported by Electroputere to Yugoslav and Bulgarian railways.

**The Romanian 060-EA and 060-EA1 group (CFR classes 40 and 41) forms Europe's largest class numerically of standard-gauge electric locomotives.**

## CLASS 42 BULGARIAN RAILWAYS (BDZ) — BULGARIA 1964

These Skoda-built locomotives had a rather startling cab design and marked one of the earliest applications of glass-reinforced plastic to locomotive construction. Ninety class 42s were built in Plzen for BDZ between 1965 and 1970, with silicon rectifiers and tap changer control. CSD classes 23 and 240 are similar to this type.

**Type:** Bo-Bo mixed-traffic
**Power:** 3200kW (4348hp)
**Supply:** 25kV 50Hz AC
**Tractive effort:** 250kN (56250lbf)
**Max. operating speed:** 110km/h (68.3mph)
**Weight:** 85 tonnes (187,425lb)
**Max. axle load:** 21.5 tonnes (47,408lb)
**Overall length:** 16.44m (53ft 8in)
**Gauge:** 1435mm (4ft 8.5in)

## PLAN MP PARCELS VANS NETHERLANDS RAILWAYS (NS) — NETHERLANDS 1964

**A pair of mPs is seen in multiple on a postal working. Netherlands Railways operated its postal services with these units radiating from a central hub at Utrecht.**

No longer a regular part of the Dutch scene, the pretty yellow-and-red electric parcels vans of Plan mP used to connect major cities in the Netherlands on postal duties, usually with two or three four-wheeled vans in tow, for which they were fitted with standard side buffers and hooked drawbars. Originally liveried dark red, the plan mPs were supplied by Werkspoor, which delivered 34 of these versatile vehicles.

Since their recent withdrawal some mPs have been used by infrastructure companies as stores and personnel carriers.

**Type:** Single-car electric parcels vans
**Power:** 1500V DC overhead line collection, four Heemaf 145kW (195hp) axle-mounted DC traction motors
**Max. operating speed:** 140km/h (87mph)
**Weight:** 54 tonnes (118,590lb) per vehicle
**Max. axle load:**
**Overall length:** 26.4m (86ft 7in)
**Gauge:** 1435mm (4ft 8.5in)

## CLASSES 279 AND 289 BO-BO SPANISH RAILWAYS (RENFE) SPAIN 1967

**On 20 October 1987, a class 279 passes Pancorbo, in the hills of Burgos province, with a freight.**

These were two similar classes of DC, dual-voltage machines utilized for operation on the Spanish 3000V system (and for cross-border work on the French 1500V system). The earlier class 279 is slightly less powerful than class 289 (introduced two years later). Both were built to a very similar mechanical design and external styling as that of single voltage class 269. Today, classes 279 and 289 belong to the RENFE Cargas freight business.

**On the same day, and at the same place, the slightly more powerful class 289 passes through.**

**Type:** Bo-Bo mixed-voltage electric
**Power:** 279 - 2700kW (3621hp); 289 - 3100kW (4157hp)
**Supply:** 1500V or 3000V DC
**Tractive effort:** Low gear - 263kN (59,175lbf); high gear - 164kN (36,900lbf)
**Max. operating speed:** Low gear - 80km/h (50mph); high gear 130km/h (81.3mph)
**Weight:** 279 - 80 tonnes (176,400lb); 289 - 84 tonnes (185,220lb)
**Max. axle load:** 21 tonnes (46,305lb)
**Overall length:** 17.27m (56ft 4in)
**Gauge:** 1668mm (5ft 3in)

## CLASS SS1 CHINESE STATE RAILWAYS CHINA 1968

Class SS1 was the first mass-produced electric locomotive built locally within China. It featured silicon rectifier and transformer tap chanter technology; however, it was otherwise based on earlier ignition rectifier locomotives imported from France (class 6Y2 of 1960 supplied by Alsthom).

Class SS1, or class 6Y1 as it was until 1968, was equipped with a 3600kW (4891hp) rheostat brake, being designed for operation through the Qinling mountain range between Chengdu and Baoji. Electrification of this 600km (375-mile) route took place between 1958 and 1975.

Mainline electric traction was inaugurated in China as late as 1960 with the 90km (56-mile) Baoji to Fungshien section that the class 6Y2 locomotives had been imported to operate. Prior to this, only mine railways were electrified. China thus started with 25kV 50Hz AC and benefited from technical developments in the rest of the world.

From 1979, the SS1 was succeeded by the higher power SS3 on the production lines of the Zhuzhou electric locomotive.

**A very clean SS1 No. 1234 stands at Lanzhou locomotive depot in 1977. Chinese locomotives are usually well maintained, both externally and internally.**

**Type:** Co-Co
**Power:** 3780kW (5136hp)
**Supply:** 25kV 50Hz AC
**Tractive effort:** 301kN (67725lbf)
**Max. operating speed:** 95km/h (59.4mph)
**Weight:** 138 tonnes (304,290lb)
**Max. axle load:** 23 tonnes (50,175lb)
**Overall length:** 20.368m (66ft 6in)
**Gauge:** 1435mm (4ft 8.5in)

## CLASS 581 JAPANESE NATIONAL RAILWAYS (JNR) JAPAN 1968

Sleeping cars have generally been considered to be specialized vehicles requiring locomotive haulage; however, since 1968, Japan has had a fleet of electric multiple-unit sleeper trains. At that time particularly, and earlier, the length of the country, especially on the main island of Honshu, made overnight trains a useful means of travel between north and south.

The class 581 was a 12-car set, and, apart from a dining car and guard's compartment, all the space was given over to sleeping compartments. The sleeping berths, arranged longitudinally and set in triple tiers, were all of the same standard, and a premium price was paid for the lowest bunk. The total number of berths is 444. With the upper-level berths folded away, the cars can also be used for daytime services, with seating accommodation for a maximum of 656 passengers. Air conditioning equipment, water tanks, etc. are fitted in the roof spaces. The driving cars at each end are not powered. The power cars are the second vehicles. Their axles, and those of four other cars, are motor-driven, giving traction from half the axles of the train, and the motors' hourly output is rated at 2800kW (3860hp).

The trains are built to the standard Japanese 1065mm (3ft 6in) gauge. Because of the different supply systems found throughout Japan, the motors were equipped to use different kinds of current: AC at 25,000V 50 or 60Hz, or DC at 1500V. An updated Class 583 sleeper train has also been produced.

Nevertheless, despite the building of the 53.85km (33.5-mile) Seikan Tunnel, the longest in the world, linking Honshu by rail to the northern island of Hokkaido, overnight sleeper services in Japan have been in a state of decline. Internal air services and the high-speed day services run on key routes by the *Shinkansen* expresses have been largely responsible.

Even with the Seikan Tunnel, a railway journey on the narrow gauge from Tokyo to Sapporo is seen as something of an ordeal, although the eventual conversion of the line to *Shinkansen* standards will change this. Holiday travellers prefer the luxury 'Cassiopeia' sleeper, running three times a week, to the more basic though comfortable accommodation to be found on class 581.

Numerous regular sleeper services still exist, including the 'Sunrise *Izumu*' between Tokyo and Izumoshi; the 'Sunrise *Seto*' between Tokyo and Takamatsu; the *Akatsuki*, Kyoto-Osaka-Nagasaki; and the *Suisei*, Shin Osaka-Kokura-Miyazaki. However, numbers of the Class 581 and 583 sleepers have been converted into commuter cars for suburban traffic.

**Type:** Twelve-car multiple-unit sleeping car train
**Power:** Twenty-four 100kW (160hp) electric motors drawing current from an overhead catenary geared to the axles of two power cars and four other cars in a 12-car set
**Tractive effort:** 142.9kN (32,140lb)
**Max. operating speed:** 72km/h (45mph)
**Total weight:** 553 tonnes (1,218,812lb)
**Max. axle load:** 12 tonnes (26,460lb)
**Overall length:** 249m (816ft 11in)
**Builder:** Nippon Sharyo, Kisha Seizo Kaisha, Kawasaki, Hitachi, Kinki Sharyo

## CLASS EF66 B-B-B JAPANESE RAILWAYS (JR) JAPAN 1968

Fifty-five class EF66 machines were supplied to Japanese Railways (JR) by Kawasaki after two years of development of the prototype (EF90 – later absorbed into the EF66 fleet as number 901). Sixteen further EF66 units of a slightly modified version were to arrive from 1989.

The middle bogie of the EF66 had mechanical levers and air suspension allowing side movements. Today, most of the EF66s operate for JR Freight on fast cargo over the Tokaido and San'yo main lines, while 13 units remain with JAR West on Tokyo Kyushu passenger duties.

**With both pantographs raised, class EF66 is seen here standing in the yards at the central Japanese city of Kyoto. Despite its weight and power, the machine's six axles give it a maximum loading of only 17 tonnes (37,385lb). One of the class's main uses is now on overnight sleeper trains.**

**Type:** B-B-B heavy freight
**Power:** 3900kW (5230hp)
**Tractive effort:** 192kN (43200lbf) at 72km/h (45mph)
**Max. operating speed:** 120km/h (75mph)
**Weight:** 101 tonnes (222,705lb)
**Max. axle load:** 17 tonnes (37,385lb)
**Overall length:** 18.2m (59ft 8in)
**Gauge:** 1067mm (3ft 6in)

## CLASS EA NEW ZEALAND RAILWAYS (NZR) — NEW ZEALAND 1968

Toshiba built EA 1 to EA 5 for the NZR South Island Otira to Arthurs Pass section, replacing the 1923 class EO. Class EA, later class EO on taking up designation of the locomotives they replaced, operated three in multiple. Electric working ceased 1998 following a tunnel ventilation system and modified U26C diesel locomotives.

**Type:** Bo-Bo
**Power:** 960kW (1285hp)
**Supply:** 1500V DC
**Tractive effort:** 103kN (23,175lbf)
**Max. operating speed:** 72km/h (45mph)
**Weight:** 55 tonnes (121,275lb)
**Max. axle load:** 18 tonnes (39,690lb)
**Overall length:** 11.6m (37ft 10in)
**Gauge:** 1067mm (3ft 6in)

## CLASS EL 14 NORWEGIAN STATE RAILWAYS (NSB) — NORWAY 1968

The electrification of Norwegian State Railways (NSB) largely took place after World War II. The main lines from Oslo to Bergen, Trondheim and Stavanger have all been worked by the class El 14 locomotives. These machines are powerful Co-Cos that are able to lift heavy passenger trains over the mountainous and curvaceous routes. The class Els have been displaced from frontline duties by successive deliveries of faster and more modern locomotives; however, they can still be seen on freight workings.

**Type:** Co-Co mixed-traffic mainline electric locomotive
**Power:** 15,000V 16.667Hz AC overhead line collection; 5080kW (6930hp); rheostatic brakes; six DC traction motors
**Tractive effort:** 350kN (78,685lbf)
**Max. operating speed:** 120km/h (75mph)
**Weight:** 105 tonnes (230,590lb)
**Max. axle load:**
**Overall length:** 17.74m (58ft 2in)
**Gauge:** 1435mm (4ft 8.5in)

**In the early Norwegian State Railways livery of dark red, this class 14 Co-Co type has bars over the cab windscreens to protect the driver from falling rocks and ice. Note also the prominent snow plough.**

## CLASS 342 SLOVENIAN RAILWAYS — SLOVENIA 1968

Slovenian railways class 342s handle mixed passenger and freight work. Built by Ansalso, class 342 was inherited from former Yugoslavian Railways.With ever-increasing freight from Koper sea port and no decision on new motive power, class 342 seems likely to remain at work all over the system on secondary passenger and freight duties.

**Type:** Bo-Bo mixed-traffic
**Power:** 2280kW (3098hp)
**Supply:** 3000V DC
**Tractive effort:** 177kN (39,825lbf)
**Max. operating speed:** 120km/h (75mph)
**Weight:** 76 tonnes (167,580lb)
**Max. axle load:** 19 tonnes (41,895lb)
**Overall length:** 17.25m (56ft 8in)
**Gauge:** 1435mm (4ft 8.5in)

## 'METROLINER' PENNSYLVANIA RAILROAD (PRR) USA 1968

Prompted by the worldwide sensation caused by the Japanese Shinkansen, which demonstrated the possibilities of trains travelling at up to 217km/h (135mph), the Pennsylvania Railroad set out to develop a high-speed rail service on its Northeast Corridor route between New York, Philadelphia and Washington DC. With the help of Federal funding, PRR developed a high-speed electric multiple unit capable of 257km/h (160mph) known as the '*Metroliner*'. By the time the train was ready to run, PRR had become part of Penn Central, and in regular service *Metroliner* EMUs were limited to 177km/h (110mph). Following Penn Central's collapse, Amtrak inherited the *Metroliner.* By the early 1980s, the original *Metroliner* EMUs had been assigned to other services and the marketing name assigned to locomotive-hauled equipment.

**Type:** High-speed electric multiple-unit train
**Power:** 11.5kV AC at 25Hz
**Tractive effort:** N/A
**Max. operating speed:** 176km/h (110mph) in revenue service; 256km/h (160mph) potential
**Weight:** 149 tonnes (328,400lb)
**Overall length:** 51.816m (170ft) for four-car set
**Max. axle load:** 19 tonnes (41,887lb)
**Gauge:** 1435mm (4ft 8.5in)

**The *Metroliner* was an American high-speed electric multiple unit inspired in part by the success of the Japanese Shinkansen. Its name was used for years after the original equipment had been reassigned to other duties.**

## CLASS 103.1 FEDERAL GERMAN RAILWAYS (DB) GERMANY 1969

**Hauling a rake of DB intercity stock, this class 103 is capable of reaching speeds up to 200km/h (125mph) on the straighter sections of main line.**

Following the assessment of four prototypes, DB started its InterCity revolution with the construction of 145 powerful passenger electric locomotives. The class 103s became favourites of railway enthusiasts because of their streamlined outline and highly competent and quiet performance in service. Painted red-and-cream to match the first-class carriages in their InterCity rakes, later versions of DB red followed.

**Type:** Express passenger electric
**Power:** 15,000V 16.67 Hz AC overhead line collection; 7440kW (9975hp); thyristor control; rheostatic braking; six frame-mounted DC traction motors.
**Wheel arrangement:** Co-Co
**Tractive effort:** 314kN (70,590lbf)
**Max. operating speed:** 200km/h (125mph)
**Weight:** 114 tonnes (250,350lb)
**Max axle load:**
**Overall length:** 19.5m (63ft 8in) up to No. 103 215, and 20.2m (66ft 3in)
**Gauge:** 1435mm (4ft 8.5in)

**Here, locomotive 103.158 stops on Cologne station with a passenger train. The last Class 103s were withdrawn from service in 2003.**

## B-B CLASS 32 BULGARIAN STATE RAILWAYS (BDZ) BULGARIA 1970

The heavily used Sofia–Plovdiv main line was electrified in 1962, using the by then international standard 25kV AC at 50Hz. This was followed by the lines from the capital to Karlova and to Russe on the Romanian border. The 79 four-car sets of class 32 went into use on intercity services between Sofia, Plovdiv and Karlova. They were single-class trains with seating capacity for 316 passengers.

**Type:** Four-car train set
**Power:** 660kW (884.4hp)
**Tractive effort:** Not known
**Max. operating speed:** 130km/h (80mph)
**Total weight:** Not known
**Overall length:** Not known
**Builder:** RVZ-Riga, Latvia

## SNCF CLASS BB15000 FRENCH NATIONAL RAILWAYS (SNCF) FRANCE 1971

The 65 members of class BB15000 are the principal 25kV AC express passenger locomotives in France. They are of the standard *monomoteur* design, the same as the 'BB7200' type, but designed for the AC electrification system. A dual-voltage version also exists, class BB22200. The BB15000s operate mainly in eastern France.

**Type:** B-B mainline mixed-traffic electric locomotive
**Power:** 25,000V 50Hz AC overhead line collection; 4400kW (5900hp); AC thyristor control; two DC frame mounted traction motors
**Tractive effort:** 294kN (66,095lbf)
**Max. operating speed:** 160km/h (100mph)
**Weight:** 90 tonnes (197,645lb)
**Max axle load:** Not known
**Overall length:** 17.48m (57ft 4in)
**Gauge:** 1435mm (4ft 8.5in)

**This BB15000 class locomotive is on foreign track at Luxembourg station. It is at the head of a train bound for Paris Gare de l'Est.**

## WAM4 Co-Co INDIAN RAILWAYS (IR) — INDIA 1971

**Type:** Co-Co multipurpose
**Power:** 2715kW (3689hp)
**Supply:** 25kV 50Hz AC
**Tractive effort:** 332kN (74700lbf)
**Max. operating speed:** 120km/h (75mph)
**Weight:** 113 tonnes (249,165lb)
**Max. axle load:** 19 tonnes (41,895lb)
**Overall length:** 18.974m (61ft 10in)
**Gauge:** 1676mm (5ft 6in)

**Chittaranjan Works has built more than 500 of these versatile and rugged engines for a variety of freight and passenger uses.**

Class WAM4 was the first wholly Indian-designed and built electric locomotive, produced after practical experience operating several imported designs (although the bogie is the Alco 'trimount' type). The design was used in further classes such as the WAG5A, WCG2 and WCAM1. Class WAM4 utilized silicon rectifiers and a high-tension traction control system, but reverted to axle-hung nose-suspended traction motors after the high maintenance costs of the spring-borne motors of earlier types had been experienced. Nearly 500 class WAM4s were built, with several variants from the basic design. Class WAM4Bs with a maximum speed of 50km/h (31.3mph) were designed for mineral traffic. WAM4Ps were 140km/h (87.5mph) passenger locomotives with control system changes to allow all parallel motor connections. There are also many depot-specific local modifications. Class WAM4 is still generally used on passenger work.

## Class ET22 POLISH STATE RAILWAYS (PKP) — POLAND 1971

**The ET22 is one of the most common types of equipment on Polish State Railways (PKP). These locomotives are usually assigned freight work, but can be used in passenger service as well.**

The most numerous electrics on the Polish State Railways are the class ET22 built by Pafawag with Dolmel electrical gear. The model entered production in 1971, and nearly 1200 were built. Each machine has six DC series-wound traction motors which can produce up to 3000kW (4020hp) of pulling power. The ET22 was designed for heavy freight service, yet some machines have been regularly assigned to passenger trains as well. Long sleeping car trains, like those that continue on points in Russia and the Ukraine, are sometimes assigned ET22 electrics. More typical tasks would be coal and iron ore trains and other heavy freight traffic on PKP routes.

**Type:** Co-Co mixed-traffic (primarily freight) electric
**Power:** 3000V DC from overhead
**Output:** 3000kW (4020hp)
**Tractive effort:** 212kN (47,600lbf) continuous TE at 50km/h (31mph)
**Max. operating speed:** 125km/h (78mph)
**Weight:** 120 tonnes (264,480lb)
**Overall length:** 19.24m (63ft 2in)
**Max. axle load:** 20 tonnes (44,080lb)
**Gauge:** 1435mm (4ft 8.5in)

## Co-Co ALGERIAN NATIONAL RAILWAYS (SNCFA) ALGERIA 1972

Co-operation between the two eastern bloc manufacturers LEW of East Germany and Skoda of Czechoslovakia resulted in these heavy mineral locomotives being built for Chemins de Fer Algeriens (SNCFA), Algeria's national railway network.

Thirty-two of these locomotives were constructed, numbered 6CE 1 to 32 and designated for mineral traffic between Djebel Onka and Tebessa, and Annaba port.

These Co-Co machines were mechanically similar to 25kV DR class 251, but electrically similar to 3000V CSD classes 181. Around half the class remain in service after introduction of class 6FE from 1992.

**Class 6 CE No. 28, one of Algerian National Railways heavy freight locomotives, plays a part in the country's minerals trade. It is seen here at the head of a coast-bound phosphates train, near the Drea Oasis, in late 1990. If necessary, an assisting engine, operating under radio control, could be cut into the middle of the train.**

**Type:** Co-Co heavy freight
**Power:** 2150kW (2880hp)
**Supply:** 3000V DC
**Tractive effort:** 241kN (54200lbf) at 32km/h (20mph)
**Max. operating speed:** 80km/h (50mph)
**Weight:** 130 tonnes (286,650lb)
**Max. axle load:** 22 tonnes (48,510lb)
**Overall length:** 18.64m (61ft 2in)
**Gauge:** 1435mm (4ft 8.5in)

## CLASS 8000 BO-BO-BO KOREAN RAILWAYS KNR SOUTH KOREA 1972

**The inwards-tilted, glare-resisting windscreen and angular front lines instantly confirm the French origins and Alsthom design of this Korean workhorse.**

**Type:** Bo-Bo-Bo heavy freight
**Power:** 3990kW (5350hp)
**Supply:** 25kV 50Hz AC
**Tractive effort:** 426kN (95850lbf)
**Max. operating speed:** 85km/h (53.1mph)
**Weight:** 128 tonnes (282,240lb)
**Max. axle load:** 21 tonnes (46,305lb)
**Overall length:** 20.73m (68ft)
**Gauge:** 1435mm (4ft 8.5in)

These 90 AC supply, DC-rectified, thyristor-controlled, rheostat-braked locomotives not only represented a significant technical achievement, but also met a demanding traction specification. KNR class 8000 locomotives were required to haul heavy loads over 1 in 40 gradients through relatively sharp curvature (for that purpose the centre bogie was permitted457mm (18in) of sideways movement). The class 8000's superstructure and body, with negative-raked cabs, is of typical Alsthom design. Class 8000 was introduced for the electrification of the 449km (279-mile) line between Seoul and Bugpyeong across the Taebaeg mountains.

## RE6/6 SWISS FEDERAL RAILWAYS (SBB) SWITZERLAND 1972

**Type:** Bo-Bo-Bo for freight and passenger mountain traffic
**Power:** 7856kW (10,665hp)
**Supply:** 15kV 16.2/3Hz AC
**Tractive effort:** 11601-11604 - 394kN (88650lbf); 11605-11689 - 398kN (89550lbf)
**Max. operating speed:** 140km/h (87.5mph)
**Weight:** 120 tonnes (264,600lb)
**Max. axle load:** 20 tonnes (44,100lb)
**Overall length:** 19.31m (63ft)
**Gauge:** 1435mm (4ft 8.5in)

A rating of 7856kW (10667hp) puts SBB Re6/6 among the most powerful locomotives of the world. The all-adhesion Bo-Bo-Bo layout combines elements of the Bo-Bo Re4/4II and Ae6/6 Co-Co. Improved curving performance with weight transfer reduction uses three Re4/4 type bogies, but keeping within Ae6/6 overall adhesive weight. While 11601 and 11602 have a body in two sections around a horizontal hinge, 11603 and 11604 had a more conventional body design that was used for the 85 production machines. Re6/6 dominated passenger and freight traffic over the St Gotthard uts from the time of their introduction until partially displaced by class 460 in the late 1990s. Re6/6s are expected to remain in traffic well into the 21st century.

**Twenty-seven years old but with that timeless look of so many Swiss electric locomotive types, an Re6/6 stops at Brig in September 1997.**

## CLASS SR1 FINNISH STATE RAILWAYS (VR) FINLAND 1973

Finland uses the Russian standard gauge of 1524mm (5ft), and its largest railway interchange partner has always been the Russian railways. In the early 1970s, when Finnish State Railways (known by the initials VR) began to electrify its main lines, it ordered its first all-electric locomotives, the class Sr1, from Russia. Mechanical and most electric components were built by Novocherkassk Electric Locomotive Works, with some working being undertaken in Finland by Oy Strömberg Ab. The first of the class was ready in 1973. With three decades of service behind it, the Sr1 class has seen its territory greatly expanded, as VR has gradually extended the reach of electrification, which uses the European standard of 25kV AC at 50Hz. They are mixed-traffic electrics, used singly and in pairs.

**Finnish State Railways (VR) uses its Sr1 electrics in both freight and passenger services. A long-distance express train approaches Helsinki's main passenger station.**

**Type:** Bo-Bo mixed-traffic electric
**Power:** 25kV AC at 50Hz
**Tractive effort:** 176.5kN (39,700lbf) at 73km/h (44mph)
**Max. operating speed:** 140km/h (87mph)
**Weight:** 84 tonnes (186,000lb)
**Overall length:** 18.96m (63ft 3in)
**Max. axle load:** 21 tonnes (46,500lb)
**Gauge:** 1524mm (5ft)

## CLASS 87 BRITISH RAIL GREAT BRITAIN 1973

**The more recent duties of class 87s were on intercity push-pull trains between London Euston and Glasgow, Manchester, Liverpool or Birmingham.**

**Type:** Bo-Bo mainline mixed-traffic electric locomotive
**Power:** 25,000V 50Hz AC overhead line collection; 3730kW (5000hp); tap-changer control; four DC frame mounted traction motors with quill drives to the axles
**Tractive effort:** 258kN (58,000lbf)
**Max. operating speed:** 175km/h (110mph)
**Weight:** 85 tonnes (187,040lb)
**Max. axle load:** Not known
**Overall length:** 17.83m (58ft 6in)
**Gauge:** 1435mm (4ft 8.5in)

When British Rail decided to electrify the northern stretches of the West Coast main line to Glasgow, more powerful electric locomotives were needed for the task. The 35 locomotives of class 87 were a direct development of the class 86 fleet. Conservatively rated, they performed well. Liveried in BR blue from the start, they later adopted InterCity colours and now carry the red Virgin Trains livery.

**Below: When first built, some class 87s were to receive pantographs with a more complex frame arrangement.**

## CLASS 381 JAPAN RAILWAYS (JR) — JAPAN 1973

Japan was an early participant in the field of tilting train technology, designed to increase speed safely on curves, while at the same time reducing the effects of centrifugal force on passengers. This was despite also being committed at this time to developing completely new tracks such as the Tokaido line, required for the super high-speed trains. In 1970, a tilting design of the 'pendulum' type was tried out on a prototype EMU three-car set, series 591. The nine-car class 381 set embodied this technology. Its body design was based on that of the class 581, but it was narrower to allow for the tilting effect. The class 381 units ran from Kyoto and Osaka on 'Ocean Arrow' services to the Pacific coast resorts of Shirahama and Shingu, until displaced in the 1990s by series 283 EMU trains.

**Type:** Express 'tilting' train set
**Power:** Six motor cars, each with four 100kw (160hp) traction motors
**Tractive effort:** N/A
**Max. operating speed:** 120km/h (75mph)
**Total weight:** 342t (753,802lb)
**Max. axle load:** 9.75t (21,490lb)
**Overall length:** 191,700mm (628ft 11in)

## CLASS 6E BO-BO SOUTH AFRICAN RAILWAYS — SOUTH AFRICA 1973

**Class 6E1 No. 1678, of a batch built 1977 and 1979. With a total of 960, this variant of 6E was the most numerous SAR electric class. The plain livery and the decals do not seem to suit the bodywork particularly well.**

Improvements in motor design and insulation materials led to the greatly uprated class 6E having a 75 per cent higher continuous tractive effort rating than the preceding class 5E. Mechanically the axle-hung nose-suspended mounting is retained in a revised bogie design. The 80 class 6E E1146–1225 are equipped with an air suspension between bogies and body, but operate freely in multiple with classes 5E, 5E1 and 6E1.

**Type:** Bo-Bo universal traffic
**Power:** 2252kW (3020hp)
**Supply:** 3000V DC
**Tractive effort:** 193kN (43400lbf) at 41km/h (25.5mph)
**Max. operating speed:** 112km/h (70mph)
**Weight:** 89 tonnes (196,245lb)
**Max. axle load:** 22.5 tonnes (49,613lb)
**Overall length:** 15.495m (50ft 6in)
**Gauge:** 1067mm (3ft 6in)

## CLASS 1044 AUSTRIAN FEDERAL RAILWAYS (ÖBB) — AUSTRIA 1974

Built in Austria to a Swedish design concept, the 140-odd class 1044 locomotives are among Austria's most powerful locomotives. They can be seen all over the country on both passenger and freight, and almost monopolize the principal InterCity and EuroCity expresses. Liveried in ÖBB's red colour, their distinctive outline is also common in southern Germany where they have been seen as far north as Munich and Frankfurt.

**Type:** Bo-Bo mainline mixed-traffic electric
**Power:** 15,000V 16.67Hz AC overhead line collection; 5300kW (7105hp); thyristor control; rheostatic braking; four frame-mounted DC traction motors
**Tractive effort:** 314kN (70,590lbf)
**Max. operating speed:** 160km/h (100mph)
**Weight:** 83 tonnes (182,275lb)
**Max. axle load:** Not known
**Overall length:** 16m (52ft 6in)
**Gauge:** 1435mm (4ft 8.5in)

**These 5350kW (7105hp) Bo-Bos were Austria's most powerful locomotives when introduced. They are used all over the country in mixed traffic.**

**This class 1044 heads a regional passenger train in the 1980s peaches-and-cream livery.**

## CLASS 181.2 FEDERAL GERMAN RAILWAYS (DB) GERMANY 1974

With France and Luxembourg as neighbours, it is only sensible that Germany's cross-border trains should be worked by locomotives compatible with each country's electrification systems in order to avoid locomotive changing at border stations. It is therefore surprising that, for many years, Federal German Railways (DB) took relatively little advantage of this technically feasible facility. A class of 25 dual-voltage Bo-Bos operates from locations such as Frankfurt-am-Main to Strasbourg and Metz in France and also into Luxembourg from Koblenz.

**Federal German Railways earlier dual-voltage electric locomotives all had a characteristic exterior shape, including ribbed bodysides.**

**Type:** Bo-Bo mainline mixed-traffic dual-voltage electric
**Power:** 15,000V 16.667Hz AC and 25,000V AC 50Hz AC overhead line collection; 3200kW (4290hp); rheostatic braking; four DC traction motors
**Tractive effort:** 285kN (64,070lbf)
**Max. operating speed:** 160km/h (100mph)
**Weight:** 83 tonnes (182,275lb)
**Max. axle load:** Not known
**Overall length:** 17.94m (58ft 10in)
**Gauge:** 1435mm (4ft 8.5in)

## CLASS 250 EAST GERMAN RAILWAYS (DR) GERMANY 1974

The former *Deutsche Reichsbahn* class 250 electric freight locomotives are a further example of an East German electric locomotive class that was to find great favour in western Germany following reunification. Now classified by DB as '155' (there is already a class 150 electric freight class from the former DB), the '250s' were DR's principal electric freight locomotive type. As such, they worked all over East Germany (the German Democratic Republic) on electrified main lines on heavy freight loads.

They were among DR's first types to use thyristor electronic traction control and have a very high tractive effort. The rather austere locomotive bodies are liveried now in DB Cargo red.

After the collapse of heavy freight traffic due to economic conditions in the German Democratic Republic, surplus class 155s have found useful work in western Germany and can be seen in the Ruhr and Rhein areas and in the south around Nürnberg and Munich. The class is displacing earlier DB locomotives of classes 150 and 140.

**Type:** Co-Co mainline heavy freight electric
**Power:** 15,000V 16.67Hz AC overhead line collection; 5400kW (7240hp); thyristor control; six axle-hung traction motors
**Tractive effort:** 465kN (104,535lbf)
**Max. operating speed:** 125km/h (78mph)
**Weight:** 123 tonnes (270,120lb)
**Max. axle load:** Not known
**Overall length:** 19.6m (64ft 1in)

## CLASS WCAM1 INDIAN STATE RAILWAYS INDIA 1974

Indian railways class WCAM1 was the first dual-voltage model from CLW (Chittaranjan Locomotive Works), using mechanical parts from class WAM4. The DC and DC networks meet at Virar on the Bombay (Mumbai) to Ahmedabad line, and the WCAM1 locomotive is not normally found on other routes in India.

Class WCAM1s have separate AC and DC pantographs. Under the DC 1500V supply, class WCAM1 does not perform very well and uses series parallel resistance control. This has been limited in practice just to series connections, restricting the top speed running to just 75km/h (46.8mph). The 25kV supply is transformed and rectified to 1500V; however, again, the control system can cause difficulties, with practical running limited in each of the top notch of each series, series parallel and parallel connections. Fifty-three of these locomotives were produced, and they are numbered in the high 21000 series.

**Different examples of Indian paint finish can be seen in this shed view. Mumbai was the operating centre of this rugged but not particularly driver-friendly class.**

**Type:** Co-Co multi purpose dual voltage
**Power:** AC 2715kW (3689hp); DC 2185kW (2969hp)
**Supply:** 25 kV 50Hz AC and 1500 V DC
**Tractive effort:** AC 332kN (74700lbf) DC 277kN (62325lbf)
**Max. operating speed:** AC 110km/h (68.8mph) DC 75km/h (46.8mph)
**Weight:** 113 tonnes (249,165lb)
**Max. axle load:** 19 tonnes (41,895lb)
**Overall length:** 20.95m (68ft 4in)
**Gauge:** 1676mm (5ft 6in)

## CP CLASS 2601 PORTUGUESE RAILWAYS PORTUGAL 1974

**Type:** B-B mainline mixed-traffic electric
**Power:** 25,000V 50Hz AC overhead line collection; 2940kW (3940hp); tap-changer control; two frame-mounted monomotor DC traction motors
**Tractive effort:** 205kN (64,200lbf) passenger gearing; 245kN (55,000lbf) freight gearing
**Max. operating speed:** 160km/h (100mph) passenger gearing; 100km/h (62mph) freight gearing
**Weight:** 78 tonnes (171,295lb)
**Max. axle load:** Not known
**Overall length:** 17.5m (57ft 5in)
**Gauge:** 1668mm (5ft 6in)

French visitors to Portugal must feel at home when confronted with CP's principal electric locomotive class of the 1970s. These Alsthom-designed locomotives are very similar to SNCF's class BB15000 in France. They have the same monomotor layout, in CP's case with changeable gear ratios for passenger and freight working. The class 2601 locomotives even have the same exterior design, with forward-leaning cab windscreens. Twelve were built in France, the remainder in Portugal by Sorefame. The locomotives operate express passenger trains throughout the electrified network in Portugal. They see some freight service though this tends to be the preserve of the more modern class 5600 Bo-Bos. Portugal's general locomotive livery is orange with white diagonal stripes on cab fronts.

**The class 2601 B-Bs have worked trains such as the Sud Express, as well as the Alfa expresses between Lisbon and Porto. These machines are painted orange with white warning stripes.**

## ER200 14-CAR SET RUSSIAN RAILWAYS RUSSIA 1974

Intended for use on the Moscow to Leningrad (St Petersburg) route, ER200 started design work as long ago as 1965. The prototype set was built from 1972, but by 1990 had proved unreliable in service. The full trains were intended to be 14 cars, each of two driving trailers and 12 motor coaches, with the high installed power useful for accelerating between speed checks and numerous freights.

**Type:** Express EMU
**Power:** 960kW (1304hp) per motor coach
**Supply:** 3000V DC
**Tractive effort:** not applicable
**Max. operating speed:** 200km/h (125mph)
**Weight:** 58 tonnes (127,890lb) motor; 48 tonnes (105,840lb) trailer
**Max. axle load:** 14.5 tonnes (31,973lb) motor
**Overall length:** 26.5m (86ft 6in) per car
**Gauge:** 1524mm (5ft)

## CLASS 350 SLOVAK RAILWAYS (ZSR) SLOVAKIA 1974

Known as 'gorillas' from their external styling, the two ES499.0 prototypes were the first dual-voltage machines for Czechoslovak Railways. Eighteen more followed in 1976 with those in service passing to ZSR. No. 350001 has been modified for 160km/h (100mph) operation, and the rest of the class are likely to follow.

**Type:** Bo-Bo express passenger
**Power:** 4000kW (5435hp)
**Supply:** 25kV 50Hz AC or 3000V DC
**Tractive effort:** 210kN (47250lbf)
**Max. operating speed:** 140 or 160km/h (87.5 or 100mph)
**Weight:** 89 tonnes (196,245lb)
**Max. axle load:** 22.5 tonnes (49,613lb)
**Overall length:** 16.74m (54ft 8in)
**Gauge:** 1435mm (4ft 8.5in)

## GE E60 AMTRAK USA 1974

In 1972, Amtrak ordered the first of 26 new electrics from General Electric which were intended replacements for Amtrak's inherited GG1 fleet. The new locomotives were designed for high-speed passenger service and planned for 192km/h (120mph) operation. Two varieties were delivered between 1974 and 1975: seven E60CPs which featured a steam generator to provide heat for older passenger stock and 19 E60CHs that used headend power for modern passenger stock such as Amtrak's Budd-built Amfleet cars. Problems with the E60's ability to track at high speeds limited the locomotives to just 137km/h (85mph), forcing Amtrak to look overseas for a practical high-speed electric. In the 1980s, Amtrak sold many of its E60s, yet some have remained on its roster and are still used (in 2002) for heavy long-distance trains.

**Type:** Co-Co passenger electric
**Power:** Alternating current: 12.5 at 25Hz; and 25kV at 60Hz
**Tractive effort:** 334kN (75,000lbf) to 364.4kN (82,000lbf)
**Max. operating speed:** 137km/h (85mph)
**Weight:** 176 tonnes (387,900lb)
**Overall length:** 21.717m (71ft 3in)
**Max. axle load:** 29 tonnes (64,650lb)
**Gauge:** 1435mm (4ft 8in)

**Although largely supplanted by AEM-7s after 1981, a few of Amtrak's General Electric-built E60 electrics remain in passenger service on the Northeast Corridor. They are often used to haul heavy long-distance trains.**

## CLASS 20 CO-CO BELGIAN NATIONAL RAILWAYS (SNCB) BELGIUM 1975

**In their last years, the SNCB class 20 locomotives are often used for carriage shunting at Brussels Midi, as well as on freights from Antwerpen.**

The 25 class 20 locomotives were built in Belgium between 1975 and 1977. They were SNCB's most powerful class until the arrival of class 13 in 1997. The 20s operated passenger trains for two decades on the Brussels–Luxembourg axis, as well as freight out of the port of Antwerpen (Anvers or Antwerp). Not always reliable technically, they have recently been drafted to less prominent duties. They have always been painted dark green.

**Type:** Co-Co mainline mixed-traffic electric
**Power:** 3000V DC overhead line collection; 5200kW (6970hp); thyristor control; rheostatic braking; six frame-mounted DC traction motors
**Tractive effort:** 314kN (70,590lbf)
**Max. operating speed:** 160km/h (100mph)
**Weight:** 110 tonnes (241,570lb)
**Max. axle load:** Not known
**Overall length:** 19.5m (63ft 8in)
**Gauge:** 1435mm (4ft 6in)

## CLASS V63 HUNGARIAN STATE RAILWAYS (MÁV) HUNGARY 1975

Known locally as '*hifi*' because of the stacked appearance of the electronic control racks, or '*gigant*', due to its size and power, the Hungarian class V63 was the most powerful locomotive operated by the MÁV until the 'Taurus' was introduced in 2002.

Production of class V63 started in 1980 leading to a total of 56 built by Ganz Mavag. These locomotives were mainly deployed east of Budapest on international freight and passenger traffic, where some workings take them to Bratislava in Slovakia.

The V63s use thyristor controls of Ganz's own development line – the 2575kW (3500hp) rheostatic brake is also under thyristor control. Eleven units of the class have been upgraded to 160km/h (100mph) to become class V63.1, and 60 locomotives in all are in current traffic.

**Class V63.021 is pictured below. While it is true that the MÁV electric livery has changed little in 20 years, its application to the long, plain but well-balanced lines of this big engine is nonetheless very effective.**

**Type:** Co-Co express passenger and heavy freight
**Power:** 3680kW (5000hp)
**Supply:** 25kV 50Hz AC
**Tractive effort:** 442kN (99,450lbf)
**Max. operating speed:** 120 to 160km/h (75 or 100mph)
**Weight:** 116 tonnes (255,780lb)
**Max. axle load:** 19.5 tonnes (42,998lb)
**Overall length:** 19.54m (63ft 9in)
**Gauge:** 1435mm (4ft 8.5in)

## CLASS E656 BO-BO-BO STATE RAILWAYS (FS) ITALY 1975

**Type:** Bo-Bo-Bo heavy freight and express passenger
**Power:** 4800kW (6522hp)
**Supply:** 3000V DC
**Tractive effort:** 131kN (29500lbf) at 103km/h (64mph)
**Max. operating speed:** 160km/h (100mph)
**Weight:** 120 tonnes (264,600lb)
**Max. axle load:** 20 tonnes (44,100lb)
**Overall length:** 18.29m (59ft 8in)
**Gauge:** 1435mm (4ft 8.5in)

Known as '*caimano*', or 'alligator', the class E656 represents the final development of traditional DC motored articulated body electric locomotives by FS (Italian state railways), and it is also the last three-bogie design. This mechanical arrangement originated from the E625 prototypes of 1927 introduced with the very first Italian 3000V DC electrified route between Foggia and Benevento. Previous mainline electrification used a two contact wire three-phase system with synchronous traction motor locomotive types such as the rigid-framed E550 and E331. The DC Bo-Bo-Bo design

**On 5 September 1993, E 656.061 arrives at Monfalcone with a Trieste–Udine service. The long grades on this line require powerful haulage.**

layout was built in large numbers, from the E626 production batch derived from the E625 prototypes (448 total built), through E636 (469 built), E645, E646 to E656 (211 built). The three two-axle bogie layout was demanded by the sharply curved nature of parts of the FS network, assisting with guiding the locomotives through curves while reducing rail and wheel wear and weight transfer difficulties on graded mountain lines. Italian and Swiss railways faced similar grades and curves on their Alpine routes, with higher speed curvature being a particular difficulty. The DC electrification system of FS did not need the bulky transformer required by the AC system in Switzerland, where (because of its weight) the transformer had to occupy a central position in the locomotive body, precluding articulation. Italian engineers had no such restrictions in their machines, hence the attraction of this design. In class E656, the six fully suspended, DC, series-wound traction motors are double-armature machines geared to a common hollow-axle drive arrangement. Double-armature traction motors were relatively outdated technology, but their use allowed more flexible permutations of traction motor connections and economical running notches. Motor connections are possible in the following formats:
(i) all 12 motors in series with five weak field stages
(ii) series grouping of six plus six, and five weak field stages
(iii) parallel grouping of four plus four plus four, with three stages of field weakening
(iv) a further parallel grouping of three plus three plus three plus three, also with three weak field stages.

**With the massive control tower in the background, a Class E656 backs into its platform at Milan Centrale to take up its train. The articulated electric locomotive has a long use history of use on the FS system.**

Constructed by Caseralta, Casertane, Reggianne, Sofer and TIBB with electrical equipment from Ansaldo, Asgen, Ercole, Marelli, Italtrafo and TIBB, the E656 perhaps represents one of the ultimate stages of straight DC electric traction designs. In later production batches, design changes introduced electronics such as static inverters (replacing rotating motor generator sets for auxiliary functions). Division of FS into business sectors has divided the 458-strong class E656 between express passenger services (154 locomotives), regional passenger (77), regional passenger equipped for push-pull working (58), and freight (169). In recent years, E656 has been reduced to 150km/h (93.8mph) maximum speed and is no longer used on fast intercity passenger trains, although it is still used on heavier, slower duties.

## PLAN Y0 'SPRINTER' CITY PENDEL EMU NETHERLANDS RAILWAYS (NS) NL 1975

This high-performance EMU for high-density traffic was initially deployed by NS on the Zoetermeer Stadslijn in Den Haag. Talbot-built with Oerlikon electrics, the two-car set's 'Sprinter' name derives from its high acceleration. In the eight class Y0 and 15 Y1 sets, 1280kW (1739hp) is distributed over all axles. From 1994, they were modified as 'Spitspendel' (peak shuttle), with fewer seats but increased standing room. Later they were further adapted for short distance work.

**Type:** High-density suburban EMU
**Power:** 1280kW (1739hp) all axles motored
**Supply:** 1500V DC
**Tractive effort:** N/A
**Max. operating speed:** 125km/h (78.1mph)
**Weight:** 105 tonnes (231,525lb) two cars
**Max. axle load:** 13.2 tonnes (29,106lb)
**Overall length:** 52.22m (170ft 5in)
**Gauge:** 1435mm (4ft 8.5in)

## CLASS 363 SLOVENIAN RAILWAYS SLOVENIA 1975

Slovenian railways class 363 have typical French-designed negative-raked cabs similar to SNCF class CC6500. Known as 'Brigitte', they have two-speed monomotor bogies with separate gearing for freight or passenger duties. Significant freight from the Adriatic sea port of Koper is shifted by class 363, with most trains requiring a banker locomotive up the heavy gradients from sea level. Intercity passenger services (centred on Ljubljana) are also hauled by class 363.

**Type:** Co-Co electric
**Power:** 2750kW (3736hp)
**Supply:** 3000V DC
**Tractive effort:** 131kN (29475lbf)
**Max. operating speed:** 125km/h (75mph)
**Weight:** 114 tonnes (251,370lb)
**Max. axle load:** 19 tonnes (41,895lb)
**Overall length:** 20.19m (65ft 11in)
**Gauge:** 1435mm (4ft 8.5in)

## CLASS RC4 STATE RAILWAYS (SJ) SWEDEN 1975

**Type:** Bo-Bo mainline mixed-traffic electric
**Power:** 15,000V 16.67Hz AC overhead line collection; 3600kW (4825hp); thyristor control; four DC traction motors
**Tractive effort:** 290kN (65,200lbf)
**Max. operating speed:** 135km/h (84mph)
**Weight:** 78 tonnes (171,295lb)
**Max axle load:** Not known
**Overall length:** 15.52m (50ft 11in)
**Gauge:** 1435mm (4ft 8.5in)

Possibly the most successful electric locomotive family in northern Europe, the Rc4 is one of a group of six classifications of basically identical locomotives that have different traffic characteristics. Over 360 of classes Rc1 to Rc6 were built from 1975, of which currently 130 are class Rc4. These straightforward Bo-Bos work almost all passenger and freight trains throughout Sweden, the Rc4 variety being specifically thyristor-controlled mixed-traffic machines.

Visually distinctive by virtue of their ribbed bodysides, these locomotives have also been an export success for Sweden. Ten were ordered by ÖBB in Austria (these have lately been sold to a Swedish railway), there are some in the United States, and a large number were built under licence in the former Yugoslavia, some of which are in use now in Serbia, Croatia and Macedonia. Romania has 130, and a group of Croatian locomotives has been sent on loan to Turkish State Railways. These last are all 25kV locomotives.

**This is a SJ class Rc2 Bo-Bo, the basis for many export locomotives and a higher speed version of which became class Rc4.**

**This Swedish State Railways Rc4 is seen at the head of a typical Swedish passenger train of ribbed-sided stock. Note the smart orange livery, which has recently been replaced by light blue.**

## CLASS 22200 FRENCH NATIONAL RAILWAYS (SNCF) FRANCE 1976

France's electrified networks at 1500V and 25kV make it essential that through trains have dual-voltage traction. The 205 locomotives of class 22200 are a dual-voltage version of classes BB7200 and BB15000 (15000 + 7200 = 22200). In effect, this is a chopper-controlled DC locomotive carrying a transformer and solid state rectifiers that are switched into use when under 25kV AC wires.

**Several of SCNF's class BB22200 were modified for use through the Channel Tunnel before BR's own class 92 locomotive had become available.**

**Type:** B-B mixed-traffic dual-voltage electric locomotive
**Power:** 1500V DC and 25,000V 50Hz AC overhead line collection; 4360kW (5845bhp); AC transformer/rectification; DC chopper control; two DC frame mounted monomotor traction motors
**Tractive effort:** 294kN (66,095lbf)
**Max. operating speed:** 160km/h (100mph)
**Weight:** 90 tonnes (197,645lb)
**Max axle load:** Not known
**Overall length:** 17.48m (57ft 4in)
**Gauge:** 1435mm (4ft 8.5in)

## CLASS BB7200 FRENCH NATIONAL RAILWAYS (SNCF) FRANCE 1976

These 240 modern mixed-traffic electrics are used on DC electrified main lines, particularly in southeast France. Although of monomotor type, they do not have a gear change mechanism. The electronically controlled traction system sets up automatically the required characteristics for fast passenger or heavy freight work. There is an AC version (class BB15000), as well as a dual-voltage version (class BB22200).

**Type:** B-B mainline mixed-traffic electric locomotive
**Power:** 1500V DC overhead line collection; 4040kW (5415hp); DC chopper control; two DC frame mounted traction motors
**Tractive effort:** 288kN (64,745lbf)
**Max. operating speed:** 160 or 200km/h (100 or 125mph)
**Weight:** 84 tonnes (184,470lb)
**Max axle load:** Not known
**Overall length:** 17.48m (57ft 4in)

## ETR 401 STATE RAILWAYS (FS) ITALY 1976

The concept of the tilting train began in the late 1960s, with work in Great Britain, Canada, Italy, Japan and Sweden. The curves on many lines meant that there were frequent speed restrictions, which reduced the average speed of trains even when they were capable of high speeds. The solution was to incorporate a tilting mechanism in the bogies, so that as the train entered a curve, the carriage bodies were automatically tilted inwards, enabling the train to run 35–45 per

**Standing at platform 1 of Rome Termini, ETR 401 forms the 15.20 crosscountry express to Ancona, on 19 April 1978. The set has recently been refurbished as a historic unit.**

cent faster in safety and with no discomfort to passengers. The British APT, 'Advanced Passenger Train', was extensively tested during the 1980s and ran on relief services between London and Glasgow between 1983 and 1985. But design problems persisted and, in the end, through lack of capital to invest in the project, it was abandoned. The first prototype of an Italian tilting train, Y 0160-71-99, a single-unit vehicle, was tested on the twisting Trofarello–Asti line in Piedmont and also on the high-speed Rome–Naples main line. It led to the building of ETR 401, a four-car set. After many tests, this train was acquired by the FS and, from 1976, was put into revenue-earning service on the Rome–Naples route as a luxury high-speed express.

First-class only, it seated 120 passengers, and the third car was fitted out as a bar-restaurant. Despite the success of this unit, it remained a one-off, and development of the concept did not really get under way until 1985. Britain, having abandoned the APT, sold its tilting technology to Italy. The traction equipment used on ETR 401 was now wholly redesigned. In 1988, a new train, ETR 450, was put into service, incorporating the work of both Italian and British designers. While ETR 401 had required a gyroscope and accelerometer to be fitted to every bogie, with consequent expense and risk of individual units failing to function, ETR 450 had these fitted only on the end bogies of the train. On all other bogies, the tilt mechanism operated automatically, in simultaneous conjunction with the master units.

The ETR 401 train has recently been refurbished, and work is also going ahead in Britain to restore the APT-P train.

**Type:** Four-car tilting electric train
**Power:** N/A
**Tractive effort:** 250kN (56,215lbf)
**Max. operating speed:** 171km/h (106mph)
**Total weight:** not known
**Max. axle load:** N/A
**Overall length:** 26.9m (88ft 4in)
**Builder:** FIAT, Turin

## Class E1100 Co-Co Moroccan Railways — Morocco 1977

A significant breakthrough by Hitachi, these 22 machines supplied to Morocco were the first from the Japanese locomotive industry to the African continent. Traditional builders were from France or the United Kingdom due to the region's history and influence of those colonial powers. Algeria and Morocco had already broken the mould with electric locomotives from East Germany and Poland, respectively. When class E1100 was introduced, three-quarters of all freight tonne kilometres turned around phosphates traffic, which these machines were designed to meet. E1100 electric braking in the form of rheostats and low 100km/h (62.5mph) speed with correspondingly high tractive effort make these machines entirely appropriate for heavy mineral workings. The E1100s are similar mechanically to JNR class EF81.

**In the hinterland of Casablanca, E1115 heads a long train of modern phosphate wagons from the mining district to the sea coast.**

**Type:** Co-Co heavy mineral traffic
**Power:** 3000kW (4020hp)
**Supply:** 3000V DC
**Tractive effort:** 314kN (70650lbf)
**Max. operating speed:** 100km/h (62.1mph)
**Weight:** 120 tonnes (264,600lb)
**Max. axle load:** 20 tonnes (40500lb)
**Overall length:** 19.7m (64 ft 7in)
**Gauge:** 1435mm (4ft 8.5in)

## CLASS 150 BO-BO CZECHOSLOVAK RAILWAYS (CSD) CZECHOSLOVAKIA 1978

**Type:** Bo-Bo express passenger
**Power:** 4000kW (5435hp)
**Supply:** 3000V DC
**Tractive effort:** 150 - 138kN (31050lbf) at 101.2km/h (63.3mph); 151 - 123kN (27675lbf) at 113.9km/h (71.2mph)
**Max. operating speed:** 150 - 140km/h (87mph); 151 - 160km/h (100mph)
**Weight:** 82 tonnes (180,810lb)
**Max. axle load:** 20.5 tonnes (45,203lb)
**Overall length:** 16.74m (54ft 8in)
**Gauge:** 1435mm (4ft 8.5in)

**Above: Formerly class E.499 of the Czechoslovak Railways, and built by Skoda, it was developed from the famous class 140 of the 1950s.**

CD class 150 is a DC version of the dual-voltage class 350, but is externally identical and also known as '*gorila*'. Built by Skoda as CSD class E499.2, all 27 machines passed to Czech Railways (CD). They are used on heavier daytime and overnight passenger and mail trains on the Praha Olomouc Bohumin route, including EC trains towards Poland, and through to Kosice in eastern Slovakia on 'Kosican' and 'Odra' expresses.

Series conversion to 160km/h (100mph) has proved a rather protracted process, with only around a dozen treated by 2002; however, all class 150s are expected to be treated in time.

**Seen here in the standard two-tone livery applied to DC locomotives, the class 150 has had various colour schemes applied in the past. This one minimizes the visual effect of the side-screens.**

# Trains à Grande Vitesse (TGV) French National Railways (SNCF) France 1978

The fastest trains in the world operate in France and now a little beyond its borders. This came about from a genuine railway capacity problem. The Paris–Lyon–Méditerranée (PLM) main line from Paris through Dijon, Lyon and Avignon to Marseilles and the French Riviera had become severely pressed with heavy traffic. Future traffic growth needed additional tracks. The alternatives were to quadruple the PLM main line between Paris, Dijon and later Lyon, or construct a new railway on a different alignment. The latter alternative was agreed.

SNCF boldly specified that the new high-speed line, designed for an ultimate top speed of around 300km/h (187mph) (the *Ligne à Grande Vitesse*, or LGV, in French) would run from Paris through to Lyon with very few intermediate stations. Its curves were gentle, with large superelevation angles and with some vertical gradients steeper than 33 per cent (1 in 30).

The first group of production trains for the Paris–Lyon LGV were eight-coach articulated trains with a power car at each end. The power cars are streamlined, single-ended Bo-Bo electric locomotives with body-mounted electric motors driving the axles of the bogies through cardan shafts. The outer end bogies of each carriage rake also are driven, each by two motors. The trains were liveried in a striking bright orange colour only recently been supplanted by the grey-and-blue colours of later TGVs.

The Paris–Lyon TGV service's runaway success, which made a huge and seemingly permanent hole in airline carryings between the two cities, led to rapid expansion of

**Designed for very high speeds, the sharp lines of the front end of the original TGV trains also proved to be an excellent marketing image for the new fast services, attracting passengers to the service and cementing its success.**

**Each TGV Atlantique set consists of two power cars flanking 10 articulated carriages.**

TGV routes. The Atlantique scheme took TGVs westwards from Paris towards Le Mans and Nantes, with TGVs running on conventional railways as far as Brittany, Bordeaux and the Spanish border. These trains were 10-car sets with no motors on the carriages themselves, the milder gradients enabling two power cars to cope. TGV Atlantiques have a top speed of 300km/h (187mph). The Paris–SudEst sets were built for 280km/h (175mph); however, they have since been upgraded for the higher speed.

The LGV Nord route links Paris with Lille and the Channel Tunnel, and with Brussels in Belgium. For the Lille services, and for trains using the new links around Paris that join up the Nord, SudEst and Atlantique lines, the TGV Réseau series was produced (eight-car sets with two power cars). Some Réseau sets have the ability to run under not only the SNCF electrification voltages of 1500V DC and 25kV AC, but also Italy's 3000V DC. Others have an additional voltage of 15kV AC enabling them to operate to Swiss cities. Expansion of traffic on Paris–SudEst caused SNCF to order a fleet of double-deck TGVs, the only double-deck high-speed trains in the world.

A successful TGV service group is the Thalys scheme joining Paris with Brussels, Amsterdam and Köln (Cologne). The Thalys sets have a unique maroon-and-grey livery and have led to a dramatic increase in travel, particularly on the Paris–Brussels section. Other recent developments are new routes to the Mediterranean coast and soon to Strasbourg. The world rail speed record of 515km/h (322mph) is held by TGV Atlantique set No. 325. The following details refer to TGV SudEst sets.

**Type:** High-speed articulated electric trains
**Power (per train):** 1500V DC and 25,000V 50Hz AC overhead line collection; 6300kW (8445hp); AC transformer/rectification; 12 DC body-mounted traction motors
**Wheel arrangement:** Bo-Bo + Bo-2-2-2-2-2-2-2-Bo + Bo-Bo
**Max. operating speed:** 300km/h (187mph)
**Weight:** 65 tonnes (142,745lb) power car; 44 tonnes (96,625lb) end carriage; 28 tonnes (61,490lb) intermediate carriage
**Overall length:** 22.15m (72ft 8in) power car; 21.845m (71ft 8in) end carriage; 18.7m (61ft 4in) intermediate carriages
**Gauge:** 1435mm (4ft 8.5in)

**The great commercial success of the TGV trains has meant that traffic on the Paris–Lyon service is so buoyant that double-deck trains are needed to cope with the high demand.**

## CLASS 7E Co-Co SOUTH AFRICAN RAILWAYS (SAR) SOUTH AFRICA 1978

Thyristor technology class 7E were ordered by SAR for the important newly electrified 25kV route between Ermelo to Richards Bay, linking Transvaal coalfields with deep sea ports with heavy loads. Assembly was by UCW in South Africa with locally produced electrical equipment from Siemens and Brown Boveri. Further units are designated 7E2, with 67 and 64 each in traffic in 2002, all assigned to 'Coallink' traffic.

**Engine change: No. 7008 of class 7E is attached to the Trans-Karoo Express at Beaufort West, midpoint between Cape Town and De Aar, on 24 November 1988.**

**Type:** Co-Co heavy freight
**Power:** 3000kW (4020hp)
**Supply:** 25kV 50Hz AC
**Tractive effort:** 300kN (67400lbf) at 35km/h (21.8mph)
**Max. operating speed:** 100km/h (62.1mph)
**Weight:** 124 tonnes (273,420lb)
**Max. axle load:** 21 tonnes (46,305lb)
**Overall length:** 18.465m (60 ft 7in)
**Gauge:** 1067mm (3ft 6in)

## CLASS 9E Co-Co SOUTH AFRICAN RAILWAYS (SAR) SOUTH AFRICA 1978

The South African Iron & Steel Industrial Corporation (ISCOR) operated a 864 km (540mile) route moving iron ore between Sishen and Saldanha. The line is electrified at 50kV, reducing installation capital costs; however, as a result of this, the body height allowable is reduced to about two-thirds height at one end in order to give adequate clearances for the pantograph and equipment.

The traction motors of these locomotives are axle-hung, nose-suspended, separately excited, DC machines. Class 9E are single-ended, intended for routine operation of three units hauling a 20200-tonne (19,882-ton) train weight. Originally, 31 locomotives were ordered, followed by an additional six class 9E1 with certain differences of detail, and operations of the route were transferred from the Iron & Steel Industrial Corporation to South African Railways (later Sport).

**Type:** Co-Co heavy freight
**Power:** 3696kW (5021hp)
**Supply:** 50kV 50Hz AC
**Tractive effort:** 382kN (85,900lbf)
**Max. operating speed:** 90km/h (56.2mph)
**Weight:** 168 tonnes (370,440lb)
**Max. axle load:** 28 tonnes (61,740lb)
**Overall length:** 20.12m (65ft 8in)
**Gauge:** 1067mm (3ft 6in)

## AEM-7 AMTRAK USA 1979

**Seen at Washington Union Station in October 2001, Amtrak 918 wears a Spartan livery that reflects the change to the Acela name for North East Corridor services.**

By the late 1970s, Amtrak's venerable former Pennsylvania Railroad GG1 electrics were nearly worn out, and the GE E60s built to replace them had been deemed unsuitable for high-speed service. Amtrak needed a new electric for its New Haven–New York–Washington DC route and turned to European designs for a practical solution. It tested French and Swedish electrics and decided upon a variation of the Swedish Rc-4 built by ASEA. Amtrak's AEM-7s were built starting in 1979 by General Motor's Electro-Motive Division under licence from ASEA. The AEM-7 closely resembles its Swedish antecedent, but is a heavier locomotive and designed to operate much faster than the Rc-4. Top speed on the North East Corridor was 200km/h (125mph).

**Type:** Bo-Bo, high-speed electric locomotive
**Power:** AC - 12.5V at 25Hz; 25kV at 60Hz
**Tractive effort:** 237kW (53,300lbf)
**Max. operating speed:** 200km/h (125mph)
**Weight:** 90.47 tonnes (199,500lb)
**Overall length:** 15.583m (51ft 2in)
**Max. axle load:** 22.6 tonnes (49,875lb)
**Gauge:** 1435mm (4ft 8.5in)

**Amtrak's AEM-7s were derived from the Swedish Rc4. For two decades, these locomotives ruled Amtrak services on the North East Corridor. Today, they still run regularly between Boston, New York and Washington DC. Several suburban commuter railways have also bought AEM-7s.**

## CLASS 269 B-B SPANISH RAILWAYS (RENFE) SPAIN 1980

**Type:** B-B multipurpose
**Power:** 3100kW (4155hp)
**Supply:** 3000V DC
**Tractive effort:** Varies from highest gear 143kN (32175lbf ) to lowest gear 263kN (59175lbf)
**Max. operating speed:** Varies from 80km/h (50mph) low gear to 160km/h (100mph) high gear
**Weight:** 88 tonnes (194,040lb)
**Max. axle load:** 22 tonnes (48,510lb)
**Overall length:** 17.27m (56 ft 8in)
**Gauge:** 1676mm (5ft 6in)

Spanish Railways (RENFE) class 269 is a Japanese product built locally in Spain under Mitsubishi licence by CAF, with Westinghouse electrical parts. Class 269 features two gear monomotor bogies leading to several 'as built' versions of the class and several subsequent modifications in traffic. Original

**Uncompromisingly angular in outline, No. 269.236 sets off with a train of tank cars; a match-wagon has been placed between the the locomotive and the lead car.**

class 269.0 were 80/140km/h (50/87.5mph), class 269.2 100/160km/h (62.5/100mph) and 269.5 90/160km/h (56.2/100mph). They were deployed on freight, passenger and intermodal, and freight and intermodal duties, respectively. Further changes have created further subclasses 269.7 of original 269.2 geared for 120km/h (75mph) only for intermodal traffic, and 269.9 also from original class 269.2 fixed at 140km/h (87.5mph) for overnight passenger service. The latter changes have taken place for the business divisions, optimizing their respective fleets. Class 269 seems likely to remain Spain's default motive power for passenger and freight.

**On passenger service, No. 269.259, is seen here at Port Bou, frontier station on the Mediterranean side between Spain and France. A change of gauge still remains between the Iberian systems and the rest of the European network.**

## CLASS 21 AND 27 BELGIAN NATIONAL RAILWAYS (SNCB) BELGIUM 1981

These two classes, each consisting of 60 locomotives, are of identical exterior appearance and interior layout. Class 21 is a lower powered version of class 27. Whereas class 27s are used mainly on express passenger and heavy freight, class 21 tends towards more secondary passenger work and freights.

**Class 21 Bo-Bo No. 2120 is seen on a typical duty with type M2 push-pull suburban carriages.**

**Type:** Bo-Bo mainline mixed-traffic electric locomotive
**Power:** 3000V DC overhead line collection; 4380kW (5870bhp) class 27, 3310kW (4435bhp) class 21; chopper control; four frame mounted DC traction motors
**Tractive effort:** 234kN (52,600lbf)
**Max. operating speed:** 160km/h (100mph)
**Weight:** 85 tonnes (186,665lb) class 27; 84 tonnes (184,470lb) class 21
**Max axle load:** Not known
**Overall length:** 18.65m (61ft 2in)
**Gauge:** 1435mm (4ft 6in)

## CLASS 1141/2 CROATIAN RAILWAYS (HZ) YUGOSLAVIA 1981

**Type:** Bo-Bo mixed-traffic
**Power:** 4080kW (5471hp)
**Supply:** 25kV 50Hz AC
**Tractive effort:** 132kN (29700lbf) at 103km/h (64.4mph)
**Max. operating speed:** 120 or 140km/h (75 or 87.4mph)
**Weight:** 78 to 82 tonnes (171,990lb to 180,810lb)
**Max. axle load:** 20.5 tonnes (45,203lb)
**Overall length:** 15.47m (50ft 5in)
**Gauge:** 1435mm (4ft 8.5in)

Croatian railways (HZ) class 1141 were former Yugoslavia railways (JZ) class 441. Several subclasses evolved, but the design is based on ASEA prototype Rb1, broadly similar to SJ class Rc1. Ordered from the 50Hz Group and constructed by SGP in Austria, the first 80 units were imported, followed by 35 kits for assembly in Yugoslavia by Rade Koncar, with production of wholly Zagreb-built machines from 1970 onwards. Variations to the original class 441 were subclasses 441.0 as the basic 120km/h (75mph) type; 441.3 with rheostatic braking and multiple working (26 built); 441.4 as class 441.3, but with flange lubrication (34 built); 441.5 class 441.0 with flange lubrication (32 built); 441.6 140km/h (87.5mph) (24 built. but some converted to class 441.7); and finally 441.7 as 441–6, but capable of multiple working (55 built). Following the disintegration of Yugoslavia, class 441 is today with various operators: Croatia railways (HZ, *Hrvatske Zeljeznice*) has 94; Bosnia (ZBH, *Zeljeznice Bosne i Hercegovine*) has 29; Macedonia (MZ, *Makedonske Zelenice*) has 8; and there are 96 with the remnant JZ *Zajednica Jugoslovenskih Zeleznica*.

**Pictured here at Zagreb's main station, class 1141.224 is seen heading an express. Following the collapse of the former state of Yugoslavia, locomotives of this class are distributed throughout several different countries.**

## NS CLASS 1600 NETHERLANDS RAILWAYS (NS) NETHERLANDS 1981

The very French-looking NS class 1600 B-Bs haul InterCity trains from Amsterdam to Heerlen and Maastricht, and local and commuter trains around the Randstad cities. The 58 locomotives of class 1600 are similar to the SNCF class BB7200 described in this book. The recent creation of operating company NS Reizigers has caused the last 25 of the fleet to be renumbered as class 1800.

**Type:** B-B mainline mixed-traffic electric locomotive
**Power:** 1500V dc overhead line collection; 4400kW (5900hp); dc chopper control; two dc frame mounted traction motors
**Tractive effort:** 294kN (66,095lbf)
**Max. operating speed:** 160km/h (100mph)
**Weight:** 83 tonnes (182,275lb)
**Max axle load:**
**Overall length:** 17.48m (57ft 4in)
**Gauge:** 1435mm (4ft 8.5in)

## CLASS 243 EAST GERMAN RAILWAYS (DR) GERMANY 1982

**This class 143 (formerly DR class 243) is working a push-pull S-Bahn suburban train in western Germany.**

The class 243 electric locomotive must be regarded as *Deutsche Reichsbahn*'s (DR) most successful electric locomotive. Totalling 647 locomotives, these thyristor-controlled machines have been in great demand in west Germany since reunification and have been absorbed by DB as its class 143. Operated as mixed-traffic locomotives, the 143s can be seen in all electrified areas of the former DR.

They are still common on express passenger trains, as well as lighter freights and on local suburban push-pull workings. Their usefulness has enabled DB to scrap many of its own postwar electric locomotives of classes 140 and 141.

**Type:** Bo-Bo mixed-traffic electric
**Power:** 15,000V 16.67Hz AC overhead line collection; 3540kW (4745hp); thyristor control; rheostatic braking; four DC traction motors with direct drive to axles
**Tractive effort:** 248kN (55,755lbf)
**Max. operating speed:** 120km/h (75mph)
**Weight:** 82 tonnes (180,080lb)
**Max. axle load:** Not known
**Overall length:** 16.64m (54ft 7in)
**Gauge:** 1435mm (4ft 8.5in)

## CLASS EM NEW ZEALAND RAILWAYS (NZR) — NEW ZEALAND 1982

Forty-four two-car units of this type were supplied to NZR in 1982–83, displacing locomotive haulage and older English Electric Dm-class units, which from then on were only used to supplement peak-hour services on the suburban lines around Wellington. The Em class ran on all lines except the Johnsonville branch. The two-car basic unit could seat 70 in the power car and 78 in the trailer. A new blue livery is currently being applied to the stock.

**Type:** Suburban multiple-unit two-car set
**Power:** Four 400kW (535hp) traction motors, driving each axle in the power car, supplied with 1500V DC via overhead catenary
**Tractive effort:** Not known
**Max. operating speed:** 100km/h (62mph)
**Total weight:** 35.9 tonnes (79,159lb)
**Max. axle load:** Not known
**Overall length:** 20.7m (67ft 11in)
**Builder:** Ganz-Mávag, Budapest, Hungary. Electrical equipment by GEC, England

**The deep front window settings and the slightly recessed doors are hallmarks of the Em design. As on some other systems, the livery has sometimes been replaced by overall advertising.**

## CLASS 250 C-C SPANISH RAILWAYS (RENFE) — SPAIN 1982

Spanish Railways Red Naçional de los Ferrocarriles Españoles (RENFE) class 250 are an unusual amalgam of German design and construction, running on French-inspired monomotor bogies. Built by Krauss Maffei and CAF with Brown Boveri electrical parts, the last five built form class 250.6 with DC chopper controls, reflecting the heavy weight of early power electronics systems.

**Type:** C-C electric
**Power:** 4600kW (6169hp)
**Supply:** 3000V DC
**Tractive effort:** Low gear 316kN (71,100lbf); high gear 197kN (44,325lbf)
**Max. operating speed:** Low gear 100km/h (62.1mph); high gear 160km/h (100mph)
**Weight:** 124 or 130 tonnes (273,420lb or 286,650lb)
**Max. axle load:** 22 tonnes (48,510lb)
**Overall length:** 20m (65ft 3in)
**Gauge:** 1668mm (5ft 6in)

## CLASS 251 B-B-B SPANISH RAILWAYS (RENFE) SPAIN 1982

Thirty of these six-axle three-bogie locomotives were built to a similar design to Japanese railways class EF66 by Mitsubishi CAF Macosa Westinghouse consortium. At one time this class could be found on heavy international and overnight passenger work, but today RENFE has assigned these unmistakeable locomotives to cargo, where they operate in the lower speed 100km/h (62mph) higher tractive effort gear.

**Type:** B-B-B freight
**Power:** 4650kW (6236hp)
**Supply:** 3000V DC
**Tractive effort:** Low gear 349kN (78,525lbf); high gear 216kN (48,600lbf)
**Max. operating speed:** Low gear 100km/h (62.1mph); high gear 160km/h (100mph)
**Weight:** 138 tonnes (304,290lb)
**Max. axle load:** 23 tonnes (50,715lb)
**Overall length:** 20.7m (67ft 6in)
**Gauge:** 1668mm (5ft 6in)

**In its days as an express passenger locomotive, a class 251 heads a Talgo rake of low-profile carriages near Almagro, on the Madrid to Cadiz line.**

## CLASS V46 BO-BO HUNGARIAN STATE RAILWAYS (MÁV) HUNGARY 1983

Manufactured by Ganz-MÁVAG between 1983 and 1992, these 60 centre cab machines are used for passenger and freight shunting work, empty passenger stock movements and light freight work across the MÁV electrified network.

**Here, a class V46.023 engages in moving empty coaching stock on 28 March 1994. The locos big windows allow for good all-round vision when carrying out shunting work.**

**Type:** Bo-Bo
**Power:** 820kW (1114hp)
**Supply:** 25kV 50Hz AC
**Tractive effort:** 153kN (34425lbf) at 71km/h (44.4mph)
**Max. operating speed:** 80km/h (50mph)
**Weight:** 80 tonnes (176,400lb)
**Max. axle load:** 20 tonnes (44,100lb)
**Overall length:** 14.4m (47ft)
**Gauge:** 1435mm (4ft 8.5in)

## SJ CLASS X10 STATE RAILWAYS (SJ) SWEDEN 1983

Being largely electrified, Sweden's local rail services require use of many electric multiple units (EMUs), particularly around major cities such as Stockholm, Göteborg, Västerås and Malmö. SJ has over 100 of these modern two-car units. There are also around 80 units in the hands of private operators which include those around Stockholm and Malmö. They are basically short distance commuter trains with minimal facilities. More advanced versions exist as classes X11 to X14 for longer-distance routes. These have more spacious seating, toilets and fewer entrance doors.

**Many of Sweden's State Railways SJ class X10 suburban electric multiple units are working services that are supported financially by local authorities. These authorities usually insist on their own colours being applied to the trains in their particular areas, as seen in the photograph below.**

**Type:** Two-car electric multiple unit suburban trains
**Power:** 15,000V 16.67Hz AC overhead line collection; 1280kW (1715hp); axle-mounted traction motors
**Max. operating speed:** 140km/h (87mph)
**Weight per vehicle:** Not known
**Overall length:** Not known
**Gauge:** 1435mm (4ft 8.5in)

## SKODA 27E BO-BO-BO CZECHOSLOVAK RAILWAYS (CSD) CZECHOSLOVAKIA 1984

Skoda 27E is a large, special-purpose locomotive for open cast mining operations in the huge Czech brown coal workings in northwest Bohemia. The city of Most was physically relocated in the 1970s to make way for these extensive mines on which the former communist economy depended for coal-fired power generation. The 27E is a robust three-section unit used over temporary rails on a soft base, where tracks are moved as mining progresses. Equipped with slow speed controls for 0.5 to 3km/h (0.25 to 1.9mph) loading operations directly under dragline excavators, top loading wagons require locomotives to have four roof-mounted side collectors where the supply contact wire is displaced. Conventional pantographs are carried for normal running. Water spray gear and large intake air filters are standard in the dusty environment. Ninety units dating from 1984 to 1989 are used by mining concerns Mostecká uhelná spolecnost and Sokolovská uhelná around Most and Sokolov.

**Type:** Bo+Bo+Bo special purpose mines
**Power:** 2520kW (3424hp)
**Supply:** 1500V DC
**Tractive effort:** 314kN (70650lbf) at 28.7km/h (17.9mph)
**Max. operating speed:** 65km/h (40.6mph)
**Weight:** 180 tonnes (396,900lb)
**Max. axle load:** 30 tonnes (66,150lb)
**Overall length:** 21.56m (70ft 4in)
**Gauge:** 1435mm (4ft 8.5in)

## CLASS 163 BO-BO CZECHOSLOVAK RAILWAYS (CSD) CZECHOSLOVAKIA 1984

Known collectively as '*persching*' or 'missile', Czech and Slovak classes 162, 163, 263, 362 and 363 from Skoda share interchangeable components. Classes 163/263/363 are 120km/h (75mph) maximum speed; 162 and 362 are 140km/h (87.5mph). Class 162 and 163 are 3000V DC supply, 263 25kV 50Hz AC, 362 and 363 dual voltage. Production of the 120km/h (75mph) versions ran to 179 363s, 12 263s and 120 163s. The second 60 163s were victims of politics – neither CD nor ZSR was able to take them for financial reasons. Eventually CD took 40 and ZSR 11; nine were disposed of to Italy's Ferrovie Nord Milano (FNM). The 140km/h (87.5mph) 362001 appeared in 1990, while 60 class 162s were built the same year. Initially CD required more 140km/h (87.5mph) machines for the Praha Brno corridor when EuroCity services began in 1993–4, so a bogie exchange between seven 363s and 162s created 140km/h (87.5mph) 362s and 120km/h (75mph) 163.2s. ZSR followed suit similarly in 1999–2000.

**Type:** Bo-Bo universal traffic
**Power:** 3060kW (4158hp)
**Supply:** 3000V DC or 25kV 50Hz AC
**Tractive effort**: 209kN (47025lbf)
**Max. operating speed:** 120 or 140km/h (75 or 87.5mph)
**Weight:** 85 to 87 tonnes (187,425lb)
**Max. axle load:** 22 tonnes (48,510lb)
**Overall length:** 16.8m (55ft 2in)
**Gauge:** 1435mm (4ft 8.5in)

**In CD livery, a class 163 nears Prague with a passenger train. Although designated for universal traffic, they are usually employed on passenger service.**

# RBDe 560 NPZ TRAIN SWISS FEDERAL RAILWAYS (SBB) SWITZERLAND 1984

The *Pendelzug*, or shuttle train – a three- or four-car unit with power car and driving trailer at opposite ends – was an established concept in Switzerland and Germany; the NPZ was the *Neue Pendelzug*, an up-to-the-minute version. Four prototype trains were tested from 1981 on the Thun–Berne and Fribourg–Biel lines. Between 1984 and 1996, 132 sets were built, and they ran on all divisions of the Swiss Federal Railways (SBB).

Six sets were adapted to run under the French 25kV catenary, as well as on the Swiss system, forming Regio runner services across the border between Basel and Mulhouse. These were classed as RBDe 562.

**An SBB *Pendelzug* unit stops in Rothenburg station on its way to Sempach, on 7 May 1999. The influence of modern European tram or streetcar design is evident in the construction of these sets.**

**Type:** Interurban multiple-unit train
**Power:** 1650kW (2211hp) 15kV 16.67Hz
**Tractive effort:** 166kN (37,326lb)
**Max. operating speed:** 140km/h (87mph)
**Total weight:** 70 tonnes (154,350lb)
**Max. axle load:** Not known
**Overall length:** Not known
**Builder:** Not known

## CLASS 11 INTERCITY — BELGIUM/NETHERLANDS 1985

**The SNCB locomotives and NS carriages on the Brussels–Antwerp–Amsterdam push-pull trains are liveried in a smart maroon-and-yellow style.**

For the hourly push-pull InterCity trains between Amsterdam and Brussels via Antwerp. NS provide the rolling stock and SNCB provide the locomotives. Both are liveried in the same smart maroon-and-yellow style. The class 11 locomotives are very similar to SNCB class 21 but have a lower top speed and are dedicated to the Brussels–Amsterdam duty cycle.

**Type:** Bo-Bo express passenger push-pull electric locomotive
**Power:** 1500V and 3000V DC overhead line collection; 3310kW (4435hp); chopper control; four frame mounted DC traction motors
**Tractive effort:** 234kN (52,600lbf)
**Max. operating speed:** 140km/h (87mph)
**Weight:** 85 tonnes (186,665lb)
**Max. axle load:** Not known
**Overall length:** 18.65m (61ft 2in)
**Gauge:** 1435 (4ft 8.5in)

## CLASS EP09 BO-BO POLISH STATE RAILWAYS (PKP) — POLAND 1985

One of the most impressive parts of the Polish State Railways (PKP) network is its high-speed line southwest from Warsaw to Katowice and Kraków. This line, along with the main line connecting Warsaw with the German capital, Berlin, runs some of Poland's fastest passenger trains. The EP09 electrics were introduced in 1985 and travel at speeds up to 160km/h (100mph). They were built by Pafawag and feature a more angular appearance than earlier electrics. Unlike most PKP electrics which are painted in a two-tone green livery, the EP09s are dressed in brown and yellow. They are used on trains such as the *Berolina* and *Varsovia* that run between Berlin and Warsaw via Poznan.

**Polish State Railways (PKP) EP09-014 catches the spring sun in April 2002 at the main station in Kraków. This type of electric is used to haul Poland's fastest passenger trains.**

**Type:** Bo-Bo electric, 3000V DC overhead
**Power:** 2920kW (3914hp)
**Tractive effort:** N/A
**Max. operating speed:** 160km/h (100mph)
**Weight:** N/A
**Overall length:** N/A
**Max. axle load:** N/A
**Gauge:** 1435mm (4ft 8.5in)

## CLASS 6E1 SOUTH AFRICAN RAILWAYS (SAR) SOUTH AFRICA 1985

**With combined tractive effort of 386kN available, class 6E1 Nos. 1324 and 1527 are lined up for freight duty in Germiston yard, outside Johannesburg, on 4 February 1978.**

SAR class 6E1 differs from the previous class 6E, with the air suspension system replaced by low-level inclined rods taking buffing and drawbar loads between body and wheels. The rods are clearly visible in pairs, appearing as a low V shape upwards from the bogie centres. No fewer than 859 6E1s were constructed with the number series E1226 to E1599 and E1601 to E2085. E1600 was a 25kV prototype development test loco. In 2001, Spoornet commenced a major rebuilding programme to convert 6E1 into a new class, 18E.

**Type:** Bo-Bo universal traffic
**Power:** 2252kW (3020hp) continuous
**Supply:** 3000V DC
**Tractive effort:** 193kN (43400lbf) at 41km/h (25.5mph)
**Max. operating speed:** 113km/h (70.6mph)
**Weight:** 89 tonnes (196,245lb)
**Max. axle load:** 22 tonnes (48,510lb)
**Overall length:** 15.495m (50ft 6in)
**Gauge:** 1067mm (3ft 6in)

## CLASS 3500/3600 BO-BO-BO QUEENSLAND RAILWAYS AUSTRALIA 1986

This was the third of three classes of Bo-Bo-Bo electric locomotives for freight traffic on Queensland Railways. Following the 3100/3200 and 3300/3400 classes, the 50-strong class 3500/3600 was built by Clyde and Walkers with ASEA electrical equipment and are in operation around the southern area of the coal field basin. Of the locomotive classes, 3200, 3400 and 3600 are the GE Harris Locotrol equipped versions of, respectively, 3100, 3300 and 3500. Locotrol allows helper locomotives to be distributed along the train remotely controlled from a single driver in the lead unit.

**Type:** Bo-Bo-Bo freight
**Power:** 2900kW (3870hp)
**Supply:** 25kV 50Hz AC
**Tractive effort:** 260kN (58500lbf) at 40km/h (25mph)
**Weight:** 110 tonnes (242,550lb)
**Max. axle load:** 18.5 tonnes (41,625lb)
**Overall length:** 20.02m (65ft 4in)
**Gauge:** 1067mm (3ft 6in)

**In an even more formidable combination of high power, Queensland Railways Nos 3546 and 3503 head for Gladstone, south of Rockhampton, with a train of loaded coal hoppers, on 16 March 1997.**

## CLASS 46 BULGARIAN STATE RAILWAYS (BDZ) BULGARIA 1986

The 45 members of Bulgaria State Railways (BDZ) class 46 were supplied by Electroputere, derived from the basic 060EA model and similar Romanian railways class 46. Actually, 46 machines were built, as the original 46.001 was severely damaged in an accident. A complete new structure was supplied for a second loco also numbered 46.001.

**Type:** Co-Co heavy freight and passenger
**Power:** 5100kW (7000hp)
**Supply:** 25kV 50Hz AC
**Tractive effort:** 280kN (63000lbf)
**Max. operating speed:** 130km/h (81.3mph)
**Weight:** 126 tonnes (277,830lb)
**Max. axle load:** 21 tonnes (46,305lb)
**Overall length:** 19.8m (64ft 8in)
**Gauge:** 1435mm (4ft 8.5in)

## CLASS 120.1 FEDERAL GERMAN RAILWAYS (DB) GERMANY 1987

Following operation of five prototypes, the class 120 production run came to 60 locomotives. These modern machines work mainly InterCity push-pull services all over Germany and are rated to operate at up to 200km/h (125mph). They are equipped to work over DB's new high-speed lines (*Neubaustrecke*), which shorten some journey times considerably. Use of push-pull for IC and EC (EuroCity) trains enables quick turnarounds at intermediate terminal stations such as Frankfurt-am-Main, Stuttgart and Leipzig. The class 120s also work some freights.

**This class 120 Bo-Bo seen at Cologne main station is working a push-pull InterCity train. The class is also programmed to work night freights.**

**Type:** Bo-Bo mainline mixed-traffic electric
**Power:** 15,000V 16.67Hz AC overhead line collection; 5600kW (7500hp); thyristor control; four DC traction motors
**Tractive effort:** 347kN (78,010lbf)
**Max. operating speed:** 200km/h (125mph)
**Weight:** 84tonnes (184,470lb)
**Max. axle load:** Not known
**Overall length:** 19.4m (63ft 8in)
**Gauge:** 1435mm (4ft 8.5in)

## CLASS E492 STATE RAILWAYS (FS) ITALY 1987

Mainland Italy's electrified railway is a substantial network of 3000V DC established through the 1950s and 1960s, some of which was converted from the earlier three-phase AC system. It was planned to electrify the island of Sardinia at 25kV 50Hz AC with 25 locomotives built in advance. The project was halted after six passenger class E492s had been built, and 19 mixed-traffic class E491s were stored.

**Type:** Bo-Bo passenger and freight
**Power:** E491 3130kW (4197hp); E492 – 3510kW
**Supply:** 25 kV 50Hz AC
**Tractive effort:** E491 – 228kN (51300lbf); E492 – 199kN (44775lbf)
**Max. operating speed:** E491 – 140km/h (87.8mph); E492 – 160km/h (100mph)
**Weight:** 86 tonnes (189,630lb)
**Max. axle load:** 21.5 tonnes (47,408lb)
**Overall length:** 17m (55ft 6in)
**Gauge:** 1435mm (4ft 8.5in)

## CLASS RE4/4, LATER 456 SCHWEIZERISCHE SÜDOSTBAHN (SOB) SWITZERLAND 1987

The new SOB company (formed in 2001) is a merger of the former *Schweizerische Südostbahn* (SOB) and *Bodensee Toggenburg Bahn* (BT) companies with 120km (75 miles) of standard-gauge track electrified at 15kV 16.67Hz AC. BT tracks made up the eastern section of the Romanshorn-Rapperswil-Lucerne route, and its six Re4/4 locomotives are used on through services running partly over SBB tracks, partly over former SOB lines, as well as BT's own route.

**Type:** Bo-Bo universal electric
**Power:** 3200kW (4348hp)
**Supply:** 15kV 16.67Hz AC
**Tractive effort:** 255kN (57,375lbf)
**Max. operating speed:** 130km/h (81.3mph)
**Weight:** 68 tonnes (149,940lb)
**Max. axle load:** 17 tonnes (37,485lb)
**Overall length:** 14.8m (48ft 4in)
**Gauge:** 1435mm (4ft 8.5in)

**An SBB class Re4/4 III of 1971 vintage moves an international freight through Bellinzona. The *Südostbahn* operated Re locomotives of this type.**

## CLASS RBDE4/4 SWISS FEDERAL RAILWAYS (SBB) SWITZERLAND 1987

Nicknamed 'Kolibri' because of their colourful livery, this series of power cars works local and regional services. They are termed *Neue Pendel Zug* (new push-pull train), or NPZ. Cabs are full width, and the cars are gangwayed at the inner ends. A pair of these vehicles can work as EMUs with several older, refurbished intermediate trailers. They can be seen on the north side of Lake Geneva and elsewhere.

**Type:** Stopping train electric multiple-unit power car
**Power:** 15,000V 16.67Hz AC overhead line collection; 1650kW (2210hp); electronic traction control; four bogie-mounted traction motors
**Tractive effort:** 166kN (37,318lbf)
**Max. operating speed:** 140km/h (75mph)
**Weight:** 70 tonnes (153,725lb)
**Max. axle load:** Not known
**Overall length:** 25m (82ft)

**SBB operates numerous electric railcars that can be formed with trailers into unit trains. The RBe4/4 series developed from this 1960s railcar into the modern RBDe4/4 described here.**

## E43000 BO-BO-BO TURKISH STATE RAILWAYS (TCDD) TURKEY 1987

TCDD, the state railway operator in Turkey, electrified the main Ankara to Istanbul line in stages between 1989 and 1994. The 45 class E43000 machines were built for this project by Tülomsas and Toshiba. These three-bogie machines are derived from typical Japanese designs and are equipped with two alternative drive gear ratios, allowing 120km/h (75mph) for passenger trains or a lower 90km/h (56.3mph) speed, but correspondingly higher tractive effort for freight work. E43000s require two pantographs for through operation along the whole length of the route due to two different electrical gauge clearances. In the early days of the 25kV electrification around Istanbul, a wide 1950mm (76.8in) pantograph head was adopted as it was thought crosswinds in the coastal region would deflect the contract wire. Later schemes used a smaller clearance and allowed a narrower, 1600mm (63in) head.

**Type:** Bo-Bo-Bo
**Power:** 3180kW (4320hp)
**Supply:** 25kV 50Hz AC
**Tractive effort:** 275kN (61875lbf) maximum
**Max. operating speed:** 120km/h (75mph)
**Weight:** 120 tonnes (264,600lb)
**Max. axle load:** 20 tonnes (44,100lb)
**Overall length:** 18.2m (59ft 8in)
**Gauge:** 1435mm (4ft 8.5in)

**The class 43000 looks impressively long in this station shot, although it was little longer than some Bo-Bo units, and many C-C and Co-Co locomotives exceeded it in length. A degree of sideplay was allowed in the middle bogie.**

## CLASS AM86 BELGIAN NATIONAL RAILWAYS (SNCB) BELGIUM 1988

Belgian railways operate regular interval EMU services on all passenger railways. A batch of 52 two-car sets introduced in 1988 have two unusual features. The cab front and bodyside cladding is all plastic, and the cab windscreens have a prominent frame that has earned these units the nickname 'snorkels'. The AM86s can be seen in Brussels, Antwerp, Charleroi, Hasselt and Leuven.

**The class AM96 units are clad in plastic instead of steel or aluminium, and are known as 'snorkels' as a result.**

**Type:** Two-car electric multiple-unit stopping trains
**Power:** 3000V DC overhead line collection; four axle-mounted 172kW (230bhp) traction motors under one power car
**Max. operating speed:** 120km/h (75mph)
**Weight:** 59 and 48 tonnes (129,570 and 105,410lb) per vehicle
**Max. axle load:**
**Overall length:** 26.4m (86ft 7in) per vehicle
**Gauge:** 1435mm (4ft 8.5in)

## CLASS BB26000 FRENCH NATIONAL RAILWAYS (SNCF) FRANCE 1988

**Type:** B-B mixed-traffic dual-voltage electric locomotive
**Power:** 1500V DC and 25,000V 50Hz AC overhead line collection; 5600kW (7500bhp); AC transformer/rectification to DC; three-phase conversion from DC; two AC synchronous traction frame mounted monomotor traction motors
**Tractive effort:** 320kN (71,940lbf)
**Max. operating speed:** 200km/h (125mph)
**Weight:** 9 1tonnes (199,845lb)
**Max. axle load:** Not known
**Overall length:** 17.48m (57ft 4in)
**Gauge:** 1435mm (4ft 8.5in)

In the late 1980s, SNCF took a technological step forwards with its general-purpose B-B 'Sybic' design. These were the first electric locomotives in France to use a three-phase traction system in which single-phase AC received from the pantograph was transformed as usual, then rectified to DC (except under 1500V DC catenary, when the DC current is used as supplied), then split electronically into three phases, enabling far simpler design, construction and maintenance of the traction motors.

The 234 BB26000s are used as mixed-traffic machines on most French main lines. By virtue of the design of their traction electronics, they have a versatile range of outputs and are as much at home on 200km/h (125mph) passenger expresses as on heavy freight trains.

**The class 26000 are France's first electric locomotives with three-phase AC electric motors, enabling much simpler maintenance.**

## BR CLASS 91 BRITISH RAIL GREAT BRITAIN 1988

As part of the electrification from London King's Cross to Edinburgh and Leeds, British Rail selected a push-pull formation for its high-speed trains. The BREL-built, GEC-equipped locomotives have a streamlined cab at one end, the other end having a blunt and smaller cab for infrequent movements. The trains were designed for a maximum of 225km/h (140mph) operation, but the required resignalling did not take place.

**The class 91 Bo-Bos have a novel form of traction motor drive wherein the motors are hung below the vehicle body and drive through cardan shafts.**

**Type:** Bo-Bo high-speed passenger electric
**Power:** 25,000V 50Hz AC overhead line collection; 4540kW (6085bhp); thyristor control; four DC underframe mounted traction motors driving through cardan shafts
**Tractive effort:** Not known
**Max. operating speed:** 200km/h (125mph)
**Weight:** 80 tonnes (184,470lb)
**Max. axle load:** Not known
**Overall length:** 19.405m (63ft 8in)
**Gauge:** 1435mm (4ft 8.5in)

## CLASS 442 BRITISH RAIL — GREAT BRITAIN 1988

When British Rail electrified the London Waterloo to Bournemouth main line in 1967, it provided a fleet of mainly rebuilt locomotive-hauled stock for its trains. It did, however, use new electric traction equipment. These became life-expired in less than 20 years.

Their replacements for the rebuilt locomotives were 24 new trains of high specification. The class 442 'Wessex Express' units are five-car buffet sets with BR mark 3 carriage bodies riding on air-sprung bogies. The electric traction equipment for the new class 442 was salvaged from the older Bournemouth sets, as it was more than capable of many decades of further use.

Introduction of these trains was paralleled by extension of electrification to Weymouth. Internally, they are comfortable if somewhat high-density in their second-class seat layout.

In the late 1990s, the class 442s were refurbished to an even higher standard, and the outside of the trains was painted in South West Trains' striking livery.

**In the red, white and blue livery of BR's Network SouthEast sector, a class 442 'Wessex Express' five-car electric multiple unit approaches Raynes Park on a morning train travelling from Weymouth to London Waterloo.**

**Type:** Five-car electric multiple unit express trains
**Power:** 750V DC conductor rail collection, camshaft motor control; four axle-mounted 300kW (400bhp) traction motors under one centrally located power car
**Tractive effort:** Not known
**Max. operating speed:** 160km/h (100mph)
**Weight per vehicle:** 35 to 54 tonnes (76,860 to 118,590lb)
**Overall length:** 23.15m (75ft 9in) outer cars; 23m (75ft 6in) inner cars
**Gauge:** 1435mm (4ft 8.5in)

## CLASS EF30 BO-BO-BO NEW ZEALAND RAILWAYS (NZR) — NEW ZEALAND 1988

Following the withdrawal of the EO (former EA) class from the Otira–Arthur's Pass route, the engines of this class became New Zealand's only electric locomotives. Twenty-two were supplied by Brush of Loughborough, England, in 1988–89, following the electrification of the 1065mm (3ft 6in) gauge 'Main Trunk' route between Auckland and Wellington to 25kV AC, which was completed in 1980.

The triple bogie format helped to spread the weight of these heavy locomotives. With a power output of 2984kW (4000hp), the EF30s are also the most powerful locomotives ever to have operated on New Zealand Railways.

Like all of New Zealand's locomotives, they do mixed-traffic duty, hauling the 'Overlander' express between the cities of Auckland and Wellington, but more often employed on express and bulk freight trains.

Originally referred to as EF30, they are nowadays more usually known simply as class EF. After the privatization of New Zealand Railways, the EFs continue to run under the new dispensation; however, the future of all long-distance passenger services is currently in jeopardy, and their work may be restricted to freight operations in the future.

Eighteen of the class remain in action; No. 30036 was written off following an accident at Oio, while three other locomotives are currently in store.

**Type:** Heavy mixed-traffic locomotive
**Power:** Six traction motors developing 2984kW (4000hp), supplied with current at 25kV AC, 50Hz, via overhead catenary
**Tractive effort:** Not known
**Max. operating speed:** 105km/h (65mph)
**Total weight:** 107 tonnes (235,935lb)
**Max. axle load:** 18 tonnes (39,690lb)
**Overall length:** 19.6m (64ft 4in)
**Builder:** Brush, Loughborough, Great Britain

## CLASS X2000 TILTING TRAINS STATE RAILWAYS (SJ) SWEDEN 1989

Sweden was one of the first two European countries seriously to adopt the tilting train concept. Its main lines are very curvaceous as a result of the country's topography, which is generally hilly with hard, rocky mountains and substructure. The principal cities are hundreds of kilometres apart, necessitating lengthy journey times for conventional trains. The cost of building new railway routes on alignments more suitable for high-speed trains would be prohibitive in Sweden in view of the extremely hard rock through which tunnels and cuttings would need to be built. Sweden is therefore an ideal country for the use of tilting train technology on its existing mainline routes.

The act of tilting the carriage body around its centre of gravity as a train rounds a curve in the track puts much less lateral centrifugal force on the passengers. They thus do not experience significant discomfort, even though the train is running through curves at speeds much higher than the speeds permitted for conventional trains. The higher curving speeds are still technically safe in that the train will not derail or turn over. Tilting is therefore purely to enable faster running round curves and yet to maintain passenger comfort at acceptable levels. The body tilt is achieved by hydraulic rams acting on a swing cradle between the body underframe and the bogie frame, reacting to impulses from sensing mechanisms on the leading bogie of the vehicle or on the carriage in front of it. A tilt angle of up to eight degrees from the vertical permits the train to run through a curve at a maximum speed 20 to 30 per cent faster than conventional trains without passenger discomfort. Tilting on the X2000s does not compensate for all lateral forces. It is understood that passengers expect to feel some lateral force as a train rounds a bend, and thus only 60 to 70 per cent of the lateral imbalance is compensated for by the body tilt angle at any time. Nonetheless, journey time reductions of 10 to 20 per cent are possible depending on the characteristics of each route.

The SJ class X2, later marketed as the 'X2000' trains, are seven-car units with a power car at one end and a passenger-carrying driving trailer at the other end. The power car in these formations does not carry passengers and does not tilt in curves. Thus the driver and any railway staff in this vehicle experience the full lateral forces of higher speed curving. All the trailer cars tilt, however, and on Swedish mainline tracks this is a more or less continuous feature of the journey. The well-controlled tilting of these trains is not intrusive to passengers, who experience a generally smooth and comfortable ride. Indeed, these trains are extremely comfortably furnished and are a credit to SJ and the manufacturers.

The 'X2000' trains are easily recognizable in service from their sharply pointed cab fronts, which give them a stylish appearance. Later batches have been built for less prestigious routes, and these include a number of four- or five-car units nominated as InterRegio units. The main lines on which the class X2000 series can be seen include Stockholm to Göteborg, Copenhagen (Denmark) through the Øresund link to Malmö and Stockholm, Stockholm to Sundsvall, Göteborg to Malmö, and Stockholm to Oslo (Norway).

**Type:** Seven-car tilting express passenger electric trains
**Power:** 15,000V 16.67Hz AC overhead line collection, thyristor control; four body mounted traction motors in power car only delivering 3260kW (4370hp) in total
**Tractive effort:** Not known
**Max. operating speed:** 200km/h (125mph)
**Weight per vehicle:** Not known
**Max. axle load:** Not known
**Overall length:** Not known
**Gauge:** 1435mm (4ft 8.5in)

**With the non-tilting power car leading, a X2000 train crosses a bridge on its way out of Stockholm Central on an fast InterCity working. The trailer vehicles on these excellent trains have tilt capability.**

## CLASS 1700 NETHERLANDS RAILWAYS (NS) NETHERLANDS 1990

The NS class 1700 B-Bs, introduced nine years after the successful Alsthom class 1600 on which they are based, are passenger locomotives used on InterCity trains throughout the Netherlands and on double-deck suburban push-pull trains in the Randstad (Amsterdam, Rotterdam and Utrecht) area. The 81 locomotives of this class are a thyristor-controlled development of the earlier design. They are liveried in NS overall yellow with dark grey roofs and underframes.

**Type:** B-B mainline passenger electric locomotive
**Power:** 1500V DC overhead line collection; 4400kW (5900hp); DC thyristor control; two DC frame-mounted traction motors
**Tractive effort:** 294kN (66,095lbf)
**Max. operating speed:** 160km/h (100mph)
**Weight:** 83 tonnes (182,275lb)
**Max. axle load:** Not known
**Overall length:** 17.48m (57ft 4in)
**Gauge:** 1435mm (4ft 8.5in)

**An NS class 1700 Alsthom B-B electric locomotive. This type is commonly used on InterCity trains on the north-south axis in the Netherlands.**

## CLASS RE450 SWISS FEDERAL RAILWAYS (SBB) SWITZERLAND 1990

Bucking the trend towards multiple units for suburban operations on the majority of systems, the 115-strong class 450 of SBB are dedicated to push-pull locomotives deployed exclusively on S-Bahn duties in the Zurich region. Passengers arriving at Zurich airport are likely to find themselves continuing their journey towards the city centre on a class 450. Generically of type Re4/4, these machines were to have been numbered in the 10500 series before SBB introduced the computer numbering system for new types. Three-phase asynchronous traction motors from ASEA Brown Boveri are mounted in SLM shifting axle bogies. Class 450 is interesting in that it is a single-ended design with the cabless end adjacent to the passenger cars, although otherwise working as a conventional push-pull train.

**On line S3 of the Zürich suburban network, hauling double-deck push-pull fitted stock, Class Re 450.005 4 emerges from the partly underground Stettbach station.**

**Type:** Bo-Bo push-pull suburban passenger
**Power:** 3200kW (4348hp)
**Supply:** 15kV 16.67Hz AC
**Tractive effort:** 240kN (54000lbf)
**Max. operating speed:** 130km/h (81.2mph)
**Weight:** 78 tonnes (171,990lb)
**Max. axle load:** 19.5 tonnes (42,998lb)
**Overall length:** 18.4m (60ft)
**Gauge:** 1435mm (4ft 8.5in)

## CLASS 470 CZECH RAILWAYS (CSD) — CZECHOSLOVAKIA 1991

This prototype design, a five-coach double-decker suburban electric multiple unit, first appeared in 1991. Class 470 has not gone into production, being superseded by the revised layout and improved technology of class 471. Two complete sets were constructed consisting of a class 470 Bo-Bo 1104kW (1500hp) single-deck motor coach sandwiching three class 070 double-deck trailers with a seating capacity of 602 (second class). These multiple units were ordered by the former Czechslovak state railway system CSD. The division to form the Czech Republic and Slovakia delayed the project, while rapid developments in electronic traction control systems quickly overtook class 470's design, with its heavy single-deck motor coaches and large equipment areas. All 10 cars were acquired by Czech Railways and remain in normal passenger service working on the Prague-Kolin-Pardubice route.

**Type:** Five-car double-deck prototype EMU
**Power:** 2208kW (300hp)
**Supply:** 3000V DC
**Tractive effort:** N/A
**Max. operating speed:** 120km/h (75mph)
**Weight:** 317 tonnes (698,985lb)
**Max. axle load:** 16 tonnes (35,280lb)
**Overall length:** 132m (430ft 8in)
**Gauge:** 1435mm (4ft 8.5in)

## CLASS 401 INTERCITY EXPRESS FEDERAL GERMAN RAILWAYS (DB) — GERMANY 1991

Germany's approach to higher speed passenger train operation has been cautiously determined, when compared with the fast expansion that occurred in Japan and France. Nonetheless, DB now has quite an extensive network of high-speed services. DB has consistently developed its mainline infrastructure to exploit the maximum possible speeds that can be operated on each section of each route. Thus conventional main lines are already equipped over many stretches for speeds of up to 200km/h (125mph). Classes 103 and 120 electric locomotives were built with this speed capacity, as were the newest machines of class 101 (see below).

When it became clear that journey times could not adequately be improved without radical measures, DB decided on a programme for construction of new railways to bypass main lines on which curves or heavy traffic prevented high-speed operation. These are called the *Neubaustrecke* (new build stretches). They cover sections between Mannheim and Stuttgart, a long one from Hannover south to Würzburg, and (built since German reunification) a fast line linking Berlin Spandau with Wolfsburg, approaching both Hannover and Braunschweig. A further high-speed route has just opened between Cologne and Frankfurt-am-Main. These lines are designed for trains running at 300km/h (187mph) or more.

The first InterCity Express (ICE) trains are numbered within the class 401 series. They consist of two power cars with 12 excellent passenger carriages between them. The power cars are of Bo-Bo arrangement with a streamlined front end and are gangwayed at the rear. The carriages each run on two bogies (that is, they do not repeat the articulation of the French TGVs), and the whole formation is able to operate at 280km/h (175mph). Internally, the trains are spaciously laid out, more so than most other European trains apart from perhaps those in Finland. The seats are comfortable, and second class is the equal of many railways' first class when it comes to comfort. The first-class section is extremely well equipped. The trains have interior maps that illuminate to show progress along the route. All have a restaurant car.

The ICE trains are liveried in a simple off-white livery with a red stripe below the windows. This livery has since been adopted for DB's IC and EC stock as well. In addition to the 60 class 401 ICEs are four further ICE types. There are some half-units of class 402 that have streamlined driving trailers at one end. These enable services to split en route and serve multiple destinations. Later units now being supplied for the Cologne–Frankfurt high-speed line are the ICE3 group, which have their traction equipment scattered along the train instead of concentrated in end power cars. These are designed for 300km/h (187mph) operation. Among their services is that from Amsterdam to Cologne which includes a small number of ICE3s owned by Netherlands Railways.

**Type:** High-speed passenger electric trains
**Power:** 15,000V 16.67Hz AC overhead line collection; 4800kW (6430hp) per power car; four body-mounted traction motors in each power car
**Tractive effort:** Not known
**Max. operating speed:** 280km/h (175mph)
**Weight per vehicle:** 80 tonnes (175,685lb) power cars; 52 to 56 tonnes (114,195 to 122,980lb) trailer cars
**Max. axle load:** Not known
**Overall length:** 20,560mm (67ft 5in) power cars; 26,400mm (86ft 7in) trailer cars
**Gauge:** 1435mm (4ft 8.5in)

**The streamlined InterCity Express trains of DB are liveried in white overall with a red flash running the length of the train. This style has since spread to all DB InterCity trains as well.**

## CLASS 252 BO-BO SPANISH RAILWAYS (RENFE) SPAIN 1991

Another member of the Siemens 'Eurosprinter' family the 75-strong RENFE class 252 contains machines of both standard and broad gauge, and single- and dual-voltage operation. As delivered from 1991 to 1994, the first 15 had 1435mm (4ft 8.5in) bogies for 220km/h (137.5mph) Talgo operation over the Madrid to Sevilla AVE high-speed line.

The remaining locomotives were 1676mm (5ft 6in) and 160km/h (100mph). Only the first 31 machines are dual voltage and adaptable between gauges. Most are now converted to the wider gauge; the remainder are for DC and wide gauge only.

**RENFE class 252.049 stops with a passenger train in Alicante in June 1997, en route to Valencia.**

**Type:** Bo-Bo universal electric
**Power:** 5600kW (7609hp)
**Supply:** 3000V DC and 25kV 50Hz AC
**Tractive effort:** 300kN (67500lbf)
**Max. operating speed:** 220km/h (137.5mph)
**Weight:** 90 tonnes (198,450lb)
**Max. axle load:** 22.5 tonnes (49,613lb)
**Overall length:** 20.38m (66ft 6in)
**Gauge:** 1435 or 1676mm (4ft 8.5in or 5ft 6in)

## CLASS X12 STATE RAILWAYS (SJ) SWEDEN 1991

The quality of the class X10 EMUs was sufficient to enable SJ to develop a superior version for lightly loaded InterCity type journeys. The X12 is a two-car adaptation that includes better seating, toilets and fewer access doorways. Currently, SJ has 18 of these, while the remaining seven or so are run by private operators.

**Type:** Two-car InterCity electric multiple units
**Power:** 15,000V 16.67Hz AC overhead line collection; 1280kW (1715bhp); axle-mounted traction motors
**Tractive effort:** Not known
**Max. operating speed:** 160km/h (100mph)
**Weight per vehicle:** Not known
**Max axle load:** Not known
**Overall length:** Not known
**Gauge:** 1435mm (4ft 8.5in)

## CLASS RE 460 SWISS FEDERAL RAILWAYS (SBB) SWITZERLAND 1991

SBB class Re 460 form the backbone motive power for the 'Bahn 2000' concept of increasing speed and capacity of the Swiss intercity network. Ordered first in 1987 (delivery completed by late 1996) the original plan was for 75 multiple-unit fitted machines designed for heavy freight traffic over the St Gotthard route and around 30 for express passenger duties from a total order of 119. Subsequent reorganization and division of SBB into business units have effectively reversed the position today, with 79 belonging to the passenger business and 40 to SBB Cargo. Although not a member of the European Union, SBB carries substantial trans-Alpine transit cargo between Italy and France and Germany. The St Gotthard route between Erstfeld and Chiasso is a key freight corridor, but also a constraint on loads, with 2.6/2.8 per cent grades on the northern climb and 2.1/2.6 per cent on the southern ascent. It may seem odd that SBB built the lower rated 6100kW (8288hp) class 460 two decades after 7900kW (10734hp) class Re6/6,

**Here, a Class 460 Bahn 2000 engine passes through a village outside Berne.**

**Engine no. 460.005-2 stops to allow passengers to board in St. Gallan, Switzerland, in April 1996.**

but two Re6/6s in multiple exceed the drawbar strength limit. The 1300-tonne maximum load of two class 460s with 12200kW (16576hp) combined is the same as the standard so-called 'Re10/10' 12550kW (17052hp) combination of Re6/6+Re4/4 normally used. Freight trains of 2000 tonnes (1968 tons) may be worked at Erstfeld, and, to overcome the 1300-tonne (1280-ton) limit south of there, one Re4/4 or Re6/6 as banker or pusher increases allowed train weight to 1600 tonne (1575 tons), but 2000 tonnes requires the load to be divided with a mid-train helper.

SBB started tests in 1998 using the US-developed GE Harris Locotrol system of radio control of locomotives distributed in the train. SBB Cargo is equipping around half its class 460s with the system, as well as more than 60 Re4/4s and Re6/6s. A further advantage was an increase in the downhill running speed. Freight trains ascended the Gotthard run at the ruling 75km/h (48.8mph) line speed, but descending maintained a lower average speed by alternate periods of 40 and 75km/h (25 and 48.8mph) working, allowing the brakes to cool. Locotrol allows for full control of the braking on the mid-train helpers so that the full electric braking capacity of all locomotives in the train is used to maintain 75km/h downhill.

Multiple-unit operation of four class 460 has been permitted in low-lying regions since 1999. 'Bahn 2000' passenger rolling stock is a mix of tilting EMU trains, new driving trailers for converting existing coaches to push-pull working, and new double-decker trains also for push-pull mode. The 60 IC-Bt driving trailers ordered in 1994 from Schindler have cabs identical to class 460 both in design and driving positions. Many Swiss intercity services reverse at Zurich main station with push-pull operation, saving eight locomotives and 60 coaches as a result of the reduced turnaround. All these trains are worked by class 460 as far as possible, with high-capacity, 14-coach, 928-seat trains working on the Geneve to St Gallen, St Gallen to Brig, Basel to Chur, Basel to Interlaken and Lucerne to Zurich Flughafen services. All these reverse in Zurich Hbf. Class 460 also operate with the new Schindler-supplied IC2000 double-deck sets formed of coaches seating up to 86 first class and 113 second class (totalling 755).

Another important Swiss freight corridor is the Lotschberg route operated by the independent BLS. Class 465 is a higher powered derivative of the class 460. Eight were delivered in 1994, essentially for replacement of elderly Ae4/4 and Ae8/8 machines of 1940s vintage. A further 10 were received in 2000 for operation by BLS (but for legal reasons are funded by SBB) for an increase in RoLa truck-carrying trains.

**Type:** Bo-Bo universal locomotive
**Power:** 4800kW (6522hp)
**Supply:** 15kV 16.2/3Hz AC
**Tractive effort:** 275kN (61875lbf)
**Max. operating speed:** 230km/h (143.8mph)
**Weight:** 81 tonnes (178,605lb)
**Max. axle load:** 20 tonnes (44,100lb)
**Overall length:** 18.5m (60ft 4in)
**Gauge:** 1435mm (4ft 8.5in)

## CLASS 6FE CO-CO ALGERIAN NATIONAL RAILWAYS (SNTF) ALGERIA 1992

Algeria state railways SNTF (Société Nationale des transports Ferroviaires) ordered 14 of these freight locomotives from GEC Alsthom and ACEC to partially replace the 20-year-old class 6CE units. They are used for movement of phosphates and ore across eastern Algeria between Djebel Onka and Tebessa, and Annaba port.

**Type:** Co-Co
**Power:** 2400kW (3261hp)
**Supply:** 3000V DC
**Tractive effort:** 266kN (59,850lbf)
**Max. operating speed:** 80km/h (50mph)
**Weight:** 132 tonnes (291,060lb)
**Max. axle load:** 22 tonnes (48,510lb)
**Overall length:** 17.48m (57ft)
**Gauge:** 1435mm (4ft 8.5in)

## CLASS 127 PROTOTYPE FEDERAL GERMAN RAILWAYS (DB) GERMANY 1992

In the early 1990s, prototype designs were produced to demonstrate the effectiveness of modern three-phase electronics in traction systems. These enable input from AC or DC supplies to be converted to three phases of DC at variable frequencies and voltages. No. 127 001 came from Krauss Maffei with Siemens electrical equipment. Marketed as the 'EuroSprinter', this type formed the basis of DB's class 101.

**Type:** Bo-Bo mainline mixed-traffic electric prototype
**Power:** 15,000V 16.67Hz AC overhead line collection; 5600kW (7500bhp); three-phase control; four body-mounted traction motors
**Tractive effort:** Not known
**Max. operating speed:** 220km/h (137mph)
**Weight:** 84 tonnes (184,470lb)
**Max axle load:** Not known
**Overall length:** 20.38m (66ft 10in)

## CLASS 323 BRITISH RAIL GREAT BRITAIN 1992

**Class 323 units in the grey-and-green livery of West Midlands Passenger Transport Executive (PTE) operate suburban services for Central Trains in the district around Birmingham.**

Among the suburban EMUs in Britain, the class 323s are unusual in several ways. They are the only inner suburban type to use the longer carriage body length of 23m (75ft) that had previously been a feature only of InterCity stock.

The class 323s use aluminium alloy body construction, not unique but at that time not common in the United Kingdom, and they have a gated thyristor control system that feeds variable voltage rectified current to the four DC traction motors on each outer power car.

With a 145km/h (90mph) top speed, they are also well suited to longer distance and outer suburban work that requires running on the densely trafficked main lines found around Birmingham and Manchester. Another attribute is that the class is the first EMU type to obtain a systemwide (as opposed to localized) certificate for operation on Railtrack tracks, under the scheme for vehicle acceptance following privatization of British Rail.

**Type:** Three-car suburban electric multiple units
**Power per three-car set:** 25,000V 50Hz AC overhead line collection; 1168kW (1565hp); eight axle-mounted traction motors
**Tractive effort:** Not known
**Max. operating speed:** 145km/h (90mph)
**Weight:** 39 and 41tonnes (86,525 and 90,040lb) per vehicle
**Overall length:** 23.4m (76ft 9in)
**Gauge:** 1435mm (4ft 8.5in)

**A class 323 EMU is seen here leaving Manchester Piccadilly carries the colours of the Great Manchester PTE.**

## CLASS 465 'NETWORKER' BRITISH RAIL — GREAT BRITAIN 1992

Between them ABB and GEC Alsthom built a total of 247 four-car units to British Rail's class 465 'Networker' EMU specification, and Alsthom also supplied 43 two-car units. So tightly was the specification drawn up that the appearance of both manufacturers' designs is almost identical.

These 'Networker' EMUs have four traction motors on each driving power car and the ability to regenerate current for return to the conductor rail.

**Type:** Four-car and two-car suburban electric multiple units
**Power per unit:** 750V DC conductor rail collection; 1120kW (1500hp); four axle-mounted traction motors per power car
**Tractive effort:** Not known
**Max. operating speed:** 120km/h (75mph)
**Weight:** 29 to 39 tonnes (65,185 to 87,810lb) per vehicle
**Max. axle load:** Not known
**Overall length:** 20.89m (68ft 6in) end power cars; 20.06m (65ft 10in) intermediate trailers
**Gauge:** 1435mm (4ft 8.5in)

**On a four-track outer suburban section in north Kent, a 'Networker' class 465 EMU heads towards London. These units were built by Adtranz and Alsthom to outwardly similar designs.**

## CLASS 787 KYUSHU RAILWAY — JAPAN 1992

Kyushu, the southernmost of Japan's main islands, has its own railway system, organized on a north–south basis between the major cities of Fukuoka, Kumamoto and Kagoshima. Class 787 seven-car trains, seen as technically innovative on introduction, with thyristor phase-controlled DC motors, run two regular express services.

**Type:** Long-distance express train set
**Power:** Not known
**Tractive effort:** Not known
**Max. operating speed:** 130km/h (81mph)
**Total weight:** Not known
**Max. axle load:** Not known
**Overall length:** Not known
**Builder:** Not known

## CLASS E1300 B-B MOROCCO STATE RAILWAYS (ONCFM) MOROCCO 1992

At high speed on level track, one of the 1992 Alsthom-MTE batch of Class E1300 hauls the Marrakesh–Casablanca express near Berrechid.

Morocco State Railways – Office National des Chemins de Fer du Maroc (ONCFM) – took delivery of two small batches of electric locomotives through the 1990s from GEC Alsthom, based on the successful French railways (SNCF) class BB7200. The first 18 came from Alsthom MTE from 1992, geared for 160km/h (100mph) passenger work (class E1300). The later nine class E1350s received in 1999 from GEC Alsthom SCIF were geared for 100km/h (62.1mph) freight work.

Unlike the majority of French-built monomotor bogie-fitted electric locomotives, both the Morocco types and the French BB7200 were permanently set in a single gear, whereas other designs change between two gear ratios as appropriate for freight or passenger. Class E1350 replaced elderly class E900 machines on phosphates traffic, working train loads of 4680 tonnes (4606 tons), and this accounts for approximately two-thirds of all traffic in Morocco.

**Type:** B-B electric
**Power:** 4000kW (5435hp)
**Supply:** 3000V DC
**Tractive effort:** E1300 - 275kN (61875lbf); E1350 - 330kN (74250lbf)
**Max. operating speed:** E1300 - 120km/h (75mph); E1350 - 160km/h (100mph)
**Weight:** 85.5 tonnes (188,528lb)
**Max. axle load:** 21.5 tonnes (47,408lb)
**Overall length:** 17.48m (57ft)
**Gauge:** 1435mm (4ft 8.5in)

## CLASS 100 AND 252 AVE SPANISH RAILWAYS (RENFE) SPAIN 1992

For the AVE high-speed line between Madrid and Sevilla, RENFE has 18 Alsthom TGV-style eight-car articulated trains, class 100. These trains give exemplary service reliability.

Eleven class 252 'EuroSprinter' locomotives work Talgo trains on the AVE line. The Talgo trains pass through automatic gauge-changing equipment when leaving the high-speed line at Cordoba to join the broad-gauge route to Malaga. A broad-gauge version of class 252 exists, 63 of which operate elsewhere in Spain.

**Type:** High-speed electric passenger train
**Track gauge:** 1435mm (4ft 8.5in) AVE, and 1668mm (5ft 6in)
**Power per train:** 25,000V 50Hz AC and 3,000V DC overhead line collection; 8800kW (11,795hp); body mounted traction motors, cardan shafts to driven axles
**Tractive effort:** Not known
**Max. operating speed:** 300km/h (187mph)
**Weight:** 65 tonnes (142,745lb) per power car
**Max axle load:** Not known
**Overall length per unit:** 22.15m (72ft 8in) power car; 21.845m (71ft 8in) end carriage; 18.7m (61ft 4in) intermediate carriages

## EUROSTAR EUROSTAR CONSORTIUM BELGIUM, GREAT BRITAIN AND FRANCE 1993

The introduction of the Eurostar service from London's Waterloo International terminus to Paris and Brussels on 14 November 1994 heralded the arrival of a new era of rail travel. The speed and comfort offered by the Eurostar enables rail to compete directly with Europe's airline network, establishing a high-quality train service linking the three capital cities.

Acknowledged as one of the most complex trains in the world, the class 373 Eurostar sets work from three different power systems, enabling them to operate regular services within the three countries. The trains operate on the 750V DC third rail system within the United Kingdom, 25kV AC overhead within the Channel Tunnel, France and Belgium, and can utilize the 3000V DC overhead system in Belgium, with some sets equipped to work off the 1500V AC overhead system within France for SNCF services.

After the signing of the Anglo-French Fixed Link Treaty on 29 July 1987, lengthy consultation began between the three main railway companies concerned: British Rail (UK), SNCF (France) and SNCB (Belgium) to consider suitable train types. The first serious proposal to build a tunnel

**The concept of the Eurostar was to provide a stylish, quality rail service to compete direct with the European airline network. While it has proved very successful, operations have never – to date – fulfilled its original aspirations.**

under the English Channel had been put forward as long ago as 1802. After numerous false starts, the building of the Channel Tunnel began on 1 December 1987. The service tunnel breakthrough came on 1 December 1990, with the two rail tunnels meeting in May and June the following year. The trains had to be capable of working over the different railway systems of the countries concerned, each of which had their individual operational rules and restrictions. The most obvious area of conflict was that of the gauge envelope, with the UK network utilizing a more restricted space between its trains and structures in comparison to those elsewhere in Europe, which follow the more spacious Berne gauge.

A design consortium was formed, led by GEC-Alsthom, builders of the highly successful French TGV-type trains. The TGV was used as the mechanical prototype for the new train; however, the outline obviously had to be designed to fit within the gauge restrictions in the United Kingdom. Axle loadings were to be kept down to 17 tonnes (37,485lb), to enable the sets to work over existing TGV tracks. An articulated 20-car set was selected to enable the vehicles to be lower slung, with body-mounted traction motors to help reduce track wear. The original contract was signed in Brussels on 18 December 1989. Each 20-car set consists of two twin 10-coach formations, comprising a driving power car plus nine passenger vehicles. A full set provides seating for 794 passengers – 210 first and 584 standard class. Seating is 2 +1 in first class and 2 + 2 in standard, with a mixture of face-to-face and unidirectional seats.

Eurostar sets were constructed at several plants in Europe and then put together at Belfort in France or Washwood Heath, Birmingham, in the United Kingdom. The first set was built at Belfort in 1992, commencing test running in January the following year. Its initial test runs under power were between Strasbourg and Mulhouse. In June 1993, the set arrived in the United Kingdom for tests on the DC system. The Eurostar sets have to be capable of working from AC and DC power supplies obtained from the third rail or overhead systems. Manual changeover by the driver between the different power supplies takes place while the train is on the move, with the train entering neutral sections.

France's second set was delivered for testing in May 1993, commencing high-speed running tests on the Paris–Lille route in July that year. In these tests, the set reached the maximum speed of 300km/h (186mph) for the first time. The initial UK-built set was delivered from Washwood Heath to London's dedicated Eurostar maintenance base, North Pole International Depot, in October 1993. Situated alongside the Great Western main line just a few minutes outside Paddington station, the site is almost three kilometres (1.86 miles) in length. The depot is divided into different sections for routine servicing and heavier maintenance/repairs. The servicing shed is the longest depot building in the United Kingdom and can accommodate a full 20-car set. The maintenance workshop can only handle half-sets. North Pole also houses the International Supply Centre for the entire Eurostar fleet. An extensive number of parts are stocked, and spare cab fronts can be seen from the adjacent main line.

The sets use the 750V DC system on the main line, but the 25kV AC overhead system is used within the depot. Conventional locomotives and/or barrier vehicles fitted with Scharfenberg couplings are also used for stock movements within the depot and for rescue purposes away from the depot. Service inspections are usually made to each unit at daily, weekly, four-weekly, three-monthly, six-monthly and 18-monthly intervals. The other Eurostar maintenance depots are Landy (Paris) and Forest (Brussels). The expected life of Eurostar sets is predicted to be 15 years.

From their introduction, the Eurostar sets appeared in a striking white and blue livery with yellow ends, plus the distinctive Eurostar

**The Eurostar's design had to fit within the gauge restrictions in the United Kingdom and be capable of operating on different power systems in the countries it serves. The resulting Class 373 Eurostar sets (above) are acknowledged as one of the most complex trains in the world. Some spare Eurostar sets have appeared in GNER's dark blue livery (below) for use on that company's 'White Rose' services.**

branding on the cabsides. Full train-length advertising liveries appeared on the side of some of the Eurostar sets during 1999.

The Royal opening of the Channel Tunnel rail link took place on 6 May 1994, with Her Majesty the Queen travelling in set No. 373004 from London Waterloo to Coquelles, to meet the President of France, François Mitterrand. Official services commenced on 14 November 1994, initially with two trains a day in each direction, linking Waterloo International with Paris Gare du Nord and Brussels Zuid/Midi. Initial journey times were three hours London–Paris and three hours 15 minutes London–Brussels. From February 1996, more than 250 trains ran each week between the three capitals. Some of the services make stops at Calais Fréthun and Lille in France, and from 8 January 1996 the second UK Eurostar station was opened at Ashford International in Kent. Eurostar carried its one millionth passenger on 23 May 1995, its second millionth on 31 August and its three millionth on 23 December 1995. By February 1996, it had run 10,000 trains since its inception in November 1994. Eurostar UK (originally European Passenger Services) bought 18 of the total 38 sets, with French Railways (SNCF) having 16 and Belgian Railways

(SNCB) four. Plans to introduce Regional Eurostar services to and from UK destinations including Edinburgh, Glasgow, Manchester, Milton Keynes and Peterborough have failed to materialize. It was intended that these would use 16-coach shorter sets – designated Class 373/2 'North of London' sets – comprising two twin-sets of a power car, plus seven passenger vehicles. The regional sets were subsequently put into store.

In 2000, however GNER (UK) hired two of these sets for its London King's Cross–York 'The White Rose' service. Additional sets have subsequently been hired – with some repainted into GNER's dark blue livery – and, from the summer 2002 timetable, services were switched to a London–Leeds 'White Rose' service, with York losing these impressive trains. Likewise in France, SNCF has used some of the under-utilized 20-coach sets for domestic services.

**Until the independent Channel Tunnel Rail Link in the United Kingdom was completed, the Eurostars had to share the existing railway infrastructure in the southeast of England. This saw them working alongside veteran trains on busy commuter routes.**

**Type:** Anglo-Belgian-French Channel Tunnel express passenger train
**Power:** 25kV AC overhead; 750V DC third rail; 3000V DC overhead (some sets also equipped for 1500V overhead DC use)
**Tractive effort:** Not known
**Weight:** 829.2 tonnes (1,828,064lb)
**Max. axle load:** Not known
**Max. operating speed:** 300km/h (186mph)
**Overall train length:** 381m (1250ft)
**Gauge:** 1435mm (4ft 8.5in)

## Channel Tunnel's Shuttle Class 9000

GREAT BRITAIN AND FRANCE 1993

The motive power for the Channel Tunnel's Shuttle Tourist car-carrying trains and Shuttle lorry-carrying freight trains is two of the powerful Bo + Bo + Bo (tri-Bo) electric locomotives – one at the front and rear of each train. The 38 class 9000 locomotives were built by Brush Traction at Loughborough (UK) from 1992, using electrical equipment from ASEA Brown Boveri. Shuttle freight services began on 19 May 1994.

Each locomotive is 22m (72ft 2in) long, 4.2m (13ft 9.5in) in height above the rail and 2.97m (9ft 9in) in width. Although they have smaller loading gauges than the Shuttle wagons they power, they are still too large to run on the UK mainline system. Each locomotive delivers 5595kW (7500hp) and is capable of hauling a full 2400-tonne (2362-ton) train under its own power in the event of a failure by the other locomotive, a characteristic which is seen as critical when operating through the Channel Tunnel. The power supply is 25 kV taken from the overhead on both sides of the Channel and through the Channel Tunnel itself.

The Bo + Bo + Bo wheel arrangement is not generally found on the either the British or French railway systems, but has been used, for example, extensively on the Italian network. Six axles were considered necessary on the Shuttle locomotives to give sufficient adhesion (some gradients being as steep as 1 in 90) and reduce wear on the curves on the reversing loops at Folkestone and Coquelles. Although the three bogies are basically the same, the central one has more lateral movement. The locomotives have a maximum speed of 160 km/h (100mph), with a normal operating speed of 140km/h (87 mph). Each locomotive has three two-axle bogies – all six bogies are powered and use 25 kV AC electric current from overhead catenary. Both friction and electrical regeneration braking systems are used.

The driver sits in the cab of the leading locomotive with the train captain based in the cab of the rear

locomotive. The captain is also trained to drive a Shuttle (either half or the whole of the train) in emergency situations. The rear of each class 9000 locomotive has a small driving cab for use in light running or for remote shunting.

One half of the fleet faces east to west and the other half in the opposite direction. They are all allocated to the Coquelles depot within the Eurotunnel terminal in France. The original fleet of 38 locomotives (Nos 9001–9038) was delivered to Coquelles before the Channel Tunnel was opened, delivery being by road and sea. No. 9030 was withdrawn following involvement in the Channel Tunnel fire in November 1996, being replaced by a new locomotive, No. 9040. There is no No. 9039.

After the Channel Tunnel's opening, additional locomotives

**The height difference between the Channel Tunnel's Shuttle class 9000 locomotives and the dedicated vehicles is very clearly illustrated in this view. These locomotives are too large to operate on the UK main line.**

were ordered to meet unexpected traffic growth. The 9100 series (9101–13) has driving controls only at the leading end (that is, without the small driving cab at the flat end) and other modifications including revised footstep arrangements for the driver's cab. In 1999, an order was placed for the 9700 series locomotives (9701–9707), these having a higher power output but within the same body style, intended exclusively for Shuttle Freight traffic.

The locomotives are finished in Eurotunnel grey and white livery. Class 9000 locomotives carried a green and blue band at cantrail height as part of the original Le Shuttle branding, but this finish was replaced by the Eurotunnel colour scheme. As they do not run on the UK mainline system, they do not require yellow warning panels on the cab ends. The first of the locomotives to receive a name was No. 9012 'Luciano Pavarotti', named after the opera singer.

Operating between the Folkestone terminal in Britain and Calais terminal in France, a full-length road vehicle carrying Tourist Shuttle comprises two locomotives, 24 carriages, two loading carriages and two unloading carriages. The capacity of these sets is 180 cars, or 120 cars and 12 coaches (or 36 minibuses). The lorry/HGV transporting Freight Shuttles are able to carry 44-tonne (97,020lb) vehicles. A full 730m (2395ft) long train is made up of one locomotive at each end, one club car, one off-loading wagon, 14 HGV transporter wagons, one loading wagon, another off-loading wagon, a further 14 HGV transporter wagons and one more loading wagon. Each of the HGV transporter wagons will normally accommodate one HGV. Terminal to terminal travelling time for Shuttle services is 35 minutes.

**Type:** Shuttle Channel Tunnel locomotives
**Power:** 25kV AC overhead, asynchronous three-phase, ABB 6PH, 5595kW (7500hp)
**Tractive effort:** 400kN (90,000lbf)
**Max. operating speed:** 160km/h (100mph)
**Weight:** 132 tonnes (291,060lb)
**Max. axle load:** Not known
**Overall length:** 21.996m (72ft 2in)
**Gauge:** 1435mm (4 ft 8.5in)

## CLASS 92 BRITISH RAIL — GREAT BRITAIN 1993

**Type:** Co-Co mainline mixed-traffic dual-voltage electric locomotives
**Power:** 25,000V 50Hz AC overhead line collection and 750V DC conductor rail collection; 5040kW (6755hp) on AC, 4000kW (5360hp) on DC; three-phase asynchronous control; six traction motors
**Tractive effort:** 400kN (89,925lbf)
**Max. operating speed:** 140km/h (87mph)
**Weight:** 126 tonnes (348,650lb)
**Max axle load:**
**Overall length:** 21.34m (70ft 1in)
**Gauge:** 1435mm (4ft 8.5in)

The advent of the Channel Tunnel with its 25kV railway electrification, separated from BR's 25kV network by the Southern Region 750V DC conductor rail system south of London, meant that it was necessary to have dual-voltage locomotives that could operate in France, in the Channel Tunnel and on BR's third rail and 25kV lines for international freight trains.

The 46 Brush Traction class 92 locomotives are able to operate on all these systems, including reacting to the different signalling systems of each railway (except that of SNCF). The class 92 locomotives were designed not only for freight, but also for overnight international sleeping car passenger trains. The latter need evaporated when the market was deemed to be insufficient.

**Brand-new class 92 Co-Co dual-voltage electric No. 92 026 stands outside its place of manufacture, the Adtranz works at Crewe.**

## CLASS 5601 PORTUGUESE RAILWAYS (CP) — PORTUGAL 1993

As Portugal's electrified network gained short extensions and traffic grew, there was a growing need for more powerful electric locomotives. CP's choice was the Krauss Maffei/Siemens 'EuroSprinter' design of Bo-Bo mixed traffic locomotive. Class 5601 locomotives are the main haulers of heavy freight in Portugal and share express passenger train working with the Alsthom '2601' locomotives.

**Type:** Bo-Bo mainline mixed-traffic electric
**Track gauge:** 1668mm (5ft 6in)
**Power:** 25,000V 50Hz AC overhead line collection; 5600kW (7500bhp); three-phase control; four body-mounted traction motors
**Tractive effort:** Not known
**Max. operating speed:** 200km/h (125mph)
**Weight:** 88 tonnes (193,255lb)
**Max axle load:** Not known
**Overall length:** 20.38m (66ft 10in)

## CLASS 3300 BO-BO-BO QUEENSLAND RAILWAYS (QR) — AUSTRALIA 1994

Queensland Railways class 3300/3400 is one of three similar six-axle Bo-Bo-Bo machines built for the 1980s electrification around coalfields largely opened up for export business in the 1970s. Trains are operates from Blackwater and Rockhampton, and up to five locomotives use Locotrol radio control of two or three mid-train helpers.

**Type:** Bo-Bo-Bo electric freight
**Power:** 3000kW (4020hp)
**Supply:** 25kV 50Hz AC
**Tractive effort:** 260kN (58,500lbf) at 40km/h (25mph)
**Max. operating speed:** 80km.h (50mph)
**Weight:** 113 tonnes (249,165lb)
**Max. axle load:** 19 tonnes (41,895lb)
**Overall length:** 20.55m (67ft)
**Gauge:** 1067mm (3ft 6in)

## CLASS 61 BULGARIAN STATE RAILWAYS (BDZ) — BULGARIA 1994

Built by Skoda BDZ, class 61 is a low-powered centre cab electric locomotive designed for station pilot, empty stock, shunting and transfer duties around main passenger stations and freight yards. Class 61's design is based on development with CSD thyristor control locomotive 209001 dating from 1990.

**Type:** Bo-Bo electric switcher
**Power:** 960kW (1304hp)
**Supply:** 25kV 50Hz AC
**Tractive effort:** 122kN (27,450lbf)
**Max. operating speed:** 80km/h (50mph)
**Weight:** 74 tonnes (163,170lb)
**Max. axle load:** 18.5 tonnes (40,793lb)
**Overall length:** 14.4m (47ft)
**Gauge:** 1435mm (4ft 8.5in)

## CLASS S699 CO-CO CZECH RAILWAYS (CD) — CZECH REPUBLIC 1994

Asynchronous motor locomotives conceived by Czechoslovakian State Railways (CSD) for 95km/h (59.4mph) freight and 155km/h (96.9mph) passenger operation, neither ZSR nor CD needed them when the working prototypes appeared in 1994. They now work in industrial service in northwest Bohemia shifting brown coal.

**Type:** Bo-Bo-Bo prototype
**Power:** 5220kW (7092hp)
**Supply:** 3000V DC
**Tractive effort:** 575kN (129,375lbf)
**Max. operating speed:** 95km/h (59.4mph)
**Weight:** 120 tonnes (264,600lb)
**Max. axle load:** 20 tonnes (44,100lb)
**Overall length:** 20.346m (66ft 4in)
**Gauge:** 1435mm (4ft 8.5in)

## Class Sr2 Electric FINNISH STATE RAILWAYS (VR) FINLAND 1994

In 1995, VR (Finnish State Railways) ordered a fleet of modern double-ended electric locomotives based on the Swiss Lok 2000, which is now used by SBB (Swiss Federal Railways) as Class 460 and Bern-Lötschberg-Simplon(BLS) as its Class 465. The VR Sr-2 differs from its Swiss counterparts in several ways. Externally, the Sr-2 lacks the skirting exhibited by the Swiss models. Electrically, the Sr-2 is designed to work from 25kV at 50Hz, instead of 15kV 16.66Hz. Finnish drivers sit on the right-hand side; in Switzerland, drivers sit on the left. As this was written in 2002, VR had ordered 46 Sr-2s, but fewer than 30 were actually in service. They are used in both express long-distance passenger services and freight services.

**Finnish State Railways (VR) 3220 is seen at Oulu in September 2001 after hauling an express train from Helsinki. Although presently VR electrification ends at Oulu, it is being extended further north.**

**Type:** Bo-Bo mixed-traffic electric
**Power:** Maximum output for 1 hour 6000kW (8054hp); continuous output 5000kW (3725hp)
**Tractive effort:** 300kN (67,500 lbf) starting TE; 240kN (54,000lbf) continuous TE
**Max. operating speed:** N/A
**Weight:** 83 tonnes (183,015lb)
**Overall length:** 13m (45ft 3in)
**Max. axle load:** 20.75 tonnes (45,754lb)
**Gauge:** 1524mm (5 ft)

## Class IRM NETHERLANDS RAILWAYS (NS) NETHERLANDS 1994

The first 80 class IRM double-deck 'Regio Runner' units were delivered by Talbot and de Dietrich in three-car and four-car formations. These are being extended to four- and six-car trains, respectively. Used on regional and InterCity services, they can be seen on almost all NS's main lines, often in multiple. Each driving car has a power bogie at the non-driving end, giving four traction motors for a three- or four-car set.

**Type:** Double-deck express electric multiple units
**Power per power car:** 1500V DC overhead line collection (25kV to be added); 604kW (810hp); two traction motors in one bogie
**Tractive effort:** Not known
**Max. operating speed:** 160km/h (100mph)
**Weight per vehicle:** 50 to 62 tonnes (110,680 to 136,595lb)
**Max. axle load:** Not known
**Overall length:** 27.28m (89ft 6in) driving cars; 26.5m (86ft 11in) intermediate cars

## Class Ge 4/4III Bo-Bo RHAETISCHE BAHN (RHB) SWITZERLAND 1994

The *Rhaetische Bahn* (RhB) operates a 276km (173-mile) system energized at 11,000V AC. Class Ge4/4III is in some ways a scaled-down SBB class 460 for the narrow gauge and features GTO technology and self-steering bogies to reduce rail wear on tight curves. Originally, nine units (641 to 649) were built. These were later supplemented by 650 to 652 for the new Veriena tunnel route opened in 1999.

The three extra Ge4/4IIIs allowed the frequent car-carrying shuttle service through the 19km (11.9-mile) tunnel to be started, while the new route allows a reduction in overall journey time to the important resort of St Moritz.

Near-identical locomotives have been delivered to Biere Apples Morges (BAM) around Lausanne in Switzerland's west as its 21 and 22, and also to the Montreux Oberland Bernois (MOB), where its 8001 to 8004 can accept 15kV, as well for possible workings to Interlaken (if dual gauging takes place as planned).

**Type:** Bo-Bo
**Power:** 1700kW (2310hp)
**Supply:** 11kV 16.67Hz AC
**Tractive effort:** 170kN (38250lbf)
**Max. operating speed:** 100km/h (62.1mph)
**Weight:** 62 tonnes (136,710lb)
**Max. axle load:** 15.5 tonnes (34,178lb)
**Overall length:** 16.05m (52ft 4in)
**Gauge:** 1000mm (3ft 3in)

**In a winter scene, a GE 4/411, in Furka-Oberalp livery, stands at the head of a shuttle car transporter train, the specialist service for which these relatively lightweight locomotives were designed.**

## CLASS 325 ROYAL MAIL GREAT BRITAIN 1995

**Type:** Four-car postal electric multiple units
**Power per unit:** 25,000V 50Hz AC overhead line collection and 750V DC conductor rail collection; 980kW (1315hp); four axle-mounted traction motors
**Tractive effort:**
**Max. operating speed:** 160km/h (100mph)
**Weight per vehicle:** 29 to 50 tonnes (65,185 to 112,000lb)
**Max. axle load:** Not known
**Overall length:** 20.35m (66ft 9in)
**Gauge:** 1435mm (4ft 8.5in)

The concept of fast EMUs for carrying mail is not uncommon on European continental railways, but was not the case in the United Kingdom until the arrival of the class 325 units. These 16 four-car dual-voltage units were built by

**A twelve-car formation of three class 325 postal EMUs speeds along Britain's West Coast main line between Crewe and London, heading for the new distribution depot at Willesden.**

ABB and owned by Royal Mail and are the first trains to have been accepted for operation on Railtrack lines after privatization. Each vehicle was designed for speedy loading and unloading of wheeled postal containers. Each car can carry 12 tonnes (26,460lb) load. Fitted for dual-voltage operation, the 325s can work on the East Coast and West Coast main lines and run through via the West London line to the conductor rail electrified area south of the River Thames. Many services operate as 12-car formations.

Based on the successful dual-voltage class 319 passenger units operated by Thameslink, there is one intermediate non-driving power car with four traction motors.

## BVmot EMU HUNGARIAN STATE RAILWAYS (MÁV) HUNGARY 1995

**Hungary's first home-built EMU was the MÁV BVmot. Here No. 018 is seen standing outside Budapest Déli station.**

**A Hungarian Railways (MÁV) BVmot power car: a striking livery and the names of great Hungarians were given to the BVmot units, Nos 001–003; however, their service performance did not live up to the external message.**

Three of these four-car express electric multiple units are in Hungarian State Railways (MÁV) service. Intended for use on intercity services, their maximum speed is 160km/h (100mph). The design of the BVmot EMU consists of one motor coach with four powered axles in Bo-Bo wheel arrangement, and three trailers. A 1845kW (2505hp) electric dynamic brake is fitted. Design and construction was by Ganz-Hunslet, the partnership formed by involvement of the UK Hunslet company and Ganz of Budapest, the latter formerly the state concern Ganz-MAVAG.

Internally appointed to the highest European standards of intercity comfort, class BVmot sets had not proved reliable in revenue earning service, and often all three units are out of service. Initially work was between Budapest and Szeged, while, by 2002, they were deployed on the Budapest Kaposvar and Nagykanizsa route. So far no production-built models of any intercity electric multiple unit for MÁV has followed on from these prototypes.

**Type:** Four-car prototype express EMU
**Power:** 1755kW (2385hp) per unit
**Supply:** 25kV 50Hz AC
**Tractive effort:** N/A
**Max. operating speed:** 160km/h (100mph)
**Weight:** 68 tonnes (149,940lb) motor coach; 206 tonnes (454,230lb) complete unit
**Max. axle load:** 17 tonnes (37,485lb)
**Overall length:** 103.2m (336ft 8in) complete unit
**Gauge:** 1435mm (4ft 8.5in)

## CLASS 471 EMU CZECH RAILWAYS (CD) CZECH REPUBLIC 1996

Class 471s are double-deck flexible formation sets with class 971 driving trailers and class 071 trailers. The initial order from Moravskoslezská vagonka a.s. was for six three-car and four two-car sets of aluminium construction under Swiss licence, and Skoda electrical systems. The 550mm (21.7in) lower floor height suits the low station platforms on the CD system. Class 471 currently runs between Pardubice and Praha.

**Type:** Double-decker suburban EMU
**Power:** 2000kW (2717hp) per motor coach
**Supply:** 3000V DC
**Tractive effort:** N/A
**Max. operating speed:** 140km/h (87.5mph)
**Weight:** 66 tonnes (145,530lb) motor coach
**Max. axle load:** 17 tonnes (37,485lb)
**Overall length:** 26.4m (86ft 2in) per coach
**Gauge:** 1435mm (4ft 8.5in)

## CLASS SA DANISH RAILWAYS (DSB) DENMARK 1996

Replacement units for suburban services around Copenhagen, the 60 class SAs are single-axle eight-car units in the same unit length as a conventional four-car set. Each intermediate car is carried on a single axle and is supported by the end of the adjacent vehicle. These novel units are proving successful and popular with passengers.

**Type:** Suburban eight-car articulated electric multiple unit
**Power:** 1500V DC overhead line collection; 1720kW (2305bhp) per unit
**Tractive effort:** Not known
**Max. operating speed:** 120km/h (75mph)
**Weight:** Not known
**Max. axle load:** Not known
**Overall length:** Not known

## CLASS WCAM-3 INDIAN RAILWAYS INDIA 1996

A modern design for dual voltage (DC and AC) developed by Bharat Heavy Electrical Limited (BHEL), class WCAM3 uses mechanical and electrical components common to other Indian Railways designs, but with technology updates. The traction motor is the same force-ventilated Hitachi 630kW (856hp) nose-suspended axle-hung type as on class WAP4, but mounted in high-adhesion bogies trucks.

**Type:** Co-Co mixed-traffic
**Power:** 3432kW (4600hp) DC; 3730kW (5000hp) AC
**System:** 1500 V DC and 25 kV 50Hz AC
**Tractive effort:** 254kN (57200lbf) DC; 327kN (73480lbf) AC
**Max. operating speed:** 105km/h (65.6mph)
**Weight:** 113 tonnes (249,165lb)
**Max. axle load:** 19 tonnes (41,895lb)
**Overall length:** Not known
**Gauge:** 1676mm (5ft 6in)

## THALYS VARIOUS RAILWAYS FRANCE/BELGIUM/GERMANY/NETHERLANDS 1996

**A new Thalys set, No. 4321, is seen here standing in the Gare du Nord, Paris, on 8 July 1997, about to depart on a Brussels and Amsterdam service. SNCF No. 15.014 can be seen on the left.**

'Thalys' has no literal meaning. It is a brand name designed for easy pronunciation and recall in the languages of the countries through which Thalys trains operate. They bear no logos or markings of names of the participating railway systems: SNCF (France), SNCB/NMBS (Belgium), NS (Netherlands) or DB (Germany). Linking the cities of Paris, Brussels, Amsterdam and Cologne, the operation is a semi-privatized commercial operation. Services started running in June 1996, initially linking Paris, Brussels and Amsterdam, and known as PBA. December 1997 saw the opening of the high-speed line through Belgium (previously Thalys services had operated over conventional 160km/h (100mph) lines). At the same time ,services started running through to Cologne. As early as April 2001, the airline Air France withdrew its flights between Paris and Brussels because of loss of passengers – it was carrying just 450 per day compared to 13,700 by Thalys. Fifty per cent of Thalys passengers are carried on this section with a journey time of just 1hr 33mins at an average speed of 222km/h (138.8mph). By 2002, Thalys had six million passenger journeys per annum. Originally a single type of train set referred to as PBKA was to have been ordered. Twenty-seven 10-vehicle train sets of a new type were ordered, but delays affecting design and production caused this to be altered to 10 PBA and 17 PBKA sets. PBA sets are three-voltage unit versions of the earlier SNCF TGV second-generation 'Réseau', allowing Thalys to commence operations on schedule. PBKA sets are third generation with single-deck trailers, but motor coaches identical to SNCF 'Duplex' sets that work in France with double-deck cars. PBA and PBKA are both formed in 10-car trains configured power car plus eight trailers plus power car, with a total of 377 seats. A quick and easy aid to recognition without knowing

**In February 1999, a gleaming Thalys train passes Brussels Schaerbeek, heading for the new high-speed line towards Lille and Paris.**

the detailed differences are PBA sets are numbered in the 4500 series and driving cabs have split windscreens. PBKAs have 4300 series numbers and no division of the cab windscreen. The PBKA fleet contract was placed in January 1994 by SNCF, SNCB/NMBS, NS and DBAG from a consortium led by GEC Alsthom and including De Dietrich of France and AC EC Transport and Bombardier Eurorail of Belgium, with traction motors supplied by Holec from Netherlands. Final ownership is SNCF six sets, NS two and SNCB nine, with DB financing but not actually owning two sets. The fleet list is 4311 to 4317; 4321 and 4322 DB; 331 and 4332 NS; and 4341 to 4346 SNCF. The SNCF sets are based at Paris le Landy; other sets are all at Brussels Forest. All are capable of operation under the four traction supply voltages of France, Germany, the Netherlands and Belgium and also five different signalling and safety systems (France has different systems for high speed and conventional lines). It was the additional weight of the four voltage systems and signalling equipment, along with the requirement to keep within the French 17-tonne (37,485lb) axle load limit for LGV lines, that caused the initial delay in the design of these trains. There are some restrictions when operating in the Netherlands, where maximum speed is limited to 160km/h (100mph), and power is limited to 3680kW (5000hp) from the 1500V DC supply. The 10 PBA sets are not equipped for operation into Germany.

**Type:** High-speed intercity train set
**Power:** 8800kW (11956hp)
**Supply:** 25kV 50Hz AC or 1500V DC or 3000V DC or 15kV 16.7Hz AC
**Tractive effort:** N/A
**Max. operating speed:** 300km/h (187.5mph)
**Weight:** 388 tonnes (855,540lb) 10-car set
**Max. axle load:** 17 tonnes (37,485lb)
**Overall length:** 200,190mm (653ft 2in) 10-car set; 22,150mm (72ft 3in) motor coaches; 18,700mm (61ft 0in) trailers
**Gauge:** 1435mm (4ft 8.5in)

## CLASS EL 18 NORWEGIAN STATE RAILWAYS (NSB) NORWAY 1996

Norwegian State Railways (NSB) had a need to replace many older locomotives in the 1990s, and it purchased 22 locomotives to a design already operating successfully as class 460 on the Swiss Federal Railways. With their streamlined appearance and ribbed sides, these locomotives are among the quietest in the world. They are used on the Oslo–Bergen main line and to Trondheim and Stavanger.

**Type:** Bo-Bo mainline mixed-traffic electric prototype
**Power:** 15,000V 16.67Hz AC overhead line collection; 5400kW (7240hp); three-phase control; four body-mounted traction motors
**Tractive effort:** 275kN (61,820lbf)
**Max. operating speed:** 200km/h (125mph)
**Weight:** 80 tonnes (175,685lb)
**Max. axle load:** Not known
**Overall length:** 18.5m (60ft 8in)
**Gauge:** 1435mm (4ft 8.5in)

**The streamlined appearance and ribbed sides of Norway's class El 18 Bo-Bos give away their Swiss class 460 ancestry. The El 18 pictured here has just arrived at Oslo's Ost station.**

## CLASS 13 BELGIAN NATIONAL RAILWAYS (SNCB) BELGIUM 1997

To replace the oldest members of its electric fleet, SNCB ordered 60 class 13 locomotives. These are a dual-voltage mixed-traffic design using three-phase AC traction equipment. The locomotives are to be seen on the push-pull intercity trains from Oostende through Brussels to Eupen, and will later work the Oostende–Cologne trains as far as Aachen. Otherwise, class 13 is mostly employed on freight.

**Type:** Bo-Bo mainline mixed-traffic electric
**Power:** 3000V DC and 25,000V 50cHz AC overhead line collection; 5000kW (6700bhp); three-phase AC control; four frame-hung traction motors
**Tractive effort:** 288kN (64,745lbf)
**Max. operating speed:** 200km/h (125mph)
**Weight:** 90 tonnes (197,650lb)
**Max axle load:** Not known
**Overall length:** 19.11m (62ft 8in)

## CLASS SS8 BO-BO CHINESE RAILWAYS CHINA 1997

Two prototypes for this class were developed in 1994 at Zhuzhou Works, and the class was series built from 1997. China railways class SS8 'Shaoshan 8' series was originally built for the Guangshen high-speed line and currently serves on electrified trunk routes. About 200 units are in service – the design is still in production and available for export.

**Type:** Bo-Bo
**Power:** 3600kW (4891hp)
**Supply:** 25kV 50Hz AC
**Tractive effort:** 126kN (28350lbf)
**Max. operating speed:** 170km/h (106.3mph)
**Weight:** 88 tonnes (194,040lb)
**Max. axle load:** 22 tonnes (48,510lb)
**Overall length:** 17.516m (57ft 2in)
**Gauge:** 1435mm (4ft 8.5in)

## Class 101 Federal German Railways (DB) Germany 1997

*Deutsche Bundesbahn*, as DB was known in the years before German reunification, set up in the 1970s its range of InterCity services of locomotive-hauled stock that connected the principal cities in West Germany by regular-interval, clockface-timed fast trains. These standard formations included at least two first-class coaches, a bar-restaurant vehicle and up to nine second-class coaches. A feature of these trains, achievable because of the reliability of their timekeeping, was a series of cross-platform interchanges. For example, each half-hour on the stretch between Mainz and Dortmund, two InterCity trains arrive within two or three minutes of each other on opposite tracks across an island platform at *Köln Hauptbahnhof* (Cologne main station), enabling passengers to change trains quickly and easily.

The same two trains then take different routes – one via the Ruhr towns, the other via the Wupper valley – and meet again across a platform at Dortmund where further interchange takes place.

Reliability in operation was helped by provision of excellent locomotives in the form of the famous class 103 Co-Co electrics described elsewhere in this book. More modern locomotives of class

**Above: The class 101 is a very versatile locomotive design. It reliably heads up push-pull InterCity and many EuroCity trains throughout the country and beyond its borders.**

**Because of their widespread and indeed almost ubiquitous exposure all over the country, DB utilizes the class 101s to carry advertising, much of which may be considered offensive to the eye.**

120 later joined the fleet, enabling the InterCity services to expand further in destinations and frequency. The 120s had the additional feature of being able to work trains in push-pull mode, for which DB provided a fleet of streamlined driving trailer second-class coaches.

One of the effects of German reunification was the inclusion of Berlin, Leipzig and Dresden in the InterCity network, adding in particular Leipzig to the many stations at which some InterCity trains needed to reverse. Others were Frankfurt-am-Main, Stuttgart and Munich. Some services from Munich to Frankfurt have also to reverse at Nürnberg.

The 145 class 103 locomotives needed replacement as their life expiry drew close, bearing in mind that they had run possibly the highest mileage in service of any electric locomotives in the world during their active and reliable 30-year life span. Meanwhile, locomotive manufacturer Adtranz had produced its three-phase express prototype No. 128 001. This machine had been extensively tested on DB metals and had clearly impressed.

*Deutsche Bahn* (the combined German railway system following reunification) ordered 145 new, high-powered Bo-Bos of class 101 from Adtranz to replace the 103s, and deliveries began in 1997. These are extremely capable machines, modern in electrical concept having three-phase traction equipment, and they are equipped for push-pull operation. Each traction motor is fed from a dedicated three-phase power converter, enabling the input to each motor to be optimized for adhesion and load conditions. Traction motors are mounted on the locomotive body and drive individual axles through cardan shafts. The locomotives are in DB's latest shade of red (*verkehrsrot* – traffic red), set off by twin white blocks on the cab front either side of the DB logo. This colour scheme enables the locomotives' simple, streamlined shape to be emphasised. The same cannot be said for the many advertising liveries which DB has been fortunate (financially) to be asked to apply to many of the fleet. One of them asked if the viewer had a headache (advertising a popular painkiller) – the livery itself could easily have provoked one!

The 101s have taken over all regular InterCity and EuroCity (EC) services in Germany, other than those rostered for the class 120s. The 101s are seen as far afield as Vienna in Austria and are now DB's flagship locomotive class.

**Type:** Bo-Bo mainline express passenger electric
**Power:** 15,000V 16.67Hz AC overhead line collection; 6400kW (8780hp); three-phase control; four body-mounted traction motors
**Tractive effort:** 300kN (67,440lbf)
**Max. operating speed:** 220km/h (137mph)
**Weight:** 87 tonnes (191,060lb)
**Max. axle load:**
**Overall length:** 19.1m (62ft 8in)
**Gauge:** 1435mm (4ft 8.5in)

## HEATHROW EXPRESS CLASS 332 HEATHROW EXPRESS — GREAT BRITAIN 1997

**One of the 160km/h (100mph) Heathrow Express trains boards passengers at London's Paddington station. The airport service offers a journey time of 15 minutes, every 15 minutes.**

The scheme to link the London West End with Heathrow Airport by fast 'overground' train was finally realized in 1998. A new branch line peels south off the main line from Paddington soon after Hayes & Harlington station. The branch then goes quickly underground to avoid the airport runways, and it has two stations serving the airport's Terminals 1, 2 and 3, and Terminal 4.

The service has a journey time of 15 minutes and a frequency of one train every 15 minutes. To achieve this journey time. a top running speed of 160km/h (100mph) was specified. Fourteen four-car EMUs were delivered in 1997 and 1998 by Siemens, having been assembled at the CAF factory in Zaragoza, Spain.

All the units are fully air conditioned, and there is first-class accommodation in one driving car on each set. Internally, they feature television monitor displays for passengers which relay news and travel information.

**Type:** Airport express four-car electric multiple unit
**Power per unit:** 25,000V 50Hz AC overhead line collection; 1400kW (1875bhp); four traction motors
**Tractive effort:** Not known
**Max. operating speed:** 160km/h (100mph)
**Weight:** 36 to 49 tonnes (78,620 to 107,200lb)
**Overall length:** 23.74m (77ft 11in) end cars; 23.15m (75ft 11in)
**Gauge:** 1435mm (4ft 8.5in)

**The Siemens designed and built class 332 Heathrow Express trains have a streamlined front end with curved cab windscreens. More than half of the service's drivers are female.**

## CLASS DD-AR (7800) NETHERLANDS RAILWAYS (NS) NETHERLANDS 1997

Central Holland is a buoyant part of the Netherlands economy, as it contains the capital city, Den Haag (The Hague); the largest cities, Amsterdam, Rotterdam and Utrecht; and some significant industrial towns including Hoogovens and Haarlem. In common parlance, Amsterdam, Rotterdam and Utrecht are grouped under the name Randstad and contain the heaviest concentration of population in the Netherlands. The Randstad also includes the Netherlands' principal international airport, Schipol near Amsterdam.

Netherlands Railways (*Nederlandse Spoorwegen*, NS) is key to the continued effective functioning of this area. There is very heavy commuting all round and within the Randstad, with journeys being made in all directions at peak times, and the railway handles a high proportion of this traffic.

The recent need has been to ensure that this traffic flow continues unimpeded, despite ever-increasing passenger numbers. To achieve this, in the past 50 years, NS has developed a highly sophisticated, dense network of suburban rail services. These services are run largely by electric multiple units that can split and join frequently by virtue of their reliable and robust Scharfenberg automatic couplers – and they have expanded track capacity.

Since 1985, NS has coped with continuing increases in traffic on its commuter services in the major cities by adding double-deck suburban carriages to its carriage fleet. The first 15 or so sets were locomotive-hauled push-pull trains which were powered by class 1700 locomotives, and they were intended for outer-suburban work from Amsterdam.

However, from 1992, came 79 inner-suburban sets of three and four double-deck coaches intended for peak and other workings around the Randstad area. These sets were initially also powered by class 1700 electric locomotives.

These double-deck carriages make use of the very large NS loading gauge to form what are among the largest cross-section vehicles in Europe. Thus, although they have two storeys, these carriages have plenty of circulating room and headroom, as well as being able to carry 576 seated passengers in just four carriages. They follow the 'French' layout of double-deck stock with stairways at each end of the double-floor section leading to a circulating platform and entrance doorways above the bogies. This means that the doorways are at high platform level to suit Dutch station standards, yet the lower deck floors are well below platform level and the upper decks are considerably higher.

The cab fronts of these Dutch sets are neatly designed with backward-sloping windscreens. Unlike other NS multiple units, they have side buffers because they are locomotive-hauled stock. All the carriages are painted NS yellow with dark grey roofs and black cab windscreen surrounds, together with three blue diagonal stripes on the bodysides.

By 1997, NS began to receive deliveries of 50 powerful driving power cars of type mDDM to replace the class 1700 locomotives on a large proportion of these trains. The power cars are unusual in a number of ways. They are ostensibly double-deck vehicles, but the passenger accommodation is all on the upper deck. The upper deck is lower than the top decks on the carriages that they haul and propel. Below the upper deck on each power car are compartments for electrical equipment that have side-opening hatches. Unlike any other EMU power cars in the world known to the author, these have a Bo-Bo-Bo triple-bogie arrangement.

At face value, this would seem to be over-provision for the movement of only three or four trailer carriages. Presumably, however, they could be used for longer train sets if so required in the future if the Dutch travel network continues its seemingly relentless expansion.

**Type:** Bo-Bo-BO suburban electric multiple-unit power car
**Power:** 1500V DC overhead line collection; 2400kW (3215hp); six traction motors
**Tractive effort:** Not known
**Max. operating speed:** 140km/h (87mph)
**Weight:** Not known
**Max. axle load:** Not known
**Overall length:** 26.4m (86ft 7in)

## WL86 2XBO-BO RUSSIAN STATE RAILWAYS (RZD) RUSSIA 1997

Struggling to move on after decades of mass producing outdated and inefficient designs, the Russian Kolomna factory (known today as '*Kolomensky Zavod*') has devised a range of electric locomotives to break away from the Soviet concept of simply creating multi section units for ever-increasing power outputs.

Five models of the WL86 2xBo-Bo have been developed, of which four exist in prototype form. EP100 and EP101 are DC types for 200 and 160km/h (125 and 100mph), with EP200 and EP201 being corresponding AC versions.

All the models are based on a common, generic mechanical design, running on two unusual four-axle bogies. Rheostatic braking of 8000kW (10870hp) capacity and a 1200kW (1630hp) train hotel supply also unusually feature in this model.

Apart from the EP200 prototypes and a pre-series batch of eight EP101 supplied to Russian railways (RZD), it remains to be seen whether any production versions will result in the face of growing interest in the market from other world suppliers – especially as the four-axle bogies found on these locomotives are unlikely to prove acceptable in any other part of the world.

**Type:** Bo-Bo-Bo-Bo
**Power:** EP100/101 - 9600kW (13133hp) EP200/201 - 8000kW (10870hp)
**Supply:** 3000V DC or 25kV 50Hz AC
**Tractive effort:** 235kN or 284.5kN (52875lbf or 63900lbf)
**Max. operating speed:** 160 or 200km/h (100 or 125mph)
**Weight:** 180 tonnes (396,900lb)
**Max. axle load:** 22.5 tonnes (49,616lb)
**Overall length:** 25m (81ft 6in)
**Gauge:** 1524mm (5ft)

## SIEMENS 'TAURUS' AUSTRIAN FEDERAL RAILWAYS (ÖBB) AUSTRIA 1998

Developed from its 'Eurosprinter' family, the Siemens 'Taurus' first appeared in Austria, where ÖBB gave it the name. German DB class 152 is based on the 'Eurosprinter' – Austrian railways ordered 400 further derivatives, technically similar, with the distinctively styled cabs, brake discs mounted on separate shafts (DB class 152 has axle-mounted discs) and lower track force bogies. Track force proved to be a problem, and ÖBB subsequently banned DB class 152 from Austria. DB converted 25 class 152s order into class 182 'Taurus' type units to maintain through operations.

Siemens' own Dispolok fleet has the type as ES64U2, in use with operators such as Netlog, while HUPAC has acquired its own. The German units are 15kV, as is ÖBB class 1016; however, class 1116 is for dual 15kV and 25kV operation. Ten similar dual voltage units are operated by Hungarian Railways (MÁV), class 1047 and five by GySEV class 1047.5.

The design is likely to find wider application, with Slovakian, Czech, Slovenian and Romanian railways showing interest.

**Type:** Bo-Bo universal
**Power:** 6400kW (8696hp)
**Supply:** 15kV 16.7Hz or 25 kV 50Hz AC (1500V and 3000V DC planned)
**Tractive effort:** 300kN (67500lbf)
**Max. operating speed:** 230km/h (143.8mph)
**Weight:** 85 tonnes (187,425lb)
**Max. axle load:** 21.5 tonnes (47,408lb)
**Overall length:**
**Gauge:** 1435mm (4ft 8.5in)

## CLASS DDJ1 EMU CHINESE RAILWAYS — CHINA 1998

Class DDJ1 electric train sets are the first high-speed – i.e. above 200km.h (125mph) – trains developed within China. They are formed of a Bo-Bo power car, four single-deck and one double-deck intermediate, and one single-deck driving trailer. Seating 438 passengers in all, class DDJ1 entered service in 2000.

**Type:** High-speed EMU
**Power:** 3600kW (4892hp)
**Supply:** 25kV 50Hz AC
**Tractive effort:** N/A
**Max. operating speed:** 220km/h (137.5mph)
**Weight:** 440 tonnes (970,200lb)
**Max. axle load:** 20 tonnes (44,100lb)
**Overall length:** 176m (574ft 3in) per unit
**Gauge:** 1435mm (4ft 8.5in)

## PRIMA FRENCH NATIONAL RAILWAYS (SNCF) — FRANCE 1998

PRIMA from the French Alsthom traction group is a range of modular locomotive designs for both electric and diesel. Models are configurable as universal or multipurpose applications, or tailored to operator's specific requirements. In the electric field, Alsthom is marketing the PRIMA against German industry with Siemens' 'Eurosprinter' model and Bombardier's (formerly ADtranz) Octeon range.

The basic PRIMA range currently consists of the four-axle EL4200B configured for 140km/h (87.5mph) general freight, EL4200B configured for 220km/h (137.5mph) express passenger, the four-axle EL6000B for 220km/h heavy international passenger, and the six-axle EL6300C for 140km/h heavy freight haulage. A double-unit Bo-Bo rated at 9600kW (13,043hp) geared down to 100km/h (62.1mph) is also available for special heavy work over difficult routes. All locomotives offered may be adapted to work off one or any of the four main European electric traction supply systems in any permutation. The ability to operate from 25kV 50Hz AC (France, Luxembourg, Denmark, Hungary, Czech Republic, Slovakia, Bulgaria, Greece, Romania) or 15kV 16.67Hz AC (Germany, Austria, Switzerland, Sweden, Norway) or 3000V DC (Belgium, Italy, Spain, Czech Republic, Slovakia, Poland) or 1500V DC (France, Netherlands) is an inbuilt design feature. The Alsthom ONIX traction package using IGBT technology drives asynchronous traction motors in both electric and diesel variants, while a DC traction motored option is also available to the diesel packages. PRIMA is designed to meet all European environmental concerns including energy use, exhaust and noise emissions. Supplementing this electrical interoperability is construction modularity of four- or six-axle bogies and variable body length. The same mechanical components feature in the diesel electric series such as the DE32B in the United Kingdom or DE43 for Iran. To date, orders for electric locomotives from the PRIMA range have come only from the freight business division of French state railway operator SNCF.

With more than 1000 ageing electric locomotives to be replaced, the initial order was for more than 400 machines, of which 120 were quickly confirmed. Starting with deliveries in 2001, SNCF Fret has 140km/h (87.5mph) Bo-Bos on order with three different voltage permutations – 90 dual-voltage 1500V DC and 25kV 50Hz AC (class BB27000), 29 triple-voltage 1500V DC, 25kV 50Hz AC and 15kV 16.2/3Hz AC (class BB37000) and a single class BB37500 for triple-voltage operation from 1500V DC, 3000V DC and 25kV 50Hz AC. By mid-2002, sufficient BB27000s had been delivered to Avignon depot to displace the last ageing CC7100 machines from traffic. Delivery of new dedicated freight locomotives marks a step change in SNCF motive power policy, as the previous trends were to cascade older designs from passenger work to freight.

BB27000s are configured to perform with 4200kW (5706hp) continuous power output in the entire range from 57 to 140km/h (87.5mph), continuous tractive effort 250kN at 57km/h (35.6mph) and a maximum effort of 350kN under ideal 36 per cent adhesion conditions. Locomotives are equipped with both rheostatic and regenerative dynamic braking. These machines are dedicated to freight traffic, so no provision is made for electric train auxiliary or hotel power. In 2001, a further 180 options were taken up for delivery between 2003 and 2007. No diesel locomotives have yet been ordered by SNCF, but the series has scored a number of export orders. Versions built at Belfort are being delivered to Iran, Israel, Sri Lanka and Syria with Ruston RK215 engines. EMD 710 engines were specified for Israel and the United Kingdom and are being built at Valencia in Spain.

**Type:** Bo-Bo or Co-Co universal design range
**Power:** Options up to 6300kW (8560hp) per unit
**Supply:** Any or all of 1500V DC or 3000V DC or 25kV 50Hz AC or 15kV 16.2/3Hz AC
**Tractive effort:** Variable
**Max. operating speed:** Configurable up to 230km/h (143.8mph)
**Weight:** Configurable Bo-Bo up to 90 tonnes (198,450lb) or Co-Co up to 135 tonnes (297,675lb)
**Max. axle load:** Configurable up to 22.5 tonnes (49,613lb)
**Overall length:** Variable
**Gauge:** 1435mm (4ft 8.5in)

## CLASS H561 BO-BO GREEK STATE RAILWAYS (OSE) — GREECE 1998

The first main line electric locomotives to be delivered to Greece state railways Organismos Sidirodromon Ellados (OSE), forerunners of a much larger fleet. The first six class H561 were delivered to for work on the 76km (48 mile) section between Thessalonaki and Idomeni on the border with Macedonia. Options exist for 24 more of these 'Hellas Sprinter' editions of the successful Siemens 'Eurosprinter' model that are likely to be taken up at some time in the near future for electrification of the 511km (319 mile) main line between Athens and Thessalonaki.

The route is currently undergoing major upgrading works for a distance of 200km/h (125mph), running including significant sections of route on new alignment, double tracking and resignalling. Electrification should follow on completion of the civil engineering work.

**Type:** Co-Co heavy freight and passenger
**Power:** 5000kW (6793hp)
**Supply:** 25kV 50Hz AC
**Tractive effort:** 300kN (67500lbf)
**Max. operating speed:** 200km/h (125mph)
**Weight:** 90 tonnes (198,450lb)
**Max. axle load:** 22.5 tonnes (49,613lb)
**Overall length:** 20.38m (66ft 6in)
**Gauge:** 1435mm (4ft 8.5in)

## CLASS 3000 BO-BO LUXEMBOURG RAILWAYS (CFL) — LUXEMBOURG 1998

Luxembourg railways (CFL) class 3000 and Belgium railways (SNCB) class 13 are identical dual-system AC/DC locomotives. They are used for high-speed passenger and heavy freight within both networks and cross-border work into France. Built by ACEC with Alsthom electrical equipment, the 3000's unusual cab styling reduces the aerodynamic effect of the overhead wire pantograph when passing trains at high speed. CFL class 3000 largely replaced the original electric locomotives of Luxembourg, class 3600.

**Type:** Bo-Bo universal
**Power:** 5200kW (7065hp)
**Supply:** 25kV 50Hz AC or 3000V DC or 1500V DC
**Tractive effort:** 288kN (64800lbf)
**Max. operating speed:** 200km/h (125mph)
**Weight:** 90 tonnes (198,450lb)
**Max. axle load:** 22.5 tonnes (49,613lb)
**Overall length:** 19.11m (62ft 4in)
**Gauge:** 1435mm (4ft 8.5in)

**A Class 3000 engine no. 3015 carries a passenger train near Montenach, on the French-Luxembourg border, in September 2000.**

## FLYTOGET AS CLASS BM71 NORWEGIAN STATE RAILWAYS (NSB) NORWAY 1998

When Norway built a new airport at Gardemoen to Oslo's northeast, it came with a well-aligned railway branch line. Sixteen new three-car EMUs were delivered to provide a fast journey. Air-conditioned with high-quality interior accommodation, they have semi-streamlined fronts ends that have a rather blunt appearance and are liveried in grey.

**Type:** Airport express three-car electric multiple unit
**Power per unit:** 15,000V 16.67Hz AC overhead line collection; 1950kW (2615hp); traction motors
**Tractive effort:** Not known
**Max. operating speed:** 210km/h (130mph)
**Weight:** Not known
**Max axle load:** Not known
**Overall length:** Not known

## EU43 POLISH STATE RAILWAYS (PKP) POLAND 1998

In the late 1990s, PKP ordered a small fleet of dual-voltage electrics from ADtranz Pafawag Works in Wroclaw (now Daimler Chrysler Rail Systems) for cross-border work into Germany. Based on Italy's class E.412, these were to be classed EU43 for use on international through trains, but difficulties have delayed implementation in regular service, despite testing of the E.412 in Poland.

(Statistics based on Italian class E.412 electric)

**Type:** Bo-Bo dual voltage electric, 3000 volt DC and 15 kV 16 2/3Hz AC
**Power:** N/A
**Tractive effort:** N/A
**Max. operating speed:** 200km/h (125mph)
**Weight:** N/A
**Overall length:** N/A
**Max. axle load:** N/A
**Gauge:** 1435mm (4ft 8.5in)

## HHL ELECTRIC AMTRAK USA 1998

In conjunction with Amtrak's long-awaited electrification of its Boston, Massachusetts, to New Haven, Connecticut, segment of the Northeast Corridor route, Amtrak ordered additional electric locomotives. The HHL (sometimes listed as HHP-8) is a double-ended, streamlined machine with the cab and nose sections using the same style as the high-profile *Acela Express* six-car 240km/h (150mph) train sets. 'HH' in the designation signifies 'high-horsepower'. At the time of writing, 15 locomotives, Nos 650–664, had been built by a consortium of Alsthom and Bombardier, which also built the *Acela Express* trains. The HHLs are rated at 5968kW (8000hp), allowing them to handle longer consists than the AEM-7 electrics. The first HHLs were built in 1998.

**Amtrak's HHLs are used on heavy Northeast Corridor trains. Although they share styling with the *Acela Express* trains, these locomotives are double-ended, not permanently coupled to tilting train sets.**

**Type:** Bo-Bo high-speed electric locomotive
**Power:** 12kV AC at 25Hz, 12kV AC at 60Hz, 25kV AC at 60Hz
**Output:** 5968kW (8000hp)
**Tractive effort:** N/A
**Max. operating speed:** 200km/h (125mph)
**Weight:** 100 tonnes (220,500lb)
**Max axle load:** Not known
**Overall length:** N/A
**Gauge:** 1435mm (4ft 8.5in)

## DSB/SJ CLASS ET EMU ØRESUND LINK DENMARK/SWEDEN 1999

July 2000 saw the opening of the Øresund link connecting Sweden and Denmark. Øresund is the second of three fixed links in the region linking Denmark, Sweden and Germany. The earlier Storebælt link connects the two principal parts of Denmark, the western mainland area with the eastern island where Copenhagen is situated. The Øresund link connects the same eastern section of Denmark with Sweden. The third connection, the Fehmarn Belt link, is at the planning stage and will link Denmark with Germany.

For passenger traffic over the Øresund link, fast high-performance three-car electric multiple units were jointly ordered by Denmark and Sweden state railways, DSB and SJ. The original order placed with ADtranz was for 27 sets with a further 18 options. Seventeen sets were to be owned by DSB as class ET and 10 by SJ as class X31. Options and revision to orders have been taken up to a total of 44, with 20 sets for DSB and 20 for SJ. The steel-bodied cars are part of the ADtranz (subsequently taken over by Bombardier) AIM modular electric multiple unit concept, but with rubber ring ends making them similar in appearance to earlier units delivered to DSB. The pressurized rubber end seals encase the front end connection, with a folded back driver's position when units are connected. This was devised because of the need to divide and combine portions en route, but still keep large gangways throughout the combined train length.

The design first appeared on DSB IC3 articulated diesel sets of 1989 found on all daytime intercity trains in Denmark before the Storebælt link opened. DSB IR4 units of 1996 are four-car electric versions for the Storebælt link rated at 1680kW (2283hp). Class ET for the Øresund link are much more highly rated, with 2120kW (2880hp). Denmark's railways are electrified at 25kV 50Hz AC, while Sweden uses 15kV 16.67Hz AC, so class ET sets are dual supply with automatic voltage detection and switching equipment. Up to five units may operate in multiple.

The Øresund link itself is a combined road and rail structure with both tunnel and bridge. Westwards from Sweden is initially over a bridge section. The gradients either side of the high bridge are one of the ruling design requirements with 1.25 per cent grades on the Swedish side and 1.55 per cent on the Danish side. Continuing west, the line crosses the 4055m (2.52-mile) long artificial island of Peberholmen (created using material dredged from the tunnel works). The tunnel is a submerged concrete box containing the two rail tracks and two roadways consisting of 20 sections, each 175m (571ft) long. Service over the link connects Copenhagen and Helsingor in Denmark with Helsingborg and Malmo in Sweden. A shuttle service running every 20 minutes is operated from 0500 to 2400 daily, of 30 minutes duration with four intermediate stops. IC3 diesel units operate over the link on EuroCity services from Hamburg. Freight traffic is to be operated by DSB Gods class EG and DB Cargo class 185. SJ has no suitable dual-voltage locomotives.

**Type:** Three-car express EMU
**Power:** 2120kW (2880hp)
**Supply:** 25kV 50Hz AC or 15kV 16.67Hz AC
**Tractive effort:** N/A
**Max. operating speed:** 180km/h (112.5mph)
**Weight:** 153 tonnes (337,365lb)
**Max. axle load:** 19 tonnes (41,895lb)
**Overall length:** 78.9m (257ft 6in) three-car unit
**Gauge:** 1435mm (4ft 8.5in)

## CLASS EG Co-Co DANISH RAILWAYS (DSB) DENMARK 1999

In all, thirteen heavy freight locomotives, with a further seven options not yet taken up, were supplied by Siemens and Krauss-Maffei of Germany to Denmark in 1999–2000. Ordered in 1997, class EG are to the requirements of the cargo division of Danish State Railways, DSB Gods, for heavy freight over the Great Belt fixed link. Such a link had been under discussion for several decades, one of three in the region planned to connect Denmark, Sweden and Germany. Serious design work on the Great Belt, or Storebælt, link started in 1965, but works were frozen in 1978, only restarting in 1986 when the formal go-ahead was finally given.

The major infrastructure works for the Storebælt link were completed towards the end of 1996 and consisted of three principal sections, the 6.6km (4.2-mile) long west bridge, a 3km (1.9-mile) crossing of Sprogo island and the 8km (5-mile) east tunnel. The suspension bridge is supported by 85cm (33in) thick cables made up of 115 million metres (around 72 miles) of wire, while the twin bore tunnel is immersed on the sea bed.

The Great Belt links two sections of Denmark, the large eastern island Sjelland area with the western mainland Jylland area. The capital city of Copenhagen and the country's main airport are located in Sjelland, with a large demand for increased rail and road links. Rail traffic connecting the two parts of Denmark was traditionally borne by rail ferries, restricting freight traffic to around 20 trains per day. Opening of the link would provide DSB with a through international rail link to partner EU countries through Germany, with accompany substantial increases in freight traffic expected.

The new rail works were an extension of the existing 25kV 50Hz AC network centred on Copenhagen. Passenger traffic is handled by new class IR4 articulated electric multiple units trains based on the successful IC3 diesel trains. Perhaps surprisingly, some weekends peak traffic on the link is operated by class ME diesel electric locomotives.

Domestic passenger journey times are reduced by some one to two hours, with a route capacity of 140 trains. Up to 100 freight train paths are available for use.

The Great Belt link officially opened for rail traffic in April 1997, with an initial service of 40 freight trains removed from the Korsor to Nyborg ferries directly closed by the fixed link. Freight trains were increased by 50 per cent just two months later by diversion of freight away from the Rodby to Puttgarten ferry, although the latter remains in use for now for passenger trains. On opening, existing EA class locomotives were used in multiple pairs or triplets to overcome the heavy gradients. The new EGs are capable of working a 2000-tonne (1969-ton) load at 120km/h (75mph) on level track, as well as working the same load over the 1.6 per cent (1 in 64) grades of the Storebælt. EG are members of the Siemens 'Eurosprinter' family, with external body styling similar to DB cargo class 152.

Unlike other 'Eurosprinters', class EGs are Co-Co machines. Other contemporary European types are of four axle Bo-Bo layout. The six-axle layout was demanded by the load and gradient profile of both the Storebælt and Øresund links. The Øresund link was opened between Denmark and Sweden in 2000, leading to the expansion of the EG operation, enabling through freight from Malmo in Sweden using the Øresund to access and cross Denmark for the Storebælt link to Germany and the rest of Europe. Through operation to Hamburg started in 2002.

Dual-current equipment is a necessary attribute on the class EG machines, as DSB uses 25kV, while the SJ in Sweden and the DB in Germany use 15kV.

**Type:** Co-Co heavy freight, dual-voltage
**Power:** 6500kW (8832hp)
**Supply:** 25kV 50 AC or 15kV 16.67Hz AC
**Tractive effort:** 400kN (90000lbf)
**Max. operating speed:** 140km/h (87.5mph)
**Weight:** 129 tonnes (284,445lb)
**Max. axle load:** 21.5 tonnes (47,408lb)
**Overall length:** 20.95m (68ft 4in)
**Gauge:** 1435mm (4ft 8.5in)

**No. 3103 is one of Denmark's most powerful locomotives and can operate into both Germany and Sweden on heavy freight.**

## 'JUNIPER' EMUs GATWICK EXPRESS GREAT BRITAIN 1999

'Juniper' is a brand name for three classes of electric multiple units that were ordered for use by train operating companies after the privatization of British Rail. The train operators and the leasing companies that put up the finance for such new builds were keen to take advantage of supplier's new standard designs that would have longer term benefits in reducing production costs. 'Junipers' that have been supplied to date are two classes for the DC network south of the River Thames and one for an AC application in the Strathclyde

**The striking nose cone and the red roofs of the Gatwick Express EMUs make them more visible from the air, so the term 'Gatwick Express' is painted on the roof of each power car.**

suburban area around Glasgow in Scotland.

The first Alsthom 'Junipers' to enter fleet service were the eight class 460 'Gatwick Express' units. These are eight-car sets of air-conditioned stock designed to impress foreign visitors arriving at Gatwick Airport who want a fast run to London Victoria. Because of the standardized body style of the 'Juniper' breed, originally proposed for suburban use, the wide entrance doors are at front and back positions on the bodysides. This actually helps handling heavy luggage, but would not otherwise be suitable for what is supposed to be an intercity-quality train. Five of the eight carriages are powered, each with two traction motors on one bogie. One power car is a baggage car for the heaviest luggage items. These units have regenerative brakes. The 'Gatwick Express' sets carry a striking red-and-grey livery with red roofs.

The South West Trains class 458s are 30 four-car sets intended for suburban use out of London Waterloo to destinations such as Windsor, Reading and Alton. Unlike the class 460s, these units have retractable gangways in the front ends so that they can be fully gangwayed when working in multiple. They are liveried in a truncated version of the South West Trains colours that look so good on class 442 express sets.

ScotRail has 40 three-car 'Juniper' class 334 suburban units working in the Glasgow area. These are similar to the 458s, but have full-width driving cabs and non-gangwayed. (All 'Junipers' are gangwayed within the units.) A new feature for the United Kingdom is the use of CCTV monitors inside the driving cabs of these units to enable the driver to watch passengers board and alight so that he can shut the doors safely without leaning out of his cab window or leaving his cab. These units work out of Glasgow to Paisley, Ayr and Largs, and are also being introduced on the cross-city lines that serve Dumbarton and Helensburgh. ScotRail has specified a livery that is based on the Strathclyde Passenger Executive's maroon-and-cream style, but in more modern layout with a blue flash along the sides.

Introduction of the 'Junipers' has been a long, drawn-out process. Each group of stock has had to pass Railtrack's vehicle acceptance process, but, in addition, have proved to possess a degree of unexpected unreliability in operation. Programmes of modifications have been undertaken, partly at the supplier's factory at Washwood Heath, Birmingham, and also at maintenance depots. The Gatwick sets are currently in service, but are backed up by three of the old class 73/2 hauled sets of mark 2 carriages. Introduction of the ScotRail units is well advanced; however, the class 458 is only just reaching the point of introduction as a fleet.

**Type:** Eight-car ('460'), four-car ('458') and three-car ('334') electric multiple unit
**Power per unit:** 750V DC conductor rail collection classes 458 and 460, and 25,000V 50Hz AC overhead line collection class 334; three-phase AC traction control; four (class 334), six (class 458), or 10 (class 460) 270kW (360bhp) axle-mounted traction motors
**Tractive effort:** Not known
**Max. operating speed:** 160km/h (100mph)
**Weight:** 34 to 45 tonnes (75,000 to 101,470lb)
**Max axle load:** Not known
**Overall length:** 21.16m (69ft 5in) end cars, 19.94m(65ft 5in) middle cars
**Gauge:** 1435mm (4ft 8.5in)

**Class 458 Juniper EMU No. 8006 awaits departure from London's Waterloo station.**

## *ACELA EXPRESS* AMTRAK USA 1999

In the late 1990s, after years of discussion and planning, Amtrak finally electrified all the way to Boston, Massachusetts, and ordered all-new high-speed train sets to operate on the Boston–New York–Philadelphia–Washington DC Northeast Corridor route. For years, Amtrak trains would change from diesel to electric locomotives at New Haven, Connecticut. New Haven Railroad had overcome the need to change engines by using the dual-mode FL9, but the advantage of using this type was greatly diminished when Amtrak took over and began running most Boston to New York trains through to Washington DC.

In December 2000, Amtrak introduced its Acela Express service using high-powered six-car tilting train sets that can operate at speeds up to 240km/h (150mph). These use Bombardier's tilting

**America's fastest train is Amtrak's *Acela Express*, which reaches a top speed of 240km/h (150mph). One of these streamlined trains is seen at Washington Union Station.**

system (originally devised for the Canadian LRC trains) and an Alsthom electrical propulsion system similar to that employed on the French TGV.

Although the Boston–Washington route is now entirely electrified, there are still several different electrification systems in place on various sections of the line as a result of complex history of the route. As a result of this, the *Acela Express* needs to adjust to different voltages and frequencies as it travels along the Northeast Corridor. Each train has a semi-permanently streamlined locomotive power car at each end.

**Type:** Eight-piece/six-car high-speed electric train
**Power:** 12kV AC at 25Hz, 12kV AC at 60Hz, 25kV AC at 60Hz
**Output:** 9200kW (12,337hp)
**Tractive effort:** 222kN (50,000lbf) starting TE
**Max. operating speed:** 240km/h (150mph)
**Weight:** 566 tonnes (1,248,000lb) for whole train set
**Train length:** 202.082m (663ft) for whole train set
**Power car length:** 21.209m (69ft 7in)
**Max. axle load:** N/A
**Gauge:** 1435mm (4ft 8.5in)

***Acela Express*** **trains can operate up to 240km/h (150mph) on certain portions of the Northeast Corridor between New London, Connecticut, and Boston, but are restricted to slower speeds leaving Washington Union Station.**

## IORE Co-Co LUOSSAVAARA KIRUNAVAARA AKTIEBOLAGET (LKAB) SWEDEN 2000

IORE locomotives form the traction element of a major rail logistics investment made by the Swedish iron ore concern Luossavaara Kirunavaara Aktiebolaget (LKAB). Deregulation of railway traffic allowed LKAB to seize the opportunity of reducing transport costs, and it was granted ore traffic rights in January 1993. The company began operations in July 1996 through two subsidiary concerns, MTAB Malmtrafik i Kiruna AB (MTAB) and Malmtrafikk AS (MTAS) (based in Sweden and Norway, respectively).

MTAB and MTAS carry 20 million tonnes (19.685 million tons) of iron ore products from Kiruna and Malmberget mines to Narvik and Luleå sea ports, and from the concentrating and palletizing plants in Svappavaara. Between 10 and 12 trains operate

**The IORE locomotives work in back-to-back pairs producing 10800kW (14675bhp) and will soon be hauling trains weighing 8100 tonnes (7972 tons) in total.**

between Kiruna and Narvik, and one for Luleå every 24 hours. In addition, four each operate between Malmberget and Luleå, and Kiruna and Svappavaara in the same period. Key objectives were fewer, longer and heavier trains by investment in new locomotives and wagons based around an increase in axle load to 30 tonnes (66,150lb).

Ore mined in Australia, Brazil, Canada and South Africa by LKABs' competitors is from large open-cast workings, whereas the Swedish ore is from more expensive and complicated deep underground mines. Rail transportation costs per tonne kilometre were also some two to four times those of overseas rivals, who could run trains loaded up to 150–250 cars of 30-plus tonnes (66,150-plus pounds) axle loading. In June 1998, LKAB approved 1.1 billion Swedish Kronor of capital expenditure for rolling stock replacement consisting of nine locomotives from ADtranz (Germany) and 209 ore wagons from Transwerk (South Africa).

Designated Uanoo, the new wagons feature low track force bogies of South African design and 100-tonne (220,500lb) payload to replace existing 80-tonne (176,400lb) Uad type wagons. The effect of the new wagons is to make substantial savings in all aspects of the rail operation. Each train set is increased from 52 to 68 cars, a decrease in the number of trains from 7000 to 4000 per year, a decrease in the total number of wagons by 250 and an increase in train speed from 50km/h (31.3mph) to 60km/h (37.5mph), saving an estimated 45 per cent in costs per tonne kilometre. With transport operating costs at the same level as those of the competition, LKAB has the potential to increase annual production to 30 million tonnes (29.53 million tons). Despite the increase in train weight, overall locomotive requirements are lower because the distance travelled per year by each locomotive has reduced. This also means only nine locomotives are required, compared to 19 previously.

Ordered from ADtranz, which was subsequently taken over by Bombardier, the first IORE locomotive was delivered from the Kassel works in Germany in August 2000. Delivery of the remaining eight will take place over an extended period from 2002–4. After commissioning and test running, IORE 1 entered regular traffic in 2002, hauling older Uad wagons. In late 2000, a pre-series batch of 68 new wagons was made for trial running.

Initially, the IORE locomotives will run unballasted with overall weight of 300 tonnes (661,500lb) over the 12 axles until infrastructure changes have been made allowing the full tractive effort potential of 1350kN to be exploited with the full 30-tonne (66,150lb) axle load. One three-phase asynchronous traction motor is suspended on each axle, with three axles per bogie and each bogie with one water-cooled GTO inverter. ADtranz MITRAC diagnostics and information systems are fitted, as is adhesion control. Regenerative braking is fitted, expected to yield a 30 per cent saving in energy consumption. The electrical braking system is of 10800kW (14675hp) maximum power rating with a maximum braking effort of 750kN. The nine IORE machines are expected to replace the 15 7176kW 9750hp class Dm3 triple units dating from 1969–70 taken over from SJ and six El15 10190kW (7500hp) single units operated in pairs (acquired from NSB and built in 1967).

**Type:** Double Co-Co for heavy mineral traffic
**Power:** Twin unit 10,800kW (14,675hp)
**Supply:** 15kV 16.67Hz AC
**Tractive effort:** Twin unit unballasted 1200kN (270,000lbf); ballasted 1350kN (303,750lbf)
**Max. operating speed:** 80km/h (50mph)
**Weight:** Twin unit 300 tonnes (661,500lb) (excluding ballast); 360 tonnes (793,800lb) (including ballast)
**Max. axle load:** 25 tonnes (55,125lb) (excluding ballast); 30 tonnes (66,150lb) (including ballast)
**Overall length:** Twin unit 45.8m (149ft 5in)
**Gauge:** 1435mm (4ft 8.5in)

## IMU 120 Interurban Train — AIRTRAIN CITYLINK — AUSTRALIA 2001

Opened in May 2001, this line links Brisbane Airport both with the city and with the holiday resort of the Gold Coast to the south. Running to the same 1067mm (3ft 6in) gauge as the Queensland Railways, the trains operate an integrated service both with the QR Cityrail and the outer suburban systems. For 8.5km (5.3 miles), the track is carried on a concrete viaduct 12.5m (41ft) high. Four three-car interurban EMU sets have been built with stainless steel bodies: a driver-motor 'A' unit, trailer car, and driver-motor 'B' unit, carrying up to 222 passengers. The power cars have IGBT AC traction systems. Electropneumatic brakes are controlled by microprocessors.

Four trains per hour run between the airport and the city, a 22-minute journey, and alternate trains continue to Robina on the Gold Coast. Frequency and train length can be stepped up as traffic increases.

**Type:** Interurban three-car train
**Power:** Eight three-phase asynchronous traction motors of 180kW (241.2hp), supplied by 25kV 50Hz AC overhead catenary
**Tractive effort:**
**Max. operating speed:** 140km/h (87mph)
**Total weight:** 130 tonnes (286,650lb)
**Max. axle load:** 14 tonnes (30,870lb)
**Overall length:** 72.6m (238ft 4in)

## Class 146 Electric Locomotives — FEDERAL GERMAN RAILWAYS (DB) — GERMANY 2001

Germany has been replacing hundreds of its older electric locomotives in recent years after the 'coming of age' of machines delivered in the 1950s and 1960s. Among the new classes is a successful mixed-freight locomotive classified 145 of which an initial order of 80 has been delivered. A derivative of class 145 is class 185, designed for dual-voltage operation on 15kV and 25kV so as to be able to work into France and other neighbouring countries. There will eventually be 400 locomotives of class 185. Another derivative of class 145, class 146, has emerged for the specific duty of powering regional push-pull trains, particularly modern double-deck stock. These have settled in on workings, for example, between Aachen to Cologne and Bielefeld. Like the other new DB locomotives, they carry its latest livery of *verkehrsrot* (traffic red).

**Type:** Bo-Bo regional passenger push-pull electric
**Power:** 15,000V 16.6Hz AC overhead line collection; 4200kW (5630hp) continuous rating; electronic control; rheostatic braking; four traction motors with direct drive to axles
**Tractive effort:** 260kN (58,450lbf)
**Max. operating speed:** 160km/h (100mph)
**Weight:** 86 tonnes (188,860lb)
**Max axle load:**
**Overall length:** 18.9m (62ft)

## 'Pendolino' Class 390 — VIRGIN TRAINS — GREAT BRITAIN 2001

**Type:** High-speed electric nine-car tilting trains
**Power:** 25,000V 50Hz AC overhead line collection.; two Alsthom ONIX 800 power packs each on seven power cars, totalling 5950kW (7975bhp) continuous rating; rheostatic and regenerative braking; two underfloor traction motors on each power car, each with cardan shaft drive to nearest axle.
**Tractive effort:** Not known
**Max. operating speed:** 225km/h (140mph)
**Weight per vehicle:** 50 to 62 tonnes (109,805 to 136,155lbf)
**Overall length:** 23.05m (75ft 7in) driving cars; 23.9m (78ft 5in) intermediate cars
**Gauge:** 1435mm (4ft 8.5in)

Many commentators have described Britain's West Coast main line (WCML) as the busiest in the country. It certainly carries heavy long-distance passenger and local traffic, and much freight. Linking London with Glasgow and Edinburgh in Scotland, and with branches reaching Manchester, Liverpool and Birmingham, the WCML was electrified between 1960 and 1974. Long-distance passenger services today are locomotive powered, mainly in 175km/h (110mph) push-pull formations at hourly or more

frequent intervals (half hourly to Birmingham), and they are operated by Virgin Trains. The long section to Scotland beyond Lancaster is extremely curvaceous, although the line is laid with sweeping rather than sharp curves, and body tilt will achieve large reductions in train times.

As part of its franchise commitment, the Virgin Trains offered to replace all its WCML rolling stock with a fleet of 53 tilting trains designed to operate at high speeds up to 225km/h (140mph). To achieve this speed and to reduce journey times by at least 25 per cent overall, the infrastructure owner has to upgrade the WCML track and signalling, a

**Tilting the body of a high-speed train such as a 'Pendolino' enables it to travel around curves about 25 per cent faster than conventional trains both safely and with no effect on passenger comfort because of centrifugal forces.**

**Above: The striking and friendly frontal aspect of the Virgin 'Pendolino' trains is expected to attract many new travellers to rail. The trains are designed for 225km/h (140mph) and have body tilt.**

major project that has become difficult to manage. The upshot is that Railtrack has not been able to deliver the planned top speed for the route, forecasting only a maximum of 200km/h (125mph) for the foreseeable future.

Thus Virgin is seeking a further order to expand the class 390 fleet in order to cope with the current longer journey times and lower utilization. As an example of the speed gains to be made, however, the trip from London Euston to Manchester Piccadilly is currently a 2hr 40min journey; with tilting. Even at 200km/h (125mph) maximum speed, this will be reduced to two hours only.

The class 390 train has seven cars with traction motors, two with pantographs for current collection which also carry the transformers, and includes first- and standard-class accommodation, plus a buffet which is accessible to all passengers, and there are also restaurant facilities in first class. Traction motors are distributed throughout the train. This arrangement spreads the weight along the train and minimizes the axle load, despite the overall heavy weight of the carriages.

Like the German ICE tilting diesel train described earlier in this book, the 'Pendolino' class 390 uses tilt to enable the trains to run at faster speeds round curves without subjecting passengers to uncomfortable lateral forces. The bogies are based on the well-proven Fiat/SIG bogie which uses electric tilt actuation.

The train itself is a quality InterCity style train consisting of nine coaches, fully air-conditioned with comfortable seating, and with entertainment headphones and power points for laptop computers and other work equipment, designed to attract and keep commuters and business passengers.

Alsthom, the UK manufacturer in Birmingham, has a test track in Leicestershire which enables the two pre-production trains to be run on different types of track and under different designs of overhead catenary, and on which the tilting mechanism and the traction equipment can be fully tested. The units are maintained at a depot at Longsight in Manchester.

When all the '390s' have been placed in service, Virgin will be able to offer a 20-minute interval service between London and Birmingham, a half-hourly service to Manchester and an hourly one to Liverpool and to Glasgow/ Edinburgh, almost doubling the present service it has in place.

## 8600 SERIES DUBLIN AREA RAPID TRANSIT — IRELAND 2001

Dublin's electric suburban services, known as the 'DART' (standing for 'Dublin Area Rapid Transit') began in 1984 with services to the suburbs of Bray and Howth. In 2000 and 2001, the opening of extensions south to Greystones and north to Malahide, combined with an enormous growth in passenger numbers, required additional DART cars and two new types of EMU were added to the fleet.

One type of new EMU used was the 8500-8600 series cars built in by Mitsui in Japan. These semi-permanently coupled pairs consist of a powered car (8500-series) and an unpowered driving trailer (8600-series). Each car has seats for 40 passengers. The first 8500-8600 cars entered service in May 2001. The other type of new DART EMU are 8200/8400 series cars built in by Alsthom in Spain.

**Dublin Area Rapid Transit often runs with capacity loads during rush hours. In 2000, two new batches of cars were delivered to ease peak crowding on the DART suburban services. Car 8606 is seen at Dublin Connolly Station.**

**Type:** Suburban passenger electric multiple-unit train
**Power:** 1500V DC from overhead wire
**Tractive effort:** N/A
**Max. operating speed:** 100km/h (62mph)
**Weight:** 39 tonnes (85,995lb) - powered car
**Overall length:** 20m (65ft 7in)
**Max. axle load:** 9.75 tonnes (21,499lb)
**Gauge:** 1600mm (5ft 3in)

# MLX01 MAGLEV PROTOTYPE TRAIN JAPANESE RAILWAYS (JR) JAPAN 2001

The French TGV has already shown that speeds in excess of 500km/h (310mph) can be attained by wheels on rails; however, in Japan, Germany and the United States, engineers have been working on a new generation of land transport which is no longer carried on wheels. The 'Maglev' system employs the principle of magnetic levitation and propulsion to move a train along a specially built track, with a resulting virtually frictionless drive. In motion, the only physical contact is made by guide-wheels holding the train in position within the trough-shaped concrete track bed. In Japan, the aim is to run a Tokyo–Osaka service in one hour, compared to the 2.5hrs taken by the *Shinkansen* train. This requires a speed of 500km/h (310mph). On the 18.4km (11.4mile) test track in Yamanashi prefecture, the five-car MLX01 prototype has already attained a speed of 552km/h (324.4mph) – on 14 April 1999. Two types of ground coils fitted in the track sides transmit power for levitation/lateral guidance, and for propulsion, when the current is on.

The development of Maglev towards a practicable system has been hugely expensive and beset by many technical problems. The superconducting magnets fitted to the train to power its linear synchronous motor are extremely sensitive to external disturbances, which can reduce or eliminate power. In many ways, the designers are probing new frontiers of railway technology while also borrowing from other fields, as in the aerodynamic braking of trains, with vanes raised from the carriage roofs. And so, despite enormous investment, it remains to be seen whether Maglev will become a standard or join the 'atmospheric railway' and 'hovertrain' among other lost causes in the long story of railway development.

**Type:** Magnetic levitation train
**Power:** Not known
**Magnetomotive force:** 700kA
**Tractive effort:** N/A
**Max. operating speed:** 500km/h (310mph)
**Total weight:** Not known
**Maximum axle load:** N/A
**Overall length:** Not known

**The scale of infrastructure needed by Maglev is seen in this shot of the test track, taken on 18 June 1998, with a Maglev unit crossing the test track's bowstring-arched concrete viaduct.**

**The control centre for the Maglev test operations rises above the tracks at Tsuru City, Yamanashi Prefecture. From such a base, driverless trains would be monitored and controlled over hundreds of kilometres of track.**

## CLASSES 4023/4024 'TALENT' AUSTRIAN FEDERAL RAILWAYS (ÖBB) AUSTRIA 2002

Being delivered to Austrian Federal Railways (ÖBB) by Bombardier and ELIN in 2002 are a group of 11 three-car (class 4023) and 40 four-car (class 4024) electric multiple units (EMUs). These are based on the German 'Talent' type of articulated diesel multiple unit.

These electric versions for Austria are to be utilized for two purposes: local services around Salzburg (the three-car sets) and for replacing older class 4030 EMUs on the Viennese S-Bahn suburban services.

As with the diesel versions, these trains have a low floor section for passenger access from low platforms. Thus the interior of both EMUs includes, at the end of each unit, a section reached by steps from the lower floor. The raised section is situated over the power bogies and equipment.

In outline, the trains are streamlined, and they are being equipped for fast running up to 160km/h (100mph). This is not unknown for outer suburban stock, as in Britain where the class 321 EMUs, for example, have the same high top speed.

**Type:** Local (three-car) and suburban (four-car) articulated electric multiple units
**Power (per unit):** 15,000V 16.67Hz AC overhead line collection; 2000kW (2700hp); traction motors with direct drive to axles
**Tractive effort:** Not known
**Max. operating speed:** 160km/h (100mph)
**Weight:** Not known
**Max axle load:** Not known
**Overall length:** Not known

## CLASS 680 CZECH RAILWAYS (CD) CZECH REPUBLIC 2003

The Vienna–Prague–Berlin route is part of European Corridor IV, with a top speed of 160km/h (100mph). Higher speed is unlikely for many years, but 230km/h (143.8mph) is possible with tilting trains. Czech Railways originally ordered such trains in 1995, but the project has been delayed. At the time of writing, seven units of seven cars were confirmed for delivery in 2003. Slovakia Railways is interested in similar trains for the Bratislava–Kosice route.

**Type:** EMU tilting, express passenger, multi-voltage
**Power:** 4000kW (5500hp) projected
**Supply:** 3000V DC or 25kV 50Hz AC or 15kV 16.67Hz AC
**Tractive effort:** N/A
**Max. operating speed:** 230km/h (143.8mph) projected
**Weight:** Not known
**Max. axle load:** 13.5 tonnes (29,768lb) projected
**Overall length:** Not known
**Gauge:** 1435mm (4ft 8.5in)

# 'TRANSRAPID' MAGNETIC LEVITATION TRAINS TRANSRAPID CONSORTIUM GERMANY 2003

**The Transrapid magnetic levitation train offers an increase in train speed to 500km/h (310mph), well beyond that currently achievable by conventional rail systems, with economic energy use.**

Ever since 1934, man has had a vision of being able to use magnetism to enable a 'hover train' to travel at vastly faster speeds than conventional trains. In that year, Hermann Kemper patented his idea in Germany for the magnetic levitation of trains. He was so far ahead of time that it took another 30 years before the concept became experimental reality. Indeed, there were simultaneous developments as researchers in the United Kingdom were also developing a magnetic levitation train, and their work culminated in the building of the Maglev shuttle between Birmingham Airport and International station, only recently withdrawn after over two decades of not entirely fault-free service.

In 1971, Messerschmitt-Bölkow-Blohm (MBB) demonstrated a passenger-carrying vehicle on a 660m (2165ft) long track near Munich. Known as 'Transrapid 02', the vehicle used an asynchronous 'shortstator' linear motor in which what would have been the commutator coils of a conventional rotating motor were laid out in a line along the track, thus creating an early 'linear motor'. The system used opposing electromagnets to create the lift and guidance forces that kept the vehicle out of physical contact of the track.

Other systems were being studied as well. AEG-Telefunken/BBC/Siemens built a 900m (2953ft) test track at Erlangen to develop an electrodynamic levitation system using superconductor coils and tried out a vehicle in 1972. Two years later, Thyssen Henschel and the Technical University of Braunschweig (Brunswick) developed a 'longstator' system in which the roles of the coils in the vehicle and along the track were reversed. This arrangement was approved in 1977 by Germany's Federal Ministry of Research and Technology as the model for further research and development. That decision gave the boost for the Magnetbahn Transrapid consortium to be formed. A much longer test track (eventually totalling 31.5km – 19.6 miles) began operation at Emsland in north Germany (adjacent to the railway line between Rheine and Emden) in 1980. The test track has a straight central section with two large radius loops, one at either end. Its capability is to test trains at up to 450km/h (280mph), whereas later versions of the Transrapid train are proposed for up to 500km/h (310mph).

The principle of Transrapid is that a train without rolling steel wheels on steel rails can have no distinct moving parts and has to face only air and wind resistance in its forward motion. Attached to the bottom outer edges of each carriage body are long structures that appear to envelop the sides of the track beam. This structure carries two sets of electromagnets. Facing upwards underneath each side of the track are the lift magnets that attract the stator laid out along the underside of the track beam. When operating, these lift the vehicle towards the track magnets so that it is suspended in midair. On each side of the track is a reaction rail, in effect a long plate that forms the outer face of the track beam. Facing this rail on the vehicle structure is a series of drive magnets that provide the forward movement force by means of harmonic waves in the propulsion magnetic field acting on the rail. This arrangement has all the active electromagnets on the rail vehicle, much cheaper than having elongated electromagnets laid out along long lengths of the tracks.

The company states that the power used to keep the train in its levitated state is less than that needed to operate its air-conditioning system. Forward movement is easy to achieve, and acceleration can be as fast as 0 to 300km/h (185mph) in 5km (3miles). By comparison (according to data supplied by Transrapid International), a conventional DB ICE train needs 31km (19miles) to accelerate to the same speed. The test trains at Emsland have run more than 800,000km (500,000 miles) in proving the reliability of the equipment. These trials include a longest nonstop run of 1665km (1040 miles) and a longest day's operation of 2460km (1538miles). The company states that the ride is comfortable and not subject to the normal jolts and bumps that conventional trains suffer in reacting to general railway track misalignments. It is possible also to produce freight vehicles that can carry up to 19 tonnes (41,895lb) of goods.

Transrapid International claims to have a proven product that can link cities at speeds much faster than can be achieved by conventional railways, opening up the possibility, for example, of all key German cities being brought to within one to three hours journey time of each other. The Transrapid company believes that the cost of installation of its track, raised or 'at grade', is not much different from that of a conventional new high-speed railway.

Thus, when German reunification brought the urgent need to improve communications across what was once the German internal border, or 'Iron Curtain', a Maglev railway was considered for the link from Hamburg to the revived capital, Berlin. Urgency was the keyword. *Deutsche Bahn* (DB) had put in hand the upgrading of the existing railway line and soon had agreement also to build a high-speed line between the two cities. Being now part of the Transrapid consortium, DB was very interested in the potential of Maglev lines to speed up intercity travel in the long term and wanted to be part of the revolution if it took place. In 1994, the Federal Government passed a law enabling the planning of high-speed Maglev routes in Germany. DB decided it would purchase and operate the new Hamburg–Berlin Transrapid line.

Although the reasons for cancellation were confused in public announcements, in January 2000 all parties involved agreed that the Berlin–Hamburg Maglev line would in fact not proceed. One can only surmise that the costs were beginning to escalate and that the need to operate rail vehicles beyond both points (for example, to run high-speed trains from Hamburg to, say, Dresden and Prague via Berlin) would be frustrated by the relatively short trunk Hamburg–Berlin section being a non-conventional system.

However, in Munich, the local authority is supporting a 37km (23-mile) Transrapid link to the international airport, and in the Rhein-Ruhr region there is strong enthusiasm for a Transrapid line connecting Dortmund with Essen and Düsseldorf. Both these projects appear feasible, so we may look out for announcements about progress in the next few months or years. There are also signs of interest in the United States for a Transrapid route in Pittsburgh and one to link Washington DC with Baltimore. The Netherlands Government is also balancing the possibility of using a Transrapid track against a proposal for a conventional high-speed line linking Amsterdam/Rotterdam with northern Germany.

It is in China, however, that the first commercial exploitation of the Transrapid system is already under construction. Work commenced in 2001 on building the track for the Shanghai Airport link. In June 2002, the first Maglev vehicle section left the Thyssen-Krupp factory in Kassel for shipment to Shanghai in China, where it arrived on 9 August.

**Type:** Magnetic levitation high-speed trains
**Track:** Steel or concrete beams carrying levitation stator magnets and longstator propulsion reaction rail
**Power:** Electromagnetic levitation and longstator propulsion
**Max. operating speed:** up to 500km/h (310mph)
**Weight:** 53 tonnes (116,400lb) per vehicle
**Overall length:** 27m (88ft 7in) end cars; 24.8m (81ft 4in) intermediate cars – up to 10 cars per train

**The first commercial use of Transrapid levitated trains is in China for the link to Shanghai Airport.**

# GLOSSARY

**Timothy Hackworth's final design: the Stockton & Darlington Railway's *Derwent* of 1845. The brakes on the water-tender can be seen clearly.**

**'A' and 'B' units:** A linked pair of diesel or electric locomotives, in which only the first, 'A', has a driving cab. This is sometimes referred to as a 'cow and calf' unit. Some are A-B-A, three units with a driving cab in each 'A' locomotive.

**AC:** Alternating current; an electric current that reverses its direction flow at regular intervals, known as cycles.

**ACFI:** *Acronym of the Société Auxiliaire des Chemins de Fer et de l'Industrie*, a French manufacturer of auxiliary equipment, especially feed-water heaters.

**Adhesion:** The ability of locomotive driving wheels to turn without slipping on the rails.

**Adhesion factor:** The ratio of the locomotive's tractive effort to its adhesive weight.

**Adhesive weight:** The proportion of a locomotive's or power car's weight resting on the driving wheels.

**Adriatic:** A name sometimes applied to a 2-6-4 locomotive.

**Anti-vacuum valve:** Also known as a snifting valve; it introduces air into the steam passages when a locomotive's steam is shut off. The valve prevents a partial vacuum forming, which would otherwise suck ash from the smoke-box into the steam passages.

**Atlantic:** A 4-4-2 locomotive (see Wheel Arrangement), so called from the Atlantic Coast Line of the United States, which first built them.

**AVE:** The Spanish high-speed rail link which runs between Madrid and Sevila.

**Axle load:** The weight placed on the track by a pair of wheels with an axle between them. Maximum axle load is that of the wheels supporting the greatest individual weight.

**Backhead:** The rear end of a boiler, on which are mounted the controls of a steam locomotive. Also known as Backplate.

**Baltic:** A locomotive consisting of 4-6-4 wheel arrangement; also known as a Hudson in the United States.

**Banker:** An additional engine used to help push a train up a gradient, or 'bank'. Also known as a Pusher, or Helper.

**Bar frame:** A structure of joined bars of iron or steel, supporting a locomotive boiler, typical of American and German practice.

**Bearing:** The point at which a turning axle or other turning part meets the supporting frame or part.

**The replica of the 1835 *Der Adler*. The small diameter of early boilers is apparent. The inside cylinders' ends can be seen below the smoke-box.**

**Berkshire:** A locomotive of 2-8-4 wheel arrangement, named after the Berkshire Mountains in the United States.

**Beyer Garratt:** A Garratt articulated locomotive built by the firm of Beyer Peacock.

**Bissell truck:** A single axle for the leading carrying wheels which could pivot and thus lead the engine into a curve. It was patented by the US inventor Levi Bissell in 1858.

**Blinkers:** The British name for the smoke deflectors that are fitted to the side of the firebox or the chimney.

**Blower:** A steam vent which is fitted to the blast-pipe and controlled by the driver, and which creates a draught when the engine is stationary and no exhaust draught is available. The blower's function is to keep the fire hot and to prevent a 'blow-back' of steam into the firebox.

**Bogie:** A wheeled under-carriage for an engine or railway vehicle. It is attached to a pivot or slide which allows it to turn or move sideways independently.

**Boiler:** The long metal barrel, filled with tubes for water, steam and fire exhaust, in which steam is generated by means of the firebox situated at one end.

**Boiler pressure:** The maximum pressure, expressed in pounds per square inch (psi), or kilograms per square centimetre (kg/cm²), of steam within the boiler before the safety valve opens to release excessive pressure.

**Bonnet unit:** A diesel or electric locomotive which has a bonnet end which protrudes below the level of the windscreen.

**Led by No. 201, four Fell engines of the New Zealand Railways can be seen here slogging with an excursion train up the Rimutaka incline in October 1955.**

**Booster:** An auxiliary engine fitted to a steam locomotive's trailing wheels (or sometimes to the tender wheels). A booster can be used to provide extra tractive power on starting or on severe grades. It is used only at low speeds.

**Boxpok:** A type of wheel cast as a solid block with a pattern of holes, rather than spokes.

**Brick arch:** An arch of fire-resistant brick built across a firebox, deflecting the path of gases and thus securing more adequate heating work, as well as providing the opportunity for the admixture of supplementary air supply.

**Brotan boiler:** A boiler with a firebox lined with water-tubes; developed by Johann Brotan on the Austrian Imperial Railways.

**Büchli drive:** A type of electric power transmission developed by Brown Boveri, in Switzerland, providing direct drive to the wheels while enabling them to move vertically and horizontally.

**Buffer beam:** The metal plate found across the front end of the frame, to which the buffers are fitted.

**Buffers:** The spring-loaded shock absorbers which are fitted to each end of a locomotive in the United Kingdom and in various other countries.

**Cab forward:** A locomotive with a cab at the front end only.

**Cab unit:** A diesel locomotive in which the cab sides extend to the outside of the frame, with no external walkway.

**Camelback:** A steam locomotive with the driving cab placed over the boiler.

**Caprotti valve gear:** A patent valve gear developed by the Italian engineer Arturo Caprotti, driven by a rotating shaft rather than by rods and levers, and normally operating poppet valves.

**Cardan shaft:** A driving shaft with a universal coupling at one or both ends.

**Carrying wheels:** The non-coupled or non-powered wheels of a locomotive.

**Catenary:** The structure of poles and wires which are used supply electric power to electrified trains.

**Clack valve:** A one-way valve, used for admitting water to a locomotive boiler.

**Clerestory:** A raised central roof section which as small vertical windows or ventilators at the sides.

**Compound expansion:** The use of steam first in high-pressure, then in low-pressure cylinders before it is ejected through the chimney.

**Conjugated valve gear:** The operation of a three-cylinder locomotive using only two external sets of valve gear; conjugated levers set ahead of the cylinders actuate the middle piston's valve.

**Connecting rod:** The rod joining the piston rod to the driving axle crank, via the cross-head.

**Consolidation:** A locomotive of 2-8-0 wheel arrangement.

**Counterpressure brake:** A means of supplementing the wheel brakes on a steam locomotive, by bringing the engine into midgear and then reverse, the cylinders then acting as compressors and absorbing power from the driving wheels (the Riggenbach system). The Le Chatelier system allowed for the admission of very hot water to the cylinders, which then vaporized under pressure.

**Coupled wheels:** Engine wheels which are joined by coupling rods.

**Crank:** An arm attached at right angles to an axle or rotating spindle, to which a rod may be joined.

**Cross-compound:** A two-cylinder compound arrangement; high-pressure on one side, low-pressure on the other.

**Crosshead:** The linking piece between the piston and the connecting rod; it slides backwards and forwards while held in place vertically by a guide bar or bars.

**Crown sheet:** the top of the firebox in a steam boiler. Although the whole of the back end of the boiler is referred to as the firebox, in fact there is a space between the crown sheet and the boiler top, in which much of the locomotive's steam is generated.

**Cut-off:** A term used to express the amount of steam admitted to the cylinder, in relation to the position of the piston. Steam supply can be cut off, by adjustment of the valve gear, when the piston has travelled a certain distance. Cut-off is expressed as a proportion of the piston's travel. On starting, maximum cut-off is applied, with steam admitted for around 75 per cent of the piston stroke. In full forward motion, cut-off may be reduced to around 15 per cent. The degree to which cut-off can be altered and the fineness of gradation depend on the type of valves and valve gear utilized.

**Cylinder:** The part of the engine where the drive is generated: a solidly cast metal unit bored out to a set diameter. Inside the cylinder, the power of steam or combustion is

**No. 4003, one of the nine Chicago & North Western 4-6-4s of class E-4, built by Alco in 1938, stops at Omaha, Nebraska, on 25 April 1942. With a maximum 21kg/cm² (300psi) boiler pressure, these had the highest tractive effort of any American 'Hudson'.**

**Originally built in 1929 as Nigel Gresley's unique four-cylinder compound no. 10,000, this 4-6-4 was rebuilt as British Railways no. 60700 with a three-cylinder simple. Here, the locomotive is leaving York bound for London's King's Cross station in July 1952.**

converted into motion by pushing the piston. This power can be measured as indicated horsepower.

**Dabeg:** A French producer of locomotive components, including feed-water heaters and valve gear.

**DC:** Direct current; an electric current that flows continuously in a single direction.

**Decapod:** A locomotive with 10 coupled wheels; the name is usually used for a 2-10-0.

**Diesel-electric:** A diesel-powered locomotive or power car that transmits its power to electric motors.

**Diesel-hydraulic:** A diesel-powered locomotive that transmits its power to the wheels by means of a hydraulic system.

**Diesel-mechanical:** A diesel-powered locomotive that transmits its power to the wheels by a direct mechanical method.

**dmu:** Diesel multiple unit; a set of carriages of which two or more are motor-driven, with a driving position at each end of the set.

**Dome:** A feature of most but not all steam locomotives, normally to provide a location for steam collection well above the boiler water-level, and where the steam is admitted through a valve (controlled by the regulator handle in the driving cab) into the main steam pipe.

**Double chimney:** A locomotive chimney with two exhaust blast-pipes inside.

**Double heading:** The use of two engines to pull a train.

**Down:** The direction leading away from the major terminus of a railway, hence 'down line', 'down train', etc.

**Drawbar:** The part of a locomotive's frame to which the draw-hook is attached. The horsepower exerted at the drawbar is an important means of assessing a locomotive's performance.

**Drawgear:** Also known as draftgear; the drawhook and the shock-absorbing, load-bearing attachments which prevent it being jerked severely.

**Driving car:** The front (or rear) car of a multiple-unit set, with a driving position. It is not necessarily a power car.

**Driving wheels:** Engine wheels driven directly from the cylinders of a steam engine or the motors of diesel and electric engines. Often used to refer to coupled wheels.

**Dynamic braking:** In a diesel-mechanical or diesel-hydraulic locomotive, the use of the engine compression or torque convertor to slow the train, and so to save subsequent wear on the wheel-brakes.

**Eccentric:** A mechanism for converting rotary motion into reciprocal motion, widely used on internally fitted valve gears, like Stephenson's link motion.

**EMD:** The Electromotive Division of General Motors, formed to construct diesel-electric locomotives.

**emu:** Electric multiple unit; a set of carriages of which two or more are powered by electric motors taking power from an outside supply, with a driving position at each end.

**Mexican narrow gauge: two US-built 2-8-0s, Nos 262 and 279, of the Mexican National Railways, seen here in the yard at Ameca, in March 1966.**

**Feed-water:** The water supplied to the boiler for conversion into steam.

**Feed-water heater:** Preheating the feed-water speeded up the steam-generation process. As a result, there were numerous patent systems used by locomotive builders.

**Footplate:** The floor level of an engine's driving cab.

**Frame:** The structural bed of a locomotive, resting on the axles. It may be inside the wheels or outside them, or, in the case of a double frame, with the wheels placed in between.

**Franco-Crosti boiler:** A boiler with a large drum or drums attached or incorporated, in which exhaust gases, drawn backwards from the cylinders, preheat the feed-water. It was developed by the Italian engineers Attilio Franco and Piero Crosti.

**Garratt locomotive:** An articulated locomotive in which the boiler is mounted on a frame under which two engine units are pivoted.

**Gauge:** The width between the rails. Standard gauge is 1435mm (56.5in). Narrow-gauge lines are less than this; broad-gauge lines are wider.

**GEC:** Acronym for General Electric Company, a US manufacturer of electric motors and locomotives.

**Giesl ejector:** A form of blast system and chimney which was devised in 1951 by the Austrian engineer Dr A. Giesl-Gieslingen.

**Grate area:** The surface space of the firebox floor in a steam locomotive.

**Hammer blow:** The force exerted by the thrust of a connecting rod on the crank; it is transmitted to the rail by the turning of the driving wheel.

**Headcode:** An arrangement of lamps, discs, letters and numbers, or other items, on the front of a locomotive, normally indicating the type of train or the route to be followed.

**Heating surface:** The combined surface area of the firebox and the boiler tubes.

**Helper engine:** See Banker.

**Hood unit:** A diesel or electric locomotive with walkways alongside the 'hood' covering the power unit, as well as a full-width driving cab.

**HST:** High Speed Train, the British 200km/h (125mph) set.

**Hudson:** A locomotive of 4-6-4 wheel arrangement.

**ICE:** Inter-City Express, a service operated by the *Deutsche Bundesbahn*.

**Injector:** Invented by the French engineer Henri Giffard in 1859, this device forces water from the tank into a steam boiler; it can be driven by live steam or by exhaust steam that has already passed through the cylinders.

**Inside bearings:** Wheel bearings fitted on the axle on the inner side of the wheel.

**Inside cylinders:** Cylinders which are fitted within a locomotive's frame.

**Kylchap chimney:** A widely used patent steam exhaust system developed by the Finnish engineer Kylälä and the French Chapelon, between 1919 and 1926.

**Lap:** In steam locomotives, an expression defining the length

**A Thai Railways postwar 4-6-2 of Series 821-50, at Thung Song on 1 January 1974. The smoke deflectors bear a New Year message.**

**The Western Pacific Railroad's 'California Zephyr' stands in the yard at Oakland, California, in September 1960. At the head is an EMD FP7A triple set, led by unit 805A. These locomotives carried steam generators and 17,730 litres (3900 gallons) of water for train heating.**

of a valve face and the extent to which it overlaps the edges of the admission ports when in midposition.

**Lead:** In steam locomotives, a term defining the extent to which the valve is open to steam admission when the piston has reached the end of its stroke.

**Lenz valve gear:** A form of valve gear which uses an oscillating cam shaft and poppet valves; it was developed by the Austrian engineer Dr Hugo Lenz.

**Limited:** Used of trains, it means an express with limited accommodation, which should be booked in advance.

**Loading gauge:** The limits of height and width imposed by fixtures of a railway track, e.g. platforms, bridges, tunnels.

**Mechanical stoker:** A power-operated system for feeding coal into a locomotive firebox; a mechanical stoker is usually a revolving spiral within a large-diameter steel tube.

**Mikado:** A locomotive of 2-8-2 wheel arrangement.

**Mixed traffic:** Designation of a locomotive designed for both passenger and freight work.

**Mixed train:** A train with both passenger and goods vehicles.

**Mogul:** A locomotive of 2-6-0 wheel arrangement.

**Monomotor bogie:** A bogie which is driven by a single electric motor.

**Mother Hubbard:** A name for 'Camelback' locomotives.

**Motion:** The system of rods and cranks that operates the valve gear.

**Mountain:** A locomotive of 4-8-2 wheel arrangement; these locomotives are known as 'Mohawks' on the New York Central Railroad.

**Multiple-unit:** Two or more locomotives or power units operated in combination by a single driver.

**Non-adhesive weight:** The proportion of a locomotive's or power car's weight that is supported by its carrying (non-driving) wheels.

**Northern:** A locomotive of 4-8-4 wheel arrangement.

**Outside bearings:** Wheel bearings attached to the frame on the outer side of the wheel.

**Outside frame:** A locomotive frame whose edges are outside the wheels.

**Pacific:** A locomotive of 4-6-2 wheel arrangement.

**Pannier tank:** A tank engine whose tanks are attached to the upper flanks of the boiler side.

**Pantograph:** The extendable overhead power collector which is mounted on the roof of an electric locomotive or power car.

***Pendelzug:*** A shuttle train, in Germany and Switzerland.

**Pilot:** American term for the cow-catcher.

**Two single-cab GE 7800 units of the Virginian Railway hauling a train of empty coal trucks westbound up New River, near Narrows (where their power was generated) in August 1951.**

**Pilot engine:** The front engine of a double-headed steam-hauled train.

**Piston valve:** A device which is used for controlling the admission and exhaust of steam to and from a cylinder. The piston valve is normally formed from two short pistons attached to a rod, the movement of which is operated by the engine's valve gear.

**Plate frame:** A locomotive frame made of riveted steel plates, typical of British construction.

**Pony wheels:** A single set of trailing wheels which is set behind the coupled wheels, as in a 4-4-2.

**Poppet valves:** Spring-mounted valves which are derived from those used in internal combustion engines, often vertically set.

**Power car:** In a multiple-unit train, the power car is the car, or one of the cars, in which the motors are fitted.

**Power classification:** A notation system which is used to grade the power of locomotives.

**Prairie:** A locomotive of 2-6-2 wheel arrangement.

**Prime mover:** In a diesel-electric locomotive, the prime mover is the diesel engine, which provides the initial source of motive power.

**Priming:** In a steam locomotive, priming is the siphoning of water into the steam collection pipe, with consequent deleterious effect on steaming capacity and also possible damage. This is often caused by impurities or chemicals which result in the boiler water foaming up.

**Pullman:** A luxury carriage built for and leased by the Pullman Car Company; often used to refer to a train which is made up of such cars.

**Quill drive:** A form of traction via sprung members fixed to a driving wheel; the name originates from a misreading of German *Feder* which means both 'quill' and 'spring'.

**Rack and pinion:** A system to maximize adhesion on steep gradients, with a toothed wheel or wheels on the locomotive or power car engaging with a toothed rail laid between the running rails. There are several different systems.

**Railcar:** A self-propelling vehicle which is able to carry passengers or light goods items.

**Reciprocating motion:** A backwards-forwards motion, as in the movement of pistons in a steam locomotive.

**Rectifier:** A device to convert an AC electric supply to DC current for the traction motors.

**Regenerative braking:** A form of dynamic braking in electric locomotives, in which the motors can be switched to work as generators, producing current which can be fed back into the power catenary, or dissipated via resistance banks.

**Regulator:** The device controlling the flow of steam from the boiler to the cylinders; a regulator is one of the chief driving instruments of a steam locomotive.

**Reverser:** The device that sets the valve gear for forward or reverse motion in a steam locomotive: another of the chief driving instruments. It may be manual or power operated.

**Rheostatic braking:** A form of dynamic braking in diesel-electric locomotives, in which the traction motors can be switched to work as generators, creating current which is dissipated in resistance banks.

**Road engine:** A locomotive that hauls trains on the open track.

**Road switcher:** A locomotive that works both as a road and a yard engine.

**Running gear:** The framework and wheels of a diesel or electric locomotive.

**Running plate:** The decking along the sides of some locomotives, accompanied by a handrail.

**Saddle tank:** A tank engine whose water tank is mounted over the boiler.

**Safety valve:** An automatic valve which opens to release steam if the boiler pressure reaches the boiler's maximum operating pressure.

**Sandwich frame:** A type of locomotive frame made of hardwood, often oak or teak, reinforced by thin metal plates on each side.

**Santa Fe:** A 2-10-2 locomotive which derives its name from the Atchison Topeka & Santa Fe Railroad.

**Saturated:** A term applied to an engine, or its steam, when there is no superheater fitted and the steam remains in a saturated state.

**Selkirk:** A 2-10-4 locomotive of the Canadian Pacific Railway.

**Shoe:** The device for picking up electric current from a third-rail supply system. A brake shoe is the brake block which is applied against the wheel rim.

**Chicago skyscrapers dominate the background as a Metra-liveried EMD F40 PHM-2 locomotive runs a two-deck cross-city service.**

**Two of the Union Pacific's General Electric Co-Co units, U30C No. 2851 and No. 2462 of C30-7, the type that supplanted the 'U-boats', at the depot in Cheyenne, Wyoming, on 13 October 1983.**

**Shunter:** The British term that is used for a switching engine which is used to remarshal trains and move rolling stock in station yards.

**Side tank:** A tank engine whose water tanks are at the boiler sides, from the running plate upwards.

**Simple expansion:** Also known as single expansion: this term refers to the use of steam only once, at uniform pressure, in the cylinders, before it is exhausted through the chimney.

**Skyline casing:** A sheet-metal shrouding found along the boiler top of a steam locomotive; skyline casing provides an air-smoothed covering for the dome, safety valves and other fittings.

**Slave unit:** A diesel or electric engine with no driving facility; a slave unit is operated as supplementary motive power to another engine.

**Slide valve:** A device for controlling the admission and exhaust of steam to and from a cylinder: shaped as a flat rectangle and operated by the engine's valve gear.

**Smoke deflectors:** Side screens fixed to the side of the smoke-box, or to the chimney sides, in order to help lift smoke upwards and keep the driver's view clear.

**Steam chest:** The steam reservoir immediately adjacent to the cylinders.

**Steam drier:** A device that is intended to prevent steam from

**This photograph shows a Volk's electric railcar no. 8 at the Aquarium Terminus in Brighton, November 1938. The Volk's Electric Railway, which ran along the seafront at Brighton, was first opened on 3 August 1883.**

**A line-up of ÖBB electric, diesel and steam traction at Hieflau, Austria, on 30 December 1970. Electric B-B 1042.55 stands at the platform, next to diesel 20.1502 and 'Kriegslok' 2-10-0 No. 52.836.**

condensing (rather than expanding) in the cylinders. There were several patent forms of the steam drier, all of which were overtaken by the superheater.

**Superheater:** A set of tubes which reheat steam that has passed through the boiler tubes, raising its temperature to 'superheated' level so that it does not condense when admitted to the cylinders.

**Switcher:** American term for a shunting engine.

**Tank engine:** A steam locomotive carrying its coal and water supply within its own frame: the tank engine has no tender.

**TEE:** Acronym for Trans-Europ Express, an international network which was formerly operated by several European countries.

**Tender:** The coal (or oil) and water-holding vehicle attached to a locomotive. Note that, in German, *Tenderlokomotive* means tank engine.

**Texas:** A 2-10-4 locomotive (Selkirk on the CPR).

**TGV:** Acronym for *Train à Grand Vitesse*, French 'High Speed Train' set.

**Thalys:** A meaningless 'Euro-term' and brand name for the TGV sets which operate between the cities of Paris, Amsterdam and Cologne.

**Thermic syphon:** A water-tube, usually in the shape of an inverted Y, which passes diagonally upwards through the firebox and helps to circulate and heat water more rapidly.

**Thyristor:** A semiconductor current rectifier, in which the flow of current between two electrodes is triggered by a signal at a third electrode.

**TIA:** Acronym for *Traitement Intégrale Armand*, a patent process which purifies locomotive feed-water.

**Tractive effort:** Usually expressed in pounds/kilos as 'nominal tractive effort', it is worked out by a mathematical formula to establish the theoretical backward push exerted on the rail by the driving wheels with the locomotive in full gear and (in the case of steam) usually with 85 per cent of the maximum boiler pressure, assuming no friction anywhere other than between wheels and rail.

**Trailing wheels:** Wheels of a locomotive positioned to the rear of the coupled wheels.

**Transformer:** A device which is used to regulate the voltage of electric current.

**Transmission:** The means by which the power developed by an engine is passed to the driving wheels.

**Travel:** In valve gear, travel is the distance moved by the valve as it opens and closes the steam ports.

**Truck:** American term for a wheeled undercarriage attached to a locomotive or railway vehicle, allowing for pivoted or lateral movement to assist with negotiation of curves and alterations in gradient.

**Turbo-charging:** In a diesel engine, the use of engine exhaust to increase pressure in the cylinders.

**Universal engine:** A locomotive adaptable to all forms of freight and passenger train work.

**Up:** The direction leading towards the major terminus of the line, hence the terms 'up line', 'up train', etc.

**Valve gear:** The arrangement of rods and cranks by which the driver of a steam engine controls steam flow in and out of the cylinders, and sets the engine in forward or reverse motion. More than a hundred versions were developed, although Stephenson's in the 19th and Walschaerts' in the 20th century were by far the most common.

**Vanderbilt tender:** A tender formed from a cylindrical water tank with a coal bunker mounted on its forward end.

**Well tank:** A tank engine whose water tank is contained within the frame.

**Wheel arrangement:** There are several standard notations for describing locomotive types, based on the number of driving and carrying wheels, or the number of wheels in motor bogies. That for steam locomotives (developed by F. M. Whyte in the United States in 1900) is based on a sequence of coupled wheels with carrying wheels in front and behind. Thus a 'Pacific' is a 4-6-2. Where there are no carrying wheels, a zero is used, as in 0-10-0. To denote a tank engine, T is added, as in 4-4-2T. For semi-articulated locomotives, such as Mallets, each set of coupled wheels is shown separately, as in 4-8-8-2. Articulated locomotives, such as Garratts, are normally treated as two separate but linked engines, as in 4-6-2+2-6-4. France and some other

**Pictured here is General Electric CM22-7i Co-Co unit No. 4540 of the Thai Railways, as newly delivered in 1996. These locomotives run the Haat Yai–Bangkok express services.**

**The TGV (*Train à Grand Vitesse*) concept has been applied in a variety of different ways since its inception. Here a double-deck set, unit 219, arrives at the Gare de Lyon, Paris.**

countries note the number of axles, rather than wheels, and with them a 'Pacific' is a 231, and a 'Mogul' a 130. Both diesel and electric locomotive types, and steam locomotives in Germany and some other countries, are denoted by a letter code based on the number of coupled or combined-drive axles, with 'A' standing for a single driving axle, 'B' for two axles, and so on up to 'F', for six axles.

The majority of modern locomotives have powered bogies of either four or six wheels. Outside the United States, a small 'o' used to be (and sometimes is still) added when the axles have separate rather than combined drive. Thus Bo-Bo denoted a locomotive with two two-axle bogies, each axle driven independently; and B-B implied that one power unit drove both axles. Digits from 1 upwards were used to show the position of non-powered carrying axles. Thus a German 4-4-0 steam locomotive is 2B. A two-axle bogie with one powered axle is denoted A1. A three-axle bogie with a central carrying axle is denoted A1A. A four-axle bogie with a single carrying axle in front, and three combined driving axles, is denoted 1C, and an engine mounted on two such bogies is 1C-C1. The power cars of almost all modern multiple-unit trains run on two four-wheel bogies with independent drive on all axles. Although technically this is Bo-Bo, it is increasingly often referred to simply as B-B.

Rack wheels fitted to locomotives are sometimes denoted as 'z' (from German *Zahn*, 'tooth'). A locomotive with three coupled axles and two rack axles would be C-2z.

**Yard engine:** Used to indicate an engine that operates only in shunting yards.

**Amtrak's 'Acela Express' unit 2004, capable of 240km/h (150mph), photographed at Old Sambrook, Connecticut. Although a TGV 'lookalike', its TGV elements are limited to traction and bogie components.**

# INDEX

# PICTURE CREDITS

**Milepost 92½:** 7, 8, 14(t), 15(b), 16(tl), 24(t), 28(t), 32(all), 33(both), 35(m), 35(b), 36(t), 36(b), 37(t), 39, 41(b), 43(t), 45(t), 46, 51(t), 52, 54(both), 56(b), 58(m), 59(both), 60(both), 62(t), 64, 66(both), 67(both), 68, 69, 71(both), 74(t), 75(b), 77(m), 78, 80, 81(t), 82(m), 83(t), 84(b), 86(t), 87(b), 88(t), 90(both), 92(b), 93(t), 95, 96, 97, 98(all), 101(m), 101(b), 102(b), 103(both), 105(t), 106(m), 107, 110(b), 111(t), 115(t), 116(b), 121(t), 122, 123(all), 126(t), 128, 129, 131(tr), 132(both), 133(br), 134(m), 135(m), 136(t), 137(b), 138(both), 140, 141(b), 143(m), 144(both), 145(b), 147, 148(tr,b), 149(b), 150(t), 151(t), 153, 154(both), 155, 157, 160(both), 162, 164, 166(t), 169(b), 170, 171(b), 172, 173(t), 174(all), 175(b), 177(b), 178(b), 179(r), 182(t), 185(both), 186(b), 189(t), 190(b), 194(b), 196(b), 197(t), 198(both), 199(t), 200(t), 201(b), 204(b), 206(both), 207(both), 208(t), 208(b), 209(b), 210(t), 216(t), 216(m), 216(b), 217(t), 218(t), 2196(b), 220(t), 222(all), 224(both), 226(t), 227(t), 228(t), 229(t), 231(b), 234(both), 235(both), 236(tl,tr), 237(b), 238(b), 239(t), 241(t), 245, 247(r), 248, 249, 250, 253, 257, 263(b) 267(both), 270(b), 273(both), 276(t) 277(both), 278(t), 281(b), 282(b), 283(t), 286(t), 287(both), 288(b), 290(t), 294(t), 296(both), 298(b), 300(t), 301(both), 302(t), 309(both), 310(b), 311(t), 317(b), 318(b), 319, 320(t), 323, 329(b), 330(b), 332(t), 332(m), 333(both), 334(t), 336(b), 337(b), 338(b), 339(t), 340(m), 341(b), 342(b), 343(b), 346(t), 347(b), 348(b), 350(b), 351(t), 353(t), 354(both), 355(t), 355(b), 356(t), 356(b), 357(both), 358(t), 359(b), 360(t), 362(both), 363(b), 365(t), 366(t), 367, 368, 369(b), 375(b), 376, 380, 383, 385(b), 389, 390(t), 390(b), 395(b), 398, 400, 401, 406 (t), 408 (b), 410, 412 (b), 414(b), 415 (t), 416 (t), 417, 421 (b), 423 (b), 424, 425 (t), 427(b), 429(b), 432(b), 433, 434(b), 435(t), 436(t), 438(t), 440(t), 441(b), 442(t), 443(b), 444(t), 447(t), 448(both), 450, 453(both), 454(b), 455, 457(m), 458(both), 459(t), 459(b), 461, 436(t), 464, 465(b), 466(t), 467, 468(b), 470(t), 472(b), 473(t), 473(b), 474(t), 476(b), 477, 478, 480(t), 481(b), 482(t), 482(b), 484(t), 484(b), 485(b), 490(b), 491, 494, 495, 496(b), 497, 501(t) 502(t), 502(b), 508, 511, 512, 514, 518(b), 520, 521, 522, 523, 524(both), 526, 528(both), 533, 534

**Milepost/Brian Solomon:** 258, 294(b), 295(b), 330(b), 347(b), 367

**Cassell/Milepost 92½:** 1, 9, 12(b), 15(ml), 16(tr), 16(b), 17(t), 18(b), 19(b), 20(t), 20(b), 21(b), 22(m), 23(t), 25, 28(b), 29(b), 31, 34, 38(b), 40(b), 45(b), 51(b), 55(b), 57(b), 58(t), 58(b), 62(b), 65(t), 72(t), 72(b), 73(b), 76(b), 77(t), 77(b), 84(t), 85(t), 89(t), 92(t), 94(t), 104, 108(t), 109(b), 110(t), 121(m), 124(b), 139(t), 139(m), 142(t), 149(m), 150(b), 156, 159(b), 161, 165(b), 167(t), 169(t), 194(t), 200(b), 211, 213, 214(t), 218(b), 223(b), 226(b), 236(b), 243, 288(t), 317(t), 381, 418, 423(t), 430(b), 456(t), 457(b)

**Millbrook House:** 12(t), 13(t), 13(b), 14(b),15(t), 15(mr), 17(b), 18(t), 19(t), 21(t), 22(t), 22(b), 23(b), 24(b), 26(t), 26(b), 27, 29(t), 35(t), 36(m), 37(b), 38(t), 40(t), 41(t), 42(t), 42(b), 43(b), 47, 48(t), 48(b), 49(all), 50, 53, 55(t), 56(t), 57(t), 61, 63(t), 63(b), 65(b), 70, 73(t), 74(b), 75(t), 76(t), 76(m), 79(t), 79(b), 81(b), 82(t), 82(b), 83(b), 85(b), 86(b), 87(t), 88(b), 89(b), 91(t), 91(b), 92(m), 93(b), 94(b), 99(all), 100(both), 101(t), 102(t), 105(b), 106(t), 106(b), 108(b), 109(t), 111(b), 113(t), 113(b), 114(all), 115(b), 116(t), 117(tr), 117(tl), 118(t), 119(t), 119(m), 119(b), 120, 121(b), 125(all), 126(b), 127(t), 127(b), 130, 131(tl), 131(b), 133(t), 133(bl), 134(t), 134(b), 135(t), 135(b), 136(b), 137(t), 139(b), 141(t), 142(b), 143(t), 143(b), 145(t), 146(t), 146(b), 148(tl), 149(t), 151(b), 152(t), 152(b), 158(t), 158(b), 159(t), 163, 165(t), 166(b), 167(b), 168(t), 168(b), 171(t), 173(b), 175(t), 176, 177(t), 178(t), 179(l), 180(t), 180(b), 181, 182(b), 183(t), 184, 187, 188, 189(b), 190(b), 191, 195(t), 195(b), 196(t), 197(b), 199(b), 201(t), 202(t), 202(b), 203(t), 203(b), 204(t), 205(t), 205(b), 208(m), 209(t), 210(b), 212(t), 214(m), 214(b), 215(t), 215(b), 217(b), 219(t), 220(b), 221(t), 221(b), 223(t), 225, 227(b), 228(b), 229(m), 229(b), 230, 231(t), 232(t), 232(b), 233, 237(t), 238(t), 239(m), 239(b), 240, 241(b), 242, 244, 251, 252, 254, 255, 259(t), 263(t), 264(t), 264(b), 265, 266(both), 269, 272(t), 274(b), 275(t), 275(b), 276(b) 278(b), 279(t), 279(b), 282(t), 283(b), 284, 285(t), 286(b), 290(b), 291(t), 292, 293, 298(t), 302(b), 303(b), 304, 305, 306(t), 307, 308(t), 308(b), 311(b), 312(t), 313(t), 313(b), 314(t), 314(b), 315, 318(t), 322(t), 322(b), 324(b), 325(t), 326, 329(tl), 330(t), 331(t), 335(b), 336(t), 337(t), 338(t), 340(t), 340(b), 342(t), 343(t), 344(t), 349, 350(t), 374(b), 382, 384, 385(t), 386, 391(b), 393(t), 393(b), 394(t), 394(b), 395(t,m), 404, 405, 406(b), 407(t), 407(b), 411(b), 412(t), 415(b), 416(b), 419(t), 420(t), 422(b), 423(m), 426(t), 426(b), 428, 429(t), 430(t), 431, 436(m), 437, 438(b), 440(b), 442(b), 449(b), 456(b), 457(t), 460, 462(t), 463(b), 465(t), 466(b), 471(b), 475, 481(t), 486, 490(t) 492(t) 492(b), 493, 498, 499, 501(b), 503, 507, 515(t) 518(t), 525, 529, 530, 531, 532(t), 535(t)

**Brian Solomon:** 246, 247(l), 259(b), 261, 262, 268(t), 268(b), 270(t), 271, 272(b), 274(t), 280(t), 280(b), 281(t), 289, 295(t), 303(t), 310(t), 312(b), 316, 320(b), 321(t), 324(t), 325(b), 327(t), 327(b), 328(t), 328(b), 329(tr), 332(b), 334(b), 335(t), 339(b), 345, 346(b), 347(t), 348(t), 351(b), 352(b), 353(b), 358(m), 360(b), 361, 363(t), 364, 365(b), 366(b), 369(t), 370, 371, 374(t), 377(t), 378, 387, 392(t), 403(b), 408(t), 409(t), 409(b), 419(b), 432(t), 441(t), 443(t), 444(b), 445, 446(b), 452(t), 468(t), 469, 472(t), 474(b) 480(b), 487, 489, 496(t), 500, 504, 506(b), 515(b), 516(t), 516(b), 519, 527, 535(b)

**Science and Society Picture Library:** 388, 403(t), 414(t), 425(b), 435(b), 439, 532(b)

**Mary Boocock:** 285(b)

**Colin Boocock:** 291(b), 297, 300(b), 306(b), 321(b), 341(t), 352(t), 358(b), 359(t), 373, 375(t), 377(b), 396, 399, 421(t), 422(t), 447(b), 470(b) 488(t), 506(t)

**Adrian Senn:** 413, 411, 479, 483, 488

**TRH Pictures:** 6, 10, 11, 118(b), 124(t), 186(t), 212(b), 256, 331(b), 344(b), 391(t), 402, 452(b), 462(b), 471(t), 485(t)

**Alvey & Towers:** 392(b), 434(t), 446(t), 449(t), 449(m), 451, 467(t), 505

**Petr Kaderavek:** 513